W9-BNR-259

Crucible of Power

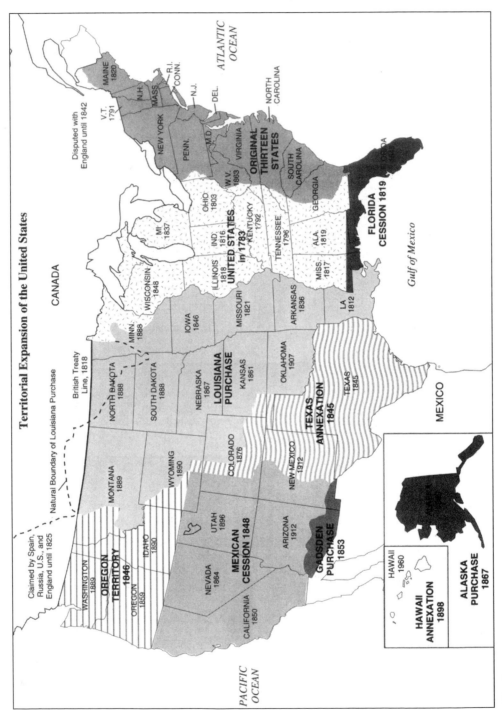

Territorial Expansion of the United States

Map 1

Crucible of Power

A History of U.S. Foreign Relations
Since 1897

HOWARD JONES

SR BOOKS

Lanham • Boulder • New York • Toronto • Oxford

Published by SR Books
An imprint of Rowman & Littlefield Publishers, Inc.
A wholly owned subsidary of The Rowman & Littlefield Publishing Group, Inc.
4501 Forbes Boulevard, Suite 200
Lanham, MD 20706

PO Box 317
Oxford
OX2 9RU, UK

Copyright © 2001 by Scholarly Resources Inc.

All rights reserved. No part of this publication may be reproduced,
stored in a retrieval system, or transmitted in any form or by any
means, electronic, mechanical, photocopying, recording, or otherwise,
without the prior permission of the publisher.

British Library Cataloguing in Publication Information Available

Library of Congress Cataloging-in-Publication Data

Jones, Howard, 1940–
    Crucible of power : a history of U.S. foreign relations since 1897 /
Howard Jones.
        p.   cm.
    Includes bibliographical references and index.
    ISBN 0-8420-2918-4 (pbk.)
    1. United States—Foreign relations—20th century.   2. United States—
Foreign relations—20th century—Decision making.   I. Title.

E744 .J669   2001
327.73—dc21   2001020991

Printed in the United States of America

∞ ™ The paper used in this publication meets the minimum requirements of
American National Standard for Information Sciences—Permanence of Paper
for Printed Library Materials, ANSI/NISO Z39.48-1992.

In Memory of Howie

ABOUT THE AUTHOR

Howard Jones received a Ph.D. from Indiana University and taught at the University of Nebraska before coming to the University of Alabama in 1974. He is now University Research Professor in the Department of History. A recipient of both the John F. Burnum Distinguished Faculty Award for teaching and research and the Blackmon-Moody Outstanding Professor Award, he teaches courses in American foreign relations and the U.S.-Vietnam War.

He is the author or editor of more than a dozen books, including *To the Webster-Ashburton Treaty: A Study in Anglo-American Relations, 1783–1843* (1977)—recipient of the Phi Alpha Theta Book Award and nominated for the Pulitzer Prize and the Stuart L. Bernath Book Award; *Mutiny on the Amistad: The Saga of a Slave Revolt and Its Impact on American Abolition, Law, and Diplomacy* (1987, revised 1997)—used in writing the screenplay for Steven Spielberg's movie "Amistad" and a selection of Book-of-the-Month Club, History Book Club, and Quality Paperbacks Book Club; *"A New Kind of War": America's Global Strategy and the Truman Doctrine in Greece* (1989)—nominated for the Harry S. Truman Book Award and for the Phi Alpha Theta Book Award; with Randall B. Woods, *Dawning of the Cold War: The United States' Quest for Order* (1991)—nominated for the Warren F. Kuehl Award and for the George Louis Beer Prize; *Union in Peril: The Crisis over British Intervention in the Civil War* (1992)—a History Book Club Selection and winner of the Phi Alpha Theta Book Award; with Donald A. Rakestraw, *Prologue to Manifest Destiny: Anglo-American Relations in the 1840s* (1997)—recognized by *Choice* magazine as one of the "Outstanding Academic Books" for 1997; and *Abraham Lincoln and a New Birth of Freedom: The Union and Slavery in the Diplomacy of the Civil War* (1999)—nominated for the Lincoln Prize and the Bancroft Prize. He has published articles in several journals, the most recent in the *Journal of American History* as the centerpiece of a forum and entitled "Cinqué of the Amistad a Slave Trader? Perpetuating a Myth." He is presently completing a book entitled *Death of a Generation: John F. Kennedy and Vietnam.*

CONTENTS

LIST OF MAPS

ACKNOWLEDGMENTS

This book, like most publications, has benefited from the contributions of others. Superb suggestions have come from both undergraduate and graduate students here at the University of Alabama, as well as from numerous friends in the profession along with the anonymous readers of the manuscript. In particular, I wish to thank Carol Jackson Adams, John Belohlavek, Kinley Brauer, Susan Brewer, Douglas Brinkley, Paul C. Clark, Robert A. Divine, Robert H. Ferrell, Mark Gilderhus, Paul Grass, Mary Ann Heiss, Peter Hill, Tim Johnson, Tim Maga, Pete Maslowski, Forrest and Ellen McDonald, Teresa Peebles, Donald A. Rakestraw, Guy Swanson, and Randall B. Woods for their encouragement along with many useful comments. For helping me through the countless trials and tribulations of securing the illustrations, I thank Scott Keller and Nancy Smelley. No one can write a book without the gift of time. For affording me that precious commodity, I express sincere gratitude to Kay Branyon, Loretta Colvin, Julie P. Moore, Nancy (again), and Fay Wheat.

On a more personal level, I wish to express appreciation to the most important people in my life—my family. Only these loved ones understand the time and solitude required in research and writing, and only they were willing to put up with my short temper and abrasive behavior as I attempted to make sense out of my many meaningless sentences and hopelessly tangled paragraphs. To my parents, to my spouse and closest confidante, Mary Ann, to my daughters Deborah and Shari, to Howie, whose brief life provided us with lasting memories, and to the lights of our lives—my grandchildren, Ashley and Timothy—I extend heartfelt gratitude for your patience and, most important, your love.

Howard Jones
Tuscaloosa, Alabama, Fall 2001

PREFACE

The central theme of America's foreign relations has been the long and steady rise of the republic to world power, followed by its gradual assumption of the position it occupies today: the first among several prominent nations. The history of U.S. foreign affairs comprises a fascinating account of a growing empire based on principles of self-government that made it unique from the Old World. In no way can a history of the United States stand as complete without the incorporation of its foreign policy. And yet, in too many instances this part of the nation's history has not received its due. In a finely crafted television documentary of the Civil War, for example, foreign affairs won barely a mention—despite all manner of documentation establishing the Lincoln administration's feverish concern about preventing a British intervention that could have profoundly affected the outcome of the war and impeded the growth of the United States to world power.

Washington's leaders have been fairly consistent in promoting the national interest as they perceived it. Whereas European diplomats talked almost exclusively of power relationships, strategic considerations, economic interests, and imperialist aims, Americans emphasized, along with those same realities, certain ideals that made their country exceptional: natural rights; the republican ideas of popular rule, free trade, neutral rights, and freedom of the seas; a missionary spirit that permeated its expansionist impulse; the separation of political and economic concerns in foreign policy; and freedom from Old World political and military entanglements. At the same time, however, they recognized that their major objective was to protect the nation's vital interests.

This work seeks to demonstrate the complexities involved in the decision-making process that led to the rise and decline of the United States (relative to the ascent of other nations) in world power status. It focuses on the personalities, security interests, and expansionist tendencies behind the formulation and implementation of U.S. foreign policy. It highlights the intimate relationship between foreign and domestic policy. It gives due attention to the historical antecedents of the nation's twentieth-century foreign policy. And it relies on the natural chronology of events to organize and narrate the story as the nation's leaders saw it. Policymaking cannot take place in a vacuum. Events occur concurrently and day after day, only at times appearing to be manageable. No one should expect contemporary leaders in Washington to grasp the intricate relationships among events and peoples world-wide that we as historians—with the advantage of hindsight—attempt to do.

Only a narrative approach can uncover the tangled and often confusing nature of foreign affairs. The compartmentalization of individual topics in thematic chapters tends to impose a design on these events that did not exist. A topical approach can create the illusion that history takes place in a well-ordered fashion, making policymakers vulnerable to unwarrantable criticisms for failing to discern "patterns" of behavior or "lessons" in history. Should readers recognize that events are largely uncontrollable, they will understand the plight of policymakers who daily encounter a kaleidoscopic array of problems rarely susceptible to simple analysis and ready solution. If readers come to realize that the outcome of events is not inevitable and that the complexity of history makes decision-making a difficult process, this book will have served its purpose.

Hopefully this work will stand on the strengths of readability, organization, accuracy, and fairness. My intention is to offer a straightforward, balanced, and comprehensive history of the major events in the nation's foreign affairs, from the American Revolution to the present. Readers wanting more detailed accounts should examine the many fine articles and monographic studies cited in the "Selected Readings" following each chapter. For citations (and summations) to these and numerous other historical works, they should consult the superb *Guide to American Foreign Relations since 1700*, edited by Richard Dean Burns and soon to be available in a revised, updated version. Also invaluable is the four-volume *Encyclopedia of U.S. Foreign Relations*, edited by Bruce W. Jentleson and Thomas G. Paterson. Finally, they should read the first-class journal of our profession, *Diplomatic History*, which features articles that often stand at the cutting edge of the field.

CHAPTER 1

U.S. Imperialism and the New Manifest Destiny, 1897–1900

Background

During the late 1890s the entire demeanor of the United States dramatically changed as it became deeply involved in the Caribbean, Pacific, and Asia in a surge of national feeling that became known as the "new manifest destiny." Whereas the expansionist drive of the 1840s had spent itself within the continental United States, the great industrial, technological, and commercial advances of the post–Civil War era turned U.S. interests toward distant shores. Expansion was inevitable and relentless, according to Secretary of State John Hay. "No man, no party, can fight with any chance of final success against a cosmic tendency; no cleverness, no popularity avails against the spirit of the age."

By the 1890s any U.S. interest in the actual annexation of territory had given way to "informal empire," or commercial penetration that led either to economic dominance without direct political controls or to the acquisition of colonies having no prospect of statehood. The expansionist mood was not national, partly because of the lack of cohesion in the political parties, and partly because of the general fragmentation still evident from the Civil War. Anti-imperialist feelings ran strong, especially among Americans who rec-ognized their nation's limitations outside the hemisphere, but also among those who feared the incorporation of nonwhite peoples and worried about the negative effects of imperialism on democratic institutions. But the economic hard times of the decade dictated a search for new commercial outlets, not so much for acquiring sources of raw materials as for securing markets capable of absorbing the United States's excess stock of manufactured goods. Although business and government did not jointly orchestrate a push toward expansion, commercial interests often had the Washington government's tacit support in searching for investment fields and foreign markets that would promote the good of the economy and hence safeguard the national interest.

During the last third of the nineteenth century some Americans had already taken the lead in trying to revive the spirit of expansion. Church groups called for increased missionary work among the primitive areas of the world and soon found themselves with unnatural allies. The English philosopher Herbert Spencer and the Yale sociologist William Graham Sumner, both using Charles Darwin's ideas of evolution, advocated the theories of Social Darwinism and Anglo-Saxon superiority in encouraging Americans to believe that the strong would survive and that the only limitations on

1

growth were self-imposed. Darwin wrote that "there is apparently much truth in the belief that the wonderful progress of the United States as well as the character of the people are the results of natural selection" and that the American nation was "the heir of all ages."

A number of Americans helped to popularize these ideas, including historian John Fiske, Reverend Josiah Strong, intellectual Brooks Adams, political scientist John Burgess, and public figures such as William H. Seward, Ulysses S. Grant, James G. Blaine, and, the most outspoken of all, the wealthy and flamboyant New Yorker Theodore Roosevelt. Brooks Adams and Roosevelt often gathered at Henry Adams's (Brooks's brother) house in Washington, discussing these ideas and developing into a tightly knit group that advocated commercial and territorial expansion as the chief means toward building a stronger nation and guaranteeing national security. Historian Frederick Jackson Turner suggested the imminence of increased international involvement in 1893 when he declared before the American Historical Association that the American frontier was closed; the end of free land, he seemed to assert, portended expansion abroad. Philosophers, missionaries, naval officers, business leaders, farmers—all warned that U.S. hesitation on the international front would concede Africa, Asia, and the Pacific to European powers.

The United States's growing export trade necessitated a larger navy to defend projected sea lanes. During the Civil War, Union naval commanders had become aware of the need for coaling stations in the Caribbean and Pacific. Afterward, many Americans supported the ideas of Captain Alfred T. Mahan of the navy, who in his seminal work, *The Influence of Seapower upon History, 1660–1783* (1890), called for overseas bases, expanded commerce, and an isthmian canal—but only after the United States had built a navy strong enough to protect its possessions. Ironically, Mahan's initial influence was greatest in Great Britain, Germany, and Japan. But even before his great work appeared, his ideas had attracted con-

Alfred T. Mahan
His writings on seapower influenced the thinking of the Germans, Japanese, and Americans—in particular, Theodore Roosevelt. *Contact print from Frances Benjamin Johnson negative; Library of Congress.*

siderable interest. One of the founders of the Naval War College in the United States, Rear Admiral Stephen B. Luce, was a major advocate of Mahan's ideas and helped establish the modern U.S. Navy. Mahan soon became an instructor among the first faculty at the War College and continued to spread his ideas in the years afterward, with notable impact on Theodore Roosevelt. Congressional and popular support for a navy had been negligible before the mid-1880s, primarily because relative peace in Europe had allowed security to develop in the Western Hemisphere through only minimal effort. Thus, while other nations built steel ships, the United States continued to repair sails, replace rotted wooden hulls, and deploy ironclads for inland duties. But growing international rivalries in Europe forced a change in America's world outlook. Interest in steel battleships soon grew so rapidly in the United States that within a decade its fleet ranked seventh in the world.

U.S. expansionists encountered many obstacles. Anti-imperialist groups, led by Senator Carl Schurz, writer Mark Twain, and newspaper editor E. L. Godkin, were more interested in bettering America's domestic institutions than in acquiring territories. Despite a growing race for European partition of Africa by the last years of the century, Americans lacked the naval power to show anything more than mild interest in that continent as a potential trade outlet or source of private adventure. Some Americans simply opposed the addition of dark-skinned peoples to the United States. Godkin fought against the acquisition of Santo Domingo because, he declared, that country had 200,000 "ignorant Catholic Spanish negroes" who might expect U.S. citizenship. Others argued that the establishment of colonies necessarily ruled out self-government and often led to competition that caused wars.

Political considerations had also blocked any interest in expansion. The United States could not make any firm moves toward world involvement until 1896, when the Republicans won the White House and both houses of Congress and soon banded together behind a new kind of foreign expansion built upon a two-headed missionary and commercial impulse. The expansionist Democratic party had been able to gain control of the presidency on only two occasions between 1865 and the first part of the new century. Even then, its standard bearer both times, Grover Cleveland, opposed imperialism. By 1897, however, the United States was ready to assume a global role under Republican leadership.

Several factors combined to push U.S. interests beyond its present borders. One catalyst was the desire to act before European powers incorporated everything of value. Expansionist Senator Henry Cabot Lodge of Massachusetts exuberantly declared in 1895 that "the great nations are rapidly absorbing for their future expansion and their present defense all the waste places of the earth. It is a movement which makes for civilization and the advancement of the race. As one of the great nations of the world," he warned, "the United States must not fall out of the line of march." Another impetus to U.S. expansion was commercial—encouraged by the Panic of 1893 and the ensuing economic depression. Still another was the adventuresome feeling of seeing the American flag flying over some foreign shore. Perhaps most important, however, was the growing understanding among Americans that their security was integrally related to events beyond their continental borders.

As in the 1840s the United States sought to harmonize realistic expansionist aims based on commercial and security considerations with idealistic goals focusing on the exportation of democracy and humanitarianism. And, as in the earlier period, Americans colored their realistic drive for imperialism—or empire—with idealistic labels emphasizing "destiny," "progress," and the spread of "civilization." Encouraged by the warlike jingoes and the sensationalist news stories carried by the burgeoning "yellow press," the United States entered a war with Spain in 1898 that resulted in the republic's first acquisition of an overseas colony and helped to end the divisive legacy of the Civil War. The war with Spain also furthered the decline of American isolationism and, because the British found themselves without an ally in this period and tended to take the side of the Americans against Spain, tightened the growing Anglo-American rapprochement. At virtually the same time—and not by sheer coincidence—Americans turned greater attention toward Asia for both realistic and idealistic reasons. The overseas expansion of the late 1890s alerted the world that the United States was about to become a great power.

Final Overture to Imperialism: Cuba and the Yellow Press

The renewed insurrection in Cuba in February 1895 led the United States into the imperialist age. Three years earlier, a Cuban exile in the United States had established the Cuban Revolutionary Party, whose goal was to overthrow Spanish rule on the island. The United States's official concern over Cuba had meanwhile declined when Spain abolished slavery and promised other reforms after the Ten Years' War had ended in 1878. In 1890 the U.S. Congress passed the McKinley Tariff, which stimulated the island's sugar industry, and the following year the United States agreed to permit tariff-free entry of the Cuban product. But the economic boom proved temporary, because the Panic of 1893 and Democratic control of Congress led to a new tariff setting high duties and virtually slamming the door on Cuban sugar imports. The ensuing depression in Cuba plus accumulated political and economic grievances set off the insurrection in 1895.

Led by General Máximo Gómez, the Cuban rebels proclaimed a republic on the eastern end of the island and proceeded to extend control over most of the surrounding region. The war was actually a resumption of the Ten Years' War, because the Spanish peace had promised much and delivered little. The Cubans had supposedly won amnesty and certain governmental rights, but the changes proved to be only a façade and the problems that had caused the long conflict persisted. Spain had not fulfilled its assurances of relief, and the bulk of the island's revenues went either toward paying Cuba's debt or directly into Spain's coffers. Cuba's complaints went unheeded by Spanish officials on the island, and Gómez, a hardened veteran of the Ten Years' War, retaliated with a "scorched-earth" policy, which entailed dynamiting passenger trains and burning the Spanish loyalists' property and sugar plantations—including many owned by Americans. Gómez intended to make the island a liability for the Spanish and force its independence or to bring about U.S. intervention in its behalf. By late 1896 the guerrilla forces controlled nearly two-thirds of the island, with the Spanish hovering along the coast and in the cities.

The Cuban war took an even uglier twist in February 1896, when Spain's new captain general on the island, Valeriano Weyler, sought to destroy the rebels' rural quarters by dividing the island into districts and establishing reconcentration centers. His directives herded all inhabitants of central and western Cuba into the towns, which Weyler barricaded with trenches rimmed by barbed wire and reinforced with soldiers in guardhouses overlooking the encampments. Nearly half a million Cubans, young and old, male and female, were quartered in hot, unsanitary, and sparsely provisioned barbed wire enclosures; anyone refusing to go along was shot. By the spring of 1898 the reconcentrado policies of "Butcher" Weyler, as he was soon called, led to widespread hunger and disease that took the lives of thousands of the captives (mostly women and children), a large proportion of the Cuban population.

The realities of the reconcentration camps were harsh enough, but the sordid episode soon fell prey to a major development in U.S. news reporting known as "yellow journalism." William Randolph Hearst had bought the struggling *New York Journal* in late 1895 and prepared to challenge Joseph Pulitzer's *New York World* for top circulation in the country. Dramatic headlines, lurid and exaggerated stories, creative writing, graphic detail, suggestions of sexual misconduct by Spanish officials—all ploys became acceptable means for selling newspapers. Hearst hired the famous portrait artist of the Indian and American West, Frederic Remington, to visit Cuba and bring back drawings illustrating the fighting. When Remington soon notified Hearst of his inability to locate the war, the newspaper owner shot back: "You furnish the pictures and I'll furnish the war." Spain emerged in the yellow press as the sole perpetrator of atrocity in Cuba, arousing strong sentiment for U.S. intervention to ensure the island's independence.

Day after day the *Journal* and *World* competed with each other for the most spectacular coverage. Hearst's paper set the tone by describing "Weyler the soldier[,] . . . Weyler the brute, the devastator of haciendas, the destroyer of families, and the outrager of women. . . . Pitiless, cold, an exterminator of men." The *Journal* saw no way "to prevent his carnal, animal brain from running riot with itself in inventing tortures and infamies of bloody debauchery." Pulitzer's *World* retaliated in kind, writing of "blood on the roadsides, blood in the fields, blood on the doorsteps, blood, blood, blood! The old, the young, the weak, the crippled—all are butchered without mercy." It finally asked, "Is there no nation wise enough, brave enough, and strong enough to restore peace in this bloodsmitten land?"

Not to be outdone, Hearst's *Journal* exploited sex to sell copy. His press picked up the story of a young Cuban girl named Evangelina Cisneros, who was thrown into prison, allegedly after fending off the advances of her male Spanish captors. Thousands of American women responded to Hearst's appeal for help by signing petitions in her behalf and dismissing the Spanish minister's claim that Hearst had fabricated the story. Shortly afterward, a reporter for Hearst's paper made his way to Havana, freed Evangelina by sawing through the jail bars, and, after disguising her as a boy, brought her to the United States. The *Journal* proudly sported the headline: "An American Newspaper Accomplishes in a Single Stroke What the Best Efforts of Diplomacy Failed Utterly to Bring about in Many Months." Washington, D.C., and New York City's Madison Square Garden hosted great receptions in her honor, and the governor of Missouri mockingly suggested that Hearst send 500 reporters to liberate the entire island of Cuba.

In the same vein, another headline event drew attention to a group of females removed from a U.S. vessel. Spanish officers had boarded the ship as it prepared to leave Havana, allegedly to search three young Cuban women suspected of carrying rebel mail packets. Highlighting the inflammatory story was Remington's fabricated sketch of a nude female suspect standing before leering Spanish officers. The

Journal indignantly asked: "Does Our Flag Protect Women?"

The yellow press deepened U.S. concern for Cuba. The United States already had economic interests in the war's outcome. Investors had sunk nearly $50 million in sugar and tobacco production and in iron and manganese mines and other enterprises, and trade between the countries had reached as high as $100 million in an exceptional year. These businesses drastically declined during the revolution. In the meantime, the Cuban war became a heavy expense for the U.S. government. Spanish officials on the island arrested Americans who had become naturalized Cubans, and the United States felt bound to secure their freedom. U.S. naval vessels meanwhile patrolled the Atlantic coast to halt illegal arms shipments to the Cuban rebels. In an attempt to end the hostilities, humanitarians, religious leaders, Americans with economic stakes in Cuba, and a large number of daily newspapers from both political camps became allies in denouncing Spanish oppression and urging reform. Few considered annexation of the island as a solution. Intervention ists wanted an independent Cuba, not a transfer of title to Washington.

The Cleveland administration resisted the growing popular clamor for intervention in Cuba. Yet it could not ignore the pressure from a Republican Congress to recognize Cuban belligerency. The White House had several options. It could recognize the Cuban belligerents, although Secretary of State Richard Olney warned that such a policy would prevent Americans from securing damage claims from Spain after the war. Recognition of Cuban independence posed another possibility. Both the president and Olney feared that the Cubans were unfit to govern themselves, however, and that the ensuing anarchy would invite Old World intervention. Besides, Spain might declare war and force U.S. involvement on the ground that a Spanish effort to defeat a newly independent Cuba would constitute an infraction of the Monroe Doctrine. The third possibility was the only feasible choice: Exert pressure on the Madrid government to permit the Cubans a degree of autonomy within the empire that would undermine native resistance. In April 1896 Olney sent a note to Spain urging reforms on the island.

But popular sentiment for the rebels continued to grow in the United States, forcing Congress to pass a resolution extending recognition to Cuban belligerency. The resulting anti-American demonstrations in Spain exploded in violence when 15,000 people stoned the U.S. consulate in Barcelona and destroyed the American flag. Despite widespread support for Cuba in the United States, Cleveland warned that should Congress declare war on Spain, he as commander in chief of the armed forces would refuse to send Americans to fight. Spain did not implement Washington's reform recommendations, and the administration did not want war. Yet the president had to protect U.S. interests in Cuba. While Congress called for stronger measures, the U.S. consul general in Havana repeatedly urged annexation. With Cleveland's Democratic party disintegrating on the eve of the presidential election of 1896, his administration could do little about the Cuban problem. The situation on the island had to await a new president.

The Cuban Prologue to War

In November 1896 the Republican party, led by William McKinley of Ohio, won the White House on a platform stressing expansion. Four years earlier the Republicans had resurrected the term "manifest destiny" and incorporated it into their campaign. Although the presidential race of 1896 had centered on currency and tariff issues, the Republicans called for a strong foreign policy that rested on an expanded naval power. Their platform advocated the acquisition of Hawaii, the use of U.S. influence to bring peace and independence to Cuba, the construction of a Nicaraguan canal under U.S. ownership and control, and the establishment of a naval base in the West Indies. Although McKinley agreed

with Alfred T. Mahan's ideas about the need for a stronger navy, he was not an imperialist. He assured anti-imperialist Carl Schurz that his administration would permit "no jingo nonsense." McKinley's first secretary of state, John Sherman, declared his opposition "to all acquisitions of territory not on the mainland."

The new administration, however, quickly realized that the Cuban issue was again approaching crisis intensity and could force U.S. intervention in the name of humanity. Spain had not implemented needed reforms, and in June 1897 the Washington government sent a note to Madrid protesting Weyler's tactics. The following month the administration instructed the new U.S. minister in Spain, Stewart Woodford, to demand Spanish withdrawal from Cuba. By the autumn, prospects for reform looked brighter when a liberal government took over in Madrid after a shocking incident—the assassination of the prime minister. The new ministry called Weyler home, assured Washington of an end to reconcentration policies, and guaranteed more autonomy to the islanders through the popular election of legislatures. President McKinley told Congress in his annual message in December that the United States should give the reforms a chance. Yet if they yielded no results, he warned, intervention might take place because of "our obligations to ourselves, to civilization and humanity."

By early 1898 Spain's promised political reforms had still not materialized, and in January the United States sent the battleship *Maine* to Cuba as a show of force to persuade the Spanish to grant the changes necessary to end the war. The Cuban rebels had elevated their demands for autonomy to independence, putting Madrid's ministry in an uneasy position between them and Spanish loyalists in Cuba who rioted that same month over the question of autonomy. Such a concession, the loyalists feared, would promote the election of a legislature injurious to their interests on the island. Besides, the granting of Cuban independence could bring down the ministry at home. Meanwhile the *Maine,* anchored in

Havana harbor, became a symbol of U.S. imperialism and a veritable announcement of deepening intervention by Washington. A close adviser to the president prophetically warned that sending the vessel to Cuba was like "waving a match in an oil well for fun."

While tensions grew over the *Maine*, a crisis developed when the Department of State in Washington received a copy of a private letter written in late 1897 from the Spanish minister in the United States, Enrique Dupuy de Lôme, to a friend in Cuba. De Lôme opposed war with the United States and had become frustrated over the events that seemed to be leading irrevocably to conflict. Already reputed to be arrogant and cynical, he confirmed these observations by indiscreetly describing McKinley as "weak and a bidder for the admiration of the crowd, . . . a would-be politician who tries to leave a door open behind himself while keeping on good terms with the jingoes of his party." Worse, de Lôme suggested that his government simply reject the Cuban demand for autonomy and consider economic reprisals, which, to many Americans, proved Spain's lack of sincerity about seeking peace.

By the time the de Lôme letter reached Washington, it had become a *cause célèbre* because a rebel partisan had somehow gotten hold of it and shared it with a number of Americans, including William Randolph Hearst. The same day the state department received the missive, February 9, the letter appeared in the *New York Journal* under the carefully crafted headline, "Worst Insult to the United States in Its History." Madrid's unavoidable decision to recall de Lôme, who had already packed his bags, further exacerbated the dangerous situation by removing Spain's chief spokesman for peace in the United States. During the next critical weeks Spain had no minister in Washington to vent Americans' anger.

Less than a week later, on the night of February 15, the *Maine* blew up in Havana harbor, sending more than 260 U.S. officers and men to their watery graves as the 7000-ton

battleship crumpled and sank. Americans blamed Spain. In their anger, they failed to consider that such an act meant certain war with the United States—a calamity the Spanish could *not* have wanted. But emotions swept aside reason as the *New York Journal* trumpeted these headlines: "The Warship Maine Was Split In Two By An Enemy's Infernal Machine"; "The Whole Country Thrills With War Fever"; "The Maine Was Destroyed By Treachery." Two days after the incident, the *Journal* included a diagram on the front page allegedly showing the placement of a mine that sank the ship. To right this great wrong, the paper offered $50,000 for information on the assailants.

President McKinley agreed with his secretary of the navy, John D. Long, that the explosion was an accident and hoped to calm Americans by arranging an immediate inquiry into the tragedy. But the idea persisted that a mine had blown up the magazines on the *Maine*. On March 6, 1898, the president asked Congress for $50 million in arms appropriations and just as quickly received approval. The Madrid government, according to Woodford, found this measure difficult to believe. On March 28 the U.S. court of inquiry, comprised of American naval officers, published its findings on the explosion: Although it now seems likely that an overheated boiler blew up the ship, the court in 1898 concluded that an external mine had destroyed the *Maine* but left the door open for speculation by declaring its inability to determine the guilty party. Americans did not need to know any more. The duplicity and animosity seemingly exhibited in the de Lôme letter had taken material form in this naval disaster. Theodore Roosevelt privately wrote that "the *Maine* was sunk by an act of dirty treachery on the part of the Spaniards," while Americans already were chanting:

Remember the *Maine*
To hell with Spain!

In the midst of the excitement over the *Maine*, a Republican senator, Redfield Proctor

The U.S.S. Maine—*Before and After*
An explosion sank the *Maine* in Havana Harbor on February 15, 1898, making
"Remember the *Maine!*" the rallying cry for the Spanish-American War. *National
Archives, Washington, D.C.*

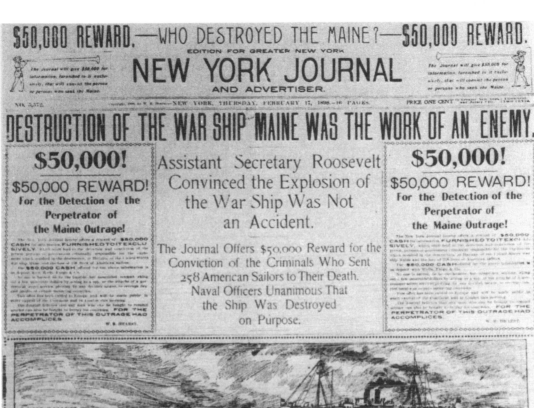

New York Journal
An example of the yellow press. No one ever claimed the $50,000 reward. *American Heritage Library*.

of Vermont, reported to his colleagues about his recent private tour of Cuba. With notable absence of passion, which paradoxically made his speech in the Senate more effective, he solemnly declared that in the outskirts of Havana, the situation "is not peace nor is it war. It is desolation and distress, misery and starvation." Thousands of Cubans lived in reconcentration camps, and "one-half have died and one-quarter of the living are so diseased that they cannot be saved." Weyler had left the island, but his replacement did not know what to do. Proctor's graphic description of the camps gave credence to the stories in the U.S. press, because he was a known opponent of war. The children wander around with "arms and chest terribly emaciated, eyes swollen, and abdomen bloated to three times the natural size. . . . I was told by one of our consuls," he continued, "that they have been found dead about the markets in the morning, where they had crawled, hoping to get some stray bits of food from the early hucksters." The greatest atrocity was "the entire native population of Cuba, struggling for freedom and deliverance from the worst misgovernment of which I ever had knowledge."

Proctor's vivid account had a major impact on Americans concerned about both humanitarian and property interests on the island. Action on behalf of Cuba's independence seemed justified as a crusade, and even U.S. business owners previously opposed to involvement recognized that the United States had to do something before the entire Cuban economy collapsed and took their investments with it. The usually unflappable *Wall Street Journal* declared that Proctor's speech had "made the blood boil." Intervention in Cuba, according to the equally cautious *Literary Digest,* was "the plain duty of the United States on the simple ground of humanity."

The Spanish-American War

President McKinley's role in these events was greater than once thought. Some contemporary observers argued that he was a gentle and

Judge
Many Americans had this image of Spain as they called for war after the sinking of the *Maine.* *Library of Congress.*

unassuming man caught up in forces beyond his control. By the spring of 1898 he could not sleep without sedatives. His mood grew irascible as his invalid wife failed in health, and he continually had to grapple with the jingoes demanding war. A friend claimed that in late March the president broke under the strain and wept over recent events. Congress, McKinley charged, was pushing the nation into war. But this was not the entire story. Nor did the full truth lay in the view of the president's harshest critics who accused him of pursuing a cold and calculating expansionist policy that included war as the final solution. The real McKinley lay somewhere between the two extremes. He sought to expand his nation's commercial boundaries; but he was not a single-minded imperialist willing to do anything to achieve this objective. He was a devout Methodist, extremely sensitive to what was going on around him; but he also believed in the use of power to spread U.S. influence as an impetus to bettering mankind. McKinley wanted the spoils but preferably not at the cost of war. When war came, however, he took command, even establishing a war room in the White House from which he helped to plan strategy and maintain control of events by keeping close contact with U.S. forces both in the Caribbean and Asia. But these behind-the-scenes activities remained hidden from public view, leaving the impression of inaction. Theodore Roosevelt and other jingoes denounced the president as weak and indecisive and regarded the Cuban conflict as a God-given opportunity to enlarge the American interest.

Political pressures and the desire for reelection in 1900 helped push McKinley toward war. Members of his party demanded war, and rival Democrats led by the outspoken and histrionic William Jennings Bryan dramatically called for an independent Cuba. Pressure in the United States for war was enormous. Secretary of War Russell Alger warned that "Congress will declare war in spite of him. He'll get run over and the party with him." A Protestant journal self-righteously declared that "if it be the will of Almighty God, that by war the last trace of this inhumanity of man to man shall be swept away from this Western Hemisphere, let it come!" When business leaders emphasized a peaceful recovery from the depression rather than a war that would bring expansion abroad, Roosevelt snorted at Ohio Senator Mark Hanna, one of their biggest spokesmen: "We will have this war for the freedom of Cuba, in spite of the timidity of the commercial interests." Exasperated with the president's apparent indecision, Roosevelt allegedly proclaimed that "McKinley has no more backbone than a chocolate eclair!"

The president staunchly searched for a way out of war and finally emerged with a policy that left room for an eleventh-hour peace. On March 27 the United States notified Spain that the president would arbitrate a settlement unless it agreed to an immediate armistice and

peace by October 1. McKinley also called for a relief program for the Cuban victims and urged the government to fulfill its assurance of ending the reconcentration camps. Though making no demand for the island's independence, the Washington administration sent a telegram to Madrid the next day referring to Cuba's freedom as the natural outcome of negotiations. The Spanish government was already tottering in early 1898 and could not risk total concession without promoting its own downfall. On March 31 it ordered the end of the reconcentration policy, promised immediate reforms in Cuba, agreed to an armistice if the rebels made the request, and offered to submit the *Maine* issue to international arbitration. But the Spanish could not condone McKinley's intervention and, all importantly, would *not* grant Cuban independence.

The same day of the Spanish reply, however, Woodford offered encouraging news by notifying McKinley that Spain's stern attitude was softening as fast as was politically possible. "I am told confidentially," Woodford wrote, "that the offer of armistice by the Spanish Government would cause revolution here." Madrid's leaders "are ready to go as far and as fast as they can and still save the dynasty here in Spain. They know that Cuba is lost." He emphasized that "no Spanish ministry would have dared to do one month ago what this ministry has proposed today." Three days later Woodford informed Washington that the pope had persuaded the Madrid government to accept an armistice. "I know that the Queen and her present ministry sincerely desire peace and that the Spanish people desire peace," Woodford declared. "If you can still give me time and reasonable liberty of action I will get for you the peace you desire so much and for which you have labored so hard."

But the counsels of war in the United States were stronger than the plaintiffs for peace, and Spain's only way out seemed to be to secure European assistance in preventing U.S. intervention in Cuba. Failure to satisfy the Washington government's expectation of

Cuban independence would lead to war with the United States; compliance meant upheaval at home. All Old World powers except Britain, which needed the United States as an ally to counter the growing German threat in the Pacific and elsewhere, expressed sympathy with Spain and accused the McKinley administration of intending to seize Spanish holdings in the Western Hemisphere. But the German foreign minister offered the Spanish ambassador a bluntly realistic appraisal of the situation that precluded European involvement. "You are isolated," he declared, "because everybody wants to be pleasant to the United States, or, at any rate, nobody wants to arouse America's anger; the United States is a rich country, against which you simply cannot sustain a war." Finally, on April 6, the ambassadors of six European governments called on McKinley and urged him to stay out of Cuba. Two days afterward the *New York World* characterized the conversation between the president and his guests in these words: "The six ambassadors remarked: 'We hope for humanity's sake you will not go to war.' McKinley replied: 'We hope if we do go to war, you will understand that it is for humanity's sake.'"

Spain's reply to the president's note of late March was unsatisfactory because it did not concede Cuban independence, and on April 11, 1898, McKinley sent Congress a message asking authorization to use force if necessary to stop the war on the island. Two days earlier the Madrid government had granted a further concession by directing the Spanish troop commander in Cuba to permit a unilateral armistice designed to bring peace. Yet such an armistice seemed hardly enough to the White House, which now considered Cuba's freedom a prerequisite to negotiations. Besides, the armistice was conditional on a Spanish decision to resume the war, and the Cuban rebels had not complied with the offer because they considered their demand for independence to be nonnegotiable. McKinley emphasized to Congress that "in the name of humanity, in the name of civilization, in behalf

of endangered American interests which give us the right and the duty to speak and to act, the war in Cuba must stop."

To counteract the "very serious injury to the commerce, trade, and business of our people, and the wanton destruction of property," McKinley asked Congress for authority "to secure a full and final termination of hostilities between the Government of Spain and the people of Cuba." Although he reminded the lawmakers to give "just and careful attention" to Spain's last-hour armistice offer, this lame plea came in the message *after* his request for arms. Given the heated atmosphere in the United States, along with Spain's past performance in failing to deliver promised reforms, most Americans regarded the armistice as another delay tactic while trying to show that they were not warmongers. McKinley had *not* asked Congress to declare war on Spain, they pointed out in drawing a distinction that in practical terms did not exist; he wanted the United States to act "as an *impartial neutral*" in ending the war in Cuba.

Congress soon approved a joint resolution in support of McKinley's request, but not until after a floor debate that took on the air of a circus. A resurgent martial spirit became conspicuously obvious in the great hall when northern congressmen sang "The Battle Hymn of the Republic" and southerners countered with "Dixie." On April 19 Congress passed a joint resolution (requiring a simple majority in each House) by the margins of 42 to 35 in the Senate and 311 to 6 in the House. The measure *directed* (not authorized) the president to use military force in securing Spain's withdrawal from Cuba and guaranteeing the island's independence. Even though no support was evident for recognition of Cuba as a republic, Congress pledged that the United States would not seek its annexation.

The last part of the joint resolution—the promise against annexing Cuba—came through the efforts of Senator Henry Teller of Colorado and seems to have passed unanimously by voice vote. The Teller Amendment proclaimed that "the United States hereby disclaims any disposition or intention to exercise sovereignty, jurisdiction, or control over said Island except for the pacification thereof, and asserts its determination, when that is accomplished, to leave the government and control of the Island to its people." Teller defended his amendment as an effort to ward off expected European charges that the United States had intervened in Cuba "for the purpose of aggrandizement." Yet he carefully added that this restriction relating to Cuba had no bearing on what the United States "may do as to some other islands," which was a thinly veiled reference to its interests in Puerto Rico and the Philippines.

Although the Teller Amendment had the appearance of altruism on the part of the United States, the realization that its sponsor was a well-known expansionist raises serious questions about motive. American sugar growers (primarily Louisiana Democrats) were among the strongest advocates of the measure, because they wanted Cuba to remain outside U.S. tariff walls and thus subject to regulation. Politics was a prime concern, because Teller was a supporter of Bryan, and Bryan's Populist and Democratic followers suspected the McKinley administration of wanting to acquire the island in an effort to protect American investments. Some legislators worried that if the United States took the island, Americans would become responsible for Cuba's debts. Finally, the promise not to annex Cuba had great appeal to racist Americans who opposed the incorporation of nonwhites into their nation. William Graham Sumner of Yale sarcastically pointed out that "the prospect of adding to the present Senate a number of Cuban senators, either native or carpetbag, is one whose terrors it is not necessary to unfold." The Teller Amendment became a convenient shield for numerous groups who opposed Cuba's annexation.

The seemingly narrow support for intervention in the upper chamber was misleading. Many of the thirty-five senators who voted in opposition actually favored intervention:

They did not like the wording of the resolution that supported the independence of Cuba without including recognition of the rebels' republican government. The McKinley administration had insisted, however, that recognition of the rebel regime would severely hamper U.S. military efforts should war develop with Spain. By 3 A.M. of April 20 (the official date remaining the 19th), Congress sent the joint resolution to the White House for the president's signature.

Events now passed quickly toward a declaration of war on Spain. That same day, April 20, 1898, the president approved the congressional resolution and insisted that "the people of Cuba are, and of right ought to be, free and independent." He then issued an ultimatum giving Spain three days to withdraw from the island. The following day word reached Washington that the Spanish government had severed diplomatic relations with the United States. On April 23 President McKinley called for 125,000 volunteers, and two days later he signed the joint resolution. The United States and Spain were at war, effective April 21.

Ideals and reality had again come together in the U.S. decision for war. For many Americans the war with Spain constituted a crusade to free Cuba from Old World oppression; for others the reasons for war were mixed. More than a few agreed with Senator George Hoar of Massachusetts, who later opposed imperialism but in 1898 wrote that "we cannot look idly on while hundreds of thousands of innocent human beings . . . die of hunger close to our door. If there is ever to be a war it should be to prevent such things as that." Protestant religious leaders prepared to convert the island's Catholic population, imperialists dreamed of empire, politicians looked forward to reelection, and business leaders formerly opposed to war now considered the commercial possibilities opened by the imminent end of Spain's colonial system. Whether or not Americans were for empire, they liked the prospect of seeing their flag waving over some tropical shore. Expansionist Senator Albert

Beveridge of Indiana rejoiced that "at last, God's hour has struck. The American people go forth in a warfare holier than liberty—holy as humanity." Irish satirist Finley Peter Dunne used his famous fictional news character Mr. Hennessy to beam forth in Irish brogue: "We're a gr-reat people." To which a fictitious Mr. Dooley agreed: "We ar-re . . . We ar-re that. An' the best iv it is, we know we ar-re."

The Spanish-American War "wasn't much of a war," Roosevelt admitted afterward, "but it was the best war we had." The Spanish were almost as sure they would lose as the Americans were certain they would win. U.S. author Sherwood Anderson remarked that going to war with Spain was "like robbing an old gypsy woman in a vacant lot at night after a fair." Ambassador to England John Hay, soon to become secretary of state, christened it "a splendid little war." Indeed it was—for the United States. Three months of uninterrupted

Map 2
Despite the prevalence of Cuba in America's explanation for war with Spain in 1898, the first battle occurred in the Philippines.

naval and land victories followed as U.S. battleships easily outmatched the antiquated vessels of the Spanish navy. Spanish officers and crew were situated far from their home base and in a state of declining morale, whereas the U.S. Navy was ready and eager, largely due to the determined efforts of Assistant Secretary of the Navy Theodore Roosevelt. The Spanish army in Cuba was larger than the U.S. force, but it was poorly provisioned, exhausted from the long guerrilla war, and cut off from Madrid by the U.S. naval blockade of the island. "We may and must expect a disaster," the Spanish naval commander wrote privately. "But . . . I hold my tongue and go forth resignedly to face the trials which God may be pleased to send me."

The first conflict in the Spanish-American War ironically occurred many miles from Cuba, when Commodore George Dewey engaged a Spanish squadron in the Philippines. The battle's location was a surprise to many, but it is clear now that the navy had earlier made secret contingency plans calling for the United States, in the event of war with Spain, to attack its fleet in Manila Bay. The moment arrived when Roosevelt became acting secretary of the navy during the hectic afternoon of February 25, 1898. He instructed Dewey to move the Asiatic Squadron from Hong Kong to Manila Bay and, when sure war was under way, to launch an offensive in the Philippines. Roosevelt immediately resigned his position to accept a commission in the army and make his mark as a "Rough Rider" at the battle of San Juan Hill, leaving the erroneous impression that he alone had engineered the Manila affair.

Near dawn of May 1, 1898, Dewey's cruisers steamed into Manila Bay and prepared for a battle that quickly took its place in mythology as well as history. His ships merely stayed out of the Spaniards' firing range, methodically and repeatedly circling past the enemy while raking its vessels, until by noon they had destroyed the entire squadron. At little cost Dewey had seized the naval station at Cavite along with Manila Bay, and the war department prepared to send an occupation force to the city of Manila. Dewey eventually encountered difficulties with German warships (more powerful than his) over blockade procedures in the Philippines, but that problem passed when it became evident that the German commander wished not to fight the Americans but to take any spoils upon their withdrawal from the islands. Indeed, the German presence permitted the British commander in those same waters to cultivate, however inadvertently, the Anglo-American rapprochement. In seeking to view the U.S. assault, he had moved his vessels in such a position that they were stationed between those of Germany and those of the United States, thereby giving rise to the legend that the British had warded off a German attack on the U.S. fleet. Dewey could remark after his triumph in Manila: "If I were a religious man, and I hope I am, I should say that the hand of God was in it."

Dewey's victory at Manila Bay revived the expansionists' arguments for Hawaii, which the Senate had shelved the previous March in light of the approaching war with Spain. On June 16, 1897, President McKinley had agreed to a treaty of annexation, and sent it to the Senate that same day. In the meantime the proposal aroused opposition again. Democrats and sugar interests aligned in denouncing the treaty, as did the Japanese government, which argued that U.S. annexation would endanger the rights of Japan's 25,000 nationals on the islands and disrupt Pacific affairs. Roosevelt would not have hesitated. He told Mahan that "if I had my way we would annex those islands tomorrow [and] . . . hoist our flag over the island leaving all details for after action." The Department of State assured Japan that annexation would not infringe upon its rights, but it also informed the U.S. naval commander in Honolulu that if he detected any evidence of Japanese aggression, he was to raise the U.S. flag and proclaim Hawaii a protectorate. Japan withdrew its protest in December 1897. Troubles with Spain again delayed action, leading the Senate to adjourn before deciding on the annexation treaty.

Now, in May 1898, the United States seemed determined to hold the Philippines as the gateway to China, which, in turn, thrust Hawaii into the fore as a vital naval and coaling station en route to Asia. Hawaii would serve as a defensive outpost for the American mainland and as a guardian of U.S. interests in the Pacific and Asia. On May 4, three days after Dewey's triumph, the annexationists introduced a joint resolution in the House that soon received overwhelming approval there and in the Senate. The president signed the bill on July 7, and Hawaii became U.S. territory.

In the meantime U.S. forces had landed on Cuban shores, where they encountered no Spanish opposition and quickly collaborated with the island's insurgents. Their objective was Santiago, where demoralized Spanish forces had prepared to defend themselves against superior firepower. On July 1, about 7000 U.S. troops seized El Caney, garrisoned by 600 Spaniards. That same day, Roosevelt's Rough Riders joined the Ninth Cavalry's black soldiers in outnumbering the Spanish about seven to one and taking San Juan Hill. U.S. casualties resulting from the two battles stood at more than 1500, but they had won control of the high bluffs east and north of Santiago and were in place to begin an artillery barrage on both the city and the Spanish fleet. Santiago and 24,000 Spanish troops surrendered on July 17, 1898.

Treaty of Paris

After U.S. victories at Santiago in Cuba and in Guam, the Philippines, and Puerto Rico, the Spanish ambassador in Paris asked the French Foreign Office to intervene and arrange a peace. Instructions immediately went to the French ambassador in Washington, who signed an armistice for Spain, effective August 12.

The joy of victory was tempered by the perplexing question of what to do with the Philippines. President McKinley recognized Manila's strategic and commercial importance

Theodore Roosevelt and the "Rough Riders"
TR and his companions pose shortly after their victory at San Juan Hill in Cuba. *Library of Congress.*

Commodore George Dewey
Dewey on the bridge of the U.S.S. *Olympia* during the Battle of Manila Bay on May 1, 1898. *Naval Historical Center, Washington, D.C.*

and at first had seemed willing to allow Spain to keep all of the Philippines except for the city. But these intentions had changed during the war. The acquisitions of Hawaii and Guam provided stepping-stones to China, and the Philippines suddenly stood as the doorway into Asia. *All* areas seemed vital to trade. Assistant Secretary of the Treasury Frank Vanderlip voiced the sentiments of Asia enthusiasts when he called the Philippines the "pickets of the Pacific, standing guard at the entrances to trade with the millions of China and Korea, French Indo-China, the Malay Peninsula, and the islands of Indonesia." U.S. business leaders recognized that colonial acquisitions might safeguard economic interests in China, continually threatened by foreign powers. The *New York Journal of Commerce* warned that returning the Philippines "would be an act of inconceivable folly in the face of our imperative future necessities for a basis of naval and military force on the Western shores of the Pacific." McKinley feared that the Filipinos were unfit to govern themselves and that France or Germany would eventually subjugate them. Some time after the war he explained to a group of Methodist clergymen visiting the White House that the Philippines were "a gift from the gods" and that "there was nothing left for us to do but to take them all, and to educate the Filipinos, and uplift and civilize and Christianize them."

When the U.S. peace delegation arrived in Paris for the first session at the Quai D'Orsay Palace on September 29, its membership revealed its purpose: Four of the five men chosen by McKinley were expansionists, and the fifth ultimately became a convert. Three of them were ranking members of the Senate Foreign Relations Committee, which meant that they would also vote on the treaty when it came before the Senate. The delegation was to seek the independence of Cuba, the acquisition of Puerto Rico, and at least the island of Luzon in the Philippines, which was the site of Manila. For almost a month the Spanish and U.S. delegates discussed Cuba's fate. The Spanish actually preferred that it come

Map 3
The realities of war in Cuba were considerably different from the implications contained in Secretary of State Hay's calling it a "splendid little war."

under U.S. ownership because of the likelihood of greater protection for their subjects and property. Although the Americans appeared to stand behind the Teller Amendment for selfless reasons, they also realized that the country owning the island would inherit a debt of $400 million that Spanish officials in Cuba had run up in trying to put down the rebellion.

By late October the United States had decided to take all of the Philippines. Americans on the islands warned that separating Manila from the Philippines was ill-advised and that the islands comprised an integrated economic whole. McKinley had recently returned from the midwestern sector of the United States, where he sensed widespread support for holding on to them. Despite demands for independence made by Filipinos under insurgent leader Emilio Aguinaldo, the United States decided that the rebel government near

Manila was unstable and that continued disorder could attract German involvement. A protectorate was out of the question in view of the difficulties experienced in Samoa with the islands' regime. The war with Spain, McKinley explained, had thrust new responsibilities on the United States, and the Philippines offered a "commercial opportunity to which American statesmanship cannot be indifferent." Through his fictitious Mr. Dooley, Finley Peter Dunne questioned the wisdom of taking the islands, which "not more thin two months since ye learned whether they were islands or canned goods." But Mr. Hennessy expressed growing American sentiment in declaring: "Hang on to thim. What we've got we must hold." Dooley agreed but remarked prophetically: "We've got the Ph'lippeens, Hinnisy; we've got thim the way Casey got the bulldog—be th' teeth."

After more than two months of negotiations, the United States and Spain emerged with the Treaty of Paris in December 1898. The Spanish agreed to assume Cuba's debt and accepted $20 million from the United States for relinquishing "all claim of sovereignty over and title to Cuba," along with the Philippines, Guam, Puerto Rico, "and other islands now under Spanish sovereignty in the West Indies" (Culebra and a few small islands near Puerto Rico plus the Isle of Pines below Cuba). Inhabitants of the transferred areas were assured religious freedom, but the U.S. Congress was to determine their "civil rights and political status." The United States had not guaranteed citizenship; nor had it promised statehood. As a Puerto Rican newspaper later complained, "We are and we are not a foreign country. We are and we are not citizens of the United States. . . . The Consti-

Treaty of Paris of 1899
Secretary of State John Hay signs the ratification of the peace treaty with Spain, while President William McKinley (standing beneath the clock) and others observe. *Library of Congress.*

tution . . . applies to us and does not apply to us." For the first time in its history, the United States had become a colonial power when it acquired the Philippines and Puerto Rico.

Arguments against the treaty began early in 1899. Anti-imperialists in the United States were both angered and saddened by what they regarded as a breakdown of American idealism. The Anti-Imperialist League in Boston considered the acquisition of the Philippines a contradiction in policy because the United States had turned down the annexation of Cuba for humanitarian reasons. Furthermore, Hawaii, Puerto Rico, and Guam seemed acceptable additions because white people on the islands formed a potential political base, whereas the darker skinned Filipinos were primarily Malays whose incorporation begged lasting trouble. New Hampshire's outspoken peace advocate Lucia Mead declared that the American presence did not automatically elevate the status of native inhabitants and therefore remove the stain of imperialism. Any nation that conquers other peoples without assuring their independence was imperialist. The anti-imperialists insisted that Aguinaldo's demands for independence ensured bitter resistance to U.S. rule that would culminate in a jungle war 6000 miles from the United States.

Many opponents of the treaty insisted that absorption of peoples without their consent was a violation of the Declaration of Independence, the U.S. Constitution, and other great republican pronouncements in America's history. Senator George Vest of Missouri sponsored a resolution (which never came to a vote) "that under the Constitution of the United States, no power is given to the Federal Government to acquire territory to be held and governed permanently as colonies." Senator Hoar of the Republican party joined Democrats in proclaiming the unconstitutionality of Old World colonialism "built upon the fundamental idea that the people of immense areas of territory can be held as subjects, never to become citizens." Expansion had turned America into "a cheapjack country, raking after the cart for the leavings of European tyranny." According to another anti-imperialist, "Dewey took Manila with the loss of one man—and all our institutions." And that was not all: U.S. involvement in the Philippines was costly and would lead to international rivalries over Asia. But despite the support of William Jennings Bryan (who had soured on expansionism, even for humanitarian reasons), Andrew Carnegie, Mark Twain, and other notables, the anti-imperialists were unable to muster enough support to reverse recent events.

The imperialists' counterarguments in favor of the treaty were difficult to refute. The McKinley administration received valuable assistance from Roosevelt, Lodge, and numerous businessmen in defending the treaty as a boon to trade and the natural outcome of U.S. superiority. British poet Rudyard Kipling expressed a strong argument for expansion when he penned these lines for *McClure's Magazine* in February 1899:

> Take up the White Man's burden—
>   Ye dare not stoop to less—
> Nor call too loud on Freedom
>   To cloke your weariness.

The United States had seemingly assumed the responsibility of spreading civilization into the "backward" areas of the World. Social Darwinists hailed the fulfillment of their teachings, missionaries planned their strategy for saving the many lost souls, commercial groups looked forward to exploiting the potentially vast China market, and proponents of a larger navy at last saw their aims become possible. The United States, many Americans argued, had to redeem the sacrifice of its soldiers by keeping all the lands their blood had bought. Lest doubt remain, expansionists warned that if the United States did not take the areas, Germany, Japan, or some other power would do so. As for the danger in acquiring distant areas, Senator Beveridge of Indiana dramatically declared that "the ocean does not separate us from the lands of our duty and desire the ocean joins us, a river never to be dredged, a canal never to be repaired." He concluded that "steam joins us, electricity joins us—the very elements are in league with our destiny."

As for the constitutionality of territorial acquisitions, Connecticut Senator Orville Platt advocated a position that later became the essence of U.S. Supreme Court decisions on the matter: In the spirit of Albert Gallatin during the debate over the Louisiana Purchase, Platt declared that the United States as a sovereign nation could incorporate territory and institute the type of government it believed best suited for the people involved. But unlike Madison and Jefferson with their call for an empire of liberty, Platt insisted that the United States had no duties to ensure either citizenship or statehood. Like other imperial nations, it could add dependencies or colonies. The Supreme Court affirmed these principles in a series of *Insular* cases beginning in 1901, when it declared that the Constitution did not necessarily follow the flag—that U.S. citizenship rights did not automatically extend to territorial inhabitants.

After a bitter fight in the Senate, the Treaty of Paris won approval on February 6, 1899, by a scant single vote more than the required two-thirds majority. Just two days before the vote, conflict broke out in the Philippines between Aguinaldo's partisans and U.S. troops, and news of this development probably encouraged support for the treaty as the only alternative to seeing some other power take the islands. Several anti-imperialists became converts at the last moment, perhaps in part because of William Jennings Bryan's argument that prolongation of the war with Spain was out of the question and that the United States could grant independence to the Philippines when emotions cooled.

The Spanish-American War, though short and inexpensive compared to other conflicts, had far-reaching consequences. It climaxed the long, steady decline of Spain's empire and at the same time initiated world recognition of the United States's newly acquired power status. The war's realities became clear in pro-

portion to the growing casualty lists. More than 5000 Americans died—fewer than 400 directly attributable to battle. Most deaths resulted from malaria and yellow fever. Yet the war had redeeming features. Some Americans believed the conflict with Spain laid their Civil War to rest. Massachusetts soldiers en route to Cuba met a joyous reception in Baltimore, which sharply contrasted with the treatment accorded the state's forces in 1861 when they marched through the same city to defend Washington and a mob pelted them with stones. With "Dixie" ringing from the band in 1898, Massachusetts Senator Henry Cabot Lodge wistfully recalled years later that "it was 'roses, roses all the way'—flags, cheers, excited crowds. Tears were in my eyes. I never felt so moved in my life. The war of 1861 was over at last and the great country for which so many died was one again."

War's Aftermath: Implications for Asia

Americans could not enjoy their conquest for long; Filipino rebels and U.S. forces on the islands soon became locked in a vicious jungle combat that lasted three years. The roots of the insurrection actually wound back to the period before the U.S. war with Spain. By the time the Spanish lost Manila to U.S. soldiers in August 1898, the city stood as the only major spot in the islands not yet under rebel control. Aguinaldo, who had led an uprising in 1895 that the Spanish crushed, had believed that his homeland would receive freedom when the United States defeated Spain. His confidence seemed justified. He had returned from exile on board a U.S. ship, and Dewey had urged him to renew the struggle against the Spanish. Indeed, after the revolution had begun anew in February 1899, Congress in Washington presented a resolution for independence that failed by only a slender margin. Aguinaldo and his cohort responded by establishing a government, drawing up a constitution, and proclaiming the new Philippine Republic. Such high expectations met a cold reception in Washington. The McKinley administration's decision to retain the islands had not only strapped them around the U.S. flag, but it left their inhabitants with no rights of citizenship. To put down the ensuing Filipino insurrection, the United States dispatched 70,000 troops to the islands, a force four times larger than that used in Cuba.

The end of the guerrilla war in the Philippines came in July 1902, but only after 200,000 Filipinos and 5000 Americans had died. The United States had sent 175,000 men to the islands and expended $160 million. More than that, both sides had committed atrocities, leaving a bitter taste among Americans that doubtless contributed to the rapid demise of the expansionist spirit. The philosopher William James declared: "Here were the precious beginnings of an indigenous national life, with which . . . it was our first duty to have squared ourselves. . . . We are destroying the lives of these islanders by the thousands, their villages and their cities," he charged. "Could there be a more damning indictment of that whole bloated ideal termed 'modern civilization' than this amounts to?"

The war in the Philippines heightened the ongoing debate over the United States's increasing foreign involvement. Writer Mark Twain cynically suggested that the United States paint black over the white stripes in the American flag and replace the stars with a skull and cross bones. Yale sociologist William Graham Sumner declared with disgust, "We talk of civilizing lower races, but we have never done it yet. We have exterminated them." Perhaps the most biting indictment came from Senator Benjamin Tillman, a South Carolina Democrat, who delighted in seeing northern Republicans squirm over the Philippines: "No Republican leader will now dare to wave the bloody shirt and preach a crusade against the South's treatment of the negro. The North has a bloody shirt of its own. Many thousands of them have been made into shrouds for murdered Filipinos, done to death because they were fighting for liberty." Yet the civil gover-

Philippine Insurrection
U.S. soldiers occupying native huts during the Filipino insurrection of 1899–1902. *Library of Congress.*

nor of the Philippines and later president of the United States, William Howard Taft, urged Americans to focus on long-range objectives. The United States's goal, he insisted, was to "teach those people individual liberty, which shall lift them up to a point of civilization . . . and which shall make them rise to call the name of the United States blessed." The *New York World* moaned over the difficulties in administering "uncivilized" peoples when it addressed these lines to Rudyard Kipling:

> We've taken up the white man's burden
> 　Of ebony and brown;
> Now will you kindly tell us, Rudyard,
> 　How we may put it down?

The United States found that the acceptance of international responsibilities made it nearly impossible to lay them down. During the war it had established control over Hawaii, Guam, the Philippines, and Puerto Rico, and in mid-January of 1899 the U.S. Navy occupied Wake Island in the Pacific and proclaimed it U.S. territory. In December of that year Britain and Germany signed a treaty in Washington conceding to the United States the

Samoan island of Tutuila—home of the valuable harbor of Pago Pago—along with nearby islands known as American Samoa. The following year the native chiefs on Tutuila formally ceded their island to the United States, and four years later, in 1904, the string of small Manua Islands did the same. Expansion seemed to breed expansion, the anti-imperialists heatedly charged.

In retrospect most of the areas acquired by the United States took on the shape of a crudely shaped arrow pointing to China. The opportunities for trade with that massive land of countless peoples, according to numerous observers, were virtually endless. But Americans had long exaggerated the commercial importance of the Celestial Kingdom: By the late 1890s the China market consumed only about 1 percent of their total exports. Determined Americans believed, however, that the volume of exchange would grow in an atmosphere of equal opportunity encouraged by their own paternal interest in the Chinese people. Japan's victory in the Sino-Japanese War of 1894–1895 had demonstrated the weakness of China's Manchu dynasty, which in turn led to further outside encroachments upon its sovereignty. Spheres of influence, long-term leases, tariff controls, transportation and communication rights—all were poorly disguised imperialist measures by European nations that permitted inroads into the Chinese mainland and caused deep concern among U.S. commercial and missionary groups. Shortly after the Sino-Japanese War, Russia, Germany, Britain, France, and Japan exacted railroad and commercial concessions in China. For good reason, Americans worried that their path to the Orient lay cluttered with other countries' entrenched interests.

The United States's active involvement in China largely originated in Britain's efforts to establish an Open Door policy. Twice in less than a year's time the British had recommended a joint venture aimed at guaranteeing equal trade opportunities in China, only to have the United States turn down both proposals as a violation of its traditional isola-

tionism. But in 1899 a British visitor to Asia and member of Parliament, Lord Charles Beresford, aroused even greater U.S. interest in China through his book *The Breakup of China* and his speeches in the United States, which warned of Russian encroachments and called for the Open Door. In the meantime U.S. merchants and missionaries put pressure on the state department to adopt an active China policy. Then, during the summer of that year, a private British citizen working for China's Customs Service, Alfred Hippisley, discussed the matter with his long-time friend in the United States, William Rockhill, who was an adviser on Asia and himself a friend of Secretary of State John Hay. Hippisley did not speak in any official capacity for his government in London, but he knew of its continued interest in China. Hippisley emphasized the commercial importance of the Open Door to *both* Britain and the United States, and he warned that continued outside penetration of China would undermine the Customs Service and lead to the partitioning of the huge country. The United States should take the initiative in establishing international respect for the Open Door. Anti-British sentiment in the United States, Hippisley realized, was still too strong to permit the London government to lead the way.

Hippisley and Rockhill worked with Hay in composing a memorandum that expressed the London government's wishes, and that document became the basis of U.S. policy toward China. On September 6, 1899, Hay sent the statement in the form of a diplomatic note to the governments in Berlin, London, and St. Petersburg, and in November he sent it to Paris, Rome, and Tokyo. Patterned after the most-favored-nation principles of the earlier part of the century, Hay's circular note called for equal commercial opportunity within the various powers' spheres of influence and took a stand against outside interference with China's tariff controls. Hay did not condemn spheres of influence, nor did he attempt to safeguard China's territorial integrity. The success of his Open Door efforts depended on whether the

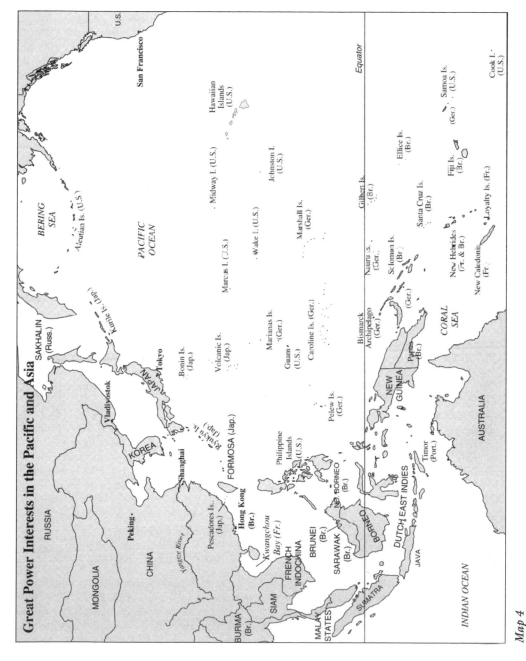

Great Power Interests in the Pacific and Asia

RUSSIA

MONGOLIA

CHINA

Peking •

SAKHALIN
(Russ.)

Vladivostok

BERING
SEA

Aleutian Is. (U.S)

U.S.

San Francisco

Yangtze River

Shanghai •

KOREA

JAPAN

Tokyo

PACIFIC
OCEAN

BURMA
(Br.)

SIAM

FRENCH
INDOCHINA

Pescadores Is.
(Jap.)

Hong Kong
(Br.)

Kwangchou
Bay (Fr.)

FORMOSA (Jap.)

Ryūkyū Is.
(Jap.)

Kurile Is. (Jap.)

Bonin Is.
(Jap.)

Volcanic Is.
(Jap.)

Marianas Is.
(Ger.)

Marcus I. (U.S.)

Wake I. (U.S.)

Midway I. (U.S.)

Johnston I.
(U.S.)

Hawaiian
Islands
(U.S.)

MALAY
STATES

BRUNEI
(Br.)

SARAWAK
(Br.)

NO. BORNEO
(Br.)

BORNEO

SUMATRA

JAVA

DUTCH EAST INDIES

Philippine
Islands
(U.S.)

Guam
(U.S.)

Pelew Is.
(Ger.)

Caroline Is. (Ger.)

Marshall Is.
(Ger.)

Timor
(Port.)

NEW
GUINEA

Papua
(Br.)

Bismarck
Archipelago
(Ger.)

Nauru Is.
(Ger.)

Solomon Is.
(Br.)

Gilbert Is.
(Br.)

Ellice Is.
(Br.)

AUSTRALIA

CORAL
SEA

New Hebrides
(Fr. & Br.)

New Caledonia
(Fr.)

Santa Cruz Is.
(Br.)

Loyalty Is. (Fr.)

Fiji Is.
(Br.)

Samoa Is.
(Ger.) (U.S.)

Cook I.
(U.S.)

INDIAN OCEAN

Equator

Map 4

By the end of the nineteenth century, numerous countries (including the United States) had made claims to parts of Asia and the Pacific.

interested powers would either publicly deny imperialist designs in China or admit to them by remaining silent. All governments sent replies to Washington, but most of them were noncommittal: They conditioned their adherence to the Open Door on the acceptance of its principles by the other parties. When Russia eventually indicated unwillingness to comply, its stand released the others from the pledge. Hay, however, simply ignored the Russian response and announced in March 1900 that the powers' *unanimous* decision to respect the Open Door had made the policy statement "final and definitive."

It would be erroneous to dismiss the United States's Open Door policy as ineffective. Admittedly, the United States lacked the military or naval might to enforce equal commercial opportunity in China, but it also recognized that the balance of power in that section of the world was so tenuous that the mere involvement of another country in Asian affairs could turn that balance either way. No one wanted war; yet no one could be sure of the other's intentions. As with the most-favored-nation approach, the United States gained equal commercial privileges in China without having to resort to military measures.

China's problems did not end with Hay's Open Door pronouncements: Continued and deepening foreign involvement ultimately led to an outbreak of fierce nationalist resistance against outsiders that became known as the Boxer Rebellion. The fast-declining Manchu dynasty, which had been in power since the mid-1600s and would finally collapse in 1911, was incapable of defending its homeland. In 1900 a secret society known as *I-ho-ch'üan* ("Righteous and Harmonious Fists"), or the Boxers, armed themselves with spears and swords and led an insurrection against foreigners in China. Hundreds of missionaries and Christian converts fell in the bloody rebellion, as the Boxers, allied with imperial soldiers and apparently encouraged by the Manchu government, laid siege on the foreigners now isolated in the legation section of Peking.

The United States decided to act when the other powers prepared to send a punitive force that would likely culminate in the permanent partition of China. To save Peking the McKinley administration in August 1900 directed 2500 soldiers from the Philippines to China, where they joined 15,000 troops from Britain, France, Germany, Japan, and Russia. Meanwhile, Hay circulated a second note affirming the Open Door policy, but with a different emphasis. Whereas the first note of September 1899 had advocated only equal commercial opportunity, the second in July 1900 urged respect for that nation's "territorial and administrative entity" and called on the interested powers to "safeguard for the world the principle of equal and impartial trade with all parts of the Chinese Empire." Hay thus widened the parameters of the Open Door to include more than trade and more than the areas in China that had come under outside control: His policy now incorporated respect for China's national independence. He did not seek a reply this time; this was to be *America's* policy—with or without the other countries' acquiescence.

Paradoxically, each foreign government deepened its involvement in China while affirming agreement with Hay's proclamation—largely to deter the others from expanding their holdings. The Open Door pronouncement of 1900 did not save China: The essential restraint was mutual distrust among the interested powers that held them all at bay. Professed adherence to the Open Door seemed wiser than to risk a world war brought on by its rivals' expansionist activities.

The U.S. policy toward China perhaps lightened the impact of the Boxer Rebellion on the growth of foreign influence in the country, but serious doubt persists about Hay's philanthropic claim that the United States sought only an "abstention from plunder" through the Open Door statement. The international expeditionary force put down the insurrection at the cost of numerous lives, and China received a huge reparations bill of about $333 million. But China had been wracked with outside intervention and internal disorder for so long that it could not pay that exorbitant amount. The United States was to receive $25 million, although it kept only $7 million to cover private damage claims and canceled the remainder. This decision bought considerable favor among the Chinese because their government used the unexpended fund to facilitate the education of their students in the United States. Meanwhile, outside intervention continued in China. In fact, in late 1900 Hay acceded to the U.S. Navy's wishes and requested a piece of territory and a naval base at Samsah Bay, located within the Japanese sphere of influence. Peking's leaders were in no position to refuse, but the Japanese government quietly yet firmly called Hay's attention to the Open Door principles. The United States dropped its request.

The United States's Open Door policy went through several shades of meaning in succeeding years, but it was above all an extension of the most-favored-nation approach of the early 1800s: a guarantee of equal commercial opportunity in China. Despite the apparently selfless aims of the first Open Door declaration of 1899, the truth is that it was largely an effort to preserve U.S. commercial interests in China. The military weakness of the United States prohibited any consideration of a stronger stand. The following year Hay's second note announced opposition to violations of China's territorial integrity, but a *statement* of policy was again the most the United States could offer. Unable to enforce the Open Door, the Washington government issued idealistic pronouncements that nonetheless affirmed its deepening realistic interests in China and the rest of Asia.

Expansion in Perspective

The United States had become an integral part of the world community by the turn of the twentieth century. Though not yet a first-rate power, it had made great strides toward that status because of the international events of the latter 1890s. The war with Spain and the liberation of Cuba, the annexation of Caribbean and Pacific islands, the colonization of the Philippines, the growing rapprochement with Britain, the Open Door in China—all entailed foreign involvements that would doubtless expand in scope. In 1899 the United States took another step toward deeper foreign involvement by participating in the First International Peace Conference at The Hague in the Netherlands. Called by the Russian czar to encourage disarmament, the meeting brought together twenty-six nations. The goal was to draw up rules of war and devise steps toward peaceful settlement of international disputes through the newly established Permanent Court of Arbitration.

European powers meanwhile worried that the United States might ally with Britain. Anglo-American rapprochement had become more of a reality after the Venezuelan episode and the rise of Germany. In addition, the British had been partial to the United States during its war with Spain, and the Americans had reciprocated by favoring Britain in its ongoing war with the Boers of South Africa. Social, political, and economic similarities underscored the growing Atlantic understanding, as did personal familial ties between the countries and shared racial views. The *Times* of London proclaimed that blood ties held the nations together, while a leading British journalist declared that his compatriots "should never stand idly by and see a hundred millions of people who speak English trampled on by people who speak Russian or French or German."

McKinley's solid reelection victory in 1900, with war hero Theodore Roosevelt at his side as vice president, assured the world that Americans were beginning to realize that their security rested, at least in part, on international events. Furthermore, victory over Spain had given Americans their first taste of empire, and the sample proved highly pleasant to their senses. They did not yet understand that following the initial thrust of power came the aftermath of responsibility.

Selected Readings

Anderson, Stuart. *Race and Rapprochement: Anglo-Saxonism and Anglo-American Relations, 1895–1904.* 1981.

Beale, Howard K. *Theodore Roosevelt and the Rise of America to World Power.* 1956.

Beisner, Robert L. *From the Old Diplomacy to the New, 1865–1900.* 2nd ed., 1986.

———. *Twelve against Empire: The Anti-Imperialists, 1898–1900.* 1968.

Braeman, John. *Albert J. Beveridge: American Nationalist.* 1971.

Brands, H. W. *Bound to Empire: The United States and the Philippines.* 1992.

———. *T.R. The Last Romantic.* 1997.

Campbell, Alexander E. *Great Britain and the United States, 1895–1903.* 1960.

Campbell, Charles S. *From Revolution to Rapprochement: The United States and Great Britain, 1783–1900.* 1974.

———. *Special Business Interests and the Open Door Policy.* 1951.

———. *The Transformation of American Foreign Relations, 1865–1900.* 1976.

Clymer, Kenton J. *Protestant Missionaries in the Philippines, 1898–1916: An Inquiry into the American Colonial Mentality.* 1986.

Cooper, John M., Jr. *The Warrior and the Priest: Woodrow Wilson and Theodore Roosevelt.* 1983.

Cosmas, Graham A. *An Army for Empire: The United States Army in the Spanish-American War.* 1971.

Craig, John M. "Lucia True Ames Mead: American Publicist for Peace and Internationalism." In Edward P. Crapol, ed., *Women and American Foreign Policy: Lobbyists, Critics, and Insiders,* 67–90. 2nd ed., 1992.

Davis, Calvin D. *The United States and the First Hague Peace Conference.* 1962.

Dulles, Foster Rhea. *Prelude to World Power: 1860–1900.* 1965.

Dunne, Finley Peter. *Mr. Dooley in Peace and War.* 1899.

Faulkner, Harold U. *Politics, Reform and Expansion, 1890–1900.* 1959.

Freidel, Frank. *The Splendid Little War.* 1958.

Fry, Joseph A. *John Tyler Morgan and the Search for Southern Autonomy.* 1992.

Gould, Lewis L. *The Presidency of William McKinley.* 1980.

———. *The Spanish-American War and President McKinley.* 1982.

Grenville, John A. S., and Young, George B. *Politics, Strategy, and American Diplomacy.* 1966.

Healy, David F. *Drive to Hegemony: The United States in the Caribbean, 1898–1917.* 1988.

———. *U.S. Expansionism: The Imperialist Urge in the 1890s.* 1970.

Hofstadter, Richard. "Manifest Destiny and the Philippines," in Daniel Aaron, ed., *America in Crisis,* 173–200. 1952.

Hoganson, Kristin L. *Fighting for American Manhood: How Gender Politics Provoked the Spanish-American and Philippine-American Wars.* 1998.

Hunt, Michael H. *The Making of a Special Relationship: The U.S. and China to 1914.* 1983.

Johnson, Robert E. *Far China Station: The U.S. Navy in Asian Waters, 1800–1898.* 1979.

Karnow, Stanley. *In Our Image: America's Empire in the Philippines.* 1989.

Kennan, George F. *American Diplomacy.* Expanded ed., 1984. Originally published as *American Diplomacy, 1900–1950.* 1951.

LaFeber, Walter. *The New Empire: An Interpretation of American Expansion, 1860–1898.* 1963.

Langley, Lester D. *The Cuban Policy of the United States: A Brief History.* 1968.

Leech, Margaret. *In the Days of McKinley.* 1959.

Linderman, Gerald F. *The Mirror of War: American Society and the Spanish-American War.* 1974.

Linn, Brian M. *The U.S. Army and Counterinsurgency in the Philippine War. 1899–1902.* 1989.

May, Ernest R. *Imperial Democracy: The Emergence of America as a Great Power.* 1961.

McCormick, Thomas J. *China Market: America's Quest for Informal Empire, 1893–1901.* 1967.

Miller, Stuart C. *"Benevolent Assimilation": The American Conquest of the Philippines, 1899–1903.* 1982.

Morgan, H. Wayne. *America's Road to Empire: The War with Spain and Overseas Expansion.* 1965.

———. *From Hayes to McKinley: National Party Politics, 1877–1896.* 1969.

———. *William McKinley and His America.* 1963.

Offner, John L. *An Unwanted War: The Diplomacy of the United States and Spain Over Cuba, 1895–1898.* 1992.

Papachristou, Judith. "American Women and Foreign Policy, 1898–1905: Exploring Gender in Diplomatic History," *Diplomatic History* 14 (1990): 493–509.

Pérez, Louis A., Jr. *Cuba and the United States.* 1997.

———. *The War of 1898: The United States and Cuba in History and Historiography.* 1998.

Perkins, Bradford. *The Great Rapprochement: England and the United States, 1895–1914.* 1968.

Perkins, Dexter. *The Monroe Doctrine, 1867–1907.* 1937.

Pratt, Julius W. *Expansionists of 1898.* 1936.

Rickover, Hyman G. *How the Battleship Maine Was Destroyed.* 1976.

Ruiz, Ramón. *Cuba: The Making of a Revolution.* 1968.

Schirmer, Daniel B. *Republic or Empire: American Resistance to the Philippine War.* 1972.

Seager, Robert, II. *Alfred Thayer Mahan.* 1977.

Smith, Ephraim K. "'A Question from Which We Could Not Escape': William McKinley and the Decision to Acquire the Philippine Islands," *Diplomatic History* 9 (1985): 363–75.

Spector, Ronald. *Admiral of the New Empire: The Life and Career of George Dewey.* 1974.

Sprout, Harold, and Sprout, Margaret. *The Rise of American Naval Power, 1776–1918.* 1944.

Tompkins, E. Berkeley. *Anti-Imperialism in the United States.* 1970.

Trask, David F. *The War with Spain in 1898.* 1981.

Weems, John E. *The Fate of the Maine.* 1992.

Welch, Richard. *Response to Imperialism: The United States and the Philippine-American War, 1899–1902.* 1979.

Williams, William A. *The Roots of the Modern American Empire.* 1969.

———. *The Tragedy of American Diplomacy.* 1959, 1962.

Young, Marilyn B. *The Rhetoric of Empire.* 1968.

CHAPTER 2

Theodore Roosevelt and the Search for World Order, 1900–1913

The United States at the Threshold of World Power

The United States and Theodore Roosevelt arrived on the international stage at the same time, a development that was not entirely coincidental. The United States was not a world power by the opening of the twentieth century, but with Roosevelt's lead it soon became the leading determinant in Caribbean matters, a force worth considering in East Asia, and more than an idle observer of European events. Meanwhile, Roosevelt promoted the growing public interest in foreign affairs by using the White House as a "bully pulpit" to dominate the U.S. scene as few leaders have done in the nation's history. He realized that world events were inseparable from the country's security. He also knew that the reform spirit of the early 1900s—Progressivism—had permeated foreign as well as domestic affairs. In foreign policy, Roosevelt first sought stability in the Western Hemisphere before working toward a world order that rested on a balance of power.

Roosevelt's background was rich and cosmopolitan. A Harvard graduate, he became police commissioner of New York City, assistant secretary of the navy, hero of the Spanish-American War, governor of New York, vice president, and, upon the assassination of McKinley in the autumn of 1901, president—an office to which he was elected in his own right three years later. Despite his active public career he found time for world travel, big game hunting in Africa, the life of a cowboy in the rugged Black Hills of South Dakota, and a continuing interest in scholarship that found him reading extensively and writing a dozen books. Roosevelt moved easily among wealthy families and intellectuals on both sides of the Atlantic, which facilitated the informal and personal brand of diplomacy he practiced while in the White House. A man of forceful personality, he relished any form of competition that resulted in efficiency and progress. Roosevelt was "pure act," Henry Adams once remarked. "Teddy," as Ohio Republican Mark Hanna sarcastically called him (behind his back), excitedly pounded his fist into his cupped left hand for emphasis and regularly appeared in cartoons highlighting his round wire-rimmed glasses, full-bristled mustache, and ever-prominent teeth. Roosevelt was a master of the strenuous life. When not behind his desk, he could be in the boxing ring, on the tennis court, demonstrating jujitsu, or on his way to Rock Creek Park, followed by panting and stiffly dressed foreign dignitaries whom he had invited for a hike.

Theodore Roosevelt
An ideal candidate for caricature. *Library of Congress.*

Roosevelt urged Americans to support their country's involvement in international affairs. The world, he believed, was divided between the civilized states and the uncivilized or backward peoples. Before becoming president, he had made his message clear to a large and cheering audience: "Exactly as it is the duty of a civilized power scrupulously to respect the rights of weaker civilized powers . . . so it is its duty to put down savagery and barbarism." As president, he emphasized to Congress in 1902 that "the increasing interdependence and complexity of international political and economic relations render it incumbent on all civilized and orderly powers to insist on the proper policing of the world." The United States, he declared through a West African proverb, needed to "speak softly and carry a big stick." An advocate of Darwinian principles, he adopted a patrician attitude toward the world's unfortunate people and in the spirit of *noblesse oblige* called on

Americans to join other Anglo-Saxons in taking up the "white man's burden" and spreading enlightenment, culture, liberty, and order.

In truth, the first decade or so of the new century stands as the era of Theodore Roosevelt. His realistic diplomacy was not new to the republic, but his verve and vitality surely marked a welcome change from the generally tired presidential administrations of the past four decades. Rarely has a White House occupant displayed such flair, exuberance, knowledge, and wit. At the heart of his spirited showmanship lay a primary concern for U.S. interests that comprised a blend of economic and strategic considerations. While president, he used almost any method short of war as an instrument of policy aimed at guaranteeing national security. "When I left the presidency," Roosevelt proudly recorded in his *Autobiography,* "I finished seven and a half years of administration, during which not one shot had been fired against a foreign foe. We were at absolute peace, and there was no nation in the world . . . whom we had wronged, or from whom we had anything to fear."

A blatant embellishment perhaps, but Roosevelt did pursue certain principles that kept the nation out of foreign entanglements conducive to war. He never pushed beyond his country's capabilities in attempting to safeguard his country's prestige. He did not believe in idle threats, because failure to deliver when challenged would destroy America's effectiveness abroad. He perceived that the United States had to adopt a foreign policy that extended only as far as the nation's military arm would permit. He wrote his close friend William Howard Taft in 1910, "I utterly disbelieve in the policy of bluff, in national and international no less than in private affairs, or in any violation of the old frontier maxim, 'Never draw unless you mean to shoot.'" To implant U.S. power and prestige throughout the world, Roosevelt sought to expand the navy. When he became president, the navy numbered less than twenty major ships, some still under construction. By 1907 it had grown to rank second in the world to

Theodore Roosevelt Wielding the "Big Stick"
All over the world, the president attempted to "speak softly and carry a big stick." *Tyler Dennett,* John Hay: From Poetry to Politics, *New York: Dodd, Mead, 1933, between pp. 394 and 395.*

Britain, and despite Germany's rapidly escalating program of naval expansion, the U.S. Navy remained in the top three (with Germany as third ranking power) on the eve of the Great War in 1914.

The United States was fortunate during the first decade of the twentieth century in that while growing in strength, it was partly isolated and largely unthreatened by outside forces. Both inside and outside the Western Hemisphere, Americans could indulge in an active foreign policy through the show of force rather than the use of force. And Roosevelt could rightfully boast afterward that during his administration the United States mediated to end one war and helped to prevent another while itself remaining at peace.

Panama Canal

Building an isthmian canal occupied much of Roosevelt's attention during his first years in office, because the Spanish-American War had revealed a security problem by demonstrating the difficulty of moving naval vessels between the Atlantic and the Pacific. The U.S. battleship *Oregon,* for example, had hurriedly left San Francisco for the Caribbean during the first

signs of trouble in 1898, but it had to steam around South America and through the treacherous Strait of Magellan before completing the arduous 14,000-mile, sixty-eight-day voyage. President McKinley reiterated the importance of a canal in his annual message to Congress in December of that year. With the annexation of Hawaii, he declared, the building of such a waterway under U.S. control had become vital to the national interest. A French corporation, the New Panama Canal Company, had taken over the bankrupted de Lesseps business along with its equipment and its Panama concessions granted by Colombia, and it now sought to sell them to the United States—for the exorbitant price of $109 million.

Immediately after the negotiations ending the Spanish-American War, McKinley instructed Secretary of State John Hay to talk with the British ambassador in Washington, Sir Julian Pauncefote, about revising the prohibitive joint construction and control provisions of the Clayton-Bulwer Treaty of 1850. The two men reached an agreement in February 1900 that allowed the United States to build and administer a canal but not to fortify it. The Hay-Pauncefote Treaty then fell into the political swirls of that year's presidential campaign. Democrats denounced the pact as a capitulation to the British, and Irish-Americans opposed it as part of the detested rapprochement with Britain. Roosevelt, at that time the highly influential governor of New York, emphasized that U.S. control of the canal was vital to the Monroe Doctrine and to the nation's security. He told the well-known naval theorist Alfred T. Mahan, "I do not see why we should dig the canal if we are not to fortify it." It was better "to have no canal at all than not give us the power to control it in time of war." Roosevelt urged his friend Senator Henry Cabot Lodge and other Republicans to insist on full U.S. control. The treaty proceedings collapsed when the London government rejected Senate amendments that would have achieved this objective for the United States.

Shortly after Roosevelt became president in September 1901, he called for new negotiations with Britain on the subject. Hay, invited to remain as secretary of state, worked closely with Lodge, and President Roosevelt publicly emphasized the necessity of establishing U.S. control of the canal. The strategy worked. In November Hay signed a second agreement with Pauncefote that permitted the United States to build the canal and, by tacit understanding, to fortify it as well. The only stipulation in the second Hay-Pauncefote Treaty was that the United States had to grant equal access to any other nation's commercial or war vessels. The British actually had little choice in signing the agreement. The outbreak of the Boer War in South Africa the previous month had found them without an ally and in need of better relations with the United States. Indeed, the United States had purposely observed a benevolent neutrality toward Britain during the war (despite the U.S. public's support for the Boers) that reciprocated its neutrality during the United States's war with Spain. The result was this important Anglo-American pact, which the Senate overwhelmingly approved in December. The second Hay-Pauncefote Treaty released the United States from the Clayton-Bulwer agreement and further stimulated the Anglo-American rapprochement.

While Hay and Pauncefote were negotiating their treaty, the Walker Isthmian Canal Commission, established during the McKinley administration, completed its two-year study of the most feasible canal route through Central America. The commission concluded, albeit with reservations, that the best route lay through Nicaragua. Engineers on the commission thought Nicaragua's rivers too shallow for a major canal, and yet that route was less expensive than one through Panama, partly because it could be a sea-level canal (whereas Panama's could not) but primarily because the New Panama Canal Company was asking too much money for the transit rights acquired from Colombia.

The Walker Commission's findings convinced the House of Representatives, making the Senate the focal point of the debate. In January 1902 the House overwhelmingly approved the Hepburn bill, which stipulated that the projected isthmian canal cut through Nicaragua. Yet final approval depended on the Senate, and there the New Panama Canal Company tried to counter the House decision by lowering its demands to $40 million, the estimated value of the company's holdings. This change, urged by Philippe Bunau-Varilla, former chief mining engineer for de Lesseps's operation and now a major stockholder in the New Panama Canal Company, would make the total expenditure for the Panama project considerably less than that required for Nicaragua. In an effort to induce the Senate to reject the House decision, the French company hired the prestigious New York attorney William Nelson Cromwell to begin a lobbying campaign in that body for Panama. Meanwhile, Bunau-Varilla worked to persuade Roosevelt, members of the Walker Commission, and leading Republican senators to change the route from Nicaragua to Panama.

As if by design, factors beyond human control also played a part in the Senate's deliberations. A volcano on the Caribbean island of Martinique had erupted, destroying a city and killing 30,000 people. Less than two weeks later Mt. Momotombo in Nicaragua rumbled menacingly and threatened to do the same. Bunau-Varilla explained how he seized the moment by hurriedly visiting stamp dealers in Washington:

> I was lucky enough to find there ninety stamps, that is, one for every Senator, showing a beautiful volcano belching forth in magnificent eruption. . . .
>
> I hastened to paste my precious postage stamps on sheets of paper. . . . Below the stamps were written the following words, which told the whole story: "An official witness of the volcanic activity of Nicaragua."

Bunau-Varilla then placed one stamp showing Mt. Momotombo on each senator's desk in the chamber.

Thus, for several reasons Congress switched its favor to Panama. Indeed, Roosevelt and Hay believed that they had an arrangement with Colombia's octogenarian scholar and dictator, José Marroquín, by which his government approved U.S. acquisition of the rights and property holdings from the New Panama Canal Company—a considerable portion of whose stock belonged to Colombia itself. The White House had therefore exerted great pressure on Congress to change the canal site to Panama. The Senate relented. It cast support for Panama in the form of an amendment to the Hepburn bill, and when the lower chamber agreed to accept the change, the bill became law with Roosevelt's signature in June 1902. Under the Spooner Amendment the president was to negotiate with Colombia for transit rights through Panama; if unable to secure an arrangement "within a reasonable time and upon reasonable terms," he could turn to Nicaragua.

Once Panama became the designated route, the last obstacle was Colombia. Hay opened negotiations with the Colombian chargé d'affaires in Washington, Tomás Herrán, who unexpectedly demanded higher yearly lease rates than those offered by the United States. When Hay irately warned that the United States would deal with Nicaragua, Herrán capitulated. In January 1903 he signed a treaty awarding the United States control of a six-mile-wide strip of land connecting the two oceans, for one hundred years, which actually was in perpetuity (forever) because it was renewable solely by the United States. For these concessions Colombia was to receive $10 million at the outset and annual payments of $250,000 to begin in nine years, the time calculated for building the canal. Less than a week after Herrán signed the treaty, he received a telegram from Bogotá directing him to delay treaty talks until new instructions arrived. But Herrán made no effort to cancel the treaty he had signed; nor did he inform Hay of the importance of the new instructions. The U.S. Senate acted quickly, approving the Hay-Herrán Treaty in March.

Colombia, however, rejected the pact. The Bogotá government, as legal sovereign over Panama, denounced the lease in perpetuity as unconstitutional and disapproved of other provisions affecting the canal zone as a violation of Colombian sovereignty. The prime reason was financial, however: Marroquín wanted more money to replenish a treasury depleted by a lengthy civil war. Colombia sought $10 million from the New Panama Canal Company's passing its concessions to the United States and eventually demanded that the United States raise the initial payment to $15 million.

The president would have none of this. Colombia's abrupt reversal of policy drew a furious reaction from Roosevelt, who thought Marroquín honor bound to comply. The president angrily told Hay that "those contemptible little creatures in Bogotá ought to understand how much they are jeopardizing things and imperilling their own future." Negotiating with Colombia was like trying to "nail currant jelly to the wall." Marroquín and his cohort were "greedy little anthropoids" who stood before the world as guilty of blackmail and robbery.

And yet, despite Roosevelt's tirade over Marroquín's behavior, Colombia had a legitimate case. Panama was a Colombian colony, and Bogotá's leaders were particularly irritated that the Hay-Herrán Treaty barred them from future negotiations over their own territory. Furthermore, the money securing the concessions could pass to the French firm without giving Colombia a share. And, as was the case with the United States, no treaty became official until ratified by the home government. Stall tactics seemed the only way out. The concessions to the French company were due to expire in October 1904, and the Bogotá government could then sell them directly to the United States—perhaps for $40 million. The congress in Bogotá, called together for the first time in years by a regime that needed popular support, denounced the Hay-Herrán Treaty, and in August 1903 the Colombian senate unanimously turned it down.

The Colombian action did not derail the effort of leaders in Washington; they became convinced that the Panamanians themselves might resolve the question by winning their independence. The decision in Bogotá had not surprised Roosevelt; Cromwell had talked with him the previous June and then followed the meeting with an assertion in the *New York World* that if Colombia rejected the pact, Panama would move for independence and grant canal rights to the United States. Roosevelt, the story claimed, supported this approach. Since becoming Colombia's possession, the Panamanians had had a long history of insurrections—over fifty of them, Roosevelt calculated—about one a year. "You don't have to foment a revolution," he flippantly remarked. "All you have to do is take your foot off and one will occur." If questions lingered over the justification for earlier revolts, none could arise now. The Hay-Herrán Treaty had conjured up the economic benefits of a canal through Panama, denied only because of Colombia's greed. After Colombia voted down the Hay-Herrán Treaty, Panamanian and U.S. inhabitants of the small province gathered privately in August. They must gain independence and negotiate another canal treaty—*before* the United States turned to Nicaragua.

Although many details remain unknown, the ensuing Panama revolution was clearly the result of a conspiracy. Numerous private discussions involving Bunau-Varilla and others took place at the Waldorf-Astoria Hotel in New York City. Bunau-Varilla, in fact, referred to room 1162 as "the cradle of the Panama Republic," because while his wife listened and sewed a flag for the new country, he pledged $100,000 for the revolution and worked with its eventual leader, Dr. Manuel Amador Guerrero, who had arrived on the scene to help formulate plans for a declaration of independence and a constitution. Though a physician, Guerrero fitted his new position well: He had interests in the Panama Railroad, which belonged to the New Panama Canal Company. The conspirators soon organized a small "patriot" force in Panama that even included 500 members of the Colombian occupation army—all suitably bribed to join the revolution.

Still, however, Colombian loyalists could easily crush the revolt unless the United States acted quickly and favorably toward the rebels. The key to U.S. policy was the Treaty of 1846 with Colombia (then New Granada), because by it the United States had guaranteed Panama's neutrality. Six times before 1903 U.S. soldiers had entered the isthmian area to restore order during insurrections—four times at Colombia's request. Now, in a strange twist that could develop only in truth rather than fiction, the Americans could argue that the threat to Panama came from *Colombia*. No one during the 1840s could have envisioned the United States protecting Panama from its proprietor; but the treaty, strictly speaking, did not prohibit such an act.

Suspicions linger over the question of U.S. complicity in the shadowy events leading to the revolution in early November 1903. One fact seems certain, however: Bunau-Varilla, in talking with Roosevelt, Hay, and other notables in Washington, could not have expected an *unfavorable* reaction to news of an impending insurrection. In October Bunau-Varilla asked the president whether he would act on

Colombia's behalf when the revolution began. "I cannot say that," Roosevelt cagily replied. "All I can say is that Colombia by her action has forfeited any claim upon the U.S. and I have no use for a government that would do what that government has done." At that, the Frenchman arose, thanked Roosevelt for his time, and left the White House, clearly satisfied that the United States would not interfere. A week after this meeting, Bunau-Varilla learned from Hay that U.S. warships were en route to Central America. Estimating their time of arrival in the city of Colón on the Caribbean side of Panama, he cabled his contacts there that the first ship, the U.S.S. *Nashville,* should be in those waters on November 2.

Thus, it was not by coincidence that the revolt took place in the early evening of the following day, November 3. When the Colombian government sent 400 additional soldiers to Colón on the Atlantic side of the isthmus, the New Panama Canal Company, whose railroad was necessary for transporting the men to Panama City, managed not to have any cars available. Commander John Hubbard of the *Nashville* then dispatched U.S. sailors to the scene, and the Colombian officer in charge, tricked into separating from his troops, accepted a bribe from the rebels' leaders and withdrew from the isthmus. Orders had reached Hubbard that day from the state department in Washington: "In the interests of peace, make every effort to prevent [Colombian] Government troops at Colón from proceeding to Panama."

The Panamanian revolution was a huge success. At the cost of only two lives (an innocent bystander and a donkey), the rebels that same day placed the Colombian general under arrest, paid the bribed Colombian officials and soldiers in a formal ceremony in Panama City, and established a provisional government. "Quiet prevails," the U.S. consul assured Washington. Manuel Amador, as planned in the New York hotel room, became president of the new republic and in a roaring speech attributed his people's freedom to the White

House. "President Roosevelt has made good. . . . Long live the Republic of Panama! Long live President Roosevelt!"

The president, however, repeatedly denied complicity and, strictly speaking, was probably telling the truth. In diplomacy, however, the line between appearances and truth is often so thin as to be indistinguishable. On several counts, the U.S. role *appeared* vital to Panama's move for independence. Three days after the revolution Roosevelt extended *de facto* recognition to Panama upon learning of the overthrow of Colombian rule only an hour before. The Washington government immediately stationed U.S. soldiers in Panama City to prevent attempts by Colombia to regain control. It seems indisputable that the Roosevelt administration was aware of the imminence of revolution and skillfully took advantage of a propitious situation. Bunau-Varilla assured suspicious inquirers that through the newspapers he had followed the *Nashville*'s route and correctly predicted its arrival time in Colón. Bunau-Varilla is "a very able fellow," Roosevelt asserted, "and it was his business to find out what he thought our Government would do. I have no doubt that he was able to make a very accurate guess, and to advise his people accordingly. In fact," the president added, "he would have been a very dull man had he been unable to make such a guess."

Questions also remain about the negotiations following the revolution. After the new republic received U.S. recognition, it appointed Bunau-Varilla as "Envoy Extraordinary and Minister Plenipotentiary" to initiate treaty discussions aimed at granting rights to build, fortify, and operate a transoceanic canal. In the meantime, the Panama government sent three emissaries—Amador and two others—to join him in Washington to complete the treaty arrangements. It also forwarded instructions forbidding Bunau-Varilla from agreeing to any terms that endangered Panama's sovereignty. Bunau-Varilla was *not* to draft any treaty without the assistance of the three emissaries: "You will proceed in everything strictly in agreement with them."

But neither the instructions nor the three Panamanians arrived in time. After Hay presented a treaty proposal much like the Hay-Herrán Treaty, Bunau-Varilla took it to his hotel room, where he worked feverishly all night and day in revising the terms to make them more attractive to the U.S. Senate. Amador and his two companions had arrived in New York City and would be in Washington the next day. Just hours before their arrival in the capital, Bunau-Varilla and Hay signed the treaty.

The Hay–Bunau-Varilla Treaty of November 18, 1903, was far more generous than the Hay-Herrán pact. The new agreement guaranteed the United States a ten-mile-wide strip of land through Panama, which became the canal zone. Although Panama retained civil control over Colón and Panama City, the United States received extremely broad powers in the zone connecting the two cities. As would have been the case with Colombia, Panama was to receive $10 million outright and $250,000 a year beginning nine years after the exchange of ratifications. Then, in the most important alterations that Bunau-Varilla inserted, the U.S. government secured *in perpetuity* "all the rights, power and authority within the Zone . . . which the United States would possess and exercise if it were the sovereign of the territory." Article I of the treaty stipulated that "the United States guarantees and will maintain the independence of the Republic of Panama." In a move strikingly similar to the status accorded Cuba under the Platt Amendment of 1901 (discussed later), the United States established a protectorate over Panama.

Six hours after Bunau-Varilla signed the treaty, he excitedly greeted the Panamanians at the train station in Washington with what he termed "the happy news": "The Republic of Panama is henceforth under the protection of the United States. I have just signed the Canal Treaty." Amador nearly fainted, and one of his companions angrily socked Bunau-Varilla in the nose.

Hay brought great pressure on the Senate for hurried approval: The Panamanian representatives, he feared, might bear treaty stipulations less favorable than those allowed by Bunau-Varilla. Senate Democrats wanted to know more about suspected White House involvement in the Panamanian uprising, but the president, despite the suspicions aroused by the *Nashville*'s convenient actions, staunchly proclaimed that "no one connected with this Government had any part in preparing, inciting, or encouraging the late revolution." It was difficult to counter this statement without documentation, and on February 23, 1904, the Senate easily approved the treaty.

Bunau-Varilla also proved instrumental in closing the deal. To ensure the treaty's passage in Panama, he sent a 370-word cable warning its new leaders that failure to approve the pact would cause Roosevelt to put an end to U.S. protection and either seize the canal zone or sign a canal treaty with Nicaragua. The Panama government immediately approved the Hay–Bunau-Varilla Treaty. What happened to the $40 million in U.S. money? The banking magnate J. P. Morgan had become financial agent for the company's holdings, which meant that he engineered the transfer of the entire treasury of the New Panama Canal Company to a list of stockholders never made public. Bunau-Varilla, however, held a large share of that stock and received an undetermined but assuredly fair share of that sum.

The United States's behavior during the Panamanian affair drew a mixed public reaction. Democrats and many others in the country denounced the president, Europeans self-righteously complained of the United States's notable lack of morality, and in succeeding years Latin Americans intensified their opposition to the Panamanian episode as the United States deepened its Caribbean involvement. If Roosevelt's supporters acted for partisan reasons, they defended their policies on a realistic ground: For security's sake, the United States *needed* a canal.

Roosevelt never shied away from upholding his actions during the Panama manipulations. To Congress in December 1903, he declared that the United States had a "mandate from

Elihu Root
Secretary of war and later secretary of state who played an integral role in Theodore Roosevelt's foreign policy. *Oscar King Davis,* William Howard Taft: The Man of the Hour, *Philadelphia: P. W. Ziegler Co., 1908, p. 20.*

civilization" to build an isthmian canal. In his *Autobiography,* he boasted that building the Panama Canal was "by far the most important action I took in foreign affairs." All of his administration's policies, he asserted, had been "carried out in accordance with the highest, finest and nicest standards of public and governmental ethics." Yet skepticism existed even among his cabinet members. In one heated meeting the president turned to Attorney General Philander C. Knox and declared that "it will be just as well for you to give us a formal legal opinion sustaining my action in this whole matter." Knox shrewdly replied: "No, Mr. President, if I were you I would not have any taint of legality about it." On another occasion Roosevelt plodded through an elaborate defense of his behavior and then turned sharply to Secretary of War Elihu Root for his reaction. The elderly man wryly commented:

"You have shown that you were accused of seduction and you have conclusively proved that you were guilty of rape."

The Panama Canal story was still not complete. Several years after ratification of the Hay–Bunau-Varilla Treaty, as the passageway neared the last stages of construction, Roosevelt gave an intriguing speech to a stadium audience in 1911 at the University of California: "I am interested in the Panama Canal because I started it," he proudly asserted. "If I had followed traditional conservative methods I would have submitted a dignified State paper of probably 200 pages to Congress and the debates on it would have been going on yet; but I took the Canal Zone and let Congress debate; and while the debate goes on the Canal does also." The stupendous engineering feat, led by George Goethals, became possible only after Dr. William Gorgas brought under control the two greatest obstacles to de Lesseps's effort: yellow fever and malaria. The Panama Canal, fifty miles long and consisting of a series of locks, opened for use in August 1914—on the eve of the Great War. It came into existence at a cost since 1904 of $352 million (four times that of the Suez Canal) and over 5600 deaths. Seven years later, after Roosevelt had died (ironically, having never seen the completed project), the United States, partly out of guilt but also because of the discovery of oil in Colombia, sent that government an additional $25 million ("canalimony," according to one critic) as recompense for its loss of Panama. In the meantime the United States expanded its involvement in Caribbean affairs in an effort to safeguard the canal from foreign encroachments.

Roosevelt Corollary

As U.S. interest in an isthmian canal had heightened after the Spanish-American War, so did the very thought of its construction underline Cuba's importance by the turn of the twentieth century. The Teller Amendment of 1898 had prohibited its annexation, but the island's location made its independence

Panama Canal under Construction
This picture demonstrates the intricate and complex process required to link the
Atlantic and Pacific Oceans. *Library of Congress.*

Panama Canal after Completion
U.S.S. *Ohio* passing Cucaracha Slide in 1915, shortly after the opening of the
Panama Canal in August 1914. *Library of Congress.*

dangerous because of possible absorption by some other power. President McKinley had warned Congress in December 1899 that Americans had "a grave responsibility for the future good government of Cuba" and that the island had to "be bound to us." The Filipino insurrection raised fears in Washington that the same could happen in Cuba. To prevent this unhappy situation, Secretary of War Root appointed General Leonard Wood as military governor of Cuba. Wood was to rid the island of yellow fever and to institute an educational program, a public works system, and an orderly government. His efforts were largely unsuccessful, but they led to a more direct U.S. involvement in Cuban affairs.

By early 1901 Root had worked with the chair of the Senate Foreign Relations Committee, Orville Platt, in drafting a congressional bill establishing a U.S. protectorate over Cuba until that island's government drew up a constitution containing certain stipulations. According to the Platt Amendment, Cuba was nominally free but could not sign a treaty or borrow money without approval from Washington. In the event of internal disorder, the United States could intervene. Finally, Cuba granted the United States "lands necessary for coaling or naval stations." The Platt Amendment became an annex to the new Cuban constitution of 1901 only under Wood's pressure and after Root's assurances that the United States would not intervene unless the Cuban government was in danger. U.S. insistence on incorporating the amendment into the Cuban constitution was attributable to Washington's concern that the Cubans could amend their constitution unilaterally; the amendment required U.S. approval before they could make changes. In May 1903 the United States and Cuba formalized the amendment into a treaty, and later that year the U.S. Navy built a base at Guantánamo Bay, located near Santiago on the southeastern side of the island. The United States was to hold this base in perpetuity.

The Platt Amendment aroused bitter opposition both inside and outside the United States. While U.S. anti-imperialists resurrected their arguments against foreign involvement, many Cubans complained that the United States had merely taken the place of their former Spanish oppressor. President Roosevelt characterized the opposition groups in the United States as "unhung traitors[,] . . . liars, slanderers and scandal mongers," and Root unconvincingly tried to establish a difference between "interventionism" and "interference" with the island's domestic affairs. U.S. intervention, he argued, would occur only to safeguard Cuba's government and preserve the island's independence—*not* to permit interference in internal matters. The United States meanwhile signed the Reciprocity Treaty with Cuba in 1902, which further tied the two peoples together by lowering duties on the island's exports to America.

In the aftermath of the Platt Amendment the United States confirmed the Cuban leaders' fears by expanding its economic and military involvement on the island. U.S. investments and trade more than quadrupled from the mid-1890s to 1913. Meanwhile, U.S. Marines repeatedly intervened because of the island's internal troubles, and in one period, from 1906 to 1909, they actually assumed control of the government. Roosevelt rigidly opposed annexation but feared that continued domestic unrest would force the United States into such a step. He could not understand why the Cubans were unable to "behave themselves." He finally turned to his friend and now secretary of war, William Howard Taft, to resolve the island's problems. As former civil governor of the Philippines, Taft recognized the importance of settling Cuba's troubles before a full-scale insurrection broke out. He served as Cuba's provisional governor for a month and upon his return home in October 1906, he left behind more than 5000 U.S. soldiers who were prepared to implement the reforms called for earlier by General Wood.

The Platt Amendment established a precedent for similar U.S. actions in other parts of the hemisphere and appears to have become

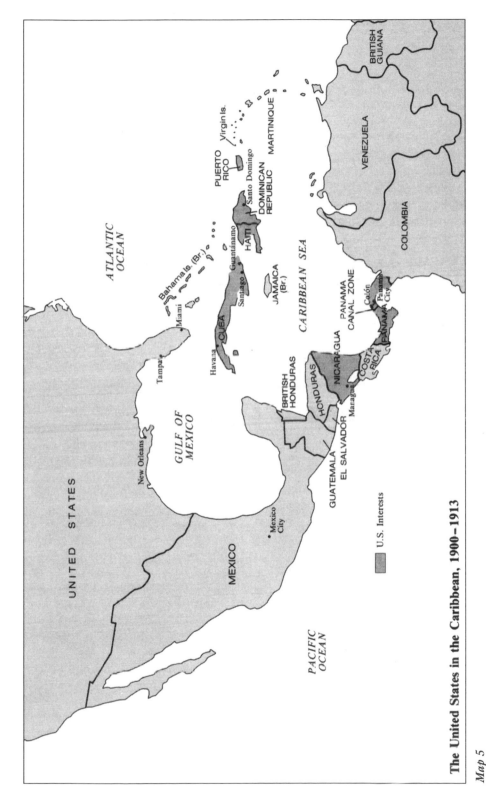

The United States in the Caribbean, 1900–1913

Map 5

In the early twentieth century, the United States announced the Roosevelt Corollary of the Monroe Doctrine and sought to "police" Central America and the Caribbean.

39

the basis of a new Latin American policy by the United States. As early as Roosevelt's first months in office, he seemed to be moving toward a major pronouncement on Latin American affairs intended to discourage Old World involvement. Negotiations over Panama and Cuba weighed heavily on his mind when, in his first annual message to Congress in December 1901, he termed the Monroe Doctrine "a guarantee of the commercial independence of the Americas." On another occasion he declared that as Voltaire had said of God, "if the Monroe Doctrine did not already exist, it would be necessary forthwith to create it." Yet Roosevelt admitted to limitations on U.S. actions. After Germany gave notice in 1901 of its intent to dispatch a punitive expedition to Venezuela, he took a stand similar to that of Secretary of State Seward during the European intervention in Mexico of the 1860s. Roosevelt asserted that the United States would not guarantee any hemispheric nation against punitive action by a non-American power unless that action involved the acquisition of territory. Roosevelt appeared to be searching for a middle ground between U.S. intervention and outright annexation. Like a watchdog, he explained, the United States would oversee Latin America's relations with the Old World.

The first test of Roosevelt's Latin American policy came in Venezuela, where Germany and Britain sought reimbursement of debts long overdue. German intentions in the hemisphere worried Americans more than did those of the British, largely because of the recent Anglo-American rapprochement but also because of recent instances of German expansionism. Kaiser Wilhelm II had tried to improve relations with the United States, but with little success. The Germans called for arbitration of the debt question by The Hague Court, but Venezuelan dictator Cipriano Castro refused the proposal. Germany and Britain then notified Washington that they were preparing to use force to collect their money, but at the same time they assured the president of having no territorial aims. Meeting no

opposition from the Roosevelt administration, they issued an ultimatum to Venezuela in December 1902 and proceeded to set up a "pacific blockade" of its main ports. But as tensions mounted, the British shelled two forts and landed troops, and the Germans sank two of Venezuela's gunboats. When U.S. popular reaction stiffened with Germany's additional bombardment of Venezuelan territory, Roosevelt insisted on arbitration. Germany and Britain agreed to his proposal but maintained the blockade. Castro, called by Roosevelt an "unspeakable villainous little monkey," had brought on a deeper European involvement in the hemisphere, provoked a challenge to the credibility of the Monroe Doctrine, and forced the United States to intervene.

British interest in maintaining the rapprochement explains that nation's retreat, but the reasons for Germany's sudden change of policy were not clear in 1902. Part of the explanation lies in the kaiser's decision to send a new ambassador to Washington. This ambassador, Hermann Speck von Sternburg, had befriended Roosevelt sometime before and now worked to defuse the dangerous situation. But there is more to the story.

In a 1916 reprinting of William R. Thayer's biography of John Hay, the author included a copy of a letter he had recently received from Roosevelt asserting that he had played a major but hidden role in resolving the Venezuelan crisis. As president in 1902, Roosevelt explained in the letter to Thayer, he became alarmed that Germany might establish a base in Venezuela that would endanger an isthmian canal and other U.S. interests. The Berlin government had at first refused the call for arbitration, according to Roosevelt, and its assurances were not convincing that any seizures of territory would be temporary. Roosevelt thereupon ordered Admiral George Dewey moved near Puerto Rico and readied for action. If Germany did not agree to arbitration within ten days, Roosevelt pointedly told von Sternburg, Dewey would go to Venezuela. The German ambassador expressed "very grave concern," Roosevelt recalled, and warned that such U.S. action would have "serious consequences." When a week passed with no reply from Berlin, Roosevelt informed the ambassador of a change in plans: Dewey would leave twenty-four hours earlier than previously announced. Germany agreed to arbitration.

Controversy exists over Roosevelt's account of his actions during the Venezuelan crisis of 1902–1903. Critics have argued that he either fabricated or embellished the story, and yet no one can deny that the actions outlined in the letter were well within Roosevelt's character and temperament. The nation's interests in the hemisphere were involved: Roosevelt recognized that a European power entrenched so close to Panama posed a potential threat to the canal as well as to the entire Caribbean. Germany did not want a confrontation with the United States, and chances are that Roosevelt may have hurried the kaiser into a decision he would have made anyway. But there is little reason to doubt the essence of Roosevelt's testimony.

In February 1903 Germany and Britain lifted the Venezuelan blockade and turned over the claims issue to the Permanent Court of Arbitration at The Hague. The British government had recognized its lack of wisdom in following Germany's lead in Venezuela, and Prime Minister Arthur Balfour had attempted to calm Anglophobes in the United States by renouncing territorial aims in the New World and recognizing the Monroe Doctrine as part of international law. The Hague Court meanwhile decided in favor of Germany and Britain, which drew a concerned reaction in the Western Hemisphere. The Department of State feared that the decision would encourage the use of force in international disputes and increase the likelihood of further European intervention in Latin America.

Seeing the danger, the Argentine minister of foreign affairs, Luis Drago, tried to reduce the chances of foreign intervention in the hemisphere. He had opposed the use of force in collecting debts from Venezuela, and in 1902 he notified the Roosevelt administration that the loss of investments was a risk business leaders took in any transactions, including those outside their country. The Drago Doctrine, as his argument became known, was incorporated into international law at the Second Hague Conference of 1907. The United States approved but added the stipulation that intervention was acceptable only if the debtor nation either rejected arbitration or refused to abide by the arbitrator's decision.

A second debt problem in the hemisphere, this one in the Dominican Republic, led the Roosevelt administration to issue a formal statement on its Latin American policy. The Dominican government owed nearly $32 million to a host of countries, including Germany and the United States (a company in New York holding U.S. and British funds). Over the years the Dominicans had repeatedly assured creditors of remuneration from customs collections, but with no results. Internal disorder had rocked the Dominican Republic since the 1890s, and though some Americans pondered annexation, Roosevelt privately declared, "I have about the same desire to annex it as a gorged boa constrictor might have to swallow a porcupine wrong-end to." Both American and European business leaders exerted pressure on the U.S. government to act, and although Roosevelt hesitated, he recognized that the Venezuelan arbitration award had established a precedent for the forceful collection of debts.

Roosevelt prepared to deal with the Dominican situation through a policy later known as the Roosevelt Corollary of the Monroe Doctrine. In May 1904 he indicated the direction of his thinking in a letter to Secretary of War Root, when he pledged U.S. friendship to any nation that acted responsibly in international affairs. He went on to advise Congress in December that the United States had to keep order in the hemisphere. "Chronic wrongdoing may in America, as elsewhere, ultimately require intervention by some civilized nation, and in the Western Hemisphere the adherence of the United

States to the Monroe Doctrine may force the United States, however reluctantly, in flagrant cases of such wrongdoing or impotence, to the exercise of an international police power."

Later, to the Senate, Roosevelt elaborated on his congressional message. Under the Monroe Doctrine, the United States could not allow any European country to "seize and permanently occupy the territory of one of these republics; and yet such seizure of territory, disguised or undisguised, may eventually offer the only way in which the power in question can collect any debts, unless there is interference on the part of the United States." The president used the situation in the Dominican Republic as the occasion to announce the Roosevelt Corollary, a unilateral statement asserting U.S. police control over the hemisphere.

In December 1904 the United States opened negotiations with the Dominican Republic to resolve the debts controversy. The resulting agreement authorized the New York company to administer the country's customs offices at two ports until the claimants received monetary satisfaction. European creditors immediately objected, arousing concern in the Roosevelt administration that its action would set off a race for the remainder of the offices. The Dominican government, as a result of the urgings of the U.S. minister in that country, asked the United States to take over all customs offices and allocate the funds in such a way as to meet the republic's financial obligations at home and abroad. Democrats and others in the United States questioned the constitutionality of such a measure, but Roosevelt sent the proposed agreement to the Senate in January 1905. Under the arrangement, he was to appoint an American to handle receivership duties. Whereas 45 percent of collected funds would go to the Dominicans, most of the remainder would go into a trust fund in a New York bank, reserved for the republic's creditors. Should the Senate oppose the agreement, the balance of the customs revenues would go to the Dominican government as well. The

Senate, however, adjourned in March without approving the pact.

Roosevelt was furious and in April 1905 negotiated an executive agreement with the Dominicans that did not require Senate approval and rested on a *modus vivendi* (temporary arrangement pending final settlement). Although the Democrats denounced his action as unconstitutional, the executive agreement remained in effect until February 1907, when the Senate finally caved in and approved a treaty granting legal standing to the American whom Roosevelt had already sent as customs collector. The Dominicans' creditors scaled down their demands, and the government secured a new bond in the United States to cover the debt and establish a public works program on the island. Root, by that time secretary of state, defended the pact in the Senate by declaring that the Panama Canal, then under construction, placed Latin American countries "in the front yard of the United States" and forced it "to police the surrounding premises" in the interest of hemispheric stability and trade.

The Dominican Republic approached economic and political soundness during the following years, but renewed insurrections soon forced the United States to broaden its involvement in the island's affairs. In late 1911 the president of the Dominican Republic was assassinated, and the next year rebels from neighboring Haiti raided and pillaged at will. Customs offices under U.S. control had to shut their doors, and in September 1912 a U.S. commission and several hundred marines arrived to restore order. By December the U.S. force had achieved some stability, but sporadic outbreaks of violence caused the Washington government to continue military occupation of the island into the early 1920s.

President Taft followed Roosevelt's example in using the Monroe Doctrine as the basis of his Latin American policy when during his administration of 1909 through 1913 the United States deepened its economic influence in Nicaragua through "dollar diplomacy." Defined by Taft as "substituting dollars for bullets," the term was new, but the idea behind it was not. Foreign policy and commercial interests had long been supportive of each other, but in this period the Washington government worked ever more closely with the nation's financial and industrial concerns in seeking out new foreign markets. Taft expressed dissatisfaction with the military thrust of Roosevelt's Caribbean policy, recognizing that such a stance would hurt the U.S. reputation throughout Latin America and provide substance for his administration's critics. He insisted that dollar diplomacy "appeals alike . . . to idealistic humanitarian sentiments, to the dictates of sound policy and strategy, and to legitimate commercial aims." During his presidency, U.S. investments and foreign policy became virtually inseparable as the economic and strategic objectives of business and government leaders often ran parallel.

When in late 1911 the Nicaraguan government threatened to cancel mine concessions to the United States and executed two Americans for aiding an ongoing revolution, the Taft administration sent marines to help bring about a new regime. The Senate in Washington opposed a treaty with Nicaragua that, like a pact negotiated with Honduras that same year (also defeated by the Senate), would have authorized a U.S. loan and placed the United States in charge of customs. Such a treaty, Democratic senators argued, would lead to an unwarrantable and dangerous extension of U.S. power. In addition, many senators feared that the president had assumed excessive authority in making treaties. But the state department became party to an agreement involving Nicaragua and various New York banks, which established a receivership similar to that set up for the Dominican Republic. Another revolution in Nicaragua in late 1912 prompted the Washington government to send out more than 2000 marines, who put down the insurrection, forced the rebel leaders out of the country, and stationed a small legation guard in the capital of Managua that remained off and on until 1933.

Although the United States had intended its Nicaraguan involvement to safeguard the areas surrounding the Panama Canal, its policies left a long-standing feeling of distrust throughout Latin America.

The Alaskan Boundary Dispute

U.S. diplomatic activities were not confined to the southern half of the hemisphere: The discovery of gold in the Klondike River area of northwest Canada in 1896 set off a boundary dispute between Alaska and British Columbia that reached dangerous proportions during Roosevelt's presidency. The best route into the area lay through the panhandle of southern Alaska, and the Canadians found a way to claim that narrow strip of territory. They suddenly argued that the original line in the Anglo-Russian Treaty of 1825, which ran thirty miles inland from the Pacific and became the basis of the U.S. purchase of Alaska more than forty years later, did not follow the twisting contours of the coast but moved due south. If that claim were correct, the United States would lose commercial control over the Alaskan interior, because Canada would own the headwaters of the larger coves and harbors cutting into North America.

Controversy intensified during the summer of 1898. In June the Canadians claimed the largest bay in the region, the Lynn Canal, which flowed by three settlements and connected with harbors (Pyramid, Dyea, and Skagway) providing access to the gold fields and the sea. The Canadian government was willing to negotiate, but only if the Americans first accepted its claim to Pyramid Harbor. Secretary of State Hay bitterly condemned the claim: "It is as if a kidnapper, stealing one of your children, should say that his conduct was more than fair, it was even generous, because he left you two."

Hay proposed the establishment of a joint commission to settle the Alaskan boundary dispute, but both nations soon became preoccupied with other more pressing matters: the United States with its war with Spain, and

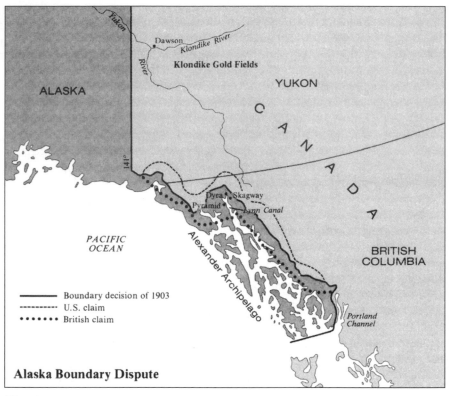

Alaska Boundary Dispute

———— Boundary decision of 1903
----------- U.S. claim
•••••• British claim

Map 6
President Theodore Roosevelt resorted to a joint commission in settling the dispute,
but only after he had used various pressures to ensure a favorable outcome.

Britain with its growing problems with the Boers in South Africa. In the meantime the McKinley administration quieted the Alaskan situation by agreeing to Canada's temporary use of the land at the opening of the Lynn Canal. When Hay recommended the commission approach to Roosevelt shortly after his arrival in the White House, the new president expressed concern. He feared that arbitration would lead to a compromise whereby the United States lost territory that the Canadians had no right to have. In March 1902, however, Roosevelt felt compelled to act because rumors had spread that gold might also be discovered in the disputed territory and force another crisis. To Hay in July, he termed the Canadians' claim "an outrage pure and simple. . . . To pay them anything where they are entitled to nothing would in a case

like this come dangerously near blackmail." As tensions mounted in the disputed area, Roosevelt dispatched 800 additional troops to keep order.

Late that same year the Canadians saw no support coming from England and retreated from their demands, indicating that their only concern now was to save face. If the United States agreed to arbitration, they would accept a decision roughly corresponding with the U.S. position. Canada had no choice. British leaders in London were worried that the Alaskan issue might endanger the Anglo-American rapprochement. British foreign secretary Lord Henry Lansdowne expressed the general feeling among his countrymen: "America seems to be our only friend just now, and it would be unfortunate to quarrel with her."

In late January 1903 Britain agreed to Hay's joint-commission proposal. The resulting Convention of 1903 called for "six impartial jurists," three American and three British to comprise an Alaskan Boundary Tribunal that would gather in London and settle the matter by majority vote. Little imagination was needed to predict the outcome. "In this case," Hay confidently remarked, "it is impossible that we should lose, and not at all impossible that a majority should give a verdict in our favor." To the commission Roosevelt appointed his friend Senator Henry Cabot Lodge of Massachusetts, Elihu Root, then the president's secretary of war, and a former senator from Washington, George Turner. None of the men fitted the category of "impartial jurists," but appointing them was politically important because their support for the U.S. boundary claims was well known. The British king appointed a commission consisting of two Canadians and the lord chief justice of England, Richard E. W. Alverstone. Both Alverstone and his Canadian companions understood that the maintenance of good relations with the United States was more important than a breakdown over Alaska's boundary. But they also knew that failure to gain something in the proceedings would pit them against an angry populace at home.

In late 1903 the Alaskan Boundary Tribunal met in London. After weeks of bitter discussions the two Canadians refused to compromise, as did the three Americans, and the outcome rested with England's Lord Alverstone. Roosevelt meanwhile exerted pressure by letting it be known that a decision against the United States would lead to U.S. military occupation of the disputed territory while the army itself drew the boundary. The London government decided to accept the U.S. interpretation of the line. Despite Canada's threats of secession, Alverstone voted with the three Americans in October 1903. Although he succeeded in reducing the width of the coastal award, he secured for Canada only two of four small islands in dispute. The United States had a clear victory. Alverstone insisted that he had decided solely on the basis of "the law and the evidence," and yet if so, the law and the evidence conveniently fitted a decision dictated by his country's need to maintain the rapprochement with the United States.

East Asia

U.S. attention had in the meantime turned toward East Asia, where growing problems would lead to the Russo-Japanese War of 1904–1905. China remained a major concern, because outside powers had expanded their claims in defiance of the Open Door declarations of 1899 and 1900. Russia had joined European powers in obstructing Japan's attempt in 1895 to secure a lease on the Liaotung Peninsula in southern Manchuria and had refused to withdraw its soldiers from Manchuria after the Boxer Rebellion of 1900. Indeed, the Russians were now building a railway through northern Manchuria and into Vladivostok, which was their major port in north Pacific waters. They had also won the right to construct and control another railroad connecting Harbin with Port Arthur in the south, where they would soon have a naval base. These advances into Manchuria threatened Japan's interests both there and in Korea, the latter traditionally regarded as "a dagger pointed at the heart of Japan." The Japanese had gradually extended control over Korea since the end of the Sino-Japanese War in 1895, and they had negotiated an alliance with Britain in 1902 admitting to each party's special interests in China. What was more important, in exchange for Japan's support of Britain in Europe, the British recognized Japan's political, commercial, and industrial concerns in Korea. The Anglo-Japanese Alliance offered Japan some guarantee that war with Russia would not necessarily lead to French intervention on behalf of their Russian ally. After Japan failed to negotiate a favorable settlement with Russia over Manchuria and Korea, the Japanese navy launched a surprise attack on Port Arthur in February 1904 that wiped out Russia's Pacific fleet. Two days later Japan declared war.

Americans initially joined the Roosevelt administration in praising the Japanese in their war with Russia. "Was not the way the Japs began the fight bully?" remarked Root. Roosevelt wrote his son less than a week after the Port Arthur attack that "I was thoroughly pleased with the Japanese victory for Japan is playing our game" in trying to halt the Russians. The Washington government of course maintained official neutrality, but it favored Japan out of expectations that its leaders would respect the Open Door in China. The president's distaste for Russian leadership and supposed backwardness was as well known as his favor for Japan's industriousness and efficiency. He was determined that France, Russia's ally, and Germany, which supported Russia in Asia, would not deny Japan the spoils of war. Roosevelt realized that the outcome of the Russo-Japanese War would determine the balance of power in that part of the world and hence affect U.S. interests—particularly in China and the Philippines.

Russia was irate over the U.S. reaction to the war. The Russians were unaware of the change in attitude in the United States brought by their expansionist policies in East Asia and by their harsh treatment of Jews and political opponents at home. Roosevelt privately considered Czar Nicholas II "a preposterous little creature," yet dangerous because he could close Manchuria to the outside world. Japan, Roosevelt believed, might preserve the Open Door and safeguard U.S. interests both in China and the Philippines. Gradually, however, this hope disappeared as Japan unexpectedly and overwhelmingly won the war by 1905 and soon posed a new danger on the Pacific horizon.

The Russo-Japanese War of 1904–1905 proved enormously expensive, even to the victorious Japanese—so costly that the Japanese minister in Washington, Kogoro Takahira, privately asked Roosevelt in the spring of 1905 to intervene and bring the warring powers to the peace table. Russia could not sustain the war because of growing internal problems that would culminate in revolution during the au-

tumn of that same year and because of pressure from France. The Paris government was more concerned about a concurrent crisis with Germany over Morocco than about Russia's plight in East Asia. Roosevelt's condition for intervention was a guarantee for the Open Door policy, which Japan gave but Russia did not. Roosevelt recognized the important role thrust upon him: If he played the balance-of-power game adeptly, he might keep the advantage from shifting too far toward Tokyo and thereby preserve U.S. interests in that part of the world.

Peace talks began on a U.S. naval base in Portsmouth, New Hampshire, during August 1905, and only after considerable difficulty did the peace-making teams manage a settlement. Japan demanded that Russia pull out of Manchuria, give up the Liaotung Peninsula and the South Manchurian Railroad from Harbin to Port Arthur, recognize Japanese hegemony in Korea and on Sakhalin Island off the north Chinese mainland, and pay $600 million in reparations. The discussions stalemated when Russia refused to relinquish Sakhalin and turned down the reparations demand. Fearing that Nicholas would rather resume the war than yield to Japan, Roosevelt sought a compromise calling for Russia to receive the northern half of Sakhalin and Japan the rest and for the two powers to agree "in principle" to a reparations bill. After a carefully crafted discussion led by the U.S. ambassador to St. Petersburg, George Meyer, the czar accepted the first part of the plan, but he still refused to pay war damages. Japan eventually gave up that demand. Resumption of the war to obtain reparations, it realized, would cancel their worth, cause permanent injury at home, and therefore cost more than peace. Japan also discerned a change in U.S. public opinion. Whether owing to the demands and seeming arrogance of the Japanese delegates at Portsmouth or to the Russians' repeated warnings that Japan was the real threat to peace, the Americans' ardor for the Japanese had noticeably cooled.

The antagonists finally came to terms with the Treaty of Portsmouth on September 5, 1905. Japan regained what it had lost in the war with China in 1894–1895: the Liaotung Peninsula, which was the site of Port Arthur, Dairen, and the South Manchurian Railroad. Russia also recognized Japan's special interests in Korea and south Sakhalin. Manchuria returned to China's civil jurisdiction, and all Japanese and Russian soldiers were to withdraw except those needed to guard the railroad. Russia remained a prominent force in the region by retaining the northern half of Sakhalin and the Chinese Eastern Railway in upper Manchuria, but Japan emerged from the Russo-Japanese War as the dominant power in East Asia.

The results of the Portsmouth Conference were mixed. U.S. relations hardened with both Russia and Japan as those countries searched for a scapegoat to explain their failures in the war. Whereas the Russians claimed they could have won the war had the Americans not intervened, the Japanese people, heavily burdened by taxation, blamed their leaders in Tokyo along with the U.S. government for failing to win an indemnity and other concessions. Violent antigovernment and anti-American demonstrations broke out in Tokyo and other cities. In February 1906 the United States protested commercial discrimination in Japanese-controlled areas in Manchuria; the Japanese, it became clear, had no intentions of respecting the Open Door. While Japanese-American relations rapidly deteriorated, Roosevelt accepted the Nobel Peace Prize in 1906 for his efforts at Portsmouth (and in settling the Moroccan dispute, as discussed later).

Not all results of the Russo-Japanese War were self-evident: Another outgrowth of the conflict was the Taft-Katsura "agreed memorandum" of late July 1905. This secret document tied the United States to Japan (and with Britain too, because of its alignment with Japan in 1902). A year earlier Roosevelt had agreed to recognize Japan's special interests in Korea, and in midsummer of the following year Secretary of War Taft, en route to the Philippines, repeated the assurance in a conversation in Tokyo with Prime Minister Taro Katsura. Japan's ongoing conquests in the war with Russia during the spring of 1905 had caused concern in Washington over the Philippines, and through this informal understanding the United States agreed to drop claims to Korea in exchange for Japan's renunciation of "any aggressive designs whatever" on the islands. Roosevelt approved the memorandum, and within a year the United States closed its legation at Seoul and conducted Korean business through the government in Tokyo.

The Taft-Katsura understanding signaled a retreat on the Open Door, but the United States had no choice. Root explained years afterward that "all we might have done was to make threats which we could not carry out." Such a move would have violated one of Roosevelt's maxims: "I never take a step in foreign policy unless I am assured that I shall be able eventually to carry out my will by force."

Americans were soon to perceive Japan as a threat to their interests at home and abroad. By 1905 about 100,000 Japanese were in the United States. They settled mostly along the west coast, where their presence reminded Californians of recent troubles with Chinese coolies who had flocked into the United States to work as cheap labor on the transcontinental railroad completed in 1869. But the Japanese soon totaled almost a tenth of the state's population and aroused deep racial animosities. Congress barred further Chinese immigration into the United States during the 1880s but did not extend the measure to include the Japanese. In 1900 the Tokyo government had prohibited its laborers from entering the United States, but this ruling proved easy to circumvent as Japanese immigrants continued in through Hawaii, Mexico, and Canada. California became the focal point of Japanese immigration, and whether for racial or economic reasons (or both), the state's inhabitants protested that Orientals were undermining the economy by working for lower wages than whites would accept. Japan's recent victory over Russia and the inflammatory articles in the U.S. press stirred up a hotbed of emotions over an alleged "yellow peril" that needed only a catalyst to set off trouble.

That catalyst came in October 1906, when the San Francisco school board acted on the separate-but-equal principle of the *Plessy v. Ferguson* Supreme Court case of 1896 in restricting the city's ninety-three Japanese children to an Oriental Public School already attended by Chinese and Korean youths. This school board decision, weakly based on the arguments that the Japanese youths were overaged and overcrowding the classrooms, drew strong complaints locally and in Japan from the Japanese press and public, who felt humiliated at seeing the United States treat their people as racial inferiors.

Roosevelt immediately detected a threat to his foreign policy. Though also concerned about the vast influx of Japanese into the United States, he feared that ill feeling over the school situation might hurt relations with Japan and thus endanger U.S. interests in the Philippines and Hawaii. Roosevelt publicly denounced the school board's decision as a "wicked absurdity" while exerting pressure on what he called the "idiots of the California legislature" to halt their racially discriminatory policies. He also recommended that the U.S. Congress enact laws naturalizing those Japanese who had made the United States their permanent home. But when he waved the big stick, he succeeded only in fanning the wrath of Californians.

The president lacked the constitutional power to act in this state matter, and he again resorted to personal diplomacy. He arranged for the transportation of San Francisco's mayor and entire school board to Washington, where he discussed the matter with them in the Oval Office. There, in February 1907, the president convinced the school board to withdraw the segregation order in exchange for his promise to halt the flow of Japanese into the United States. Through a series of diplomatic notes in late 1907 and early 1908, he secured an informal "gentlemen's agreement" with Japan whereby its government voluntarily restricted the immigration of laborers into the continental United States, and then he approved a U.S. policy prohibit-

ing their indirect entrance through Hawaii, Mexico, and Canada. Again, to avoid political wrangling in the Senate, the president implemented the arrangement through executive agreement.

Roosevelt recognized the possibility of future problems with Japan in the Pacific and decided to send the U.S. fleet on a world cruise to demonstrate its strength, allow crew members to gain firsthand experience at sea, and encourage Congress to appropriate money for a larger navy. In July 1907 the administration announced that the "Great White Fleet"—sixteen battleships and their escorts—would leave the Atlantic for a practice cruise around the world. East Coast Americans complained about being left defenseless, and the chair of the Senate Committee on Naval Affairs piously notified Roosevelt that no funds for the enterprise were available. The president crisply replied that he had enough finances on hand to move the navy to the Pacific, and that if Congress wanted to leave the ships there, that was its decision. Congress allotted the money.

In December 1907 the Great White Fleet steamed out of Hampton Roads and eventually around Cape Horn, arriving in Lower California and preparing to cross the Pacific and honor invitations from Japan, Australia, and other countries. The Japanese, perhaps wanting a closer view of U.S. naval power, welcomed the men from the ships with throngs of youths along the roadsides waving small U.S. flags and singing the National Anthem in English. After a three-day visit in Japan, the fleet departed, making its way through the Suez Canal, European waters, and the Atlantic before returning home safely and without incident in February 1909.

The cruise drew a mixed assessment. The president proclaimed it "the most important service that I rendered to peace." And evidence does suggest that the Tokyo visit cleared the air between the nations. Yet a rise in naval armaments programs took place in Japan, Germany, and other countries—perhaps partly in response to the cruise. In the spring of

1908 the U.S. Congress approved the construction of additional battleships. The cruise also demonstrated the nation's need for Pacific naval bases near East Asia, especially to enhance the security of the Philippines.

The visit of the U.S. fleet to Tokyo probably stimulated the Root-Takahira agreement of November 1908. On the day of the fleet's departure from Japan, the Tokyo government reversed a previous stance and instructed its new ambassador in Washington, Kogoro Takahira, to propose an arrangement with Secretary of State Root that would recognize both the status quo in the Pacific and the Open Door in China. The Root-Takahira agreement thus guaranteed U.S. interests in the Philippines, but it constituted a tacit admission to Japan's dominance in Korea and Manchuria and hence a violation of the Open Door. In a weak effort to safeguard the Open Door, the agreement also called on each signatory to preserve "by all pacific means" the "independence and integrity of China and the principle of equal opportunity for commerce and industry of all nations in that Empire."

Controversy developed over the measure shortly after Roosevelt likewise enacted it through executive agreement. China was irritated at not having participated in the negotiations. The interested European powers approved the agreement only because East Asia seemed left open for exploitation. Americans praised it for safeguarding the Open Door in China and their own control over the Philippines, however, and the Japanese were pleased because respect for the status quo meant their continued economic control over Manchuria. Yet many Americans were concerned that the agreement only implicitly won Japan's assurances against interfering with U.S. interests in the Philippines and Hawaii—and at the huge cost of accepting Japan's deepening entrenchment in Manchuria.

If Root allowed questions to remain about the sanctity of the Open Door, it was a result of Roosevelt's guidance. The president realized that the United States lacked the military strength to stop Japanese expansion in China.

He later explained to Taft, himself then president, that "if the Japanese choose to follow a course of conduct [in Manchuria] to which we are adverse, we cannot stop it unless we are prepared to go to war, and a successful war about Manchuria would require a fleet as good as that of England, plus an army as good as that of Germany." The Open Door "completely disappears as soon as a powerful nation determines to disregard it."

Taft did not fare as well as his predecessor did in East Asian affairs. He followed dollar diplomacy in China as he had done in Latin America, but before his presidency was over, his East Asian policies proved disillusioning to the Chinese and threatening to Japan. Whereas Roosevelt had recognized power realities and tried to mollify the Japanese through concessions disguised as treaties, Taft sought a stronger policy based on economic means. To strengthen U.S. interests and promote orderly development overseas, Taft and his secretary of state, Philander C. Knox, attempted to use U.S. investments as a mechanism for undercutting outside influence in China. Shortly after Taft's arrival in the White House, he demanded that the Chinese government permit U.S. banking interests to participate in a consortium (international association of banking interests) with England, France, and Germany. This consortium would arrange a loan enabling China either to buy the Manchurian railroads from Russia and Japan or to build competing railways and drive the others into bankruptcy. Such a so-called neutralization scheme posed a direct challenge to Japan's interests. But continued unrest in China made the Manchurian venture too risky for U.S. bankers. Taft's East Asian policies succeeded only in driving Russia and Japan closer together, and by the time he left office four years later, the Open Door in China, both in the commercial and territorial sense, was nearly shut.

The Algeciras Conference

One last matter further illustrated Roosevelt's belief that U.S. interests reached beyond the

Western Hemisphere: his decision to mediate the 1905 Franco-German crisis over Morocco. The year before, France had approved British claims in Egypt for reciprocal recognition of its rights in the North African country of Morocco. The Germans decided to test the Anglo-French Entente, or understanding. With France's ally Russia at war with Japan, Kaiser Wilhelm II arrived in the Moroccan capital of Tangier in March 1905 and delivered a belligerent speech praising the sultan as "an absolutely independent sovereign" and demanding German rights in that country. The French turned him down, and war seemed imminent. Although the British prepared to support the French, the premier in Paris declared that his country was not ready for war and could not depend on Russian assistance along with British support. The cabinet forced a change in the foreign ministry, and France moved to conciliate the Germans.

The Berlin government asked Roosevelt to call a meeting with Russia and Germany to resolve the Moroccan question. Roosevelt agreed, though reluctantly, because he recognized that a European war would affect everyone, including the United States. The French were also wary about a conference in which they could gain nothing and probably would *lose* territory in a predictable compromise solution. Roosevelt finally convinced them to attend. In the meantime, according to contemporary U.S. accounts that their German colleagues disputed, Wilhelm offered assurances that in case of serious disagreements at the conference, he would accept whatever decision Roosevelt considered fair. Roosevelt justified his decision to intervene on three bases: (1) a commercial convention in 1880 that the United States had signed in Madrid affecting Morocco, (2) his desire to prevent the country's partition, and (3) his wish to preserve the principle of the Open Door. Realizing the opportunity to reset the European balance of power, Roosevelt agreed to send representatives to a conference in the small Spanish coastal town of Algeciras, located near Gibraltar.

The Algeciras Conference opened in January 1906 and closed with a treaty in April. Henry White, ambassador to Italy and the ranking member of the U.S. delegation, managed to reconcile the disagreements between the opposing parties without capitulating to Germany's demand for Morocco's partition. By the General Act of Algeciras, Morocco's territorial integrity remained intact, although France and Spain won the right to establish controls over that country's police force. Germany had suffered a severe defeat—and not only at the treaty table. The crisis drove France and England closer together and convinced many Americans that the Berlin government wanted war.

Roosevelt later claimed to have been highly instrumental in resolving the crisis. When the Germans opposed French and Spanish control over the Moroccan police force, Wilhelm gave in only after being warned of the publication of his alleged promise to abide by the president's decisions. To soothe the German emperor, Roosevelt asserted that he had flattered him with the "sincerest felicitation" on his policy that had been "masterly from beginning to end." Yet to a friend Roosevelt boasted, "You will notice that while I was most suave and pleasant with the Emperor, . . . when it became necessary at the end I stood him on his head with great decision." As mentioned earlier, Roosevelt soon received the Nobel Peace Prize for his roles in the Algeciras and Portsmouth settlements.

Americans generally praised Roosevelt's efforts in the success of the Algeciras Conference, although they warned that the U.S. involvement did not signal a break with traditional isolationism from European political or military affairs. The Senate approved the pact in December 1906, but only after attaching an amendment reiterating opposition to Old World entanglements. A number of Americans insisted that their country's security was too much to risk for guaranteeing the sanctity of a North African state neither commercially nor strategically important to the United States. Yet Roosevelt's participation in the Algeciras proceedings constituted a warning to the Old World that the United States was prepared to make decisions affecting the balance of power outside the Western Hemisphere.

A Final Analysis

Theodore Roosevelt sought to promote the national interest by leading the United States in a new and more assertive style of foreign policy. In the Western Hemisphere, he worked to safeguard U.S. military and economic interests by building the Panama Canal and by claiming the right of intervention in Latin American affairs through the Roosevelt Corollary. Outside the hemisphere, he strengthened the Anglo-American rapprochement, mediated the Russo-Japanese War, facilitated a resolution of the Moroccan crisis at the Algeciras Conference, helped engineer a Second Peace Conference at The Hague in 1907, and enhanced the stature of the U.S. Navy by sending a fleet around the world. Not all his moves were popular. Three times he bypassed the Senate in negotiating treaties through controversial executive agreements, and critics would denounce his rough-riding arrogance toward those peoples who did not fit his definition of "civilized." And yet no one could deny that the president, for good or ill, had moved the United States into the same international arena occupied by imperial powers more accustomed to such status.

Roosevelt had demonstrated an understanding of the intricacies of balance-of-power relationships, both on the continent of Europe and in regard to the way European matters affected East Asia and hence the world power system. Americans remained reluctant to become involved in international politics, but Roosevelt had made great advances in shaping a national mood more receptive to major-power status. By the time he left the political scene, the United States had solidified its security in the Western Hemisphere and set the path toward a deepening involvement in international affairs.

Selected Readings

Anderson, Stuart. *Race and Rapprochement: Anglo-Saxonism and Anglo-American Relations, 1895–1904.* 1981.

Beale, Howard K. *Theodore Roosevelt and the Rise of America to World Power.* 1956.

Blum, John M. *The Republican Roosevelt.* 1954.

Brands, H. W. *T.R. The Last Romantic.* 1997.

Burton, David H. *Theodore Roosevelt: Confident Imperialist.* 1968.

Campbell, Alexander E. *Great Britain and the United States, 1895–1903.* 1960.

Campbell, Charles S. *Anglo-American Understanding, 1898–1903.* 1957.

Chessman, G. Wallace. *Theodore Roosevelt and the Politics of Power.* 1969.

Coletta, Paolo E. *The Presidency of William Howard Taft.* 1973.

Collin, Richard H. *Theodore Roosevelt, Culture, Diplomacy, and Expansion: A New View of American Imperialism.* 1985.

———. *Theodore Roosevelt's Caribbean: The Panama Canal, the Monroe Doctrine, and the Latin American Context.* 1990.

Conniff, Michael L. *Panama and the United States.* 1992.

Cooper, John M., Jr. *The Warrior and the Priest: Woodrow Wilson and Theodore Roosevelt.* 1983.

Daniels, Roger. *The Politics of Prejudice: The Anti-Japanese Movement in California and the Struggle for Japanese Exclusion.* 1962.

Davis, Calvin D. *The United States and the First Hague Peace Conference.* 1962.

———. *The United States and the Second Hague Peace Conference: American Diplomacy and International Organization, 1899–1914.* 1976.

Dennett, Tyler. *John Hay.* 1933.

Dyer, Thomas G. *Theodore Roosevelt and the Idea of Race.* 1980.

Esthus, Raymond A. *Double Eagle and Rising Sun: The Russians and Japanese at Portsmouth in 1905.* 1988.

———. *Theodore Roosevelt and Japan.* 1966.

———. *Theodore Roosevelt and the International Rivalries.* 1970.

Gould, Lewis L. *The Presidency of Theodore Roosevelt.* 1991.

Graham, Terence. *The "Interests of Civilization": Reaction in the United States against the Seizure of the Panama Canal Zone, 1903–1904.* 1983.

Griswold, A. Whitney. *The Far Eastern Policy of the United States*. 1938.

Harbaugh, William H. *The Life and Times of Theodore Roosevelt*. 1975 ed.

Hart, Robert A. *The Great White Fleet: Its Voyage around the World, 1907–1909*. 1965.

Healy, David F. *Drive to Hegemony: The United States in the Caribbean, 1898–1917*. 1988.

———. *The United States in Cuba, 1898–1902*. 1963.

Hogan, J. Michael. *The Panama Canal in American Politics*. 1986.

Hunt, Michael H. *The Making of a Special Relationship: The United States and China to 1914*. 1983.

Iriye, Akira. *Across the Pacific*. 1967.

———. *Pacific Estrangement: Japanese and American Expansion, 1897–1911*. 1972.

LaFeber, Walter. *The Clash: A History of U.S.-Japanese Relations*. 1997.

———. *Inevitable Revolutions: The United States in Central America*. 1993 ed.

———. *The Panama Canal: The Crisis in Historical Perspective*. 1989 ed.

Langley, Lester. *The Banana Wars: An Inner History of American Empire, 1900–1934*. 1983.

Leopold, Richard W. *Elihu Root and the Conservative Tradition*. 1954.

Major, John. "Who Wrote the Hay–Bunau-Varilla Convention?", *Diplomatic History* 8 (1984): 115–23.

Marks, Frederick W., III. "Morality as a Drive Wheel in the Diplomacy of Theodore Roosevelt," *Diplomatic History* 2 (1978): 43–62.

———. *Velvet on Iron: The Diplomacy of Theodore Roosevelt*. 1979.

McCullough, David G. *The Path Between the Seas: The Creation of the Panama Canal, 1870–1914*. 1977.

McKee, Delber L. *Chinese Exclusion versus the Open Door Policy, 1900–1906*. 1976.

Miller, Edward S. *War Plan Orange: The U.S. Strategy to Defeat Japan, 1897–1945*. 1991.

Millett, Allan R. *The Politics of Intervention: The Military Occupation of Cuba, 1906–1909*. 1968.

Miner, Dwight C. *The Fight for the Panama Route*. 1940.

Mitchell, Nancy. "The Height of the German Challenge: The Venezuela Blockade, 1902–3," *Diplomatic History* 20 (1996): 185–209.

Munro, Dana G. *Intervention and Dollar Diplomacy in the Caribbean, 1900–1921*. 1964.

Neu, Charles E. *An Uncertain Friendship: Theodore Roosevelt and Japan, 1906–1909*. 1967.

———. *The Troubled Encounter: The United States and Japan*. 1975.

Ninkovich, Frank. "Theodore Roosevelt: Civilization as Ideology," *Diplomatic History* 10 (1986): 221–45.

O'Brien, Thomas F. *The Revolutionary Mission: American Business in Latin America*. 1996.

Papachristou, Judith. "American Women and Foreign Policy, 1898–1905: Exploring Gender in Diplomatic History," *Diplomatic History* 14 (1990): 493–509.

Penlington, Norman. *The Alaska Boundary Dispute: A Critical Reappraisal*. 1973.

Pérez, Louis A., Jr. *Cuba and the United States*. 1997.

———. *Cuba under the Platt Amendment, 1902–1934*. 1986.

Perkins, Bradford. *The Great Rapprochement: England and the United States, 1895–1914*. 1968.

Perkins, Dexter. *The Monroe Doctrine, 1867–1907*. 1937.

Pratt, Julius W. *America's Colonial Experiment*. 1950.

———. *America and World Leadership, 1900–1921*. 1967. Originally published as *Challenge and Rejection*. 1967.

Pringle, Henry F. *Theodore Roosevelt*. 1931.

Randall, Stephen J. *Colombia and the United States: Hegemony and Interdependence*. 1992.

Scholes, Walter V., and Scholes, Marie V. *The Foreign Policies of the Taft Administration*. 1970.

Schoonover, Thomas. "Max Farrand's Memorandum on the U.S. Role in the Panamanian Revolution of 1903," *Diplomatic History* 12 (1988): 501–6.

———. *The United States in Central America, 1860–1911*. 1991.

———, and Langley, Lester D. *The Banana Men: American Mercenaries and Entrepreneurs in Central America, 1880–1930*. 1995.

Tilchin, William N. *Theodore Roosevelt and the British Empire*. 1997.

Tompkins, E. Berkeley. *Anti-Imperialism in the United States: The Great Debate, 1890–1920*. 1970.

Trani, Eugene P. *The Treaty of Portsmouth*. 1969.

Varg, Paul A. *The Making of a Myth: The United States and China, 1897–1912*. 1968.

Vevier, Charles. *The United States and China, 1906–1913*. 1955.

CHAPTER 3

Woodrow Wilson and Missionary Diplomacy
PROLOGUE TO U.S. ENTRY INTO WORLD WAR I, 1913–1917

A Sense of Mission

U.S. diplomacy veered sharply toward the goals of idealism and internationalism during the two presidential terms of Woodrow Wilson. By the time his administrations came to a close, the United States had delved deeply into East Asian and Latin American affairs, entered a world war that Wilson called a crusade for democracy, and engaged in two military interventionist episodes in Russia in 1918 and 1920 that took on dangerous political overtones. In the meantime global problems resulted from the breakup of colonial empires and the place of new nations in the postwar world. These struggles and the search for an effective world peace organization based on the principle of collective security served as repeated reminders of the constant strain between the ideal and the real. At first the president attempted to reconcile the two elements, because he believed that reform in international affairs would, in turn, safeguard U.S. security. But he ultimately became committed to idealistic objectives emphasizing the exportation of a highly moralistic democracy, a path that allowed him no room for compromise. Indeed, Wilson's sense of mission pressed him to intervene in other countries' affairs and it proved dangerous to the U.S. interest.

Critics have highlighted arrogance and hypocrisy in Wilson's missionary diplomacy; others have been more sympathetic to his aims and have noted a sincere struggle to impose his Christian and democratic ideals onto the realities around him. As in all complex situations, the truth probably lies somewhere between the two extremes. Wilson was born the son of a Presbyterian minister in Virginia just before the Civil War, and he came to hate war almost to the point of being a pacifist. He earned a doctorate in political science at Johns Hopkins University, wrote numerous books, and became president of Princeton University and then a successful governor of New Jersey before winning the White House in 1912. In that bitterly contested campaign, he received only 42 percent of the popular vote but emerged triumphant over two opposing candidates—incumbent William Howard Taft on the Republican ticket and Theodore Roosevelt as standard bearer of the newly formed Progressive party, which had split from the Republicans after a bitter convention in Chicago. Wilson's Democratic administration ended sixteen years of a Republican-controlled presidency, and he looked forward to implementing domestic reforms under his New Freedom program. It would be ironic, he remarked, if foreign affairs occupied his time in office.

Wilson and Taft
Presidents Wilson and Taft at Wilson's inauguration in March 1913. *Library of Congress.*

Cold and aloof, Wilson was a moralist, a legalist, a rationalist, an egotist, and a strict Calvinist who survived a series of small strokes that began as early as 1896. These qualities combined to persuade the stern-minded Wilson that Providence had reserved a special place in history for the United States, and that he as president was responsible for ensuring the fulfillment of enlightened democratic objectives. Whereas Theodore Roosevelt's philosophy is capsulized in the words inscribed near his grave, "Keep your eyes on the stars and your feet on the ground," Wilson came to believe that the United States, with his guidance, could reach the stars. Roosevelt and Wilson shared similar beliefs in U.S. superiority, but Wilson went farther than merely carrying a stick and hoping others would follow; he *wielded* the stick and, like the Spanish conquistadors of old, brought both spiritual teachings and a sword. In Latin America and Europe, he believed that his mission as the chief steward of righteousness was to establish order by spreading democracy—often with military force.

Attempted Renunciation of Dollar Diplomacy in East Asia and Latin America

Wilson's initial objective in foreign affairs was to break with his predecessor's policy of "dollar diplomacy" in East Asia and Latin America and replace the economic emphasis with moral values. In this regard, he reflected the Progressive reform spirit of the times when, a week after his inauguration, he publicly expressed opposition to special interest groups who might in foreign affairs exploit those countries experiencing internal disorder. Wilson's public statements attracted considerable attention because he released them to the press rather than through the state department. His views also won particular repute because of the efforts of his outspoken secretary of state, William Jennings Bryan, who had won the position as a political plum for his long-time service to the Democratic party. Bryan was a fundamentalist in religion who knew little about foreign affairs but strongly supported Wilson's ideas during the early days of the administration. Although Bryan worked to promote world peace through conciliation or "cooling-off" treaties, he was a mere figurehead in the state department and soon resigned the position. His superior, Bryan complained, controlled foreign affairs, even to the point of hammering out dispatches on his own typewriter. Whereas Taft sought to substitute dollars for bullets, Wilson and Bryan intended to undercut the alleged heartlessness of business by accompanying money with morals.

And yet the Wilson administration wavered in its policies toward dollar diplomacy in China, largely out of concern about Japanese and Russian advances in the troubled area. China remained vulnerable to outside intervention, despite the final 1911 collapse of the aging Manchu dynasty in revolutionary upheaval and the rise of a republic led by Sun Yat-sen, a doctor educated in the United States. The new president used the newspapers to allege that U.S. loans violated China's "administrative independence" and encouraged outside interference in its affairs. His refusal to endorse China's financial proposals was welcome news to U.S. investors, because it freed them from a failing enterprise that had come under the domination of Japanese and Russian businesses. Yet Wilson became apprehensive that the United States's economic withdrawal would endanger the Open Door by leaving China for Japan and Russia to plunder. He also agreed with his former graduate student colleague at Johns Hopkins, the historian Frederick Jackson Turner, who had argued that the American frontier was gone and that a new era in history awaited the United States. Wilson believed that government must work with business in finding new world outlets for production. That goal in mind, he reversed his stand on East Asia toward the end of the decade and placed pres-

William Jennings Bryan
Wilson's first secretary of state who negotiated a number of conciliation treaties before resigning during the *Lusitania* controversy. *Library of Congress.*

sure on mystified U.S. bankers to join a four-power consortium in China. But the effort could do little to slow the economic penetration of either Japan or Russia.

U.S. relations with Japan remained uncertain upon Wilson's ascension to the presidency. Californians feared the "yellow peril" so much that their Republican-dominated legislature had considered prohibiting the Japanese from owning agricultural land. When the Democrats won the White House in 1913, the central obstacle to the measure, party loyalty, was gone, and the Republicans in California prepared such a bill. Wilson urged them to reconsider because of the probable international impact: Mass demonstrations against the proposal had already taken place in Japan. But the bill was a concern of the state of California, and he could do no more because of restrictions inherent in the federal system of government. Avoiding a direct reference to the Japanese, California enacted a law barring land ownership by aliens ineligible for citizenship, even though Bryan had visited the state's capital in April 1913 and urged the governor and legislators to oppose such a measure. Despite talk of war in both Japan and the United States, the crisis passed when Bryan convinced the Japanese ambassador in Washington that California's actions did not reflect a national policy of discrimination.

The Great War beginning in Europe during August 1914 preoccupied the Western nations and provided an opportunity for Japan to expand its influence in China. During the following January, after Japan had entered the conflict on the Allies' side and seized German holdings in East Asia and the Pacific, the Tokyo government secretly made "Twenty-one Demands" on China that, if accepted, would have converted that country into a Japanese protectorate. The Peking government leaked the demands to Washington, whereupon the United States warned the Japanese that it opposed the use of force in China. The Tokyo government retreated from its most extreme claims, although it secured most of the others because China had no choice.

Two years later, in 1917, the United States's entry into the Great War encouraged Japan to seek additional concessions in China. When Britain and France sent missions to the United States in the spring of that year to discuss the war effort, the Tokyo leadership ordered a special emissary, Viscount Kikujiro Ishii, to persuade the new secretary of state, Robert Lansing, to recognize Japan's interests in China. In November 1917 Japan and the United States signed the Lansing-Ishii Agreement, which allowed China to retain its "territorial sovereignty" in exchange for U.S. admission to Japan's "special interests" in China. Lansing interpreted these interests as economic and growing out of geographical contiguity or proximity; the Japanese read them as "paramount" and hence considered themselves under no restrictions as to defini-

tion. Although the Chinese protested, their interests were sacrificed in the greater aim of establishing good wartime relations between Japan and the United States.

The Wilson administration's major efforts toward eliminating dollar diplomacy took place within the Western Hemisphere. U.S. concern over Latin America had increased with the imminent completion of the Panama Canal. Respect for the Monroe Doctrine was vital, the president emphasized, as was the welfare of Latin American people long victimized by oppressive regimes. Before Wilson left the White House, the United States had purchased the Danish West Indies and expanded its involvement in Panama, Nicaragua, Haiti, the Dominican Republic, and Mexico. In numerous instances marines had occupied countries, partly to impose democracy through the establishment of "protectorates" but also to safeguard U.S. economic and strategic concerns in the Caribbean.

The Taft administration had left its successor a major problem in Central America: the Panama Canal Tolls Act of 1912, which established regulations for the great waterway but exempted U.S. intrastate shippers from toll exactions. U.S. businesses dispatching goods between Atlantic and Pacific coastal cities would not have to pay for use of the canal. Wilson's antitrust stand might have influenced his initial support for the act, because the huge transcontinental railroads would have to scale down rates to counter the wider competition from smaller shipping lines. He came to realize, however, that the toll measure threatened the Anglo-American rapprochement by violating the Hay-Pauncefote Treaty with Britain. That pact of 1901 contained assurances that all nations would pay the same toll charges. The Taft administration had argued that the treaty referred to nations other than the United States and that the toll clause fit with longstanding U.S. prohibitions against the participation of foreign shippers in the American coastal trade. Other proponents of the toll exemption flatly declared that the nation building the canal should enjoy special privileges.

Tempers flared as the British protested the Tolls Act as a breach of faith and called for arbitration. The Senate in Washington, however, refused to approve the suggestion. The U.S. ambassador to London, Walter Hines Page, warned the White House that the British people considered the U.S. stand "dishonorable," and he admitted that he found it difficult to refute the charge. "We made a bargain— a solemn compact—and we have broken it," Page declared. "Whether it were a good bargain or a bad one, a silly one or a wise one; that's far from the point."

Wilson dropped his support for the exemption clause when relations with Britain seemed endangered and U.S. honor came into question. In March 1914 he appeared before Congress and called for repeal of the measure. The United States, he declared, was "too big, too powerful, too self-respecting a Nation to interpret with too strained or refined a reading the words of our own promises just because we have power enough to give us leave to read them as we please." Wilson may have hoped that removal of the exemption clause would elevate the United States into a position of moral leadership in the world; he doubtless thought the act might persuade the British to follow his moralistic policy in Mexico (discussed later). After heated debates in the Senate, Congress approved his request in June 1914 but reserved the right to restore the exemption clause at any time. The president's action succeeded in protecting national honor while maintaining the rapprochement with Britain.

As the Panama Canal neared completion, Americans became increasingly anxious lest another nation build a competing waterway through Nicaragua. A few weeks before Wilson's inauguration, the Taft administration had begun negotiations with that country, intending to gain perpetual and exclusive rights to construct a canal and to set up a ninety-nine-year lease on two strategic islands for the purpose of building naval bases. For these concessions the United States was to pay $3 million, which Nicaragua would use to reimburse U.S. bankers for past loans. The Senate in Washington, however, refused to approve the pact because of its blatant approval of U.S. intervention. Although the new president was at first inclined to oppose this agreement as another instance of dollar diplomacy, he realized the danger of a competing canal under foreign ownership and instructed his secretary of state to reopen the discussions. In February 1916 Bryan signed the pact with the Nicaraguan minister in Washington, Emiliano Chamorro.

The Bryan-Chamorro Treaty drew a mixed reception. On the one hand, it bolstered Nicaragua's finances and would help the United States ward off suspected European interests in the isthmus. On the other hand, it caused widespread consternation in Costa Rica, El Salvador, and Honduras, whose leaders complained that Nicaragua had permitted concessions belonging to them. Indeed, the recently established Central American Court of Justice heard their case and decided in their favor, only to have Nicaragua and the United States ignore the ruling. Like Taft, Wilson approved U.S. control over Nicaragua's finances and maintained a small contingent of marines to enforce policy. The United States's protectorate status over Nicaragua lasted until 1933.

Haiti also became a major U.S. concern after the outbreak of war in Europe in 1914. European investments in Haiti were high, causing Americans to fear that revolutionary disorder in that Caribbean country would invite foreign intervention. Haiti usually met its interest payments on debts, but by the early 1900s its government defaulted because of recurring domestic trouble that undermined the island's already weak financial structure. Americans were worried that Germany might seize Haiti's harbor of Môle Saint Nicolas and threaten the Panama Canal. When France and Germany sent soldiers to restore order, the Wilson administration became anxious that their stay might become permanent.

The president also feared that continued troubles in Haiti could encourage the ongoing insurrection in its Dominican neighbor, and he prepared to follow Roosevelt's earlier interventionist policies in the Caribbean. The United States requested permission from the Haitian government to send an adviser on financial affairs and establish a customs receivership. It also wanted to oversee elections and receive assurances that Môle Saint Nicolas would not pass to another government. These moves met such savage opposition from the Haitians that by late July of 1915 the United States had to send more than 2000 marines to restore order. The state department meanwhile drew up a treaty virtually assigning Haiti's financial affairs to the United States and claiming the right of intervention through a general clause allowing it to guarantee "a government adequate for the protection of life, property, and individual liberty." The U.S. military government in Haiti lasted until 1934, although customs controls continued another seven years.

Growing unrest in the Dominican Republic caused the United States to adopt policies there that were similar to those in Haiti. In 1911 revolutions broke out again, and the Dominican government had to borrow a huge sum, which caused another debt problem encouraging to foreign intervention. A U.S. treaty established a financial adviser, broadened receivership powers over domestic and customs revenues, and set up a constabulary or state police force. Three years later the Wilson administration authorized Americans to supervise the approaching elections. But when the new Dominican president took office, he rejected the U.S. treaty. In the spring of 1916 the country sank deeper into revolution. The United States sent marines in May, and when another Dominican president refused the U.S. treaty, Wilson ordered the installation of a military government run by the navy department in Washington. For six years, while the Dominican legislature stood in adjournment, the marines discharged cabinet responsibilities, and U.S. engineers worked to improve the country's roads, schools, and sanitation facilities. To the very end, however, the Dominicans bitterly resisted U.S. intervention.

The war in Europe also caused concern that Germany would defeat Denmark, seize its West Indies possessions (Virgin Islands), and endanger the Panama Canal. To prevent this potential threat, the United States negotiated a treaty with Denmark in the summer of 1916 that permitted purchase of the islands. The Danish government had little choice. The Wilson administration had already warned that if Germany made a move toward the islands, U.S. forces would seize them.

The Wilson administration's Caribbean policy was, of course, based on protecting U.S. commercial interests, but its more immediate concern was to safeguard the hemisphere and the Panama Canal from European intervention. The president first sought treaties, but, when necessary, he resorted to military force. Critics charged the White House with too readily assuming that domestic unrest constituted an automatic invitation to Old World involvement. In emphasizing the external dangers caused by revolutions in the Caribbean countries, they asserted, the Wilson administration overlooked genuine internal problems and ignored the people's protests against U.S. policy. They were not reassured by the administration's weak attempts to salve these hard feelings in the Caribbean with offers of economic assistance conducive to democratic reforms. In truth, the United States sought legitimate commercial and security interests in Latin America, but its apparent high-handedness left a legacy of bitter distrust throughout the southern half of the hemisphere.

Missionary Diplomacy in Mexico

Wilson's policy in Mexico, though partly determined by concern for the Panama Canal, was more the product of a struggle over what he perceived as morally correct behavior in foreign affairs. Mexico had been unique among Latin American governments in that since 1877 it had remained fairly stable under the iron rule of Porfirio Díaz and thus suitable for foreign investments. But by the turn of the century his long-standing dictatorship had begun to weaken. In 1910 a young nationalist visionary, Francisco Madero, led the "Constitutionalists" in an uprising driven by a call for democratic and economic reforms, and in spring of the following year he forced the nearly senile Díaz into exile. But Madero's reform program endangered foreign holdings in Mexico because it would unseat the conservative landed classes, create massive disorder, and discourage continued investment. By 1913, nearly 50,000 Americans had investments in Mexico, valued at almost $2 billion (much of that money in oil), a figure surpassing that of all other countries combined. Indeed, Americans owned more than 40 percent of all properties in Mexico—which exceeded those owned by the Mexicans themselves. The revolutionaries blamed the United States for Mexico's ills and for losses of U.S. property and life, but President Taft refused to get involved.

A month before Wilson's inauguration, the U.S. ambassador in Mexico, Henry Lane Wilson (no relation to the president), gave tacit support to an overthrow of the government led by one of Madero's own generals, Victoriano Huerta. Ambassador Wilson regarded Madero as a threat to stability and hence an obstacle to investment; other critics considered him unbalanced because of his spiritual beliefs. Huerta, however, was a favorite of conservative interests and amenable to dollar diplomacy. When he asked the U.S. ambassador what to do with Madero, Henry Lane Wilson discreetly advised him to take whatever steps were necessary to bring peace to Mexico. Huerta thereupon forced his rival's resignation and, early on a February morning in 1913, had Madero and his vice president shot to death during an alleged escape attempt.

Huerta won recognition from most foreign governments, but Taft held back until the new regime agreed to resolve damage claims questions with the United States. The proposed *quid pro quo* fell through partly because Taft's

Francisco Madero and Victoriano Huerta
Madero, the democrat, murdered by Huerta, who headed what President Wilson called "a government of butchers." Madero: *Library of Congress;* Huerta: *National Archives, Washington, D.C.*

Venustiano Carranza
The white-bearded and bespectacled leader of the Constitutionalist party sits among his followers. *Library of Congress.*

presidential administration ended, but also because a former governor of the northern province of Coahuila and follower of Madero, the white-bearded, bespectacled, and scholarly looking Venustiano Carranza, had taken up the Constitutionalists' mantle to lead a rebellion against Huerta. With U.S. property and lives victimized by both sides in the ensuing civil war, Taft bequeathed the matter to his successor.

President Wilson's Mexican policy marked a revolutionary new direction in U.S. foreign affairs because it exemplified the most flagrant features of "missionary diplomacy." Whereas previous presidential administrations had extended *de facto* recognition to foreign regimes that had achieved control, Wilson flatly rejected Huerta and called for the formulation of moral judgments regarding what constituted a "good" government. The president refused to extend recognition to Huerta be-

cause he had risen to power over Madero's body, was of poor moral character, and did not advocate reform. In March 1913 Wilson issued a press release declaring that the United States would extend recognition only to those Latin American governments built on "orderly processes of just government based upon law, not upon arbitrary or irregular force." The British argued that Huerta was a stabilizing force who would keep Mexico safe for investors. Wilson countered that Huerta headed "a government of butchers," which made it incumbent upon the United States to protect the Mexican people from their ruler. The British, he declared sarcastically, should stop allowing oil interests to control their policies and follow the U.S. lead. To a British citizen in the United States, Wilson self-righteously declared, "I am going to teach the South American republics to elect good men!"

President Wilson then added a dangerous moral dimension to his country's Mexican policy when he denounced Huerta as a drunken "brute" and called for his resignation. By late summer of 1913 he had recalled Ambassador Wilson from Mexico City and removed him from the diplomatic service because of his involvement with Huerta's rise to power and because of his open opposition to the president's new policies in Mexico. President Wilson now relied almost exclusively on special agents, who often did not know much about Mexico or the Spanish language, but were his close and trusted acquaintances. Before an audience in Mobile in late October, Wilson insisted that "morality," not "material interest," had to guide U.S. policy. The United States "will never again seek one additional foot of territory by conquest. She will devote herself to showing that she knows how to make honorable and fruitful use of the territory she has."

Wilson's rhetoric only seemed to mark an end to U.S. territorial imperialism in Latin America. His words actually contained an even more dangerous element in that they offered no guarantees against interventionism in the name of righteousness. The irony is that Wilson's diplomacy was potentially more entangling than that of either Roosevelt or Taft. Whereas compromise and retreat can characterize a foreign policy built on realistic interests, those necessary give-and-take attributes of effective diplomacy cannot coexist with a policy resting on absolute standards of right and wrong. A moral crusade could lead to a sweeping interventionist effort conducive to native resistance or outright war.

One of Wilson's emissaries, John Lind, reached Mexico's shore, appropriately enough, on board a U.S. ship of war. This venture marked the first diplomatic effort for Lind, former governor of Minnesota, who was further hampered by his reputation as a notorious opponent of Catholicism now entering an overwhelmingly Catholic nation. In early August 1913 Lind first threatened Huerta if he rejected mediation by the president, and

then backed off with a proposal to help Huerta put down the revolution—on the condition that he then withdraw from public affairs. For Huerta to receive U.S. recognition and assistance, he had to arrange an immediate cease-fire and sponsor a free election—*without* participating as a candidate. The Mexican minister of foreign affairs, Federico Gamboa, regarded the choice of Lind and his arrival by warship as a calculated insult. He then bitterly denounced Lind's proposal as an attempt by the U.S. president to "veto" elections in Mexico. Wilson reacted decisively. He cut off arms sales to Mexico, warned Americans to return home, and, in a path-breaking move, went before Congress to declare that the United States would follow a policy of "watchful waiting."

The Wilson administration tried to persuade the European governments to join in supporting Carranza, who claimed to favor Madero's reform program. Huerta did nothing to placate the United States. He arranged a congressional election in October, but on election eve he seized dictatorial power after ordering the imprisonment of more than 100 opposition members of the legislature. When the election took place (with British assistance) and clearly confirmed Huerta's control, Wilson angrily countered with another special agent to offer aid to Carranza in upper Mexico. But Carranza also opposed U.S. intervention. The following month, Wilson informed the other countries having interests in Mexico that he intended to isolate Huerta and force him from office. Should political and economic pressure fail, he ominously declared, the United States's "duty" was to use "less peaceful means to put him out."

Wilson's note aroused little support in Europe but gradually drew Britain into his camp. The British at first hesitated to alienate Huerta, primarily because they ranked second only to the Americans in Mexican investments and were heavily dependent on that country's oil. Yet the imminent threat of Germany and the need for continued friendship with the United States gradually forced a change in

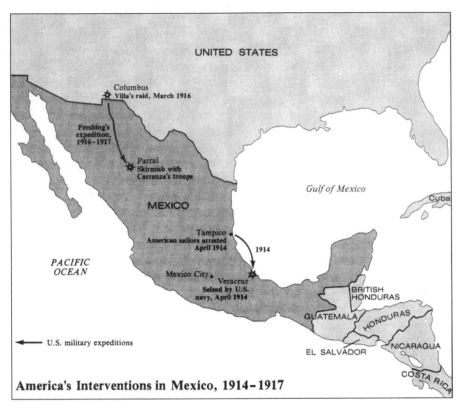

UNITED STATES

Columbus
Villa's raid, March 1916

Pershing's
expedition,
1916-1917

Parral
Skirmish with
Carranza's troops

MEXICO

Gulf of Mexico

Cuba

Tampico
American sailors arrested
April 1914

1914

PACIFIC
OCEAN

Mexico City
Veracruz
Seized by U.S.
navy, April 1914

BRITISH
HONDURAS

GUATEMALA

HONDURAS

EL SALVADOR

NICARAGUA

COSTA RICA

← U.S. military expeditions

America's Interventions in Mexico, 1914-1917

Map 7
The United States and Mexico almost went to war more than once in this brief
period.

British policy. They recalled their minister, Sir Lionel Carden, who had opposed the U.S. policy in Mexico, and now likewise encouraged Huerta to resign.

Wilson ignored growing discontent at home with his Mexican policy and, with recently won British support, prepared to move against Huerta. He issued a formal call for Huerta's resignation in November 1913 and the following February lifted the arms embargo to allow sales to Carranza. U.S. criticism persisted. Some observers warned that Wilson's policy encouraged a climate of unrest ill-suited for investment; others ridiculed its pious morality and called for decisive military action. More than seventy Americans had died in the Mexican civil war since 1913, causing more than a few in the United States to demand armed intervention to restore order.

Trouble erupted in the booming east coast oil town of Tampico on April 9, 1914, when Huerta's forces arrested seven U.S. sailors and an officer for loading gasoline onto their whaleboat, which was then docked in a canal running close to Huerta's defense lines against the rebels. Given the tense situation, the arrests constituted a mistake in judgment, which the Mexican officer in charge realized immediately. He released the Americans and personally apologized, but this was not enough for Rear Admiral Henry Mayo. The granite-faced U.S. squadron commander pompously demanded a formal, written apology, punishment of the officer responsible, and a twenty-one-gun salute to the U.S. flag—all within twenty-four hours. The Mexican general wrote his regrets for the incident, and Huerta publicly renounced his men's actions, but he refused to approve a salute to the flag (by a people, he noted with sardonic humor, whom the United States did not recognize as a country) unless the Americans reciprocated in kind.

Wilson regarded the Tampico incident as an opportunity to facilitate a change of government in Mexico, and on April 20 he asked Congress for authorization to use military force in taking the port at Veracruz and deposing Huerta by denying him outside help. He felt thoroughly justified. Messages from Veracruz, though garbled and mistaken, reported that Mexican forces had captured "marines" and "paraded" them down the streets in an effort to humiliate the United States. Bryan supported Mayo's demands as a way of regaining national honor, and just two days later Congress responded favorably to the president's request. In the meantime Wilson had been awakened early in the morning of April 21 to learn that a German steamship was en route to Veracruz carrying weapons and ammunition for Huerta. Rear Admiral Frank Fletcher, then stationed at Veracruz, received telephoned orders from the White House to seize the city's port and customs house.

U.S. military intervention in Veracruz had the potential to cause war. About 800 troops arrived in the city on April 21, where they met unexpected and effective resistance from former prisoners of the town's jails, who had been released and armed by a local officer from Huerta's army. Mexican regulars had pulled out, but the ensuing street fighting in the waning hours before nightfall led to a number of casualties on both sides. The next day 3000 more marines landed. U.S. and Mexican death tolls climbed as the conflict raged for days. Wilson's policy drew criticism from all sides. Huerta's opponents joined other Latin Americans, investors from the United States, and numerous observers elsewhere in denouncing the Wilson administration for using military force over such a small matter. The London *Economist* chided the United States for justifying such rash and irresponsible action "on points of punctilio raised by admirals and generals." If the Washington government persisted in "this return to mediaeval conditions it will be a bad day for civilization."

The truth is that the occupation of Veracruz was an act of war, despite Wilson's argument that his quarrel was with Huerta, not Mexico. The president failed to realize that his interventionist policy made the United States a greater threat to Mexico than did its own internal strife. His efforts, no matter how well-intentioned, had united the Mexican people against him.

Wilson had created a situation that was injurious to U.S. prestige no matter what action he took. Withdrawal without reparations would be humiliation, and war with Mexico was sheer aggression; he had no honorable way out. Carranza warned of war with the United States, and the U.S. and European press condemned the invasion. Wilson admitted to his personal physician that he was shocked and guilt-ridden as the number of U.S. casualties grew to 90 (including 19 dead) and those of Mexico reached 321 (including 126 dead). In doing what he thought was morally right, he had earned the animosity of nearly everyone.

In late April, with almost 7000 U.S. forces in Mexico, Wilson accepted a mediation offer from the "ABC Powers" of Argentina, Brazil, and Chile. The following month the three Latin American nations sponsored a conference in Niagara Falls, Canada, bringing together delegates from Huerta's government and from the United States. Carranza declined to attend on the ground that outsiders were attempting to determine his country's domestic affairs. The Niagara talks deadlocked when Wilson forbade his representatives to discuss U.S. withdrawal from Mexico and then demanded that Huerta renounce his position in favor of a provisional regime under Carranza's Constitutionalist party. The Niagara Conference broke up in July without any substantial results.

As fate would have it, Huerta's regime collapsed soon afterward, leaving the mistaken impression in the United States that the conference had achieved its objectives. In mid-July, about two weeks after adjournment, heightened pressure from Carranza and the White House combined with Huerta's dire financial situation and dwindling popular support to drive him from office. After he fled Mexico to seek asylum in Spain, Carranza's forces marched triumphantly into Mexico City on August 20, 1914.

The civil war in Mexico did not end with Carranza's rise to power. Promised reforms did not materialize, and Carranza soon faced armed resistance from within his own ranks—from Emiliano Zapata in the south and from Pancho Villa in the north. When Villa claimed to support U.S. policies toward Mexico, Wilson decided to withhold recognition from Carranza's government and give Villa time to broaden his influence. Partly to return Mexico's attention to internal troubles, Wilson ordered U.S. soldiers home from Veracruz in late November 1914. The following month Villa's forces marched into Mexico City, making it appear that Wilson's watching and waiting had brought success. But Carranza's army soon rallied and drove Villa back into the north.

Carranza, Wilson moaned, "will somehow have to be digested." In October 1915 Secretary of State Robert Lansing called another conference of the ABC Powers and they, along with Bolivia, Guatemala, and Uruguay, proposed that the United States extend *de facto* recognition to Carranza's government. The United States complied that same month and permitted the sale of arms to Carranza's forces while denying them to his opposition.

But U.S. recognition of Carranza did not settle the disorder in Mexico, because Villa bitterly resented Wilson's "betrayal" and sought to entangle Carranza and the United States in war. In January 1916 Villa and his followers stopped a train in northern Mexico where they shot sixteen young U.S. engineers on board (sparing one to tell the story) who had received Carranza's assurances of safe passage. Three months later Villa crossed the U.S. border before daybreak and raided and burned the town of Columbus, New Mexico, killing nineteen Americans.

News of Villa's attack on U.S. territory brought an immediate White House response: Wilson ordered General John J. ("Black Jack") Pershing to head a "punitive expedition" of 7000 soldiers to capture Villa. Carranza disapproved but had no choice. He accepted the "invasion" with the face-saving stipulation that in the future, *both* nations had the right to pursue bandits across the border. The U.S. force entered Mexico in mid-March and ultimately trudged through 350 miles of desert without even seeing its prey.

Instead of resolving the problem, the Pershing expedition created an even larger one: Carranza complained of the growing size of the army and demanded its immediate withdrawal. The invasion force had nearly doubled in number to 12,000, and trouble had erupted. In April, Americans exchanged fire with Mexicans belonging to Carranza's army in the town of Parral, killing two Americans and forty Mexicans. This incident soon led Wilson to send 150,000 National Guardsmen to patrol the border. In late June, at Carrizal, the two armies clashed again, with a dozen Americans killed and twenty-three taken captive. War seemed unavoidable.

Despite the incontestable failure of the expedition, Wilson at first refused to order Pershing home. The president's hesitancy was due partly to his unwillingness to admit error, but it was also attributable to the negative effect that such a move could have on the presidential election at home in November. The White House turned down a mediation offer from Latin America but agreed to Carranza's call for a face-saving joint investigatory commission. Although the commission failed to find a solution, the U.S. representatives recommended that Wilson recall the soldiers (now derisively called the "Perishing Expedition") and leave Mexican concerns to Carranza. U.S. entry into another war—the European war—seemed imminent in early February 1917, and the president finally ordered Pershing to leave Mexico.

Alvaro Obregon, Gen. Francisco Villa, and Gen. John J. Pershing
The euphoric days before President Wilson extended recognition to Carranza.
Otis Aultman Collection, El Paso Public Library.

As the last of the U.S. soldiers came home, Wilson's Mexican policy lay in shambles. The revolution continued, Carranza resented the United States and leaned toward Germany in the European war, and Villa still hawked the border, flouting his own country's government as well as that of the United States. In March a new U.S. ambassador arrived in Mexico, assigned the awesome responsibility of repairing relations.

The United States extended *de jure*, or lawful, recognition to the Carranza regime in late August 1917, although the move came too late to placate most Latin American nations. Wilson remained reluctant until the final moment but had to relent because the United States had entered the European war the previous April and could not allow troubles with Mexico to continue. The president had averted war with Mexico; he had accepted mediation; he had favored a government in Mexico that

professed interest in reform. Yet his policy in Mexico was paternalistic and arrogantly self-righteous, which left him open to severe criticism as the apostle of Americanism who piously expressed opposition to military force but sent more marines to Latin America than did either Roosevelt or Taft.

Missionary Diplomacy in Europe

The Great War of 1914 through 1918 ultimately dominated Americans' attention, convincing them that modern war was worldwide and total and that only through a reassertion of ideals could the world avoid another such calamity. The first sign of changing times came when the United States found itself unable to remain neutral while trading with both sides during the European conflict. No longer could one distinguish between contraband and noncontraband. In modern warfare, *any*

Map 8
By the summer of 1914, according to Colonel House, Europe was a
"powder keg" ready to explode. In less than three years, the United States
was also involved in what became known as the Great War.

item benefiting the enemy was subject to con-
fiscation, thereby making freedom of the seas
one of the first casualties of the Great War.
Wilson's moral stance helped to stir up an
international crusade for humanitarian reform
and the establishment of permanent world
peace. Combined with numerous other factors, his idealism helped to promote the U.S.
entrance into the war.

On June 28, 1914, a young Serbian nationalist shattered the uneasy peace in Europe
when he shot and killed the heir to the Austro-
Hungarian throne, Archduke Franz Ferdinand,
in the streets of Sarajevo in Bosnia. The shots
fired in the Balkans echoed throughout the
world, tearing down the illusion of security
afforded by the intricate system of alliances and
armaments and setting off a series of events

that led to world war. With the full support of
Germany, Austria-Hungary presented the Ser-
bians with an ultimatum, which, in turn,
caused the Russians, backed by France, to
mobilize on behalf of their fellow Slavs. By
early August Austria-Hungary and Russia had
declared war on each other, and Germany and
France did the same shortly thereafter. When
Germany prepared to march through neutral
Belgium to strike France, the British abided
by their pledges to Belgian neutrality and their
entente with France to declare war on Germany. The guns of August soon led to a division of the warring camps between the Allies
(Britain, France, and Russia, later joined by
Japan and Italy) and the Central Powers (Germany and Austria-Hungary, later joined by
Bulgaria and Turkey). It took four years of all-

out fighting and more than ten million deaths to settle the war.

World War I was a total war in every respect. It brought down old empires resting on raw power and raised new ones grounded in a mixture of military and economic hegemony. The global upheaval that grew out of the shots fired in Sarajevo led to nationalist movements that reshaped the world socially, politically, and economically. The war also brought a coalition of science and industry that resulted in the most destructive weaponry ever seen. Submarines, tanks, airplanes, improved machine guns, howitzers, the "Big Bertha" cannon, naval blockades, the heavily armed dreadnoughts or battleships, poison gas, trench warfare, a massive flu epidemic, and other diseases—all caused astonishing casualties on both sides. In the first full year of the war, France's casualties numbered 1.3 million, Germany's 848,000, and Britain's 313,000. By war's end the Allies had amassed a casualty rate of more than 50 percent; that of the Central Powers was more than 67 percent. In addition to the deaths of soldiers, another 20 million civilians died in the war and soon afterward.

The German invasion of Belgium seemed particularly atrocious. When the Berlin government first sought permission to march through that country en route to attack France, the Belgian king indignantly replied, "Belgium is a nation, not a thoroughfare." Britain's appeal to treaty guarantees of Belgium's neutrality reportedly brought the ill-advised remark from German Chancellor Theobald von Bethmann Hollweg that the British were going to war over a mere "scrap of paper." In early January 1915 the editor of *Life* magazine declared that for Americans "the great, clear issue of this war is Belgium. If we see anything right at all in this matter," the article continued, "Belgium is a martyr to civilization, sister to all who love liberty or law; assailed, polluted, trampled in the mire, heelmarked in her breast, tattered, homeless."

Americans varied in their reaction to the outbreak of war, although most regarded the conflict as peculiarly European and of no direct concern to them. Wilson later declared that "America did not at first see the full meaning of the war. It looked like a natural raking out of the pent-up jealousies and rivalries of the complicated politics of Europe." It was "a war with which we have nothing to do, whose causes cannot touch us." Some U.S. representatives abroad had been unaware of the serious nature of tensions in Europe. The minister to Belgium, Brand Whitlock, had been writing a novel when the assassination took place and later admitted, "I had never heard of Sarajevo. I had not the least idea where it was in this world, if it was in this world." Colonel Edward House, Wilson's closest confidant, had considered the situation in Europe to be a "powder keg" long before the autumn of 1914 and had tried to convince the German ambassador in Washington to join the United States and other world powers in keeping the peace by civilizing backward peoples and ensuring investment. The U.S. ambassador to London, Walter Hines Page, agreed. As late as the summer of 1914, House sought support for his proposal in Berlin and other European capitals. The assassination abruptly ended his hopes.

President Wilson's official policy toward the European war was neutrality, but his people were deeply divided in sentiment. In August 1914 he announced a proclamation of neutrality and later that month urged Americans to be "impartial in thought as well as in action." The United States, he asserted, must set an example for peace. But problems were clear at the outset. The United States was a nation of immigrants having close ties to their homelands. Many Americans felt social, political, economic, and cultural affinities with the British and French; a great number were pro-German, including Americans of German and Irish descent, along with others who for one reason or another were opposed to Russia. The "hyphenates," whether German-Americans, Irish-Americans, or whatever national origin, had pronounced views on the war that were impossible to neutralize.

Colonel Edward House
House was President Wilson's closest confidant until their break during the Versailles Treaty proceedings. *National Portrait Gallery.*

Although most Americans favored the Allies for personal reasons, Wilson and nearly all members of his administration had a broader rationale that rested on realistic interests: They feared that German victory would set back democracy in favor of world militarism. Wilson's scholarly writings had long reflected his sympathies for Britain's parliamentary and constitutional form of government, and he soon joined House and Page in believing the war a battle between good and evil. Robert Lansing, then legal counselor in the state department, was stronger in opinion: He considered Germany's defeat so important that he *wanted* the United States to intervene on the side of the Allies. Page, author and editor, was perfectly acclimated to British life and got along well with Foreign Secretary Sir Edward Grey. In fact, Page did not like the firm legal pronouncements contained in state department dispatches and at times toned them down to avoid antagonizing his host government.

Propagandists in England cultivated Americans' long-time distrust of Germany, which became more widespread after the invasion of Belgium. During the first days of the war, the British cut the Atlantic cable connecting Germany with the United States, meaning that direct information on the European conflict came only from Allied sources. U.S. relations with Germany had been uneasy before 1914, encouraging British propagandists to play upon this and early events of the war to foster an unfavorable image of the Germans among influential U.S. journalists, politicians, ministers, and educators. According to postwar evidence, the British government had engineered a careful propaganda campaign designed to create sympathy for the Allies. Such efforts included writing letters, circulating books and pamphlets favorable to Britain, and sponsoring speakers who emphasized Anglo-American similarities in culture based on familial ties.

British efforts to deepen anti-German feeling found a fairly receptive audience in the United States. Americans had long been suspicious of German motives in both hemispheres, and now Kaiser Wilhelm II became the "Beast of Berlin," determined to stamp out democracy everywhere. Cartoonists portrayed the German "Hun" as an animalistic killer of men, women, and children, a savage despoiler of religion, education, and culture, and a fierce advocate of militarism and barbarism. Always caricatured wearing a handlebar mustache, high black boots, and spiked helmet, the Hun leered as he goose-stepped across civilization, bayoneting babies, raping and mutilating women, gathering the helpless for labor gangs, loading corpses as fodder for soap factories, and executing resisters such as the celebrated British nurse Edith Cavell, who actually was a spy. German armies left behind countless bodies, burned out church buildings and schools, and razed libraries such as the magnificent one at the University of Louvain in Belgium. Herbert Hoover, a young mining engineer and later president of the United States, headed a U.S. relief group in Belgium whose stories convinced many Americans that German expansion and militarism had interlocked to spawn a brutal imperialism that used war as its only instrument of policy.

The Wilson administration insisted that the European conflict was subject to the restrictions of international laws guaranteeing the rights of neutrals. If so, the most recent set of codes, contained in the Declaration of London in 1909, should have been the guide to all nations' behavior in the war. But the big powers had not ratified the measure, and it had never gone into effect. The British had refused because the Declaration's maritime provisions favored neutral nations and those with small navies. Hence, the guarantees outlined in the Declaration of Paris of 1856, now outmoded, were the only so-called rules in effect when the war began in 1914. According to this nineteenth-century program, neutral flags bonded the safety of ocean cargoes; contraband was strictly war materiel; neutral vessels could carry noncontraband goods ("free ships, free goods") to and from belligerent ports; and blockades must pose an "imminent danger" to ships seeking entry into those closed waters. Neutral rights seemed clear in theory but became muddled in the reality of war. Neither belligerent could permit neutral ships to pass through the war zone without searching them for contraband, and the very nature of modern, full-scale war forced a generalized definition of contraband that included *all* items benefiting the enemy. Britain controlled the seas and, without actually proclaiming a blockade, succeeded in closing European ports. Their naval commanders followed visit-and-search procedures reminiscent of maritime tactics that a century before had caused war between the English-speaking peoples.

Neutral rights became a major issue when Germany's invasion of France deadlocked in trench warfare at the Marne River in the autumn of 1914 and made the central question in the war whether one side could tip the balance by depriving the other's access to the sea. The London government announced in November that in reply to the Germans' decision to mine the open seas, it had decided to lay mines in the North Sea to force Germany into submission. Neutrals wishing to use these waters had to obtain directions from Britain for safe passage. Despite complaints that the North Sea was not territorial waters, the British declared it a "military area" automatically closed to neutral traffic. Because Germany did not have free use of the Atlantic Ocean, the Central Powers' only recourse was an appeal to international law.

The United States found itself between the antagonists, but more immediately affected by the British because their navy controlled the seas. Britain broadened the definition of contraband to include any goods helpful to the enemy, except for cotton, which for a while remained on the free list because of US pressure. The Royal Navy also searched US mail and interrupted neutrals' use of their own ports and coastlines. In March 1915 the London ministry made it official: Naval commanders would seize all goods "of enemy destination, ownership, or origin." The stalemate at the Marne had emphasized the importance of neutral trade, but Britain so narrowed the "rights of neutrals" that the term lost its meaning.

The strains on Anglo-American relations were serious, but they never broke. Part of the explanation lies in Britain's carefully crafted foreign policy. Foreign Secretary Grey explained after the war that his objective had been "to secure the maximum of blockade that could be enforced without a rupture with the United States." Although Bryan was secretary of state, Lansing played an integral role in maintaining the Atlantic relationship. The tragic death of President Wilson's first wife in early August 1914 had left him in such utter despondency that most of the nation's initial policies toward the war fell into the hands of Lansing, who firmly supported the Allies. Indeed, the administration perhaps left the door open for British maritime infractions when, in December 1914, it admitted that "imperative necessity to protect their [the

Allies'] national safety" might justify actions that in other contexts were illegal.

As Lansing conceded, his country's diplomatic notes to England were often designed to leave the impression of protest without reaching the level of an ultimatum; chances were, he believed, that the United States might join the Allies and be expected to use the very tactics it now condemned. After the war Lansing explained in his memoirs that the notes sent to Britain were "long and exhaustive treatises which opened up new subjects of discussion and rarely ever closed those in controversy. Short and emphatic notes were dangerous. Everything was submerged in verbosity. It was done with deliberate purpose." Such an approach "insured continuance of the controversies and left the questions unsettled, which was necessary in order to leave this country free to act and even to act illegally when it entered the war."

To finance the war effort the Allies initially hoped to draw on monetary accounts owed by the United States in Europe, but these were quickly exhausted, and Britain and France had to seek direct U.S. loans. When the financially powerful J. P. Morgan and Company in New York sought the state department's position on the matter in August 1914, Bryan frowned on loans to belligerents as a violation of neutrality. "Money," he wrote the president, was the "worst of all contrabands because it commands all other things." Yet Bryan failed to recognize that both precedent and law stood on the side of the Allies' request. Belligerents in the past, including the Union and Confederate governments during the American Civil War, had financed their efforts through money borrowed from neutral nations. U.S. bankers had loaned money to Japan during its war with Russia in 1904 and 1905. Bryan finally realized that his policy was legally unsound and that the munitions traffic benefited both the United States and the Allies. A state department spokesman had also convincingly argued that whereas loans by neutral governments were a violation of neutrality, loans by private

individuals were not. Bryan relented in October 1914 but stipulated that the administration would approve "credits," not loans, thus maintaining the fiction of avoiding financial involvement in the war.

The *Lusitania* Crisis

The Berlin government had meanwhile adopted new maritime tactics designed to break the deadlock in the trenches. On February 4, 1915, it announced that in two weeks it would begin a policy of "unrestricted submarine warfare" (firing without warning) on enemy ships entering a "war zone" surrounding the British Isles. The wisdom of this decision was questionable. Britain and France combined had nearly five times more submarines than Germany. At the time of the announcement the Germans had twenty-one U-boats, only four of which were functional, and even though that number grew to more than 125 within three years, logistical difficulties made it impossible to send more than a third to sea at one time. Germany nonetheless ordered submarine commanders to sink all intruders on sight and warned neutrals to stay out of the war zone for fear of being mistaken as an enemy. Citizens from neutral nations, Germany declared, should not book passage on liners belonging to belligerents. Within a week Wilson warned that the United States would hold Germany to "strict accountability" for any harm to Americans. The Washington government would adopt all measures needed "to safeguard American lives and property and to secure to American citizens the full enjoyment of their acknowledged rights on the high seas."

Germany's use of the submarine reinforced the growing conviction that existing maritime codes of international law were outdated by the time of the Great War. Traditional practice called for belligerent vessels to stay just beyond the three-mile zone while patrolling ports. But Britain soon argued that because of long-range guns and German submarines, it must station its vessels on the high seas. The

British then used the doctrine of "continuous voyage" (defining a cargo's status by determining the ship's *ultimate* destination, a policy used by the British during the War of 1812 and by the Union in the Civil War) to justify seizures of U.S. commercial vessels en route to other neutral nations, which in turn might allow cargoes to enter Germany in their own ships. Past practice also permitted a belligerent to search a neutral's cargo at sea; if suspected of carrying contraband, the ship went to a prize court for adjudication. But modern merchant vessels were larger, and boarding parties needed more time for inspecting cargo and papers. The submarine forced a change in this procedure. Nothing was more inviting to the enemy than to find its opponent motionless at sea; the British therefore decided that a careful and safe examination of cargo could take place only within their harbors. Such a policy caused resentment among neutrals, because it meant delay, broken contracts, and

financial losses. Although some U.S. merchants suspected their British competitors of pressing the London government into this policy, the crucial factor was the submarine.

German maritime policies likewise upset Americans, but much more so because use of the submarine increased the chances for loss of life. The fragile submarine was incapable of meeting the requirements of international law without risking destruction. It had to rely on the element of surprise. Slow to surface, slow to move, and even slower to submerge, the U-boat seldom fired its torpedoes with great accuracy: They had to hit their target at almost a ninety-degree angle to be most effective. The U-boat commander could not adhere to maritime rules calling for him to warn a vessel before attack; British naval and merchant marine commanders were under orders to ram or shell enemy submarines because of their known vulnerability. Indeed, the mere toss of a hand grenade could prove disabling. The

German U-boat
A crowd inspects a German U-boat stranded on the south coast of England during the Great War. *Library of Congress.*

submarine could not withstand deep-water pressure, and its small size made it impractical to take on passengers from a ship about to be destroyed. Regardless of these realities, the German U-boat raised the specter of barbarism. Wilson later drew a clear distinction between German and British policy when he declared that "property rights can be vindicated by claims for damages when the war is over, and no modern nation can decline to arbitrate such claims; but the fundamental rights of humanity cannot be. The loss of life," he emphasized, "is irreparable."

During the first two months of unrestricted submarine warfare, the Germans sank about ninety vessels in the war zone, including the British *Falaba,* with the loss of one American. They also torpedoed (without sinking) a U.S. oil tanker, the *Gulflight,* with several casualties. But no attack aroused as much furor and righteous indignation among Americans as the Germans' sinking of the British luxury liner *Lusitania* on May 7, 1915. Experts considered the vessel unsinkable because it had 175 watertight compartments, could outrun any submarine, and was so huge—a seventh of a mile long, the largest passenger liner afloat. For eight years it had crossed the Atlantic with record speed. Its owner, the Cunard Line, had used government funds in building this model vessel, and in return builders had made the *Lusitania* readily adaptable to gun fittings. Half of its crew were members of the naval reserve. On the outside the *Lusitania* was a lavish showcase of wealth and splendor; with its four smokestacks silhouetted against the sky it suggested a portrait in motion. But on the inside the reality of war rested quietly below its decks. As 1257 passengers and 702 crew members moved from stem to stern during the Atlantic voyage, they walked above a cargo of foodstuffs and contraband that included more than a thousand cases of empty shrapnel shells, nearly twenty cases of nonexplosive fuses, and more than four million rounds of rifle ammunition. As the *Lusitania* prepared for departure from New York

harbor it carried both "babies and bullets," according to a state department member.

The Imperial German Embassy in Washington had on the morning of May 1 warned Americans through fifty newspapers not to travel on the *Lusitania,* which was about to leave New York. Next to the advertisement for the Cunard Line, the embassy ran a "Notice" reminding readers that ships entering the war zone around the British Isles were subject to attack. But instead of frightening passengers, the announcement took on a perverse kind of fascination by spurring excitement about seeing a submarine on the trip overseas. Captain William Turner of the *Lusitania* scoffed at the danger. "Do you think all these people would be booking passage on board the *Lusitania,*" the veteran seaman asked journalists, "if they thought she could be caught by a German submarine? Why it's the best joke I've heard in many days, this talk of torpedoing!" Nearly 200 Americans joined the other passengers boarding the ship. No word of caution came from the government in Washington. Such a warning would violate freedom of the seas, Wilson reminded Bryan, who had expressed fear that American travel on belligerent ships would cause trouble. The agent for the Cunard Line in the United States dismissed the German warning as a cheap scare tactic. "The truth is that the *Lusitania* is the safest boat on the sea. She is too fast for any submarine. No German war vessel can get her or near her."

The *Lusitania* left New York for Liverpool just past noon on May 1, with a crew that numbered fewer than the maximum and was of less than top caliber because the more experienced sailors had been assigned to the Royal Navy. Five days later the *Lusitania* was nearing Ireland when Turner received a message out of Queenstown (present-day Cobh): "Submarines active off south coast of Ireland." U-boats had sunk two vessels in those waters earlier that day, but Turner failed to follow standing orders in such conditions. He did not avoid headlands, nor did he steer the great vessel into the deeper mid-channel waters and maintain full speed and a zigzag course.

The British warning had been accurate: Lieutenant Walter Schwieger commanded a U-boat in the shallow waters off the Irish coast. He remained below during the morning of May 7 because of fog and the presence of British patrol ships, but he surfaced before 2 P.M. and sighted a large ship with four smokestacks on the distant horizon. Heading toward the vessel, he submerged to its side and fired a single torpedo. The starboard watch on the *Lusitania* sounded a warning as he saw the projectile cutting a trail of foam and bubbles in the water. But despite a full minute's notice, his warning went unheeded because Turner was not on deck as he should have been in those waters. Thirty seconds before impact, another lookout shouted the warning and Turner managed to reach the bridge just before the torpedo struck. Schwieger's log recorded the drama:

> . . . four funnels and two masts of a steamer. . . . Ship is made out to be large passenger steamer . . . Clean bow shot at a distance of 700 meters. . . . Torpedo hits starboard side right behind the bridge. An unusually heavy explosion takes place with a very strong explosion cloud (cloud reaches far beyond front funnel). The explosion of the torpedo must have been followed by a second one (boiler or coal or powder?). . . . The ship stops immediately and heels over to starboard very quickly, immersing simultaneously at the bow. . . . The name *Lusitania* becomes visible in gold letters.

In just eighteen minutes a single torpedo had driven the mighty *Lusitania* from serenity to total confusion and then, finally, headlong into the deep. Passengers frantically tried to board lifeboats, only to find that the rapid and extreme list to starboard swung some of the craft helplessly away from deck, while those lifeboats on the opposite side of the ship were bounced to bits against the hull. A lone torpedo revealed that the greatly heralded engineering genius of the *Lusitania*'s construction—the watertight compartments—proved to be its fatal flaw. The sealed off damaged section confined the sea water to starboard, as the system was supposed to do;

but by preventing the tremendous volume of inrushing water from dispersing evenly throughout the hull, the enormous concentration of weight helped drag the vessel to its side and ultimately to the bottom. Even the outer longitudinal bulkheads running fore to aft, filled with coal for ballast, contributed to the ship's undoing. Great torrents of water gushed into the long channels, expanding the weight of the coal and further dragging down the vessel. Nearly 1200 perished, including 128 Americans, as the *Lusitania* briefly stood on its bow on the ocean floor and, with rudders jutting above the shallow waters, seemed to heave and sigh before disappearing sullenly beneath the surface.

U.S. reaction to the sinking of the *Lusitania* was a mixture of stunned disbelief and marked revulsion. Many Americans called it an atrocity. The *Nation* of New York proclaimed it "a deed for which a Hun would blush, a Turk be ashamed, and a Barbary pirate apologize. To speak of technicalities and the rules of war, in the face of such wholesale murder on the high seas, is a waste of time." The "law of nations and the law of God have been alike trampled upon. . . . The torpedo that sank the *Lusitania* also sank Germany in the opinion of mankind." Germany, the magazine continued, "has affronted the moral sense of the world and sacrificed her standing among the nations." Evangelist Billy Sunday called it "Damnable! Damnable! Absolutely hellish!"

A cabinet meeting had just broken up when Wilson received the news; though shocked and indignant, he did not want to respond publicly until he had had time to consider his stance and that of fellow Americans. On May 10 in Philadelphia, after allowing his compatriots' emotions to simmer for three days, he delivered an address that he thought was a reflection of the popular mood. "There is such a thing as a man being too proud to fight. There is such a thing as a nation being so right that it does not need to convince others by force that it is right." The following morning he informed his cabinet that he would send a note to Berlin demanding recognition of

New York Times *on the* Lusitania
Although the Germans' sinking of the *Lusitania* was not an immediate cause of the U.S. entry into
World War I, it remains one of the worst maritime tragedies of all time. *New York Public Library.*

Americans' rights to cross the sea and a renunciation of further sinkings of unarmed vessels.
Bryan argued that in the interests of neutrality, the White House should send a similar
note to Britain warning against its violations
of the United States's maritime rights. Wilson
rejected Bryan's proposal. On May 12 the
London government tried to ensure U.S.
entry into the war by releasing the Bryce
Report, a document supposedly given the
stamp of veracity by having the name of the
respected writer and diplomat Viscount James
Bryce affixed to it. The report graphically
depicted the German atrocities allegedly committed in Belgium and France.

But the highly anticipated decision for war
did not come. The following day, the United

States informed Germany that it expected
indemnities for the *Lusitania*'s victims. Roosevelt was livid with the Wilson administration's apparent inaction; but he was one of
only a few Americans who demanded war.
Most were appalled by the disaster but admitted that passengers on the *Lusitania* had traveled at their own risk.

The Berlin government was divided in reaction to the *Lusitania* incident, but it soon
termed the sinking an act of self-defense
because of the munitions aboard. Chancellor
Bethmann Hollweg had long dreaded the possibility of a submarine forcing war onto the
United States and attempted to defuse this
dangerous situation by avoiding a direct reply
to Wilson's note. Yet he posed questions that

the United States had to confront. Indeed, many of the charges made by the Germans have since been substantiated. The *Lusitania,* according to the German note, was a virtual ship of war because it was fitted for arms, carried munitions and other war materiel, and was under orders to ram submarines. The sinking was "self-defense," and Germany recommended arbitration.

The Wilson administration at first was incredulous with the German response but then decided, over Bryan's vehement objections, to send a second and more sternly worded note to Berlin. A heated debate then developed in the cabinet over Bryan's proposal to send a note to London as well. When his colleagues voted down the idea, Bryan bitterly accused them of favoring the Allies. This was an "unfair and unjust" remark, the president shot back in the raw atmosphere. Bryan had no choice but

to resign. The second *Lusitania* note, Bryan explained, criticized Germany too sharply; the administration sent no equivalent warning to Britain; Wilson had refused to warn Americans against traveling on belligerent ships; and the president had continually ignored him in formulating policy. Bryan privately told Wilson that "Colonel House has been Secretary of State, not I, and I have never had your full confidence." The president, then experiencing another of a prolonged series of blinding headaches, found some relief in replacing Bryan with Lansing. The new secretary of state openly sided with the Allies and believed that the United States would ultimately enter the war on Britain's side.

By late summer of 1915, changed conditions in the United States led the Washington government to authorize loans to the Allies. Bryan was gone, Lansing favored loans, and

"He's Such an Impulsive Chap!"
The kaiser pleads his case before Uncle Sam for using the submarine. *New York World.*

Robert Lansing
Secretary of state who openly favored the Allies
in the Great War. *Library of Congress.*

the country was in severe economic straits. War loans would stimulate the U.S. economy and prevent a depression, Lansing argued along with Secretary of the Treasury William McAdoo. Wilson was convinced. He permitted the Morgan company to underwrite a huge loan to the Allies, and soon U.S. merchants were providing munitions as well. The decision had quick results at home. By the end of the year the United States had taken a major turn toward economic recovery.

Britain's control of the seas caused a built-in bias in U.S. commercial activity that further endangered relations with Germany. As munitions sales climbed, German complaints became louder. *The Fatherland,* which was the major German-American propaganda organ in the United States, remarked that "we [Americans] prattle about humanity, while we manufacture poisoned shrapnel and picric acid for profit. Ten thousand German widows, ten thousand orphans, ten thousand

graves bear the legend 'Made in America.'" Lansing denied that the administration favored the Allies. If one belligerent enjoyed geographical, military, or naval advantages, he insisted, "the rules of neutral conduct cannot be varied so as to favor the less fortunate combatant." His analysis revealed the danger inherent in a neutral's wish to trade with both belligerents. By the spring of 1917 the United States had loaned the Allies $2.3 billion and the Germans only $27 million. The advantage belonged to the maritime power, and that was Britain.

Germany had reason to complain about U.S. wartime commercial policies. Britain's decision to arm its merchant ships raised legitimate questions about whether these vessels should enter neutral ports; yet the Washington government merely labeled these measures "defensive" and permitted their entry. Regarding munitions sales, the Wilson administration explained that no law prevented private Americans from selling war materiel to belligerents. In fact, the state department argued, a ban on such sales would help the Germans and therefore constitute a violation of neutrality because they had more munitions plants than did the Allies. Germany could legally buy these same goods, of course, but it had to come to the United States to get them. Surely it was not the United States's fault that Britain controlled the seas. A U.S. embargo on the munitions trade would aid Germany, whereas the continuation of such sales helped the Allies. No middle ground existed. Profits dictated the sale of these goods, and Congress refused to alienate its constituency by ending the lucrative business. The Wilson administration ignored Germany's complaints—a silence that itself signaled tacit approval of the arms traffic.

Germany had meanwhile undergone a quiet retreat on its maritime policies, but the United States did not know that, and relations continued to deteriorate. A month after the *Lusitania*'s sinking, the Berlin government secretly directed U-boat commanders to refrain from attacking passenger liners without warning. The ensuing calm at sea did not stop Americans from exerting pressure on the Wilson administration to exact reparations for past damages. Roosevelt ridiculed "Professor Wilson," and one U.S. newspaper played upon John Paul Jones's famous words by facetiously declaring that "we have not yet begun to write." Despite Berlin's secret orders, a submarine commander in August 1915 torpedoed the *Arabic,* a British passenger vessel en route to New York, and two more Americans died.

The following month the British secret service intercepted and turned over to the Americans information revealing Austro-Hungarian attempts to instigate strikes in munitions plants. Lansing ordered the expulsion of the Austro-Hungarian ambassador for possessing such materials. The Washington government also published documents confiscated from a German spy in the United States that showed Germany's intentions to sabotage munitions industries. In December Lansing secured the recall of the German military and naval attachés. When in 1916 the Black Tom munitions factory in New Jersey exploded with a loss of over $20 million, Americans blamed German conspirators.

U.S. emotions over the *Arabic* episode seemed dangerous enough to prompt the German ambassador in Washington, Count Johann von Bernstorff, to take an unauthorized action in an attempt to halt his country's perilous submarine policy. On September 1, 1915, without first securing approval from his home government, he released a statement later known as the "*Arabic* pledge": "Liners will not be sunk by our submarines without warning and without safety of the lives of noncombatants, provided that the liners do not try to escape or offer resistance." The note did not mention merchant ships, and the United States's continued protests led the Berlin government to announce in early October that orders to U-boat commanders "have been made so stringent that a recurrence of incidents similar to the *Arabic* case is considered out of the question."

On February 4, 1916, almost nine months after the *Lusitania*'s sinking, the German government expressed regret and agreed to make reparations, which it did during the early 1920s. Germany never admitted to wrongdoing, refused to offer an apology, and continued its calls for arbitration. Yet no popular clamor for war developed in the United States, and the drawn-out exchanges of notes allowed passions to calm while leaving the misleading impression that Wilsonian diplomacy had achieved a major victory. The White House chose to regard the promise of indemnification as satisfactory and dropped the matter.

The Decision to Intervene

The United States made several attempts in early 1916 to mediate an end to the war. House spent two weeks in London trying to determine acceptable conditions for peace, but he departed for Berlin with nothing substantial to offer. The German response was the same. Moving on to Paris, House later recorded in his diary that he went beyond his instructions in assuring the French that "in the event the Allies are successful during the next few months I promised that the President would *not* intervene. In the event that they were losing ground, I promised the President *would* intervene." House did not tell Wilson that he had made these assurances to France. He then returned to London and met again with Grey. The president had authorized House to guarantee his country's "moral force" against the Central Powers if they rejected peace talks, but when Grey recorded his conversation with House, the moral assurances seemed to include physical force as well. According to the House-Grey memorandum of February 22, "President Wilson was ready, on hearing from France and England that the moment was opportune, to propose that a conference should be summoned to put an end to the war. Should the Allies accept this proposal, and should Germany refuse it, the United States would [probably] enter the war against Germany."

Wilson approved the essentials of the House-Grey memorandum, but he had carefully added the word "probably" (in brackets) in the sentence, thereby nearly ensuring U.S. entry into the war. The Allies, however, turned down Wilson's proposal, perhaps because the insertion of "probably" as a qualifier made it appear indecisive, but undoubtedly more because they hoped to win the war without being bound to the president. Yet the Allies had secured moral support. The British interpreted the message as a sign that U.S. objections to their maritime actions were more form than substance.

Some congressional members had meanwhile grown suspicious that Wilson sought to enter the war, and they tried to enact legislation barring citizens from traveling on armed belligerent ships. They were particularly concerned about a new twist in Germany's submarine policies. In February 1916 the Berlin government had announced that its U-boats had orders to sink armed merchant vessels without warning. Texas Representative Jeff McLemore sponsored a bill warning Americans not to travel on such ships, and about a month afterward Oklahoma Senator Thomas Gore did the same. The Gore-McLemore resolution attracted widespread interest in Congress, although Wilson indignantly regarded it as an infringement of the executive's authority over foreign policy, a slur on U.S. honor, and a violation of international law. He sent an emotionally charged letter to the chair of the Senate Foreign Relations Committee on February 24, asserting that he could not "consent to any abridgement of the rights of American citizens in any respect. . . . Once accept a single abatement of right," he warned, "and many other humiliations would certainly follow, and the whole fine fabric of international law might crumble under our hands piece by piece." White House pressure paid off. Congress tabled the Gore-McLemore resolution.

On March 24, 1916, the crisis pitch built again as a German submarine torpedoed and severely disabled the *Sussex,* an unarmed French passenger ship passing through the English Channel. No Americans were among the nearly eighty who lost their lives in the attack, but four were injured. The German commander evidently thought the vessel a British minelayer, because in outline from a distance the *Sussex* looked like one. In fact, his belief that he had hit a warship led Berlin's leaders to deny that a submarine had attacked an unarmed vessel. This seemingly flagrant lie infuriated the Wilson administration and the American people, causing many, including Lansing and House, to push for a break in diplomatic relations.

Americans regarded the *Sussex* incident as an infraction of the German promises given after both the *Lusitania* and *Arabic* sinkings. The president faced enormous pressure to break relations with Germany, but he knew that his country was currently in trouble with Mexico and that his people were not united on maritime issues. On April 18 Wilson sent an ultimatum to Berlin warning that if it did not halt "submarine warfare against passenger and freight-carrying vessels," the United States would "sever diplomatic relations with the German Empire altogether."

Germany's reply to Wilson's note came on May 4 in the form of the so-called "*Sussex* pledge," which only *seemed* encouraging. Germany guaranteed that merchant ships would "not be sunk without warning and without saving human lives, unless these ships attempt to escape or offer resistance." But it conditioned this promise upon the United States's success in convincing Britain to lift its blockade. Should this plan fail, "the German Government would then be facing a new situation, in which it must reserve itself complete liberty of action."

The war, of course, had dictated this German response. On the one hand, Germany could not be too rigid because its military offensive in Europe was grinding down in devastating losses at Verdun; on the other hand, Germany could not forgo its most effective weapon—the submarine. The United States had little chance of persuading the British to drop the blockade, but the general impression among Americans was that Wilson had forced the Berlin government to call off the submarines. The truth was that his ultimatum had surrendered the diplomatic initiative to Germany. Should its submarine policies continue, the United States would face the unhappy choice of submission or war.

Like a seesaw, U.S. relations with Britain deteriorated in almost direct proportion to their improvement with Germany after the *Sussex* crisis. The United States again considered mediation in the summer of 1916, but the time was not auspicious because Britain was preparing to open an offensive in the west, and France was engaged in the mighty defense at Verdun. Both Allied belligerents hoped to gain a stronger military position before agreeing to peace negotiations. When the French lines held against the Germans and the British met defeat on the Somme River, neither government expressed interest in ending the war. U.S. relations with Britain had meanwhile hardened as the London government brutally put down an Irish rebellion in April 1916 and soon imposed greater restrictions on neutrals' trade with the Central Powers.

In July 1916 the British infuriated Americans by releasing a "blacklist" of more than eighty business leaders or companies in the United States that traded with the enemy. The president, Ambassador Page in London, the *New York Times,* and other Americans considered the blacklist a monumental mistake. Wilson told House: "I am, I must admit, about at the end of my patience with Great Britain and the Allies. This blacklist business is the last straw." Congress tried to counter the blacklist by authorizing the president to close U.S. ports to British subjects adhering to their government's policy of boycotting blacklisted companies. It also passed the Naval Act of 1916 in response to Wilson's challenge to build a navy larger than Britain's that would allow Americans to "do what we please." The president reacted furiously to the blacklist, because such a measure compromised the principle of freedom of the seas, infringed on the rights of citizens, and was economically harmful to the United States. His protests

were somewhat effective. The British soon shortened their blacklist.

In the midst of these growing problems, Wilson sought reelection in 1916 on a platform highlighting the claim, "He Kept Us Out of War." Former president Theodore Roosevelt had returned to the Republican fold but failed to win the nomination from those who remembered the 1912 debacle and were now reluctant to support a candidate so ardently in favor of armed intervention in the war. Instead, the Republicans nominated an associate justice of the Supreme Court, Charles Evans Hughes, who faced the unenviable task of attracting the German-American vote while condemning the wartime actions of their homeland and urging greater preparedness in a nation preferring peace. The Democrats, meanwhile, promised continued neutrality and adopted practically the entire slate of reform programs contained in the Progressive party platform in 1912, thereby drawing Roosevelt's erstwhile supporters along with those opposing war. Wilson won the narrowest of victories.

After Wilson's reelection, he tried again to intervene for peace. Notes went to both belligerents, inquiring about their objectives in the war and urging negotiations. But before he could act, the Berlin government announced interest in a peace conference. Germany had recently improved its military position by defeating Russia on the Eastern Front, crushing Rumania, winning control of the Balkans, and holding back French and Belgian forces in the west. If Wilson at this point showed interest in the German offer, the impression would be that he and the Germans had acted in collusion against the Allies; yet if he refused, an opportunity for peace might escape. The president went ahead with his notes on December 18. Leaders in London and Paris were not interested. Indeed, they were bitterly offended by Wilson's cutting assertion that "the objects which the statesmen of the belligerents on both sides have in mind in this war are virtually the same." The Allies found it difficult to believe that the United States did not find justice in their cause. One British spokesman called Wilson an "ass," and another declared that everyone was "mad as hell." The king, his nerves shattered by the war, wept over Wilson's inability to understand that democracy itself was at stake.

On January 22, 1917, Wilson appeared before the Senate to push his mediation efforts and call for "peace without victory" and the establishment of a world organization to maintain that peace. The previous May he had recommended such an organization in a speech before the League to Enforce Peace. The United States should be a member, but only if peace terms were reconcilable with its postwar aims of peace without victory, freedom of the seas, reductions in arms, and self-government for all peoples. But the belligerents had come too far and lost too much to accept a stalemate. Wilson nonetheless insisted on "equality of nations" as the avenue to lasting peace. For a third time he offered U.S. mediation; and for a third time both sides refused.

Germany had already decided to resume unrestricted submarine warfare on February 1, 1917, so the United States had little chance to secure the peace and earn a seat at the victors' conference table without entering the war. German-American relations had improved during the months since the *Sussex* incident and the announcement of the British blacklist; Bethmann Hollweg and other moderates in Berlin urged great care in matters affecting U.S. neutrality. Only the United States could save the Allies, they declared, and the German high command should gear its policy toward preventing U.S. involvement in the war. But the moderates in Berlin lost the initiative to Admiral Alfred von Tirpitz and other hard-line military and naval leaders who were unwilling to compromise on war issues. The submarine, they confidently argued, would force British capitulation *before* the United States could mobilize for war.

Ambassador Bernstorff in Washington likewise tried to convince his superiors in Berlin that unrestricted submarine warfare would force the United States into the war and perhaps ensure Allied victory. The *Sussex* pledge, he insisted, should determine his nation's maritime policies; in time Wilson would persuade the Allies to retreat from their extreme conditions for peace. But Bernstorff was unsuccessful and on January 31 notified Lansing that Britain's naval actions had forced his home government to resume unrestricted submarine warfare the following day. Several members of Berlin's high command recognized that the decision was a gamble, because they feared that the United States could enter the war before Britain's defeat. But the German admiralty discounted the threat of U.S. intervention. The United States's munitions trade with the Allies, one admiral underlined, would not affect the course of the war because Britain controlled the seas, and as belligerent vessels U.S. ships could carry no more goods than they did as neutrals. Proponents of the new policy considered it the only way to end Britain's blockade and bring victory. Besides, German naval officers believed that their U-boats could cut off U.S. shipments of war materiel and break British resistance in six months. Matters could not be worse with the United States in the war, German Field Marshal Paul von Hindenburg remarked to Bethmann Hollweg, as they solemnly surveyed mounting casualty lists from trench warfare.

Wilson's previous pronouncements against Germany's use of the submarine necessitated a strong response to the new policy, and on February 3 the United States took a pivotal step closer to war: It broke diplomatic relations with Germany. Wilson still had hopes for peace. Should the United States enter the conflict, he realized, no disinterested civilized nation would be left to construct a lasting peace. Yet he also knew that the new German policy would confine U.S. ships to port, hurting the economy and endangering the national interest by giving the appearance of capitulation. Had the Germans refrained from maritime action against U.S. vessels after the new policy of February 1, the Wilson administration might have stayed out of the war.

As the final seconds of peace ticked away, Wilson perhaps hoped that the implications of ruptured relations would awaken Germany to the folly of antagonizing the United States. But both the Germans and the Americans had been moving into hard-line positions that allowed no honorable retreat. Berlin's decision to use the submarine without restrictions virtually assured U.S. participation in the war. Neither government *wanted* to fight the other, but both became locked into policies that permitted either a step backward into dishonor or a plunge forward into war.

While the Washington government anxiously awaited news from the Atlantic, still another crisis developed when Ambassador Page in London got hold of a secret telegram from German Foreign Minister Arthur Zimmermann in Berlin to his emissary in Mexico City. The so-called Zimmermann Telegram of February 24, 1917, which British Naval Intelligence had intercepted from two German transmissions, suggested that Germany might negotiate a military alliance with Carranza's government in Mexico should the United States enter the war. In exchange, Germany would aid Mexico in regaining Arizona, California, and New Mexico, the lands lost in the war with the United States ending in 1848. The telegram also hinted at persuading Japan, one of the Allies, to join the German-Mexican pact against the United States.

News of the telegram had instant impact. Such an arrangement, if consummated, posed a direct threat to U.S. security—especially in the southwest and west coast, areas hitherto untouched by Germany's war policies but traditionally concerned about Mexican and Japanese infiltration. The telegram was particularly exasperating to Wilson because, in the interest of neutrality, he had allowed both sets of belligerents to send communications through state department wires and the U.S. embassy in Berlin. He was furious and believed himself duped and U.S. honor betrayed. After the American press published the telegram on March 1, Roosevelt, still fuming over the *Lusitania* and succeeding crises, warned that

if the president did not ask Congress for war, he would "skin him alive."

The Zimmermann Telegram had deep implications for U.S. diplomacy. Perhaps the German foreign minister intended only to stir up trouble between Mexico and the United States and thus weaken U.S. effectiveness should it enter the war with Germany. But the telegram was a colossal blunder that unleashed a popular storm that Zimmermann could hardly have expected. Its contents were no different in tone and objective than other secret treaties made in Europe that had helped bring on the war. But Zimmermann's proposals struck Americans directly, rudely introducing them to the realities of world politics. The Zimmermann Telegram posed a threat to the nation's security, substantiated the image of the Hun that British propagandists had long portrayed, involved Americans heretofore insulated from the European conflict, and removed Wilson's fast waning hope for uncovering some element of decency among German leaders. The telegram helped push the United States closer to war because it substantiated charges from Atlantic Coast Americans that unrestricted submarine warfare was only one of several German threats to the nation's honor and security.

Events on the Atlantic finally forced the United States into action. A German submarine sank the British merchant vessel *Laconia* in late February, taking two Americans down with it. On March 1, the same day the Zimmermann Telegram appeared in the newspapers, Wilson asked Congress for authorization to arm the country's merchant vessels and to use "any other instrumentalities or methods" to safeguard U.S. property and lives. But he encountered strong opposition from isolationist Senators Robert LaFollette of Wisconsin and George Norris of Nebraska, who led a filibuster against the bill until Congress went out of session. The "little group of willful men," as Wilson bitterly called them, only temporarily blocked the measure, because Lansing presented a convincing legal argument for the president's right to arm the ships on his own authority as commander in chief of the armed forces. On March 12 Wilson announced that he was doing so. Within a few days news arrived that justified his decision. A German submarine had sunk an unarmed American merchant ship on March 12, the same day of his announcement, and even though no loss of life had occurred, the U-boats went on to sink three other unarmed American freighters in a three-day span from March 16 to 18, killing many aboard. U.S. ships had become prey to German submarine commanders, leaving the president no choice but to seek war.

At 8:30 on the warm, rainy evening of April 2, 1917, Wilson went before a special joint session of Congress and asked it to declare war on Germany. The Berlin government had forced the United States into this position, he explained in deeply moving terms. German submarines had waged a "war against all nations"—a "warfare against mankind."

Recent events in Russia, he added, had signaled an important change in the tenor of the war. A revolution had brought down the czar and removed the last remaining barrier to fighting a war for democracy. The idealists, Jewish-Americans, and others who had opposed Russia could now join the Allies in their struggle against "Prussian autocracy" and militarism. The United States, Wilson proclaimed, had "to vindicate the principles of peace and justice." It "shall fight for the things which we have always carried nearest our hearts—for democracy, for the right of those who submit to authority to have a voice in their own government, for the rights and liberties of small nations, for a universal dominion of right by such a concert of free peoples as shall bring peace and safety to all nations and make the world itself at last free." Wilson had a peace plan and a deep conviction that only he could guarantee its success. To do so, he must take part in the war to ensure a voice

"Exploding in His Hand"
The German attempt to arrange a pact with Mexico by the Zimmermann Telegram thoroughly alienated the American Southwest, Far West, and President Wilson. *New York World*.

at the peace conference. In a memorable statement, he declared that "the world must be made safe for democracy."

Oratory was one of Wilson's fortes, and he used that quality to advantage that day. Congress greeted his message with a moment of silence, followed by ringing applause.

A War to End All Wars

On April 6, 1917, with overwhelming congressional approval (82 to 6 in the Senate and 373 to 50 in the House), Wilson announced that the United States was at war with Germany. Idealism and realism had merged into the joint aim of fulfilling the tenets of missionary diplomacy and safeguarding the national interest. Wilson had ingeniously touched Americans' emotions by calling for a "war to end all wars" and to "make the world safe for democracy." The probability is that he believed what he said; chances are that many Americans also did. It was the only type of war a peace-loving president and nation could wage: one for world reform designed to bring permanent peace.

Selected Readings

Ambrosius, Lloyd E. *Wilsonian Statecraft: Theory and Practice of Liberal Internationalism during World War I.* 1991.

Bailey, Thomas A., and Ryan, Paul B. *The Lusitania Disaster.* 1975.

Birnbaum, Karl. *Peace Moves and U-Boat Warfare.* 1970.

Brown, Jonathan C. *Oil and Revolution in Mexico.* 1993.

Buehrig, Edward H. *Woodrow Wilson and the Balance of Power.* 1955.

Burk, Kathleen. *Britain, America, and the Sinews of War, 1914–1918.* 1985.

Calder, Bruce J. *The Impact of Intervention: The Dominican Republic during the U.S. Occupation of 1916–1924.* 1984.

Calhoun, Frederick S. *Power and Principle: Armed Intervention in Wilsonian Foreign Policy.* 1986.

———. *Uses of Force and Wilsonian Foreign Policy.* 1993.

Clements, Kendrick A. *The Presidency of Woodrow Wilson.* 1992.

———. *William Jennings Bryan, Missionary Isolationist.* 1983.

———. "Woodrow Wilson's Mexican Policy, 1913–1915," *Diplomatic History* 4 (1980): 113–36.

———. *Woodrow Wilson: World Statesman.* 1987.

Clendenen, Clarence C. *The United States and Pancho Villa.* 1961.

Clifford, J. Garry. *The Citizen Soldiers: The Plattsburg Training Camp Movement, 1913–1920.* 1972.

Cohen, Warren I. *The American Revisionists: The Lessons of Intervention in World War I.* 1967.

Conyne, G. R. *Woodrow Wilson: British Perspectives, 1912–21.* 1992.

Coogan, John W. *The End of Neutrality: The United States, Britain, and Maritime Rights, 1899–1915.* 1981.

Cooper, John M., Jr. *The Vanity of Power: American Isolationism and World War I, 1914–1917.* 1969.

———. *Walter Hines Page: The Southerner as American, 1855–1918.* 1977.

———. *The Warrior and the Priest: Woodrow Wilson and Theodore Roosevelt.* 1983.

Curry, Roy W. *Woodrow Wilson and Far Eastern Policy, 1913–1921.* 1957.

Devlin, Patrick. *Too Proud to Fight: Woodrow Wilson's Neutrality.* 1974.

Gaddis, John L. *Russia, the Soviet Union, and the United States: An Interpretive History.* 2nd ed., 1990.

Gardner, Lloyd C. *Safe for Democracy: The Anglo-American Response to Revolution, 1913–1923.* 1984.

Gilderhus, Mark T. *Diplomacy and Revolution: U.S.-Mexican Relations under Wilson and Carranza.* 1977.

———. *Pan-American Visions: Woodrow Wilson in the Western Hemisphere, 1913–1921.* 1986.

———. "Wilson, Carranza, and the Monroe Doctrine: A Question in Regional Organization," *Diplomatic History* 7 (1983): 103–15.

Gregory, Ross. *The Origins of American Intervention in the First World War.* 1971.

———. *Walter Hines Page: Ambassador to the Court of St. James's.* 1970.

Grieb, Kenneth J. *The United States and Huerta.* 1969.

Haley, P. Edward. *Revolution and Intervention: The Diplomacy of Taft and Wilson with Mexico, 1910–1917.* 1970.

Healy, David F. *Drive to Hegemony: The United States in the Caribbean, 1898–1917.* 1988.

———. *Gunboat Diplomacy in the Wilson Era: The U.S. Navy in Haiti, 1915–1916.* 1976.

Heckscher, August. *Woodrow Wilson.* 1991.

Hill, L.D. *Emissaries to a Revolution: Woodrow Wilson's Executive Agents in Mexico.* 1973.

Hunt, Michael H. *The Making of a Special Relationship: The United States and China to 1914.* 1983.

Jonas, Manfred. *The United States and Germany, A Diplomatic History.* 1984.

Joseph, Gilbert M. *Revolution from Without: Yucatán, Mexico, and the United States, 1880–1924.* 1982.

Kaplan, Edward S. *U.S. Imperialism in Latin America.* 1997.

Katz, Friedrich. *The Life and Times of Pancho Villa.* 1998.

———. *The Secret War in Mexico: Europe, the United States, and the Mexican Revolution.* 1981.

Kaufman, Burton I. *Efficiency and Expansion: Foreign Trade Organization in the Wilson Administration, 1913–1921.* 1974.

Kennan, George F. *American Diplomacy.* Expanded ed. 1984. Originally published as *American Diplomacy, 1900–1950.* 1951.

Killen, Linda. *The Russian Bureau: A Case Study in Wilsonian Diplomacy.* 1983.

LaFeber, Walter. *The Clash: A History of U.S.-Japanese Relations.* 1997.

Langley, Lester D. *The Banana Wars: An Inner History of American Empire, 1900–1934.* 1983.

Levin, N. Gordon, Jr. *Woodrow Wilson and World Politics: America's Response to War and Revolution.* 1968.

Link, Arthur S. *The Higher Realism of Woodrow Wilson and Other Essays.* 1971.

———. *Wilson: Campaigns for Progressivism and Peace.* 1965.

———. *Wilson: Confusions and Crises, 1915–1916.* 1964.

———. *Wilson: The New Freedom.* 1956.

———. *Wilson: The Struggle for Neutrality, 1914–1915.* 1960.

———. *Woodrow Wilson and the Progressive Era, 1910–1917.* 1954.

———. *Woodrow Wilson: Revolution, War, and Peace.* 1979. Rev. ed. of *Wilson the Diplomatist: A Look at His Major Foreign Policies.* 1957.

———, ed. *Woodrow Wilson and a Revolutionary World, 1913–1921.* 1982.

May, Ernest R. *The World War and American Isolation, 1914–1917.* 1959.

May, Henry. *The End of American Innocence.* 1959.

Millis, Walter. *Road to War: America, 1914–1917.* 1935.

Munro, Dana G. *Intervention and Dollar Diplomacy in the Caribbean, 1900–1921.* 1964.

Nordholt, Jan Willem Schulte. *Woodrow Wilson.* 1991.

O'Brien, Thomas F. *The Revolutionary Mission: American Enterprise in Latin America, 1900–1945.* 1996.

Pearlman, Michael. *To Make Democracy Safe for America.* 1984.

Quirk, Robert E. *An Affair of Honor: Woodrow Wilson and the Occupation of Veracruz.* 1962.

Reed, James. *The Missionary Mind and American East Asia Policy, 1911–1915.* 1983.

Rosenberg, Emily S. *Spreading the American Dream: American Economic and Cultural Expansion, 1890–1945.* 1982.

Safford, Jeffrey J. *Wilsonian Maritime Diplomacy, 1913–1921.* 1978.

Schieber, Clara E. *The Transformation of American Sentiment Toward Germany, 1870–1914.* 1923.

Schmidt, Hans. *The United States Occupation of Haiti, 1915–1934.* 1971.

Schoultz, Lars. *Beneath the United States: A History of U.S. Policy Toward Latin America.* 1998.

Seymour, Charles. *American Diplomacy during the World War.* 1934.

Smith, Daniel M. *The Great Departure: The United States and World War I, 1914–1920.* 1965.

———. *Robert Lansing and American Neutrality, 1914–1917.* 1958.

Smith, Robert F. *The United States and Revolutionary Nationalism in Mexico, 1916–1932.* 1972.

Stevenson, David. *The First World War and International Politics.* 1988.

Tansill, Charles C. *America Goes to War.* 1942.

Thompson, John A. *Reformers and War: American Progressive Publicists and the First World War.* 1987.

Tien-yi, Li. *Woodrow Wilson's China Policy, 1913–1917.* 1952.

Tuchman, Barbara W. *The Guns of August.* 1962.

———. *The Zimmermann Telegram.* 1958.

Weinstein, Edwin A. *Woodrow Wilson: A Medical and Psychological Biography.* 1981.

CHAPTER 4

World War I and the League of Nations, 1917–1921

The United States at War

The pace of events picked up quickly after the United States declared war on Germany in April 1917. Austria-Hungary and Turkey broke relations with the United States, and even though Congress never declared war on Germany's allies Bulgaria or Turkey, it did so on Austria-Hungary in December. The governments of Britain, France, Italy, and Belgium sent missions to Washington to discuss the military role of their new ally, but were surprised to learn that U.S. soldiers would not simply mesh with the frontal ranks on the battle scene. The head of the American Expeditionary Force (AEF), General John J. Pershing, staunchly opposed the use of his men within foreign units under foreign command. The United States would maintain its national identity and long-time opposition to entangling alliances by entering the war as an "associated power."

Though not technically an "ally," the United States did as much for its "associates" in the war as if a formal alignment existed. It continued loans to the Allies, set up a War Industries Board to supervise the production of war materiel, and ordered the navy to shift construction emphasis from battleships to destroyers and submarine chasers. The navy

also cooperated with the British in using the convoy system and laying mines along the narrow entrances to the North Sea, closing it to German submarines.

The speed with which the United States sent soldiers to Europe suggested that unrestricted submarine warfare was the Germans' biggest mistake of the war. At the time of the U.S. declaration of war, the U.S. Army numbered 130,000, with 180,000 National Guardsmen in reserve. Some of the men had had military experience in Cuba, the Philippines, or Mexico, but few were ready for combat on the Western Front. The U.S. Navy, the Germans thought, would be of little value in the war, and the U.S. "air service" was a mere adjunct of the army and had no planes fitted with machine guns capable of challenging those of the enemy. But the United States surprised the Germans with the rapidity of its mobilization program. The Allies requested a million U.S. troops by the close of 1918, and the United States not only had that many men in Europe more than six months before the target date, but it doubled that number by the following October.

The United States was not as ill-prepared for war in 1917 as the Germans had calculated. Theodore Roosevelt and activist organizations had been exerting pressure on

British General Douglas Haig and Pershing
At Chaumont, France, during World War I. *Library of Congress.*

Congress for military expansion since 1914. President Wilson had not ignored the need for military readiness. He had tried to persuade Congress in December 1915 to expand the army and navy, but peace groups fought the measure as an unwelcome boon to big business and a threat to civil liberties and social reform programs. Early the following year Wilson took his case to the American people and, with the continuous bad news of submarine warfare as background, convinced Congress in May 1916 to approve the National Defense Act. It enlarged the U.S. Army and National Guard and established summer training camps to build a manpower reserve. By the following autumn Congress had also expanded the navy and merchant marine.

In Wilson's war message of April 1917 he had asked for 500,000 additional soldiers, and Congress responded the following month with the Selective Service Act. It required the registration of all males between eighteen and forty-five years of age and by war's end had created a fighting force of nearly five million men. They went through six months of training with seventeen-hour days, usually using broom handles, shovels, and sticks as substitutes for rifles. Indeed, some men never held a rifle until they arrived in France, and officers most often came from upper-class families and learned their responsibilities in ninety-day training sessions. Nearly 400,000 black troops experienced "Jim Crowism" in a war intended "to make the world safe for democracy." Segregated training camps led to outbreaks of violence, followed by courts-martial of more than 100 black soldiers and thirteen executions by hanging. In the war, 200,000 blacks fought in Europe primarily as separate units, many of them winning citations for bravery from France. When the war came to a close, American deaths totaled 112,000, more than one-half of them attributable to a massive flu epidemic in 1918 and other diseases.

The first U.S. troops reached France in early July 1917. But before General Pershing would send the "Doughboys" to battle, as the infantrymen were called (derived from "adobes," then "dobies," in referring to U.S. infantry along the Rio Grande who were dusted white from adobe soil), he insisted on a change in Allied strategy and objectives. Trench warfare had caused too many needless deaths, he argued; open-field combat was essential to victory. Pershing wanted two additional months of training time to introduce his men to trench warfare and poison gas. In October 1917 the first Americans died in combat. The following spring the AEF fought alongside Allied soldiers on the Western Front under command of Marshal Ferdinand Foch of France.

U.S. wartime diplomacy included an effort to isolate Germany by persuading Austria-Hungary to drop out of the conflict. A major weak spot in the Central Powers seemed to be Austria-Hungary. Almost as soon as the Vienna government declared war on Serbia in 1914, it wanted to withdraw. In late 1916 Emperor Francis Joseph died, and his successor wanted a face-saving peace. The Dual Monarchy quickly eroded as numerous minority groups became more restless and soldiers increasingly deserted the ranks. Wilson sought to exploit these openings by arranging Austria-Hungary's withdrawal from the war before it collapsed from within. His strategy was unsuccessful, largely because the proximity of German soldiers made it dangerous to give in to the Allies, whereas the continuation of war encouraged the drive for independence among various nationalities who took advantage of the monarchy's vulnerability. By the summer of 1918 the Austro-Hungarian empire lay in pieces.

Wilson announced his goals for the postwar world on January 8, 1918, when he delivered his much-heralded Fourteen Points address before Congress. Certain guarantees, he in-

Navy Recruiting Posters
Inaugurating the democratic crusade. *National Archives, Washington, D.C.*

sisted, were essential to a peace settlement: freedom of the seas, arms limitations programs, economic interdependence based on the removal of barriers to trade, fair settlement of colonial claims, the restoration of Belgium, and the right of the Russian people to self-determination. The president argued that to avert wars stemming from secret alliances, the nations must agree to "open covenants, openly arrived at." Many observers assumed that this phrase meant an end to secret negotiations, but this was not so. Wilson recognized the necessity of private discussions but opposed secret agreements that went into effect without appearing before the world in final, published treaty forms. The fourteenth point was indispensable: the establishment of a "general association of nations" to guarantee "political independence and territorial integrity to great and small states alike."

Wilson had several reasons for this address. His peace program greatly differed from that of the Allies, as made clear by the Russian revolutionists' recent publication of the Allies' secret London agreements with the czar in 1915. Under these, France was to receive Alsace-Lorraine and the Saar Valley, whereas the German area west of the Rhine River, containing nearly five million people, was to become an independent buffer zone. Italy was to receive guarantees to the Brenner Pass in the Tyrol, which necessitated Austria-Hungary's release of Trieste and Trentino (or South Tyrol) and other lands along the top of the Adriatic Sea. Japan would gain Germany's possessions in the North Pacific and its economic rights in the Shandong [Shantung] Peninsula in China. Russia was to assume control over Constantinople and other parts of the Ottoman (Turkish) Empire in Asia Minor. The remainder of Turkey would go to Britain, France, Italy, and Greece. In the Fourteen Points address, Wilson sought to boost Allied morale, arouse popular support for just war aims, and undermine the enemy's will by offering a humane peace.

Wilson was also concerned about Russia's staying in the war. A seemingly liberal provisional government under lawyer Alexander Kerensky had replaced Czar Nicholas II after his fall in March 1917 but now seemed on the verge of collapse. Despite Allied hopes that the Russians would continue their war against Germany, they had lost the will to fight. Vladimir Lenin, exiled by the czar, had returned to Russia in early 1917 declaring that his people needed "peace, bread, and land." In early November he and Leon Trotsky led the Bolsheviks (or Communists) in a revolution that threw out the provisional government and established a new regime of Soviets (working-class committees). Wilson and the Allies saw the new ideology as a threat to capitalism and government stability. Their more immediate concern, however, was that the Bolsheviks would lead their country out of the war.

To keep Russia in the war, Wilson hoped that his liberal peace program would appeal to the Bolsheviks, who had called for self-determination and no exchange of territories or payments of indemnities. The Allies feared that the new Russian leaders, now engaged in a civil war, might sign a separate peace with

The Confusion of War
U.S. traffic jam northwest of Verdun. *National Archives, Washington, D.C.*

Germany. Colonel House was in Europe in late 1917 and urged the Allied governments to counter the Bolshevik offer with one designed to keep Russia in the war, but neither France nor Italy would retreat on territorial or other claims. Allied leaders had already lost a large number of men and could not return from the battlefront empty-handed.

The United States had to take the initiative regarding Russia, and Wilson was not disposed to ignore the opportunity. He praised the Bolsheviks' suggestions for peace and declared his country's wish to help the Russian people achieve "liberty and ordered peace." Point six urged the withdrawal of occupation armies from Russia followed by that country's entrance "into the society of free nations under institutions of her own choosing." The world's treatment of the Russians, Wilson warned, would be the "acid test" of its "good will."

Wilson's peace program became effective wartime propaganda through the efforts of the American Committee on Public Information, headed by George Creel. The committee circulated more than sixty million copies of the president's Fourteen Points throughout the world, and the Allies dropped 100,000 pamphlets a day into Germany and Austria-Hungary. Translations of the peace offer called for fair and honorable terms and no "unconditional surrender." They emphasized that the United States's conflict was with the "military masters" in Berlin, not the German people with whom the United States felt only "sympathy and friendship." The United States was certain that the German people's interests lay in accepting Wilson's generous peace rather than in following their government's disastrous war. Wilson intended that his Fourteen Points weaken resistance to the Allies by ensuring a new world order after the war.

Despite Wilson's efforts, Russia and Germany concluded a separate peace in the spring of 1918, helping to bring on the Allies' darkest moments in the war. The Bolsheviks had signed an armistice with Germany in mid-December 1917, raising the specter of a peace on the Eastern Front that would free forty German divisions for action on the Western Front. Wilson tried again in February and March of 1918 to discourage the possibility of peace negotiations between Germany and Russia, when he approved the Bolsheviks' opposition to exactions based on the war and reiterated his call for self-determination. But on March 3 they negotiated the Treaty of Brest-Litovsk, by which the Russians made peace at the heavy cost of transferring to German control almost a third of their population and over a million square miles of territory between the Baltic and Black seas. As the West feared, the Germans launched a major offensive that same month of March and by late May had pushed the Allies back to the Marne River, not fifty miles from Paris.

The devastating German assault destroyed Wilson's hopes for peace without victory. To a huge crowd in Baltimore, he declared that "Germany has once more said that force, and force alone, shall decide whether Justice and Peace shall reign. . . . There is, therefore, but one response possible from us: Force, Force to the utmost." On July 4 he asserted that "the Past and Present are in deadly grapple, and the peoples of the world are being done to death between them. . . . There can be no compromise." The small number of American Doughboys already in France helped resist this onslaught at Saint-Mihiel and Belleau Wood, until at Château-Thierry in June the Allied and Associated Powers finally blunted the enemy drive.

Meanwhile, Western concern had grown over events in Russia itself. Britain and France had convinced the United States in July 1918 to join them in an international military expedition at Murmansk and Archangel in extreme northwestern Russia, which aimed at diverting German troops back to the Eastern Front and protecting Russian military goods and railroads from German takeover. Wilson declared that the U.S. forces, 5000 of them, had orders to avoid military involvement in the ongoing Russian civil war. During a terrible winter characterized by little daylight in this far northern

Map 9
The U.S. involvement in Russia during the revolution remains a source of controversy.

area and by temperatures hovering consistently around fifty below zero, 139 Americans died for a cause never fully explained to them. Others' morale sank to the point of a near mutiny before they were finally called home after little or no success in June 1919.

About the same time of the intervention in northwestern Russia, Wilson again relented to French and British pressure and sent more than 9000 U.S. troops to Vladivostok in the frozen northland of Siberia. These troops were to assist the return to the Western Front of a Czech legion of 40,000 soldiers who had joined the now defunct Russian army in an effort to secure a homeland in Austria-Hungary. The Czechs intended to make the long journey back to Europe via Vladivostok, the Pacific Ocean, transcontinental United States, and Atlantic. Another objective became clear to the Wilson administration: U.S. intervention might slow the imperialistic drive of Japan, which was especially concerned about securing China and halting the spread of Bolshevism. In subsequent months the Tokyo government sent an unusually large contingent of nearly 73,000 men to Siberia for the ostensible reasons of protecting the Trans-Siberian Railroad and helping those people in the region who opposed the Germans.

But as the international force moved into Siberia, the interventionist issue became enormously complicated and heavily tainted with politics. Since mid-1918 the Czechs had been fighting the Bolsheviks for control of the Trans-Siberian Railroad, which meant that Allied assistance to the Czechs now implied opposition to the Bolshevik "Reds" in their civil war against the "Whites." Indeed, by the time the Czechs left Siberia, the European war was over. Wilson had meanwhile stipulated no U.S. intervention in Russia's internal affairs, but for various unexplained reasons his orders arrived late. A few Americans had already joined British and French soldiers in fighting the Bolsheviks for control of the railroad. Furthermore, in what turned out to be a lost cause, Wilson worked with the Allies in attempting to bring down Lenin by supporting the anti-Bolshevik leader of the White Russians, Admiral A. V. Kolchak, in establishing a constitutional government favorable to the West. An interventionist effort initially driven by allegedly strategic and humanitarian purposes had taken on a political cast. The United States, critics would later charge, had sought to steer the Russian Revolution into democratic channels.

Whatever the primary motive for the U.S. intervention in Siberian Russia, thirty-six Americans died before the bewildered remainder returned home in early 1920. Japan's contingent stayed until late 1922. In the meantime a "Red Scare" broke out in the United States in 1919 and 1920, leading to mass arrests of aliens suspected of Bolshevism and reinforcing Washington's decision to deny recognition to the victorious Bolshevik regime. Wilson, it is now clear, regarded Bolshevism as a "poison" and castigated its supporters for dropping out of the war, implanting a dictatorship, and calling for an international revolution of the world's working class. Wilson also wanted to maintain good relations with the Allies and protect the Open Door in China by stopping the Japanese advance into Siberia. Questions linger about U.S. intervention, but it is certain that the episode left a legacy of deep distrust in Russia.

Meanwhile, all along the Western Front the war's fortunes had turned against the Germans by July 1918. The Allies and more than a million U.S. soldiers rebuffed the murderous German assault at Château-Thierry. In their massive Meuse-Argonne offensive of late September the Allies used a new weapon—the tank—to split the Hindenburg Line and provide the mobility and protection needed for the foot soldiers to approach the borders of Belgium and Germany. The head of the German army, General Erich Ludendorff, saw the end coming and urged his government to ask for peace.

On October 4, while Americans were fighting in the Argonne Forest, the German chancellor appealed to Wilson for an armistice based on the Fourteen Points. The president,

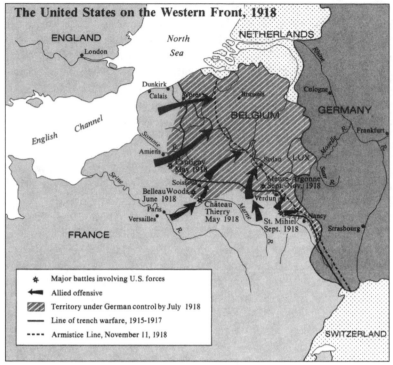

The United States on the Western Front, 1918

Map 10
The arrival of the American Expeditionary Force (or "doughboys") broke
the stalemate along the Western Front and ultimately led to Allied victory.

however, proved more difficult to deal with than the Germans had expected. He first wanted them to admit defeat and accept a cease-fire that would prevent them from beginning the war anew. The Germans should not totally disarm, Wilson told House, because if the balance tipped too far toward the Allies, real peace would become almost impossible. Finally, the Berlin government had to change hands before the United States could consider an armistice.

Ensuing pressure on Kaiser Wilhelm II forced his abdication in early November 1918, and on the day he fled the country a provisional government took over in Germany. With mutinies spreading among German soldiers and violence rocking the nation's cities, the German high command recognized that morale was shattered and the war was over. The kaiser's armies were in a fairly sound mil-

itary position along the Western Front, but any attempt to continue the war, combined with the country's internal strife, could lead to an Allied invasion and a vindictive peace. Bulgaria had quit the war in late September, Turkey did the same a month afterward, and Austria-Hungary followed suit in early November. Germany had no alternative but to sue for peace. When the Germans laid down their arms, the AEF held more than one-fifth of the Western Front. U.S. military forces and materiel had turned the long stalemate into an Allied victory.

But problems suddenly developed among the victorious powers: The Allies bitterly opposed a generous peace based on Wilson's Fourteen Points. The British adamantly resisted freedom of the seas, and the French demanded heavy war reparations that would crush Germany once and for all. U.S. pressure

America Goes to War
U.S. forces moving into the Argonne Forest, September 1918. *National Archives, Washington, D.C.*

convinced both Allies to compromise but caused considerable ill will. House, still in Europe, warned that the United States would sign a separate peace with Germany and cut back postwar economic assistance to Britain and France. He also discussed the effects of the president's publicizing the Allies' war aims. Britain and France reluctantly accepted Wilson's conditions but inserted two qualifications: The *Allies* were to define "freedom of the seas," and Germany had to make indemnities "for all damage done to the civilian population of the Allies and their property." On these unhappy notes, the antagonists took the first major steps toward ending the war. Wilson, however, had emerged as the chief architect of peace.

On November 9, 1918, the Germans received notification through the prearmistice agreement that the Fourteen Points would provide the basis for peace. Marshal Foch would meanwhile determine the military terms of the cease-fire. He and Pershing set severe military and naval conditions that denied Germany any possibility of rejecting treaty terms. The French were to occupy all territories west of the Rhine River, and Germany was to relinquish its fleet, its largest weapons, and a huge number of locomotives and box cars. At 5 A.M. on November 11, 1918, German representatives signed armistice papers in Foch's headquarters in a railway car in the Compiègne Forest.

The Paris Peace Conference

The Allies' disgruntlement over the way the war ended left considerable apprehension about the kind of peace lying ahead. Roosevelt and many other Americans were dissatisfied because the Allied and Associated Powers had not invaded Berlin and hanged the kaiser. But whatever complaints arose, Wilson had won the opportunity for achieving his central objective in entering the war: to sit at the peace table and draft a peace treaty preventing future wars. The United States would participate in the talks scheduled to begin in Paris in 1919, and Wilson's Fourteen Points would be the basis of those discussions.

The previous October Wilson had called on Americans to elect a Democratic Congress that would allow him, he declared, to "continue to be your unembarrassed spokesman in affairs at home and abroad." Republicans angrily denounced this move as sheer demagoguery because it unfairly implied that only the Democrats were patriots. The Republicans were particularly furious because they had rallied around Wilson's plea for a political truce during the war, only to have Wilson now break it. For whatever reasons, the voters returned a Republican majority in both chambers (the Senate by only two seats). The results would compromise Wilson's position at Paris by suggesting to his European counterparts that he did not represent the majority of his own people and was certainly not an emissary for the world. Roosevelt put it bluntly: "Mr. Wilson has no authority whatever to speak for the American people at this time. His leadership has just been emphatically repudiated by them."

Wilson compounded his first political error by announcing a week after the armistice that he personally would lead the U.S. peace delegation to Paris. Some immediately questioned the legality of a president's leaving the country while in office; but they were never able to cite a law upholding their point. Confidants warned that Wilson would become involved in heated debates over details and that his idealistic aims would suffer if he failed to win on all points. Secretary of State Lansing added that Wilson's image as the world's moral leader could remain intact only if he stayed above such matters. If he operated from the White House, he could avoid petty, selfish quarrels and make decisions without coming under the personal pressure of negotiators in Paris. Many in Congress argued that domestic matters demanded his attention and that he should send a delegation, not lead it. Most of all, if he stayed home he could maintain contact with public opinion. Wilson countered that he could not entrust the issues

to someone else. The meeting was among heads of state, he declared. "I must go."

Wilson's selection of members of the American Peace Commission also hurt his program. No Republican of political weight sat on it; no senator received an invitation. The president headed a delegation of loyalists: House; Lansing; General Tasker Bliss, who was the U.S. representative on the Supreme War Council in Paris that had coordinated the Allied effort; and Republican Henry White, a career diplomat who had helped negotiate the Algeciras settlement of 1906 but wielded no party influence. Wilson did not confer with members of the Senate Foreign Relations Committee before choosing the delegation, and he did not consult them before leaving for Paris. Had he done so, he would have been well advised to have made room for one of the following: Senator Henry Cabot Lodge, who was to become chair of the powerful Foreign Relations Committee on March 4, 1919, but who carried the weighty burden of being an archenemy of the president; Elihu Root, an elder statesman with considerable diplomatic experience; William Howard Taft, former president; and Charles Evans Hughes, loser of the close presidential contest of 1916 and respected member of the Republican party. All but Lodge had indicated interest in Wilson's peace program and his call for a league of nations. The president, however, insisted on managing the commission his own way. He had lost touch with political reality, because even if he were successful in Paris, he still had to guide the treaty through the Senate in Washington. Many in the United States recognized the approaching trouble. A U.S. editor wittily described the commission in this manner:

Name	Occupation	Representing
Woodrow Wilson	President	Himself
Robert Lansing	Secretary of State	The executive
Henry White	None	Nobody
Edward M. House	Scout	The executive
Tasker H. Bliss	Soldier	The commander-in-chief

Humorist Will Rogers expressed the situation more succinctly when he wryly commented that Wilson had told the Republicans: "I tell you what, we will split 50-50—I will go and you fellows can stay."

The American Peace Commission, along with numerous technical advisers and a cargo of books, reports, maps, and other scholarly materials, pulled out of New York harbor on board the one-time German luxury liner *George Washington* on December 4, 1918. The group seemed prepared for anything. At Wilson's urgings, House had earlier established "The Inquiry," a team of historians, economists, geographers, bankers, and other specialists who had spent more than a year in New York City formulating recommendations on the issues that probably would dominate the negotiations. They had compiled nearly 2000 detailed reports for the U.S. delegates to study and later drafted parts of the treaty with Germany.

After a nine-day voyage the Americans arrived in France, where they received a tumultuous welcome that only temporarily hid the troubles lying ahead. Wilson toured the continent for a month, examining the war's destruction and learning with immense gratification that he had become the Messiah to the people of Europe. In Paris a woman wrote: "Wilson, you have given back the father to his home, the ploughman to his field. . . . You have saved our fiancés; love blooms again. Wilson, you have saved our children. Through you evil is punished. Wilson! Wilson! Glory to you, who, like Jesus, have said: Peace on Earth and Good Will to Men!" Wilson believed his mission just: He had a universal mandate from the people to oppose the selfish ambitions of Allied leaders and achieve lasting peace. He still did not understand that the peace desired by the victors did not rest on the precepts of the Sermon on the Mount but on the wrath that God promised to wrongdoers. Germany was not to be forgiven; Germany was to receive everlasting punishment.

The Paris proceedings were chaotic from beginning to end. Angry crowds hovered around the scene of the meetings—the French Foreign Office—shouting at the peacemakers, peering through keyholes, banging on the doors and windows, throwing rocks on the roof, demanding revenge. Inside the high-ceilinged halls, speakers could not be heard more than a few rows from the front because of poor acoustics, continual loud talk, and wandering, noisy delegates. Most of the thirty-two Allied and Associated Powers, including Britain's four dominions and India, sought security and expansion—not the moralization of the world. The several hundred delegates held ten plenary or general sessions from January through June of 1919 but found that the size of the gathering made it difficult to conduct business. At first the "Supreme Council," or "Council of Ten," composed of two members each from Britain, France, Italy, Japan, and the United States, handled the major issues in secret and then sent reports to the plenary sessions for final decisions. But this procedure proved cumbersome. By March the "Big Four," or "Council of Four" (Britain, France, Italy, and the United States), took care of important business, many times without the presence of secretaries. Fifty-two commissions handled the detailed work of meetings and drafted most of the treaty.

All the while, hundreds of reporters swarmed outside the building, anxiously seeking any news. In a surprise ruling on the opening day of the conference, they had been denied entrance. Rather than gathering first-hand information, the reporters had to depend on a messenger who came out and read a terse and uninformative summary of each day's proceedings. The results were predictable: bitter competition for scraps of news, rumors converted into fact by the printed page, and dark suspicions of the actual transactions inside the chambers.

The general feeling at first was that the work of the conference was preliminary to a final round of negotiations between the victors and the vanquished. As in many instances of opening bargaining sessions, demands were extreme but expectedly open to modification

Hall of Mirrors, Palace of Versailles
Signing the Treaty of Versailles, June 1919. *From the painting by Sir William Orpen, reproduced by courtesy of the Imperial War Museum, London, England.*

and alteration. Sometime in the course of the meetings, however, these assumptions fell aside, the harsh preliminary terms remained, and the German representatives (denied any participation in the talks) had only the choice of accepting them or renewing the war. The Treaty of Versailles (signed at the Trianon Palace in Versailles), as German leaders would proclaim, was a *Diktat,* a dictated peace that warranted revenge. Whereas Wilson fought for national self-determination and a league of nations built on the Fourteen Points, the French were interested only in security and revenge, and that necessitated harsh conditions for Germany. Thus did the severe terms contained in the preliminary peace eventually become the Treaty of Versailles.

One of the most serious obstacles to Wilson's program was the Allies' secret territorial arrangements made in London in 1915. The European powers involved were infuriated

when the Bolsheviks published copies of the secret treaties found in the Russian Foreign Office, and yet, except for the Japanese claim to Shandong, Wilson had been aware of these agreements shortly after the United States entered the war. He never discussed them, however, probably to avoid any U.S. commitments while hoping to use his nation's vast economic strength to win a fair peace. The French had even recommended the suspension of all secret agreements, but Wilson chose not to accept this offer and ultimately hurt his own cause of self-determination.

But the central problem in Paris was the Allies' vengeful spirit. The other members of the Big Four—Premier Georges Clemenceau of France, Prime Minister David Lloyd George of Britain, and Vittorio Orlando of Italy—had promised their people that they would avenge German wrongs. Seventy-seven-year-old Clemenceau—heavily mustached, wearing a black skullcap, and appropriately called "The Tiger"—made no effort to conceal his rabid hatred of the Germans. During the Franco-Prussian War of 1870 and 1871 he had watched the enemy invade Paris and had seen his people barely survive. In the Great War, at the ripened age of seventy-two, he had again stood helpless as the Germans invaded and humiliated his beloved country. French casualty lists had ballooned to nearly four million, including one-half of the country's men between the ages of twenty and thirty-two. The physical destruction was especially awesome because the bulk of the war's worst fighting took place in France.

Clemenceau, presiding officer of the conference, personified the Old Order of Europe and had no stomach for Wilson's idealisms. "God gave us the Ten Commandments, and we broke them," he snarled. "Wilson gives us the Fourteen Points. We shall see." Lloyd George, a consummate politician appropriately dubbed the "Welsh wizard," wanted to maintain Germany's capacity to buy British goods without allowing it to threaten the balance of power that he hoped to bring about through the reconstruction of France. Like

Clemenceau, he became exasperated with Wilson, declaring him "the most extraordinary compound I have ever encountered of the noble visionary, the implacable and unscrupulous partisan, the exalted idealist and the man of rather petty personal rancour." Orlando's concern was simple: Secure the regions just above Italy. Recent congressional elections did not allow Wilson to claim popular leverage at home; the Big Three refused to give him the lead in Paris.

The first formal meeting in Paris took place on January 12, with Russia noticeably absent. None of the countries represented in Paris had extended recognition to the Bolshevik government, and they now refused to invite Russia to the proceedings. France charged that the Russians' withdrawal from the war and separate peace with Germany cost them any right to participate in peace talks. Wilson and Lloyd George thought it unwise to draw new boundaries in Europe without Russia's participation, but they finally retreated, justifying their decision on the basis of the civil war still raging between the Reds and the Whites. In January Wilson urged those in Paris to call on the Russian antagonists to accept a cease-fire and meet with the Allies and the United States to work out a peace agreement. Although the Reds showed interest, the Whites, encouraged by the French, refused to attend.

Wilson did not give up. With Lloyd George's approval, he directed William Bullitt, a twenty-eight-year-old attaché from the American Peace Commission, to accompany the well-known journalist Lincoln Steffens on a secret mission to Moscow to discuss armistice terms with Lenin. Bullitt was inexperienced, liberal, and so anxious to please that he exceeded his instructions. He authorized the withdrawal of Allied forces from Russia if the Bolsheviks would assure their enemies sufficient territory to allow the war to wind down. Lenin agreed to these and other favorable conditions, but before Bullitt could return to Paris the newspapers learned of his mission. The resulting

Big Four
From left to right: George (England), Orlando (Italy), Clemenceau (France), and Wilson (United States). *National Archives, Washington, D.C.*

cry of protest caused Lloyd George to disavow the mission, and Wilson pleaded a severe headache and flu (which probably was true, because he experienced a physical and nervous collapse a day or so later). He shuffled off Bullitt to talk with House. Bullitt was bitterly disillusioned by this cold treatment and by news of the harsh peace conditions the Allies were preparing to impose on Germany. He resigned his commission and went home. The Russians were not in Paris, but the specter of bolshevism clouded all discussions.

Wilson recognized that the intense hatred resonating throughout Paris made the establishment of a league of nations *within* the treaty text vital to peace. His counterparts insisted on drawing the peace treaty first, but he was worried that if business took place in that order, the delegates would dismiss the league in their haste to divide the spoils of war. After considerable debate he won his way. Wilson's struggle for the league took place concurrently with his attempt to establish the principle of self-determination during the discussions of colonies and the birth of new nations. The Allies' commitments to Japan and Britain's promises to its dominions proved the primary barrier to Wilson's call for an "absolutely impartial adjustment of all colonial claims." The most he could get was the "mandate system," whereby former German and Turkish possessions would come under the trusteeship of league members until the freed territories were capable of governing themselves. Wilson had intended that small neutral nations such as Switzerland should administer the mandates, but the former colonies instead went to the victorious powers. He had been unable to budge the Allies from their territorial commitments, and that made a league of nations even more essential.

Wilson had to compromise on territorial questions to save the league. More than one million square miles of territory changed hands, which itself was a violation of self-determination. The mandate system and the establishment of new states left the erroneous impression that Wilson's assurances of self-

determination had prevailed. Yet under the mandates, the Allied powers won most of their territorial demands, whereas the fledgling independent states were weak and susceptible to outside influence. A saving factor was that in the end most European peoples were aligned with those of similar nationalities. Adoption of the league, Wilson hoped, would remedy the remaining ills.

The president won a big victory when the Paris delegates agreed in late January to incorporate the league covenant into the treaty's text. He chaired the League of Nations Commission that wrote the covenant and, along with House, who composed its draft, completed the document in ten days of enormous pressure. In addition to an Assembly comprised of all League members, the central governing body was to be a council of five permanent members from the major powers (the Big Four and Japan), along with representatives elected from other member states on a rotating basis. Article Ten of the covenant, the president proclaimed, provided the major safeguard against war because it established the principle of collective security. According to terms, League members would "respect and preserve as against external aggression the territorial integrity and existing political independence of all Members of the League." In cases of aggression the Council would "advise upon the means by which this obligation shall be fulfilled." While the Paris delegates studied the draft set before them on February 14, the president prepared to return home to take care of executive responsibilities and outline the contents of the League covenant to his people.

Stringent opposition to the Paris negotiations greeted Wilson upon his arrival in the United States in late February. Before leaving Europe he had had cables sent to members of the Senate Foreign Relations and House Foreign Affairs committees, asking them to refrain from making public comments about the matter until he could discuss the peace program with them. But one member—isolationist Senator William Borah of Idaho—

had already begun criticizing Wilson's work in Paris. Weeks before the president sent the treaty to the Senate, Borah had secured a copy and read the entire text into the *Congressional Record*. Upon his arrival in Boston, Wilson attacked those who failed to recognize that the United States had a mission to guarantee freedom to all people. By the time the congressional committees met with him at a White House dinner on February 26, the atmosphere was tense. Several members were absent, most conspicuously Borah, who had pointedly turned down the invitation. Wilson was aware of the congressmen's concern that the League requirement to protect all members' integrity would endanger their nation's independence of action, and he knew that the isolationist tradition determined the sentiments of numerous Americans outside Congress. In a lengthy, acrimonious session, he defended the covenant and argued that collective security was the only way to stem aggression and guarantee world peace. Supporters thought he had fared well; anti-League congressmen came away unconvinced. Republican Senator Frank Brandegee of Connecticut remarked, "I feel as if I had been wandering with Alice in Wonderland and had tea with the Mad Hatter."

By early March the battle lines were becoming clear. League skeptics were beginning to gather around Senator Lodge of Massachusetts, a close friend of Roosevelt's (who had died that previous January) and new chair of the Foreign Relations Committee. The impending struggle over the League seemed to draw out the antagonists by design. Wilson and Lodge were bitter personal and political enemies; each held high academic degrees that perhaps encouraged a sense of jealousy. Although both were internationalists, the president held a Ph.D. in political science from Princeton and supported U.S. involvement in an organization based on collective security. Lodge had a Ph.D. in history from Harvard and saw little in the past to justify a departure from independent U.S. action in foreign affairs. Wilson's enemies regarded him as strait-

Elihu Root and Henry Cabot Lodge
On the way to testify before the Senate Foreign Relations Committee. *International Photo News Service.*

laced and stubborn; Lodge's enemies compared his mind to the New England farmland: "Naturally barren, but highly cultivated."

The day before Congress closed its session on March 4, Lodge persuaded thirty-nine Republican senators (more than the third necessary to defeat a treaty) to sign a Round Robin statement declaring that "the constitution of the League of Nations in the form now proposed . . . should not be accepted by the United States." Once the United States signed a peace treaty with Germany, "the proposal for a League of Nations to insure the permanent peace of the world should then be taken up for careful and serious consideration." The warning was clear: The Senate would not approve a treaty that included the League covenant in its text. And yet, Wilson knew, the Senate had never before refused a peace treaty. That same evening he assured an assembly in New York's Metropolitan Opera House that the Senate would approve the

League. The covenant, he declared, would be so tightly woven into the treaty text that a vote against the League would defeat the entire treaty. Even the senators, he felt confident, would not tear down the structure of peace to get at the League.

Wilson returned to Paris in mid-March, indignant over what he considered to be the petty behavior of Lodge and his colleagues; yet he realized that they were a formidable political bloc that could wreck the League. A bipartisan group of League supporters, including former President Taft, had talked with Wilson about making changes in the covenant to ensure Senate approval, and upon his return to Paris, he called a meeting of the League of Nations Commission. Wilson suggested four revisions: (1) League members could pull out after a two years' notice; (2) domestic matters, including tariffs and immigration, would not come under League jurisdiction; (3) no member could be required to assume mandate responsibilities; and (4) the League had no power that could endanger the Monroe Doctrine. But Wilson opposed any alterations in Article Ten; to change it, he believed, would destroy the League. Wilson was irritated that during his time home, the Paris conferees had set the League aside for other matters and that House and Lansing had given in to some of the other delegates' demands. He was determined to carry the fight to the end.

Wilson's most formidable opponents in Paris were the French. Clemenceau had demanded the Saar Basin and its coal deposits, German reparations for *all* costs of the war (not merely damages), and, to achieve security against future German invasion, French occupation of German lands west of the Rhine River as a buffer state. Wilson argued that the French demands violated self-determination because the areas in question were Germanic. Clemenceau objected. To House he impatiently declared, "I can get on with you. You are practical. I understand you, but talking to Wilson is something like talking to Jesus Christ!" Indeed, according to one account, Wilson lamented, "If I didn't feel that I was

the personal instrument of God I couldn't carry on." During the most heated arguments over France's demands in early April, Wilson became extremely ill with influenza. But despite fits of coughing and a temperature soaring to 103°, he rose from his sickbed to shout "No!" to demands made by Clemenceau, Orlando, and Lloyd George as they sat in the study adjoining his bedroom.

Perhaps Wilson's threat on April 7 that he would return home for good was decisive, because shortly afterward Clemenceau agreed to a compromise. France got Alsace-Lorraine, but the Rhineland, along with a belt of territory about thirty miles wide on the eastern side of the river, was to be permanently demilitarized and occupied by Allied forces for fifteen years, thereby creating the buffer zone that the French wanted on both sides of the Rhine. France also won the coal mines of the Saar, although the basin would come under League supervision for fifteen years. Afterward a plebiscite would determine whether the Saar would become French or German or remain under international direction. For these terms, Wilson and Lloyd George agreed to a joint security pact guaranteeing their military aid if Germany attacked France. But the Senate in Washington later refused to vote for the proposal, thus releasing the British from any obligation. France received neither the Rhineland nor the security guarantees.

Italy's demands similarly challenged the principle of self-determination. Under the secret London agreements of 1915 Italy was to receive areas in the Alps containing more than 200,000 Germans of Austrian descent. Italy also wanted the city of Fiume, which now constituted a vital outlet to the Adriatic Sea for the new state of Yugoslavia. Whereas most residents of the city were Italian, the majority of people in its outlying districts were Slavs. These demands had not been part of the secret pact of 1915, and Wilson fought them as violations of self-determination. He had earlier approved Italy's claim to the South Tyrol up to the Brenner Pass as important to security, and he later accepted the argument for Trieste. But Wilson refused to consider Italy's demand for Fiume. When he appealed directly to the Italian people, he infuriated Orlando and his colleague. They stalked out of the hall and returned home, where their people and parliament exuberantly praised them and bitterly assailed the U.S. president. The Fiume question remained unsettled at Paris and a continuing source of great national anger.

Japan also presented serious problems. It sought the Germans' holdings in the North Pacific as well as their economic concessions in China's Shandong Peninsula, and it also hoped to persuade the Allied powers to include in the League covenant a declaration of racial equality. The British dominions, however, led the opposition to such a statement: Australia and others had passed discriminatory legislation against Asians and did not want such a precedent set in Paris. But because Wilson chaired the committee that voted down the Japanese request, the United States drew the blame. The Japanese therefore became adamant about acquiring Germany's rights in Shandong. They argued that a secret treaty with Britain in 1917 guaranteed them the peninsula and Germany's Pacific islands, in exchange for their support of Britain's claim to Germany's islands in the South Pacific. In the Twenty-One Demands of 1915, the Japanese noted, China had ceded all rights that Japan secured from Germany in the war, and Britain and France had secretly assured Japan that they would support that claim. The Chinese were furious, because they argued that the concessions to Japan had come only under duress and that Shandong housed thirty million Chinese people and was the birthplace of Confucius. Wilson was concerned about self-determination and did not want China to lose what the Germans had originally taken by force; but he was also worried that Japan might join Italy in leaving the conference and thereby abort the League of Nations.

The delegates attempted to draw a compromise on the Japanese demands. Japan received the mandate over Germany's islands in the North Pacific—the Marshalls, Carolines, and Marianas—and it won Germany's

economic rights in Shandong in exchange for a promise (honored in 1923) that Japan would "hand back the Shantung Peninsula in full sovereignty to China retaining only the economic privileges granted to Germany." China later refused to sign the treaty. Indeed, its terms hurt Wilson's image as the defender of self-determination. The American press criticized the president's treatment of China, even though he considered the concession another part of the price necessary to win the League. The Shandong settlement, Wilson later remarked, "was the best that could be had out of a dirty past."

On the German question Wilson sought a fair settlement that did not contain the seeds of another war; but he likewise had to give in to the Allies' demands that Germany accept full blame for the war and agree to pay reparations for *all* damages. "If we humiliate the German people and drive them too far," he warned, "we shall destroy all form of government, and Bolshevism will take its place." His counterparts at the conference believed differently. France and Britain wanted Germany to sign a statement assuming total responsibility for the war and its aftermath. The "war guilt" clause, Article 231 of the treaty, was an admission that Germany and its cohort had caused "all the loss and damages" incurred by the Allies "as a consequence of the war imposed upon them by the aggression of Germany and her allies." The facts do not support this allegation, but the Germans were forced to sign: They had laid down their arms in accordance with the armistice and the Allies had not. Wilson went along with the Allies because he felt confident that the League of Nations could resolve these problems later on.

The reparations demands caused deep German resentment, toward both the Allies and Wilson. Besides believing the terms excessive, the Germans had trusted Wilson, who in February 1918 had promised "no punitive damages." Germany's agreement to the armistice had rested on this assurance, although the Allies asserted that their conditions for the restoration of German-occupied territories had included reparations "for all damages done to the civilian population of the Allies and their property by the aggression of Germany."

At first Wilson refused to consider the proposition, but Lloyd George argued that the Germans should assume responsibility for pensions and other payments to Allied soldiers and their families as "damages done to the civilian population." This interpretation greatly increased the amount Britain and its allies would receive, but Wilson acquiesced—perhaps with the understanding that this would not raise the *total* assessment on Germany but would increase the percentage *within* the sum awarded to the British. In actuality, the Allies greatly elevated the overall damage claim by tacking on pensions and similar allotments to other charges that they set.

The Paris delegates could not agree on a reparations figure and turned over the matter to a Reparations Commission. Two years later, in 1921, the commission set the figure at $33 billion—thirty-three times the amount levied on France in 1871 after its war with Prussia.

One cannot evaluate the impact on Germany of the reparations charge without considering the other parts of the treaty that restricted its ability to pay. Germany was to give up all colonies, most of its merchant vessels, a great part of its industrial and agricultural resources, and its rich deposits of coal in the Saar and iron ore in Lorraine. East Prussia was separated from Germany by the Polish Corridor, which granted Poland passage to the sea through an area that had belonged to Germany for hundreds of years. Furthermore, the German port of Danzig in the Corridor was to become a free city under League supervision. Finally, about seven million German-speaking Austrians were denied unification with Germany because of French opposition. Germany was to surrender more than six million people (a tenth of its total) and one-eighth of its territory.

The Germans were allowed into the treaty proceedings (which had now moved to Versailles) after the delegates had negotiated the terms and were given the document to sign, not to discuss. In an extremely tense plenary session in the Trianon Palace on May 17, 1919, Clemenceau handed the treaty to Count Ulrich von Brockdorff-Rantzau, head of the 160-member German delegation. As he did so, the French leader spat out in cold, biting language that "it is neither the time nor the place for superfluous words. . . . The time has come when we must settle our accounts. You have asked for peace," Clemenceau concluded. "We are ready to give you peace."

In a shocking move, the Germans had decided not to rise in receiving the document from Clemenceau now standing before them, nor did they assume the demeanor of a defeated people. Instead, Brockdorff-Rantzau defiantly declared that he and his colleagues had not read the treaty but knew that it was harsh. Despite claiming that his country was under "no illusions" about having lost the war and now stood powerless before its conquerors, the truth was that he believed the war had ended in a stalemate. Why should he and other members of his delegation assume the appearance of criminals standing before a judge? In a remark aimed at Lloyd George and that pushed the prime minister even closer to Clemenceau's hard-nosed position, Brockdorff-Rantzau asserted that "hundreds of thousands" of German civilians had died since Armistice Day because the Allies had unfairly maintained the blockade during the peace talks. And although the conquerors actually had demanded that Germany join its allies in accepting full blame for the war, Brockdorff-Rantzau mistakenly thought they wanted the Germans to admit that "we alone are guilty of having caused the war." He sternly insisted that "Such a confession in my mouth would be a lie."

Clemenceau, now red-faced and staring intently down at his adversary, somehow kept his composure as the last German words reverberated throughout the totally silent hall. At last he asked, "Has anybody any more observations to offer? Does no one wish to speak? If not, the meeting is closed."

The German response may have been far more costly than anyone realized at the time. Wilson had not been happy with the peace terms and might have tried again for compromise had Brockdorff-Rantzau appeared repentant. But the bitter attack drove Wilson and his fellow peacemakers together in defense of their treaty. "Isn't it just like them!" Wilson disgustedly remarked to Lloyd George about the Germans. Numerous members of the Allied delegations, particularly the British, were clearly displeased with the treaty. Indeed, those who drafted the document had done so in independent groups, many under the erroneous assumption that their requirements were for bargaining purposes and subject to revision as the negotiations progressed. But they were surprised when drafted articles came together in treaty form, thereby creating a severe total package that prevented an equitable adjustment of claims in line with the Fourteen Points. Lloyd George felt justified in slamming the door on Germany. He had angrily broken a small knife in his hands as he listened to the German response. "It is hard to have won the war and to have to listen to that." Even the slightest show of conciliation by the Germans at this crucial juncture might have led to more talks and an easing of terms.

On May 29 the Germans delivered their written response to the Versailles Treaty. They bitterly denounced the entire document instead of specific sections and thereby put the delegates on the defensive by suggesting that they were evil and vindictive. Most of the negotiators rallied around Clemenceau, and nearly all terms remained unchanged. The Germans had the choice of signing the treaty or resuming the war. The latter was unthinkable: Their will was broken, they had disarmed although the Allies had not, and Foch had promised to carry renewed fighting into Berlin. On June 23, 1919, less than two hours before the armistice was to expire, Germany agreed to terms. Five days later the signing ceremony took place in the Palace of Versailles's Hall of Mirrors—not by coincidence the same place where the Prussians had humil-

iated the French by announcing the creation of the German Empire after their conquest of France in 1871. Germany had lost both the war and the peace.

Most of Germany's people directed their bitterness toward France and Britain, but many regarded Wilson as central to the humiliation. On seeing the treaty, General Ludendorff remarked, "If these are the peace terms, then America can go to hell." The head of the German ministry, Philipp Scheidemann, snapped that "President Wilson is a hypocrite and the Versailles Treaty is the vilest crime in history." Especially sobering was the assessment offered by a socialist newspaper in New York. It called the settlement a "peace that passeth all understanding" and issued the prophetic warning: "Accept it, children, with faith and resignation—and prepare for the next Armageddon."

The Treaty Fight in the United States

When Wilson made his second and final return to the United States in July he found that even worse days lay ahead: Opposition to the League was growing. On July 10 he turned over the treaty package to the Senate with assurances that "the hand of God" had shaped the peace. He later told the French ambassador in Washington that he would reject any amendments to the treaty. "I shall consent to nothing. The Senate must take its medicine." To a journalist he sternly emphasized that "*the Senate is going to ratify the treaty.*"

U.S. opposition to the League came from varied sources. Politics was important, because Republicans did not want Democrats to enter the campaign of 1920 with the League of Nations as an asset and Wilson as standard bearer for a third time. Numerous ethnic groups criticized the treaty. German-Americans denounced the terms, Italian-Americans insisted on Fiume, Irish-Americans wanted freedom from Britain, and other minorities wondered what had happened to self-determination. Racist fears also shaped reactions to the League. Missouri Senator James Reed snidely remarked: "Think of submitting questions involving the very life of the United States to a tribunal on which a nigger from Liberia, a nigger from Honduras, a nigger from India . . . each have votes equal to that of the great United States."

The spirit of Progressive reform also permeated the arguments of those isolationists who fought the League. Nebraska Senator George Norris believed that the proposed organization lacked the means for preventing war and claimed it would further big power interests. Long-time reform Senator Robert LaFollette of Wisconsin warned that the League's authority to halt aggression could be used to put down colonial rebellions against repressive governments. Article Ten of the covenant, Borah declared, would send "our boys to fight throughout the world by order of the League." It also set back self-determination by authorizing the use of military force in protecting the interests of imperial powers. Big business would combine with bankers to run the organization. "If the Savior of men would revisit the earth and declare for a League of Nations," Borah stubbornly proclaimed, "I would be opposed to it."

The emotions of war had raised hopes for a better world, and, as is often the case, the postcrusade attitude had turned from idealism toward reality. Bitter disillusionment followed in its wake. The interventionists had only temporarily shelved isolationism, because the Fourteen Points had not transformed the world. Renewed war in Europe seemed likely, and Americans had had enough experience with the Old World to seek the sanctity afforded by two oceans. Article Ten, they feared, required the United States to forgo sovereignty in the interests of internationalism. The sacrifices Wilson had sought had not made the world safe for democracy, nor had they ended the threat of war. The intriguing question is whether many Americans might have accepted a compromise between the programs advocated by Wilson and Lodge. Neither man, however, seemed willing to consider any con-cessions that might alter his own conception of internationalism.

The Senate was deeply divided over the League. The Republican party held the majority by only a two-vote margin. Sixteen of the forty-nine Republicans opposed the League with or without changes and were called the "irreconcilables." Led by Borah, Norris, and LaFollette, they were referred to as "bitter-enders" or the "Battalion of Death." The remainder of the party broke into roughly three degrees of reaction. Perhaps as many as ten favored moderate revisions but would support the League; and nearly eighteen aligned with Lodge, chair of the Foreign Relations Committee and recently chosen majority leader, in wanting major alterations as a condition for joining the organization. The rest fell somewhere between the two groups. Lodge recognized that the Senate Democrats had mixed feelings and would give varying levels of support to amendments he might propose. Should the treaty pass, he wanted enough changes to protect the United States from outside interference in its affairs.

Lodge's motives for opposing the League are uncertain. Some have attributed them to his loyalty to Roosevelt, who consistently opposed Wilson, others to Lodge's own deep animosity toward the president. Yet more was probably involved. Lodge had always been an ardent nationalist and imperialist who would predictably harbor doubts about U.S. participation in an international organization built on collective security. It is unclear whether he intended to destroy Wilson's League of Nations from the first or merely to insert revisions making it safe for U.S. membership. He proposed a series of "reservations" that he claimed would safeguard the constitutional role of Congress in foreign policy. Such amendments, he realized, would necessitate new negotiations with the European powers for acceptance, whereas reservations would go into effect with or without their approval. Article Ten was the central threat. If Congress *specifically* retained the power to approve any U.S. action, Lodge seemed amenable to the

League. As chair of the Senate Foreign Relations Committee, he helped pack it with members unfriendly to the League. Ten of the seventeen members were Republicans, including Borah and five other irreconcilables, and only one of the remaining four Republicans favored the treaty without change. Among the seven Democrats, one had a record in foreign policy of supporting Lodge more than Wilson.

Perhaps at first Lodge saw little chance of defeating the League but hoped that its support would diminish with the passage of time. He realized that the introduction of amendments would lead to lengthy hearings and tie up the League proposal in committee. In the meantime, the treaty's opponents could remind Americans of Old World dangers. When the treaty came before the Foreign Relations Committee, Lodge read all 264 pages of the text into the official record, a stall tactic that required two weeks, drove everyone (including the stenographers) out of the room, and prevented the hearings from beginning until July 31. Six more weeks would pass as sixty witnesses gave testimony that filled 1200 pages of the record. Some people, such as Secretary of State Lansing, were informative; others spoke for minority groups and used the occasion to air grievances about the treaty. The most damaging testimony came from William Bullitt, who had resigned the Paris peace commission in disgust when Wilson ignored his negotiations with Lenin. Bullitt caused a sensation when he told the Senate committee that Lansing had privately described the League as "entirely useless" and said that if the Senate understood the treaty's implications, it would vote down Wilson's program. If Lodge's methods were transparent in motive, they were working. By the autumn of 1919 the treaty seemed to be losing popularity.

The culmination came with a tense three-hour public meeting in the White House on August 19 between the president and Lodge's Foreign Relations Committee. Wilson told the senators that he was agreeable to incorporating explanatory sections into the general peace pact, but he would not accept them as formal terms. Such a measure, he asserted, would alter the proposal and necessitate another series of negotiations with the Allies to secure their approval. Yet it was unclear where to insert these interpretive provisions. When Wilson refused to attach them to the ratification resolution, the Senate considered his position unreasonable.

Wilson refused to compromise on Article Ten. The deals he had accepted in Paris had sapped his reservoir of concessions, leaving him in no mood to grant more in the United States. Should Congress specifically assert the right to determine whether to defend another country, he believed, the move would tear the heart out of the League and provide no collective leverage against aggression. Yet he understood that the war had greatly damaged the military capacity of the Allied governments and that if the United States decided against intervening in a given situation, the other four members would hesitate to act. He also knew that according to the Constitution, only Congress could declare war. If Wilson thought all these things privately, he could not express them publicly. He came close to an admission during his speeches on behalf of the League in the autumn of 1919. Article Ten, he explained, bound the United States morally but not legally to use military means in enforcing League decisions. But this statement impressed many as a confusing attempt to use expediency in achieving his goals. He could not explicitly guarantee U.S. protection from the decisions of the League Council.

Wilson was a political warrior and would not submit to the Senate's wishes: He would take his case to the people. Though sixty-three years of age, in failing health, and both mentally and physically exhausted by his long fight for domestic reform, the war effort, and the peace ordeal in Paris, he ignored his doctor's warnings and set out in September on a grueling 8000-mile speaking tour through the old northwest, upper Mississippi valley, and west coast. In these centers of isolationist sentiment he delivered more than thirty major speeches as well as numerous short addresses along the way (from the rear of the train). He consistently warned that the Senate's failure to approve the pact would betray the millions of boys who died in the war, encourage a resurgence of international aggression, and require another U.S. intervention in European affairs. Those who opposed the treaty, he emotionally charged, were traitors to humanity. Isolationist senators such as Borah and California's Hiram Johnson became alarmed over the large and enthusiastic crowds gathering to hear the president and began speaking in the same places a day or so later in an attempt to dismantle his efforts. Wilson appeared to win converts among the people, but his derogatory remarks about League opponents in the Senate only hardened their positions and ensured a more difficult struggle for acceptance of his position in that body—the only battleground that could ultimately decide the issue.

Wilson's health finally broke under the excessive heat and pressure of countless speeches, press conferences, and interviews. Excruciating headaches pounded at him as in Paris, and he experienced a noticeable trembling of the body and severe loss of emotional control that suggested a resurgence of the small strokes that had hit him in earlier years. Yet he seemed willing to sacrifice his life for the treaty. In Pueblo, Colorado, on September 25, a huge crowd greeted him with a ten-minute standing ovation. He tearfully urged support for the League as humanity's last hope for peace, but at the close of his address he was so mentally and physically drained that he turned ashen on the platform and later collapsed on the train. Rushed back to Washington, he suffered a life-threatening stroke a few days afterward that paralyzed the left side of his body and made him a virtual invalid.

Wilson's stroke isolated him and seems to have stiffened his resistance even more to compromise. For nearly eight months he did not see his cabinet, and during the first few weeks of his convalescence no one except his doctor and his wife was able to talk with him. The former Edith Bolling Galt, whom he had married in December 1915, had sole access to

the president and decided which papers and eventually which people got into his room. By early 1920 House and Lansing had suggested compromises to save the League, and for that they completed their fall from grace that had begun in Paris when Wilson suspected them of making concessions to their European counterparts during his brief return home. Everyone had betrayed him, Wilson came to believe, but he would not forsake the great cause. When rumors spread about whether the "sick man" in the White House was steering the ship of state, Senate Republicans sent a committee to inquire about his health. Senator Albert Fall headed it and declared, "Well, Mr. President, we have all been praying for you." Wilson snapped back, "Which way, Senator?"

After considerable wrangling in the Senate, Lodge emerged in November with fourteen reservations (coincidental with Wilson's Fourteen Points?) that had to precede passage of the treaty. More discussions and changes followed before the Republicans, supported by more than a few Democrats, signified approval. Before Wilson left Washington for the western speaking tour, he had offered a few compromise terms through Senate Minority Leader Gilbert Hitchcock, who then proceeded to add one provision that dealt with Britain's right to more than one vote because of its dominions. Yet even though Wilson's attempts were similar to those offered by Lodge, they failed to resolve objections over the voting dispute, Article Ten, the Monroe Doctrine, the League's relation to domestic matters, and withdrawal of membership. All five issues had come before the Senate in November. By this time, however, even the moderates had promised to support Lodge's program. His second reservation related to Article Ten and guaranteed no U.S. action without the consent of Congress. His fifth reservation protected the Monroe Doctrine from any arbitral or investigative procedure under the League. The sixth refused U.S. approval of Japan's rights in Shandong, and the last, the fourteenth, renounced U.S. subjection to a League decision in which "any member of the league and its self-governing dominions, colonies, or parts of empire, in the aggregate have cast more than one vote." Lodge had inserted still another safeguard in the introduction to the Senate resolution: Ratification of the treaty required approval of all fourteen reservations by three of the four "principal allied and associated powers" (Britain, France, Italy, and Japan). It seemed highly unlikely that either Britain or Japan would accept Lodge's reservations.

That same month of November Wilson informed members of his party that a vote for the Lodge reservations was a vote against the League. Still bedridden, he wrote Hitchcock that the Democrats must defeat the treaty containing the reservations. Hitchcock warned that fellow party members would not do this unless Wilson permitted some changes in his treaty proposal. "Let Lodge compromise!" Wilson snorted. "Well, of course, he must compromise also," Hitchcock declared, "but we might well hold out the olive branch." The president quickly replied, "Let Lodge hold out the olive branch." On November 19, 1919, the Senate voted against two versions of the League covenant. The first bill contained Lodge's reservations, and all Democrats but four followed the president's bidding and banded with the irreconcilables to defeat it in two roll calls. After considerable discussion the Senate decided not to vote on Hitchcock's suggested changes, and the second bill, that without reservations, likewise failed to pass. Perhaps a few of those who supported the League but voted against it hoped their move might lead to a coalition of moderates that could pass a compromise treaty. Others doubtless feared the president's wrath should they break party ranks. Enormous White House pressure had maintained party unity against amendments to the treaty, but with the bizarre result that Democrats joined Republicans (including the irreconcilables) in ensuring its defeat. Republicans self-righteously noted that Wilson had blocked U.S. membership in the League, not they. Brandegee, an irrecon-

cilable, turned to Lodge and smugly remarked, "We can always depend on Mr. Wilson. He never has failed us."

By early 1920 the treaty's supporters believed it wise to accept the Lodge reservations and save the League; but they could not overcome Wilson's opposition. Colonel House, Herbert Hoover (who had accompanied the U.S. peace mission to Paris as a technical adviser), William Jennings Bryan, and William Howard Taft called for compromise, and Britain and France gave indications that they would accept a treaty with or without reservations. Wilson still opposed changes. He wrote a letter to those at the Jackson Day dinner on January 8 stating that Lodge's reservations would kill the treaty and that the presidential election later that year should be "a great and solemn referendum" on the people's will. He had even considered making a far-fetched proposal that senators opposed to the treaty should resign and run for reelection in 1920 on the League issue. If most of them won, he and his vice president would resign after he took steps to ensure that a Republican completed his term in the White House.

The negative votes on the treaty in November did not close the issue. The great majority of senators claimed to favor a League with reservations, and they faced pressure from numerous Americans interested in the treaty. Nearly thirty national organizations, boasting twenty million members, sent delegates to Lodge to demand acceptance of the treaty. But when he considered a compromise, Borah and other irreconcilables abruptly killed that thought by warning that they would unseat him as party majority leader. The treaty came before the Senate for the last time on March 19, 1920. Now laden with fifteen reservations (the new one calling for Ireland's independence), it failed again, this time by a close margin of forty-nine to thirty-five. Despite pressure from Wilson's cabinet members, twenty-one Democrats broke with the president to support this proposal; had seven more done so, the treaty would have passed. Yet even then, Wilson would have refused to ratify the resolution.

Legacy: The League and the Presidential Election of 1920

Despite Wilson's claim that the presidential election of 1920 was a referendum on the treaty, the issues were too muddled to draw reliable conclusions. The Democrats, led by Governor James Cox of Ohio, called for "immediate ratification of the treaty without reservations," although their candidate left the door open for compromise. The Republican platform supported "agreement among the nations to preserve the peace of the world" but not at the cost of "national independence." Party nominee Warren G. Harding, who as a senator had favored the League with reservations, became increasingly vague on the matter and thereby prevented the race from focusing on the League. The Republicans could not express interest in the League without driving out the irreconcilables, and yet their candidate had supported the treaty with the Lodge reservations. Harding declared in the campaign that he favored an "association of nations" but fuzzily suggested one greatly improved over Wilson's proposal. As the contest wore on he became more outspoken against U.S. membership in the League. A month before election day Harding told a crowd in Des Moines, Iowa, that Cox "favors going into the Paris League and I favor staying out."

If Harding did not confuse voters, a public declaration by thirty-one well-known Republicans on behalf of both the League *and* Harding surely did. A week after the candidate's renunciation of U.S. membership in the organization, these Republicans (including Herbert Hoover, Charles Evans Hughes, Elihu Root, and Henry L. Stimson) explained that if Harding won the election, he should persuade other nations to strike Article Ten from the League covenant as a condition to U.S. membership.

There is no way to determine the meaning of the election. A vote for Cox could have meant support for the League; a vote for Harding could have indicated either favor for Root and the others who supported the League or favor for Borah and the irreconcilables who opposed it. Harding won by a landslide, and even while the irreconcilables proclaimed the treaty issue dead, the thirty-one Republicans who signed the public statement looked forward to dropping Article Ten and joining the League. Two of them became members of the new president's cabinet (Hughes as secretary of state and Hoover as secretary of commerce), but when the administration later seemed to move toward League membership, the isolationists in the Senate warned that if the president did not back off they would fight every part of his administration's program. Harding beat a strategic retreat.

In April 1921 Harding announced to Congress that he would not support U.S. membership in *any* organization of nations. Such a move, he explained, would betray "the deliberate expression of the American people in the recent election." Congress officially ended the war in July, and the following month it concluded the Treaty of Berlin with Germany that tied the United States to all parts of the Versailles Treaty *except* the League. Despite Harding's assurances about a popular mandate against the League, the vote in 1920 was more a call for a return to "normalcy" than a verdict on the League. Americans were tired of crusades. Wilsonian reformism at home and abroad had lost the election and then took the League down with it.

Selected Readings

Ambrosius, Lloyd E. *Wilsonian Statecraft: Theory and Practice of Liberal Internationalism during World War I.* 1991.

———. *Woodrow Wilson and the American Diplomatic Tradition: The Treaty Fight in Perspective.* 1987.

Bailey, Thomas A. *Woodrow Wilson and the Great Betrayal.* 1945.

———. *Woodrow Wilson and the Lost Peace.* 1944.

Blumenthal, Henry. *Illusion and Reality in Franco-American Diplomacy, 1914–1945.* 1986.

Burk, Kathleen. *Britain, America, and the Sinews of War, 1914–1918.* 1985.

Calhoun, Frederick S. *Power and Principle: Armed Intervention in Wilsonian Foreign Policy.* 1986.

Chambers, John W. *To Raise an Army.* 1987.

———. *Woodrow Wilson and the Lost Peace.* 1944.

Clements, Kendrick A. *The Presidency of Woodrow Wilson.* 1992.

———. *Woodrow Wilson: World Statesman.* 1987.

Clifford, J. Garry. *The Citizen Soldiers: The Plattsburg Training Camp Movement, 1913–1920.* 1972.

Coffman, Edward M. *The War to End All Wars: The American Military Experience in World War I.* 1968.

Conyne, G. R. *Woodrow Wilson: British Perspectives, 1912–21.* 1992.

Coogan, John W. *The End of Neutrality: The United States, Britain, and Maritime Rights, 1899–1915.* 1981.

Cooper, John M., Jr. "The British Response to the House-Grey Memorandum: New Evidence and New Questions," *Journal of American History* 59 (1973): 958–71.

———. *Walter Hines Page: The Southerner as American, 1855–1918.* 1977.

———. *The Warrior and the Priest: Woodrow Wilson and Theodore Roosevelt.* 1983.

Egerton, George W. *Great Britain and the Creation of the League of Nations: Strategy, Politics and International Organization, 1914–1919.* 1978.

Esposito, David M. *The Legacy of Woodrow Wilson: American War Aims in World War I.* 1996.

Ferrell, Robert H. *Ill-Advised: Presidential Health and Public Trust.* 1992.

———. *Woodrow Wilson and World War I, 1917–1921.* 1985.

Fic, Victor M. *The Collapse of American Policy in Russia and Siberia, 1918.* 1995.

Fleming, Denna F. *The United States and the League of Nations, 1918–1920.* 1932.

Floto, Inga. *Colonel House in Paris: A Study of American Policy at the Paris Peace Conference, 1919.* 1973.

Foglesong, David S. *America's Secret War Against Bolshevism: U.S. Intervention in the Russian Civil War.* 1995.

Gaddis, John L. *Russia, the Soviet Union, and the United States: An Interpretive History.* 2nd ed., 1990.

Gardner, Lloyd C. *Safe for Democracy: The Anglo-American Response to Revolution, 1913–1923.* 1984.

Garraty, John A. *Henry Cabot Lodge: A Biography.* 1968.

Gelfand, Lawrence E. *The Inquiry: American Preparations for Peace, 1917–1919.* 1963.

George, Alexander L., and George, Juliette L. *Woodrow Wilson and Colonel House: A Personality Study.* 1956.

Goldhurst, Richard. *The Midnight War: The American Intervention in Russia, 1918–1920.* 1978.

Gregory, Ross. *Walter Hines Page: Ambassador to the Court of St. James's.* 1970.

Hagan, Kenneth J. *This People's Navy: The Making of American Sea Power.* 1991.

Hawley, Elis W. *The Great War and the Search for a Modern Order: A History of the American People and Their Institutions, 1917–1933.* 1979.

Heater, Derek. *National Self-Determination.* 1994.

Heckscher, August. *Woodrow Wilson.* 1991.

James, Clayton D., and Wells, Anne Sharp. *America and the Great War.* 1998.

Jonas, Manfred. *The United States and Germany, A Diplomatic History.* 1984.

Kaufman, Burton I. *Efficiency and Expansion: Foreign Trade Organization in the Wilson Administration, 1913–1921.* 1982.

Kennan, George F. *American Diplomacy.* Expanded ed. 1984. Originally published as *American Diplomacy, 1900–1950.* 1951.

———. *The Decision to Intervene.* 1958. Vol. II of *Soviet-American Relations.*

———. *Russia Leaves the War.* 1956. Vol. I of *Soviet-American Relations.*

Kennedy, David M. *Over Here: The First World War and American Society.* 1980.

Kettle, Michael. *The Allies and the Russian Collapse.* 1981.

Killen, Linda. *The Russian Bureau: A Case Study in Wilsonian Diplomacy.* 1983.

Knock, Thomas J. *To End All Wars: Woodrow Wilson and the Quest for a New World Order.* 1992.

Kuehl, Warren F. *Seeking World Order: The United States and International Organization to 1920.* 1969.

———, and Dunn, Lynne K. *Keeping the Covenant: American Internationalists and the League of Nations, 1920–1939.* 1997.

Kuhlman, Erika A. *Petticoats and White Feathers: Gender Conformity, Race, the Progressive Peace Movement, and the Debate over War, 1895–1919.* 1997.

Lentin, Antony. *Lloyd George, Woodrow Wilson, and the Guilt of Germany: An Essay in the Prehistory of Appeasement.* 1985.

Levin, N. Gordon, Jr. *Woodrow Wilson and World Politics: America's Response to War and Revolution.* 1968.

Link, Arthur S. *The Higher Realism of Woodrow Wilson and Other Essays.* 1971.

———. *Woodrow Wilson: Revolution, War, and Peace.* 1979. Rev. ed. of *Wilson the Diplomatist: A Look at His Major Foreign Policies.* 1957.

———, ed. *Woodrow Wilson and a Revolutionary World, 1913–1921.* 1982.

Livermore, Seward W. *Politics Is Adjourned: Woodrow Wilson and the War Congress, 1916–1918.* 1966.

Long, John W. "American Intervention in Russia: The North Russian Expedition, 1918–19," *Diplomatic History* 6 (1982): 45–67.

Lowry, Bullitt. *Armistice, 1918.* 1996.

Maddox, Robert J. *William E. Borah and American Foreign Policy.* 1969.

Martin, Laurence W. *Peace without Victory: Woodrow Wilson and the British Liberals.* 1958.

Mayer, Arno J. *Political Origins of the New Diplomacy, 1917–1918.* 1959.

———. *Politics and Diplomacy of Peacemaking: Containment and Counterrevolution at Versailles, 1918–1919.* 1967.

McCartin, Joseph A. *Labor's Great War: The Struggle for Industrial Democracy and the Origins of Modern American Labor Relations, 1912–1921.* 1997.

McFadden, David W. *Alternative Paths: Soviets and Americans, 1917–1920.* 1993.

McKay, Ernest A. *Against Wilson and War.* 1996.

Mee, Charles L., Jr. *The End of Order: Versailles, 1919.* 1980.

Murphy, Paul L. *World War I and the Origin of Civil Liberties in the United States.* 1979.

Nelson, Keith. *Victors Divided: America and the Allies in Germany, 1918–1923.* 1973.

Osgood, Robert. *Ideals and Self-Interest in America's Foreign Relations: The Great Transformation.* 1953.

Parrini, Carl. *Heir to Empire: United States Economic Diplomacy, 1916–1923.* 1969.

Peterson, H. C., and Fite, Gilbert C. *Opponents of War, 1917–1918.* 1968.

Pratt, Julius W. *America and World Leadership, 1900–1921.* 1967. Originally published as *Challenge and Rejection.* 1967.

Rhodes, Benjamin D. *The Anglo-American Winter War with Russia, 1918–1919: A Diplomatic and Military Tragicomedy.* 1988.

Rosenberg, Emily S. *Spreading the American Dream: American Economic and Cultural Expansion, 1890–1945.* 1982.

———. *World War I and the Growth of United States Predominance in Latin America.* 1987.

Safford, Jeffrey J. *Wilsonian Maritime Diplomacy, 1913–1921.* 1978.

Salzman, Neil V. *Reform and Revolution: The Life and Times of Raymond Robins.* 1991.

Schaffer, Ronald. *America in the Great War: The Managed Society.* 1991.

Schmitt, Bernadotte E., and Vedeler, Harold C. *The World in the Crucible, 1914–1919.* 1984.

Schwabe, Klaus. *Woodrow Wilson, Revolutionary Germany, and Peacemaking, 1918–1919: Missionary Diplomacy and the Realities of Power.* 1985.

Seymour, Charles. *American Diplomacy during the World War.* 1934.

Sharp, Alan. *The Versailles Settlement: Peacemaking in Paris, 1919.* 1991.

Smith, Daniel M. *The Great Departure: The United States and World War I, 1914–1920.* 1965.

Smith, Tony. *America's Mission: The United States and the Worldwide Struggle for Democracy in the Twentieth Century.* 1994.

Smythe, Donald. *Pershing: General of the Armies.* 1986.

Somin, Ilya. *Stillborn Crusade: The Tragic Failure of Western Intervention in the Russian Civil War, 1918–1920.* 1996.

Stallings, Laurence. *The Doughboys: The Story of the AEF, 1917–1918.* 1963.

Stevenson, David. *The First World War and International Politics.* 1988.

Stone, Ralph. *The Irreconcilables: The Fight against the League of Nations.* 1970.

Thompson, John A. *Reformers and War: American Progressive Publicists and the First World War.* 1987.

Thompson, John M. *Russia, Bolshevism, and the Versailles Peace.* 1966.

Tillman, Seth P. *Anglo-American Relations at the Paris Peace Conference, 1919.* 1961.

Trani, Eugene P. "Woodrow Wilson and the Decision to Intervene in Russia: A Reconsideration," *Journal of Modern History* 48 (1976): 440–61.

Trask, David F. *The AEF and Coalition Warmaking, 1917–1918.* 1993.

———. *Captains & Cabinets: Anglo-American Naval Relations, 1917–1918.* 1972.

———. *The United States and the Supreme War Council: American War Aims and Inter-Allied Strategy, 1917–1918.* 1961.

Tucker, Spencer C. *The Great War, 1914–1918.* 1998.

Unterberger, Betty M. *America's Siberian Expedition.* 1956.

———. *The United States, Revolutionary Russia, and the Rise of Czechoslovakia.* 1989.

———. "Woodrow Wilson and the Bolsheviks: The 'Acid Test' of Soviet-American Relations," *Diplomatic History* 11 (1987): 71–90.

Vaughn, Stephen. *Holding Fast the Inner Lines: Democracy, Nationalism, and the Committee on Public Information.* 1980.

Walworth, Arthur. *America's Moment, 1918: American Diplomacy at the End of World War I.* 1977.

———. *Wilson and the Peacemakers: American Diplomacy at the Paris Peace Conference, 1919.* 1986.

Weinstein, Edwin A. *Woodrow Wilson: A Medical and Psychological Biography.* 1981.

Widenor, William C. *Henry Cabot Lodge and the Search for an American Foreign Policy.* 1979.

Woodward, David R. *Trial by Friendship: Anglo-American Relations, 1917–1918.* 1993.

CHAPTER 5

The Independent Internationalism of the United States, 1921–1933

War's Legacy: The Myth of Isolationism

Of all nations in the Western world, only the United States emerged from World War I stronger than it was when the war began. Germany lay devastated and humiliated; the Austro-Hungarian empire had been dismembered; the Russian empire, upon the triumph of the Bolsheviks, had seen czarist tyranny replaced by civil war, economic chaos, and government by terror. The "victors" in Europe—Britain, France, and Italy—had suffered awesome destruction of property while accumulating public debts of unprecedented and unmanageable proportions. Both sides had lost numerous young men: nearly ten million killed, another twenty-one million wounded, and countless more demoralized and disillusioned. The United States, by contrast, lost comparatively few soldiers in combat. Although nearly 50,000 died and another 200,000 were wounded, for most of the 4.8 million Americans who volunteered or were drafted for military service, the war was at worst a nuisance and at best an exhilarating experience.

Economically, the war had transformed the United States into the leading power in the world. The war had brought not mass destruction but a huge increase in productive capac-

ity, together with profits in the form of many billions of dollars owed by the Allies for war materiel furnished by the United States. Indeed, the United States changed from a debtor to a creditor nation for the first time in its history, and New York City replaced London as the financial nerve center of the world. U.S. investors became prominent in industries all over the globe: oil in Iraq, rubber in Liberia and Malaya, Ford Motor Company in Russia, General Electric and General Motors in Germany, and untold other business ventures in Europe, Asia, and Latin America. During the postwar decade, the United States assumed its dominant international position by producing seventy percent of the world's petroleum, forty percent of the world's coal, and nearly fifty percent of the world's industrial output.

In these circumstances the United States found itself thrust into a role it was altogether unable and somewhat unwilling to play: that of world leader. In this role the Americans failed, but not (as historical myth would have it) for want of trying. Despite the emphasis on domestic and hemispheric affairs, the refusal to join the League of Nations and the World Court, the influence of vociferous isolationist and pacifist groups, and the bungling of financiers, the United States took the initiative in trying to establish international peace and order through nonmilitary means. Increasing numbers of private advisers in all specialties worked closely with government officials in developing a relationship that writers later called "corporatism." Economic diplomacy—the attempt to construct an international commercial network intended to guarantee peace through interdependence among nations—became the chief means toward building a new world order. Although U.S. leaders were moderately successful in the Western Hemisphere, they failed outside the Americas—partly because of naiveté and inexperience, and partly because of social, economic, and political forces unleashed by the Great War that lay beyond the capacity of any nation to manage. Only upon the collapse of the world economy between 1929 and 1933 did the United States retreat into a shell of irresponsibility.

Superficially, it does seem that the United States embraced isolationism in 1921. When a reporter asked President Warren G. Harding about European affairs, he brusquely replied, "I don't know anything about this European stuff." Perhaps victimized by catchy statements depicting his looks as his only presidential qualification, Harding became a veritable instrument for caricature in the hands of sharp-witted and satirical journalists such as Henry L. Mencken. More than once Harding substantiated Mencken's description of the president's public statements as "Gamalielese"—particularly when he misread his own campaign speech by calling for a "return to *normalcy*" and thereby contributed a new word to the dictionary. "Keep Warren at home," warned Senator Bose Penrose of Pennsylvania when Harding's election in 1920 seemed certain. "Don't let him make any speeches. If he goes out on a tour, somebody's sure to ask him questions, and Warren's just the sort of damn fool to try to answer them."

Harding's successors, Republican presidents Calvin Coolidge and Herbert Hoover, fared little better in the face of political punsters and domestic and foreign factors lying beyond their own control. Coolidge was impeccably honest and coldly straitlaced in puritan outlook and demeanor. However, he often chose to confront crises by taking long naps in the White House, which, combined with his eternally tired disposition, caused many observers to believe that his virtue was his only asset. "Silent Cal," according to quipster Will Rogers, "don't say much, but when he does, he don't say much." Coolidge certainly regarded business as the bedrock of U.S. success, but he clearly lacked the ability to inspire listeners and repeatedly demonstrated his failure to understand the enormity of events occurring all around him. As the economy dipped in the days before its collapse, he blandly told his people, "The future may be better or worse." He was certain of one thing, however: "When people are thrown out of work, unemployment results." Thus, by logical extension he sagely observed, "The final solution for unemployment is work." Hoover likewise was cold and aloof, never succeeding in proving to Americans that he cared about their welfare. Although he was brilliant and known as the "great engineer," it was his particular misfortune to enter the White House just in time to receive full blame for the Great Depression. As a highly successful and idolized businessman before and during the "Roaring Twenties," he became part of that same fallen idolatry after the great stock market crash of October 1929. All three Republican presidents of the decade seem to have followed the same ostrich-like pattern of devoting their attention to promoting the interests of domestic businesses, leaving foreign affairs to their able secretaries of state.

But this assessment does not entirely fit either the presidents or the international events of the 1920s. Harding, Coolidge, and Hoover supported all types of nonmilitary pursuits aimed at securing world peace. As Republicans, they believed in laissez-faire government and economics both at home and abroad: Private enterprise, not state-run corporations or nations, held the key to economic expansion in both domestic and foreign affairs. Their emphasis on economic diplomacy led them to favor an independent form of internationalism and to help only those nations who first took steps to help themselves. Furthermore, their interest in encouraging private business enterprise abroad received special impetus from the Webb-Pomerene Act of 1918, which exempted U.S. firms from antitrust legislation and thereby opened the door for cooperative commercial pursuits. The following year, the Edge Act went into effect, permitting U.S. banks to establish branch offices in foreign countries. Congress also approved legislation allowing American businesspeople to take tax credits for foreign investments. During Harding's administration, the commerce department under Hoover's leadership furnished business entrepreneurs with information essential to commercial expansion outside the United States.

The Harding administration realized that the old world order had brought a devastating war, and it worked to build a new international system resting on U.S. ideas and dedicated to peace. The president's secretary of state—Charles Evans Hughes, a legal expert and internationalist who had been a reform governor of New York and candidate for the presidency in 1916—now sought a *"Pax Americana"* based on reason and not brawn. But it was probably Hoover in commerce who best exemplified the Republican party's philosophy in foreign affairs. A former mining engineer and self-made multimillionaire, he became internationally known after his wartime food relief activities in Belgium and Russia and his work as a reparations adviser at the Paris peace conference. Now, in the postwar period, he urged the United States to accept the responsibility of world leadership and help build a new order for peace based on free enterprise. Washington's policymakers must work with private businesses along with agricultural and labor groups in fostering economic expansion on a worldwide basis as the mainspring for stability and peace. In 1921 Hoover explained, "I am thus making a plea for individualism in international economic life just as strongly as I would make a plea for individualism in the life

of our own people." As Hughes and Hoover insisted, freedom in the international sphere was inextricably related to freedom at home.

It would be misleading to assume that government and business were in total harmony in foreign affairs and that the Republican administrations of the 1920s were unified in seeking a business-led foreign policy. Hoover's commercial attachés, for example, became so influential that the state department and career Foreign Service officers became concerned about losing control over foreign policy. Hughes's prodding led Hoover to agree in 1923 to direct all foreign business arrangements to the ambassador, who reported to the secretary of state. And the following year, Foreign Service officers took another step toward regaining control over foreign policy when Congress passed the Rogers Act, which combined the diplomatic and consular branches of the state department. Despite these and other problems along the way, the Republican administrations of the decade felt confident that their particular brand of diplomacy would lead to economic interdependence among nations and lessen the chance for war.

Latin America

The various presidents of the 1920s sought to secure the Western Hemisphere and undercut European economic influence (particularly that of the British) by working toward better relations with the Latin American states, which were still in disarray after the interventionist policies of Presidents Roosevelt, Taft, and Wilson. Widespread pressure had grown throughout Latin America for the renunciation of U.S. interventionism and the conversion of the Monroe Doctrine into a multilateral instrument of policy. The timing seemed propitious. The wartime defeat of Germany had eased fears of outside control of the Panama Canal, allowing the United States to reconsider its relationship with Latin America. The destruction of the Great War had forced Britain, the United States's long-time commercial competitor in the hemisphere, to curtail its expansionist activities. In addition, many Americans regarded trade and investment as fundamental to world peace. Others simply opposed their government's long-standing interventionist policies in the Caribbean. During the 1920s the United States embarked on an uncertain course in hemispheric affairs aimed at allaying the ill feelings generated by the Monroe Doctrine, Roosevelt Corollary, and Wilson's missionary diplomacy.

Only on the surface did relations between the Americas appear to improve. During the decade the United States signed a treaty with Colombia compensating that country for the Roosevelt administration's manipulative acquisition of canal rights in Panama, offered assurances in Rio de Janeiro that it sought no more territory in Latin America, and withdrew its military forces from the Dominican Republic while taking slow but certain steps toward the same objective in Nicaragua, Haiti, and Cuba. In addition, the United States settled long-standing problems with Mexico emanating from its new constitution of 1917, which had condoned government expropriations of oil and minerals belonging to Americans by declaring all land, water, and subsoil materials freed from foreign ownership or control. After considerable controversy the United States and Mexico signed the Bucareli Agreements of 1923. This settlement authorized U.S. recognition of the Mexican government in exchange for continued U.S. ownership of oil companies acquired before 1917 and provided indemnification for those Americans who lost agricultural lands to expropriation. Four years later, in response to Mexico's revocation of these foreign ownership rights in favor of fifty-year leases, the Coolidge administration sent Wall Street banker Dwight W. Morrow as ambassador. He soon established considerable goodwill by arranging for visits by Will Rogers and Charles Lindbergh, the latter of whom had recently won folk hero status by flying solo across the Atlantic to Europe. Morrow succeeded in negotiating a compromise that recognized the validity of oil lands owned before 1917 and established leases on those afterward.

President Wilson had assured the Latin Americans that the United States would never again seek territorial acquisitions to the south, but he had not renounced the spread of U.S. influence through economic means. During the 1920s the United States exercised great control over many noneconomic aspects of Latin American affairs by approving the efforts of private U.S. investors and owners of railroads, electric utilities, and numerous other economic enterprises. Brazilian coffee; Chilean copper, iron, and nitrate; Cuban sugar; Honduran fruit; Peruvian copper and vanadium; Uruguayan meats; Venezuelan oil—all these commodities and more came under the control of U.S. business people and investors supported by favorable Washington legislation. As early as the dawn of the decade, seventy-five percent of the Latin American states fell under the economic sway of more than a thousand U.S. run businesses. American investments doubled between the outbreak of the Great War and the eve of the Great Depression, as Standard Oil of New Jersey, International Telephone and Telegraph, United Fruit Company, and numerous other U.S. businesses vastly extended their holdings in the southern half of the hemisphere. Not by coincidence did U.S. exports to Latin America triple in volume during the same period. And not by coincidence did resentment grow in Latin America over this new form of U.S. imperialism, which, like the old form, rested on territorial expansion and removed more wealth than it returned.

Through an intricate web of influence that went beyond purely economic matters, the United States managed to dominate Latin American affairs without incurring all the usual political and administrative trappings. But the Latin American people realized that economic control provided the basis for political and military control as well. "If anti-American critics wish to describe this as our 'imperialism,'" U.S. ambassador to Chile William Culbertson smugly remarked, "let them make the most of it."

Latin Americans resented not only the expanding U.S. economic influence within their borders but also the continued military interventionism based on the Monroe Doctrine. In the Dominican Republic, U.S. marine and naval forces had run the government since 1916, but in 1924 the Republicans brought this occupation to an end and proclaimed this move a signal of a new goodwill policy toward Latin America. In the course of this occupation, however, U.S. military officials on the island had facilitated the rise to power of dictator Rafael Trujillo, who offered the surety of domestic order and became president after the violent and fraudulent election of 1930. In neighboring Haiti, U.S. Marines governed from 1915 to 1934, leaving behind many notable improvements in everyday life but failing to resolve the island's economic destitution. Furthermore, the Americans bequeathed a legacy of ill will emanating from their brutal suppressions of domestic disorder and the rampant Jim Crowism they transported to the island.

Nicaragua posed a major problem in U.S.-Latin American relations that involved Mexico as well. U.S. military forces had run Nicaragua from 1912 until their departure in 1925. But they returned the next year. Bolsheviks had caused new troubles in Nicaragua, the Coolidge administration declared, even though no evidence has appeared to support this allegation. In reality, members of the traditionally anti-American Liberal party in Nicaragua had banded under César Augusto Sandino, who had seen firsthand the arrival of U.S. troops in Mexico in 1914 and now sought to drive this new American contingent out of his native Nicaragua. Using Mexico as a base of military operations, the Sandinistas launched a guerrilla war on U.S. marine camps as well as the U.S.-supported Conservative party then in power. After years of bitter fighting (including in 1927 the first use of U.S. planes in dive-bombing assaults in the hemisphere), the U.S. Marines were unable to capture Sandino. In 1933, after special negotiator Henry L. Stimson had arranged the Peace of Tipitapa in 1927, they again withdrew. The Liberals and Conservatives soon called a truce, but the situation remained explosive—particularly after

the U.S.-trained National Guard led by Anastasio Somoza assassinated Sandino and two close allies.

With the festering problems in Nicaragua and Mexico serving as a backdrop, the Sixth Inter-American Conference took place in Havana in 1928, where even the personal appearance of President Coolidge to address the opening session did little to ease tensions. When El Salvador introduced a resolution declaring that "no state may intervene in the internal affairs of another," the head of the U.S. delegation, former Secretary of State Hughes, fought against its passage but found only four Latin American states (three of them under U.S. military occupation) willing to support him. Although he succeeded in tabling the resolution, the victory came at tremendous cost. Both Mexico and Argentina had supported nonintervention, and only silence had greeted Hughes's defense made in language strikingly reminiscent of the hated Roosevelt Corollary: "We do not wish to intervene in the affairs of any American Republic," Hughes assured his listeners. "We simply wish peace and order and stability and recognition of honest rights properly acquired so that this hemisphere may not only be the hemisphere of peace but the hemisphere of international justice."

In November 1928 President-elect Hoover had just returned from a lengthy goodwill tour of Latin America that set the tone for what would later be called the Good Neighbor policy. He furthered this feeling in his inaugural address by indicating interest in ending the presence of U.S. Marines in the Caribbean. Indeed, in 1930 the government published a 236-page treatise written by Undersecretary of State J. Reuben Clark, entitled a *Memorandum on the Monroe Doctrine*. Although the document was ambiguous in wording, it repudiated the Roosevelt Corollary and seemed to ensure an end to military intervention in Latin America. In reality the Clark memorandum only renounced intervention based on the Monroe Doctrine, retaining by implication the right to secure the acquiescence of other states in the hemisphere before intervening on the basis of the U.S. national interest. Yet the United States appeared to have reversed past policies, even while continuing to spread influence in the hemisphere by nonmilitary means.

When the Great Depression deepened unrest in Latin America and helped set off numerous domestic insurrections, Hoover dropped Wilson's moral approach to recognition and returned to the traditional principles of *de facto* recognition. By the early 1930s relations with Latin America had improved, however slightly.

Peace Through Disarmament and Outlawing War

In matters outside the hemisphere the United States sought to safeguard autonomy in action by avoiding anything that suggested an official connection with the League of Nations, including formal participation in the so-called World Court. The United States had initially proposed that kind of institution—a court of international law, not of arbitration—at the First Hague Conference in 1899 and again at the Second Hague Conference in 1907. But the tribunal established at The Hague rested on arbitration. The covenant of the League had authorized its Council to create a court of international law separate from the League, and in May 1922 the Permanent Court of International Justice, or World Court, came into existence. Soon afterward Secretary of State Hughes persuaded President Harding to ask the Senate to approve U.S. membership, but the chair of the Foreign Relations Committee after Lodge's death, the irreconcilable isolationist William Borah, led a successful fight against the proposal. Membership in the Court, he warned, would lead the United States into the League and thus into dangerous political and military ventures. Similarly, the Senate blocked various other state department efforts to promote U.S. participation in League affairs.

Despite the Harding administration's initial attempts to ignore the League, Hughes sent observers to its meetings in Geneva, and the United States took part in its business related to social work, drug control, efforts to halt the white slave traffic, and arms limitations talks. Moreover, Hughes, Secretary of State Frank B. Kellogg, and other Americans served on the World Court over the years. In addition, the Republican secretaries of state worked to negotiate bilateral and multilateral arbitration and conciliation treaties outside the framework of the League of Nations, all with a view toward establishing world order through law.

But the United States aimed its most important international initiatives at disarmament. Conventional wisdom of the time held that the Great War had resulted from the armaments race in Europe during the decade or so before 1914. It followed logically from that premise that if the major powers reduced their military establishments, international tensions would decline in direct proportion to the rise of international trust, thereby enhancing the prospects for a lasting peace. So thinking, the United States initiated and participated in half a dozen international disarmament conferences during the 1920s and early 1930s.

The first of these conferences arose from the threat of a postwar naval armaments race in East Asia that involved the United States, Britain, and Japan. The U.S. Navy ranked second in the world to the British and posed a threat to the Japanese by expanding its fleet in the Pacific and building a base at Pearl Harbor. Japan stood third in the world in naval power after the war, and by 1921 it devoted a third of its budget to expanding its fleet. This ambitious program bolstered rumors that the Japanese intended to fortify mandated German islands in the Pacific, and it contributed to the Washington navy department's call to build a larger fleet. Meanwhile, the British alienated Americans by their recent renewal of the Anglo-Japanese Alliance of 1902 and their attempts to establish oil rights in the Middle East. Yet both the United States and Britain were reluctant to enter an expensive naval race.

Borah and Stimson
Borah was an "irreconcilable" who bitterly oppposed Wilson's League of Nations and later disagreed with the Franklin D. Roosevelt administration's warnings of the German threat during the 1930s. Stimson advocated non-recognition of Japan's holdings in Manchuria in the early 1930s, later called for an oil embargo on Japan, and then served in Roosevelt's cabinet as secretary of war. *Library of Congress.*

Japan was in a precarious position after the Great War and did not trust its former allies' intentions in East Asia. France had joined the United States and Britain in assigning more naval vessels to the region, and should the three nations reach an understanding, Japan would stand alone. Its suspicions of the Western powers were not unwarranted. The Versailles proceedings had left a legacy of deep resentment in Japan. Not only had the Western powers refused to issue a statement upholding racial equality, but they had appeared reluctant to recognize Japan's growing hegemony in East Asia. Problems had already developed over China, Shandong, Siberia, and the Japanese mandates in the Pacific. Moreover, the British were under pressure from both the United States and Canada to terminate their 1902 alliance with Japan. To win relief from

that obligation, British Prime Minister David Lloyd George had to give Japan something in return—perhaps further concessions in East Asia and the Pacific Ocean. The time was opportune for arms limitations talks.

In late 1920 Borah introduced a resolution calling for a disarmament conference bringing together the United States, Britain, and Japan. Such a move, he argued, would reduce arms expenditures and promote peace. Although Harding favored naval expansion, he changed his stand after Congress overwhelmingly approved the Borah resolution. Moreover, Hughes argued that such a conference would not only slow down Japan's military growth (including a possible abrogation of the Anglo-Japanese pact) but provide the United States with the opportunity to take advantage of the Tokyo government's desire to rely on U.S.

banks in developing Korea and Manchuria. In exchange for New York capital to finance its East Asia enterprises, Japan would have to abide by the Open Door in China—or so Hughes hoped. Furthermore, such an arrangement might safeguard U.S. interests in the Philippines, Guam, and Samoa. With all these objectives in mind, the president announced a meeting on naval disarmament to convene in Washington in November 1921. France and Italy were also to receive invitations, and when the British recommended that the delegates focus on the Pacific and East Asia, it became necessary to include China as well as those countries with holdings in the area—Belgium, Portugal, and the Netherlands.

On November 12, 1921, Hughes opened the first plenary session of the Washington Naval Conference with a stunning proposal: "The way to disarm is to disarm," he declared. He then designated *specific* arms limitations and cutbacks, which included a ten-year holiday on the construction of capital ships—those huge battleships or cruisers of more than 10,000 tons and fitted with a minimum of eight-inch guns. To fulfill these requirements, he explained, the United States would have to scrap thirty such vessels, Britain nineteen, and Japan seventeen. In half an hour Hughes had called for junking nearly two million tons of ships, a figure that a British journalist asserted to be more "than all the admirals of the world have sunk in a cycle of centuries." A U.S. journalist wrote that Hughes's recommendations had caused one British admiral to come "forward in his chair with the manner of a bulldog, sleeping on a sunny doorstep, who had been poked in the stomach by the impudent foot of an itinerant soapcanvasser."

Hughes's shocking speech drew thunderous applause and even tears from observers who sensed a monumental step toward the end of war. A British newsman wrote, "It is an audacious and astonishing scheme, and took us off our feet. The few men to whom I spoke babbled incoherently. What will they say in London? To see a British First Lord of the Admiralty, and another late First Lord, sit-

ting at a table with the American Secretary of State telling them how many ships they might keep and how many they should scrap, struck me as a delightfully fantastic idea."

The first major settlement at the Washington Naval Conference was the Four-Power Treaty among the United States, Britain, Japan, and France. Signed on December 13, 1921, it achieved one of the United States's major objectives by terminating the Anglo-Japanese Alliance of 1902. It also won Japan's assent to later disarmament terms by assuring the status quo in the Pacific. Hughes had made it clear that the Anglo-Japanese pact seemed directed at the United States, and he argued that Japan could now give it up because Germany and the Soviet Union were no longer threats in East Asia. The Four-Power Treaty left the implication of armed cooperation when the signatories promised to "communicate with one another fully and frankly in order to arrive at an understanding as to the most efficient measures to be taken, jointly or separately, to meet the exigencies of the particular situation." Because each nation guaranteed respect for the others' Pacific holdings, the unquestioned advantage went to Japan—the power that employed the largest fleet and claimed the most possessions in the Pacific at that time. The Senate later hesitated to approve the pact out of fear that a deeper commitment could entail a military involvement that violated the tenets of isolationism, but it finally acquiesced after attaching an amendment guaranteeing that the United States would make "no commitment to armed force, no alliance, no obligation to join in any defense."

On the day the Washington Naval Conference adjourned, February 6, 1922, the delegates agreed to their second important pact—the Five-Power Treaty providing terms for disarmament. The United States, Britain, Japan, France, and Italy approved a ten-year moratorium on the building of capital ships and set a maximum tonnage on aircraft carriers. Hughes worked out an intricate ratio plan on battleships and battle cruisers with the number "1" as the base that was equivalent to about 100,000 tons. He called for a comparative relationship of 5:5:3:1.75:1.75, with the United States and Britain occupying the two top positions in capital ships and aircraft carriers, and with Japan next, followed by France and Italy. After the ten-year period the signatories could replace the older vessels, but only to a maximum size of 35,000 tons and with guns having bores no larger than sixteen inches. The plan worked to the United States's advantage, because the provision cleverly included ships already completed plus those under construction. Had the plan applied only to those already built, Britain would have led the way; had it included those completed, under construction, and planned, Japan would have approached the strength of the United States.

Japan initially opposed the Five-Power Treaty. The Japanese ambassador to the United States bitterly labeled it "Rolls-Royce-Rolls-Royce-Ford," but U.S. military intelligence had earlier learned through breaking Tokyo's secret diplomatic codes that the Japanese would accept the ratio plan if the British and Americans promised no new fortifications or reinforcements in their Pacific holdings. Indeed, the British and Americans had already done so under the Four-Power Treaty. Thus would the British continue to lack important bases north of Singapore and the United States west of Hawaii, thereby leaving Japan secure from attack and supreme in its home waters.

France was also displeased with the ratio arrangement. It wanted a navy large enough to protect its coastal areas and overseas possessions, but it had another consideration even more important: Germany. The French sought to base disarmament figures on their security needs against Germany, which would have meant doubling their allotment of capital tonnage. France was still upset over the decisions by the United States and Britain not to ratify the Security Pact negotiated at Versailles in 1919 and remained determined to build a defense system in Europe strong enough to contain the Germans. Britain, however, forced

the French into accepting the treaty terms by leaking their demands and thus exposing their self-interests to worldwide condemnation. The French relented, but with the stipulation that the ratio plan would have no bearing on lesser craft. The Five-Power Treaty therefore carried a near fatal weakness: It set no maximum tonnage on vessels outside the "warship" category—submarines, destroyers, and small cruisers. Within a year the naval race resumed as nations sought to acquire smaller vessels not included in the Five-Power Treaty.

On February 6, 1922, the delegates in Washington signed their third agreement—the Nine-Power Treaty (the Big Four plus Belgium, China, Italy, the Netherlands, and Portugal), which affirmed the Open Door in China. All signatory powers promised to "respect the sovereignty, the independence, and the territorial integrity of China," but the treaty included a potential loophole that permitted intervention: China must "develop and maintain . . . an effective and stable government." These assurances included equal commercial opportunity, because Hughes inserted the words of the secret protocol attached to the Lansing-Ishii Agreement of 1917. That protocol guaranteed against any power "taking advantage of conditions in China in order to seek special rights or privileges which would abridge the rights of subjects or citizens of the friendly States, and from countenancing action inimical to the security of such States." Yet the Nine-Power Treaty did not seek to correct past violations of China's sovereignty, and it contained no provision for enforcement. The Open Door depended solely upon the signatories' honoring their pledges.

The Washington Naval Conference led to other agreements that did not become part of the treaties. Japan consented to terminate its military occupation of Shandong and allowed Chinese control over the major railroad running through the peninsula. Thus, Japan fulfilled its assurances given at Versailles in 1919, even though maintaining political and economic influence on the Chinese mainland. More than a year after the Washington Naval

Conference, Japan annulled the Lansing-Ishii Agreement, which had approved its "special interests" in China. Japan also granted the United States cable, missionary, and property rights on the small Pacific island of Yap in exchange for U.S. recognition of Japan's mandates over Germany's former Pacific possessions—the Carolines, Marianas, and Marshalls. Finally, Hughes informed the Japanese that the United States refused to accept any arrangement that "might impair existing treaty rights or the political or territorial integrity of Russia." Japan thus agreed to withdraw from Siberia and the northern half of Sakhalin Island, which it did in 1922 and 1925, respectively.

The Washington Naval Conference of 1921 and 1922 consisted of a series of compromises, even though the agreements were a tacit recognition of Japan's superiority in the Pacific and East Asia. The United States and Britain could not alter the strategic situation without a costly arms program, and even then Japan's geographical location and recently gained mandates over the surrounding Pacific islands gave it an overwhelming advantage in East Asia. And yet the United States had diminished the threat to the Open Door in China by securing the abrogation of the Anglo-Japanese Alliance and at least momentarily maintaining its own hold on the Philippines, Guam, and Samoa.

If relations with Japan improved because of the conference, they soured soon afterward. In 1924 the U.S. Congress capitulated to enormous pressures from racists and passed the Johnson Immigration Act barring entry to "aliens ineligible to citizenship" (the Japanese and other Asians). When the act went into effect the Japanese declared it "National Humiliation Day" at home.

Subsequent efforts at disarmament failed to match even the modest successes of the 1921–1922 conference. President Coolidge invited Britain, France, Italy, and Japan to meet with the United States in Geneva during the summer of 1927. France and Italy declined to attend, however, and Britain and the United States soon engaged in such intense disagreements over their needs for "domestic safety" and the definition of large and small vessels that Japan itself tried to mediate. After six weeks of heated discussions the Geneva Conference broke up, leaving hardened Anglo-American relations and a dying faith in disarmament as a means toward peace. The following year, in Coolidge's Armistice Day address, he chastised those nations that "made agreements limiting that class of combat vessels in which we were superior, but refused limitation in the class in which they were superior."

Renewed disarmament efforts at the London Naval Conference of 1930 affirmed that trying to control the amount of arms was an attack on the symptoms of trouble and not the actual trouble: the distrust and insecurity caused by competing imperial interests. In April, after three months of discussions, the United States, Britain, France, Italy, and Japan reached agreements that again offered only the illusion of peace. First, the United States won parity, or equality, with Britain on all vessels, even though this arrangement entailed the *addition* of U.S. armaments rather than actual disarmament. Second, the powers saved considerable money by agreeing to a five-year extension of the ten-year moratorium on the replacement of capital ships, which the Five-Power Treaty of 1922 had provided. Third, Japan won parity with Britain and the United States in submarines and made substantial gains on them in cruisers and destroyers. Fourth, the powers passed the so-called escalator clause, which provided that a signatory nation could expand its fleet beyond the limiting terms drawn in London if it felt threatened by any nation not party to this treaty.

Suspicions and ill feelings were rife at the London Conference. The United States rejected French demands for guarantees of military security prior to participating in disarmament efforts, and both France and Italy refused to approve the final cruiser arrangements. Nonetheless, the Senate in Washington overwhelmingly approved the pact in July 1930, although it also passed a resolution freeing the United States from any secret terms.

The great powers attempted disarmament two more times. Nearly sixty nations assembled at the World Disarmament Conference in Geneva in 1932, only to adjourn without success two years later in the face of growing troubles in Europe and East Asia. As stipulated at the London Conference of 1930, the nations met again in London in 1935, but when Japan failed to win naval parity with the United States and Britain, its delegates walked out of the proceedings. Insecurity and distrust in both Europe and East Asia continued to obstruct the hopes for disarmament.

As the tough-minded approach to a peace grounded in power politics was running its futile course, a soft approach, based on goodwill, was taking its place. This was the movement to prevent war by universal renunciation. Naive as the notion of "outlawing" war may appear in retrospect—and as it appeared to realists at the time—it had one strong argument in its favor: *Realpolitik* had been tried and had led to the catastrophe of world war. It is not certain whose brainchild the goodwill movement was. Besides its support from an assortment of intellectuals, socialists, and pacifists, the leading exponent of outlawing war was a Chicago lawyer, Salmon Levinson, who backed the idea financially and won the endorsement of Senator Borah. Other leaders in the movement included Nicholas M. Butler, the president of Columbia University, and one of its faculty members, James T. Shotwell, noted professor of international relations and trustee of the Carnegie Endowment for International Peace. Shotwell won the attention of French Foreign Minister Aristide Briand and induced him to make such a proposal in the spring of 1927. In early April Briand extended a public invitation to the United States, through the Associated Press, to join France in a bilateral treaty renouncing war. His letter declared that France was "ready publicly to subscribe, with the United States, to any mutual engagement tending, as between those two countries, to 'outlaw war,' to use an American phrase."

But Briand's seemingly idealistic gesture had a basis in *realpolitik:* He hoped to pull the United States into France's defense system against Germany. The French defense alliance already included Belgium, Czechoslovakia, Poland, Rumania, and Yugoslavia. His proposal would not bind the United States to intervene in a Franco-German war. Rather, a joint renunciation of war would prohibit the United States from retaliating against France should it violate neutral rights in a war with Germany. Briand spoke with the world stature of having recently won the Nobel Peace Prize for the 1925 Treaty of Locarno guaranteeing peace along Germany's western borders, and he now declared that U.S. cooperation with France "would greatly contribute in the eyes of the world to broaden and strengthen the foundation upon which the international policy of peace is being raised."

Secretary of State Kellogg was furious with Briand's specious tactics. Kellogg had been a moderate critic of Wilson's League of Nations and since that time had moved closer to Borah's noninterventionist camp. The seventy-year-old Kellogg was physically small, blind in one eye, and burdened with a twisted and perpetually shaking hand. A corporate lawyer who had acquired a reputation for trust-busting under Theodore Roosevelt, he went on to become a senator and then ambassador to Britain. Kellogg was short on temper, long on stubbornness, and an accomplished practitioner of expletives when on a rampage. The time had come to put all these qualities into play. The French foreign minister had already won the support of U.S. peace groups, who now urged Kellogg to accept the French offer. But the secretary of state saw through Briand's cover and rigidly opposed any arrangement hinting at a European alliance. He initially ignored Briand's plea but came under enormous pressure to accept it from the *New York Times* and numerous public figures and organizations. Still, he refused.

Then, as if by design, the image of Franco-American friendship received a sudden boost when Lindbergh made his solo flight across the Atlantic and landed in Paris in May 1927. Petitions containing two million signatures soon rolled into Washington, all calling on the United States to join the French move against war. Faced with such popular pressure, Kellogg had no choice but to agree to talk about Briand's invitation. In compliance with Kellogg's change of heart, the French foreign minister in June handed the U.S. ambassador in Paris a draft of the proposed treaty, which he called a "Pact of Perpetual Friendship."

In late December 1927 Kellogg found a way out of an imbroglio that could entangle the United States in Europe's political and military affairs. The Senate Foreign Relations Committee informed him that it would approve a general treaty renouncing war, but not one with France alone. Kellogg therefore presented a counterproposal to Briand that rested on a well-known principle in diplomacy: The more parties to a treaty, the less binding it becomes. Briand's proposal was so laudable, Kellogg loftily declared, that France and the United States should invite all nations to join. Thus would Kellogg's crafty arrangement remove all dangers of European involvement. The United States would retain the right to defend itself and the Monroe Doctrine while accepting no responsibility for enforcing the pact against any signatory who violated it. To eliminate doubt, the Senate Foreign Relations Committee emphasized that "the treaty does not provide sanctions, express or implied."

The idea of such a worldwide multilateral pact won immediate support in Washington, and after Kellogg sent the proposal to Briand in late December, the two nations made arrangements for a widely publicized conference in Paris to outlaw war. The French foreign minister was irate with Kellogg's maneuverings but had no choice. As a winner of the Nobel Peace Prize, Briand could not publicly refuse a general declaration renouncing war. After three months of delay Briand agreed to the proposal, but with reservations designed to safeguard what he called his country's right of "legitimate self-defense."

Frank B. Kellogg
Secretary of state who negotiated the Pact of Paris outlawing war in 1928. *Painting by Alexius de László de Lonbos, U.S. Department of State.*

On August 27, 1928, the representatives of fifteen nations gathered in Paris and in an elaborate ceremony signed the Kellogg-Briand Pact, or Pact of Paris, which renounced war as "an instrument of national policy" and supported "pacific means" in resolving "international controversies." Afterward the signatories invited other nations to join the pact, and sixty-two governments ultimately did so—including Germany, Italy, Japan, and the Soviet Union. The U.S. Senate approved the treaty almost unanimously.

The much-heralded results of the peace proceedings were misleading and, in the retrospect of World War II, leave the ghostlike impression of mindless participants engaged in a cruel charade. Missouri Senator James Reed dismissed the pact as an "international kiss," and Senator Carter Glass of Virginia offered the most truthful assessment even as he voted for it. "I am not willing that anybody in

Virginia shall think that I am simple enough to suppose that it is worth a postage stamp in the direction of accomplishing permanent peace." He warned that "it is going to confuse the minds of many good and pious people who think that peace may be secured by polite professions of neighborly and brotherly love." The Senate was not naive. Nor was President Coolidge, who signed a naval appropriations bill for the construction of fifteen large cruisers less than a month after he ratified the pact outlawing war.

In a final bit of irony, Kellogg received the Nobel Peace Prize for his part in negotiating the Pact of Paris.

The War Debts-Reparations Problem

Even while the Republican administrations of the 1920s sought to knit together a world economic community, both kinds of peace seekers—realists and idealists—overlooked the fundamental acquisitive causes of wars among nations to appeal, instead, to the nations' better instincts. But the proposed peace plans failed to come to grips with the gravest international problem of the period: the financial dislocations that were impelling the world toward another calamity, the collapse of the very international economic order that the United States sought to construct. Leaders in every nation were unable to deal with this danger, partly because the forces behind it were so large as to be invisible, and partly because the leaders were shortsighted.

The international economic disorders of the postwar period were extremely complex. Wartime destruction of physical property in Europe was so great that under the best of circumstances, only with great difficulty could its economies have regained their capacity to feed, clothe, and house their citizens. And circumstances were hardly the best. The major obstacle to recovery was the burden of debts owed by governments to their own citizens, to other governments, and to private creditors in other countries. Britain, France, and Italy owed large

sums to their citizens who had bought government bonds, and in addition they owed nearly $10 billion to the U.S. government and several billion more to New York banks. The debts of the former Allies to their own citizens might have been scaled down in both interest and principle, or the debts might have been effectively repudiated by inflating them out of existence, had their citizens been willing to tolerate such courses. The debts due the United States were another matter. Had American markets been open to the Allies' manufactured goods and farm products, international obligations might have been met by exports to the United States. But American producers, fighting the challenges posed by low-cost foreign producers, demanded an increased protective tariff and got it in the Fordney-McCumber Act of 1922. Its high tariff schedules precluded the possibility of Europe's paying its U.S. debts by normal means.

But the former Allies had an abnormal means at their disposal, and they seized upon it. The French, bitter over the destruction of lives and property inflicted by the Germans, remembered that Germany had extracted a huge reparations settlement from them after the Franco-Prussian War. Forgetting that the result had been an international economic depression, they demanded that Germany pay for all damages resulting from the Great War. The delegates at Versailles had agreed to reparations in principle, and in April 1921 the Allied Reparations Commission fixed Germany's obligation at the astronomical sum of $33 billion. The result seemed appropriate to its makers. If Germany met its reparations payments on schedule, France, Britain, and Italy could meet their obligations to the United States on schedule.

The flaw in this simple sounding arrangement was that Germany was unable to pay, on schedule or otherwise. Like the victorious powers in the war, its productive capacity had been devastated, and its economy was weakened further by the ill-advised course its postwar Weimar Republic government followed in trying to cope with internal financial obligations. In a word, that course was to inflate its currency by printing unsecured paper money at an ever-increasing rate. International depreciation of German currency inevitably followed. The German mark, which before the war had been at 4.2 to the U.S. dollar, fell to 162 to the dollar by the end of 1921, and to 7000 by the end of 1922. A year later it took 4 trillion marks to make a dollar, and Germany's traditional frugal middle class had been wiped out.

Belatedly, the United States acted to reduce the burden of both debts and reparations, though as a matter of principle it refused to agree to a total cancellation. "They hired the money, didn't they?" Coolidge snorted. During the Paris peace talks of 1919 President Wilson had rejected suggestions to cancel war debts, despite arguments by some congressional members that such a move would add to the U.S. contribution to victory, ensure better international relations, and avert Allied bankruptcy. Had not the Allies expressed extreme bitterness over the United States's tardy entrance into the war and the relatively small amount of destruction it experienced? Wilson and others realized that to cancel the European debt meant that the American taxpayer would have to assume the Allied debt by meeting the Treasury's bond obligations. For a time, support in this stand came from the British, who twice in 1920 opposed cancellation in the interest of European recovery. But this position soon changed. The Allies came to believe that the credits advanced by the United States should be its shared costs in victory. If the United States canceled British obligations, Britain would do the same for France, which in turn might lower its reparations demands of Germany. The United States, however, refused to link war debts with German reparations, and debt cancellation was out of the question.

The United States made several attempts to ease the war debt obligations. In the summer of 1921 President Harding recommended this approach, and the following February Congress established the World War Foreign Debt Commission to work out details. Congress stipulated no debt cancellations but agreed to a lowered interest rate and an extended maturity date. The debtor nations still could not meet these terms. In early 1923 the United States again agreed with Britain to lower the interest rate and not to exact full return for sixty-two years. But the other chief debtors—France, Italy, and Belgium—refused the arrangement because they first wanted reparations from Germany, which had defaulted on its payments in 1922. The international financial situation grew worse, and by 1925 the Foreign Debt Commission was willing to go much farther. In spring of the following year it scaled down the debts by drastic margins. The Commission canceled four-fifths of the Italian debt and nearly two-thirds of the French, and it reduced interest to a nominal rate. Even then the French called the United States "Uncle Shylock," and cartoonists changed the stars on Uncle Sam's hat to dollar signs. The debts remained beyond the Allies' ability to pay unless they received reparations payments from Germany.

In 1924 the United States tried to solve the German problem with the Dawes Plan. The occasion for the U.S. intervention in the matter presented itself when Germany first defaulted on reparations payments and France and Belgium retaliated by occupying the industrialized Ruhr Valley in January 1923. Secretary of State Hughes had already suggested that an investigative team scale down the reparations bill in accordance with Germany's capacity to pay. His recommendation now won approval, and the Reparations Commission established a committee to devise the terms. European treasury officers and private U.S. business leaders worked with the state department to select Republican Charles G. Dawes, a Chicago banker, to head the committee. The Dawes Plan of September 1924 reduced Germany's reparations payments to 2.5 billion marks over the succeeding fifty years and established a system of yearly reparations payments without setting a deadline for the fulfillment of obligations. To stimulate economic recovery, the act permitted private investments in Germany of $200 million, with the amount split evenly between U.S. and foreign banks. The purpose of the plan was to save the German economy by tying reparations to the nation's financial recovery.

The Dawes Plan worked fairly well for five years, but the European economy still threatened to collapse under the burdens of debts and reparations. In 1929 Germany's creditors sought a final resolution of the question through the Young Plan. Owen D. Young, chair of both General Electric and RCA, also acted in a private capacity in heading a committee that lowered the reparations bill to a little more than $8 billion plus interest and which gave Germany fifty-nine years to make payments at a lowered interest. The Young Plan also provided (without official U.S. concurrence) that reductions in war debts would have a proportional effect on reparations. Europe had succeeded in linking debts with reparations despite U.S. efforts to keep them separate. The number of annual reparations payments as well as the total amount paid nearly equaled that sum owed the United States in European wartime credits.

The Dawes and Young Plans created a shaky, circular financial system whereby the United States furnished much of the money Germany used for reparations payments to the Allies, who in turn used the money to meet war debt obligations to Americans. From 1924 to 1931 Germany received $2.25 billion in U.S. loans; Germany paid the Allies $2.75 billion in reparations; and the Allies paid the United States $2 billion for war debts. The system worked as long as foreign recipients of U.S. loans and investments could meet interest payments and return some of the principal. But ultimately the United States's debtors could satisfy their obligations only by selling goods and services in the foreign markets, especially in the United States.

The onset of the Great Depression forced a reconsideration of the reparations and debts issues. After the stock market crash of 1929 President Hoover tried to protect U.S. businesses through a higher tariff, making the specious argument that there was no connection between tariff duties and the European debtors' capacity to pay. Over the objections of more than a thousand economists, he signed the Hawley-Smoot Act into law in June 1930. The highest tariff in the country's history, it further damaged the international financial situation and alienated European nations opposed to the country's nationalistic economic policies. Hoover then believed it wise to temporarily suspend the collection of both war debts and reparations, which in itself was a tacit admission that the European governments would not give up reparations demands without an accompanying release from debt collections. All governments concerned immediately approved, and in December 1931 Congress implemented a one-year moratorium with the understanding that payments would resume when the moratorium expired the following December. Had the United States opposed this measure, the results would have been German default on private U.S. loans, the destruction of U.S. bankers' collateral in Germany, and widespread bank closings in the United States. Still, the moratorium was only temporarily effective: It could not protect U.S. investments from the effects of the Depression.

The European nations finally acted on their own. The debtor governments came to believe that the United States would cut the debts figure if they reduced the German reparations bill. With this hope in mind, they gathered in Lausanne, Switzerland, in the summer of 1932 and authorized Germany to cancel ninety percent of its bill if the United States would reciprocate with equivalent reductions in war debts. This proposal caused a furor in Washington. Despite Hoover's warnings that U.S. failure to comply would end all payments, Congress insisted on maintaining the original reparations figure. He then appealed to President-elect Franklin D. Roosevelt to ask Congress to revive the War Debt Commission and scale down debts. Roosevelt refused to do so.

On December 15, 1932, the moratorium expired and the United States notified the European debtors that payments were due. Most governments met their obligations for a short while, but then sent only token sums. Finally, even these payments stopped. By mid-1934 all debtor nations except Finland had defaulted.

Crisis in Manchuria

Total economic collapse had taken place in every industrialized nation by the early 1930s, leading to the Great Depression and increasing the likelihood of massive international unrest conducive to war. Unemployment ranged from twenty-five percent in the United States to eighty percent in Germany; probably half of the world's industrial workers were out of work, and farmers were no better off. In short, the banking and monetary systems of every nation lay in ruins. All this was calamitous enough in its own right. But what was more, the dire economic situation posed a threat to world peace, because in Japan, Germany, and Italy powerful groups came to believe that the solution to economic problems was foreign conquest. The result was fierce competition for markets and resources that constituted a race for empire and created an intense atmosphere that encouraged war.

Japan was the first to succumb to the illusion of resolving its economic problems by building an empire. The Japanese wanted China's northern province of Manchuria in order to absorb their overflowing population, supply markets for cotton and silk, furnish mineral resources, and provide a buffer against the Soviets. Among the chief proponents of this expansionist position was the Japanese army, which had become more democratized after the Great War. Indeed, it had turned into a haven for young, spirited peasants who had moved into officer positions and who now emerged as super-patriots determined to make Japan a world power. Their initial objective was to bring about a "Showa restoration," which called for a moral rebirth of the nation

built on returning power to the Showa, the name for Emperor Hirohito. Although Japanese emperors had never possessed the power that this new group attributed to them, the belief, however mythical, was strong enough among the youthful soldiers to instill a deep sense of loyalty to one another and to the throne. But the younger officers had been unable to wrest control from the civilian moderates, who had insisted on abiding by the arms control agreements reached at the London Naval Conference of 1930. Politicians had hurt the nation, the militarists believed; these young officers sought to restore the nation's world prominence by first establishing hegemony in Manchuria.

The time was opportune for Japan to begin such a move, largely because civil war in China during the 1920s again invited outside intervention. Americans had initially sympathized with the nationalist uprising against the Manchu dynasty that began in 1911. Under the leadership of Sun Yat-sen, the Guomindang (Kuomintang) or Nationalist People's Party promised modernization through extensive reforms. Yet when Americans joined other Western nations in refusing to aid the rebels, Sun turned to the Soviet Union. The Soviets, hoping to restrain Japan and the West, sent special agent Michael Borodin (a former school principal in Chicago) and other advisers to instruct the Chinese on how to strengthen the Nationalist party. But Sun Yat-sen died in 1925, before he could unite the country with the aid of Chinese Communists now allowed into the party. The Nationalists in Shanghai, however, rebelled and attacked foreign holdings and foreigners—including Americans and Christian missionaries. The new leader of the Guomindang armies, General Jiang Jieshi (Chiang Kai-shek), then turned northward, seizing nearly half of China from the independent war lords. The Washington government sent soldiers and warships to protect its holdings and citizens. In 1926 and 1927 Jiang ordered the Soviet advisers out of the country and prepared to purge the Nationalist party of the Communists. After the massacre of thousands of Communist party members and supporters, their leader, Mao Zedong (Mao Tse-tung), fled south to establish a rebel government in central China. From there he carried on a civil war that lasted over the next two decades.

Japan could not allow the Chinese Nationalists to regain control in Manchuria. Although the Soviet Union's sphere of interest in the north had diminished after the Bolshevik Revolution, the Japanese meanwhile had pulled out of Shandong, Siberia, and northern Sakhalin and had terminated the Lansing-Ishii Agreement of 1917. Jiang's forces continued their move northward and in the Yangtze Valley established a new government at Nanking. Two years later, in 1928, they took over the ancient imperial capital at Peking and changed its name to Peiping (to mean "Northern Peace" rather than "Northern Capital"). That same year the United States signed a treaty acknowledging China's control over tariffs and securing most-favored-nation treatment in return. The treaty did not renounce the principle of extraterritoriality, but its very signing signaled a major concession because it constituted U.S. recognition of the Nationalist government.

The Japanese were worried about the United States's growing economic influence in China, even though the image loomed larger than the reality. By 1930 only one percent of U.S. investment overseas was in China, and during the previous seven years the United States had exported only three percent of its goods to China. Trade with Japan was twice as large. Still, the myth persisted of a boundless "China market." The United States's long-time pro-Chinese sentiment helped to override the shortcomings of the trade, and Jiang won favor because he opposed communism and was a Christian. Another attraction was his marriage to a Chinese businessman's daughter: Madame Jiang had a U.S. education and strong links with influential Americans having interests in China. The dangers of growing Soviet and U.S. involvement in China unsettled the

Japanese. When a change in Manchuria's government implanted a ruler favorable to the Nationalists, the Open Door seemed to have been slammed shut.

By the summer of 1929 China's relations with the Soviet Union had deteriorated to the breaking point. Fighting broke out when the Nationalists tried to gain control of the Chinese Eastern Railway and reestablish their country's authority in upper Manchuria. The Japanese feared that the Chinese might do the same with the South Manchurian Railway and other Japanese holdings in Manchuria. Worse, the Soviets might take everything. Secretary of State Stimson, the former secretary of war under Taft and troubleshooter in Nicaragua, had reminded both antagonists of the Kellogg-Briand Pact against war, but the Soviets had claimed self-defense as they invaded Manchuria in August. In November Stimson sent a circular letter urging the two nations to end the conflict. Through the combined efforts of the League of Nations and the United States, the nations accomplished a cease-fire in Shanghai in May 1931. The Soviets, however, had emerged triumphant.

The end of the Sino-Soviet clash did not resolve the tensions in China, because a number of incidents occurred as Japan's militarists sought to expand into Manchuria. In the summer of 1931 the Japanese press accused the Chinese of executing one of Japan's undercover army officers in Manchuria. Japanese moderates tried to resolve the matter peaceably, despite the army's call to take Manchuria. But shortly before midnight on September 18, 1931, an explosion ripped apart a small section of the South Manchurian Railway outside the capital at Mukden. The Japanese accused the Chinese of sabotage, although it is likely that young Japanese officers of the Guandong (Kwantung) or Manchurian Army fabricated the story to justify occupation of the entire province. Japanese forces, without orders from either the premier or the Foreign Office, quickly seized the Chinese barracks in Mukden along with other important positions near the railroad.

Jiang's government in China appealed to both the United States and the League for help. The Japanese had violated the League's assurances of security, the Nine-Power Treaty of 1922 guaranteeing the Open Door in China, and the Kellogg-Briand Pact outlawing war—even though they dismissed the events in Manchuria as mere "incidents" and not acts of war. The Mukden incident, it appeared, provided a dangerous example of unchecked aggression that could spur on similar actions by other countries in other areas of the world.

The Hoover administration was reluctant to act. Stimson wanted decisive U.S. action but drew no support from the president. Stimson had been a colonel in World War I and remained a firm believer in the use of force in international affairs. Never one to believe that the Japanese were racially equal to white people, he was convinced that they (and other Orientals) would buckle under to the use of force. He realized that Japan was dependent on U.S. oil and other goods, and he argued for an economic boycott. But his suggestion met staunch opposition from President Hoover, who disliked Stimson's combative style and feared that economic pressure by the United States would lead to war.

The League responded to Jiang's pleas with a toothless warning to the Japanese to pull out of the troubled region. The two key members of the League, Britain and France, hesitated to cut off trade in depression times. Both preferred giving in to Japan rather than draw some retaliatory action by the Tokyo government that endangered their own holdings in East Asia. Stimson realized that his only recourse was to notify the Japanese of his government's disapproval of their actions and hope that this mild expedient would be enough to curtail further advances. Stimson urged the two nations to stop fighting and sent an observer to the League discussions on the matter. But this latter move, primarily symbolic in origin, had little impact because the U.S. representative was under orders to participate only when the Council focused on

the relationship of the Kellogg-Briand Pact to the crisis. When the Council proposed sending an investigative commission to Manchuria, Japan protested. Moderates in Tokyo assured both the United States and the League that the Japanese government would restrain its army. The Council nonetheless set a deadline of November 16 for Japan's withdrawal from the railroad area.

But the Japanese military prepared instead to take all of northern Manchuria. By the winter of 1931–1932 Japanese forces threatened to expand along the South Manchurian Railway and into the Soviet sphere—that part of upper Manchuria adjoining the Soviet section of the Chinese Eastern Railway. Another Russo-Japanese war seemed certain. The League Council meanwhile reconvened on November 16, the date set for Japan's departure from Manchuria. In response to this modest threat, the Japanese two days later seized an area above the Chinese Eastern Railway in preparation for a grand sweep across Manchuria.

Japan's thrust into Manchuria soon came, and on January 7, 1932, the United States lamely responded with the Stimson Doctrine of nonrecognition. When the Japanese won Chinchow in southern Manchuria, they broke the Chinese army's last point of resistance. The secretary of state accused the Japanese of violating their nonaggression pledges and, probably under Hoover's prodding, declared that the United States refused to recognize governments established by force. In a stance consistent with that of the Wilson administration, the United States again departed from the principles of *de facto* recognition. Stimson firmly believed in abiding by treaty obligations and blasted the Japanese for violating the Open Door in China and the Kellogg-Briand Pact against war. Although he would have preferred the use of force, he realized that such a response was out of the question because of popular opposition to such a move, the absence of U.S. military leverage in that part of the world, the refusal of either Britain or France to join the nonrecognition stand, and

Map 11
Japan's invasion of Manchuria in 1931–1932 was the high point of its expansionist activities before December 1941.

Hoover's aversion to war. The president, a Quaker who thought nonmilitary correctives the adequate remedy for world problems, saw no alternative to nonrecognition despite his fears that the Japanese had begun a concerted drive to take all of China.

As in the Wilson presidential years, moral pressure failed because those exerting it—this time the Hoover administration—lacked the will and the means for enforcement. In late January Japan retaliated against a Chinese boycott on its goods by bombarding Shanghai, which led the United States to send additional military forces to join the small number already in the city. Yet U.S. soldiers were not under orders to fight the Japanese. Stimson later explained that his hope had been to remind them of America's "great size and military strength." Japan "was afraid of that, and I was willing to let her be afraid of that without telling her that we were not going to use it against her." The bluff did not work. It seems clear that Japan had no pattern for conquest and that its officers merely reacted to situations as they developed. But the newsreels, pictures, and firsthand accounts of the bombings in Shanghai caused worldwide revulsion. Japan's assault on that great city posed a threat to British interests in the Yangtze Valley and raised demands for Japanese-Chinese negotiations.

As Japan's forces continued to spread into Manchuria, it became increasingly evident that the United States's nonrecognition policy had proved ineffective. Ignoring an aggressor seldom reforms him, U.S. diplomat Hugh Wilson noted almost a decade after the Stimson Doctrine. "If the nations of the world feel strongly enough to condemn," he asserted, "they should feel strongly enough to use force. . . . To condemn only merely intensifies the heat. . . . Condemnation creates a community of the damned who are forced outside the pale, who have nothing to lose by the violation of all laws of order and international good faith." Indeed, nonrecognition constituted an admission to Japan's upper hand in East Asia, because the Washington government had virtually announced its inability to take any decisive action. Events in Manchuria exposed the fatal flaw in the peacekeeping treaties of the 1920s: The West lacked the will to enforce them. The United States's aversion to force, its lack of military power in East Asia, and the Great Depression dictated a policy of inaction that masqueraded behind the mask of nonrecognition.

The Japanese restructured Manchuria into the puppet regime of Manchukuo ("country of the Manchus") in mid-February 1932 and drew only another restrained response from the United States. Within a week Stimson sent a public letter to Borah, chair of the Senate Foreign Relations Committee, which called on other nations to support the nonrecognition policy and strongly implied that if Japan continued its aggressions in China, the United States might terminate the Five-Power Treaty of 1922, fortify Guam and the Philippines, and strengthen its naval forces in the Pacific. Japan, Stimson charged, had violated "the principles of fair play, patience, and mutual goodwill." Stimson's letter had some effect. In March the League of Nations announced support for nonrecognition and ensured opposition to any matter "brought about by means contrary to the Covenant of the League of Nations or to the Pact of Paris." But the Great Depression prohibited economic or military sanctions. Japan's assault eased, however,

largely because of the costs of the expedition and the continued resistance by the Chinese. Japan withdrew from Shanghai in May 1932, but only after saving face by brutally driving out Chinese forces.

Meanwhile the League of Nations appointed a commission headed by England's Earl of Lytton to investigate the problems in East Asia. In September 1932 the Lytton Commission reported to the League that Japan was primarily responsible for the Manchurian crisis. The report admitted that China had failed to protect Japan's legitimate rights in Manchuria, but it also suggested that Japan was guilty of aggression in the Mukden incident. Manchukuo, the findings showed, was not an outgrowth of the popular will. The Japanese had stirred up resentment among dissatisfied groups in China and fomented a drive for independence. The Lytton Commission recommended that Manchuria receive autonomy but remain under Chinese political control, and it called on the withdrawal of Japanese and Chinese soldiers and the establishment of a gendarmerie, or local police force, to restore order in the province. The two governments would then sign a treaty guaranteeing Japanese interests and peaceful settlement of disputes. Thus, the commission sought to maintain Chinese authority in Manchuria without endangering Japan's legitimate economic concerns. Two weeks after Lytton submitted his findings to the League, Japan pointedly extended formal recognition to Manchukuo.

On February 24, 1933, the League of Nations adopted the Lytton Report. The leader of the Japanese delegation, Yosuke Matsuoka, left no doubt about his anger when he emotionally declared to the Assembly that his country's position was similar to that faced by Christ as he went to the cross. Japan then served the stipulated two-year notice of withdrawal from the League.

Impact of the Manchurian Crisis

Stimson was pleased that the League's adoption of the Lytton Report virtually meant acceptance of the doctrine of nonrecognition, and yet this so-called triumph for U.S. policy left a dangerous legacy. Stimson's appeals to morality had increased Japan's animosity toward the United States, deepened its already embittered reaction to the Open Door, and made the United States its central obstacle to expansion in East Asia. Furthermore, nonrecognition had underlined the United States's reluctance to act forcefully. By announcing a stand of opposition and then doing nothing to enforce it, the United States had inadvertently encouraged Japan to take actions that set an example of aggression unchallenged by the West. The only question remaining was whether other imperialist nations would follow that example.

Selected Readings

Adler, Selig. *The Isolationist Impulse: Its Twentieth Century Reaction.* 1957.

———. *The Uncertain Giant: 1921–1941, American Foreign Policy between the Wars.* 1965.

Aldcroft, Derek H. *From Versailles to Wall Street, 1919–1929.* 1977.

Barnhart, Michael. *Japan Prepares for Total War: The Search for Economic Security, 1919–1941.* 1987.

Brandes, Joseph. *Herbert Hoover and Economic Diplomacy: Department of Commerce Policy, 1921–1928.* 1962.

Buckingham, Peter H. *International Normalcy: The Open Door Peace with the Former Central Powers, 1921–1929.* 1983.

Buckley, Thomas H. *The United States and the Washington Conference, 1921–1922.* 1970.

Burner, David. *Herbert Hoover.* 1978.

Calder, Bruce J. *The Impact of Intervention: The Dominican Republic during the U.S. Occupation of 1916–1924.* 1984.

Carroll, John M. "American Diplomacy in the 1920s," in Carroll, John M., and Herring, George C., eds. *Modern American Diplomacy,* 53–70. 1986.

Cohen, Warren I. *America's Response to China: An Interpretive History of Sino-American Relations.* 2000.

———. *Empire Without Tears: America's Foreign Relations, 1921–1933.* 1987.

Costigliola, Frank. *Awkward Dominion: American Political, Economic, and Cultural Relations with Europe, 1919–1933.* 1984.

———. "The United States and the Reconstruction of Germany in the 1920s," *Business History Review* 50 (1976): 477–502.

Current, Richard. *Secretary Stimson: A Study in Statecraft.* 1954.

DeBenedetti, Charles. *Origins of the Modern American Peace Movement, 1915–1929.* 1978.

DeConde, Alexander. *Herbert Hoover's Latin American Policy.* 1951.

Delpar, Helen. *The Enormous Vogue of Things Mexican: Cultural Relations Between the United States and Mexico, 1920–1935.* 1992.

Dingman, Roger. *Power in the Pacific: The Origins of Naval Arms Limitation, 1914–1922.* 1976.

Doenecke, Justus D. *When the Wicked Rise: American Opinion-Makers and the Manchurian Crisis of 1931–1933.* 1984.

———, and Wilz, John E. *From Isolation to War, 1931–1941.* 1991.

Dunne, Michael. *The United States and the World Court, 1920–1935.* 1988.

Ellis, L. Ethan. *Republican Foreign Policy, 1921–1933.* 1968.

Fanning, Richard W. *Peace and Disarmament: Naval Rivalry and Arms Control, 1922–1933.* 1995.

Fausold, Martin L. *The Presidency of Herbert C. Hoover.* 1985.

Feis, Herbert. *The Diplomacy of the Dollar: The First Era, 1919–1933.* 1950.

Ferrell, Robert H. *American Diplomacy in the Great Depression: Hoover-Stimson Foreign Policy, 1929–1933.* 1957.

———. *Frank B. Kellogg and Henry L. Stimson.* 1963.

———. *Peace in Their Time: The Origins of the Kellogg-Briand Pact.* 1952.

———. *The Presidency of Calvin Coolidge.* 1998.

Filene, Peter. *Americans and the Soviet Experiment, 1917–1933.* 1967.

Fleming, Denna F. *The United States and World Organization, 1920–1933.* 1938.

Foster, Carrie A. *The Women and the Warriors: The U.S. Section of the Women's International League for Peace and Freedom, 1915–1946.* 1995.

Foster, Catherine. *Women for All Seasons: The Story of the Women's International League for Peace and Freedom.* 1989.

Gaddis, John L. *Russia, the Soviet Union, and the United States: An Interpretive History.* 2nd ed., 1990.

Glad, Betty. *Charles Evans Hughes and the Illusions of Innocence: A Study of American Diplomacy.* 1966.

Goldman, Emily O. *Sunken Treaties: Naval Arms Control between the Wars.* 1994.

Grieb, Kenneth J. *The Latin American Policy of Warren G. Harding.* 1976.

Grover, David H. *American Merchant Ships on the Yangtze, 1920–1941.* 1992.

Guinsburg, Thomas N. *The Pursuit of Isolationism in the United States Senate from Versailles to Pearl Harbor.* 1981.

Hall, Linda B. *Oil, Banks, and Politics: The United States and Postrevolutionary Mexico, 1917–1924.* 1995.

Hawley, Ellis W. *The Great War and the Search for a Modern Order: A History of the American People and Their Institutions, 1917–1933.* 1979.

Hodgson, Godfrey. *The Colonel: The Life and Wars of Henry Stimson, 1867–1950.* 1990.

Hogan, Michael J. *Informal Entente: The Private Structure of Cooperation in Anglo-American Economic Diplomacy, 1918–1929.* 1977.

Hu, Shizhang. *Stanley K. Hornbeck and the Open Door Policy, 1919–1937.* 1995.

Iriye, Akira. *After Imperialism: The Search for a New Order in the Far East, 1921–1931.* 1965.

Johnson, Robert D. *The Peace Progressives and American Foreign Relations.* 1995.

Jonas, Manfred. *The United States and Germany, A Diplomatic History.* 1984.

Josephson, Harold. "Outlawing War: Internationalism and the Pact of Paris," *Diplomatic History* 3 (1979): 377–90.

Kamman, William. *A Search for Stability: United States Diplomacy toward Nicaragua, 1925–1933.* 1968.

Kuehl, Warren. F., and Dunn, Lynne K. *Keeping the Covenant: American Internationalists and the League of Nations, 1920–1939.* 1997.

Langley, Lester D. *The Banana Wars: An Inner History of American Empire, 1900–1934.* 1983.

Leffler, Melvyn P. *The Elusive Quest: America's Pursuit of European Stability and French Security, 1919–1933.* 1979.

Linn, Brian M. *Guardians of Empire: The U.S. Army and the Pacific, 1902–1940.* 1997.

Lower, Richard C. *A Bloc of One: The Political Career of Hiram W. Johnson.* 1993.

Macaulay, Neill. *The Sandino Affair.* 1967.

Maddox, Robert J. *William E. Borah and American Foreign Policy.* 1969.

McNeil, William C. *American Money and the Weimar Republic.* 1986.

Meyer, Lorenzo. *Mexico and the United States in the Oil Controversy, 1917–1942.* 1977.

Miller, Edward S. *War Plan Orange: The U.S. Strategy to Defeat Japan, 1897–1945.* 1991.

Morison, Elting E. *Turmoil and Tradition: The Life and Times of Henry L. Stimson.* 1960.

Moser, John E. *Twisting the Lion's Tail: American Anglophobia between the World Wars.* 1999.

Munro, Dana G. *The United States and the Caribbean Republics, 1921–1933.* 1974.

Murray, Robert K. *The Harding Era.* 1969.

Neu, Charles E. *The Troubled Encounter: The United States and Japan.* 1975.

Neumann, William L. *America Encounters Japan: From Perry to MacArthur.* 1963.

O'Connor, Raymond G. *Perilous Equilibrium: The United States and the London Disarmament Conference of 1930.* 1962, 1969.

Ostrower, Gary B. *Collective Security: The U.S. and the League of Nations during the Early Thirties.* 1979.

Parrini, Carl P. *Heir to Empire: United States Economic Diplomacy, 1916–1923.* 1969.

Pease, Neal. *Poland, the United States, and the Stabilization of Europe, 1919–1933.* 1986.

Pelz, Stephen E. *Road to Pearl Harbor: The Failure of the Second London Naval Conference and the Onset of World War II.* 1974.

Pérez, Louis A., Jr. *Cuba and the United States.* 1997.

———. *Cuba Under the Platt Amendment, 1902–1934.* 1986.

Rappaport, Armin. *Henry L. Stimson and Japan, 1931–1933.* 1963.

Rosenberg, Emily S. *Spreading the American Dream: American Economic and Cultural Expansion, 1890–1945.* 1982.

Salisbury, Richard V. *Anti-Imperialism and International Competition in Central America, 1920–1929.* 1989.

Schmidt, Hans. *The United States Occupation of Haiti, 1915–1934.* 1971.

Schmitz, David F. *Thank God They're on Our Side: The United States and Right-Wing Dictatorships, 1921–1965.* 1999.

Schulzinger, Robert D. *The Making of the Diplomatic Mind: The Training, Outlook and Style of*

United States Foreign Service Officers, 1908–1931. 1975.

Sharbach, Sarah E. *Stereotypes of Latin America, Press Images, and U.S. Foreign Policy, 1920–1933.* 1993.

Shewmaker, Kenneth E. *Americans and Chinese Communists, 1927–1945: A Persuading Encounter.* 1971.

Smith, Robert F. *The United States and Revolutionary Nationalism in Mexico, 1916–1932.* 1972.

Spinelli, Lawrence. *Dry Diplomacy: The United States, Great Britain, and Prohibition.* 1989.

Steward, Dick. *Trade and Hemisphere: The Good Neighbor Policy and Reciprocal Trade.* 1975.

Thorne, Chistopher. *The Limits of Foreign Policy: The West, the League and the Far Eastern Crisis of 1931–1933.* 1972.

Trachtenberg, Marc. *Reparation in World Politics: France and European Economic Diplomacy, 1916–1923.* 1980.

Tulchin, Joseph S. *The Aftermath of War: World War I and U.S. Policy Toward Latin America.* 1971.

Vinson, John C. *The Parchment Peace: The United States Senate and the Washington Conference, 1921–1922.* 1956.

Walker, Thomas W. *Nicaragua: The Land of Sandino.* 1981.

Weatherson, Michael, and Bochin, Hal W. *Hiram Johnson: Political Revivalist.* 1995.

Wheeler, Gerald E. *Prelude to Pearl Harbor: The United States Navy and the Far East, 1921–1931.* 1963.

Wilson, Joan Hoff. *American Business and Foreign Policy, 1920–1933.* 1971.

———. *Herbert Hoover: Forgotten Progressive.* 1975.

———. *Ideology and Economics: U.S. Relations with the Soviet Union, 1918–1933.* 1974.

Wood, Bryce. *The Making of the Good Neighbor Policy.* 1961.

CHAPTER 6

The Coming of World War II, 1933–1939

Franklin D. Roosevelt as Diplomat

On March 4, 1933, Franklin D. Roosevelt took the oath as president of the United States and soon began an activist, personal form of diplomacy that was to be the hallmark of his administration's foreign policy. He really had no philosophy of foreign policy, however, except that he believed in a strong navy and acted primarily out of concern for domestic needs. A New York patrician and a Harvard graduate, he had been assistant secretary of the navy under President Wilson, and as a vice-presidential candidate in 1920 had supported both the Versailles Treaty and the League of Nations. But early in his 1932 campaign for the presidential nomination he had won the backing of influential newspaper publisher William Randolph Hearst, an isolationist and Democrat, only by publicly renouncing support for U.S. membership in the League. The only chief executive to win election for four terms, Roosevelt proved to be, in a sense, a singular combination of his distant cousin and idol Theodore Roosevelt and former President Wilson. Theodore Roosevelt exemplified a zest for life and office that was contagious and yet tempered by the hard reality of politics; Wilson personified a strict morality that prohibited any compromise of ideals. Franklin D. Roosevelt somehow combined the reality and the ideal to ultimately seek world order through a "policeman" approach led by the United States, which Wilson once told him was "the only nation that all feel is disinterested and all trust."

Pragmatic, charismatic, and even enigmatic, Roosevelt brought to the presidency an unusual mixture of realism and idealism, of straightforwardness and cunning, and of cosmopolitan outlook and yet genuine national concern, while utterly defying his enemies with his uncanny political ability and warm, personal charm. Roosevelt, Hoover once grumbled, was "a chameleon on plaid." Roosevelt stamped his personality, as both the "lion" and the "fox," onto his tenure in the White House, twelve years that have rightfully become known as the "Roosevelt Era" in U.S. history.

Like most dominant figures, Roosevelt nearly always aroused strong feelings of either love or hate while becoming a top personality in a world then characterized by forceful and charismatic international leaders. Stricken with infantile paralysis in 1921 at the age of thirty-nine, he had astounded his contemporaries by refusing to compromise with his inability to walk and pursuing a political career that took him to the highest office in the land. Roosevelt firmly believed in maintaining his country's world responsibilities, but he had

Herbert Hoover and Franklin D. Roosevelt
At Roosevelt's first inaugural, March 4, 1933. *International Photo News Service.*

to exercise extreme caution in following an internationalist course because of his people's disillusionment resulting from U.S. entry into World War I.

Although Roosevelt usually took the lead in making foreign policy, he shrewdly recognized that the realities of domestic politics and public opinion prohibited him from venturing too far ahead of his constituents. Even so, in European affairs he often ignored his secretary of state, Cordell Hull, who frequently had to learn secondhand what the administration's policy was toward that part of the world. Except in matters affecting Latin America and Asia, Roosevelt sought advice primarily from four colleagues: Henry Morgenthau, secretary of the treasury and long-time friend and neighbor in New York; Harry Hopkins, secretary of commerce and head of various New Deal programs until he became the president's chief aide and confidant after the outbreak of war in Europe in 1939; Sumner Welles, ambassador to Cuba and later undersecretary of state whom Hull detested; and William Bullitt, Wilson's embittered peace emissary dur-

ing the Russian civil war and the nation's first ambassador to the Soviet Union. Through sheer force of character and personality, Roosevelt relegated others in his administration to live and work in his long shadow.

The Good Neighbor Policy in Latin America

Problems stemming from the Great Depression dominated Roosevelt's first two terms in office, although his domestic reform efforts were integrally related to foreign affairs. During the early 1930s fascism spread in Asia and Europe. In China, the Japanese completed their hold on Manchukuo by inserting their own people in key governmental positions. Meanwhile, German Nazi party figure Adolf Hitler achieved dictatorial powers as the führer, or leader. His demagogic tactics were to exploit widespread unrest in his country resulting from the Depression, inflame anti-Semitic and anti-Communist feelings, and encourage mass hatred for the Versailles Treaty and the "November criminals" of Germany

Franklin D. Roosevelt and Cordell Hull
As secretary of state for over a decade, Hull dealt primarily with Latin American and Asian affairs, while Roosevelt focused on Europe and the Atlantic. *National Archives, Washington, D.C.*

who had, he bitterly charged, sacrificed their homeland in agreeing to terms. Likewise, in Italy Fascista Benito Mussolini led his army of Black Shirts into dictatorial power by clamping down on communism and socialism while bringing about a tough kind of domestic stability that rested on his brutal suppression of strikes and other internal disorders. But despite these potential threats to world peace, Roosevelt's central concern remained internal reform; even in foreign policy he sought to build sufficient international trade primarily to promote the United States's domestic recovery. Consequently, his administration's initial priority was to establish a network of reciprocal trade treaties designed to benefit the United States. The focus of attention became Latin America, and the leader in formulating such a policy was Hull.

Roosevelt's first attempt to enhance trade and better relations with Latin America lay in broadening his predecessor's Good Neighbor policy by moving away from the use of force. And yet, also like his predecessor, the president could not abandon all involvement in light of external threats to the hemisphere that would, in turn, endanger U.S. interests. Roosevelt, too, found it more advantageous to his country to emphasize a multilateral relationship with Latin America based on economic ties rather than adhere to the long-standing unilateral interventionist policy of the Monroe Doctrine, which had come to rest mainly on military means.

Although Roosevelt did not refer to any particular area of the world, he declared in his inaugural address that "in the field of world policy I would dedicate this Nation to the policy of the good neighbor—the neighbor who resolutely respects himself and, because he does so, respects the rights of others." Such a move was easier now for the Washington government because in Latin America during the immediate aftermath of World War I, the British challenge had dissipated, the German threat had ended, and the U.S. Navy reigned supreme. Examples of the new direction in Latin American policy came in the early 1930s with the withdrawal of U.S. Marines from Haiti and Nicaragua (discussed in the previous chapter). Although domestic instability characterized a number of Latin American states on the eve of Roosevelt's new policy, he hoped to restore order chiefly by economic measures.

To increase trade throughout the hemisphere, the United States attempted to win the trust of Latin Americans at the Seventh International Conference of American States in Montevideo, Uruguay, in December 1933. Hull had called for reciprocal trade agreements to erase the damaging effects on Cuban sugar of the high Hawley-Smoot Tariff of 1930, but on his arrival as chair of the U.S. delegation in Montevideo, he encountered angry crowds in the streets waving signs proclaiming "Down with Hull." After extending personal goodwill assurances to each country's delegation, he went before the assembly to deliver a strong statement against foreign intervention and then signed a convention declaring that "no state has the right to intervene in the internal or external affairs of another." Even so, Hull upheld the tradition of his predecessors by stipulating that in the interests of self-defense, the United States could intervene "by the law of nations as generally recognized and accepted." Two days after the conference, Roosevelt eased some of the apprehension about Hull's qualification by publicly declaring that "the definite policy of the United States from now on is one opposed to armed intervention." The U.S. Senate overwhelmingly approved the Montevideo convention, offering hope for improved relations with Latin America.

While in Montevideo, Hull also moved toward the establishment of reciprocal trade agreements that would affect not only Latin America but all other interested nations in the world. Advocates pointed out that during the nineteenth century, tariffs were lower than at any time in history and so was, not coincidentally, the number of wars. Skeptics countered that low tariffs had no bearing on world peace and attributed the absence of a major war to British naval dominance and the world's preoccupation with industrial expansion. Still, Hull thought it worthwhile to pursue a program of commercial expansion and won executive approval to proceed.

As a southern senator and a Wilsonian in foreign affairs, Hull had long favored low tariffs and greater economic interdependence among nations as vital tools for removing the causes of war. He noted in his memoirs that "it seemed virtually impossible to develop friendly relations with other nations in the political sphere so long as we provoked their animosity in the economic sphere. How could we promote peace with them while waging war on them commercially?" Ironically, the major obstacle in 1933 was Roosevelt's New Deal program, because it necessitated a high tariff to protect the nation's economy. Yet such a drive for national self-sufficiency, Hull believed, encouraged international divisiveness, lessened the chances for raising living standards all over the world, and promoted "the economic dissatisfaction that breeds war."

Hull was a stubborn backwoods Tennessean with a characteristic lisp in his sermonic pattern of speech. He kept battering away at the president in a high, piercing tone until his superior gave in to the principles of commercial reciprocity. "We must eliminate these twade baayuhs heah, theah and ev'ywheah," according to Hull's opponents in mimicking language and with hands flailing in further imitation of his animated demeanor. One factor encouraging a change in the president's stance was the conference in Montevideo, because those in attendance overwhelmingly supported lower tariffs on a reciprocal basis. But even more important were Hull's persistent arguments for the interlocking nature of trade and peace. Protracted world economic disorder, he warned, encouraged dictatorships and made people susceptible to tyrannical ideologies such as communism. As Hull told a congressional committee, world trade "is not only calculated to aid materially in the restoration of prosperity everywhere, but it is the greatest civilizer and peacemaker in the experience of the human race."

Congress responded with the Reciprocal Trade Agreements Act of June 1934, which sought to stimulate foreign purchases of U.S. goods through tariff reductions and proved particularly effective in Latin America. To remove the issue from politics, the act authorized the president to take the initiative in lowering tariffs on a reciprocal basis up to fifty percent through three-year bilateral executive agreements based on the most-favored-nation principle. Thus, the president gained enormous power in economic diplomacy because the agreements went into effect without Senate approval while automatically extending to each party the lowest tariff rates awarded anyone else. By 1940 the Executive Office achieved a highly favorable balance of trade for the United States by negotiating bilateral treaties on a reciprocal basis with more than twenty nations. Indeed, U.S. participation in Latin America's trade grew from one-third to almost one-half. But even though the treaties drove down duties and encouraged international trade, they did not stop the events leading to war.

Roosevelt's Good Neighbor assurances particularly suggested the need for a drastic change in U.S. relations with Cuba, because that uneven relationship still rested on the interventionist rights contained in the hated Platt Amendment of 1901. The timing was opportune. The Platt Amendment had become an expensive and irksome burden for the United States, and it was a highly unpopular symbol of U.S. imperialism to Cubans.

For another reason as well, the time seemed right for change in Cuba: Economic hard times on the island, exacerbated by the Hawley-Smoot Tariff, had fomented a revolution against the dictator Gerardo Machado in late 1933. U.S. ambassador Sumner Welles secretly worked to undermine the government and install his favorite, Carlos Manuel de Céspedes, as president. But Céspedes proved colorless, and within a month the Cuban army, led by young Sergeant Fulgencio Batista, overthrew the hapless ruler and replaced him with Ramón Grau San Martín. A liberal-minded professor of biology at the University of Havana, Grau immediately alienated Welles by abrogating the Platt Amendment, suspending loan payments to New York's Chase National Bank, and expropriating U.S.-owned sugar plantations. Although the new provisional president acted in the name of nationalism, Welles thought him a friend of the Communists—a charge never substantiated.

The Good Neighbor policy underwent a critical test in Cuba. Even though the Roosevelt administration had turned away from the use of force, it could not permit an internal problem on the island to threaten U.S. interests. The first challenge to the nation's new policy came when Welles requested military intervention. Even though the request met a strong rebuff in Washington, Roosevelt approved sending nearly thirty warships as a show of force. Although Hull dismissed them as "little vessels" sent for the "moral effect" of protecting American lives, the administration offered economic assistance to Batista, who had no qualms about shifting allegiances and leading a coup against Grau in January 1934 that forced him to flee to Mexico.

A conservative and head of the Nationalist Party, Carlos Mendieta, became provisional president, but Batista held the real political and military power. As head of the Cuban army, Batista quickly restored order to the island, and the United States extended recognition to the Mendieta regime within a week of his taking office. A commercial treaty soon followed that reduced the U.S. tariff on sugar under the auspices of the Reciprocal Trade Agreements Act. In addition, the Export-Import Bank, a government agency established that same year of 1934 to promote foreign commerce, threw open its coffers to the new regime. The United States abrogated the Platt Amendment in May, although strong economic ties remained and Cuba allowed the United States to retain its naval base at Guantánamo.

The World Economic Conference in London

A second broad attempt by Roosevelt to deal with the Great Depression resulted from his predecessor's promise that the United States would attend a forthcoming World Economic Conference in London, called to stabilize the international currency situation. Numerous studies had linked the seriousness of the Depression to high tariffs, war debts, the termination of foreign loans, and the decision by Britain, France, and other nations to leave the gold standard. The last measure posed a special threat to world stability because it blocked the convertibility of paper money by permitting great fluctuations in exchange rates. Without a common medium of exchange, the world's trade would virtually cease.

From the international point of view it seemed economically and politically sound to return to the gold standard. The move, its proponents argued, would stabilize the currency and stimulate global trade. Having a gold standard prevented nations from meeting their debt obligations simply by printing more money and thereby causing rampant inflation: The amount printed had to be in proportion to their supply of gold. Even more compelling, according to supporters, a return to the gold standard discouraged the huge spending necessary to military buildups and thereby decreased the likelihood of war. Roosevelt appeared to agree on these points, although he refused to permit any negotiation of war debts: "That stays with Poppa— right here," he declared.

In the spring of 1933 the representatives of eleven nations met with the president in Washington and departed with his assurance that international monetary stabilization would be the priority of the upcoming conference. The gathering in London, Roosevelt had asserted, would "establish order by stabilization of currencies. It must supplement individual domestic programs for economic recovery by wise-considered international action." Britain and all other nations must return to the gold standard.

But soon after the Washington meeting, additional economic reversals in the United States forced it off the gold standard as well. Roosevelt feared that if the dollar was tied to gold and hence to the unstable nature of international trade, he would lose control over his domestic recovery program. The gold standard dictated a balanced budget based on greatly restricted expenditures, he knew, and this approach would seriously hamper internal reform programs. Furthermore, the dollar's purchasing power had risen with the Depression, forcing debtors into the undesirable position of having to honor loan commitments made when the dollar was not worth as much. Thus, Roosevelt sought to devalue the dollar to the level of the previous decade, but he could not do this if U.S. currency was dependent on the prevailing rate of international exchange. Roosevelt had to be free to manipulate the value of the currency within the United States in an effort to create public building projects—even to the point of accepting an unbalanced budget by raising U.S. prices (by printing more currency) or incurring great debts. Defensible as the policy was, his error lay in adopting it *after* the U.S. delegation, led by Hull, had left for England.

In mid-June the U.S. delegates assembled in London with those of sixty-three other nations, all hoping to remove barriers to international trade. Trouble developed two weeks later, however, when the White House sent a telegram announcing its decision to abandon the gold standard. Hull was as shocked as the others attending the conference. He had been ready to present a proposal for lowered tariffs through reciprocity arrangements, but his entire program now came into danger because of the president's decision. In Roosevelt's note to the U.S. delegation on July 3, he expressed opposition to international currency stabilization and emphasized the need for domestic recovery. "The sound internal economic system of a nation," he insisted, "is a greater factor in its well-being than the price of its currency in changing terms of the currencies of other nations." The United States would not become a party to reciprocal tariff agreements, nor would it stay on the gold standard. If the dollar were convertible into other currency, he reasoned, the nation's domestic purchasing power would be at the mercy of the irregularities of world trade.

The London Conference was already facing high obstacles to success, primarily because of competing national interests, but Roosevelt's action virtually jettisoned the entire effort. The European delegations hotly warned Hull that the step would hamper trade by guaranteeing a sharp rise in the costs of foreign goods. France, Italy, Belgium, and other nations demanded stabilization through a return to the gold standard. When their efforts proved fruitless, they accused the United States of subverting the conference and angrily called for adjournment.

Hull's cause was not helped by the antics of a pivotal member of the U.S. delegation, Key Pittman. The influential chair of the Senate Foreign Relations Committee, he called for the monetization of silver—which, not by coincidence, was a chief resource of his home state of Nevada. The senator also went on wild drinking bouts (in a country not under the stringencies of Prohibition—as was the United States) and, like a man possessed, on one occasion shot out street lights in London with a six-shooter. In still another escapade, he brandished a whiskey bottle in one hand and a bowie knife in the other and, while buck naked, chased a terrified colleague down the hall of their London hotel, yelling at him to support the silver standard.

In this chaotic atmosphere, Hull somehow managed to keep the conference going for three more weeks, until late July, when it broke up in failure. Currency stabilization remained elusive, although one can cynically argue that the outcome of the conference helped to end the war debt issue. Afterward only Finland made its payment in December, and in the following year, 1934, Congress passed the Johnson Act prohibiting loans to nations already in default. A year later British, French, and U.S. central banks entered an informal agreement fixing currency values; but no permanent currency stabilization on a global scale seemed possible. The Roosevelt administration's strongly nationalistic stance on these monetary matters undercut such efforts and deepened European hostility toward the United States.

U.S. Recognition of the Soviet Union

A third administration program designed to alleviate the economic situation at home, but also carrying foreign policy objectives, was the decision to extend diplomatic recognition to the Soviet Union. Many in the Western world abhorred the harsh methods used by the Bolsheviks in their rise to power in 1917, and the United States joined other nations in refusing to grant diplomatic recognition throughout the succeeding decade when the new Moscow regime called for world revolution, denounced capitalism, expropriated private properties, and repudiated the debts of the czar and the provisional government. The United States's official reason for nonrecognition related to the more than $600 million owed Americans and their government, but another consideration was equally important. The radical, atheist, and anticapitalist nature of the Soviets' revolutionary system aroused deep suspicions among Americans, who linked their distrust of the Bolsheviks with the Red Scare of 1919–1920.

Some Americans, however, had expressed concern about the welfare of the Soviet people after the devastating effects of the Great War and sought to extend economic aid. Famine had swept the huge country in 1921, and Russian author Maxim Gorky led others in requesting humanitarian help from the United States. That same year, Herbert Hoover, as secretary of commerce in the Harding administration, signed an agreement with the Soviet Union that authorized relief assistance. Hoover had long argued that such an approach would undercut revolutionary forces in the Soviet Union and enhance U.S. influence in that huge country. Within three years the American Relief Administration raised $50 million from Americans and the Washington government to help the Soviet people. Another benefit seemed clear. The head of the relief program in the Soviet Union, Colonel William Haskell, boasted in 1923 that U.S. efforts had destroyed communism in that country.

But nonrecognition had not forced changes in Soviet behavior, and polls revealed a surprising amount of popular support for reversing the policy. In addition, pressure for U.S. recognition had developed among business leaders interested in the Soviet market and among liberals who thought it no concern of the United States what kind of regime the Soviets had. During the 1920s General Electric, Du Pont, Ford, and other U.S. companies signed commercial agreements with the Soviet Union that dramatically increased trade. But after the stock market crash of 1929, exchanges dropped and leading business figures urged diplomatic recognition in an effort to revive commerce. As was the case with the mythical "China market," they confidently spoke of unlimited commercial gains derived from the Soviet Union without explaining how its people would pay for U.S. goods.

Other proponents of Soviet recognition feared German and Japanese imperialist expansion and hoped that a revitalized Soviet Union could help to restore a power balance to the world. After supporting the decision not to invite the Soviets to either the Versailles proceedings in 1919 or the Washington Conference of 1921–1922, many Americans had finally realized the impracticality of ignoring a nation whose actions had great impact on both Europe and Asia.

Some influential members of the state department, however, had ideological reasons for rigidly opposing recognition. A specialist on Russia and head of the state department's East European Affairs division, Robert Kelley, had argued in 1929 that the chief obstacle to recognition was "the Bolshevik world revolutionary purpose" espoused by the Comintern (Communist International). From this purpose stemmed those actions ill-befitting a responsible member of the community of nations. He had already persuaded his superiors to set up a departmental program to train a group of experts to recognize the revolutionary threat posed by the Soviets. Among the experts emerging from this new program were George F. Kennan and Charles E. Bohlen, both extraordinarily gifted young men who strongly distrusted the Soviets and later played integral roles in constructing the United States's Cold War policy.

Despite stringent opposition from the state department and numerous other groups in the United States, Roosevelt moved ahead in his efforts to grant recognition to the Soviet Union. He felt it prudent to use any means available for ridding the world of the economic crisis while slowing the spread of Germany and Japan. The establishment of trade would benefit both the United States and Soviet Union, and diplomatic cooperation might help to keep the peace when the delicate fiber woven together at Versailles seemed to be unraveling everywhere. How embarrassing it was that when Japan rolled into Manchuria in 1931, the Hoover administration could not engage in any joint deterrent action with the Soviet Union because the United States (alone among the important countries) had still not established diplomatic relations.

In a move demonstrating Roosevelt's personal approach to foreign affairs, he insisted that the arrangement for discussions take place under his own direction. Rather than work through the state department and Foreign Service officers (whom he dismissed as spoiled and effeminate), he chose to keep the matter secret by relying on Secretary of Commerce Henry Morgenthau and William Bullitt, the special assistant to the secretary of state. In October 1933 Roosevelt arranged a secret meeting between his personal emissaries and the head of the Soviet Information Bureau in Washington, Boris Skvirsky. Bullitt remained frustrated by his inability to negotiate a settlement with Lenin in 1919 and now was gratified to have a second chance to establish relations. When Skvirsky asked, "Does this mean recognition?" Bullitt replied, "What more can you expect than to have your representative sit down with the President of the United States?"

A few days afterward the White House received a favorable response to its overtures, and Roosevelt publicized the news by releasing the recent correspondence with the Soviets' titular president, Mikhail Kalinin. Roosevelt called for personal discussions with the Soviets, and Kalinin accepted. The Soviet Union's motives were partly commercial, but it was also concerned about halting Japan's recent spread into China. In addition, Soviet leader Joseph Stalin had become deeply concerned about the German Nazis, especially after they had recently forced members of the German Communist party into concentration camps and declared the party illegal. Among Stalin's reactions was an order to Communists in the West to align with non-Communists in "popular fronts." Another expedient was to work with the Western governments themselves. Any Soviet-American agreement, of course, would rest solely on mutual need.

Negotiations were stiff and uncertain when they opened in Washington in November 1933. The Soviet commissar for foreign affairs, Maxim Litvinov, arrived in the United States on November 7, prepared to begin discussions the next day and supremely confident that his country would receive immediate recognition. But this was not to be so. After two days of talks with Hull (who soon had to leave for the Montevideo conference), Bullitt, Morgenthau, and other administration leaders, the two sides failed to reach any agreement. Litvinov, one wag had put it, was so slick that he could "come out dry from the water." Recognition, the Soviet envoy seemed to believe, should come without any concessions from his country. As the discussions became cooler and cooler, Litvinov declared that he wanted to talk with the president.

The icy atmosphere abruptly changed when Roosevelt agreed to meet with Litvinov for one hour on November 10. The introduction took place in the White House Blue Room, where Roosevelt jokingly remarked that the most appropriate meeting place might have been the Red Room. Despite the attempted humor, the talks did not go well until the two men moved from specifics to generalities. Litvinov stipulated the granting of recognition prior to the discussions, but Roosevelt realized that to do so would give away his major bargaining card. As the tension mounted, the president finally drew laughter from Litvinov when he recommended that the two men meet privately so "they could, if need be, insult each other with impunity."

With the tension broken, Roosevelt and Litvinov made substantial progress toward resolving the problems that obstructed recognition. That evening, in a three-hour meeting, they reached agreements over matters relating to propaganda, subversion, and religious liberties, and then, in another two-hour discussion on November 12, resolved the issue of Americans' legal rights in the Soviet Union. Yet the two men still could not settle the war debts issue. Litvinov denied responsibility for the money sought by the United States and argued that the czar and provisional government should have paid off the debts before their fall to the Bolsheviks. Three days later, however, Roosevelt and Litvinov informally agreed to a debt resolution at some future date, by which the Soviets would pay upward to $150 million of a debt that the state department indignantly declared was four times higher.

Following a White House party on the evening of November 16, Roosevelt and Litvinov reached a formal agreement that they signed shortly before 1:00 A.M. the following morning. The United States extended recognition to the Soviet Union in return for its promise to halt subversion and propaganda against the United States, guarantee civil and religious liberties to Americans in the Soviet Union, and resolve the debts and claims questions at a later time. That same day, November 17, Roosevelt notified the press of the agreements, while highlighting the concession of religious freedom, and announced the beginning of formal Soviet-American relations.

To his cabinet later on, the president lightheartedly boasted of his diplomatic prowess. On the matter of religious freedom in the Soviet Union, he claimed to have told Litvinov: "You know, Max, your good old father and mother, pious Jewish people, always said their prayers. I know they must have taught you to say prayers." By this time, Roosevelt continued, "Max was red as a beet and I said to him, 'Now you may think you're an atheist . . . But I tell you, Max, when you die . . . you're going to be thinking about what your father and mother taught you.'" With that, Roosevelt smugly declared, Litvinov "blustered and puffed and said all kinds of things, laughed and was very embarrassed, but I had him."

In Moscow, Stalin was restrained but pleased with the outcome of the discussions, while in Washington the state department was guardedly optimistic. Yet despite commercial treaties with the Soviet Union in 1935 and 1937 (financed by the Export-Import Bank), trade actually declined because its people lacked the means to buy U.S. goods and in turn did not have items attractive to U.S. consumers. Moreover, the Soviets did not fulfill their pledge for religious freedom and did not meet their debt obligations. Finally, the establishment of Soviet-American diplomatic relations did nothing to curtail Japan's expansion in East Asia.

The United States sent Bullitt as its first ambassador to the Soviet Union, but within two years he resigned the position in disgust. His initial optimism had quickly vanished because of ill treatment characterized by recurring insults, the Soviet government's oppressive policies, and a general atmosphere of suspicion and secrecy. Furthermore, the Soviets refused to honor their huge debt to the United States on the ground that their financial obligations to Britain and France were even greater. Despite the Soviets' pledge against anti-American propaganda, U.S. Communists appeared in Moscow and criticized the United States during a meeting of the Comintern Congress in 1935. Bullitt's hopes for socialist reform in the Soviet Union disappeared as numerous political assassinations intensified into the bloody purges of the mid-1930s that Kennan, Bohlen, and other members of the embassy staff witnessed. Bullitt returned home in 1936, a bitterly disillusioned archcritic of the Soviet Union, before going to France as ambassador.

Rise of the Dictators and U.S. Neutrality

The rise of the dictators by the mid-1930s eventually forced a change in U.S. foreign pol-

icy. The nation's disillusionment over interventionism at first, however, deterred any action stronger than economic or moral pressures. In Japan, Germany, and Italy, powerful spokesmen for nationalism and imperialism had come to the front, driven by the hatreds resulting from unfair treatment at Versailles and the economic hardships born of the Great Depression. Western leaders had shown little will to resist any aggressively expansionist moves, as evidenced by their refusal to take action against Japan's penetration into Manchuria. Such an example of unchecked aggression brought predictable results. Japan's success in Manchuria encouraged other would-be expansionists to adopt the same tactic in resolving their nation's economic problems and enhancing its worldwide prestige.

Shortly after the West's weak response to Japan's growing influence in East Asia, Germany's interests in Europe expanded under Hitler's lead. While in prison during the early 1920s, he had written *Mein Kampf* ("My Struggle"), which set out his aims for Germany under the banner of the National Socialists, or Nazi party. He became chancellor in January 1933 and the following year took on full dictatorial powers by declaring a state of national emergency resulting from an alleged Communist threat at home. Determined to achieve *Lebensraum* ("living space") for his people, he called for a Pan-German movement to regain territories lost at Versailles in 1919. He quickly established one-party rule, stripped Jews of citizenship and blamed them for many of the nation's ills, installed a central state, and called for immediate arms equality with other nations.

Roosevelt became alarmed by Germany's expansionist activities and attempted to mobilize some form of nonmilitary resistance. He first tried to arrange a compromise disarmament program and a general nonaggression agreement. He then proposed consultation with other powers if a crisis ensued and agreed not to interfere with the League of Nations if it imposed sanctions on an aggressor. Thus, Roosevelt made cooperation with the League conditional upon a general disarmament plan. But Hitler testily announced that Germany would not agree to a smaller armaments program than that of other nations, and in October 1933 he withdrew Germany from both the League of Nations and the Geneva Disarmament Conference. Ambassador William Dodd wrote from Berlin that the Germans were confident that the United States would not intervene, even if they sought to surround the Soviet Union by taking the Polish Corridor, Lithuania, Latvia, and Estonia. Most German people, Dodd declared, would support Hitler even in "outright conquest."

Hitler sounded the death knell of the Versailles Treaty when he announced in March 1935 that Germany intended to expand its military establishment. He first planned a rearmament program that entailed compulsory military training aimed at creating an army of 500,000—five times larger than that allowed by the treaty. This move was justified, he declared, because the other powers had not fulfilled their pledges for general disarmament. Britain, France, and Italy protested but took no further action. In June, the British approved Germany's decision to build a navy more than a third the size of their own—much bigger than permitted by the Versailles Treaty.

Americans did not approve of Germany's military buildup but believed that their government should stay out of European affairs and allow Britain and France to deal with the problem. Disillusionment with the Great War had set in, arousing U.S. hostility to any measure leading to European entanglements. Revisionist historians had meanwhile absolved Germany of total responsibility for the war and argued that President Wilson's pro-Ally policies had resulted from the work of propagandists and business interests. The United States's noninterventionist attitude was also attributable to domestic reformers who feared that involvement in another war would end the New Deal and squelch civil liberties at home. Those who condemned U.S. entry into the Great War as a monumental mistake included the renowned scientist Albert Einstein,

the airplane pilot and folk hero Charles Lindbergh, the noted historian Charles A. Beard, Senators William Borah and George Norris, and a number of outspoken groups on the college campuses. Princeton University students founded an organization called the Veterans of Future Wars and morbidly declared that since most soldiers would die in the next conflict, each participant should receive a $1000 bonus as a prerequisite for going to war. Other antiwar groups circulated posters displaying the horrors of war under the label, "Hello Sucker."

By 1934 the focus of bitterness over the Great War turned toward U.S. bankers and munitions makers who had profited from the war and then had fallen into ill repute as incompetent and greedy business moguls who had helped bring on the Great Depression. A best-selling Book-of-the Month Club selection, entitled *Merchants of Death* and written by Helmuth Engelbrecht and Frank Hanighen, argued that bankers and arms makers had exploited U.S. neutrality through war profiteering and then maneuvered the United States into the war to protect their investments abroad. Out of this book came a series of hearings by a Senate Select Committee specifically instructed to examine the authors' allegations. From autumn 1934 through 1936 isolationist and progressive crusader Senator Gerald P. Nye of North Dakota led a committee investigation of firms such as Bethlehem Steel, Du Pont, and Remington Arms. Public hearings, punctuated by dramatic revelations of huge profits from U.S. entry, suggested but never proved the widespread belief that the United States had cynically entered the war to protect its loans to the Allies.

In the midst of growing problems in Europe and East Asia, President Roosevelt came to understand the depth of isolationist sentiment when, in early 1935, he advocated U.S. membership in the World Court. He had not anticipated the angry opposition generated by the isolationist Hearst press and the outspoken radio priest, Father Charles Coughlin. The Court, like the League, was under the control of international bankers and "pluto-crats," Coughlin declared. Soon the opposition to the Court swelled to include those Americans who were bitter over unpaid war debts, fearful that European entanglements might draw them into another war, shocked by the Nye Committee's disclosures, and concerned about the totalitarian direction the United States was taking under the New Deal. Thousands of telegrams poured into Washington, carried in wheelbarrows into the Senate office building, warning against membership in the Court. On January 29, only fifty-two senators voted for U.S. membership, which meant that the thirty-six who voted against the move left the Roosevelt administration seven votes short of the necessary two-thirds majority.

The president was livid but realistically acknowledged the strength of the non-interventionists. Some Americans, he angrily charged, were "willing to see a city burn down just so long as their own houses remain standing in the ruins." To a senator, the president wrote, "As to the 36 Gentlemen who voted against the principle of a World Court, I am inclined to think that if they ever get to Heaven they will be doing a great deal of apologizing for a very long time—that is if God is against war—and I think He is." But Roosevelt recognized the futility of pursuing an internationalist course. In another letter he observed, "We shall go through a period of non-cooperation in everything . . . for the next year or two."

The first evidence of this growing isolationist sentiment came during the Ethiopian crisis of 1935, which resulted in the United States's lame declaration of neutrality toward Italian aggressions. Fascist leader Benito Mussolini had postured and strutted for thirteen years about making Italy into a global power. Already he had established control over the weak East African states of Somaliland and Eritrea; now he sought oil concessions from neighboring Ethiopia as part of his bizarre fantasy of restoring the Roman Empire. After fighting erupted in December 1934 near the common border of Ethiopia and Italian Somaliland, Mussolini prepared to use full military force.

The United States reacted with its first declaration of neutrality. By the summer of 1935 the Roosevelt administration wanted authority to determine the aggressor in a conflict and send aid to the victim. But Congress rejected this suggestion as dangerously interventionist and passed instead the Neutrality Act of August, which clearly mirrored the prevailing disenchantment during the United States's neutrality era in the period before entering the Great War. Was not Walter Millis correct in asserting in that year's best-selling *Road to War: America, 1914–1917* that U.S. trade with the Allies had made it "a silent partner of the Entente"? The act of 1935 instituted an impartial arms embargo and authorized the president to warn Americans traveling on belligerent ships that they did so at their own risk.

The overall effect of the neutrality measure was self-defeating: It assured Mussolini that the United States would do nothing for Ethiopia. The president signed the bill but warned that it "might drag us into war instead of keeping us out."

In October 1935, after the rainy season, Italian military forces stormed into Ethiopia and drew only a restrained response from Washington. Roosevelt declared a state of war between the antagonists and cut off trade to both by invoking the Neutrality Act, but he did have the consolation of knowing that Ethiopia's remote location would have prevented large shipments of U.S. goods anyway. Another aspect of the administration's neutrality stand offered no solace, however: The U.S. government could not halt the private sale of oil to Italy because that product was not on the arms or munitions list. U.S. oil was fueling the aggression. Roosevelt could only announce a "moral embargo" on oil and other goods, somehow hoping that U.S. business leaders would themselves voluntarily restrict the flow. The appeal had little impact. U.S. trade with Italy, especially in oil, actually increased during the African crisis.

Europe's reaction to Ethiopia's plight only appeared to be stronger than that of the United States, because the continental nations likewise refused to restrain Italy. The League of Nations labeled Italy the aggressor and imposed economic sanctions on war materiel, loans, and purchases of certain Italian goods, but the list did not include the vital ingredients of oil, steel, iron, coal, and coke. Even though the French had interests in Africa and the British were concerned about the Mediterranean and Suez Canal, neither government wanted to adopt economic policies detrimental to its people in Depression times. The Royal Navy made a show of force by moving its Mediterranean fleet to the Suez Canal and another naval contingent to Gibraltar, but the British made no effort to obstruct the passage of Italy's troops or warships. Both Britain and France were primarily concerned with Germany and seemed to consider Ethiopia a small price to pay for keeping Italy out of the German camp and thereby preventing a wider war.

In late February 1936 Congress reenacted the Neutrality Act of the previous year and then passed another measure, a second and more broadly conceived Neutrality Act. Like the first, it sent a message to aggressors that the United States intended to stay out of non-hemispheric problems. Whereas the initial act had given the president the option of widening the embargo to include any new belligerents in a conflict, the second one *required* him to do so. It also prohibited loans to belligerents but added that any American republic victimized by a non-American state would receive assistance—including war materiel. Both Neutrality Acts would expire on May 1, 1937. "Out of the mountain of discussion and turmoil," according to Undersecretary of State William Phillips's wry comment, "has come, in fact, a mouse."

The divided and weak European response to the Italian invasion of Ethiopia encouraged Hitler to believe that he would encounter no resistance to future aggressive actions on the European continent. Both the British and the French had considered imposing an oil embargo on Italy, but Hitler's repudiation of the Treaty of Versailles and other actions had caused France to shy away from any measure that might drive the two aggressors together. In March 1936, just one week after Roosevelt signed the Neutrality Act, Hitler notified the Belgian, British, Dutch, French, and Italian ambassadors in Berlin of the death of the Locarno Treaty of 1925, which had guaranteed the borders of countries to Germany's west. He then went before the Reichstag to inform the stunned legislators that German armies at that very moment were marching into the Rhineland adjoining France and Belgium, thus shattering the fragile peace assurances contained in the Locarno Pact and the Treaty of Versailles's provision for the area's permanent demilitarization. His army's actions severed the French connection with Czechoslovakia and threatened the Maginot Line, a fixed military defense network built by France following the Great War, which stretched along the Franco-German border from Switzerland to Belgium.

Hitler's reoccupation of the Rhineland had a positive impact on Mussolini's efforts in Africa. With no French support forthcoming, Britain refused to close the Suez Canal and thus ensured Italy's victory over Ethiopia. Mussolini's armies took the Ethiopian capital of Addis Ababa in early May 1936 and shortly afterward annexed the entire country. The League's sanctions expired on schedule in June and were lifted the following month. When the League refused to cancel Ethiopia's membership, Italy withdrew from the organization in July, following similar actions already taken by Japan and Germany.

The scene then abruptly shifted to Spain, where Nationalist forces under General Francisco Franco rebelled against Madrid's Republican and secular government and set off a three-year civil war that, like so many wars of this nature, invited foreign intervention. France tried to persuade the European powers to stay out of Spanish affairs for fear of causing a full-scale war. Its anxieties were not groundless. The French, British, and Soviets favored the

Republicans, or Loyalists, whereas the Germans and Italians wanted Franco to win because his regime would take an anti-French stance. Little time passed before Germany and Italy sent military assistance to Franco and the Soviet Union extended aid to the Communists, who were among the Republican forces. Britain and France countered with the International Nonintervention Committee, whose long membership roll included, interestingly enough, Germany, Italy, and the Soviet Union. Although the organization guaranteed against formal intervention in Spain, Hitler and Mussolini continued to send aid privately. The Soviet Union, Mexico, and 3000 volunteer Americans (mostly leftists and liberals) helped the Republicans. Britain and France could do nothing because they had tied their hands by establishing the Nonintervention Committee.

The United States likewise urged nonintervention in the Spanish Civil War. Although the Neutrality Acts applied only to wars between foreign nations and not to domestic conflicts, Roosevelt wanted Congress to institute a mandatory arms embargo that applied only to Spain. In early January 1937 Congress overwhelmingly passed a joint resolution to that effect, but the embargo failed to hamper Franco's rebel advances. Throughout the civil war, Roosevelt remained shackled to a rigid embargo policy that he had chosen to accept rather than engage in another fight with Congress over discretionary powers. Part of his reasoning related to his desire to win rapid passage of the embargo, but his chief concern was to avert a congressional debate. Such certain division, he knew, might stall his ongoing struggle for judicial reforms designed to liberalize the Supreme Court and give the New Deal program a chance to succeed. The strategy proved costly. The U.S. decision to stay out of the civil war hurt the Loyalists and encouraged German and Italian efforts to establish a fascist regime in Spain. The Spanish government ultimately collapsed, allowing Franco's forces to take over in 1939.

By November 1936 the dictatorships in Germany, Italy, and Japan had moved closer together. The Germans and Italians had differed with each other on only a single issue. When the Nazi party in Austria made an abortive attempt to seize the government in 1936, Mussolini sent troops to the Austrian border in an effort to prevent the Germans from establishing a stronghold at the Brenner Pass. But Hitler offered assurances that Austria would remain independent and did not express opposition to Italy's invasion of Ethiopia; in addition, both leaders favored Franco in the Spanish Civil War. Consequently, in October 1936, Hitler and Mussolini signed a pact guaranteeing cooperation toward Spain, opposition to communism, and recognition of Italy's control of Ethiopia. One month afterward, Germany and Japan allied in the Anti-Comintern Pact, which reflected the reality of Japan's deep thrust into China and both signatories' hatred for the Soviet Union. When Italy joined the pact a year later, it became the Rome-Berlin-Tokyo Axis.

War clouds over Europe, plus the growing influence of Germany and Italy in Latin America, had meanwhile caused the Roosevelt administration to tighten its hemispheric policies by reaffirming its renunciation of military intervention. In March 1936, at the height of the German and Italian crises, the United States signed a pact with Panama (not approved by the Senate until 1939) that terminated the original treaty of 1903 establishing a U.S. protectorate over Panama and renounced any right of intervention. The United States also disclaimed the right to add new territory that might become necessary to running the canal, though retaining the power to defend the waterway in the event of a crisis. In December 1936 the Inter-American Conference for the Maintenance of Peace assembled in Buenos Aires, Argentina, where Hull chaired the U.S. delegation and Roosevelt traveled 7000 miles to address the opening session on the importance of hemispheric unity. The conferees agreed to consultation in the event of a threat to peace, the United States joined others in a Declaration of Solidarity, and Hull assured nonintervention by approving the following statement: "The High Contracting Parties declare inadmissible the intervention of any one of them, directly or indirectly, and for whatever reason, in the internal or external affairs of any other of the Parties."

Although the United States had taken a stand against only military intervention, numerous Latin American states thought the policy included a ban on economic involvement as well. The agreement to consult did not specify procedural steps, but it encouraged hopes of U.S. nonintervention by helping to convert the Monroe Doctrine from unilateral to multilateral status. The pacts signed by the United States at Panama and Buenos Aires reinforced the Good Neighbor policy and strengthened relations with Latin America.

The China Incident and U.S. Neutrality

Meanwhile, in East Asia a sudden calm in Sino-Japanese relations continued uneasily throughout the first four years of Roosevelt's presidency. The new administration in Washington had supported the Stimson policy of nonrecognition of Manchukuo largely because U.S. public sentiment permitted no choice, but also because the nation's lack of military preparedness prevented anything other than veiled threats. The Roosevelt administration had extended recognition to the Soviet Union partly to slow down Japan's advances by causing concern in Tokyo about a possible Soviet-American alliance. The administration also ordered the fleet to remain in the Pacific and urged Congress to build a larger navy. Growing apprehension over its Pacific possessions guided the United States's East Asian policy, but the White House could do little else except avoid a confrontation. Indeed, Congress passed the Tydings-McDuffie Act in 1934, which assured independence to the Philippines in ten years and was therefore a virtual admission to U.S. military weakness in the region. For the time being, however, that policy seemed sufficient. In May 1933 the Japanese and Chinese agreed to a cease-fire, which established a neutral zone south of the Great Wall of China.

The Manchurian question remained unsettled, however. At a press conference in spring 1934 the Tokyo Foreign Office proclaimed that Japan's "position and mission" gave it sole responsibility for maintaining "peace and order in East Asia." A short time later its ambassador in Washington proposed a joint settlement calling for the establishment of U.S. and Japanese spheres of interest in the Pacific and cooperation in erecting "a reign of law and order in the regions geographically adjacent to their respective countries." But Japan's own "Monroe Doctrine" for East Asia, as its proponents sometimes called it, would have established Japanese control over China, with nothing of equal value going to the United States. It also would have violated the moral obligations of the Open Door. Hull turned down the proposal. Japan meanwhile gave the necessary two-year notice of abrogation of the Washington and London treaties of the 1920s and 1930s, relieving itself of restrictions on naval construction. In April 1935 Japanese Foreign Minister Koki Hirota informed the U.S. and British ambassadors in Tokyo that his government had conditioned the Open Door guarantees upon other nations' diplomatic recognition of Manchukuo; until that took place, "no dispute whatever could be entertained with regard to that country."

Peace in East Asia ended just as suddenly as it had begun: Tokyo's continued interest in northern China finally led to the outbreak of the Sino-Japanese War in 1937, a conflict that lasted until the close of World War II in 1945. Japan had called for the independence of upper China, repeatedly urging the Nanking government to extend *de facto* recognition to Manchukuo and help stamp out communism in Asia. Although the Roosevelt administration knew that these stipulations would have facilitated Japan's attempt to dominate China, it still sought to avert a collision with the Japanese and apparently would have accepted such an agreement. In mid-1937, however, Chinese and Japanese soldiers clashed at the

Marco Polo Bridge outside Beijing (Peiping) in what became known as the "China Incident." As Japanese forces pushed into China afterward, lurid stories spread of government by intimidation and assassination. U.S. newsreel cameras recorded the conflict for theaters back home, as the bombings, lootings, and burnings spread into Beijing and Shanghai and became an all-out war. The Japanese forces in northern China soon became locked in conflict with those of Nationalist Jiang Jieshi (Chiang Kai-shek) and Communist Mao Zedong (Mao Tse-tung), now temporarily in league against the common enemy.

The United States followed a mixed policy during the war in China. Its ambassador in Tokyo, Joseph Grew, considered Japan the aggressor but warned that intervention might strengthen the militarists in that country. This stance must have been difficult for him. Although he was deaf and knew only a little Japanese, he felt special ties with his host. His wife Alice was the granddaughter of Commodore Matthew Perry (who had opened Japan to the West during the 1850s) and was fluent in the language. Grew urged his home government to safeguard its 10,000 nationals and their property in China. The Washington administration sent 1200 marines to Shanghai and suggested that Americans evacuate the country. It also warned both antagonists that the United States expected damage reparations. But it made no move to uphold the Open Door principles contained in the Nine-Power Treaty of 1922.

Congress acted even more cautiously than did the president. The Neutrality Acts of 1935 and 1936 had expired on May 1, 1937, but Congress had responded to the growing crises in Europe and East Asia with a "permanent" neutrality law. Roosevelt was in no political position to ask for more control over foreign policy. His bitter fight with the Supreme Court had led opponents to accuse him of trying to establish a dictatorship bent on destroying the Constitution and the courts. Isolationist Hiram Johnson from California declared in the Senate: "I will try to prevent

the President's sinister grasp of . . . the war-making power" that, combined with the court-packing bill, would make him "an absolute dictator in fact."

The Neutrality Act of May 1, 1937, authorized the president to invoke neutrality in a foreign civil war if the sale of war materiel to either side could endanger U.S. interests. It also prohibited Americans from traveling on belligerent ships and banned loans and munitions sales. But the new legislation appeared to veer sharply from the two earlier acts by exempting Latin America from the law. It also allowed Britain and other maritime nations to pick up *nonmilitary* goods through a cash-and-carry provision that, alone among the act's provisions, would expire on May 1, 1939. The other provisions were permanent.

Both the Great War and the Great Depression had dictated this type of careful policy, because its proponents thought it would protect that nation's neutral commerce while keeping the United States out of the conflicts in Europe and East Asia. Financier Bernard Baruch had been the chief architect of the attempt to preserve neutrality without losing commercial profits. "We will sell to any belligerent anything except lethal weapons, but," he emphasized, "the terms are '*cash on the barrelhead and come and get it.*'" Close analysis reveals, however, that even this move reflected continuing concern about the alleged lessons of World War I. The new law of 1937 would prevent belligerent destruction of U.S. ships and property and avoid the granting of credits that could again drag the United States into war.

Roosevelt decided against invoking the Neutrality Act of 1937 during the East Asian crisis because such refusal tacitly allowed the Chinese to buy American arms and supplies while denying that same privilege to the Japanese, who had the cash and the naval vessels to carry off goods. The act had permitted some maneuverability by the administration. Neutrality went into effect "whenever the President shall find that there exists a state of war between, or among, two or more foreign states, the President shall proclaim such fact."

As China and Japan resumed their conflict the following July, Roosevelt did not announce neutrality on the basis that he did not "find" a war. The Japanese had not declared war, and the "incident" in China had not technically violated the Kellogg-Briand Pact. Thus could the president arrange nonmilitary aid to the Chinese. He meanwhile ordered that no government vessels could carry war materiel to either side in the conflict and cautioned private citizens against looking to Washington for protection should they violate his directives.

The irony is that U.S. efforts to maintain neutrality in 1937 constituted still another message to aggressors that the United States would not help victims and was indifferent to international affairs. As one international lawyer put it at the time, the Roosevelt administration had adopted "a policy of scuttle and run to the storm cellar." In Congress's determination to adhere to non-intervention, it enacted a law that actually encouraged a widened war in China.

On October 5, 1937, in Chicago, the isolationist center of the Midwest, Roosevelt made a public statement on the China crisis that called for a worldwide "quarantine" on aggressors. The "epidemic of world lawlessness," he warned, could lead to U.S. involvement in a world war. Though not referring to Japan or any other nation, he appeared to be considering some form of pressure on treaty violators. "The peace, the freedom, and the security of 90 percent of the population of the world," he declared, "is being jeopardized by the remaining 10 percent, who are threatening a breakdown of all international order and law. Surely the 90 percent who want to live in peace under law and in accordance with moral standards . . . can and must find some way to make their will prevail. . . . There must be positive endeavors to preserve peace." He concluded with a series of remarkably vague statements: "America hates war, America hopes for peace. Therefore, America actively engages in the search for peace."

The "Quarantine Speech" aroused a surprisingly mixed reaction. It, of course, stirred up virulent opposition among isolationists. But it also received strong praise from the *Washington Post* and the *New York Times,* along with even some mild support from the isolationist Midwest. The following day, however, the president returned to form. He evaded probing questions from the press by insisting that he had no specific program in mind to counteract Japan's aggressions in China, although his administration was searching for one.

Though without substance, the speech carried some significance. If Roosevelt was testing Americans' opinion, he must have been pleasantly surprised to find them less isolationist than he had previously thought. Yet he still refused to consider any specific plan that called for the United States to take the lead in countering the growing world crisis. The only tangible result of the speech was the president's agreement to send a delegation to a meeting with the 1922 signatories of the Nine-Power Treaty in Brussels the following month to affirm the Open Door in China. But another far more important development was quietly under way: His call for a quarantine had combined with his agreement to participate in the Brussels talks to put increased international pressure on the United States to take action against Japan.

The China crisis meanwhile deepened as the Japanese seized Shanghai and then took the capital of Nanking at the horrendous cost of 100,000 Chinese lives. Americans in China frantically complained of brutal treatment by Japanese soldiers and sent reports of bombs hitting Americans' schools and hospitals, despite the Stars and Stripes emblems painted on their roofs. A United Press International photograph captured the war's horror by showing a crying baby sitting alone among the bombed-out remnants of a railroad yard in Shanghai.

In the midst of this growing crisis, the Brussels Conference convened on November 3, 1937, to discuss the East Asian situation. By this time the list of nations in attendance had grown to nineteen, all having interests in East

Asia. Japan refused to attend but indignantly declared its actions defensive, the Nine-Power Treaty dated, and the Kellogg-Briand Pact irrelevant. Soviet representatives requested U.S. cooperation in stopping both the Japanese and Germans. But U.S. public opinion had combined with the resurgence of domestic economic problems to prevent any action that might test Soviet sincerity. At the end of three weeks of meetings, the participants went home after making a hollow plea for the Open Door in China.

In late 1937 the United States was drawn directly into the ongoing East Asian conflict when in the daytime hours of December 12, Japanese pilots bombed and sank the U.S. gunboat *Panay* on the Yangtze River in China as the sailors helped Americans evacuating the embassy in Nanking. Three Standard Oil tankers under the *Panay*'s escort also went down in the fray. Two Americans died, and thirty were wounded, including those machine-gunned as they swam for safety. The Roosevelt administration hotly demanded an apology and reparations, and the government in Japan immediately complied. The foreign minister personally apologized to Grew in Tokyo, the Japanese government paid more than $2 million in reparations, and its citizens contributed to a fund for the victims. Once again it appeared that Japanese militarists had only temporarily gotten out of hand, and within weeks the *Panay* crisis passed.

Isolationist feeling in the United States necessitated administration policies that were nonconfrontational, because despite the furor over the *Panay* incident, the public remained opposed to intervention in China. Two days afterward, isolationists in Congress supported a constitutional amendment sponsored by Indiana Congressman Louis Ludlow, which provided that except for invasion, the United States could not go to war without the majority approval of Americans as expressed in a national referendum. The president warned that such a law would strip the Executive Office of authority in foreign affairs, and even Michigan's isolationist Senator Arthur Van-

denberg proclaimed that it "would be as sensible to require a town meeting before permitting the fire department to put out the blaze." Yet support for the measure seemed formidable, and only great pressure from the White House defeated it in the House of Representatives by a slender margin.

Faced with such strong isolationist sentiment, the Roosevelt administration tried indirect means to stem the Japanese onslaught. In July 1938 it resorted to a "moral embargo," by which Hull sent a letter informing American manufacturers that the government "strongly opposed" the sale of planes to nations that bombed civilians. Most business leaders complied. The United States also helped China expand its transportation network, and it bought silver from the Chinese, which allowed them to purchase weapons and war materiel from Americans. In the meantime Congress appropriated funds to naval construction and moved toward approving the fortification of Guam and other Pacific islands as potential wartime bases. By October, however, the Chinese government had withdrawn to Chongqing (Chungking) on the upper Yangtse River, leaving Japan in control of the major ports, coastal cities, and railroads.

Japan responded to the United States's implicit warnings on November 3, 1938, when Prime Minister Fumimaro Konoye, a popular but weak figure, announced the formation of a "New Order" in East Asia revolving around Japan, Manchukuo, and China, and aimed specifically at countering "bolshevism." U.S. appeals to the Open Door and treaties involving China had no effect, although Japan conceded that U.S. recognition of the New Order would lead to increased trade. Perhaps the economic enticement was worth pursuing. In fact, U.S. commerce with China was still not large. From 1931 to 1935 about one-fifth of U.S. foreign trade went to East Asia, and Japan's share was three times that of China's. Yet many Americans either felt a moral commitment to the Chinese or continued to believe in the mythical "China market." For whatever reasons, the Washington government reaffirmed support for the Open Door and subsequent treaty rights and negotiated a loan for China through the Export-Import Bank. By the end of 1938 the lines of division were clear between the United States and Japan: The Open Door in China was incompatible with the New Order.

Crisis in Europe

In early 1938 Hitler turned toward Austria in beginning his expansionist drive to the east. He called Austrian Chancellor Kurt von Schuschnigg to his Bavarian refuge at Berchtesgaden and demanded that he award government cabinet positions to members of the Austrian Nazi party. Schuschnigg did so but called for a plebiscite that he thought would rally his people against imminent German annexation. Hitler thereupon demanded Schuschnigg's resignation and stationed troops along the Austrian border, raising the possibility of invasion and forcing the chancellor's compliance on March 11. The following day the new head of Austria, Arthur Seyss-Inquart of the Nazi party, invited German soldiers into the country, ostensibly to keep order. Over protests from London and Paris, Germany again violated the Versailles pact in announcing the *Anschluss* (annexation) of Austria on March 14, 1938. Less than a month later, Austrian voters went to the polls in a Nazi-supervised plebiscite: 99.75 percent of the ballots came out marked in favor of union with Germany.

Hitler's push eastward then focused on the Germans in Czechoslovakia, who he claimed were in need of liberation from oppressive rule. Nearly a fourth of Czechoslovakia's fourteen million inhabitants were Germans, most of whom lived in the Sudeten (south) region jutting into the republic's midsection from the southeast. Shaped like the letter V laid on its side, the Sudetenland had been stripped from Germany at Versailles and now pierced the country like a dagger to the heart. Since 1932 the Nazi party had been working for Sudeten autonomy within Czechoslovakia, preparatory for German annexation. But when Germany prepared to annex the Sudetenland, the Czechs, bolstered by a capable army and military pacts with the Soviet Union and France, declared their willingness to fight. The British intervened in September 1938.

British Prime Minister Neville Chamberlain feared a full-scale European war and worked feverishly to prevent such a calamity. His election in mid-1937 had affirmed the popularity of his "appeasement" policy, which called for satisfying Germany's just demands and thereby holding on to peace. In the campaign he had attributed Germany's aggressive actions to the unfair provisions of the Versailles Treaty and seemed willing to concede its control over German-speaking peoples in Austria, Czechoslovakia, and Poland. Once the treaty was revised and Germany got what it rightfully deserved, or so Chamberlain hoped, Hitler would join the West in opposing the Communists in the Soviet Union. Chamberlain's priority now was to prevent Czech resistance to Germany's demands.

In mid-September Chamberlain visited Hitler twice at Berchtesgaden to plead for a so-called compromise proposal that Czech President Eduard Benes had denounced as humiliating but finally accepted only under extreme British and French pressure. The Czech minister to England had bitterly complained that Chamberlain had "yet to find out that Czechoslovakia was a country and not a disease." But even the French, Ambassador Bullitt reported from Paris, thought the Versailles Treaty "one of the stupidest documents ever penned by the hand of man" and now favored "an alteration" of the Czech boundary. According to Chamberlain's proposal, every region in Czechoslovakia in which more than half of its inhabitants were German would go to Germany; an international commission would draw a new border; and the remainder of Czechoslovakia would become independent. The result of this territorial amputation would be Germany's absorption of 800,000 Czechs along with a whole line of vital military fortifications that the West would replace with

Hitler at Reichstag
Ovation for Hitler after the *Anschluss* of Austria, March 1938. *Imperial War Museum, London, England.*

only a weak "general guarantee" of security similar to that earlier accorded to Austria.

But Hitler rejected Chamberlain's proposal and demanded *all* of the Sudetenland. Furthermore, he expected an immediate withdrawal of Czech officials, and he wanted plebiscites held in areas with questionable German constituencies. If his demands were not met by October 1, he darkly warned, German soldiers would take the area. Hitler's ultimatum made war seem imminent. The Czechs mobilized, and both British and French public opinion joined them in denouncing Hitler's demands. While the Paris and London governments assured the Czechs of assistance if attacked, Mussolini promised aid to Hitler.

Under Western pressure, Hitler agreed to convene a conference at Munich in late September, at which Mussolini, Chamberlain, and French Premier Édouard Daladier would join him in dealing with the Czech crisis. Noninterventionist feeling in the United States had combined with Roosevelt's slipping political popularity due to the "court packing" bill and struggling New Deal program to preclude his taking a strong public position on European affairs, but he had sent a telegram to Hitler, Chamberlain, Daladier, and Benes, calling for negotiations intended to reach "a peaceful, fair and constructive settlement of the question at issue." Roosevelt also wrote Hitler, "Should you agree to a solution in this peaceful manner I am convinced that hundreds of millions throughout the world would recognize your action as an outstanding historic service to humanity." Publicly, the president expressed confidence in the maintenance of peace. To his cabinet, however, he had already offered a dire prognosis: The British and French would sell out the rest of Czechoslovakia and then "wash the blood from their Judas Iscariot hands."

At the Munich Conference of September 29 and 30, 1938, Britain, France, and Italy approved the transfer of the entire Sudetenland to Germany and seemingly assured peace. The outcome was virtually identical to the demands contained in Hitler's ultimatum of a few days earlier and, for the moment at least, bought peace—albeit at Czechoslovakia's expense. Chamberlain returned to London and triumphantly proclaimed to an exuberant crowd at the airport "peace with honour" and "peace for our time." Not everyone felt optimistic. Roosevelt saw the conference as only a respite between crises and wanted the West to arm. Daladier regarded the Munich proceedings as a devastating defeat for France and England and anticipated more German demands that would soon lead to war. A Conservative member of Parliament, Winston Churchill, dourly warned that this was "only the beginning of the reckoning. This is only the first sip, the first foretaste of a bitter cup which will be proffered to us year by year unless, by a supreme recovery of moral health and martial vigor, we arise again and take our stand for freedom as in the olden time."

And yet, despite all the doubts, the prognosis appeared hopeful. Had not Hitler offered assurances at Munich that the Sudetenland was "the last territorial claim which I have to make in Europe"?

But trouble continued to spread in the Munich aftermath. In early 1938, even before the ill-fated conference, Hitler had begun another round of Jewish persecutions at home that included the burning of the Great Synagogue in Munich, followed by the consignment of 15,000 Jews to the concentration camp at Buchenwald. Now, on the night of November 9, Hitler launched still another terrorist campaign against Jews. The result was "The Night of Broken Glass" or *Kristallnacht* ("Crystal Night"), which got its name from the torrent of broken glass strewn in the sidewalks from homes, shops, hospitals, schools, and synagogues smashed and burned by Nazi storm troopers wielding axes and crowbars. Perhaps as many as 60,000 more Jews were shipped off to concentration camps, even as Roosevelt and leaders of most other concerned nations declined to open their doors for refuge. Hitler then demanded all of Czecho-

slovakia, threatening to break his own assurances made at Munich. His actions soon inextricably joined the name of the conference with the term *appeasement* and made both of them forever synonymous with weakness of will in the face of aggression.

Yet another problem was the Soviet Union. That huge nation had again failed to receive an invitation to a top-level international conference that involved its own vital interests. In fact, the French and British decision to meet without the Soviets ultimately pushed Stalin closer to Hitler. The Red Armies were not prepared to resist an expected Nazi invasion, and the only alternative was to buy time through negotiation. But Stalin's bitter recriminations did not faze the West. The United States did not even have an ambassador in Moscow during these black days, and the British and French apparently thought that their decision to meet Hitler's demands had secured peace. A generation that had seen millions of its youth perish in one world war considered any chance for peace worth a try. But the British were not naive. Even while Chamberlain attempted to appease Hitler, the London government used the tenuous calm in Europe to step up its armaments program. The Munich agreement turned Germany toward the east, whether or not by French and British design as Stalin believed, and proved to be the last step before the collapse of Czechoslovakia.

While Americans deluded themselves into believing that the Munich Conference had averted war, the Roosevelt administration adopted measures suggesting its awareness of the still-imminent danger. A month before the conference, the president met with Canadian Prime Minister Mackenzie King to arrange mutual assurances of help, and in October he asked Congress to bolster the national defense. The United States began a program of airplane manufacturing and soon agreed to sell bombers to France. The Roosevelt administration meanwhile pushed ever more strongly for revisions in the neutrality laws that would permit aid to victims of aggression.

With war threatening, Latin America loomed as a potential trouble spot, and in December 1938 the Roosevelt administration sent delegates to the Eighth International Conference of American States in Lima, Peru, which focused on hemispheric cooperation against European dangers. Nazi Germany's influence in the hemisphere had quickened in 1937 (although not on the scale envisioned by the White House) as it negotiated a series of commercial and airlines agreements with Latin American states and pursued subversive activities in Argentina, Brazil, Guatemala, and Uruguay. The United States responded by using the Export-Import Bank to underwrite various building projects, particularly in Brazil, and agents of the Federal Bureau of Investigation uncovered the commercial and propaganda activities of Nazis and Communists in the hemisphere. But the Roosevelt administration especially wanted a defensive alliance against outside danger. The ensuing Declaration of Lima marked the first time that all American Republics had united in facing the rest of the world. Upon the request of any foreign minister, the others would consult about resisting "all foreign intervention or activity that may threaten them."

The growing international crisis also made the United States's ongoing problems with Mexico take on a sudden urgency. Longstanding unrest in Mexico had deepened as Nationalists in 1938 rallied behind President Lázaro Cárdenas, who introduced a social reform program and supported strong labor unions in an effort to undercut foreign corporations through the use of the strike. When U.S. oil companies rejected workers' demands for a thirty-three percent pay raise and refused to adhere to court decisions upholding the unions, Cárdenas disbanded the arrangement worked out a decade earlier by Dwight Morrow. Following the example set by Bolivia's takeover of Standard Oil a year earlier, he ordered the nationalization of Dutch, British, *and* American oil companies in Mexico.

The imminence of war in Europe drove the Roosevelt administration into making con-cessions to Mexico. Hull believed Standard Oil's unfounded claims that Cárdenas was Communist and defended the oil company's demands for compensation. But Roosevelt deferred to his ambassador in Mexico, Josephus Daniels, who had been secretary of the navy when Wilson sent military forces into Veracruz in 1914 and now seemed more determined than ever to repair relations through the Good Neighbor policy. Daniels especially feared that Hull's hard-line policies would drive Mexico into the hands of Germany, Italy, and Japan. The administration worked toward an accommodation with the Mexican government (reached in November 1941, followed by a similar arrangement between Standard Oil and Bolivia the following year), which recognized Mexico's ownership of subsoil minerals in exchange for its compensation to Americans whose properties had fallen under expropriation. To further soothe relations, Mexico soon received a $30 million loan from the Export-Import Bank.

In spring 1939 war seemed closer in Europe as Hitler and Mussolini resumed expansion. Nazi armies marched into Czechoslovakia at 6 A.M. on March 15—brazenly breaking Hitler's assurances at Munich—and that same month he intensified pressure on Poland for two areas wrested from Germany at Versailles: the port city of Danzig and "the Polish Corridor," a strip of land that connected Germany with East Prussia. The Polish government turned down his demands, and Britain and France promised support in the event of a German attack. Hitler privately remarked that "England may talk big, [but] she is sure not to resort to armed intervention in the conflict." Nor would France take action. "I witnessed the miserable worms Daladier and Chamberlain in Munich. They will be too cowardly to attack." In April Italian troops occupied Albania, leading Britain and France to offer assurances to Rumania and Greece, seemingly next in Mussolini's path.

In vain Roosevelt made still another appeal for peace. He urged Germany and Italy to join a ten-year guarantee of nonaggression against the thirty-one governments in Europe and the Near East. If such a pact transpired, Roosevelt continued, the United States would encourage negotiations aimed at scaling down armaments and reestablishing world trade. No response came from Italy, and two weeks later Hitler sarcastically announced that all thirty-one governments had assured him they trusted Germany and did not need U.S. guarantees.

The German and Italian refusals to pledge nonaggression pushed the Roosevelt administration into seeking repeal of the arms embargo. The cash-and-carry provision on nonmilitary goods would expire on May 1, 1939, and Hitler could interpret a failure to lift the arms embargo as a U.S. refusal to assist Britain and France. The president and Hull met with Senate leaders in July to warn of war in Europe and advocate U.S. help to the British and French. But isolationist William Borah obstinately replied that his own sources of information were more reliable than those of the state department, and they told him war was unlikely. Opposition to repeal of the Neutrality Act was too strong, and Congress adjourned in August without passing a new bill. Failure to reenact neutrality legislation carried another dangerous implication: Should war break out in Europe, U.S. cargo vessels were under no prohibitions against entering the combat zone.

Fear of a German assault on the Soviet Union drove Stalin into negotiations, first with neighboring states, then with Britain and France. When unsuccessful in both instances, he consulted with Germany itself. In a bitter twist of fate, failing economic plans had combined with Stalin's brutal purges of millions of his own people during the mid-1930s to weaken his country and leave him no choice. Indeed, among the casualties were one-third of his top army officers and three of five marshals. Despite bitterness with the West over Munich, Stalin tried from April through August of 1939 to secure a defensive pact with any government willing to take a stand against Germany. But Poland, Rumania, and the Baltic States realized that Soviet territorial guarantees historically translated into Soviet occupation. Stalin's overtures to Britain and France had likewise failed. In a desperate effort to buy time he entered negotiations with Hitler.

On August 23, 1939, Germany and the Soviet Union shocked the world by announcing a nonaggression pact in Moscow that achieved the inconceivable: an alliance between fascists and Communists. Three days after the two nations negotiated a commercial pact, German Foreign Minister Joachim von Ribbentrop flew to Moscow to sign a nonaggression agreement with Soviet Foreign Commissar Vyacheslav M. Molotov (successor to Maxim Litvinov, a Jew who had favored collective security). The Nazi-Soviet Pact provided that for a ten-year period neither nation would commit an act of aggression on the other and that each would remain neutral if the other became involved in a war with another country. But the pact contained a secret protocol (not discovered until after World War II) setting up German and Soviet spheres of influence in eastern Europe. In exchange for the Soviets' recognition of Lithuania as part of the German sphere, the Soviet Union would claim eastern Poland, Finland, Bessarabia (then part of Rumania), and the two Baltic states of Estonia and Latvia (both former members of the Russian empire). Germany was free to attack western Poland and then focus on France and Britain.

In retrospect, war in Europe became certain on the day the Nazi-Soviet Pact went into effect. At Munich, Britain and France had given in to Hitler's demands and successfully turned his focus east; in Moscow, Stalin skillfully used the same tactics to turn Hitler west. A member of the state department in Washington, Jay Pierrepont Moffat, recorded in his diary just after receiving news of the Nonaggression Pact that "these last two days have given me the feeling of sitting in a house where somebody is dying upstairs. There is relatively little to do and yet the suspense continues unabated." Assistant Secretary of State Adolf A. Berle, Jr. grimly observed, "I have a horrible feeling of seeing ... a civilization dying even before its actual death."

The Final Moment of Peace

While Americans' attention remained riveted on the growing crisis in Europe, Japan took advantage of the tense situation by establishing control over the islands that lay in the French and British sea lanes of East Asia. Such a move demonstrated the global nature of the crisis, because Japan's assertiveness endangered French Indochina, British and Dutch possessions in southeast Asia, and U.S. interests in the Philippines. In Asia as in Europe, Chamberlain had resorted to appeasement in favoring almost any arrangement that placated the Japanese and lessened their threat to British-controlled Hong Kong, India, and Singapore. Indeed, Roosevelt had even grown suspicious that Chamberlain intended his

policy to pressure the United States into taking on the difficult task of stopping Japanese expansion and thereby protecting the British Empire.

U.S. Ambassador Grew in Tokyo was concerned that his government might enact measures against Japan that would drive it into war against the United States. The former secretary of state, Henry L. Stimson, headed the American Committee for Nonparticipation in Japanese Aggression, which called for an embargo on oil and scrap iron. According to a poll taken that summer of 1939, eighty-two percent of Americans wanted to end the sale of war materiel to Japan. Yet the Roosevelt administration hesitated because an embargo might force the Japanese into a war that the United States was not militarily prepared to fight. On July 26, 1939, however, the state department left the impression that economic sanctions were imminent when it gave Japan

Nazi-Soviet Nonaggression Pact
Soviet Foreign Commissar Molotov signs the pact on August 23, 1939, as German Foreign Minister Joachim von Ribbentrop (behind Molotov) and Soviet Premier Joseph Stalin (to von Ribbentrop's left) look on. *National Archive, Washington, D.C.*

the required six months' notice for ending the long-standing Treaty of Commerce and Navigation of 1911.

The threatened cutoff of U.S. trade caused leaders of the Japanese army to push for an alliance with Germany that would ensure Soviet neutrality while they secured control over the oil, rice, rubber, and tin of southeast Asia. But cabinet, naval, and business figures in Tokyo feared that expansion south would lead to economic retaliation and possibly war with the United States. The hard-liners had to back off in August 1939, however, when Germany broke the Anti-Comintern Pact with Japan and joined the Soviet Union in the Nonaggression Pact. Whereas Hitler was under fewer constraints in Europe, Stalin was freer to move in East Asia. The threatened abrogation of the commercial treaty with the United States and the implications of the Nazi-Soviet Pact left Japan virtually alone and had the inadvertent effect of temporarily easing its relations with Washington.

Indeed, the autumn of 1939 seemed an opportune time for the United States to reconstruct relations with Japan. Threatened economic sanctions and the negotiation of the Nonaggression Pact isolated Japan, restrained the warlords in Tokyo, and renewed the moderates' hopes for reconciliation with the United States. But internal discussions in Tokyo were, of course, secret, and no one in Washington sensed the moment. Grew urged his home government to drop the idealism of the Open Door pledges and accept the reality of Japan's control over China. His hard-nosed proposal encountered stringent opposition from Hull, however, who remained outraged by Japan's aggressive actions in East Asia and believed the United States morally bound to protect China. Before long the secretary of state's pronouncements helped to elevate the principles of the Open Door to the status of official policy. Grew's call for accommodation on realistic terms might not have changed the course of events, but it would have provided more time for the United States to prepare for war in the Pacific.

This opportunity passed on September 1, 1939, when Hitler's armies invaded Poland. Two days later Britain and France kept their promises and declared war on Germany. World War II had begun in Europe. The U.S. ambassador in London, Joseph Kennedy, sorrowfully concluded, "It's the end of the world, the end of everything."

Selected Readings

Adams, Frederick C. *Economic Diplomacy: The Export-Import Bank and American Foreign Policy, 1934–1939.* 1976.

Adler, Selig. *The Isolationist Impulse: Its Twentieth Century Reaction.* 1957.

——. *The Uncertain Giant: 1921–1941, American Foreign Policy Between the Wars.* 1965.

Ambrose, Stephen E., and Brinkley, Douglas G. *Rise to Globalism: American Foreign Policy since 1938.* 8th ed., 1997.

Anderson, Irvine H., Jr. *The Standard-Vacuum Oil Company and United States East Asian Policy, 1933–1941.* 1975.

Atkins, G. Pope, and Wilson, Larman C. *The Dominican Republic and the United States: From Imperialism to Transnationalism.* 1998.

——. *The United States and the Trujillo Regime.* 1972.

Bailey, Thomas A. *America Faces Russia.* 1950.

Barnhart, Michael A. *Japan Prepares for Total War: The Search for Economic Security, 1919–1941.* 1987.

Bemis, Samuel F. *The Latin-American Policy of the United States.* 1943.

Benjamin, Jules R. *The United States and Cuba: Hegemony and Dependent Development, 1880–1934.* 1978.

——. *The United States and the Origins of the Cuban Revolution: An Empire of Liberty in an Age of National Liberation.* 1990.

Bennett, Edward M. *Franklin D. Roosevelt and the Search for Security: American-Soviet Relations, 1933–1939.* 1985.

——. *Recognition of Russia: An American Foreign Policy Dilemma.* 1970.

Bishop, Donald G. *The Roosevelt-Litvinov Agreements: The American View.* 1965.

Borg, Dorothy. *The United States and the Far Eastern Crisis of 1933–1938.* 1964.

Breitman, Richard, and Kraut, Alan M. *American Refugee Policy and European Jewry, 1933–1945.* 1987.

Britton, John A. *Revolution and Ideology: Images of the Mexican Revolution in the United States.* 1995.

Browder, Robert P. *The Origins of Soviet-American Diplomacy.* 1953.

Buhite, Russell D. *Nelson T. Johnson and American Policy Toward China, 1925–1941.* 1968.

Clark, Paul C., Jr. *The United States and Somoza, 1933–1956: A Revisionist Look.* 1992.

Cohen, Warren I. *The American Revisionists: The Lessons of Intervention in World War I.* 1967.

———. *America's Response to China: An Interpretive History of Sino-American Relations.* 2000.

Cole, Wayne S. *America First: Senator Gerald P. Nye and American Foreign Relations.* 1962.

———. *Charles A. Lindbergh and the Battle against American Intervention in World War II.* 1974.

———. *Roosevelt and the Isolationists, 1932–1945.* 1983.

Compton, James V. *The Swastika and the Eagle: Hitler, the United States and the Origins of World War II.* 1967.

Cronon, E. David. *Josephus Daniels in Mexico.* 1960.

Crowley, James B. *Japan's Quest for Autonomy: National Security and Foreign Policy, 1930–1938.* 1966.

Dallek, Robert. *Franklin D. Roosevelt and American Foreign Policy, 1932–1945.* 1979.

DeConde, Alexander. *Isolation and Security.* 1957.

Delpar, Helen. *The Enormous Vogue of Things Mexican: Cultural Relations Between the United States and Mexico, 1920–1935.* 1992.

Divine, Robert A. *The Illusion of Neutrality.* 1962.

———. *The Reluctant Belligerent: American Entry into World War II.* Rev. ed. 1979.

———. *Roosevelt and World War II.* 1969.

Dodd, Thomas J. *Managing Democracy in Central America.* 1992.

Doenecke, Justus D., and Wilz, John E. *From Isolation to War, 1931–1941.* 1991.

Dosal, Paul J. *Doing Business with the Dictators: A Political History of United Fruit in Guatemala, 1899–1944.* 1993.

Dozer, Donald M. *Are We Good Neighbors? Three Decades of Inter-American Relations, 1930–1960.* 1959.

Duggan, Laurence. *The Americas: The Search for Hemisphere Security.* 1949.

Dunne, Michael. *The United States and the World Court, 1920–1935.* 1988.

Feis, Herbert. *The Road to Pearl Harbor.* 1950.

Fernandez, Ronald. *The Disenchanted Island: Puerto Rico and the United States in the Twentieth Century.* 2nd ed., 1996.

Freidel, Frank. *Franklin D. Roosevelt: A Rendezvous with Destiny.* 1990.

Frye, Alton. *Nazi Germany and the American Hemisphere, 1933–1941.* 1967.

Gaddis, John L. *Russia, the Soviet Union, and the United States: An Interpretive History.* 2nd ed., 1990.

Gardner, Lloyd C. *Economic Aspects of New Deal Diplomacy.* 1964.

Gellman, Irwin F. *Good Neighbor Diplomacy: United States Policies in Latin America, 1933–1945.* 1979.

———. *Roosevelt and Batista: Good Neighbor Diplomacy in Cuba, 1933–1945.* 1973.

Griswold, A. Whitney. *The Far Eastern Policy of the United States.* 1938.

Grover, David H. *American Merchant Ships on the Yangtze, 1920–1941.* 1992.

Haglund, David. *Latin America and the Transformation of U.S. Strategic Thought, 1936–1940.* 1984.

Hearden, Patrick J. *Roosevelt Confronts Hitler: America's Entry into World War II.* 1987.

Herzstein, Robert. *Roosevelt & Hitler: Prelude to War.* 1989.

Hodgson, Godfrey. *The Colonel: The Life and Wars of Henry Stimson, 1867–1950.* 1990.

Hu, Shizhang. *Stanley K. Hornbeck and the Open Door Policy, 1919–1937.* 1995.

Iriye, Akira. *Across the Pacific: An Inner History of American-East Asian Relations.* 1967.

Jablon, Howard. *Crossroads of Decision: The State Department and Foreign Policy, 1933–1937.* 1983.

Jonas, Manfred. *Isolationism in America, 1935–1941.* 1966.

———. *The United States and Germany: A Diplomatic History.* 1984.

Kennan, George F. *American Diplomacy.* Expanded ed., 1984. Originally published as *American Diplomacy, 1900–1950.* 1951.

Koginos, Manny T. *The Panay Incident.* 1967.

Koppes, Clayton R. "The Good Neighbor Policy and the Nationalization of Mexican Oil: A Reinterpretation," *Journal of American History* 69 (1982): 62–81.

LaFeber, Walter. *The Clash: A History of U.S.-Japanese Relations.* 1997.

———. *Inevitable Revolutions: The United States in Central America.* 1984 ed.

Langer, William, and Gleason, S. Everett. *The Challenge to Isolation, 1937–1940.* 1952.

Langley, Lester D. *The Banana Wars: An Inner History of American Empire, 1900–1934.* 1983.

———. *The United States and the Caribbean, 1900–1970.* 1980.

Leutze, James R. *Bargaining for Supremacy: Anglo-American Naval Collaboration, 1937–1941.* 1977.

Linn, Brian M. *Guardians of Empire: The U.S. Army and the Pacific, 1902–1940.* 1997.

Lipstadt, Deborah. *Beyond Belief: The American Press and the Coming of the Holocaust, 1933–1945.* 1986.

Little, Douglas. *Malevolent Neutrality: The United States, Great Britain, and the Origins of the Spanish Civil War.* 1985.

MacDonald, C.A. *The United States, Britain and Appeasement, 1936–1939.* 1981.

Maddux, Thomas R. "Watching Stalin Maneuver Between Hitler and the West: American Diplomats and Soviet Diplomacy, 1934–1939," *Diplomatic History* 1 (1977): 140–54.

———. *Years of Estrangement: American Relations with the Soviet Union, 1933–1941.* 1980.

Marks, Frederick W., III. *Wind over Sand: The Diplomacy of Franklin Roosevelt.* 1988.

Marshall, Jonathan. *To Have and Have Not: Southeast Asian Raw Materials and the Origins of the Pacific War.* 1995.

Meyer, Lorenzo. *Mexico and the United States in the Oil Controversy, 1917–1942.* 1977.

Miller, Edward S. *War Plan Orange: The U.S. Strategy to Defeat Japan, 1897–1945.* 1991.

Neu, Charles E. *The Troubled Encounter: The United States and Japan.* 1975.

Neumann, William L. *America Encounters Japan: From Perry to MacArthur.* 1963.

Niblo, Stephen R. *War, Diplomacy, and Development: The United States and Mexico, 1938–1954.* 1995.

O'Brien, Thomas F. *The Revolutionary Mission: American Enterprise in Latin America, 1900–1945.* 1996.

Offner, Arnold A. *American Appeasement: United States Foreign Policy and Germany, 1933–1938.* 1969.

———. "Appeasement Revisited: The United States, Great Britain, and Germany, 1933–1940," *Journal of American History* 64 (1977): 373–93.

Pérez, Louis A., Jr. *Cuba and the United States.* 1997.

———. *Cuba Under the Platt Amendment, 1902–1934.* 1986.

Pike, Frederick B. *FDR's Good Neighbor Policy: Sixty Years of Generally Gentle Chaos.* 1995.

Plummer, Brenda G. *Haiti and the United States: The Psychological Moment.* 1992.

———. *Rising Wind: Black Americans and U.S. Foreign Affairs, 1935–1960.* 1996.

Pratt, Julius W. *Cordell Hull, 1933–1944.* 2 vols., 1964.

Propas, Frederic L. "Creating a Hard Line Toward Russia: The Training of State Department Soviet Experts, 1927–1937," *Diplomatic History* 8 (1984): 209–26.

Reynolds, David. *The Creation of the Anglo-American Alliance, 1937–1941: A Study in Competitive Cooperation.* 1982.

Rock, William. *Chamberlain and Roosevelt: British Foreign Policy and the United States, 1937–1940.* 1988.

Roorda, Eric P. *The Dictator Next Door.* 1998.

Rosenberg, Emily S. *Financial Missionaries to the World.* 1999.

Schaller, Michael. *The U.S. Crusade in China, 1938–1945.* 1979.

Schmitz, David F. *Thank God They're on Our Side: The United States and Right-Wing Dictatorships, 1921–1965.* 1999.

———. *The United States and Fascist Italy, 1922–1940.* 1988.

Schoultz, James. *Beneath the United States: A History of U.S. Policy Toward Latin America.* 1998.

Schuler, Friedrich E. *Mexico Between Hitler and Roosevelt: Mexican Foreign Relations in the Age of Lázaro Cárdenas, 1934–1940.* 1998.

Schwoch, James. *The American Radio Industry and Its Latin American Activities, 1900–1939.* 1990.

Smith, Geoffrey. *To Save a Nation: American Countersubversives, the New Deal and the Coming of World War II.* 1973, 1992.

Smith, Peter H. *Talons of the Eagle: Dynamics of U.S.-Latin American Relations.* 2nd ed., 2000.

Smith, Robert F. *The United States and Cuba: Business and Diplomacy, 1917–1960.* 1960.

Steward, Dick. *Trade and Hemisphere: The Good Neighbor Policy and Reciprocal Trade.* 1975.

Sun, You-Li. *China and the Origins of the Pacific War, 1931–41.* 1993.

Utley, Jonathan G. *Going to War with Japan, 1937–1941*. 1985.

Varg, Paul. "The Economic Side of the Good Neighbor Policy: The Reciprocal Trade Program and South America," *Pacific Historical Review* 45 (1976): 47–72.

Vieth, Jane Karoline. "The Diplomacy of the Depression," in Carroll, John M., and Herring, George C., eds., *Modern American Diplomacy*, 71–89. 1986.

Walter, Knut. *The Regime of Anastasio Somoza, 1936–1956*. 1993.

Watt, D. Cameron. *Succeeding John Bull: America in Britain's Place, 1900–1975*. 1984.

Williams, William A. *American-Russian Relations, 1781–1947*. 1952.

Wiltz, John E. *In Search of Peace: The Senate Munitions Inquiry, 1934–1936*. 1963.

Wittner, Lawrence S. *Rebels against War*. 1984.

Wood, Bryce. *The Making of the Good Neighbor Policy*. 1961.

Wyman, David S. *Paper Walls: America and the Refugee Crisis, 1938–1941*. 1968.

CHAPTER 7

From Europe to Pearl Harbor, 1939–1941

War in Europe

Although the outbreak of war in Europe had long been expected, it nevertheless came as a shock. "Everything that I have worked for," Chamberlain lamented, "has crashed into ruins." In a fireside chat, President Roosevelt asked Americans to be neutral in action but admitted that they could not be neutral in thought. That same month the foreign ministers of the American republics approved the Declaration of Panama, which warned the belligerent powers to stay out of a "safety belt" below Canada that extended 300 miles out to sea around North and South America. In mid-September Poland collapsed and soon underwent a massive terrorist campaign by Nazi SS (special security) units ordered to stamp out all opposition, whether it be Jews, Communists, or anyone associated with the old order. Finally, in accordance with the secret provisions of the Nazi-Soviet Pact of 1939, the Germans and Russians divided the country between them.

After the fall of Poland the European conflict took a surprising twist: It settled into the *Sitzkrieg* or "phony war" of winter 1939–1940 and thereby allowed the dark friendship resulting from the Nazi-Soviet Pact to show its true character. In the far north, the Soviets sought to subjugate Finland in the "winter war" as part of their effort to build a defense against a possible German assault. Roosevelt denounced the Soviets' "dreadful rape of Finland" and urged U.S. business leaders to cut off war materiel to Moscow. His "moral embargo" proved a dismal failure: American exports to the Soviet Union actually doubled at the most crucial time in the war. Congress meanwhile took stronger action by suspending Finland's World War I debt obligations and approving a huge loan. But even then, that body pursued its usual path of restraint: The credits were limited to *nonmilitary* goods and did little to stop the Soviet assault. Nor did the expulsion of the Soviet Union from the League of Nations have any positive impact. Finland capitulated under severe terms in March 1940, and shortly afterward the Soviets seized the Baltic States of Estonia, Latvia, and (in violation of the Nazi-Soviet Pact) Lithuania.

As in World War I, both sides tried to seize the advantage on the seas. In the Atlantic the Germans began laying magnetic mines outside British harbors—a new weapon in violation of maritime law. The Allies retaliated with an illegal blockade of Germany's exports. The older generation of Americans must have experienced a sense of *déjà vu* when their

The German Assault, 1939–1941

▨	Germany and Axis powers
▨	German occupied countries, 1941
▨	Allied countries
▨	Neutral countries
→	German advances

NORWEGIAN SEA

NORTH SEA

IRELAND

GREAT BRITAIN

London

Dunkirk

NETH.

BELG.

LUX.

Paris

FRANCE

Vichy

SWITZ.

Berlin

GERMANY

Munich

AUSTRIA

ITALY

SPAIN

Corsica

Sardinia

Rome

ADRIATIC SEA

ALBANIA

Sicily

ALGERIA

TUNISIA

MEDITERRANEAN SEA

LIBYA

DEN.

BALTIC SEA

NORWAY

SWEDEN

FINLAND

Murmansk

Leningrad

ESTONIA

LATVIA

LITHUANIA

GER.

Warsaw

POLAND

CZECHOSLOVAKIA

HUNGARY

Belgrade

YUGOSLAVIA

BULGARIA

GREECE

Athens

Crete

AEGEAN SEA

Moscow

SOVIET UNION

Stalingrad

Ukraine

Crimea

CAUCASUS MTNS.

BLACK SEA

RUMANIA

TURKEY

Cyprus (Br.)

SYRIA

LEBANON

PALESTINE

TRANS-JORDAN

EGYPT

Map 12
Except for the failure to defeat Britain, the German *Blitzkrieg* achieved a series of almost unbroken victories in the period before 1941.

government, as in 1916, protested British violations of freedom on the seas that included opening Americans' mail, searching U.S. cargo, and disrupting commercial shipments. But in 1939 and 1940 Americans were more tolerant of British infractions than they were in World War I because the aggressors this time were clearly defined.

The Roosevelt administration quickened its efforts to repeal the arms embargo and thereby allow Britain and France to acquire war materiel on a cash-and-carry basis. Such a pivotal step, the president assured fellow Americans, would help keep the United States out of the war. Isolationists repeatedly charged that financial ties had pulled the country into war in 1917 and bitterly fought any changes in neutrality legislation. To win his program, Roosevelt persuaded an influential Republican journalist from Kansas, William Allen White, to head the Nonpartisan Committee for Peace through Revision of the Neutrality Act. After a fervent White House appeal, Congress debated the proposal for six weeks before finally emerging with a revised Neutrality Act in November 1939. It revoked the arms embargo and allowed cash-and-carry basis purchases of military goods. To mollify its opponents, the bill prohibited Americans from entering combat areas designated by the president. The United States had taken a major step away from its rigid neutrality stance of the early 1930s: Britain and France could buy war goods for cash if they came and got them.

In spring 1940 the phony war came to an abrupt end when the Germans opened a mighty offensive in Europe called the *Blitzkrieg,* or "lightning war." Hitler's panzer (armor) tanks and fighter bombers led a million infantrymen in easily overrunning Denmark, Norway, Belgium, the Netherlands, and Luxembourg en route to the English Channel to destroy a large British expeditionary force sent to the continent. Britain's abortive attempt to drive the Germans out of Norway in May led to Chamberlain's fall from power, and in early June nearly 350,000 soldiers, mostly British, barely managed to evacuate

Europe in a phenomenal escape at Dunkirk. But British forces had suffered a devastating defeat and, in their haste to leave, abandoned huge supplies of heavy war machinery on the beach. Hitler's legions were now poised to invade France. With catastrophe in the offing, the new prime minister of Britain, Winston Churchill, went before Parliament on the day Dunkirk fell to exhort his countrymen in golden language that inspired generations then and afterward:

> We shall not flag or fail. We shall go on to the end, we shall fight in France, we shall fight in the seas and oceans, we shall fight with growing confidence and growing strength in the air, we shall defend our island, whatever the cost may be, we shall fight on the beaches, we shall fight on the landing-grounds, we shall fight in the fields and in the streets, we shall fight in the hills; we shall never surrender, and even if, which I do not for a moment believe, this island or a large part of it were subjugated and starving, then our Empire beyond the seas, armed and guarded by the British Fleet, would carry on the struggle, until, in God's good time, the New World, with all its power and might, steps forth to the rescue and the liberation of the Old.

The imminent fall of France stirred the United States into stronger action. After Germany attacked Denmark and Norway, the Roosevelt administration froze those two countries' assets in the United States to keep millions of dollars out of Hitler's hands. Americans were also concerned that French and Dutch possessions in the Western Hemisphere could fall to Germany and thereby endanger the Panama Canal and the United States. Congress therefore passed a resolution in June expressing opposition to the transfer of territory in the Americas "from one non-American power to another non-American power." That same month Mussolini entered the war against France and drew a bitter retort from the president. Speaking before the graduating class of the University of Virginia, Roosevelt declared that "the hand that held the dagger has struck it into the back of its neighbor." The United States, he promised, would help those people

Hitler in Paris
With the Eiffel Tower in the background, Hitler poses triumphantly on June 23, 1940, after his forces had overrun Paris. *National Archives, Washington, D.C.*

resisting aggression while itself preparing for "any emergency and every defense."

On June 22, 1940, Americans were stunned when France collapsed under the heel of the *Wehrmacht* (Nazi war machine). With a flare for dramatic vengeance, Hitler gleefully accepted the surrender in the same railway car used by the Allies in signing the armistice ending World War I. More shocks were to come as French Marshal Henri Philippe Pétain established a government at Vichy, in the southeastern part of the country, which collaborated with the Germans in an effort to avert a total Nazi takeover. Americans realized that only Britain stood between them and Germany.

In this crisis atmosphere, reports arrived in Washington of widespread German subversion in Latin America. The stories were exaggerated, because Hitler did not wish to do anything to pull the United States into the war. But he doubtless sought to create the illusion of a huge Nazi threat in the region that might, in turn, persuade the United States to reduce economic assistance for fear of its falling into the wrong hands. In July the United States became a party to the Act of Havana, which authorized the American republics to occupy any European possession in the hemisphere threatened by an outside power, thereby reaffirming the Monroe Doctrine as a multilateral pact.

During summer 1940, the Roosevelt administration moved toward more stringent action as the German *Luftwaffe* launched massive air assaults on London and other big cities in preparation for an all-out invasion. As the Battle of Britain raged both day and night, the United States increased the production of war goods, enlarged its air corps, and took steps toward creating a two-ocean navy. In August, Roosevelt met with Canadian Prime Minister Mackenzie King to establish the Permanent Joint Board on Defense. When Franco of Spain seemed ready to join the Axis in the war, Roosevelt worked with the British in exerting economic pressure on Spain to allow the Royal Navy to maintain its strategic hold on Gibraltar at the entrance into the Mediterranean. The president also won congressional approval to move the National Guard into the service of the federal government, and he sent U.S. military officers to London to discuss closer cooperation against the German navy. To win public support, William Allen White, instrumental in bringing about revision of the Neutrality Act, established the Committee to Defend America by Aiding the Allies. Polls substantiated this approach. Where eighty percent of Americans opposed going to war, nearly the same number favored helping England as the chief means of staying out of that war.

Some administration measures were of questionable propriety if not legality. The White House turned over planes to U.S. manufacturers who built aircraft for the government, with the understanding that the older models would go to the British. It also sold outdated military goods to private business leaders, who then dealt them to the British. For a time U.S. pilots flew to a point just south of Canada and abandoned their craft for the Canadians to haul across the border. British pilots were trained in Florida rather than in the harsh weather of Canada. During June alone, more than $43 million worth of cannons, machine guns, rifles, mortars, and ammunition went to Britain—without technically violating neutrality legislation.

Partly to mute criticism of his policies, but also to build bipartisan support for a third term as president, Roosevelt made changes in his cabinet. He replaced two supporters of isolationism with two leading Republican internationalists, Henry L. Stimson as secretary of war and Frank Knox as secretary of the navy.

London Under Siege
London's docks burn on September 7, 1940, as Tower Bridge escapes serious damage from German air raids. *National Archives, Washington, D.C.*

Stimson had served Taft in the same position before becoming secretary of state under Hoover, and Knox had run as vice president in 1936. Both men called for a greatly expanded U.S. military establishment and continued aid to Britain.

Roosevelt also authorized Secretary of the Interior Harold Ickes and the director of the Federal Bureau of Investigation, J. Edgar Hoover, to pursue several clandestine activities that were of dubious value and patently illegal. FBI agents wire-tapped telephones, read the mail of Americans favorable to the Axis powers, and spied on congressional members who opposed the administration's policies. Indeed, the president eventually directed the FBI to compile information proving that aviator Charles Lindbergh and other members of the isolationist America First Committee were engaged in fifth-column activities on behalf of the Nazis. "What a pity," Roosevelt angrily declared, "that this youngster has completely abandoned his belief in our form of government and has accepted Nazi methods because apparently they are efficient." Although the FBI shadowed America Firsters and fabricated letters showing their favor for the Nazis, it never substantiated White House suspicions of treason.

In still another indication of the global impact of European events, the successes of the German *Blitzkrieg* on the continent changed the tone of U.S. relations with Japan. Americans realized that Hitler's military advances had tied up the western European nations and exposed their possessions in the Pacific and southeast Asia to Japan. Should the Japanese seize the region's oil, rice, rubber, and tin, the long stalemate in China would end with Japanese victory. After the fall of the Netherlands and France, the Tokyo government demanded that Britain and Vichy France halt the flow of goods to China from Burma and Indochina and pushed for oil concessions from the Dutch East Indies. With Britain seemingly on the verge of collapse, the Japanese could move into Malaya and Singapore, leaving the United States as the only barrier to total Japanese control of Asia.

The United States tried to counter this calamity by means short of war. Its commercial treaty of 1911 with Japan had expired in late January 1940, and the state department attempted to force concessions by maintaining trade on a day-to-day basis. In an effort to deter any Japanese moves in the Pacific, the Roosevelt administration ordered the Pacific Fleet to remain at Pearl Harbor until further notice. The United States was trying to steer a dangerous course between honoring its Open Door pledges to China and pursuing policies that might lead to war with Japan.

Because Japan's war machine ran primarily on U.S. oil, demands for an embargo came from numerous officials in Washington, including Stimson, Knox, and Morgenthau. Roosevelt and Hull remained opposed for more than one reason. They still tried to treat events in Asia separately from those in Europe, declaring that the preservation of Britain and the defeat of Germany were priorities. Although this argument seemed narrow in perception, another part of their stand had more validity. Whereas the *threat* of an oil embargo might discourage Japanese expansion, its *implementation* might push Japan into the Axis alliance, drive the Japanese deeper into southeast Asia for oil, and ultimately cause war with the United States. Hull wrote in his memoirs that "our best tactic was to keep them guessing." Roosevelt's military advisers added weight to his position. They reminded him that Congress had not authorized a two-ocean navy until that year and insisted that the United States was not prepared for war in the Pacific. Chief of Naval Operations Harold Stark stressed the need for time and warned against any action that might provoke Japan.

By the autumn, however, the White House had clearly turned toward economic pressure. Late in July 1940, Stimson and Morgenthau convinced the president to tighten economic sanctions on Japan by forbidding the export of quality scrap metal and petroleum products and restricting the sale of aviation fuel outside the Western Hemisphere to Britain only. After a bitter cabinet fight the next day over the new measure, the president gave in to Undersecretary of State Welles, who warned that the step would cause war with Japan. Roosevelt agreed to restrict the embargo to include only aviation gasoline among petroleum products and only the best quality scrap iron and steel. But Japan's continued encroachments in Indochina and the United States's growing fear of a Japanese military alliance with Germany soon forced another change in administration policy. In September the White House added scrap metals and steel to the list of embargoed goods, although it still refrained from stopping the flow of oil.

Meanwhile, the increasingly desperate situation in Britain caused Roosevelt to take a bold step without first securing congressional approval: He expanded U.S. assistance through the highly controversial destroyers-bases deal of early September 1940. According to its terms, the United States traded fifty overage destroyers for ninety-nine-year leases on eight British bases in the New World that extended from Newfoundland south to British Guiana. To assure Americans that the destroyers would not be used against them, the British government publicly promised never to surrender its fleet to Germany. The arrangement, Roosevelt's critics hotly claimed, violated international law and raised serious questions about the legality of selling military items to other nations. Although the attorney general in Washington upheld the deal as a proper retaliatory measure against Germany's illegal actions, the president decided to sidestep a lengthy congressional inquiry and the necessity of Senate approval by concluding the arrangement through executive agreement. His method infuriated Congress, but that body eventually confirmed the deal by appropriating funds for provisioning the naval bases.

Although the destroyers-bases agreement did not offer as much direct assistance as Churchill wanted, it moved the two Atlantic nations closer together. Churchill privately called the exchange a "decidedly unneutral act" that was absolutely essential to British security, and Roosevelt told Congress that it was "the most important action in the reinforcement of our national defense . . . since the Louisiana Purchase." Both men were correct. In practical terms, the destroyers-bases deal constituted an integral step toward making the United States a nonbelligerent actively aiding the British in the war against Germany.

As the presidential election of 1940 loomed near, isolationists became deeply concerned that the Roosevelt administration fully intended to take the United States into the war. The destroyers-bases deal seemed to confirm their worst fears, and late in that same month of September, the White House took another step that further substantiated their charge: It won congressional approval for the Selective Training and Service Act, which instituted the nation's first peacetime military draft. To secure its passage the president relied on the public support of Stimson (a Republican) and the highly respected army chief of staff, General George C. Marshall. The act faced formidable opposition from folk hero Charles Lindbergh, who had joined the isolationists in fighting intervention through the America First Committee, established the very next day after the destroyers-bases deal.

The Democrats meanwhile broke historical precedent by nominating Roosevelt for a third term, and the Republicans turned from their outspoken isolationist constituency and put forth a proponent of internationalism: Indiana's Wendell Willkie, a wealthy business leader and liberal who approved helping the British and agreed with Roosevelt not to use either the destroyers-bases deal or the Selective Service Act as campaign issues. Both parties renounced U.S. participation in "any foreign war," although the Democrats added the all-important qualifying phrase, "except in case of attack."

As the presidential campaign wore on, however, both candidates strayed from their truce on foreign policy matters. At one point Willkie accused his opponent of secretly wanting war and promised that "if you elect me president I will never send an American boy to fight in any European war." Roosevelt retaliated in

Boston with the assurance that "I have said this before, but I shall say it again and again and again: Your boys are not going to be sent into any foreign wars." His statement raised serious questions, however, because it did not rule out war in the event of attack. "Of course we'll fight if we're attacked," Roosevelt afterward admitted. "If somebody attacks us, then it isn't a foreign war, is it?" The bluntness of his remark in Boston would later open him to charges of deception and at the time drew a bitter reaction from Willkie. Roosevelt easily won reelection, although with a smaller margin than the landslide of 1936.

Buoyed by his convincing victory, Roosevelt soon embarked on an even more controversial course in foreign affairs: lend-lease. Realizing that the British had nearly depleted their cash flow, he sought to lend or lease them any goods necessary to win the war. Both neutrality legislation and the Johnson Act of 1934 prohibited loans, so he sought another avenue through which to extend assistance.

In a fireside chat of late December 1940, Roosevelt began his campaign for lend-lease by first reassuring Americans over nationwide radio that he intended his pro-Allied policies to keep the United States out of the war. Conceding that shipments of war materiel enhanced the possibility of U.S. involvement, he quickly added that "our national policy is not directed toward war. Its sole purpose is to keep war away from our country and our people." The United States had to become "the great arsenal of democracy." In his annual message to Congress of January 1941, Roosevelt emphasized the necessity of protecting the "Four Freedoms" essential to life: freedom of speech and worship and freedom from want and fear. To guarantee these freedoms to the British people, the United States had to lend or lease any materials they needed. "I am trying to . . . eliminate the silly, foolish old dollar sign," he explained. If a neighbor's house is burning, I surely will allow him to use my garden hose. Once the fire is quenched, "he gives it back to me and thanks me very much for the use of it."

The bitterness of the debate surfaced when the president angrily denounced isolationist Senator Burton K. Wheeler's criticism of the lend-lease proposal. The Montana Democrat had declared that "the lend-lease-give program is the New Deal's triple A foreign policy; it will plow under every fourth American boy." Roosevelt sharply rebuked him. At a press conference he asserted that Wheeler's comment was "the most untruthful[,] . . . the most dastardly, unpatriotic thing that has ever been said. Quote me on that. That really is the rottenest thing that has been said in public life in my generation."

Thus, the battle lines were drawn for a vicious fight in Congress. The White House engineer for the lend-lease bill was Democratic Representative John McCormack of Massachusetts, who expressed concern that his Irish constituency in Boston would oppose a bill with his name on it that was intended to help the British. He finally managed to have the proposal designated as H.R. (House Resolution) 1776, which added a patriotic ring and averted his own political knell. Mothers marched in Washington with signs declaring "Kill Bill 1776 Not Our Boys," and Robert Taft, son of the former president and isolationist Republican senator from Ohio, asserted that "lending war equipment is a good deal like lending chewing gum. You don't want it back." Historian Charles A. Beard begged a Senate committee to "preserve one stronghold of order and sanity even against the gates of hell."

Despite this vocal opposition, lend-lease became law in March 1941. In February, Willkie had announced his support for the bill, thereby making it a bipartisan issue, and it passed Congress by a vote of 60 to 31 in the Senate and 317 to 71 in the House. On March 11 the president signed into law "An Act to Promote the Defense of the United States," which permitted the United States to "sell, transfer title to, exchange, lease, lend, or otherwise dispose of" any "defense article" or "defense information" to "any country whose defense the President deems vital to the defense of the United

States." Congress initially appropriated $7 billion for the program, but it had eventually approved more than $50 billion in lend-lease funds by the time the war was over. Of the total, Britain received $31.6 billion of goods, including nearly a million feet of fire hose in the first package alone. Isolationist Senator Arthur Vandenberg, a Republican from Michigan, charged that "we have torn up 150 years of traditional American foreign policy. We have tossed Washington's Farewell Address in the discard." Roosevelt simply called it a measure for peace.

If Vandenberg's claims were melodramatic, they were not far off the mark: The Lend-Lease Act placed the United States on an even more international course. Certainly the measure joined the destroyers-bases deal in putting a public stamp on the end of neutrality. Indeed, the Lend-Lease Act constituted an unofficial U.S. declaration of war on the Axis powers. Even while Congress debated the bill from January through March of 1941, U.S. and British military and naval staff officers were meeting privately in Washington to formulate a joint strategy in the event of U.S. entry into the war against Germany. The discussions did not go easily, particularly when it became plain that the United States opposed the retention of imperial preference (special commercial rights among members of the British Empire). But the two negotiating teams finally adopted the so-called ABC-1 staff agreements, which provided that if the United States joined Britain in the war, the newly allied forces would first concentrate on the Germans in the Atlantic while fighting a defensive war against Japan in the Pacific. After Germany's defeat, the allies would turn on the Japanese.

Passage of the Lend-Lease Act soon led to another heated argument in Congress as administration supporters called for convoys to protect ships carrying lend-lease materials. Roosevelt recognized that the United States could not escort such vessels without raising legal questions about the nation's nonbelligerent status. Indeed, the Lend-Lease Act

itself posed seemingly insurmountable obstacles to convoys. It declared that "nothing in this Act shall be construed to authorize or to permit the authorization of convoying by naval vessels of the United States . . . or . . . the entry of any American vessel into a combat area." Several members of Roosevelt's cabinet—including Stimson, Knox, Morgenthau, and Ickes—wanted the president to authorize U.S. convoys to protect British ships, but Stimson recognized that Roosevelt had created his own dilemma by assuring the nation against any action conducive to war.

Roosevelt hesitated to use U.S. convoys because he feared public disfavor, but he found an opening in the Declaration of Panama of 1939, which had proclaimed a wide security zone in the Atlantic that the American states agreed to protect. In April 1941, therefore, the president authorized a "neutrality patrol" that could police the waters beyond that zone to provide information helpful to U.S. security and to notify the British of the presence of enemy ships or planes. Although the patrols did not safeguard all lend-lease shipments, their use provided some security and eased the public outcry over convoys.

By May 1941 the United States had become an active participant in the Atlantic theater of the European war. Its navy cooperated with Britain in locating German submarines and other vessels and in April dropped its first depth charges on a U-boat. That same month the United States secured approval from Denmark's government-in-exile to occupy Greenland. Roosevelt also removed the Red Sea from the "combat zone," enabling U.S. ships to transport goods to British soldiers fighting in North Africa. In the meantime German maritime warfare became more effective as U-boats banded together in "wolf packs" to attack single vessels or convoys. On May 21, 1941, the Germans sank their first U.S. vessel, the freighter *Robin Moor.* Although no loss of life resulted, Roosevelt demanded reparations for the lost cargo. The Germans refused. In retaliation, the United States froze

German and Italian assets and closed their consulates, moves that drew similar retaliatory actions against Americans in those countries.

Growing Global Character of the War

Germany's military successes in the Balkans and North Africa had meanwhile turned attention from the United States's steadily deteriorating relations with Japan. In August 1940 Prime Minister Konoye reflected the growing influence of the hard-liners in his new cabinet when he expanded the objectives of the New Order into those of the "Greater East Asia Co-Prosperity Sphere." The new foreign minister was the outspoken Yosuke Matsuoka, a graduate of the University of Oregon who had led the walkout from the League of Nations in 1933 and whom Hull considered "as crooked as a basket of fishhooks." The minister of war was General Hideki Tojo (called "Fighting Tojo" by his young classmates) who, like Matsuoka, had long advocated military expansion. As with the New Order, Greater East Asia would have Japan, Manchuria, and China at its center, but Matsuoka emphasized that the new program would be wider in scope. It would encompass German islands mandated to Japan in 1920 (the Carolines, Marianas, and Marshalls), French possessions in the Pacific and Indochina, British Malaya and Borneo, the Dutch East Indies, Burma, Thailand (or Siam), India, New Zealand, and Australia. The foreign minister did not mention the Philippines, but he inserted a conspicuous *et cetera* at the end of the list and pointedly remarked that "this sphere could be automatically broadened in the course of time." In September, Japan began its push toward isolating China by pressing Vichy France for concessions in northern Indochina. When the United States protested, Matsuoka acidly dismissed the protest with the remark that "the Western Powers taught Japan the game of poker but after acquiring most of the chips they pronounced the game immoral and took up contract bridge."

Less than a week after Japan's gains in Indochina, delegates from Germany, Italy, and Japan gathered in Berlin and signed the Tripartite Pact of September 27, 1940, which in large part was aimed at preventing the United States from either allying with the British in the war or opposing Japan's expansionist program in Asia. The three signatories guaranteed one another's spheres of influence in Europe and Asia, which meant that Japan had won Germany's approval for moving south and its help in resolving problems with the Soviet Union in the north. Furthermore, the new allies promised to "assist one another with all political, economic and military means when one of the three contracting Parties is attacked by a power at present not involved in the European War or in the Sino-Japanese Conflict." Another article in the pact specifically exempted the Soviet Union from the warning, meaning that the United States remained the only power "not involved" in either conflict.

The three-power agreement instilled new hope in Japan's expansionist drive. An irony was still inescapable, however: Whereas Germany sought to prevent U.S. entry into the European war by diverting its attention to Asia, Japan counted on the Rome-Berlin-Tokyo Axis to keep the United States out of the Pacific. In the meantime the Japanese could encourage good relations with the Soviet Union and close the ring around China. Militarists in Tokyo were elated because the Tripartite Pact virtually reduced the Nazi-Soviet Pact to a dead letter. The new power alignment would force Jiang Jieshi into an agreement, enabling Japan to reassign its troops elsewhere. The Japanese would be free to take British, French, and Dutch possessions in Asia without encountering U.S. interference.

The Tripartite Pact was a monument to Japan's growing illusions, because it exemplified again the inseparability of Asian and European events. Roosevelt and Hull had been correct in arguing against the embargo on scrap iron: The tactic had encouraged Japan to ally with Germany and Italy, and the Axis

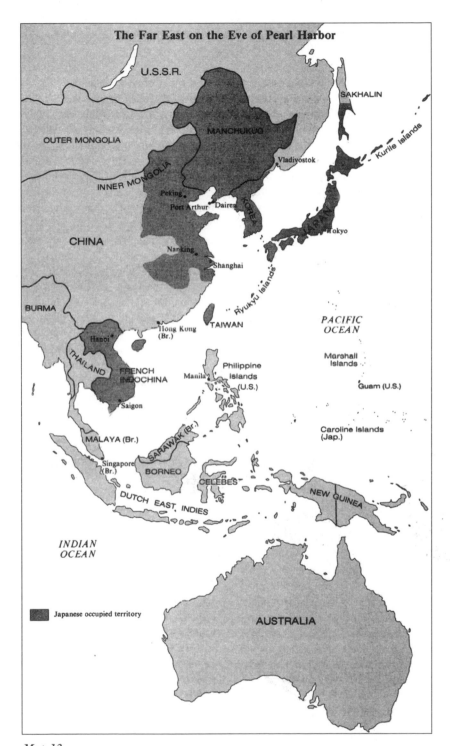

The Far East on the Eve of Pearl Harbor

Map 13

The Japanese were able to take advantage of the war in Europe to expand their holdings in Asia.

now posed a threat to U.S. interests in the Pacific. The new alliance had the potential of cutting off Britain's supplies from Asia and forcing the ill-prepared United States into the war. The Roosevelt administration was beginning to realize that support for Britain in the Atlantic necessitated protection of British and U.S. interests in Asia. The state department warned Americans to leave the region, and in November the White House approved a loan to China. U.S. policies bought time by temporarily slowing Japan's advances and helping to keep China in the war, but they also pushed the United States into a collision course with Japan.

U.S. leaders increasingly understood how the European war had automatic repercussions in Asia and the Pacific that affected America's own national security. The president had become convinced that the United States could not survive as a free and democratic society in a closed world dominated by European Nazis and Fascists combined with Japanese militarists. The Open Door principles originally applied specifically to China had taken on a generalized meaning that encompassed the globe. Roosevelt wrote Grew in Tokyo in January 1941 that "we must recognize that the hostilities in Europe, in Africa, and in Asia are all parts of a single world conflict. We must, consequently, recognize that our interests are menaced both in Europe and in the Far East. . . . Our strategy of self-defense," he asserted, "must be a global strategy which takes account of every front and takes advantage of every opportunity to contribute to our total security." The British had to have Asia's resources to keep their war effort alive in the Middle East, the Mediterranean, and Europe. As a nonbelligerent ally, the United States recognized the necessity of keeping communication and supply lines open throughout the world.

The broadly scoped U.S. policy carried dangerous implications for its relations with Japan. Less than a week after receiving Roosevelt's message, Grew noted in his diary that "there is a lot of talk around town to the effect that the Japanese, in case of a break with the United States, are planning to go all out in a surprise mass attack at Pearl Harbor." Although his report dismissed this assertion as one of many groundless rumors then circulating in Tokyo, Grew could not have known that at this very time a small circle of Japanese leaders was making plans that culminated in the attack on Pearl Harbor less than a year afterward. Grew had earlier begun to retreat from his hopes for an accommodation with the Japanese. The previous September of 1940, he had cabled Washington the famous "green light" message. Japan, he declared, was "one of the predatory powers; she has submerged all moral and ethical sense and has become unashamedly and frankly opportunist, seeking at every turn to profit by the weakness of others. Her policy of southward expansion definitely threatens American interests in the Pacific." The United States could have no distinct policy for either Europe or Asia. Every action in one region of the world profoundly affected the situation in the other.

Fear of an oil embargo caused the Tokyo government to try negotiating its differences with America. Retired Admiral Kichisaburo Nomura, a known friend of the Western powers and of Roosevelt, arrived in Washington in February as ambassador and initiated a long series of informal talks with Hull in his hotel suite. Nomura's very presence and calm demeanor set him apart from his militant countrymen. Six feet tall, he had only one good eye and walked with a limp, the result of a bomb thrown by a Chinese terrorist some nine years earlier. But despite his reputation for moderation and his desire for peace, problems quickly developed with Hull. Nomura could not understand English very well and attempted to work without a translator. When he tried to defend his country's expansionist activities in China, Hull countered with objections grounded in moral convictions that his counterpart did not understand. Even though the two men met forty times in the next nine months, they could not break the impasse over Greater East Asia and the Open Door.

While Nomura and Hull continued their conversations, still another attempt at negotiations resulted from the unauthorized intervention of a group of private U.S. citizens called the John Doe Associates. Their leaders, two Catholic missionaries, had recently returned from Japan with a liberal peace offer, allegedly from Konoye, which they were to present to Roosevelt. It pledged Japan's withdrawal from China and the Tripartite Pact in exchange for restored trading rights with the United States.

But the initial hopes in Washington quickly disappeared. After the missionaries talked with a high Japanese official sent from the War Ministry in Tokyo, they returned to Hull on April 9 with a Draft Understanding that reflected Matsuoka's hard-line views. Japan no longer offered any assurance of withdrawal from either China or the Tripartite Pact, although it did agree to abide by its obligations under the pact on one condition: *if* the United States attacked Germany. Furthermore, Japan would ease its pressure on southeast Asia *if* Washington lifted commercial restrictions and helped Japan secure raw materials in the South Pacific. Thus, the Japanese expected the United States to cut off aid to China and persuade Jiang to accept their conditions for peace. The long-standing internal conflict between moderates and hard-liners in Japan had now emerged in the form of two diametrically opposed policy statements, which led Hull to accuse the Japanese of hypocrisy and further damaged relations with the United States.

Hull was infuriated over Japan's proposals, but he decided against an outright rejection in hope of reaching a better settlement. The secretary agreed to use the terms as a *modus vivendi,* or temporary basis for settlement, but told Nomura that in return the Japanese had to accept four principles of conduct in foreign affairs: respect for the sovereignty of all nations, noninterference in their domestic concerns, recognition of equal trade opportunities, and acceptance of the status quo in the Pacific.

The two sets of demands were mutually exclusive. Nomura, however, mistakenly thought that Hull had accepted the Draft Understanding and failed to mention the four principles when he passed on the information to his government. Matsuoka and others in Tokyo therefore regarded Hull's reply as a U.S. proposal and worked out a counterplan with conditions more favorable to Japan. Hull was incredulous when he read this document in May. Japanese leaders finally came to understand that Hull's four principles were vital, but at the time they thought he had taken an abrupt change in position since talking with Nomura. Each side was bitterly disenchanted with the apparent lack of good faith shown by the other. In reality, neither Washington nor Tokyo had changed its stand; but the Doe Associates' involvement had combined with Nomura's inept diplomacy to leave mutually erroneous impressions of duplicity.

Failure of the Hull-Nomura talks led Japan to prepare for its thrust southward by first signing a nonaggression pact with the Soviet Union in April 1941. Foreign Ministers Matsuoka and Molotov negotiated a five-year agreement in Moscow guaranteeing neutrality if either party went to war. News of the agreement caused immediate concern in Washington that the Soviets would cut back on assistance to China. Roosevelt therefore approved the resignation of U.S. military personnel to establish the "Flying Tigers," a group of pilots under the alleged "private" command of Colonel Claire Chennault who sought to continue lend-lease aid to Jiang. But China was not the only country that felt the ramifications of this Soviet-Japanese pact. Mutual self-interests, of course, had brought together these long-time foes. The Soviet Union could continue shoring up its western borders against Germany while reducing the immediate likelihood of a conflict with Japan along their common eastern border of Manchukuo. The Japanese had secured their northern holdings from Soviet attack and now could turn south.

But before the Japanese could make their move, Hitler's armies shocked the world on June 22, 1941, by launching "Operation Barbarossa"—a massive invasion of the Soviet

Union that radically changed the war's complexion. His successes in Poland had freed him from the danger of a two-front war (a point emphasized in *Mein Kampf*), and with U.S. assistance helping Britain stave off invasion, he turned toward crushing the Soviet Union. "We have only to kick in the door," Hitler boasted, "and the whole rotten structure will come crashing down." Stalin was so stunned by news of the swiftly approaching German armies that he disappeared for almost two weeks, apparently because of a nervous breakdown. Democratic Senator Harry S. Truman of Missouri expressed the initial reaction of more than a few Americans when the *New York Times* quoted him as saying: "If we see that Germany is winning the war we ought to help Russia and if Russia is winning we ought to help Germany, and . . . let them kill as many as possible."

But British observers did not favor a hands-off policy toward what many Americans regarded as a contest between "Satan and Lucifer." Churchill recognized the unexpected opportunity afforded by the German assault and called for all-out assistance to the Soviets in an effort to ward off a Nazi invasion of Britain. "If Hitler invaded Hell," Churchill growled, "I would make at least a favorable reference to the Devil in the House of Commons." The British soon sent aid to the Soviet Union by sea around the northern tip of Norway and into Murmansk, and they made clear to the White House that U.S. assistance was required in protecting lend-lease imports if the program was to continue.

But as Hitler's armies rolled within sight of Moscow and Leningrad, the Roosevelt administration became hesitant about extending lend-lease assistance to what appeared to be a lost cause. Two days following the German invasion the president assured reporters that the United States would "give all aid we possibly can to Russia." But he was evasive about whether that included lend-lease. That same day the United States released $40 million in recently frozen Soviet assets and a day later permitted U.S. ships to carry goods to the Soviet Union's north Pacific port of Vladi-

vostok. In July 1941 the administration took a step that Roosevelt called "one of the most important things that have happened since the war began." To safeguard Greenland and North America from the Germans and to facilitate lend-lease assistance to Britain (which in turn might help the Soviets), he authorized 4000 U.S. Marines to occupy Iceland. Such a move enabled the U.S. Navy to escort American, Icelandic, and other vessels making the treacherous journey between the United States and Iceland, where British convoys then accompanied them to the British Isles. Finally, in late October, Roosevelt overrode the objections of military advisers and notified Stalin of the extension of lend-lease to the Soviet Union. Failure to help the Soviets, he realized, constituted assistance to the Nazis and Fascists along with their Japanese militarist allies. Most Americans set aside their aversion to communism and regarded his decision as another step toward securing their own country without having to go to war.

Germany's invasion of the Soviet Union also had a major impact on Asian affairs: Japan seized the advantage and began its drive south. The Japanese had failed to persuade the government of the Netherlands, then in exile in London, to turn over the East Indies. Members of an Imperial Conference in Tokyo decided to expand into southern Indochina and Thailand as steps toward occupying British Singapore and the Netherlands East Indies. The record of the July meeting clearly reflected the resolve of those present: "We will not be deterred by the possibility of being involved in a war with England and America." Japan then turned back to Vichy France to demand bases in southern Indochina. Whereas the earlier agreement granted Japan's access to Saigon's airfields and harbor and placed Singapore within bombing range, the new arrangement in July established a joint protectorate over all Indochina, thereby endangering U.S. interests in the Philippines.

Roosevelt believed that the German attack on the Soviet Union had opened a big debate in Japan about what policy to pursue. In July he wrote in a letter that the Japanese were having "a real drag-down and knockout fight among themselves" over whether to "attack Russia, attack the South Seas . . . or . . . sit on the fence and be more friendly with us. No one knows what the decision will be but . . . it is terribly important for the control of the Atlantic for us to help to keep peace in the Pacific. I simply have not got enough Navy to go around."

Japan's push into southern Indochina led Roosevelt to issue an executive order on July 25 that froze Japanese assets in the United States and, in so doing, inadvertently led to an oil embargo. Indeed, the embargo so vehemently opposed by the president and Hull became administration policy without specific command. A bureaucratic mixup had occurred, in which Washington's hard-liners misinterpreted Roosevelt's executive order to encompass a stoppage of oil exports. Both Americans and Japanese thought that the commercial ban included all products, even though the administration tried to repair the damage by announcing on August 1 that it would accept applications for petroleum export licenses under certain limited conditions. But it was too late. Roosevelt had left for a meeting with Churchill in the Atlantic and was not aware of the incidental oil embargo until early September, at which time he could not reverse the *de facto* policy without appearing to retreat in the face of Japanese pressure.

Whatever Japan's dilemma regarding policy, the Roosevelt administration's fumbling establishment of an oil embargo left the Tokyo government with only two options: Either cancel its plans for Greater East Asia, or seize Dutch East Indies oil as a step toward fulfilling its expansionist objectives. Eighty percent of Japan's oil came from U.S. producers, and its reserve would last no longer than eighteen months. Roosevelt knew that the freeze would force Japan's hand. He therefore nationalized Philippine armed forces into the U.S. service and called former Army Chief of Staff Douglas MacArthur out of retirement, promoting him to commanding general of the U.S. Armed Forces Far East (USAFFE). The *New York Times* called the freeze "the most drastic blow short of actual war." Grew confided to his diary: "The obvious conclusion is eventual war."

The Japanese decision to move south did not surprise the United States, because in August 1940 the Office of Naval Intelligence had cracked their highest secret diplomatic code—the Purple Cipher—and soon had a vast collection of information resulting from a code-breaking machine called "Magic." Churchill urged Roosevelt to warn the Tokyo government that any attacks on British or Dutch holdings in Asia could mean war, and even though the state department convinced the president to tone down his message, his meaning was clear. On August 17 Roosevelt warned Nomura that if Japan took "any further steps in pursuance of a policy or program of military domination by force or threat of force on neighboring countries," the United States would "take immediately any and all steps which it may deem necessary toward safeguarding the legitimate rights and interest of the United States and American nationals and toward insuring the safety and security of the United States."

Negotiations in Washington during the summer of 1941 only hardened each side's demands. Hull refused to retreat from U.S. pledges to China, and Nomura, unaware of the military's preparations in Tokyo, repeatedly sought recognition of his nation's holdings in China. Doubtless the White House toughened its policy because of the danger of a Japanese assault on the Soviet rear while the Nazis moved toward Moscow. The Japanese ambassador impressed Americans with his sincerity and integrity, and Konoye in Tokyo had a reputation for moderation. But the militarists under General Tojo were gaining control.

The Atlantic Charter and Undeclared War

From August 9 through 12, 1941, Roosevelt and Churchill secretly met for the first time to discuss a joint public declaration of war aims that might convince Americans of the issues at stake while protecting the president from the charge of having made secret commitments to the British. On a British battleship in Placentia Bay off Newfoundland, they formulated a joint public statement that ultimately guided the two Atlantic nations' policies through the end of the war.

The long-standing Anglo-American rapprochement reached its warmest point at this meeting. Roosevelt, with the help of a cane and his son Elliott, joined the British prime minister in a symbolic display of Atlantic unity after struggling across the entire length of the vessel before 1500 men standing at attention. Sunday church services on August 10 highlighted the singing of "Onward Christian Soldiers," which brought tears to the president's eyes and led him to remark to his son that "if nothing else had happened, that would have cemented us. 'Onward Christian Soldiers.' We *are,* and we *will,* go on, with God's help." Churchill saw deep meaning in the day's events. In his memoirs of the war, he noted

> . . . the symbolism of the Union Jack and the Stars and Stripes draped side by side on the pulpit; . . . the highest naval, military, and air officers of Britain and the United States grouped in one body behind the President and me; the close-packed ranks of British and American sailors, completely intermingled, sharing the same books and joining fervently together in the prayers and hymns familiar to both. . . . Every word seemed to stir the heart. It was a great hour to live.

In a press release after the conference, Britain and the United States announced their common objectives in what became known as the Atlantic Charter. These included a pledge against aggression and territorial aggrandizement; the formation of a collective security system; and assurances of self-determination of peoples, freedom of the seas, and reduced commercial restrictions. The affirmation of such idealistic principles perhaps reminded the perceptive observer of Wilson's Fourteen Points and how they had seemingly combined with the reformist tone of the New Deal. But

realistic concerns permeated the Charter: Roosevelt feared that Britain itself might reject self-determination in postwar Europe. His call for commercial freedom had met expected resistance from the British, who wanted to maintain their system of imperial preference. Out of expediency, therefore, the public declaration called for equal commercial access to the world's markets and raw materials but promised "due respect for their existing obligations." Indeed, Churchill later assured the House of Commons that the Atlantic Charter applied only to "nations of Europe now under the Nazi yoke." On Churchill's proposal for a new League of Nations, Roosevelt would make no commitment except to support "the establishment of a wider and permanent system of general security." This broad statement would perhaps avert a confrontation with U.S. isolationists.

The Atlantic Charter constituted a virtual Anglo-American alliance against the Axis and thereby eased some of the strained feelings resulting from the negotiations over the destroyers-bases deal and the lend-lease agreements. Churchill was optimistic about imminent U.S. involvement in the conflict. He wrote afterward that "the fact alone of the United States, still technically neutral, joining with a belligerent Power in making such a declaration was astonishing. The inclusion in it of a reference to 'the final destruction of the Nazi tyranny' . . . amounted to a challenge which in ordinary times would have implied warlike action." To his war cabinet, he privately declared that Roosevelt had assured him that "he would wage war, but not declare it, and that he would become more and more provocative" by looking "to force an 'incident' . . . which would justify him in opening hostilities." If Churchill's rendition of the conversation was accurate, the president had taken his nation to the brink of war.

In September those attending an Inter-Allied Meeting in London announced formal approval of the Atlantic Charter, and the Soviets soon agreed to a limited acceptance of its principles. Two weeks before the Placentia

Roosevelt and Churchill
Aboard H.M.S. *Prince of Wales* off Newfoundland in August 1941 as they
formulate the Atlantic Charter. Left to right: Admiral Ernest J. King, General
George C. Marshall, General Sir John Dill, Admiral Harold A. Stark, and
Admiral Sir Dudley Pound. *National Archives, Washington, D.C.*

meeting, Roosevelt's chief aide, Harry Hopkins (despite an ongoing bout with stomach cancer that would eventually take his life), made the long and arduous journey to Moscow and returned with an optimistic report that the Soviets would survive the German onslaught. Churchill and Roosevelt sent a communiqué to Stalin, praising his "splendid defense" against Hitler and guaranteeing their assistance. And yet, the idea of self-determination held no attraction to Stalin, who certainly opposed the right of neighboring countries in eastern Europe to choose governments alien to Soviet interests. Had not Poland provided a thoroughway into his country for the Nazi juggernaut? Only the exigencies of war—the need for Anglo-American aid against the *Wehrmacht*—could persuade Stalin to mouth support for a doctrine that by its very nature posed a threat to his nation's security.

An incident involving the U.S. destroyer *Greer* soon underlined the new unity exemplified in the Atlantic Charter by causing events in the Atlantic to take on the character of an undeclared war between the United States and Germany. On September 4, 1941, a German submarine fired on the *Greer* off Iceland and drew a heated reaction from Roosevelt. Before learning the full story, he took advantage of the incident to justify extending the naval patrols to Iceland. The Germans, he declared over nationwide radio, were guilty of "piracy." If the "rattlesnakes of the Atlantic" entered U.S. waters, they did so at their own risk. The *Greer* "was carrying American mail to Iceland. . . . She was then and there attacked by a submarine. . . . I tell you the blunt fact that the German submarine fired first upon this American destroyer without warning, and with deliberate design to sink her." This incident was "one determined step toward creating a permanent world system based on force, terror, and murder." The navy now had orders to "shoot-on-sight," a decision resulting from "months and months of constant thought and anxiety and prayer." From now on, the United States would protect any ship in "our defensive waters."

But Roosevelt had revealed only carefully selected truths in an effort to manipulate public opinion in favor of a stronger policy. A British patrol plane had notified the *Greer* that a German submarine lay ten miles ahead in its path, and the destroyer had pursued it for over three hours, radioing its location to the British plane so that it could drop depth charges. At long last, the submarine commander turned in desperation and fired a torpedo at the *Greer,* missing it by a bare 300 feet. The *Greer* proceeded to drop depth charges and drew another errant torpedo. After more pursuit the *Greer* finally quit the chase and resumed its voyage to Iceland.

Roosevelt was correct in believing that Hitler sought to avert a confrontation with the United States until after his forces had defeated Britain and the Soviet Union. Isolationists, however, warned that the president would force war with Germany by his destroyers-bases deal, Lend-Lease Act, naval

patrols, public condemnations of the Nazis, and shoot-on-sight orders. Their fears were not totally unfounded. Hitler ordered his naval commanders to avoid combat with the United States *unless* the U-boats were in danger. In early October he declared that "when I see the enemy leveling his rifle at me, I am not going to wait till he presses the trigger. I would rather be the first to press the trigger." And yet Hitler considered Americans too weak to go to war. The United States was a "Jewish rubbish heap," he cynically charged, hopelessly divided by economic depression and racial impurities. As the much-heralded haven for immigrants and oppressed peoples, it had become "half Judaized, half negrified." The United States, he concluded, posed no threat to Germany.

The undeclared war meanwhile continued in the Atlantic. In mid-October 1941 a German submarine torpedoed the U.S. destroyer *Kearney* southwest of Iceland, killing eleven men and inflicting heavy damage on the vessel. Ten days later Roosevelt indignantly declared that "we have wished to avoid shooting. But the shooting has started. And history has recorded who fired the first shot." Roosevelt did not mention that the *Kearney,* like the *Greer,* had been in hot pursuit of the German submarine at the time of attack. Repeal of the Neutrality Act of 1939, he now insisted, was imperative to permit him to arm merchant ships and allow their entry into the combat zones. The day after the attack the House overwhelmingly voted to arm merchant ships, throwing the matter before the Senate. By the end of the month the Germans had sunk a U.S. tanker, and during the night of October 31 they sent down the first naval vessel, the destroyer *Reuben James,* with the loss of more than one hundred men. Despite these events, the America First Committee defiantly proclaimed that the president's request for repeal of the Neutrality Act was tantamount to "asking Congress to issue an engraved drowning license to American seamen."

By November 1941 war with Germany was a matter of time. The U.S. Navy was shooting at U-boats on sight, dropping depth charges, and dodging torpedoes in the North Atlantic. That same month Congress authorized the first lend-lease shipments to the Soviet Union, which ultimately received $11 billion in assistance under the program. Less than two weeks later Congress narrowly approved a more elastic Neutrality Act, which permitted U.S. merchant vessels to arm themselves and enter the combat zones when carrying war materiel to Britain. With attention riveted on Europe and the Atlantic, war came suddenly for the United States—some 6000 miles away at Pearl Harbor, Hawaii.

Pearl Harbor

Seen in retrospect, the Roosevelt administration's decision in July 1941 to freeze Japanese assets had set the events in motion that ultimately led to war with Japan. On September 6 in Tokyo, leaders at an Imperial Conference made a momentous decision: If the Washington negotiations did not take a favorable turn by early October, Japan would declare war on the United States, Britain, and the Netherlands. Emperor Hirohito and several high-ranking army and navy officers were not enthusiastic about the decision, but they adhered to the wishes of the Supreme Command of both services. Prime Minister Konoye had six weeks to secure U.S. concessions regarding China.

That autumn, Konoye proposed a personal meeting with Roosevelt in the Pacific to resolve their nations' problems. The idea immediately attracted Grew's support, because he thought that the stalemated war in China, the U.S. embargo, and deepening suspicions of Hitler had convinced the Japanese of the foolhardy prospect of going to war with the United States. Roosevelt favored the suggestion until he talked with Hull. The secretary of state did not believe that Konoye spoke for his more militant colleagues and warned that because the Japanese had called the meeting, a failure to reach a settlement would place the onus on the United States. *Before* such a conference,

he insisted, Japan must give a "clear-cut manifestation" of its intention to withdraw from China and Indochina. Konoye could not do this, and Roosevelt declined to meet with him without such a preliminary agreement.

A summit meeting might have bought some valuable time, but there is little reason to believe that Konoye and Roosevelt could have found some way to take the two nations off their collision course. In truth, there was no honorable way to close the huge gap between the Open Door and the Greater East Asia Co-Prosperity Sphere. Yet such a high-level meeting might have led to a temporary understanding, which would have given the United States more time to bolster its Pacific holdings. When Konoye's gamble on a meeting with Roosevelt failed, fateful events took a quicker pace. Hard-liners in Tokyo forced Konoye's resignation on October 16, and two days later their chief spokesman, General Tojo, became premier.

On November 5 another Imperial Conference led to the decision to complete preparations for war by early December but to continue the negotiations by sending another emissary, Saburo Kurusu, to join Ambassador Nomura in Washington. The Magic intercepts revealed that the men had two proposals— Plan A and Plan B—the second containing more concessions than the first, but not to be presented unless the Roosevelt administration rejected Plan A. The decoders also learned that the deadline for success in the talks was November 29. "After that," the message ominously declared, "things are automatically going to happen."

No surprises were contained in either plan presented by the Japanese envoys. On November 7 Hull immediately rejected Plan A because it again sought U.S. acquiescence in Japan's domination of Asia. Ten days later Kurusu tried to encourage a settlement when, in reference to the Tripartite Pact, he assured the president that Japan "had no intention of becoming a tool of Germany nor did she mean to wait until the United States became deeply involved in the battle of the Atlantic

General Hideki Tojo
Japanese premier from mid-October 1941
through mid-1944. *U.S. Army.*

and then stab her in the back." Nomura and Kurusu presented their final offer on November 20. Plan B called for both governments to refrain from sending troops into southeast Asia or the South Pacific, except for Indochina; to help one another acquire goods from the Dutch East Indies; and to reestablish trade relations as they were before Roosevelt froze Japanese assets—including restoration of the "required quantity of oil." Plan B also stipulated that if the United States stayed out of China, Japan would evacuate Indochina when there was either peace in China or an "equitable peace" in the Pacific. Hull rejected Plan B as "virtually a surrender."

Late in November Hull tried to gain time for the U.S. Army and Navy by advocating a truce of three months accompanied by a *modus vivendi.* According to his proposal, the United States would grant oil concessions if the Tokyo government disavowed force, ordered the evacuation of southern Indochina,

and reduced its military contingent in northern Indochina. Hull sent the paper to the Washington diplomatic representatives of Britain, China, Australia, and the Netherlands. The proposal drew no support. Jiang Jieshi complained of the lack of guarantees for China; the other leaders warned that China might pull out of the war, releasing Japanese forces for use elsewhere and taking away the major strategic point for launching an invasion of Japan if war developed. The White House dropped Hull's *modus vivendi* without forwarding it to Japan.

On November 26 Hull presented Japan with a ten-point program that comprised his government's final proposal. Japan was to withdraw from China and Indochina, virtually disavow the Tripartite Pact, recognize the Chinese Nationalist government, and join a multilateral nonaggression pact in East Asia. In return, the United States would restore trade, remove the freeze on Japanese assets, assist Tokyo in stabilizing its currency, and try to end extraterritoriality in China. Hull's proposal was not an ultimatum, but it was a clear admission to the likelihood of war. Japan could not pull out of China.

Hull realized that Japan would reject his counteroffer and that the outcome would probably be war. The following day he told Stimson: "I have washed my hands of it, and it is now in the hands of you and Knox, the army and navy." Yet the army and navy were not ready for a Pacific war. Stimson warned that among other preparations the United States needed at least three months to assemble enough B-17 long-range bombers (Flying Fortresses) to safeguard the Philippines. Hull meanwhile warned the British ambassador to expect a Japanese move "suddenly and with every element of surprise."

Magic intercepts of November 27 established Japan's decision for war, although they did not reveal where the fighting would begin. One Asian specialist in the state department remained unconvinced about the dark outlook. Stanley Hornbeck, who probably had not seen the decoded messages, believed that the Japanese were not prepared to go to war with the United States before mid-December. No one goes to war "out of desperation," he assured anxious colleagues in Washington. Japanese forces nonetheless seemed to be assembling in Indochina for an attack on at least one of several places: Singapore, Thailand, Borneo, the Dutch East Indies, or perhaps the Philippines. Roosevelt's major concern was that a Japanese attack in southeast Asia might avoid hitting U.S. possessions and make it difficult to secure a congressional decision for war.

Confusion took over at this crucial juncture. On November 28 General George C. Marshall in Washington sent an alert to Pearl Harbor. But in Hawaii, Lieutenant General Walter Short had recently worked out a new warning system based on numbers that, as fate would have it, was the exact opposite of that used by both the Pentagon in Washington and the navy in the islands under the command of Admiral Husband Kimmel. Whereas stage 1 had previously signified full alert for attack and 3 as an alert for sabotage, he reversed the numbers. Consequently, when Marshall's stage 1 warning arrived, the army mistakenly prepared for sabotage by aligning all its planes wingtip to wingtip for better surveillance and locking up all antiaircraft materiel.

Roosevelt tried several last-second measures to prevent war. He prepared a congressional message showing that a Japanese assault in southeast Asia would endanger U.S. interests and warrant retaliation. He considered a personal appeal to Emperor Hirohito, which contained assurances that no country would take Indochina if Japan agreed to withdraw. A week of debate passed before the message went to Tokyo on the evening of December 6. For the first time the United States had made a proposal to Japan that did not mention China. It came too late.

Japan's decision to attack Pearl Harbor was the product of desperation and illusion. General Tojo and his supporters regarded the United States as an aggressor because the freeze of July 1941 had left Japan with only two choices—war with the United States or retreat from China. The latter was unthinkable, because no government could survive if it gave up the vast territorial gains of the last decade. Furthermore, Japan's military machine consumed 12,000 tons of oil a day, making the U.S. embargo an act of provocation and dictating the push south for the oil of the Dutch East Indies. Japan realized that the United States had ten times the industrial might and twice the population. Yet a string of quick conquests in the Pacific might force a favorable settlement in China and southeast Asia. By that time, or so the Japanese calculated, the United States would be at war with the Germans, and it could not fight a two-front war. Concessions to Japan would be the United States's only choice.

The minister who planned the attack on Pearl Harbor was Admiral Isoroku Yamamoto, who once remarked that he enlisted in the navy "so I could return Admiral Perry's visit." Now, as commander-in-chief of the Combined Fleet, he prepared to carry out a plan he had formulated the previous January—at precisely the time Grew had detected rumors in Tokyo of a planned attack on Pearl Harbor. Yamamoto staunchly opposed a prolonged war with the United States because he knew his country could not win. Indeed, he had assured Konoye as early as September 1940 that the Japanese navy could offer six months of resistance but no guarantees afterward. U.S. military and industrial capabilities, Yamamoto realized, were too extensive for Japan to wage a lengthy war. Its priority in 1941 was to disable the U.S. Pacific Fleet and air power at Pearl Harbor and thereby facilitate the southward thrust. Such an attack would furnish time for the Japanese to seize much of Asia before the United States could recover. By then, Tokyo's leaders believed, the United States would be in the European war and would have to negotiate a treaty recognizing Greater East Asia. On December 1 the cabinet met with the emperor and approved Tojo's call for war on the United States, Britain, and the Netherlands.

While the November negotiations continued in Washington, a large Japanese carrier task force of thirty-three vessels, under command of Vice-Admiral Chuichi Nagumo, stealthily gathered in the icy cold waters around the Kurile Islands, awaiting orders from Tokyo. To make it appear that the fleet was still in home waters, the Japanese government ordered its radio operators in port to send out false messages and arranged to have large groups of sailors sent to Tokyo during their leaves.

At long last the orders came, and in the early morning of November 25, six carriers with bombers and fighter escorts, two battleships, and accompanying cruisers, destroyers, tankers, and submarines broke eastward into the rough waters of the North Pacific. Their destination was Hawaii, which entailed a radio-silent, 3000-mile journey, subject to recall in the event of a sudden breakthrough in the Washington negotiations. To avoid leaving a trail, Nagumo forbade the dumping of garbage and oil drums into the ocean. He also decreed a total blackout at night and used the highest quality fuel to reduce smoke. On December 2 the final orders came to "Climb Mount Niitaka." The next day captains announced to crews that the force would attack Pearl Harbor at dawn on December 8 Tokyo time (Sunday, December 7, in Hawaii).

Americans had lost radio contact with the Japanese fleet in the North Pacific in mid-November. Their air patrols in both the north and the south were no help. They operated only 500 miles below the Aleutians and 500 miles above Hawaii, leaving a large void between these areas. In fact, on December 7 aircraft from the U.S. Navy were not on patrol north of the islands. Nagumo's fleet simply moved due east to a spot 800 miles above Hawaii, refueled, and veered southward to a spot within flying distance of the target. As a pointed reference to history, high above the flagship *Akagi* waved the same flag that had flown over one of the battleships that had surprised the Russians in Tsushima Straits in 1905. At 6:00 A.M., just before daylight, 350

planes began taking off for the final 230 miles of their destination.

In Pearl Harbor on Sunday morning, December 7, 1941, two young radar operators on duty noted "something completely out of the ordinary" on the screen. An unusually large number of blips suggested that more than fifty planes were about 132 miles north of Oahu and rapidly approaching the islands. And yet no warning went out. The operators' superiors at first did not believe the blips were planes and later, as the signals became unmistakable, dismissed them as U.S. B-17s due to arrive that morning. Suddenly the skies were filled with hundreds of planes bearing the emblem of the Rising Sun. Encountering no opposition, the Japanese flight commander, Captain Mitsuo Fuchida, radioed back to the navy the code words signaling a full surprise: "*Tora! Tora! Tora!*" ("Tiger! Tiger! Tiger!"). Two minutes later, at 7:55 A.M., the pursuit officer at Oahu saw the first bombs fall as he went outside to watch what he presumed to be "Navy bombers in bombing practice over Pearl Harbor." Shortly after the first wave of 183 Japanese planes had pummeled Pearl Harbor, Washington received the shocking message: "AIR RAID PEARL HARBOR. THIS IS NO DRILL."

Japan's attack on Pearl Harbor proved devastating to U.S. forces. In two hours its planes swooped over the islands in two death-defying waves, sinking seven U.S. battleships and disabling another, severely damaging several cruisers, destroyers, and auxiliary craft, and ripping apart nearly eighty-five percent of the 347 U.S. Army and Navy planes as they sat clustered and helpless on the runways. The Japanese inflicted 3581 casualties, including 2403 dead. U.S. commanders had believed that aerial torpedoes could not be effective in the shallow forty-five-foot-deep channels of Pearl Harbor. But a few days before the attack, the Japanese had discovered that the attachment of wooden stabilizers to the torpedoes' fins kept them from touching the bottom and allowed them to hit their targets.

There were saving factors on the U.S. side. Because the Japanese assault had seemingly achieved their leaders' every objective, Nagumo did not order additional hits the next day while the Americans were bewildered and badly reeling. The Japanese did not even try to find Admiral William F. Halsey and his aircraft carriers, which were in the Pacific on special assignment at the time of attack. Moreover, the Japanese pilots were not under orders to hit military emplacements, fuel tanks, or submarine bases; otherwise, the United States might have been forced to withdraw the remainder of its fleet home to the west coast. Japan's small losses leave the misleading impression of a totally successful attack. The Japanese lost a mere twenty-nine planes, fifty-five men, and six submarines. But in the exuberance of praising their own performance, they did not pursue their great advantage of having caused mass confusion at Pearl Harbor. In failing to exploit what one of their squadron commanders called "the chance of a lifetime" by continuing the attack the next day,

the Japanese made perhaps their most fatal strategic mistake of the Pacific War.

Roosevelt's arch-critics would later read conspiracy into the Pearl Harbor attack. According to the "back door to war" theory, the president was unable to convince Americans that Hitler was a threat to their interests (the "front door" to war) and, never imagining the possibility of such extensive destruction, enticed a Japanese attack on Pearl Harbor (hence the "back door") by stationing the Pacific Fleet in those waters. Whether to discredit a president derisively called "that man in the White House" or to justify the long-time argument that the war did not endanger U.S. security, hard-core isolationists led the way in blaming Roosevelt for an attack that could have succeeded only by treachery and surprise.

Even though this dark-minded and sinister argument persists among a small number of writers, it has largely slipped into the intellectual vacuum it deserves. Japan's success was

Bombing of Pearl Harbor
"Day of Infamy," December 7, 1941. *National Archives, Washington, D.C.*

attributable to audacity, illogic, and mistaken assumptions, not to some presidential design to take the United States into the war through the back door. The theory's fundamental premise—that Roosevelt moved the Pacific Fleet to Hawaii to draw an attack—is flawed: The naval strength was there to *discourage* Japanese aggression. The irony, of course, is that the Japanese intention was to cripple the U.S. fleet and that the stronger it was at Pearl Harbor, the more attractive it became to a surprise attack. Another unmistakable factor was Japan's determination to launch an assault, regardless of the specious claim that the president of the United States had maneuvered Tokyo's leaders into doing so. A great number of Japanese figures felt a sense of racial superiority that impelled them to believe it possible to defeat the United States. Roosevelt's critics have failed to uncover any evidence to substantiate their charge. The great American tragedy of December 7, 1941, resulted from a faulty intelligence network, erroneous assumptions about Japan's intentions and capabilities, and numerous other errors in judgment and procedure.

This conclusion does not relieve everyone of culpability, however. Just eleven days after the attack, the *Chicago Tribune* blamed Short and Kimmel for the disaster. "It is a military maxim," the paper argued, "that there is no excuse for surprise. The service regulations of both the army and navy require every officer to take adequate precautions for the security of his own forces, regardless of orders or lack of orders from his superiors." More telling, however, is the fundamental truth that everyone from President Roosevelt on down the chain of U.S. command deserves criticism. Instead of preparing for the absolute worst-case scenario, they all assumed that the Japanese (considered racially inferior and hence incapable of such an act) would never attempt such a reckless and foolhardy venture.

Meanwhile in Washington, Nomura and Kurusu were unaware of their government's decision to attack Pearl Harbor and prepared to follow Tojo's staged directive to deliver his

official rejection of Hull's ten-point proposal at precisely 1:00 P.M., twenty minutes before the scheduled time of attack. But this plan went awry. The evening before, Magic had intercepted the first thirteen parts of the Japanese message. After denouncing U.S. policy in East Asia, the message claimed that Hull's proposal "ignores Japan's sacrifices in the four years in China, menaces the Empire's existence itself, and disparages its honor and prestige." The president read the note before his pacing and extremely agitated chief aide, Harry Hopkins, and declared that "this means war."

Shortly after breakfast on December 7, the fourteenth and final section of the message was in Roosevelt's hands. Its last paragraph was chilling: "The Japanese Government regrets to have to notify hereby the American government that in view of the attitude of the American government it cannot but consider that it is impossible to reach an agreement through further negotiations." Word immediately went to Marshall at the Pentagon, who sent an alert to both the Philippines and Hawaii—*not* by his scrambler telephone, which he regarded as insecure, but by the army's message center to avoid suggesting to Japan that the United States had broken the Purple Cipher. Then happenstance intervened on Japan's behalf. Transmitting problems developed, and the signal officer, unaware of the importance of the message, sent it by Western Union, which caused a lengthy and perhaps critical delay.

In the meantime, typing difficulties in the Japanese Embassy in Washington held off delivery of the note by Nomura and Kurusu until 2:20 P.M., Washington time—*after* the first bombs had hit Pearl Harbor, and a half hour *after* Hull had learned of the attack. When the envoys arrived in his office he did not offer them a seat. Hull went through the motions of reading the note that Magic had provided some four hours before, and then glared coldly at Nomura. "In all my fifty years of public service I have never seen a document that was more crowded with infamous falsehoods and distortions—infamous false-

Roosevelt Before Congress
Roosevelt asks Congress to declare war on Japan, December 8, 1941. *National Archives, Washington, D.C.*

hoods and distortions on a scale so huge that I never imagined until today that any Government on this planet was capable of uttering them." Raising his hand to stop whatever reply Nomura had in mind, Hull cut his eyes to the door, an unmistakable signal for the stunned envoys to leave.

The aftermath was anticlimactic. About two hours following the attack on Pearl Harbor, the Japanese government declared war on the United States. A little after 3:00 P.M., Hawaiian time, more than seven hours after the first wave of bombers, Marshall's warning message reached the desk of General Short, who forlornly sent a copy to Admiral Kimmel. The message informed the U.S. commanders at Pearl Harbor that the Japanese were delivering an ultimatum to Washington at 1:00 P.M. (8:00 A.M. in Hawaii). "Just what significance the hour set may have we do not know, but be on the alert accordingly." Kimmel angrily

crumpled the paper and threw it into the wastebasket. Washington learned later that afternoon that Japan had gone on to attack the Philippines, Thailand, Malaya, and other places in the Pacific.

Into the Abyss

President Roosevelt appeared before a solemn Congress at 12:29 P.M. on the gray-skied day following the Pearl Harbor attack. As he slowly worked his way to the rostrum of the House of Representatives, both Democrats and Republicans gave him the greatest ovation of his presidency. Among the many dignitaries in the huge and packed chamber was Mrs. Woodrow Wilson, who had attended a similar congressional session some twenty-five years before and now sat next to President Roosevelt's wife Eleanor. With movie cameras whirring and bright lights glazing the podium, the president opened the black looseleaf notebook before him and began speaking slowly and emphatically into a veritable web of microphones: "Yesterday, December 7, 1941—a date which will live in infamy—the United States of America was suddenly and deliberately attacked by naval and air forces of the Empire of Japan." After recounting the Japanese attacks on Hawaii, the Philippines, and other areas in southeast Asia, he dramatically declared that "with confidence in our armed forces—with the unbounded determination of our people—we will gain the inevitable triumph—so help us God." He concluded by asking Congress to declare war on Japan.

In a bare six minutes President Roosevelt finished a speech that launched the United States into a new era of history. Before the attack, isolationists and pacifists in the country had rigidly resisted the possibility of war; national anger and disgust over Pearl Harbor quieted them as no other single event could have done. In just thirty-three minutes on that same day of December 8, the Senate voted unanimously for war, and the House followed with only one dissent—that of Jeanette Rankin, a pacifist from Montana who had also voted against war in 1917. News soon arrived that the U.S. decision for war had come just a few hours after that of the British.

Three days later, on December 11, Germany and Italy declared war on the United States, resolving Washington's dilemma of whether to declare war on Japan's Axis partners. Both houses of Congress reacted that same day by unanimously voting for war with Germany and Italy.

Hitler's decision to declare war on the United States constitutes perhaps his biggest mistake of the war. The United States's preoccupation with Japan would certainly have freed him to focus on European affairs. Germany's declaration of war did not rest on any treaty obligations with the Japanese, because the Tripartite Pact included no such stipulation. Hitler doubtless had other reasons. The United States, the German government declared, had moved from "initial violations of

neutrality" to "open acts of war against Germany." Hitler thus posed as the chief defender of international law against alleged U.S. violations. But even more important, he thought the Japanese attack on Pearl Harbor had all but disabled the United States and that he could now win the war with Britain and the Soviet Union by closing off the Atlantic sea-lanes and thereby ending U.S. lend-lease aid. If so, he miscalculated—and badly. Hitler's call for war freed Roosevelt from enormous public pressure to concentrate solely on Japan and greatly relieved Churchill, whose priority also was the Nazis. In accordance with the ABC-1 staff agreements of early 1941, the Roosevelt administration prepared to focus first on the Axis in Europe.

Selected Readings

Ambrose, Stephen E., and Brinkley, Douglas G. *Rise to Globalism: American Foreign Policy since 1938.* 8th ed., 1997.

Bailey, Thomas A., and Ryan, Paul B. *Hitler vs. Roosevelt: The Undeclared Naval War.* 1979.

Barnes, Harry E. *Perpetual War for Perpetual Peace: A Critical Examination of the Foreign Policy of Franklin D. Roosevelt and Its Aftermath.* 1952.

Barnhart, Michael A. *Japan Prepares for Total War: The Search for Economic Security, 1919–1941.* 1987.

Beard, Charles A. *President Roosevelt and the Coming of the War.* 1948.

Blumenthal, Henry. *Illusion and Reality in Franco-American Diplomacy, 1914–1945.* 1986.

Breitman, Richard, and Kraut, Alan M. *American Refugee Policy and European Jewry, 1933–1945.* 1987.

Burns, James M. *Roosevelt: The Soldier of Freedom, 1940–1945.* 1970.

Butow, Robert J. C. *The John Doe Associates: Backdoor Diplomacy for Peace, 1941.* 1974.

———. *Tojo and the Coming of the War.* 1961.

Churchill, Winston S. *The Second World War.* 6 vols., 1948–1953.

Clifford, J. Garry, and Spencer, Samuel R., Jr. *The First Peacetime Draft.* 1986.

———. *America's Response to China: An Interpretive History of Sino-American Relations.* 2000.

Cole, Wayne S. *America First: The Battle against Intervention, 1940–1941.* 1953.

———. *Roosevelt and the Isolationists, 1932–1945.* 1983.

Compton, James V. *The Swastika and the Eagle: Hitler, the United States and the Origins of World War II.* 1967.

Dallek, Robert. *Franklin D. Roosevelt and American Foreign Policy, 1932–1945.* 1979.

Divine, Robert A. *The Illusion of Neutrality.* 1962.

———. *The Reluctant Belligerent: American Entry into World War II.* Rev. ed., 1979.

Doenecke, Justus D. *The Battle Against Intervention, 1939–1941.* 1997.

———, and Wilz, John E. *From Isolation to War, 1931–1941.* 1991.

Farago, Ladislas. *The Broken Seal: The Story of "Operation Magic" and the Pearl Harbor Disaster.* 1967.

Feis, Herbert. *The Road to Pearl Harbor.* 1950.

Freidel, Frank. *Franklin D. Roosevelt: A Rendezvous with Destiny.* 1990.

Friedlander, Saul. *Prelude to Downfall: Hitler and the United States, 1939–1941.* 1967.

Haines, Gerald K. "Under the Eagle's Wing: The Franklin Roosevelt Administration Forges An American Hemisphere," *Diplomatic History* 1 (1977): 373–88.

Heinrichs, Waldo. "President Franklin D. Roosevelt's Intervention in the Battle of the Atlantic, 1941," *Diplomatic History* 10 (1986): 311–32.

———. *Threshold of War: Franklin Delano Roosevelt and American Entry into World War II.* 1988.

Hurstsfield, Julian G. *America and the French Nation, 1939–1945.* 1986.

Iriye, Akira. *The Origins of the Second World War in Asia and the Pacific.* 1987.

Jacobs, Travis B. *America and the Winter War, 1939–1940.* 1981.

Jonas, Manfred. *Isolationism in America, 1935–1941.* 1966.

———. *The United States and Germany: A Diplomatic History.* 1984.

Jones, Howard. "One World: An American Perspective," in James H. Madison, ed., *Wendell Willkie: Hoosier Internationalist*, 103–24. 1992.

Kimball, Warren F. *The Most Unsordid Act: Lend-Lease, 1939–1941.* 1969.

LaFeber, Walter. *The Clash: A History of U.S.-Japanese Relations.* 1997.

Langer, William L., and Gleason, S. Everett. *The Challenge to Isolation, 1937–1940.* 1952.

———. *The Undeclared War, 1940–1941.* 1953.

Layton, Edwin T. *"And I Was There": Pearl Harbor and Midway—Breaking the Secrets.* 1985.

Leutze, James R. *Bargaining for Supremacy: Anglo-American Naval Collaboration, 1937–1941.* 1977.

Lipstadt, Deborah. *Beyond Belief: The American Press and the Coming of the Holocaust, 1933–1945.* 1986.

Maddux, Thomas R. *Years of Estrangement: American Relations with the Soviet Union, 1934–1941.* 1980.

Melosi, Martin. *The Shadow of Pearl Harbor.* 1977.

Miller, Edward S. *War Plan Orange: The U.S. Strategy to Defeat Japan, 1897–1945.* 1991.

Neu, Charles E. *The Troubled Encounter: The United States and Japan.* 1975.

Offner, Arnold A. *The Origins of the Second World War.* 1975.

Penkower, Monty N. *The Jews Were Expendable: Free World Diplomacy and the Holocaust.* 1983.

Prange, Gordon W. *At Dawn We Slept: The Untold Story of Pearl Harbor.* 1981.

———. *Pearl Harbor: The Verdict of History.* 1986.

Read, Anthony, and Fisher, David. *The Deadly Embrace: Hitler, Stalin, and the Nazi-Soviet Pact, 1939–1941.* 1989.

Reynolds, David. *The Creation of the Anglo-American Alliance, 1937–1941: A Study in Competitive Cooperation.* 1982.

Schneider, James C. *Should America Go to War? The Debate over Foreign Policy in Chicago, 1939–1941.* 1989.

Schroeder, Paul W. *The Axis Alliance and Japanese-American Relations, 1941.* 1958.

Smith, Geoffrey. *To Save a Nation: American Counter-Subversives, the New Deal and the Coming of World War II.* 1973.

Smith, Kevin. *Conflict over Convoys: Anglo-American Logistics Diplomacy in World War Two.* 1996.

Steele, Richard W. "The Great Debate: Roosevelt, the Media, and the Coming of the War, 1940–1941," *Journal of American History* 71 (1984): 69–92.

Sun, You-Li. *China and the Origins of the Pacific War, 1931–41.* 1993.

Tansill, Charles C. *Back Door to War: The Roosevelt Foreign Policy, 1933–1941.* 1952.

Toland, John. *Infamy: Pearl Harbor and Its After-math.* 1982.

———. *The Rising Sun: The Decline and Fall of the Japanese Empire, 1936–1945.* 2 vols., 1970.

Utley, Jonathan G. *Going to War with Japan, 1937–1941.* 1985.

Weintraub, Stanley. *Long Day's Journey into War: December 7, 1941.* 1991.

Wilson, Theodore A. *The First Summit: Roosevelt and Churchill at Placentia Bay, 1941.* 1969.

Wohlstetter, Roberta. *Pearl Harbor: Warning and Decision.* 1962.

Wright, Gordon. *The Ordeal of Total War, 1939–1945.* 1968.

Wyman, David S. *The Abandonment of the Jews: America and the Holocaust, 1941–1945.* 1984.

CHAPTER 8

Wartime Diplomacy and the Origins of the Cold War, 1941–1945

The Strange Alliance

The central thread holding together the "Strange Alliance" of World War II—primarily Britain, the United States, and the Soviet Union—was the common need to defeat Hitler. As long as the Nazis posed a threat, the Big Three overcame their individual interests and worked together. But wartime unity could not permanently dispel their fundamental social, political, economic, and cultural differences. On the one hand, the democracies still felt revulsion at Marxist revolutionary ideology, the bloody Stalinist purges of the 1930s, the Nazi-Soviet Pact, and the Soviet attack on Finland in 1939 and brutal occupation of the Baltic States the following year. The Soviets, on the other hand, distrusted capitalism, bitterly recalled the West's hostile treatment of their new regime after the Bolshevik Revolution of 1917, and remained suspicious of their Anglo-American partners throughout the war. Some Americans, to be sure, believed that wartime cooperation would smooth doubts in the period afterward; indeed, the war did temporarily set aside ideological differences, raising false hopes of world peace by leaving the erroneous impression that the problems straining the alliance were of no lasting consequence. Yet beneath the surface lay profound difficulties that erupted in angry disputes once the tide of war turned in favor of the Allies and their attention began to focus on postwar matters.

These harsh undertones became especially evident in the bitter wartime controversy over the "second front" in France. From the time of the U.S. entry into the war until the Allied invasion of Normandy on June 6, 1944, the Soviets bore the brunt of the fighting against the Nazis and continually urged the Americans and British to relieve them by opening an assault on Germany's western flank. But for military and political reasons Churchill persuaded Roosevelt to approve instead a landing in North Africa, followed by an invasion of Italy through the "soft underbelly" of Europe. U.S. military leaders questioned the strategic wisdom of the North African campaign, but when British efforts in Egypt faltered in early 1942, Roosevelt gave in to Churchill's wishes and postponed a cross-channel invasion. The second front—aimed at Germany itself—became feasible only in mid-1943, when the United States achieved military superiority and thereby became the dominant voice in the Allied war effort.

Other wartime difficulties revealed the lack of trust between the Americans and British on the one side and the Soviets on the other.

They rarely shared military strategies, strongly opposed the reciprocal use of airstrips, steadfastly refused to cooperate in accepting the surrenders of Axis powers, and constantly worried that their partners might sign a separate peace with the Germans. They also disagreed over the makeup and procedure of the projected United Nations Organization, the role of Nationalist China in the postwar world, and the amounts of lend-lease war materiel that should go to the Soviet Union. The United States and Britain also withheld from the Soviet Union their research into atomic weaponry. Indeed, in the final stages of development the United States concealed information from the British.

Despite the grand aims proclaimed in the Atlantic Charter, not one of the three powers remained faithful to self-determination. Both the United States and Britain ultimately twisted the idealistic pronouncements either to satisfy their own national interests or to meet political or military realities, even though their actions violated both the spirit and the letter of the Charter. The Soviet Union lukewarmly approved the Charter, but with the glaring exception "that the practical application of these principles will necessarily adapt itself to the circumstances, needs, and historic peculiarities of particular countries." Stalin could not reconcile self-determination with his overarching concern for security along his country's western border. Two German invasions in the twentieth century alone convinced him of the necessity of having "friendly" neighboring states.

The Soviet quest for security required expansion along its western frontier, and this forecasted a clash with the defenders of the Atlantic Charter. In late 1941 Stalin demanded that Britain recognize Soviet annexation of the Baltic States and part of Finland. When the London government passed this to Washington for consideration, the United States turned it down as a violation of the Atlantic Charter. Yet when Soviet Foreign Commissar Vyacheslav M. Molotov later demanded a piece of Rumania and recognition

of Soviet control over eastern Poland, the British agreed to a twenty-year pact by which both nations promised to "act in accordance with the two principles of not seeking territorial aggrandizement for themselves and of noninterference in the internal affairs of other States." The British were determined to maintain their empire, which meant forsaking self-determination. Americans, too, understood the importance of national security. They could not grant independence to the strategically important Pacific islands and expect to remain secure both in that area and at home.

Thus, ironically, the Strange Alliance began to disintegrate in direct proportion to its successes in the war. From the call for self-determination would come a whole new series of nation-states rising from the remains of the old colonial system, many of which wanted to act independently and became vital players in the growing bipolar struggle between East and West. National and ideological differences surfaced again among the Big Three, forcing them farther apart. Despite the widely heralded achievements of the wartime conferences at Teheran, Yalta, and Potsdam, the alliance continued its steady demise until its final collapse led to the Cold War.

Beginnings of the Wartime Alliance

Shortly after Pearl Harbor the United States moved swiftly toward closer relations with the British against the Axis. In late December Churchill crossed the Atlantic again, this time to discuss wartime strategy with Roosevelt. The visit, code-named Arcadia, led to the establishment in January 1942 of the Combined Chiefs of Staff (CCS), which was composed of the United States's Joint Chiefs of Staff and representatives of the British Chiefs, who together set up quarters in the Pentagon. Under the direction of the president and the prime minister, the CCS formulated and implemented a strategy that adhered to the earlier ABC-1 staff agreements by focusing on Germany before turning to Japan. The Americans and British did not enter a formal alliance, but the United States drafted the "Declaration by United Nations" on January 1, which established what Churchill termed the "Grand Alliance" of the United Kingdom, Soviet Union, United States, Nationalist China, and all others opposing the Axis and endorsing the Atlantic Charter. Ultimately signed by forty-seven nations, the Declaration assured wartime unity, prohibited a separate peace, and encouraged the creation of a postwar peace organization.

The Axis threat also caused the United States to seek greater unity within the hemisphere. The Roosevelt administration formalized by treaty the Act of Havana of July 1940, by which representatives from the American republics could temporarily install a provisional government in any European possession in the New World that was in danger of enemy takeover. In mid-January 1942 the American republics gathered in Rio de Janeiro and proclaimed that a violation of one nation's sovereignty was a threat to all. The United States's Good Neighbor policy perhaps paid dividends, because every Latin American republic except Chile and Argentina immediately broke diplomatic relations with the Axis. Chile did a year later, and Argentina declared war on the Axis in late March 1945.

The United States talked about raising Nationalist China to major power status, despite Churchill's strong opposition. Although Roosevelt agreed to concentrate U.S. resources in Europe and the Soviet Union, he feared a separate Sino-Japanese peace and insisted on establishing a postwar balance of power in Asia that included China as the dominant force. But the White House based its hopes on an exaggerated estimate of China that resulted from decades of self-delusion and paternal sentiment. The United States's long-standing commitment to the Open Door, combined with its determination to fit Jiang Jieshi into the mold of a capable, Christian, democratic leader, convinced Americans that China could become a postwar pillar of peace. Yet by the time the United States entered the war, China had already undergone four difficult years of

conflict with the Japanese that forced Jiang to retreat inland to Chongqing. Churchill was incredulous that the United States "rated the Chinese armies as a factor to be mentioned in the same breath as the armies of Russia." The hope of making China into a major power, he privately remarked, was "an absolute farce."

In reality, Roosevelt's China policy was primarily a matter of rhetoric, because neither U.S. military nor U.S. economic aid matched his promises. Germany was the priority in the war; until its defeat the United States intended to keep China in the war to occupy Japan.

Until mid-1943 Churchill's argument against a second front in Western Europe prevailed, largely because the British had more soldiers and materiel in the war than did the United States and was therefore in the position to determine policy. Stalin repeatedly demanded an immediate cross-channel invasion of Europe to draw the Germans out of the Soviet Union, but even though General Dwight D. Eisenhower warned that a postponed second front could drive the Soviet Union out of the war and bring the "blackest day in history," Churchill won the argument for an initial assault through southern Europe rather than its western part. The United States suspected that Britain emphasized the Mediterranean to preserve its imperial controls in the postwar period; the British insisted that their strategy was vital to softening Germany *before* an invasion through France.

The truth doubtless encompasses both arguments. Churchill was legitimately concerned about postwar arrangements in Central Europe should the Soviet armies get there first. But he also had practical wartime considerations. The deaths of thousands of British soldiers in the trenches of World War I convinced him not to be hasty about a channel assault. The lessons of Dunkirk also bore heavily on his mind. Before sending forces into France, Churchill wanted Germany reeling from a blockade, aerial bombardments, and simultaneous attacks from the south and east. In May 1942, however, Roosevelt had told Molotov in Washington that a second front

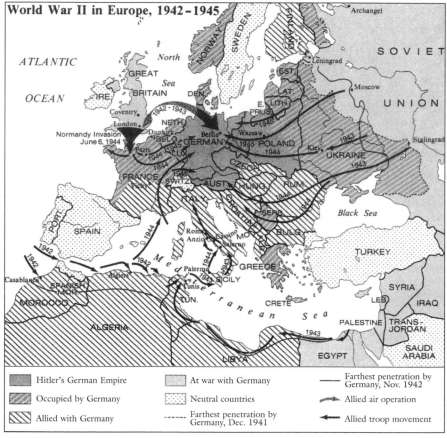

Map 14
After Germany reached its peak in territorial control in 1942, the Allies slowly turned
the tide with their victory in North Africa and invasion of Europe.

seemed possible that year. The president perhaps hoped that such a statement would postpone the delineation of boundaries until after
the war, but his assurances led to no action
and deepened Stalin's suspicions that his so-
called allies sought to prolong the Soviet-
German war to drain both countries and
benefit the West.

Britain's success in engineering Operation
TORCH in November 1942 demonstrated
how the exigencies of war often overcame the
incompatibilities of ideologies. Rather than
calling for a cross-channel attack, this strategy
entailed an Allied invasion of French North
Africa, followed by assaults on Sicily and Italy
in the summer of 1943. To achieve success,

Anglo-American forces made an arrangement
with Franco in Spain that facilitated the Allied
landing in North Africa. In the spirit of
Churchill's earlier remark about helping the
Soviets against Hitler, Roosevelt cited a Bulgarian proverb: "My children, you are permitted in time of great danger to walk with
the Devil until you have crossed the bridge."

The United States and Britain were aware
of Franco's fascist and pro-Axis neutrality, but
they also recognized that should Spain seize
Gibraltar, it could cut off the Allies from the
Mediterranean and severely hamper the North
African campaign. After assuring Franco that
they had no interest in his African possessions,
Britain and the United States furnished Spain

enough raw materials (including oil) for daily consumption and purchased Spanish ore at a higher price than market value, thereby tying the country to the Allies without giving it enough materiel to cause trouble. For added assurance, they sent a huge military contingent to prevent an assault on Allied invasion forces by Franco's 150,000 men in Spanish Morocco. After the landing in Africa, the United States stopped the oil shipments. The strategy was successful. Franco did not interfere with the North African campaign, and with each Axis defeat his alleged neutrality shifted more in favor of the Allies.

The United States also found it expedient to maintain relations with Vichy France, which had averted occupation by collaborating with the Nazis. But even though the Roosevelt administration sent lend-lease materiel to areas under Free French control, it refused to recognize the government of "Free France," then in exile in London and led by the imperious General Charles de Gaulle. The U.S. ambassador to Vichy France, Admiral William Leahy, authorized shipments of coal, sugar, and cotton to persuade the French to withhold naval assistance from the Axis.

Help from Vichy France also proved critical to the Allied invasion of North Africa, because U.S. agents in Algiers and French Morocco had made secret agreements with the French to facilitate the landing. Two days earlier General Eisenhower, who was concerned about his troops' lack of fighting experience, reached an agreement with the commander of Vichy forces in Algiers, Admiral Jean Darlan, recognizing him as French leader in North Africa in exchange for his assistance in the Allied invasion. During the expedition, in fact, Darlan ordered his men to cease firing on the Allies as they approached the shore. Soon thereafter Darlan was assassinated by a supporter of Free France. In October 1944 the Big Three realized that de Gaulle had attracted a huge following in France and recognized him as head of the provisional government.

After the successful Allied landing in North Africa, Roosevelt and Churchill met in mid-January 1943 at Casablanca in French Morocco to discuss future military campaigns and reassure the Soviets of continued Allied unity. Stalin had declined an invitation to the conference because of his preoccupation with the war at home. Roosevelt, however, took this to mean that the Soviets were concerned over the delayed second front and the Anglo-American success in North Africa. He had to convince Stalin that neither the United States nor Britain would sign separate peace treaties with Hitler's allies—a difficult goal in view of the recent Anglo-American dealings with Spain and Vichy France.

At Casablanca, Roosevelt and Churchill first decided to proceed with the invasion of Sicily and Italy. They then turned to their major concern of assuring the Soviets that they would sign no early peace with the Axis. Consequently, near the close of the conference, Roosevelt told reporters that "the democracies' war plans were to compel the 'unconditional surrender' of the Axis." In contrast with the outcome of World War I, the victors in this war intended to leave no doubts about which side had lost. Unconditional surrender, Roosevelt emphasized, did not mean "the destruction of the population of Germany, Italy, or Japan," but it did mean "the destruction of the philosophies in those countries which are based on conquest and the subjugation of other people."

The Casablanca Declaration proved integral to maintaining Allied unity. It possibly hardened Axis resistance and lengthened the war. It perhaps also helped to set the pattern for the postwar era by guaranteeing a power imbalance that the Soviet armies quickly exploited. But the immediate aim of the Declaration was to encourage continued wartime cooperation among the Allies by postponing arguments over postwar matters. The British and Americans were too dependent on the Red Army to fall out over postwar boundaries in eastern Europe. A breakdown in the alliance could have promoted independent Soviet military action in the Balkans and Central Europe. Worse, a race between the Soviets and the Anglo-Americans for military control in Europe could have caused war between members of the alliance. The Casablanca Declaration helped to hold the Big Three together.

Toward Postwar Arrangements

The Allies' successful North African campaign proved critical in turning the war in their favor by mid-1943 and, for that reason, encouraged all three powers to look more toward postwar arrangements. German forces had surrendered at Stalingrad in early February, and in mid-May both the Germans and the Italians laid down their arms in North Africa. The U.S. Navy had meanwhile pushed back the Japanese at Midway and taken the offensive in the Pacific. In summer 1943 the German attack on the Soviet Union failed, and the Allied assault on Sicily led to Mussolini's fall and the surrender of Italy in early September, followed by its turnaround declaration of war on Germany the next month.

The previous April, however, the alliance had undergone a severe test after the Germans unearthed nearly 10,000 Polish soldiers in a mass grave in the Katyn Forest close to Smolensk and blamed the Soviets for the atrocity. Stalin hotly denied the allegation and attributed the slaughter to the Nazis. And yet, evidence now shows that the *Soviets* had executed the soldiers during the spring of 1940. In 1943, however, the Americans and British chose to believe Stalin—even though he suspiciously refused to approve a request by the London Poles for an investigation by the International Red Cross. Both Churchill and Roosevelt joined the Soviet premier in opposing such an inquiry behind German lines as a "fraud" and certainly injurious to the alliance. Churchill insisted that the Germans' intention was to break up the alliance and persuaded the Poles to let the matter go because "nothing you can do will bring them [the slain soldiers] back." Stalin meanwhile took advantage of the opportunity to break relations with the London Poles and use the reestablishment of such relations as a bargaining point for better

Polish borders and a government more amenable to Soviet wishes. Not by coincidence did he also attempt to strengthen his bond with the Anglo-American allies by dissolving the Comintern in May, thereby suggesting that his country did not wish to subvert Western governments.

The war's successes, however, increasingly exposed the cracks in the alliance. By summer 1943 the Soviets were infuriated because the emphasis in lend-lease shipments had shifted to the Mediterranean and Pacific rather than to their own country. Stalin was also displeased at first with the Anglo-American attempt to negotiate a separate peace with Italy. But he did not push the issue, probably because he realized that his two wartime partners had set a valuable precedent: The armies that liberated a country from the Germans would determine its postwar status.

The most controversial issue remained the second front. Roosevelt had argued for a cross-channel invasion during spring 1943, but again Churchill refused. Although the Germans failed to take either Moscow or Stalingrad, they had overrun the oil fields of the Caucasus, killing millions of Soviet soldiers and civilians in the process. Then Stalin received word that Roosevelt and Churchill had decided in an August 1943 meeting in Quebec that the invasion would not take place until May of the following year. Stalin was angry as he wrote a note to Roosevelt: "Need I speak of the dishearteningly negative impression that this fresh postponement of the second front ... will produce in the Soviet Union?" Again, he complained to the president that "to date it has been like this, the U.S.A. and Britain reached agreement between themselves while the U.S.S.R. [Union of Soviet Socialist Republics] is informed ... as a third party looking passively on. I must say that this situation cannot be tolerated any longer."

In view of the strained relations within the alliance, the United States and Britain decided to meet with the Soviet Union in Moscow at a Council of Foreign Ministers conference in

October 1943. Hull was elderly, in poor health, and deathly afraid of flying because of claustrophobia, but he insisted on making the long trip to meet with British Foreign Secretary Anthony Eden and Soviet Foreign Commissar Molotov. Postwar questions dominated the discussions. Stalin was particularly concerned that the Italian surrender would allow U.S. and British armies to reach Central Europe before his own forces did and therefore dictate surrender terms. With his armies 600 miles away, he would find it difficult to restore the 1941 boundaries.

The Moscow Conference had several notable results. It led to the establishment of an Advisory Council on Italy, which promoted Allied cooperation and guaranteed a government "made more democratic by the introduction of representatives of those sections of the Italian people who have always opposed Fascism." The foreign ministers agreed to establish a European Advisory Commission in London to make proposals on wartime issues and work out peace arrangements. They issued a declaration calling for "a free and independent Austria," and they agreed to partition Germany among the Big Three powers until they could decide its fate. Stalin again received assurances of a second front, and he reciprocated by promising Soviet entry into the war against Japan after the European conflict was over.

The Moscow meeting also led, in October, to the Declaration of Four Nations on General Security, which was the first Allied guarantee of a postwar world peace organization. Congress in Washington had recently passed resolutions of overwhelming support for such a move, and at Hull's urgings, Molotov agreed to allow the Chinese ambassador in Moscow to join the Big Three in calling for "a general international organization, based on the principle of the sovereign equality of all peace-loving states, and open to membership by all such states, large and small, for the maintenance of international peace and security." Later, before Congress, Hull let his zeal take command of his senses when he asserted

that the Moscow Conference showed that there would "no longer be need for spheres of influence, for alliances, for a balance of power, or any other of the special arrangements through which, in the unhappy past, the nations strove to safeguard their security or to promote their interests."

The Big Three in Moscow also released a statement on German wartime atrocities, which assured punishment for crimes inflicted on peoples in countries occupied by Nazi armies—but *not* for those acts committed against their own Jewish citizens. News of Jewish persecutions in Germany had reached the United States before the war, but throughout the Great Depression Americans had opposed granting asylum to refugees while millions of Americans were unemployed. Many also were indifferent toward the Jews or were simply anti-Semitic. During the war the immigration restrictions remained in effect, because the state department feared that German or Soviet spies might easily hide among refugees.

By August 1942 the United States had received reports of the Nazis' mass extermination of Jews, but neither the state department nor the White House had an official reaction. Research later established that in Poland, at Auschwitz-Birkenau, about one million Jews perished in specially constructed gas chambers and that by autumn 1942 the Germans had killed all but 70,000 of Warsaw's 380,000 Jewish residents. In January 1944 Morgenthau (himself a Jew) persuaded the president to establish a War Refugee Board authorized to set up refugee centers in the countries bordering Germany. Roosevelt later called the Nazis' mass murders "one of the blackest crimes of all history." But he did not back his sentiments with action and, despite pressure on Americans to bomb railways leading to the extermination camps, the war department countered that this tactic would divert the military effort and delay victory—the only conceivable way to save the Jews. By the end of the war the Nazis had executed six million Jews in the Holocaust,

Buchenwald
Jewish concentration camp near Jean, Germany, liberated by U.S. troops of the 80th
Division in mid-April 1945. *National Archives, Washington, D.C.*

about sixty percent of the total number living in the European areas seized by Germany.

Inside the United States, Japanese-Americans also felt the full brunt of the war. The Pearl Harbor attack had combined with long-time racial prejudice and fear of sabotage and espionage to unleash a furious wave of anti-Japanese feeling that encompassed even those who had been born citizens of the United States. Americans throughout the nation supported President Roosevelt's executive order of February 1942, which directed the U.S. Army to evacuate and incarcerate about 110,000 Americans of Japanese ancestry. Citizens from all over the country, including every Japanese-American resident of California, Oregon, and Washington, were held in ten barbed-wire enclosures euphemistically labeled "military areas" but in reality concentration camps that stretched from the desert of California to the Arkansas swampland. Under the rubric of "military necessity," the White House condoned an action that clearly violated the due process guarantees of the Constitution. Explainable perhaps as an outgrowth of wartime hysteria, the relocation program is nonetheless difficult to justify in view of the Japanese-Americans' unquestioned loyalty to the United States and the fact that they comprised less than one-tenth of one percent of the U.S. population.

Meanwhile Roosevelt wanted to inject more life into the wartime role of China and invited Jiang to meet with Churchill and himself in Egypt's capital city of Cairo in November 1943. There, the three leaders issued the Cairo Declaration, which called for the unconditional surrender of Japan and proclaimed that "Japan shall be stripped of all the islands in the Pacific" acquired since 1914. Manchuria, Formosa, and the Pescadores would return to China, whereas Korea was to become "free and independent" in "due course." The president had earlier secured an end to extraterritoriality and other special privileges in China, and now, in December 1943, the U.S. Congress repealed exclusion laws, authorized immigration in accordance with the same quota system long applicable to Europeans, and permitted naturalization. The Cairo Declaration of unconditional surrender perhaps inspired the Japanese to fight harder, but it also raised Chinese and Korean morale, and it assured the Soviets that their allies would sign no separate peace with Japan.

Shortly after the Cairo Conference, Roosevelt, Churchill, and Stalin met, for the first time, in the Iranian capital of Teheran in late November 1943. Both military and political matters were on the agenda, but the three

leaders were as interested in examining each other as in dealing with the wartime issues. Roosevelt considered Stalin "very confident, very sure of himself[,] . . . altogether quite impressive." The president seemed to have decided to cultivate a close relationship with Stalin—even at Churchill's expense. Roosevelt refused to meet privately with the prime minister for fear that Stalin would suspect them of working together; yet he talked with the Soviet premier three times without Churchill being present. At one point in the talks, Roosevelt alleviated tension with Stalin by making fun of Churchill's British mannerisms. The premier laughed, whereas the prime minister turned red with anger. Stalin was not averse to playing a macabre game. At a dinner party he infuriated Churchill by lightheartedly suggesting that the Allies exterminate 50,000 to 100,000 German officers. When the prime

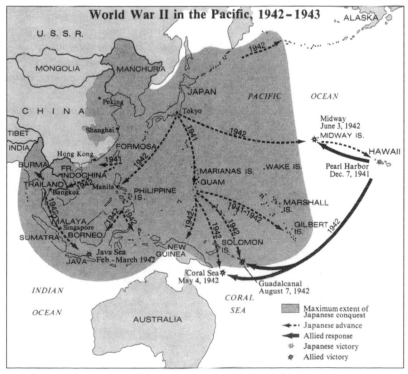

Map 15
The Japanese reached the height of their power in Asia in 1943.

minister indignantly retorted that his people could not condone "mass executions," Roosevelt remarked that surely a more acceptable figure would be 49,000. Churchill stalked from the room, later consoled by Roosevelt's assurance that he had been joking.

A number of exploratory discussions helped to establish each nation's position. Roosevelt and Churchill realized that Stalin would not risk Soviet security for the Atlantic Charter. When Roosevelt declared that numerous Americans of Baltic background sought self-determination for Lithuania, Latvia, and Estonia, Stalin refused to negotiate. He blandly asserted that these people had already voted to become part of the Soviet Union. But Americans "neither knew nor understood this," the president tried to explain. Then the U.S. government had "some propaganda work" ahead of it, Stalin crisply replied. On Poland, Stalin cited security reasons for wanting its borders moved farther west to include parts of Germany to the Oder River; in the meantime the Soviet Union would incorporate Poland's eastern territory to the Curzon Line, which included regions in White Russia and the Ukraine. Roosevelt agreed with Stalin's objectives but warned that for political reasons he could not "publicly take part in any such arrangement at the present time." The presidential election of 1944 lay ahead, he privately told the Soviet premier, and six million Polish-American voters could determine the outcome. Ever the realist, Stalin affirmed his understanding of the president's position.

The German question also caused disagreements at Teheran. Stalin wanted Germany's total dismemberment, whereas Roosevelt recommended dividing the country into five autonomous districts and setting up international supervision of the Kiel Canal and Ruhr and Saar valleys. Churchill sought to strip power from Prussia and tie the remainder of Germany to Austria and Hungary in a Danubian confederation. The three leaders decided to postpone the issue for future consideration. Although Stalin's expectations violated the Atlantic Charter's pledge against territorial changes without "the freely expressed wishes of the peoples concerned," the West felt compelled to go along because of its need for Soviet help in the war. A key consideration was the location of the Red Armies: They were already in or close to the areas in question.

Before the conference adjourned on December 1, the president called for a world peace organization led by the "Four Policemen," which implied the creation of balance-of-power relationships based on spheres of influence. Stalin shared Churchill's doubts about China's potential for playing such a critical role but agreed that any peace organization had to be "world-wide and not regional." The Soviet premier raised the possibility of establishing two regional organizations: in Europe, the Big Three plus one other nation and in Asia, the Big Three and China. Churchill was pleased with the proposed arrangements. The major threats to world peace, he believed, were "hungry" and "ambitious" nations, and he wanted "the leading nations of the world in the position of rich, happy men." Upon the president's return home, he ebulliently told Americans that he "got along fine" with Stalin and that the United States would "get along very well with him and the Russian people—very well indeed."

The major decision reached at Teheran was to implement Operation OVERLORD, the long-debated cross-channel assault on Europe. The Big Three agreed that it would begin in spring 1944 and that it would occur simultaneously with an Allied drive through southern France and a Soviet offensive from the east. Accordingly, on the morning of June 6, 1944, "D-day" began when more than 100,000 Allied forces launched a massive amphibious invasion at the heavily fortified Normandy Beach in northern France. In the east, Soviet armies initiated a major drive through Poland and the Balkans that forced the surrender of Germany's partner nations. As Allied forces liberated Nazi-held territories in their push toward Berlin, the imminent defeat of Germany further eroded the wartime alliance.

Opening the Second Front
General Dwight D. Eisenhower calls for total victory as paratroopers in England prepare to board planes taking part in the Allied invasion of Normandy Beach in France, June 6, 1944. *National Archives, Washington, D.C.*

In late August 1944, after the hard-fought Allied success at Normandy, the United States gathered with Britain, the Soviet Union, and China at Dumbarton Oaks, a Harvard-owned Georgetown estate in Washington, D.C., to make plans for a postwar United Nations Organization. Their draft charter called for a Security Council of the big powers, a General Assembly of all member nations, a Secretariat, an Economic and Social Council, and an International Court of Justice.

Disagreements immediately arose over several matters relating to the proposed United Nations (UN). The United States wanted China to become a permanent member of the Security Council, whereas Britain preferred France. The Soviet Union finally agreed to allow both China and France into the Council, provided that each of the five major permanent powers had a veto over Council proceedings. But the discussions broke down over voting arrangements in the eleven-member Council (United States, Soviet Union, Great Britain, China, France, and six seats rotated among others in the United Nations) and membership in the Assembly. The Soviets wanted permanent Council members to have the veto power on all issues, whether substantive (legal rights and principles) or procedural (rules of form). This right would include the authority to veto a discussion, an inquiry into, or proposals about resolving a dispute short of war. The Americans would approve the suspension of a member's veto on only those matters in which that member was a party. On the second issue involving the Assembly, the Soviets wanted equal representation for all their sixteen republics. This tactic (so explosive that Roosevelt code-named it the "X matter" to keep it from Americans) would counter Britain's "bloc" of voters from the Commonwealth and the United States's "bloc" of Latin American states. The conference adjourned in October without a resolution of these issues, but with a working draft of a UN charter.

The Allied military advance into Europe also raised the issue of postwar Germany, which the Americans initially tried to resolve in autumn 1944 with the Morgenthau Plan. The central debate among the Allies was whether to rebuild Germany and integrate it into the European economy or to punish and reform the country with economic reprisals, high reparations, and the establishment of a decentralized system of government. Morgenthau presented a plan to the president calling for Germany's dismemberment and the elimination of its war potential. Hull and Stimson warned that such severe treatment of Germany would prolong disorder in Europe, but in a memorandum to Stimson the president defended his position. "It is of the utmost importance that every person in Germany should realize that this time Germany is a defeated nation." He added that "I do not want them to starve to death but . . . if they need food to keep body and soul together beyond what we have, they should be fed three times a day with soup from Army group kitchens. . . . They will remember that experience all their lives."

At the Quebec Conference of mid-September, Roosevelt and Churchill temporarily seemed to support Morgenthau's recommendations for Germany when they initialed a memorandum containing the essence of his plan: "This programme for eliminating the war-making industries in the Ruhr and in the Saar is looking forward to converting Germany into a country primarily agricultural and pastoral in its character." Roosevelt, however, later retreated on his stand. Perhaps to avoid division on the eve of a presidential election, but also to mollify a deeply angered Hull who warned that a revitalized Germany was inte-

gral to a revitalized Europe, the president told Stimson that he had approved the plan "without much thought." Yet he hoped that the British "might inherit Germany's Ruhr business" to facilitate their economic recovery. Churchill likewise changed his stance. He later claimed that he had "violently opposed the idea" at first but had relented to the "insistent" demands of Roosevelt and Morgenthau. Although the two wartime leaders consummated no deal at Quebec, the prime minister perhaps was amenable to the plan in an effort to ensure the approval of nearly seven billion dollars of postwar aid tentatively offered by the United States. In any case, the Morgenthau Plan served as propaganda for the Nazis, who called it a "satanic plan of annihilation" concocted by the Jews and urged fellow Germans to resist it to the death.

In October 1944 Churchill and Stalin met in Moscow and negotiated the controversial "percentages agreement," a clear example of power politics based on spheres of influence that belied Hull's idealistic hopes earlier expressed before Congress. Churchill had warned Roosevelt that they were nearing a "showdown" with the Soviets over the Balkans and in early 1944 had urged a settlement. The president, however, was unable to attend the conference but arranged for his ambassador to the Soviet Union, W. Averell Harriman, to sit in as observer. Roosevelt was uneasy about the postwar objectives of both Churchill and Stalin. He did not favor permanent spheres of influence but would accept a temporary wartime division of authority. The problem was that as Churchill and Stalin came together that autumn, the Soviet Union held the military advantages. The Red Army controlled Rumania; the Communist partisan leader Josip Broz Tito was gaining hold in Yugoslavia (with Allied promises of support); the Soviets were assisting the Communists' spread into Bulgaria; and Greece threatened to break down in a civil war that could result in a Communist takeover. The previous June of 1944, Roosevelt had recognized prevailing realities and rejected state department advice in agreeing to Soviet control over Rumania and British hegemony in Greece, each for three months. He then notified Stalin that the United States would not be bound by any agreements reached in Moscow.

During the Moscow meeting, Churchill made a proposal that caused controversy for many years. He scratched a series of percentage figures onto a scrap of paper and shoved it across the table to Stalin. The prime minister recommended that the Soviet Union receive ninety percent control in Rumania, that Britain receive the same in Greece, that there be an even split in Yugoslavia and Hungary, and that the Soviets get seventy-five percent control in Bulgaria. The remainder would go to the "others." Stalin read the proposal, Churchill recalled, and "took his blue pencil and made a large tick upon it." Perhaps they should burn the paper, Churchill suggested. "No, you keep it," Stalin replied. Churchill's proposal demonstrated that to protect his imperial interests, he was willing to approve Soviet spheres of influence in eastern Europe.

Meanwhile the dismal performance of Jiang's Nationalist Army had proved Churchill correct in his assertion that China was not capable of becoming one of the world's Four Policemen. In July 1944, after Jiang showed increasing reluctance to fight the Japanese, Roosevelt proposed that the Chinese command go to General Joseph Stilwell, who had been chief of staff to the Nationalist Army for over two years but had failed to get along with Jiang—whom he disparagingly dismissed as "the Peanut." When Jiang delayed a response for two months, Roosevelt sent a virtual ultimatum that Stilwell insisted on delivering himself. "I handed this bundle of paprika to the Peanut, and then sank back with a sigh," Stilwell recorded in his diary. "The harpoon hit the little bugger right in the solar plexus, and went right through him." Jiang was thoroughly humiliated and demanded Stilwell's recall. The following November, after the brief replacement of Stilwell with General Albert C. Wedemeyer,

Roosevelt appointed General Patrick Hurley as ambassador to Chongqing.

A Republican and former governor of Oklahoma, Hurley was anything but a diplomat. Ignorant of China, he had some years ago committed a faux pas by thanking Jiang and "*Madame Shek*" for a gift, embarrassing the White House by his ignorance of the difference between a given name and family name. Furthermore, Hurley was loud and obnoxious, often greeting his hosts with Indian yells accompanied by flagrant violations of Asian social customs that included boisterous back slapping and vigorous handshakes. Like his predecessor, Hurley opposed communism but at first favored a coalition government comprised of Jiang's Nationalists and Mao's Communists. Then he underwent a change of heart. Against all advice and without orders, Hurley shifted the goal of his mission from mediating the dispute in China to saving the Nationalist government. The previous August, Hurley had talked with Molotov in Moscow and felt confident that the Soviets intended to help Jiang and that Mao's forces were no threat because they "had no relation whatever to Communism."

Hurley ignored his advisers. The foreign service officers around him argued that Mao's form of communism was tied to the peasants and the land and warned that refusal to help his forces would push them into the arms of the Soviet Union. Some of the so-called "China hands" had already talked with Mao and in January 1945 informed Washington that he was willing to meet with Roosevelt. Hurley, however, suspected his staff of being pro-Communist and blocked the meeting. Indeed, he accused his embassy assistant, John Paton Davies, of trying to subvert Jiang and later arranged to have Davies and a career diplomat, John Service, transferred from China.

In February, Hurley arrived in Washington, where he convinced Roosevelt to continue supporting Jiang. The Nationalist China that was to police Asia soon found itself fighting for its life at home against Mao's Communist forces.

Yalta

By the beginning of 1945, amid an exuberant air of impending Allied victory, the Big Three prepared to deal with postwar problems at a summit conference in Yalta on the Black Sea. Anglo-American forces had been fighting the Germans in the savage Battle of the Bulge in Belgium since the middle of December and were beginning to claw their way toward the Rhine. The Red Armies had pierced the German front en route to Berlin and were in control of Rumania, Poland, Czechoslovakia, Bulgaria, Hungary, and Yugoslavia. In Asia, Japan was a long way from surrender. It remained strong in the Philippines and the Marianas, and its soldiers numbered two million on the Chinese mainland and another two million at home. Japan also had more than 5000 kamikaze (suicide) planes ready for action and another 7000 in reserve.

The West was in no position to make demands in either Europe or Asia. The Soviet Union dominated the field in the West, and the Japanese remained firmly entrenched in the East. The Americans and British believed that Stalin's forces were vital to ending the war in Europe and would prove critical to the final effort in Asia. The United States had perfected no new weapons by early 1945, and its military experts anticipated a long siege of the Japanese islands that, without Soviet assistance, could last until December 1946 and cost one million American lives. In early January 1945 Churchill warned Roosevelt that "this may well be a fateful Conference, coming at a moment when the Great Allies are so divided and the shadow of the war lengthens out before us. At the present time, the end of this war may well prove to be more disappointing than was the last."

From February 4 through 11, 1945, the Big Three met for a second time, at a Crimean resort close to Yalta. The time had come to formulate postwar policy toward eastern Europe; lay plans for Germany's partitioning, occupation, and meeting of war reparations; determine voting and membership regulations for the UN organization; and finalize Soviet entry into the war in Asia. These would be difficult tasks. The idealism of the Atlantic Charter stood in stark contrast with the realities of the world situation. The Americans sought a United Nations, Soviet entry into the war against Japan, diminished Communist influence in Poland, and big power status for Nationalist China. The Soviets wanted a central voice in Poland, favorable boundaries in eastern Europe, a flattened Germany burdened with large-scale reparations, and major concessions in East Asia. The British wanted a French zone in Germany, a Poland safeguarded from the Soviet Union, and, most of all, preservation of the British Empire. The three sets of demands were incompatible.

The Yalta proceedings caused bitter controversy for years after the war. Critics accused Roosevelt of giving away huge portions of Europe and Asia to the Soviets in an unnecessary effort to persuade them to enter the war against Japan. This charge is unfounded. Actually, the Big Three had reached most of the settlements on an informal basis earlier at Teheran. Realist that he was, Roosevelt quite likely conceded eastern Europe to the Soviets as a sphere of influence because, first, he could do nothing to stop it, and second, he considered it a necessary price for securing Stalin's cooperation on other issues—most importantly a UN organization. The powers made secret agreements at Yalta that were deemed essential to the war effort, but in the years afterward these same agreements erroneously took on the appearance of Anglo-American capitulation to the Soviet Union. Most settlements were purposely vague in wording but loud in rhetoric and open to interpretations that benefited each party—and, for those reasons, predictably detrimental to peace. And finally, the Soviets refused to abide by those stipulations that were not subject to flexible readings. With Soviet armies in control of many of the disputed areas, the West could do little to change matters short of going to war. Perhaps, Roosevelt hoped, the Big Three powers could reconcile their differences through a United Nations.

Churchill, Roosevelt, and Stalin
The Big Three meet in the Crimea in February 1945 to make postwar global arrangements. *Franklin D. Roosevelt Library, Hyde Park, New York.*

The most exasperating problem at Yalta was Poland. Of eight plenary sessions at the conference, seven dealt with that question. Churchill called it "the most urgent reason for the Yalta Conference." The Soviets, he knew, regarded favorable boundaries and a strong position within the Polish government as essential to their security. Indeed, two German invasions of Stalin's homeland in the twentieth century had taken place through Poland. As he explained at Yalta, "the question of Poland is not only a question of honor but also a question of security. Throughout history, Poland has been the corridor through which the enemy has passed into Russia." Poland was a matter "of life and death for the Soviet Union."

No success could take place at Yalta without concessions to the Soviets regarding Poland. The problems in that country exemplified those that disrupted other countries after the war: Two governments claimed legitimacy, one recognized by the Soviets, the other by the West. The United States and Britain considered the London-based government-in-exile to be Poland's legitimate ruling authority; the Soviet Union supported the Lublin provisional government led by the Communists. Stalin demanded Anglo-American support for boundaries that would award Poland a section of eastern Germany along the Oder-Neisse line to compensate for the large part of east Poland that the USSR would receive as a buffer along the Curzon Line of 1919. If the Big Three drew these boundaries, Poland would lose forty percent of its territory and five million people. These expectations were in violation of the Atlantic Charter, but such an argument rang hollow because Poland was already under Red Army control.

Map 16
Stalin considered a "friendly" Poland to be vital to Soviet security.

The Yalta agreements on Poland are comprehensible only in relation to Soviet security demands and the military advantages held by its armies. Favorable boundaries and a "friendly" regime, in the eyes of the Kremlin, were vital interests. Yet the United States and Britain salvaged something. They won the establishment of the Polish Provisional Government of National Unity, which was to be a coalition of Communists from the Lublin group along with "democratic leaders from Poland itself and from Poles abroad." The Lublin government, the starting point for postwar rule, was "pledged to the holding of free and unfettered elections as soon as possible." Thus, Poland's government was to be "more broadly based" through the reorganization of the provisional government along democratic guidelines. On the boundary issue, Poland's temporary eastern border was to be the Curzon Line, but its western boundary remained uncertain. Even though Roosevelt and Churchill were receptive to the Oder River, they were unwilling to drop the line to the Western Neisse. The conferees recognized the impossibility of reaching a settlement at Yalta and decided that "the final delimitation of the Western frontier of Poland should thereafter await the Peace Conference." The Big Three never convened talks on Poland.

Americans interpreted the Yalta accords to mean that a new government in Poland would emerge, but many considered this wishful thinking. Admiral Leahy warned, "Mr. President, this is so elastic that the Russians can stretch it all the way from Yalta to Washington without technically breaking it." Roosevelt replied, "I know, Bill—I know it. But it's the best I can do for Poland at this time."

One of the chief reasons for the optimism that pervaded the Yalta Conference and a brief time afterward was Stalin's agreement to the much heralded and well-publicized "Declaration on Liberated Europe." Sponsored by the United States, it promised Big Three cooperation in forming "interim governmental authorities broadly representative of all democratic elements in the population and pledged

to the earliest possible establishment through free elections of governments responsive to the will of the people." Stalin thus consented to "free" and "democratic" governments in eastern Europe. Hope was not unwarranted, because up to this point he had seemed to keep his promises. He had honored the "percentages agreement" by not interfering with Britain's military actions in Greece during a civil war that broke out in the streets of Athens in December 1944, and his troops were marching toward Berlin to wind down the European war. Weeks after Yalta, when his lack of good faith became evident in Rumania, Poland, and other places in eastern Europe, the United States and Britain could at least point to the Yalta Declaration in condemning Soviet behavior.

The second major subject discussed at Yalta was Germany. The Big Three did not settle Germany's postwar status, but they were in no mood for conciliation and agreed to "take such steps, including the complete disarmament, demilitarization and the dismemberment of Germany as they deem requisite for future peace and security." The negotiators decided to partition Germany into four military zones, the fourth a French sector created from "within the British and American zones." It was a formula for trouble. Eastern Germany and eastern Berlin fell under Soviet occupation, western Germany and western Berlin went to the other three powers, and all four received seats on the Allied Control Commission for Germany.

For a time Stalin staunchly opposed French participation because of their quick collapse in the war, followed by the Vichy government's collaboration with the Germans. Roosevelt had earlier agreed with this view but now changed his position in hope of winning the support of the Free French leader, General Charles de Gaulle, on other postwar issues. Churchill argued that because of expected U.S. troop withdrawals after the war, his country needed a strong France to balance off Germany. To Stalin's objections, Churchill made reference to the Soviets' alignment with

Map 17
Divided Berlin.

the Germans before the June 1941 Nazi invasion, when he pointedly remarked that "every nation had had their difficulties in the beginning of the war and had made mistakes."

German reparations were also an important subject of the deliberations. Stalin demanded extensive reparations to achieve the "military and economic disarmament of Germany"; Churchill insisted on only enough reparations "to destroy the German war potential." Roosevelt and Churchill vaguely conceded to reparations "in kind" but declined to specify an amount until they could assess Germany's economic standing after the war. Roosevelt was particularly concerned about avoiding another war debts-reparations imbroglio in which, as after World War I, the United States paid much of the bill. The Big Three called for the establishment of a reparations commission. The Soviet Union and United States believed that such a commission should use as "a basis of discussion the figure of reparations as $20 billion and 50 percent of these should go to the Soviet Union." The Soviets had made this proposal some time before the conference, and even though the Yalta agreement postponed final settlements until after

future talks, Stalin probably thought he had secured his counterparts' approval of the Soviet Union's receiving $10 billion. The Big Three agreed to secrecy on all arrangements affecting Germany out of fear that the news would fuel Nazi propagandists and prolong the war.

The third matter discussed at Yalta was the projected UN organization. The Big Three had worked out a draft charter at Dumbarton Oaks, even though they had been unable to resolve voting and membership questions. Roosevelt thought the United Nations so vital that he was willing to make concessions on other issues. But Stalin's position on unrestricted use of the veto was unacceptable to Roosevelt and Churchill, who wanted the United Nations to become a forum for discussing all subjects brought before the Council. Stalin finally agreed to suspension of the veto in procedural matters, thereby guaranteeing freedom of discussion, but he retained the right of veto in substantive issues. After Stalin's concession, the United States was in a poor position to deny his request for two additional seats in the General Assembly, one for the Ukraine and the other for White Russia. To prevent political problems at home, Roosevelt secured the consent of Churchill and Stalin to two additional seats for the United States—a right it never exercised. Finally, the Big Three set the date and place for the meeting of the UN Conference on World Organization: April 25, 1945, in the United States. San Francisco became the designated location.

Questions over Nazi-liberated territories also caused division during the Yalta discussions of the United Nations. Because it seemed undesirable either to annex the areas or grant their freedom, the Big Three emerged with a solution similar to the mandate system established under League of Nations supervision: territorial trusteeships. But this agreement aroused deep concern among the British delegates, who felt their empire threatened. Churchill had told Foreign Secretary Anthony Eden that "if the Americans want to take

Japanese islands which they have conquered, let them do so with our blessing and any form of words that may be agreeable to them. But 'Hands Off the British Empire' is our maxim."

U.S. opposition to colonial rule had become increasingly evident as the war progressed toward its end. Roosevelt had made clear that British and French colonial rule violated the principle of self-determination, and Hull had earlier warned that Britain's system of "imperial preference" endangered the open world market he sought to create through reciprocal trade agreements. Indeed, Roosevelt had convinced Churchill to follow the wishes of his predecessors and support India's early independence. But the prime minister would not give up anything else. As early as November 1942—just after Operation TORCH had begun—Churchill indignantly declared before the House of Commons: "I have not become the King's First Minister in order to preside over the liquidation of the British Empire."

The United States knew that the UN trusteeships posed a potential danger to Britain's colonial concerns in the Mediterranean, Persian Gulf, and Asia. In fact, some of Churchill's wartime actions now seemed to fit a pattern designed to defend his colonial interests and the Mediterranean "lifeline." Most notable were his repeated delays on the second front, his insistence on an invasion through North Africa and Italy, and his call for Anglo-American forces to get into Central Europe before the Soviets. Churchill regarded the trusteeships as a means by which the United States intended to break up the British Empire. At one point during the Yalta proceedings he stormed, "I will not have one scrap of British Territory flung into that area. . . . I will have no suggestion that the British Empire is to be put into the dock and examined by everybody to see whether it is up to their standard." Stalin "beamed" at this tirade, Eden later recalled. The Soviet premier jumped up and excitedly paced the room, even stopping to applaud at times. The British had cause for concern. Roosevelt had secretly told Stalin of his desire to dismantle the British Empire, which included granting sovereignty over Hong Kong to China.

The fourth set of discussions at Yalta related to East Asia and proved the most controversial of all because, for military reasons, the arrangements were secret. Roosevelt had come prepared to deal with Stalin's demands regarding that region of the world. Ambassador Harriman had talked with the premier in Moscow the previous December of 1944 and realized that Stalin had raised territorial expectations to the level of demands. On December 15 Harriman forwarded them by telegraph to the White House. Consequently, Roosevelt's Yalta agreements on East Asia were the result of six weeks of studied preparation.

At Yalta, Stalin secured a favored position in East Asia in exchange for his pledge to enter the war against Japan "in two or three months" following Germany's defeat, which was the estimated time required to relocate soldiers to the East. For Stalin's promise to enter the war, the Soviet Union was to regain several possessions lost in the war against Japan in 1904 and 1905. Although the United States did not consult the Chinese before making these agreements, Roosevelt promised to secure Jiang's approval. To placate the Chinese, Stalin agreed to recognize their sovereignty over Manchuria and negotiate a treaty of aid with the Nationalist government. Jiang read the terms in June and considered them "generally OK." The Big Three guaranteed that all conditions would be "unquestionably . . . fulfilled" after Japan's surrender, but they also agreed to keep them secret because news of Soviet entry into the war might stiffen Japan's resistance. Roosevelt had warned Churchill and Stalin that any matter discussed with the Chinese became "known to the whole world in twenty-four hours."

Public reaction to the Yalta agreements was instantaneous and overwhelmingly favorable. *Time* magazine exuberantly hailed the peace conference as the "New Dawn" of civilization. The Declaration on Liberated Europe, the promise of a United Nations, the general atmosphere of good will—all made Yalta the grand climax to the greatest war ever fought. On March 1, 1945, Roosevelt, weak, pale, and drawn, appeared before Congress to report on the conference. Forced to sit in a chair for the first time during a public address because of his frail health and the weight of his steel leg braces, he triumphantly declared (though in slurred and stumbling language) that the UN discussions pointed to "the end of the system of unilateral action and exclusive alliances and spheres of influence and balances of power." Former President Hoover called Yalta a "great hope to the world," renowned writer William L. Shirer labeled it a "landmark in human history," and even the hard-nosed Churchill glossed over his real fears in assuring the House of Commons that "I know of no government which stands to its obligations . . . more solidly than the Russian government."

Indeed, it appeared that a new age had arrived, largely because the divisive Yalta discussions relating to Germany, Poland, and East Asia would remain secret for about a year. Roosevelt's confidant, Harry Hopkins, provided the most realistic assessment of the U.S. delegation's feelings at the time of the conference: "We really believed in our hearts that this was the dawn of the new day we had all been praying for and talking about for so many years. We were absolutely certain that we had won the first great victory of the peace—and, by 'we,' I mean *all* of us, the whole civilized human race." The Soviets had proved "reasonable and farseeing and there wasn't any doubt in the minds of the President or any of us that we could live with them and get along with them peacefully for as far into the future as any of us could imagine. But," Hopkins cautioned, "I have to make one amendment to that—I think we all had in our minds the reservation that we could not foretell what the results would be if anything should happen to Stalin. We felt sure that we could count on him to be reasonable and sensible and understanding—but we never could be sure who or what might be in back of him there in the Kremlin."

Truman, the Bomb, and the End of World War II

On April 12, 1945, Roosevelt suddenly died of a cerebral hemorrhage in Warm Springs, Georgia, leaving the Executive Office to Harry S. Truman. As vice president for less than four months, the former bank clerk, farmer, merchant, army captain in World War I, and senator from Missouri was unaware of the vast complexities of the war, primarily because Roosevelt had purposely kept him uninformed. Truman was a relative unknown, except that he had headed a successful wartime Senate committee charged with investigating the accusations of fraud and mismanagement in the national defense program. Brash, assertive, outspoken, unreflective, hot-tempered, lacking in vision—these descriptions and more followed him during his presidential tenure. Truman was willing to learn, however, and just as important, he was capable of making hard decisions.

The abrupt change in government leadership would eventually cause a long debate over whether ensuing events in foreign affairs might have been much different had Roosevelt lived. Some observers have noted a sharp turn by the new president toward a hard-line policy that worsened relations with the Soviet Union and helped bring on the heightened international tensions referred to as the "Cold War." Less than two weeks after becoming chief executive, Truman so severely chastised Molotov for the Soviets' infractions of the Yalta accords on Poland that the foreign minister indignantly declared, "I have never been talked to like that in my life." "Carry out your agreements," the new president shot back, "and you won't get talked to like that." Proponents of this argument also point out that those who surrounded Truman were deeply suspicious of the Soviets. Leahy considered Stalin "a liar and a crook," and Harriman in Moscow regarded the Soviets as "barbarians" not yet housebroken. Because many of Truman's advisers had also served in the previous administration, it seems that Roosevelt indeed was in firm control of foreign policy. Yet had he survived into the postwar period, the Soviet violations of treaty agreements and other understandings would have become obvious to him as well. In fact, considerable evidence shows that he had already become disenchanted with the Soviets shortly before his death, so it seems unlikely that anything but a Cold War could have developed after the end of World War II.

In one important sense, however, a change had occurred in April 1945: Roosevelt's successor listened more to his advisers, especially those in the state and war (later defense) departments. If the U.S. outlook toward foreign affairs had any consistency, it emanated from those members of the diplomatic corps and military service who had long questioned Soviet motives and continually called for a policy based on realistic self-interest. With Roosevelt at the helm, their warnings had little effect; with Truman in office, they could for-

mulate policy based on the dual premises that Stalin was not trustworthy and that he was not interested in the ideals of the Atlantic Charter. The Soviets' primary concern, Truman's advisers argued, was security. This issue necessitated Soviet control over the neighboring states of eastern Europe, either through Communist infiltration of the governments or, as a last resort, through military force. The United States, they warned, could do little to block the establishment of Soviet spheres of influence. Thus, upon Truman's elevation to the presidency, the primary shift in foreign policy direction stemmed from the growing White House reliance on state and war department advisers, who all advocated a stronger stance against Soviet aggression but one that recognized limitations on what actions the United States could take.

The new president's first major decision was to proceed with plans for the UN Conference on International Organization, scheduled in

Roosevelt and Truman
Roosevelt died in April 1945, leaving the presidency to Truman. *Library of Congress.*

San Francisco in April 1945. Unlike the Paris deliberations of 1919, the conferees this time intended to keep the drafting of the charter for the world organization separate from the peacemaking process. In this manner, the outcome of one set of agreements would not automatically determine the fate of the other. Secretary of State Edward R. Stettinius, Jr., who had succeeded Hull the previous year, headed an eight-member bipartisan delegation to San Francisco, which included the heads of the Senate Foreign Relations Committee and the House Committee on Foreign Affairs. In all, nearly three hundred delegates from fifty nations attended; but in fact the Big Four of Stettinius, British Foreign Secretary Eden, Soviet Foreign Commissar Molotov, and Chinese Foreign Minister T. V. Soong made the key decisions during the evenings spent in the Stettinius penthouse apartment high atop the Fairmont Hotel. The new president had a sense of history. His instructions to Stettinius were to "write a document that would pass the U.S. Senate and that would not arouse such opposition as confronted Woodrow Wilson."

The resultant UN Charter formalized the various compartments within the organization called for at Dumbarton Oaks and Yalta. The Security Council, comprised of the Big Five as permanent members along with six others chosen by the General Assembly for two-year terms, was to be the police force of the United Nations. The Council could render decisions that bound all members, which included making recommendations for breaking diplomatic relations and exerting economic pressure. The intention was to establish an armed force furnished by member states and under the direction of a military staff committee, but the Soviet rift with the West interfered, and the committee was never able to agree on the makeup of the force. The charter prohibited the suspension of the veto on procedural matters, which meant that small countries could take problems before the Security Council if the majority of its members agreed to hear them. The General Assembly also became an

international forum. Its members could engage in almost unlimited debate, and they could make proposals on any international issue falling within the scope of the charter.

The UN Charter also provided for numerous other organizations. The Economic and Social Council was to work under the Assembly and coordinate the work of "specialized agencies." It could "make recommendations for the purpose of promoting respect for, and observance of, human rights and fundamental freedoms for all." The Trusteeship Council, also emerging from the San Francisco meeting, aimed at the ultimate independence of colonial peoples, but its responsibilities were so vaguely worded that Britain and France managed to hold on to their empires, and the United States was able to assume control over Japan's Pacific possessions (the Carolines, Marianas, and Marshalls). According to the Charter, any area in a territory under trust could be designated a "strategic area" and placed under the auspices of the Security Council. Thus, the Council's permanent members could use the veto to maintain exclusive control over any trusteed area. Article 51 of the Charter approved the formation of regional pacts and declared that members had "the inherent right of individual or collective self-defense" in the event of attack, until the Security Council could take "measures necessary to maintain international peace and security." Finally, the Charter created the International Court of Justice, the Secretariat for dispensing administrative duties, and many other special agencies.

In contrast to Wilson's experiences with the League of Nations, the United States quickly became a member of the United Nations. In truth, of course, the UN Charter did not contain a controversial sanctioning process as did the League Charter, because the United States could veto any action deemed self-injurious. In this sense, the advocates of independent internationalism of the post-World War I period would have been pleased with the United Nations. The United States had not adopted Wilson's call for meshing Americans with other peoples in a collective security organization and had instead retained its independent position while pledging to remain involved in international affairs all over the world. To encourage acceptance at home, Truman had shrewdly avoided Wilson's mistakes by making the UN effort bipartisan in nature, thereby ensuring rapid approval at home. On June 26 the delegates signed the UN Charter. About a month afterward, the U.S. Senate approved U.S. membership by the overwhelming margin of eighty-nine to two.

While the UN Conference moved toward conclusion, Allied forces completed the military operations that led to Germany's collapse and the declaration of "V-E Day" on May 8, 1945. Combined Allied armies had penetrated Germany from the east and west, and on May 1 reports had come that the Soviets had entered Berlin and that Hitler and his bride had committed suicide in their bunker hidden deep beneath the city. Six days later the German army surrendered. In early June the Allied Control Commission began work in Berlin. The war in Europe was over.

But the war in Asia continued. On V-E Day, President Truman turned to that task when he called for the "unconditional surrender" of Japan, which he insisted did not mean "the extermination or enslavement of the Japanese people." Peace groups in Japan had gained leverage with every Allied victory, but the army and others held on. Their resistance was due partly to the fact that the Allies' call for unconditional surrender did not guarantee maintenance of the emperor, who was regarded as a godlike figure and whose preservation was the single most important stipulation in all peace efforts by Japan. U.S. peace advocates tried in June to persuade the Soviet Union to mediate an end to the war, but it refused. A U.S. invasion of Japan, supported by Soviet entry into the war, seemed necessary. Indeed, the war department had plans under way for an invasion of Japan to begin on November 1, 1945.

In the meantime, however, Soviet-American relations threatened to come apart over the lend-lease program and recent events in Poland. Shortly after Germany's defeat, the Truman administration considered the European war over and abruptly terminated lend-lease aid to the Soviet Union, a decision the president then partly reversed when the Kremlin bitterly denounced the move as White House pressure aimed at postwar concessions. The administration saw little use in trying to convince the Soviets that the sudden cutoff was attributable to the end of the war in Europe. Indeed, the U.S. termination of aid to other allies, including Britain, failed to ease Soviet resentment. Stalin denounced the cessation of lend-lease as "brutal" and indignantly warned that if the move "was designed as pressure on the Soviets in order to soften them up, then it was a fundamental mistake." In view of growing suspicions of Soviet motives in Poland, Truman persuaded the ailing Harry Hopkins to make the arduous trip to Moscow (as he had done for Roosevelt in 1941) to remove the obstructions to the war effort in Asia.

In Moscow, Hopkins assured Stalin that the cancellation of lend-lease was not an attempt to exert pressure on the Soviet Union, yet he warned that the Washington government was losing patience over the Kremlin's laxity in implementing the Yalta agreements in Poland. Stalin replied that free elections in Poland would lead to the installation of the London government-in-exile, a group opposed to the Soviet Union. "In the course of twenty-five years," he emphasized in an argument made earlier at Yalta, "the Germans had twice invaded Russia via Poland. Neither the British nor American people had experienced such German invasions which were a horrible thing to endure and the results of which were not easily forgotten. . . . Poland has served as a corridor for the German attacks on Russia. . . . It is therefore in Russia's vital interest that Poland should be both strong and friendly." Harriman had raised a point critical to understanding Stalin's views on the U.S. relation to the Polish question and therefore essential to comprehending the mutual misunderstanding

East Meets West
2nd Lt. William Robertson of the U.S. Army meets Lt. Alexander Sylvashko of the Russian Army near Torgau, Germany, on April 25, 1945, symbolizing the "Strange Alliance" that was already crumbling from within. *National Archives, Washington, D.C.*

crucial to the origins of the Cold War. The Soviet premier, Harriman explained, simply could not "understand why we should want to interfere with Soviet policy in a country like Poland, which he considers so important to Russia's security, unless we have some ulterior motive." Nonetheless, Stalin assured Hopkins that those Poles not associated with the Lublin regime could have a few ministries in the government, and he repeated his promises to enter the war against Japan and respect the Chinese Nationalist government.

Hopkins's mission to Moscow was a mild success. Before returning home, he made final arrangements for another Big Three conference, this one to be at Potsdam, outside Berlin. Hopkins's efforts temporarily eased difficulties with the Soviet Union and allowed the Allies to concentrate on Japan.

From mid-July through early August 1945, the Big Three gathered in Potsdam to finalize plans for postwar Germany and for ending the war in Asia. After Truman's first encounter with Stalin, he wrote his family that the Soviets were "pig-headed." He allegedly said about the Soviet premier that "I thought he was an S.O.B. But, of course, I guess he thinks I'm one, too." Churchill was in Potsdam until mid-conference, when his Conservative party lost the elections to the Labour party. Clement Attlee replaced him as prime minister, and Ernest Bevin succeeded Eden as foreign secretary. Before Churchill departed, he had gained a favorable impression of the new president: Truman had "exceptional character and ability with . . . simple and direct methods of speech, and a great deal of self-confidence and resolution."

On the first day of the Potsdam Conference, July 17, 1945, Truman received word that American scientists in New Mexico had successfully exploded an atomic device the previous day. The secret "Manhattan Project" had been under way since August 1942 and would so profoundly change the course of history that no one in 1945 could have guessed its impact. Problems remained in adapting the mechanism for use in a bomb and in getting the heavy apparatus airborne. Nor was there a guarantee that another detonating device would work or, if so, how soon it could be developed. But the researchers had proved the feasibility of nuclear fission, and its conceivable use as a weapon suddenly raised hopes for ending the war without a costly invasion of Japan.

On the same day that Truman learned the news, he informed Stalin that the United States had developed "a new weapon of unusual destructive force." Stalin's reply was terse: He hoped the United States would use it on the Japanese. His spy network had probably already uncovered the atomic project, but like the Americans he could not have known its potential. After the Americans at Potsdam informed Churchill of the successful test, he declared the following day that "now I know what happened to Truman yesterday. . . . When he got to the meeting after having read this report he was a changed man. He told the Russians just where they got on and off and generally bossed the whole meeting."

The development of atomic bomb potential did not enable the United States to achieve all of its objectives at Potsdam. Soviet armies were in control of eastern Europe, and local Communist party members occupied key

Churchill, Truman, and Stalin at Potsdam
The Big Three meet in Germany in July–August 1945 to discuss postwar arrangements and to call for the unconditional surrender of Japan. *Imperial War Museum, London.*

government positions in nearly all countries involved. The Soviets meanwhile made a secret arrangement with Poland's Provisional Government, which temporarily drew its western boundary at the Oder and Western Neisse rivers to compensate for Poland's territorial losses in the east resulting from the adjusted border at the Curzon Line. In regard to Germany, the Big Three followed the Yalta agreements by dividing the country into four zones with a military governor in each, but with Germany remaining "a single economic unity." The United States did not agree to any reparations figure until the Allies could ascertain how much the Germans could pay, and it denied Stalin access to Germany's industrial wealth (located in the Western zones) by authorizing each nation to exact reparations from its zone of occupation only. Truman realized that Germany was vital to Europe's economic rehabilitation and shied away from the severe proposals contained in the Morgenthau Plan; in fact, he had arranged Morgenthau's removal from the Treasury office. The Big Three would equally divide Germany's commercial and naval vessels among themselves, remove all vestiges of Nazism, and sponsor war crimes trials. Finally, they agreed to establish a Council of Foreign Ministers of the United States, Britain, the Soviet Union, and France, which would deal with matters left unresolved at Potsdam.

On July 26, 1945, the United States, Britain, and China signed the Potsdam Declaration, which repeated the call for Japan's unconditional surrender contained in the Casablanca Declaration of January 1943. Such terms entailed disarmament, the forfeiture of possessions acquired during the last half-century, an end to militarism, and the removal of any other obstacles to the planting of democracy. Allied occupation would last until there was "established in accordance with the freely expressed will of the Japanese people a peacefully inclined and responsible government." Although the Allies dropped thousands of leaflets over Japan warning that the alternative to surrender was massive destruc-

tion, Japan at first wanted to await word from the Soviet Union of possible mediation. Besides, since the Japanese had already undergone extensive bombings that were terrifying in their fiery consequences, surely they could withstand more. Finally, the Japanese cabinet yielded to the military's pressure and informed reporters that it was adopting the posture of *mokusatsu*, a term unfortunately open to two meanings. Whereas the Tokyo government intended merely to "withhold comment" on the Potsdam Declaration, Japanese newspapers read the term as a decision to ignore the warning.

Japan's apparent rejection of unconditional surrender presented the United States with a choice: Either begin a long and costly invasion of the Japanese islands or use the newly developed atomic weapon and possibly end the war quickly and with minimal loss of American lives. Truman chose the latter course. His decision was no doubt partly attributable to the bureaucratic momentum resulting from the creation and successful culmination of the Manhattan Project. It seemed inconceivable not to use the bomb after all the time and expense put into the program. Should the bomb prove successful, the United States would also gain a stronger negotiating position in the postwar world—if it could demonstrate its power, gain sole control over Japan, and end the war in Asia before Soviet entry. The president probably considered these factors; certainly he recalled the bombing of Pearl Harbor and, like other Americans, sought some measure of revenge. But he insisted that his central motive in using the new weapon was to save Americans' lives by ending the war quickly.

On August 6, 1945, just four days after the close of the Potsdam Conference, an overloaded U.S. B-29 lumbered down the two-mile runway at Tinian Island in the Marianas and struggled into the air. It was shortly before 3:00 A.M., and the B-29 was carrying a 10,000-pound bomb labeled the "Little Boy." The commander of the *Enola Gay,* Colonel Paul Tibbets, had as his destination the islands of Japan—a five-hour flight, during which two observer planes with cameras and scientists aboard followed closely behind. Tibbets had learned from a weather plane, sent a little more than an hour ahead, that the skies were clear over Hiroshima, a city of 250,000 that was a center of war production and one of Japan's regional military headquarters.

Just above the city of Hiroshima the *Enola Gay* released its cargo, which fell for nearly a minute before exploding less than half a mile above the ground. At 8:15 A.M. a blinding flash of light streaked across the sky, followed by an enormous boom and instantaneous burst of heat reaching 5400°F that scattered burning debris nearly eight miles into the atmosphere. The huge mushroom cloud, according to the plane's tail gunner, was "a bubbling mass of purple-gray smoke and you could see it had a

red core in it and everything was burning inside." Within a half hour the gigantic fireball had generated a firestorm that pelted the entire area with sheets of heavy black rain carrying radioactive materials and tossed wildly by heavy winds. By the time the world's first atomic bomb had registered its initial impact, more than eighty percent of Hiroshima's buildings in a four-square-mile area were leveled, and 80,000 men, women, and children lay dead. Countless more were injured. By the end of the year the number of deaths reached 140,000, and 60,000 more bombing victims died over the next five years.

Three days later, on August 9, the United States dropped a second atomic bomb ("Fat Man," named after Churchill) on Nagasaki, virtually destroying the city. This bomb killed

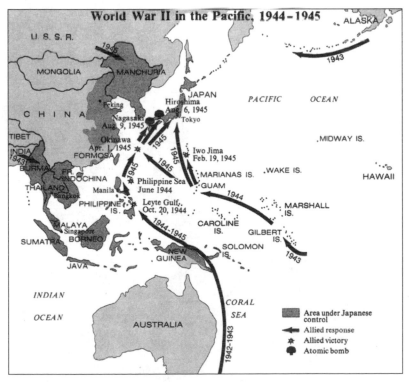

Map 18
After the Japanese were halted in the Battle of the Coral Sea, the Allies began a counterattack in mid-1942 that eventually led to the dropping of atomic bombs on Hiroshima and Nagasaki and the Japanese surrender in August 1945.

another 35,000 instantly in the firestorm and ultimately led to 140,000 deaths. "The general impression," a U.S. Navy officer observed a month later as he walked among the ruins of a city that once had 200,000 people, "is one of deadness, the absolute essence of death in the sense of finality without hope of resurrection."

News of the atomic destruction drew mixed reactions in Washington. Truman called it "the greatest thing in history," but Leahy was not so sure. "In being the first to use it," the admiral believed, "we had adopted the ethical standard common to the barbarians of the Dark Ages. I was not taught to make war in that fashion, and wars cannot be won by destroying women and children." Then and later, critics have argued that the administration should first have pursued peace talks, used conventional bombings and a blockade, awaited the outcome of a Soviet declaration of war on Japan, invaded Japan through the island of Kyushu, described

the new bomb to Japan and offered a chance to surrender, or set off a bomb in some deserted spot before an international team of observers that included Japanese representatives. Japan was so close to defeat, they asserted, that the bomb was not necessary. The administration's defenders have countered every argument with the most telling one: U.S. military experts guaranteed a long war with heavy loss of life in the event of invasion. They also noted that Soviet entry would have stiffened Japan's resistance, not broken it; that there was no assurance that the explosion of a bomb in a deserted place would have had the impact of one used in a city; that a demonstration bomb might not have detonated.

However horrendous the ultimate loss of life, the U.S. government justified use of the atomic bomb by the believed military necessity of the war. Japan had adamantly refused to surrender. The president was especially concerned

Hiroshima
After the explosion of the atomic bomb, August 6, 1945. *U.S. Air Force.*

about the projected loss of American service-men in an invasion of Japan and, as has always been the case in past wars, turned to a weap-on that seemed to offer a viable alternative. Whether the estimated American losses were one million or 40,000, the number was too high. Domestic criticisms would have reached fever pitch if Americans knew that their gov-ernment possessed a new weapon and decided not to use it in favor of a costly invasion. If the essence of military strategy is to achieve an objective in the shortest and most expeditious manner, Truman's use of the bomb was highly effective strategy. If victory in war can come through technology rather than human effort, that same strategy is even more praiseworthy. And if use of the bomb afforded the United States a stronger bargaining position with the Soviet Union in the postwar period, this was an added bonus. "The final decision of where and when to use the atomic bomb," Truman later asserted, "was up to me. Let there be no mistake about it. I regarded the bomb as a mil-itary weapon and never had any doubt that it should be used."

Japan *had* to surrender. On August 10, 1945, the day after Nagasaki's destruction, the Japanese government agreed to the terms announced at Potsdam, but with the stipula-tion that the declaration "does not comprise any demand which prejudices the prerogatives of His Majesty as a Sovereign Ruler." The Allies permitted the emperor to retain his throne, but made him subject to the control of the Allied Supreme Commander. Two days earlier the Soviet Union had fulfilled its Yalta obligations by entering the war and ordering its armies into Manchuria, Korea, and south-ern Sakhalin—exactly three months after Ger-many's surrender and almost one week before the Kremlin signed a treaty of assistance with Nationalist China. For railway and port rights in Manchuria and the maintenance of the sta-tus quo in Outer Mongolia, the Soviets agreed to help the Nationalists, promised to stay out of China's domestic affairs, and recognized Chinese sovereignty in Manchuria. The same day as the Soviet-Chinese treaty, August 14,

Nagasaki
A mushroom cloud rises more than 60,000 feet above the port of Nagasaki, where the United States dropped a second atomic bomb, August 9, 1945. *National Archives, Washington, D.C.*

the Allies agreed to accept Japan's surrender. On September 2, 1945 ("V-J Day"), aboard the U.S. battleship *Missouri* in Tokyo Bay, the Japanese formally surrendered to the Allies under the command of General Douglas MacArthur. World War II was over.

Bases of the Cold War

One of the most far-reaching effects of World War II was the bipolar division between two ideologically and culturally different systems: the United States and the Soviet Union. Hit-ler's "greatest crime," according to Harriman, was his loss on the battlefield, because it ex-posed Europe to the Soviets. In fighting the invading Nazi forces, the Soviet Union had paid dearly in population and resources and now expected generous indemnities, full equal-ity in international affairs, and absolute secu-rity along all borders. The war had devastated

MacArthur at Japanese Surrender in 1945
He later headed the American occupation of Japan before becoming commander of
UN forces during the Korean War. *National Archives, Washington, D.C.*

Europe and Asia, killing thirty-five million in Europe alone and spawning millions of refugees or "displaced persons." But the most profound fact was that of all those who died in Europe, twenty million were Soviets.

The victors were better prepared for postwar reconstruction than they had been in 1918. The UN Relief and Rehabilitation Administration (UNRRA) had come into being in Washington in November 1943 to assist the war's victims and prevent them from turning in desperation toward totalitarian political systems such as communism. Headed by and mostly financed by the United States, UNRRA lasted until the middle of 1947 and helped more than one million displaced persons in Europe and Asia, including those in the Soviet Union. In July 1944, 1300 delegates from forty-four nations had attended the UN Monetary and Financial Conference at a mountain resort in New Hampshire called Bretton Woods, where they established the International Monetary Fund and the International Bank for Reconstruction and Development, or World Bank. Dominated by Americans, the two organizations aimed to assist countries hurting from trade imbalances and to loan money for reconstruction and economic recovery. The goal was to ensure a postwar capitalist world by reestablishing financial stability and multilateral trade based on gold and the U.S. dollar.

The United States, like the Soviet Union, had political objectives in its postwar programs. Economic rehabilitation was the prerequisite to promoting the stability and order vital to preventing Europe, Asia, Africa, and Latin America from becoming breeding grounds for communism and ultimate Soviet control. The ideal of helping those ravaged by the war was compatible with the reality of stopping the postwar spread of communism and building a free market resting on U.S. trade and investments. To promote U.S. interests, Roosevelt had considered spheres of influence, assuming that the Western Hemisphere remained under U.S. dominance, and he had ordered the military to make preparations for the acquisition of Pacific bases. Postwar problems were predictable, not only because Soviet national interests competed with the dictates of the Atlantic Charter, but also because of the contradictions in U.S. policy itself.

The two most controversial aspects of World War II were the Yalta Conference and the atomic bomb, because both were integral to the outbreak of Soviet-American tensions that soon became known as the Cold War. Few wartime conferences have drawn as much praise followed by such bitter condemnation as did Yalta. Critics of the conference have overlooked the unbroken antipathy between the Soviet Union and the United States that had existed since the Bolshevik Revolution of 1917, and they have argued that Roosevelt's personal diplomacy instilled hope at Yalta for the postwar world that Truman destroyed by his unbending stance and unnecessary use of the bomb. Yet hatred of Hitler was the central bond of the wartime alliance, and the Nazis' demise in 1945 again exposed the incompatibility of capitalism and communism, of U.S. and Soviet cultures, and of the Atlantic Charter and Soviet security. Evidence lay in the mutual wartime suspicions concerning the second front and other matters. Further proof rested in the unfulfilled assurances of free and democratic elections in Poland and eastern Europe and in the bitter disagreements over Germany. The role of diplomacy would become even more vital as the mutual needs of the war only temporarily overrode these divisive feelings.

After Yalta and before the bomb, the United States believed it needed Soviet entry into the Asian war and therefore approved the so-called concessions that it could not have prevented anyway. Roosevelt could not have given away either Europe or Asia because they never belonged to him. Besides, one wonders what military action the United States would have been willing and able to carry out to remove Soviet forces already in Europe and to stop them from advancing into East Asia. The United States was not in the position to dictate terms. Churchill provided the most realistic rebuttal to critics of Yalta: "What would have happened if we had quarreled with Russia while the Germans still had three or four hundred divisions on the fighting front?"

Some critics have blamed Roosevelt for calling off the U.S. drive into Berlin for political reasons; yet it was General Eisenhower who for military reasons held back his forces at the Elbe River. Though certainly aware of the political ramifications of such a decision, he considered it far more important to save U.S. lives by bringing a rapid end to the war. Eisenhower later explained that his men were in a state of exhaustion, dangerously separated from their supply line, farther from the city than were the Soviets, and facing a much more difficult terrain. Besides, a siege of Berlin would have taken thousands of U.S. lives and yielded the same results as if they had not participated. Eisenhower was correct. The Soviet march into Berlin cost more than 100,000 soldiers' lives—all Soviets—and afterward the United States still shared in occupying the city and country.

Some observers have argued that Roosevelt should have used economic aid as a club to force political concessions; others have countered that Stalin could just as easily have made threats based on a takeover of Berlin during the Yalta proceedings. Yet the Soviet premier directed his armies to stop the thrust into the city. It is questionable why, but some believe that a major victory at this time would have raised Western fears of the Soviet Union and upset his objectives at Yalta. Britain's Sir Alexander Cadogan thought that Stalin downplayed his military successes because they "seemed to have given him the added assurance enabling him to take broad views and to be unafraid of making concessions."

Arguments also developed over the Yalta agreements relating to East Asia. It is doubtful that the Soviet Union was entitled to areas

Sands of Iwo Jima
U.S. Marines triumphantly raise the flag over the Japanese possession on February 23, 1945.
National Archives, Washington, D.C.

in that region on the basis of the war with Japan in 1904 and 1905. The Russians had been the aggressors between 1894 and 1904, and they did not have a strong argument for areas belonging to China. Recognition in 1945 of the Soviet Union's "preeminent interests" would have condoned aggression and violated the United States's open door pledges to China. Yet China did not lose territories at Yalta; *Japan* did. China actually regained sovereignty in Manchuria, whereas Outer Mongolia had been estranged from China and had tipped toward coming under Soviet hegemony for some time. Soviet assistance against Japan seemed vital in February 1945 (before development of the atomic bomb), and Americans could find no way short of war to dislodge the Red Armies from Europe and keep them out of East Asia.

In a highly dubious conclusion, the U.S. Strategic Bombing Survey declared in 1946 that Japan would have surrendered without either the bomb, Soviet entry into the war, or an all-out U.S. invasion. And yet Japanese forces numbered nearly two million, and they had at their disposal 5350 kamikaze planes, with 7000 more nearly ready for action, and 5000 additional pilots then training for duty in the Kamikaze Corps. Wartime events substantiated the military's fears about an invasion of Japan: Americans sustained extremely heavy losses in taking Iwo Jima and Okinawa, islands not even integrally connected with the Japanese homeland and yet the scenes of horrible fighting.

In 1970 Harriman made the most incisive comment about the Yalta Conference: "If we hadn't had the Yalta agreements we would have been blamed for all the postwar tensions." Many arrangements of February 1945 were products of previous understandings, but so much faith had rested in the Yalta proceedings that they offered impossible hopes. Indeed, the published achievements—the Yalta Declaration and the United Nations—heralded a new age of peace. But the issues kept secret—Poland, eastern Europe, Germany, and Asia—quickly stamped out the prospect of international harmony with the bitter disillusionment of Cold War. Had the Soviets adhered to the Yalta terms, the Anglo-Americans would have succeeded in placing restraints on Soviet expansion into Europe and East Asia. The Soviets, however, realized that these conditions endangered their security. The principle of self-determination contained in the Atlantic Charter was irreconcilable with the Soviets' drive for national safety. The only resort for the United States was to make sure that the world recognized the Soviet Union as the aggressor in the postwar period. The Yalta agreements accomplished this objective. The irony is that the United States then developed a weapon of such massive force that it won the war but subsequently drove the Soviet Union into a more aggressive drive for security through expansion. The bomb that ended World War II necessitated a UN organization to maintain world peace; at the same time the bomb left a dangerous legacy of Cold War.

Selected Readings

Abzug, Robert H. *Inside the Vicious Heart: Americans and the Liberation of Nazi Concentration Camps.* 1985.

Adams, Michael C. C. *The Best War Ever: America and World War II.* 1994.

Alperovitz, Gar. *Atomic Diplomacy: Hiroshima and Potsdam.* 1965. Rev. ed., 1994.

———. *The Decision to Use the Atomic Bomb and the Architecture of an American Myth.* 1995.

Ambrose, Stephen E. *Eisenhower.* Vol. 1: *Soldier, General of the Army, President-Elect, 1890–1952.* 1983.

———, and Brinkley, Douglas G. *Rise to Globalism: American Foreign Policy since 1938.* 8th ed., 1997.

Anderson, Terry H. *The United States, Great Britain, and the Cold War, 1944–1947.* 1981.

Bagby, Wesley M. *The Eagle-Dragon Alliance: America's Relations with China in World War II.* 1992.

Buth, Alan H. *Tracking the Axis Enemy: The Triumph of Anglo-American Naval Intelligence.* 1998.

Bauer, Yehuda. *Jews for Sale? Nazi-Jewish Negotiations, 1933–1945.* 1994.

Beaulac, Willard L. *Franco: Silent Ally in World War II.* 1986.

Beitzell, Robert. *The Uneasy Alliance: America, Britain, and Russia, 1941–1943.* 1972.

Blumenthal, Henry. *Illusion and Reality in Franco-American Diplomacy, 1914–1945.* 1986.

Boyer, Paul S. *Fallout: A Historian Reflects on America's Half-Century Encounter with Nuclear Weapons.* 1998.

Breitman, Richard. *Official Secrets: What the Nazis Planned, What the British and Americans Knew.* 1998.

———, and Kraut, Alan M. *American Refugee Policy and European Jewry, 1933–1945.* 1987.

Brewer, Susan A. *To Win the Peace: British Propaganda in the United States during World War II.* 1997.

Browning, Christopher R. *The Path to Genocide: Essays in Launching the Final Solution.* 1992.

Buchanan, A. Russell. *The United States and World War II.* 2 vols., 1964.

Buhite, Russell D. *Decisions at Yalta: An Appraisal of Summit Diplomacy.* 1986.

———. *Patrick J. Hurley and American Foreign Policy.* 1973.

Burns, James M. *Roosevelt: The Soldier of Freedom, 1940–1945.* 1970.

Butow, Robert J. C. *Japan's Decision to Surrender.* 1954.

Campbell, Thomas M. *Masquerade Peace: America's UN Policy, 1944–1945.* 1973.

Charmley, John. *Churchill's Grand Alliance: The Anglo-American Special Relationship, 1940–1957.* 1995.

Churchill, Winston S. *The Second World War.* 6 vols. 1948–1953.

Clemens, Diane S. *Yalta.* 1970.

Cohen, Warren I. *America's Response to China: A History of Sino-American Relations.* 2000.

Cole, Wayne S. *Roosevelt and the Isolationists, 1932–1945.* 1983.

Conversino, Mark J. *Fighting with the Soviets: The Failure of Operation FRANTIC, 1944–1945.* 1997.

Cull, Nicholas J. *Selling War: The British Propaganda Campaign Against American "Neutrality" in World War II.* 1995.

Dallek, Robert. *Franklin D. Roosevelt and American Foreign Policy, 1932–1945.* 1979.

Daniels, Roger. *Concentration Camps USA: Japanese Americans and World War II.* 1972.

Davis, Lynn E. *The Cold War Begins: Soviet-American Conflict over Eastern Europe.* 1974.

DeSantis, Hugh. *The Diplomacy of Silence: The American Foreign Service, the Soviet Union, and the Cold War, 1933–1947.* 1980.

Divine, Robert A. *Roosevelt and World War II.* 1969.

———. *Second Chance: The Triumph of Internationalism in America during World War II.* 1967.

Dower, John W. *Embracing Defeat: Japan in the Wake of World War II.* 1999.

———. *War without Mercy: Race and Power in the Pacific War.* 1986.

Eubank, Keith. *Summit at Teheran.* 1985.

Feingold, Henry L. *Bearing Witness: How America and Its Jews Responded to the Holocaust.* 1995.

———. *Politics of Rescue: The Roosevelt Administration and the Holocaust, 1938–1945.* 1970.

Feis, Herbert. *The Atomic Bomb and the End of World War II.* 1966. Originally published as *Japan Subdued: The Atomic Bomb and the End of the War in the Pacific.* 1961.

———. *Between War and Peace: The Potsdam Conference.* 1960.

———. *The China Tangle: The American Effort in China from Pearl Harbor to the Marshall Mission.* 1953.

————. *Churchill, Roosevelt, Stalin.* 1957.

Ferrell, Robert H. *The Dying President: Franklin D. Roosevelt, 1944–1945.* 1998.

————. *Harry S. Truman: A Life.* 1994.

————. *Harry S. Truman and the Modern American Presidency.* 1983.

————. *Ill-Advised: Presidential Health and Public Trust.* 1992.

Freidel, Frank. *Franklin D. Roosevelt: A Rendezvous with Destiny.* 1990.

Friedman, Saul S. *No Haven for the Oppressed: United States Policy toward Jewish Refugees, 1938–1945.* 1973.

Gaddis, John L. *The United States and the Origins of the Cold War, 1941–1947.* 1972.

Gardner, Lloyd C. *Architects of Illusion: Men and Ideas in American Foreign Policy, 1941–1949.* 1970.

————. *Spheres of Influence: The Great Powers Partition Europe, from Munich to Yalta.* 1993.

Gormly, James L. *From Potsdam to the Cold War: Big Three Diplomacy, 1945–1947.* 1990.

Greenfield, Kent R. *American Strategy in World War II.* 1963.

Hathaway, Robert M. *Ambiguous Partnership: Britain and America, 1944–1947.* 1981.

Helmreich, Jonathan E. *Gathering Rare Ores: The Diplomacy of Uranium Acquisition, 1943–1954.* 1986.

Henriksen, Margot A. *Dr. Strangelove's America: Society and Culture in the Atomic Age.* 1997.

Herring, George C., Jr. *Aid to Russia, 1941–1946: Strategy, Diplomacy, and the Origins of the Cold War.* 1973.

Hess, Gary R. *The United States at War, 1941–1945.* 1986.

Hildebrand, Robert C. *Dumbarton Oaks: The Origins of the United Nations and the Search for Postwar Security.* 1990.

Hilton, Stanley E. *Hitler's Secret War in South America, 1939–1945: German Military Espionage and Allied Counterespionage in Brazil.* 1981.

Holloway, David. *Stalin and the Bomb: The Soviet Union and Atomic Energy, 1939–1956.* 1994.

Hoopes, Townsend, and Brinkley, Douglas. *FDR and the Creation of the U.N.* 1997.

Hoyt, Edwin P. *Japan's War: The Great Pacific Conflict, 1853 to 1952.* 1986.

Hurstfield, Julian G. *America and the French Nation, 1939–1945.* 1986.

Iriye, Akira. *Power and Culture: The Japanese-American War, 1941–1945.* 1981.

Jonas, Manfred. *The United States and Germany: A Diplomatic History.* 1984.

Kahn, E. J., Jr. *The China Hands: America's Foreign Service Officers and What Befell Them.* 1975.

Kimball, Warren F. *The Juggler: Franklin Roosevelt as Wartime Statesman.* 1991.

————. *Forged in War: Roosevelt, Churchill, and the Second World War.* 1997.

Kolko, Gabriel. *The Politics of War: The World and United States Foreign Policy, 1943–1945.* 1968.

Koppes, Clayton R., and Black, Gregory D. "Blacks, Loyalty, and Motion-Picture Propaganda in World War II," *Journal of American History* 73 (1986): 383–406.

————. *Hollywood Goes to War: How Politics, Profits, and Propaganda Shaped World War II.* 1987.

Kurzman, Dan. *Day of the Bomb: Countdown to Hiroshima.* 1986.

LaFeber, Walter. *The Clash: A History of U.S.-Japanese Relations.* 1997.

Langer, William L. *Our Vichy Gamble.* 1947.

Larrabee, Eric. *Commander in Chief: Franklin Delano Roosevelt, His Lieutenants and Their War.* 1986.

Laurie, Clayton D. *The Propaganda Warriors: America's Crusade Against Nazi Germany.* 1996.

Levering, Ralph B. *American Opinion and the Russian Alliance.* 1976.

Lifton, Robert J., and Mitchell, Greg. *Hiroshima in America: Fifty Years of Denial.* 1995.

Lindee, M. Susan. *Suffering Made Real: American Science and the Survivors at Hiroshima.* 1994.

Lipstadt, Deborah E. *Beyond Belief: The American Press and the Coming of the Holocaust, 1933–1945.* 1993.

Liu, Xiaoyuan. *A Partnership for Disorder: China, the United States, and Their Policies for the Postwar Disposition of the Japanese Empire, 1941–1945.* 1996.

Louis, William R. *Imperialism at Bay: The United States and the Decolonization of the British Empire.* 1978.

Lukas, Richard C. *The Strange Allies: The United States and Poland, 1941–1945.* 1978.

Lundestad, Geir. *The American Non-Policy towards Eastern Europe, 1943–1947.* 1975.

Maddox, Robert J. *Weapons for Victory: The Hiroshima Decision Fifty Years Later.* 1995.

Marks, Frederick W., III. *Wind over Sand: The Diplomacy of Franklin Roosevelt.* 1988.

Mastny, Vojtech. *Russia's Road to the Cold War: Diplomacy, Strategy, and the Politics of Communism, 1941–1945.* 1979.

McCann, Frank D., Jr. *The Brazilian-American Alliance, 1937–1945.* 1973.

McNeill, William H. *America, Britain, & Russia: Their Co-operation and Conflict, 1941–1946.* 1953.

Mee, Charles L., Jr. *Meeting at Potsdam.* 1975.

Miller, Edward S. *War Plan Orange: The U.S. Strategy to Defeat Japan, 1897–1945.* 1991.

Nadeau, Remi. *Stalin, Churchill, and Roosevelt Divide Europe.* 1990.

Neuman, Robert P. *Truman and the Hiroshima Cult.* 1995.

Niblo, Stephen R. *War, Diplomacy, and Development: The United States and Mexico, 1938–1954.* 1995.

O'Connor, Raymond G. *Diplomacy for Victory: FDR and Unconditional Surrender.* 1971.

O'Neill, William. *A Democracy at War: America's Fight at Home and Abroad in World War II.* 1993.

Paz, María E. *Strategy, Security, and Spies.* 1997.

Penkower, Monty N. *The Jews Were Expendable: Free World Diplomacy and the Holocaust.* 1983.

Raack, R. C. *Stalin's Drive to the West, 1938–1945: The Origins of the Cold War.* 1995.

Reynolds, David. *Rich Relations: The American Occupation of Britain, 1942–1945.* 1995.

Rhodes, Richard. *The Making of the Atomic Bomb.* 1986.

Roeder, George H. *The Censored War: American Visual Experience during World War II.* 1993.

Sainsbury, Keith. *Churchill and Roosevelt at War: The War They Fought and the Peace They Hoped to Make.* 1994.

———. *The Turning Point: Roosevelt, Stalin, Churchill, and Chiang-Kai shek, 1943: The Moscow, Cairo, and Teheran Conferences.* 1985.

Schaffer, Ronald. "American Military Ethics in World War II: The Bombing of German Civilians," *Journal of American History* 67 (1980): 318–34.

———. *Wings of Judgment: American Bombing in World War II.* 1985.

Schaller, Michael. *The U.S. Crusade in China, 1938–1945.* 1979.

Schild, Greg. *Bretton Woods and Dumbarton Oaks.* 1995.

Sheng, Michael M. *Battling Western Imperialism: Mao, Stalin, and the United States.* 1997.

Sherry, Michael S. *The Rise of American Airpower: The Creation of Armageddon.* 1987.

Sherwin, Martin J. *A World Destroyed: The Atomic Bomb and the Grand Alliance.* 1975.

Shewmaker, Kenneth. *Americans and the Chinese Communists, 1927–1945: A Persuading Encounter.* 1971.

Shulman, Holly C. *The Voice of America: Propaganda and Democracy, 1941–1945.* 1990.

Sigal, Leon V. *Fighting to a Finish: The Politics of War Termination in the United States and Japan, 1945.* 1988.

Smith, Bradley F. *The Shadow Warriors: O.S.S. and the Origins of the C.I.A.* 1983.

———. *Sharing Secrets with Stalin: How the Allies Traded Intelligence, 1941–1945.* 1996.

Smith, Gaddis. *American Diplomacy during the Second World War, 1941–1945.* 2nd ed., 1985.

Smith, Kevin. *Conflict over Convoys: Anglo-American Logistics Diplomacy in World War Two.* 1996.

Snell, John L. *Illusion and Necessity: The Diplomacy of Global War, 1939–1945.* 1963.

———, ed. *The Meaning of Yalta.* 1956.

Spector, Ronald H. *Eagle against the Sun: The American War with Japan.* 1985.

Stoler, Mark A. *The Politics of the Second Front: American Military Planning and Diplomacy in Coalition Warfare, 1941–1943.* 1977.

Takaki, Ronald. *Hiroshima.* 1995.

Thorne, Christopher. *Allies of a Kind: The United States, Britain, and the War against Japan, 1941–1945.* 1978.

Tsou, Tang. *America's Failure in China, 1941–1950.* 1963.

Tuchman, Barbara W. *Stilwell and the American Experience in China, 1911–1945.* 1970.

Tuttle, Dwight W. *Harry L. Hopkins and Anglo-American-Soviet Relations, 1941–1945.* 1983.

Viorst, Milton. *Hostile Allies: FDR and Charles de Gaulle.* 1965.

Walker, J. Samuel. *Prompt and Utter Destruction: Truman and the Use of Atomic Bombs Against Japan.* 1997.

Wandycz, Piotr S. *The United States and Poland.* 1980.

Weigley, Russell F. *Eisenhower's Lieutenants: The Campaign of France and Germany, 1944–1945.* 1981.

Weinberg, Gerhard L. *A World at Arms: A Global History of World War II.* 1994.

Weiss, Steve. *Allies in Conflict: Anglo-American Strategic Negotiations, 1938–1944.* 1996.

Westad, Odd Arne. *Cold War and Revolution: Soviet-American Rivalry and the Origins of the Chinese Civil War, 1944–1946.* 1993.

Williamson, Samuel R., and Rearden, Steven L. *The Origins of U.S. Nuclear Strategy.* 1993.

Winkler, Allan M. *Life Under a Cloud: American Anxiety About the Atom.* 1993.

Wittner, Lawrence S. *The Struggle Against the Bomb.* 1993.

Wood, Bryce. *The Dismantling of the Good Neighbor Policy.* 1985.

Woods, Randall B. *A Changing of the Guard: Anglo-American Relations, 1941–1946.* 1990.

———. *The Roosevelt Foreign Policy Establishment and the Good Neighbor: The United States and Argentina, 1941–1945.* 1979.

———, and Jones, Howard. *Dawning of the Cold War: The United States' Quest for Order.* 1991, 1994.

Wyman, David S. *The Abandonment of the Jews: America and the Holocaust, 1941–1945.* 1984.

CHAPTER 9

Cold War and Containment in Europe and the Near East, 1945–1950

Prospectus for Trouble

Even though the United States emerged from World War II as the unquestioned leader of the world, such global stature did not automatically ensure peace and security either at home or abroad. With power came the responsibility for maintaining peace, and with global power came that same responsibility on a global scale—or so the Truman administration seemed to think. The wartime struggle for self-determination had combined with the collapse of the old colonial system and the widespread social, political, and economic dislocation resulting from the greatest war in history to cause internal turmoil in numerous countries and massive international disorder. Such havoc provided a predictable invitation to totalitarian exploitation and hence an obstacle to postwar trade, stability, and peace. The war had bequeathed a global system that stood dangerously divided between two vastly different cultures, economies, and political ideologies—those of the United States and the Soviet Union. Contrary to what followed World War I, however, the United States intended to take the lead in stimulating its own economy and establishing world order through multilateral trade, the principle of self-determination, and

a vast network of foreign aid programs and military alliances.

The bipolar power structure of the postwar world soon contributed to Americans' belief that nearly every international problem emanated from the Soviet Union. Distrust between the superpowers received impetus from the clashing ideologies of capitalism and communism. Each nation constructed exaggerated images of the other's military strength until each rival perceived the other as omnipresent and omnipotent (especially when both nations had atomic bomb capabilities). Perceptions became realities as opposing ideologies took on moral and spiritual overtones, leaving no room for compromise.

In this increasingly tense atmosphere, it is doubtful that any leaders of state could have convinced their counterparts that a push for security did not necessarily entail imperialist aggression. Some members of the Truman administration were aware of the Soviets' traditional drive westward and admitted to their postwar need for security along borders fronting Poland and much of the rest of Eastern Europe. Few were willing to retreat on the idealistic promises of the Atlantic Charter and Yalta Declaration, however, because, in short, the establishment of such ideals translated into realistic contributions to the United States's

Harry S. Truman
Among the foreign policy decisions of his administration were the Truman Doctrine, Marshall Plan, Berlin airlift, NATO, Point Four, and Korean War. *Library of Congress.*

own security. At the same time, Stalin was a realist and a nationalist rather than an ideologue committed to worldwide Communist revolution, and he refused to endanger his homeland in the name of self-determination. The Soviet Union had undergone numerous invasions along its sprawling western frontier. Because "friendly neighbors" (that is, Communist governments) were unlikely to emerge from democratic elections, he exploited local Communist movements when it was to his advantage. In two instances, however, Stalin permitted elections—in Czechoslovakia and Hungary—but only because he remained unsure of what the United States would do regarding Eastern Europe. When the White House showed no inclination to guarantee the Yalta Declaration, the chances for more elections came to an end. By 1947 the intensification of these and other conflicting interests had taken on the appellation of the "Cold War."

Fear of Soviet Communist aggression stimulated U.S. political and military intervention in postwar Europe and the Near East. By 1950 the United States had established economic, political, and military order in Europe by proclaiming the Truman Doctrine and Marshall Plan, emerging triumphant in a confrontation over Berlin that raised talk of using the bomb, and breaking with its long-standing opposition to political and military involvement on the continent by joining the North Atlantic Treaty Organization (NATO). It had also approved a peacetime draft and called for an expanded military budget based on the possibility of war with the Soviet Union. The advent of the atomic bomb had dictated actions and counteractions short of outright war, but it had also created a mind-bending paradox: The United States possessed the most powerful weapon in the world, and yet the sheer destructive power of that very bomb prohibited its use except in matters directly threatening the United States.

And therein lay the problem, according to White House advisers: The Soviets were not equipped for full-scale aggression in the immediate postwar period and consequently engaged in indirect tactics that a *New York Times* correspondent called "a new kind of war." Though possessing extensive ground forces in Eastern Europe and Germany, the Soviets lacked a strong navy and air force, did not have atomic weapons, and were reeling from crippling economic and population losses in the war. The Soviets, therefore, resorted to any means short of all-out war in achieving postwar objectives. Infiltration of a country through subversive methods and the use of its people as proxies became the hallmarks of Soviet expansion, whether for security or aggression. The primary goal was national security, which led to a series of efforts to safeguard Soviet borders that the West predictably interpreted as territorial aggressions similar to those of the 1930s. The Soviets, hurt so badly by World War II, undoubtedly wanted security above all else, even though Americans believed that Stalin's support of the Communist-led Lublin government in Poland constituted the first step in a well-organized plan of conquest. The Communists sought imperial expansion, according to Americans long reared in anti-Soviet feeling and fearful of the conspiratorial and revolutionary nature of Communist ideology. President Truman noted in 1947 that "there isn't any difference in totalitarian states. I don't care what you call them, Nazi, Communist, or Fascist."

Postwar tension mounted most immediately in Eastern Europe, but the center point of East-West rivalry was always Germany. Much like the period following World War I, Germany had lost again on the battlefield but paradoxically loomed as the most powerful country in Europe in terms of human and material resources. The Soviets, of course, remained determined to strip Germany of all power, and joining them were the French, who likewise feared another resurgence of their long-time hated neighbor. The British, however, recognized the importance of maintaining a formidable (though controlled) German presence on the continent to counter the Soviets, and they found a ready ally in the United States. Germany, located at the very crossroads of East and West in Europe, quickly became both the symbolic and the real hot spot of the Cold War.

The rapid postwar demobilization of U.S. military forces proved a vital determinant in the nation's foreign policy. Overseas troops received orders to return home soon after the fighting ended in Europe, leaving a power vacuum that Washington's policymakers feared the Soviets would fill. Americans believed that wars ended when the firing ceased, forgetting that power balances often shift as the victors tie up the loose ends of a conflict. But Americans in 1945 were in no mood for further overseas commitments. The Great Depression followed by war had sapped their willingness to sacrifice, and foreign affairs no longer had priority. The nation sought demobilization and reconversion of the economy to peacetime production. The military was severely weakened by a policy that granted the hurried discharge of soldiers through a point system based on length of service, because it meant that battle-seasoned veterans went home first. In an address at the Pentagon in 1950, General George C. Marshall recalled the military problems facing the nation during the Cold War 1940s:

> I remember, when I was Secretary of State, I was being pressed constantly, particularly when in Moscow, by radio message after radio message to give the Russians hell. . . . When I got back, I was getting the same appeal in relation to the Far East and China. At that time, my facilities for giving them hell—and I am a soldier and know something about the ability to give hell— was $1\frac{1}{3}$ divisions over the entire United States. That is quite a proposition when you deal with somebody with over 260.

For several reasons the Truman administration feared that Americans, as during the late 1920s, would reject a leadership role in international affairs after World War II. Such an inner-directed policy at first appeared feasible. President Roosevelt had left the foundations of a UN organization to keep the peace, and the United States held military predominance in the world, primarily because of the bomb. Prosperity born of war would surely combine with superior economic resources to enable the country to surge far ahead of others. Moreover, to some observers at least, the Soviets seemed to have changed. General Eisenhower had noted after visiting Moscow that "nothing guides Russian policy so much as a desire for friendship with the United States." Yet, ironically, diplomats possessed little leverage because of the sheer destructive magnitude of the bomb. What events could so directly threaten U.S. security to justify use of the bomb? Soviet-American tension was unavoidable because of differing ideologies, cultures, and definitions of security, but leaders of both nations realized that tension must never lead to war. A fine line wound its way between toughness and aggression, between security and expansion. These perilous times demanded careful leadership because the international climate of distrust made any words susceptible to misinterpretation and any events open to misperception.

The postwar world situation almost inevitably led the United States into adopting a form of economic diplomacy that gradually became military in thrust. As in the 1920s and 1930s, U.S. leaders argued that international trade was vital to the maintenance of world peace, the spread of democratic institutions, and the prevention of another postwar depression through the growth of capitalism. Truman made his position clear when he declared that "the three—peace, freedom, and world trade—are inseparable." Americans would prosper, of course, from an economically open world, but such a system would benefit others too. Yet the chief snag was that war-devastated Europeans lacked the means to buy U.S. goods. The path to peace therefore seemed to lie in an ambitious foreign aid program. By 1950, however, U.S. involvement in European and Near Eastern affairs above the Mediterranean Sea had become so military in nature that almost every action widened the division between East and West and thereby intensified the Cold War.

Onset of the Cold War

The first real sign of impending Soviet-American postwar difficulties arose at a late 1945 series of Council of Foreign Ministers' meetings. From September through October the ministers met in London to draw up peace treaties with Italy and the other former Axis states of Rumania, Bulgaria, Hungary, and Finland. Despite an agenda that related only to European matters, Soviet Foreign Commissar Molotov repeatedly protested against the United States's independent postwar occupation of Japan (discussed in the next chapter). He also wanted Italy to award the Soviet Union some territory in the Mediterranean and $100 million in reparations. U.S. Secretary of State James F. Byrnes joined the British in opposing Soviet advances into the Mediterranean and in arguing that Italy's war-ravaged economy could not permit huge reparations. He also rejected any peace terms with Rumania and Bulgaria that did not require the establishment of democratic governments. Molotov refused to give such assurances, defending his stance by pointing to the dominance of Britain in Greece and the United States in Japan. At one point during the proceedings, Molotov asked Byrnes if he had "an atomic bomb in his side pocket." The South Carolinian wittily replied, "You don't know Southerners. We carry our artillery in our hip pocket. If you don't cut out all this stalling and let us get down to work, I am going to pull an atomic bomb out of my hip pocket and let you have it." Molotov and the interpreter laughed, although Byrnes's remark suggested that the Truman administration was keenly aware of the diplomatic advantages afforded by the bomb. The conference adjourned in deadlock.

The following December 1945, at the Moscow Conference of Foreign Ministers, Soviet attitudes appeared to have softened. Byrnes agreed to recognize the Soviet-controlled Rumanian and Bulgarian governments and to recommend an Allied Control Council for Japan; Stalin accepted a more broadly based representation in Rumania and Bulgaria, promised to attend a peace conference in Paris in 1946, and consented to cooperate in the establishment of a program of international atomic supervision. The atmosphere in Moscow was less tense than it had been in London, but the Soviets' aggressive behavior had already made a distinct impression on Truman. Although he had earlier tried to mediate between growing British and Soviet animosities, he now sharply rebuked what he called Byrnes's "appeasement policy" and asserted that the secretary had "lost his nerve in Moscow." In January 1946 Truman disgustedly wrote Byrnes that he was "tired of babying the Soviets."

By early 1946 the nation's attitude toward the Soviet Union had become more rigid. Secretary of the Navy James V. Forrestal opposed any attempt to "buy understanding and sympathy" from the Soviets. "We tried that once with Hitler," he caustically remarked. Republican Senator Arthur Vandenberg of Michigan (an isolationist until Pearl Harbor) encouraged the administration to adopt a harder line toward the Soviets and recalled what happened when the West gave in to aggressors during the 1930s. In February, Americans learned that a spy ring in Canada had relayed information on atomic research to the Soviet Union. Armed with the atomic bomb, the Soviets appeared to be capable of anything.

Problems in Iran suggested the ominous direction of international affairs and soon emerged as the first major issue for the newly established UN organization. An Anglo-Soviet agreement in 1942 had approved the wartime occupation of Iran, with the stipulation that each force would withdraw six months after the fighting ended. In the meantime the British had retained their virtual monopoly on

Iranian oil production and marketing that they had held since the beginning of the century, whereas a U.S. firm had secured a small concession in 1944 and prompted the Soviets to seek the same. When a Communist-inspired revolution broke out in the northern province of Azerbaijan in late 1945, the Moscow government sent arms and troops to aid the rebels.

Iran worked with the United States in bringing the matter before the United Nations, which was then meeting in London. The Security Council turned the issue over to the Soviets and Iranians to negotiate. The Soviets demanded the permanent installation of their troops in Iran, control of a proposed oil company, and rights for the Communist Tudeh party in Azerbaijan. Iran rejected every term. When the deadline for the Soviets' withdrawal came and passed in March 1946, the West became alarmed that both countries had enlarged their armies and had brought in additional heavy military goods.

Yet neither the Soviets nor their cohort made any attempt to overthrow the Iranian government, probably because of U.S. opposition and the worldwide hostility toward the Kremlin's actions. The Soviets pulled out of Iran in May after securing certain rights for the Tudeh in Azerbaijan and gaining the assurance of oil concessions if the Iranian legislature approved (which never materialized). The following December 1946 the United States sent aid to Iran that helped to put down the unrest in Azerbaijan. Although the Soviets did not intervene, the Truman administration recognized that East-West rivalries in the Near East, as well as in Eastern Europe, could escalate tensions to a dangerous level.

In the midst of the Iranian troubles, heated rhetorical exchanges brought greater focus to the growing impasse between East and West. Stalin delivered a spirited speech praising Leninist doctrine and denouncing the West. In it he argued that a clash between communism and capitalism was inevitable and necessitated a massive Soviet military buildup. Emphasis would be on internal development through a series of five-year plans, and not on the international economic proposals worked out at Bretton Woods in 1944. Although he probably intended this speech only for domestic consumption, Americans considered it the prelude to a new wave of Soviet aggression. Indeed, Moscow's leaders began to tighten controls in Eastern Europe, and at home launched a bitter propaganda campaign against the United States and the West.

Less than two weeks later, on February 22, 1946, the American chargé in Moscow, George F. Kennan, sent his home office the famous "long telegram," an 8000-word, sixteen-page response to the state department's request for an analysis of Stalin's fiery speech. Kennan was a career diplomat who had been educated at Princeton and trained in the Foreign Service as one of the first Ameri-cans assigned to observe the Soviets from Riga in Latvia. He was also a member of the first U.S. embassy in Moscow when William Bul-litt began his nightmarish three-year stint as ambassador in 1933. For more than a decade, Kennan remained in the Soviet Union and eastern Europe, developing a warm feeling for the Soviet people while enriching his scholarly interest in nineteenth-century Russian litera-ture. But he strongly detested the revolution-ary principles of the Bolshevik Revolution and the bloody Stalinist purges of the 1930s—which he had seen firsthand.

Neither friendship nor war with the Soviets was conceivable, Kennan insisted in early 1946. The Soviets had a "neurotic" view of the world and were "committed fanatically to the belief that with [the] U.S. there can be no perma-nent modus vivendi." Their fear of "capitalist

George F. Kennan
As chargé in Moscow in 1946, he wrote the "long telegram," and as a member of the state department's Policy Planning Staff, he wrote an article entitled, "The Sources of Soviet Conduct"—both of which helped to establish him as the chief architect of America's containment policy. *Wide World Photos, New York.*

encirclement," Kennan continued, had now reasserted "the traditional and instinctive Russian sense of insecurity." Americans must work toward securing the industrial and economic nerve centers of Western Europe and Japan while preparing countermeasures short of war to discourage Soviet expansion. The president read the telegram as did many officials in the state department. Its argument confirmed what they already believed.

In March 1946 Churchill bore witness to a certain East-West confrontation when he came to the United States and delivered a blunt warning of Soviet intentions. Before a Westminster College crowd in Fulton, Missouri, and with Truman on the dais, the august and elderly British statesman dramatically proclaimed in his gravelly voice that "from Stettin in the Baltic to Trieste in the Adriatic, an iron curtain has descended across the continent." The Soviets did not want war; they sought "the fruits of war and the indefinite expansion of their power and doctrines." The only recourse was a "fraternal association of English-speaking peoples." A *Pravda* interview with Stalin soon appeared in the *New York Times*, which carried the Soviet premier's dark assertion that Churchill's appeal for an Anglo-American alliance was a "call to war" as dangerous in its racial implications as Hitler's hate-filled speeches. Surely, Stalin declared, the European nations did not want to replace the "lordship of Hitler" with the "lordship of Churchill."

Other developments pointed to continually worsening Soviet-American relations during the spring of 1946. The Soviets had wanted a huge loan from the United States for domestic reconstruction purposes, but even though Secretary of Commerce Henry Wallace and Secretary of the Treasury Henry Morgenthau favored the financial measure as a stimulus to trade and better relations, Truman opposed the action without Soviet concessions. The former U.S. ambassador to the Soviet Union, W. Averell Harriman, had won Truman's support for foreign aid as "one of the most effective weapons at our disposal."

The president later asserted that the Soviets would have to come to the United States because "we held all the cards." The United States had offered the enticement of new negotiations regarding Eastern Europe along with the possibility of Soviet involvement in the World Bank, but the Kremlin showed no interest in either idea. The first could lead to concessions to the West, and the second would entail subordination to an organization under U.S. control. But in May the Soviets suddenly reversed their position and expressed a willingness to discuss Eastern Europe. Their surprising message aroused considerable uncertainty within the Truman administration. The president's advisers did not believe that the Soviet Union was ready to retreat in Eastern Europe, and they realized that funds in the World Bank were too low to permit a major loan. The state department therefore turned down the Soviet proposal and promptly ended all loan discussions. That same month the military governor of the U.S. occupation zone in Germany, General Lucius Clay, cut off reparations from that zone to the Soviet Union until it cooperated in promoting German economic unity. The Soviets doubtless interpreted the U.S. rejection of the loan and the termination of German reparations as the first assault of a massive economic offensive by the United States.

Another major source of contention was the Truman administration's proposal for international control of atomic weaponry through the Baruch Plan. The United States, Britain, and Canada had called for an international organization to regulate atomic energy, and Truman responded by asking Undersecretary of State Dean Acheson and David Lilienthal (head of the Tennessee Valley Authority) to draw up a plan. Their proposal called for an international body to supervise both the materiel and the production process involved in developing atomic energy. In June 1946 financier Bernard Baruch, the U.S. representative on the Atomic Energy Commission (recently established by the UN General Assembly), made significant revisions in the

Acheson-Lilienthal Plan that authorized the United States to control the entire program—including peaceful research on atomic power *inside* the Soviet Union. Under what became known as the Baruch Plan, an International Atomic Development Authority was to regulate "all atomic energy activities potentially dangerous to world security" through licensing and on-site inspections. Once this agency established controls, the United States would dispose of its atomic stockpile and halt further production. The United States would give up its atomic monopoly—*after* the Soviets stopped their research and permitted on-the-spot verification. To allow the program to work, Baruch insisted on suspension of the veto in the Security Council. The choice, he declared, was "World Peace or World Destruction."

Not surprisingly, the Soviet Union rejected the Baruch Plan. The Kremlin could not approve a program of international atomic control monopolized by the United States, nor could it allow internal inspection and forgo use of the veto in such a substantive matter. The Americans, according to the Moscow government, should destroy their atomic stockpile, outlaw atomic weapons, and allow the veto to apply to atomic energy matters. After months of wrangling, the Soviet delegate in the Security Council, Andrei Gromyko, declared that suspension of the veto would lead to "unlimited interference" in "the economic life of the countries on whose territories this control would be carried out, and . . . in their internal affairs." Proponents of the Baruch Plan, Gromyko charged with considerable justification, "completely ignore national interests of other countries and proceed from . . . the interests actually of one country; that is, the United States of America."

There was little hope for international atomic energy controls. The United States could not surrender its monopoly on atomic weapons because of the strength of the Red Army, and the Soviets refused to cut back on ground forces because of U.S. possession of the bomb. One way out of this dilemma was for the West to build up its land armies; the other was for the Soviets to develop their own atomic bomb. As for the Baruch Plan, it was dead.

By autumn 1946 the Truman administration's growing hard-line approach to Soviet affairs became increasingly evident during the steadily escalating controversy over Germany. The only common ground between East and West was the belief that Germany should exist as a nation; beyond that, the two sides vehemently disagreed over nearly every issue—particularly whether its government should be democratic or Communist. After the war, and consistent with the Potsdam reparations agreements, the Soviets confiscated huge amounts of foodstuffs, carried away numerous Germans for forced labor, and dismantled and took home entire industrial plants and other materials from their eastern zone. The Soviets also refused to fulfill the wartime agreements requiring the occupation forces to send food and supplies to the other zones; but in doing so they failed to foresee the adverse effect this move would have on their interests: It forced Germans outside the eastern sector to depend on the United States for assistance.

At Stuttgart in September 1946, Secretary of State Byrnes signaled a major change in U.S. policy when he delivered a stirring speech that called for partitioning Germany between East and West. The Potsdam agreement aimed at the economic unity of Germany was not working, he declared, and more direct assistance from the United States was needed to secure the continent, restore Germany's economy, and encourage its move toward a federal system of self-government. The Truman administration had given up on uniting the country economically and now admitted to the seemingly irrevocable partition between East and West. Thus, a stalemate presented a better option than continued disagreements that might culminate in war. The punitive spirit so evident at Potsdam had given way to the overriding necessities of securing French cooperation by dropping the call for German reunification and of offering assurances to Western Germany and U.S. allies in Europe that it intended to safeguard them from Soviet communism. The U.S. and British zones should merge, Byrnes said, and the United States must stay in Europe indefinitely.

In December 1946 Britain and the United States took a big step toward an East-West partition of Germany when they combined their occupied areas into "Bizonia." The Soviet Union charged (correctly) that such a move violated the wartime agreements by promoting the permanent partition of Germany. France feared another resurrection of its long-time enemy and refused to join the merger. Although the reaction from Paris was disturbing to the Truman administration, its chief concern was the Soviet Union. "There's no way to argue with a river," Acheson later declared about negotiating with the Soviets. "You can channel it; you can dam it up. But you can't argue with it."

The Truman administration had meanwhile asked for an in-house study of the motives behind Soviet behavior and the recommended actions by the United States. The result was a lengthy report in September 1946, prepared by presidential counsel Clark Clifford, that the president considered so explosive that he collected all copies and had them locked away. The Clifford memorandum, drawing heavily from Kennan's ideas, advised the United States to prepare for atomic and biological warfare because of Soviet aggressions driven by fear of capitalist encirclement. Moreover, these Soviet aggressions would stop only if checked by U.S. counterpressure, both military and economic. The Clifford report called on the United States to prepare for a war on all fronts. "When you are faced with that kind of crisis," Clifford declared, "you come up with whatever weapons you have—political, military, economic, psychological, whatever they might be."

Secretary of Commerce Wallace was worried that the Truman administration's hardening Soviet policies would lead to war. A former member of Roosevelt's cabinet and his vice president until January 1945, Wallace remained an ardent New Deal liberal and a strong advocate of developing an economic

relationship with the Soviets. In a September 1946 speech before a huge crowd of 20,000 in New York's Madison Square Garden, he insisted that " 'getting tough' never brought anything real and lasting—whether for schoolyard bullies or businessmen or world powers. The tougher we get, the tougher the Russians will get." Americans must "get out of eastern Europe" and allow the Soviets to devise their own security apparatus. Wallace had already embarrassed the administration by repeatedly criticizing the new president's domestic and foreign policies, and after some confusion over whether the secretary had had prior approval to deliver the address, Truman secured his resignation. "The Reds, phonies and 'parlor pinks,' " the president recorded in his diary, "seem to be banded together and are becoming a national danger. I am afraid they are a sabotage front for Uncle Joe Stalin."

The Wallace episode suggested deep division within the administration over the direction of foreign policy, but this appearance quickly changed in the spring of 1947 when a sharp deterioration in U.S.-Soviet relations prompted the White House to draw the line against Soviet expansion. After another rancorous Council of Foreign Ministers' meeting in Moscow, the focus of trouble abruptly shifted from Western and Eastern Europe to the fringe area along the top of the Mediterranean—the "northern tier" of Greece, Turkey, and Iran. Rebuffed in Iran a year earlier, the Soviets now seemed determined to stage a Communist takeover in Greece and wrest the straits from Turkey.

Although it is doubtful that the Soviets were either directly involved in the Greek troubles or actually prepared to make a military move against Turkey, the heightened emotional atmosphere resulting from the believed threat encouraged perceptions that distorted reality. Evidence suggests that from mid-1945 through late 1946 the Soviets attempted a political infiltration of Greece, but even that restrained effort failed. Yet the impression remained in Washington that the Soviets exercised considerable control over events. The

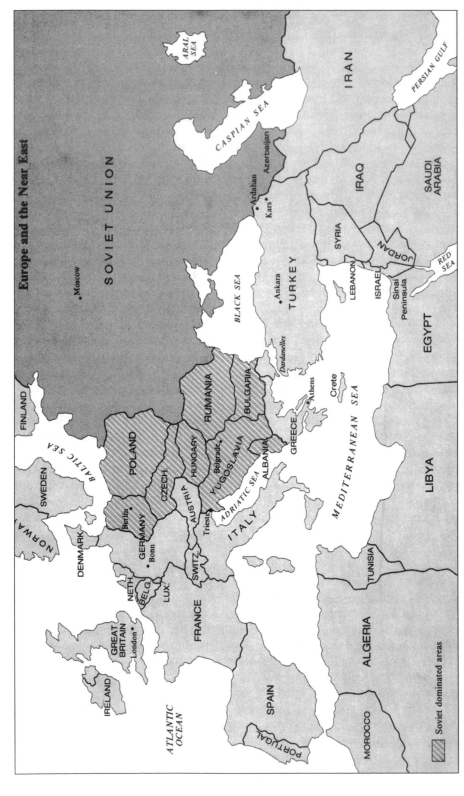

Europe and the Near East

Map 19
These areas, in particular the "northern tier" of Greece, Turkey, and Iran, became the focal points of the Cold War in the early part of the Truman administration.

Truman administration feared that Soviet success in these two ventures would provide access to the Persian Gulf, the Mediterranean, and, ultimately, the entire Middle East. The alarming prospect was that Soviet hegemony in this oil-rich region could promote the collapse of Western Europe without the firing of a single shot. Americans came to perceive Greece and Turkey as the last barrier to a catastrophic break in Britain's Mediterranean lifeline that would permit a dangerous spread of Soviet influence. The controlling power in the eastern Mediterranean would determine the fate of the World Island—that huge area adjoining the Mediterranean, the Near and Middle East, and North Africa.

Formation of the Truman Doctrine

The Truman administration's immediate concern was Greece. That small country had been under Nazi occupation until October 1944 and then had experienced sporadic outbreaks of domestic violence that took on the extreme bitterness of a vendetta. The central political issue was whether Greece would remain monarchical or adopt a democratic system of government. King George II had fled the country during World War II and established a government-in-exile, first in London and then in Cairo. The British promised to support his attempt to reoccupy the throne after the German withdrawal, but they encountered staunch opposition from a leftist and Communist-led wartime resistance group called the National Popular Liberation Army, or ELAS, and its political counterpart, the National Liberation Front, or EAM. In the period after the Germans pulled out of the country, the Greek Communist party—the KKE—boasted of building a Greater Greece. But the new state meant different things to different people. To Greek nationalists, it heralded territorial expansion northward and the enhancement of Greece as a nation; to hard-core Communists it entailed meshing the Greeks into a Balkan federation or Macedonian free state led by Slavs. EAM/ELAS enjoyed considerable popular support as long as it sustained an image of promoting purely Greek interests.

Germany's departure from Greece threatened to set off a civil war in the long-beleaguered country. Major fighting broke out between leftists and rightists in the streets of Athens by December of 1944, which led the British to send troops to aid Greek national forces in putting down what was a Communist-led rebellion. Widespread apprehension had developed over whether the Soviets would help the KKE, but they had not done so for several reasons. As pointed out earlier, during the previous October of 1944 Stalin and Churchill had negotiated the percentages agreement in Moscow, which recognized a British sphere of interest in Greece in exchange for Soviet hegemony in Rumania. Stalin abided by that agreement. According to a contemporary, the Soviet premier refused to interfere with the December uprising because he opposed spontaneous, indigenous or nationalist revolutions not susceptible to his control. It also seems likely that Stalin realized that Soviet interference in Greece on the eve of the Yalta Conference could have hurt his chances for achieving favorable postwar adjustments in Europe and Asia. For whatever reasons, he did not order the Red Army to intervene in the December revolution in Greece.

The warring parties finally arranged an uneasy truce at Varkiza in February 1946, which called first for a plebiscite to determine the people's will concerning the form of government they wanted and then the election of a constituent assembly. But during succeeding days the rightist Athens government heated the political atmosphere by brutally repressing all opposition to the monarchy. By March, when the plebiscite was to occur, the British and Americans had reversed the political procedure stipulated at Varkiza. Over KKE protests and its eventual abstention, the general election took place first, which brought in a constituent assembly favorable to the monarchy, and in the following September a plebiscite yielded the same results, seemingly demonstrating great popular support for the king's return. It is impossible to determine the legitimacy of the vote. Americans were part of an international observer team that attested to the fairness of the elections, although the Soviet press joined the KKE and others in criticizing the outcome and blasting the British-supported government in Athens as "monarcho-fascist."

It seems certain now that most of the problems in Greece were of domestic origin, but in this angry atmosphere reason gave way to emotion, causing the March elections to set off the civil war that many Americans automatically assumed was Soviet-inspired. In August 1946 the guerrillas launched a number of raids on villages and towns and received valuable assistance from the Communist regimes in Yugoslavia, Albania, and Bulgaria. For territorial ambitions rather than ideological ties, the Communist leader in Yugoslavia, Josip Broz Tito, soon furnished the bulk of the aid by providing sanctuary, material goods (both military and nonmilitary), and training and hospital facilities. Indeed, according to one of Tito's cohort, the Soviet Union itself contributed a small portion of these goods. Tito hoped to build a Balkan federation by acquiring Trieste at the top of the Adriatic Sea and annexing enough of Greece to permit access to the Mediterranean. The British, however, became convinced that aid to the guerrillas came indirectly from Moscow and warned Americans of Greece's imminent collapse to communism. Although most rebels were Greek nationalists and not Communists interested in world revolution, the West believed that Communist leadership in the uprising necessarily meant links to the Kremlin. Firsthand observations underlined that point, however unsubstantiated by concrete evidence. The U.S. ambassador to Greece, Lincoln MacVeagh, warned that Yugoslavia, Albania, and Bulgaria were Moscow's puppets and that Greece's fall would open the Mediterranean to the Soviets. By spring 1947 the United States regarded Greece as the supreme test of the Free World's will.

Turkey was also a vital part of the West's concern. Located along the Soviet border,

Turkey controlled the straits connecting the Black Sea with the Mediterranean and was vital to the Soviets' push for a warm water link to the Middle East. For two hundred years the Russians had wanted the straits. In the post–World War II period the Soviet Union sought a revision of the Montreux Convention of 1936, which had recognized Turkish control of the straits. The Soviets wanted the Dardanelles, along with the districts of Kars and Ardahan on the east side of the Black Sea, the last two of which bordered Soviet Georgia and Armenia and had been lost after World War I. During World War II the Turks had allowed Germany to use the straits to enter the Black Sea and attack the Soviet Union itself. At Yalta, Stalin declared that he could not allow Turkey to have "a hand on Russia's throat," and at Potsdam he sought to salvage the straits by opposing the U.S. call for internationalizing all inland waterways bordered by more than two countries (thereby safeguarding U.S. control over the Panama Canal and British control over the Suez Canal because both waterways touched only a single country). Turkey was anti-Soviet, Stalin told the U.S. ambassador in Moscow, and command of the straits was "a matter of our security."

A Soviet intimidation campaign against Turkey began soon after the war. Moscow's leaders launched a series of feverish propaganda attacks, and by early 1947 Soviet troops had amassed along the common border. These events suggested an imminent invasion of Turkey, causing a "war of nerves" that forced the Ankara government to assign most of its already sparse funds to military preparations.

The Turkish crisis of late 1946 did not surprise the United States. In the autumn of that year it had stationed a battleship in nearby waters to demonstrate support for Turkey and had warned the Moscow government that any move toward the straits would cause the United States to take the issue before the UN Security Council. Truman had agreed with Undersecretary of State Dean Acheson to stand firm. "We might as well find out whether

Dean Acheson
President Truman's secretary of state who became a Pulitzer-Prize winning author in 1969 for his book *Present at the Creation. National Portrait Gallery.*

bottle through which Soviet political and military influence could most effectively flow into the eastern Mediterranean and Middle East."

The twin crises along the northern rim of the Mediterranean merged into a U.S. problem in February 1947, when the British government informed the United States that it was no longer financially able to maintain long-standing commitments in Greece and Turkey. On Monday, February 24, the state department received two notes from the British ambassador announcing an end to economic assistance in Greece and Turkey on March 31 and warning that if aid were to continue the United States would have to assume the responsibility. General Marshall, who had replaced Byrnes as secretary of state in January, had already instructed Acheson to prepare an economic and military assistance plan for Greece. The task of formulating an official reaction to the notes therefore fell to Acheson, who had received word just the Friday before that the British were preparing to withdraw from Greece and Turkey. That same day he had authorized a state department policy planning group to work around the clock over the weekend to draft a favorable response to London.

Events moved quickly in Washington. The director of the newly organized Near Eastern Affairs Division, Loy Henderson, joined others in the state department in writing a plan outlining U.S. economic assistance to Greece and Turkey. From Acheson's desk the draft went before the State-War-Navy Coordinating Committee (SWNCC), which believed that economic rehabilitation in Greece could not succeed until the Athens government wound down the civil war. SWNCC therefore called for a shift in emphasis to military aid. In the meantime the Greek government followed the state department's recommendation to make a formal request for help, and Acheson easily secured Truman's support by warning that the collapse of Greece and Turkey would throw open the entire Mediterranean to the Soviet Union. "If Greece fell within the Russian orbit," Acheson told his cabinet colleagues, "not only Turkey would be affected but

the Russians were bent on world conquest now," the president declared.

With the United States firmly behind the Turks, the Soviets soon eased their demands. In September the Truman administration declared that a task force, spearheaded by the huge aircraft carrier *Franklin D. Roosevelt,* would remain in the Mediterranean on a permanent basis. When Soviet newspapers angrily called this "gangster diplomacy," Admiral William ("Bull") Halsey drew widespread U.S. support with his indignant reply: "It's nobody's damn business where we go. We will go anywhere we please." Although the crisis had passed, the White House believed this only a reprieve and would not relax its vigilance. A state department study had earlier asserted that Turkish control of the straits "constitutes the stopper in the neck of the also Italy, France, and the whole of western Europe." Congressional members from both parties received invitations to the White House to join the administration in forming a bipartisan foreign policy aimed at halting a Communist drive allegedly engineered by the Kremlin.

Although the oil of the Middle East (forty percent of the world's reserves) was a crucial factor in U.S. thinking, the administration presumed that everyone understood this fundamental truth and emphasized instead the battle with communism. Senator Arthur Vandenberg, chair of the Foreign Relations Committee, supported the approach and warned that the proposal would succeed only if the administration engaged in a major campaign designed to scare Americans about the dangers of a Communist takeover. What lay ahead, Truman remarked to his advisers, was "the greatest selling job ever facing a President."

This whirlwind of activity in Washington culminated in the Truman Doctrine. Before a joint session of Congress on March 12, 1947, the president outlined the dangers in Greece and Turkey and then pointed to the bipolarity of interests in the world. He did not specify the Soviet Union as the cause of unrest in the Mediterranean world, although the allusions were unmistakable. One set of ideas was totalitarian and repressive, Truman asserted, the other democratic and supportive of freedom. Should Greece and Turkey fall to communism, the forces of oppression could stamp out freedom in the Near and Middle East. "I believe," he emphasized in the main thrust of the Truman Doctrine, "that it must be the policy of the United States to support free peoples who are resisting attempted subjugation by armed minorities or by outside pressures." To save Greece and Turkey, Congress must support a massive military and economic aid program of $400 million, most of which would be military and go to Greece. He also sought authorization for sending military and civilian advisers to each country to administer the aid programs.

Considerable resistance immediately arose against what appeared to be a drastic shift in the nation's foreign policy. Marshall and Kennan, who had been recently recalled from Moscow to serve in the state department office, thought the anti-Communist tone of the message too severe, but the president had deferred to Clifford's advice in delivering a "blunt" statement of the U.S. position on recent events along the Mediterranean. Kennan did not perceive a military threat in either Greece or Turkey and argued that the Soviet challenge was primarily political; economic assistance offered the correct remedy. Truman's language was "grandiose" and "sweeping," Kennan warned, and would lead to a worldwide crusade that the United States was neither militarily nor economically prepared to support. When critics inquired why the United States did not act through the United Nations, Acheson explained that the situation was an emergency, that the United Nations had no funds except those provided by the United States, and that once the crisis had passed, the United Nations could assume responsibility. Vandenberg helped to ward off much of this criticism. Failure to act, he warned Congress, would encourage a "Communist chain reaction from the Dardanelles to the China Sea and westward to the rim of the Atlantic." He then sponsored an amendment assuring Americans that the United States would retreat from its commitments to the Truman Doctrine when the United Nations was able to assume them.

Others complained that the United States had made a blanket commitment to worldwide foreign aid that would ultimately bankrupt the country. Acheson countered that the Truman Doctrine applied specifically to Greece and Turkey and that the administration would consider aid to other countries only on their "individual merits." To other skeptics the administration admitted that neither Greece nor Turkey was democratic but noted that those situations might change if the United States could guarantee both nations' right to choose a government. Isolationist Republican Robert Taft insisted that the United States was taking on Britain's responsibilities; Acheson responded that whatever happened in Greece and Turkey affected the United States's own vital interests.

The arguments continued for weeks, but in May 1947 Congress approved the Greek-Turkish Aid bills in a wide and bipartisan vote. By autumn U.S. aid was en route to both countries.

Thus, by summer 1947 the United States had moved toward a more cohesive foreign policy that gradually became known as "containment," a policy that rested in part on Kennan's theories of attempting to thwart Soviet expansion through any means short of war. In July he expanded his ideas in an anonymously written article for *Foreign Affairs* magazine which he entitled, "The Sources of Soviet Conduct." Signing it "X" (a ploy that fooled few people), Kennan warned that the basis of Stalin's behavior was Marxist-Leninist ideology combined with his effort to mobilize popular support for his policies by exploiting the widespread fear of "capitalist encirclement." The Kremlin was in no hurry to achieve world conquest. Its "political action is a fluid stream which moves constantly, wherever it is permitted to move, toward a given goal." The only solution was "a long-term, patient but firm and vigilant containment." The United States had to counter the Soviets "at a series of constantly shifting geographical and political points, corresponding to the shifts and maneuvers of Soviet policy." Such a U.S. response might lead to "either the breakup or the gradual mellowing of Soviet power."

The vagueness of Kennan's argument left him susceptible to the unwarranted charge of favoring a global crusade against communism. He did not clarify whether he meant containment through military or economic means. Nor did he make clear that some areas of the world were vital to U.S. interests and that others lay on the periphery. The result was that policymakers would regard his writings as a warning that all over the world the Soviets intended to instigate crises designed to spread Communist ideology and that the United

States had to be militarily ready to halt this new form of aggression wherever it occurred.

The same month that Kennan's article appeared, Congress left little doubt about the aggressive direction of U.S. foreign policy when it passed the National Security Act. This legislation first gave statutory sanction to the Joint Chiefs of Staff and then established several advisory bodies. It created a National Security Council to advise the president on domestic and foreign policy relating to the nation's security, a secretary of defense to replace the secretary of war and coordinate control over the nation's armed forces, and the Central Intelligence Agency to gather and analyze intelligence at home. An amendment to the act in 1949 created the Department of Defense, and the CIA's activities were later expanded to include covert operations outside the country. Indeed, the secret provision condoning "sabotage" and "subversion" also instituted untruths as an official part of policy by declaring that CIA leaders were to craft their activities so carefully that if exposed there must be room for plausible denial. Containment, whether by military or economic means, or both, became the guiding principle of the administration's foreign policy.

Columnist Walter Lippmann was among more than a few Americans who opposed the doctrine of containment. He warned that it would lead to a worldwide ideological crusade because it failed to delineate which areas sought by the Soviets were of vital importance to the United States. In addition, Lippmann believed, Stalin was motivated more by historic Soviet expansionist aims than by Communist ideology. The real issue, Lippmann insisted, was a balance of power. The United States should confront the Soviets with naval bases in the eastern Mediterranean, along with other visible signs of its strength. There was danger in attempting to stop Soviet expansion with "dispersed American power in the service of a heterogeneous collection of unstable governments and of contending parties and factions which happen to be opposed to the Soviet Union." Such a policy would harden the Soviet military presence in Europe while draining U.S. resources and will. It presumed Soviet involvement in all of Europe and Asia, which in turn depended on the questionable premises that the Moscow government had the ability to coordinate its own foreign policy as well as that of its allies. Leaders in Washington and Moscow should arrange a mutual withdrawal of their military forces from Central Europe and thus defuse the dangerous situation. Containment, Lippmann concluded, was a "strategic monstrosity."

Despite the much trumpeted fears of globalism and ultimate war, Washington's policymakers had actually fashioned a program that, if carefully used, rested on the principles of flexibility and restraint. Acheson repeatedly assured congressional committees that the Truman Doctrine did not entail an automatic global commitment by the United States and that each applicant for assistance would receive consideration based on the merits of that case alone. The chief guidelines were simple: The area requesting assistance must be vital to U.S. interests and capable of salvation. Acheson also emphasized that the type of aid depended on the type of problem under advisement. Greece was in the throes of civil war and needed emergency military assistance. Indeed, the war at first went so badly for the Greek government that some Washington officials seriously considered sending U.S. combat troops. Finally, however, the Greek National Army firmed up its performance in the field as a result of the arrival of U.S. military materiel and uniformed advisers on the operational level. The Soviet threat to Turkey had already eased, permitting that government to handle many of its problems without as much direct U.S. involvement.

The Truman Doctrine eventually stabilized Greece and Turkey, thereby appearing to establish the credibility of the United States's containment policy. Nearly three hundred U.S. military and civilian advisers and a host of support personnel provided advisory assistance to the Greek army in its war against the guerrillas. U.S. advice and firepower proved

essential to the ultimate triumph of the government's forces, although Tito's independent posture in the Communist world caused a bitter rift between Yugoslavia and the Soviet Union that was also important in winding down the civil war in Greece. A year after Tito defected from the Communist Information Bureau (Cominform) in July 1948, he closed the border to Greek guerrillas and cut off assistance. The guerrillas no longer had a place of refuge and were forced to raid and pillage the Greek countryside for provisions and seize hostages as military inductees. Popular resistance to their methods grew, increasing support for the king. In October 1949 the fighting came to an end when the royalist forces, aided by U.S. napalm and navy Helldivers, scattered the guerrillas into the northern mountains of Greece and into Albania. The crisis in Turkey likewise passed as U.S. military assistance and advice bolstered the country against Soviet pressure.

Both successes were fortuitous abroad though divisive at home. In May 1948 the United States had extended recognition to the new Jewish state of Israel (discussed in a later chapter), whose creation set off the first of many postwar crises in the Middle East and thereby brought even more stature to the resolution of the Greek-Turkish problems. On the one hand, containment seemed to have yielded a monumental triumph in the Near East, and hence in the Cold War. On the other hand, the administration's success in scaring Americans into adopting such an ambitious aid program had a negative and inflammatory effect at home: It encouraged another "red scare" similar to that of 1919 and 1920. Its label during the 1950s became "McCarthyism," however, and its impact proved even more damaging to the blameless Americans caught in the accusatory fallout.

The atmosphere of McCarthyism actually began to develop during the late 1940s, when Whitaker Chambers, senior editor of *Time* and a former Communist party member, accused Alger Hiss, a state department adviser who had accompanied Roosevelt to Yalta, of being a Communist spy. A widely publicized trial followed that catapulted young Republican Representative Richard M. Nixon of California, then chair of the House Committee on Un-American Activities, into the national limelight as an anti-Communist crusader. To support the charges, Chambers escorted Nixon and a large group of reporters to his farm in Maryland, where he pulled out of a pumpkin several rolls of microfilm containing the state department documents of the late 1930s allegedly pilfered by Hiss. Though protected from the charge of espionage by the statute of limitations, Hiss was convicted of perjury in January 1950 and sentenced to five years' imprisonment for denying having been a Communist or knowing Chambers. The judicial process, however, failed to resolve the central question of whether Hiss actually was a spy. A pattern of conspiracy seemed to develop when that same month British physicist Klaus Fuchs was identified as one of several spies who had participated in developing the atomic bomb and then shared secrets with the Soviets.

Then, in February 1950, Senator Joe McCarthy of Wisconsin, desperately looking for an issue that would assure his shaky bid for reelection, appeared before a Republican Women's Club in Wheeling, West Virginia, and dramatically waved a so-called list of Communists in the state department. Although he had no such list, his theatrics caused a veritable witch-hunt that spread like wildfire throughout the country, lasting for nearly five years and ruining many innocent persons' reputations. In every walk of life, including the government, Hollywood, and the college teaching profession, Americans suspected of being anything less than fiercely anti-Communist were automatically condemned as "pinkos," "fellow travelers," or "hard-core Communists." Fear of subversion at home necessitated a stronger policy abroad, leading Americans to attribute problems in other countries to a huge monolithic form of communism emanating solely from the Kremlin, and not to difficulties arising from within

troubled countries. The forecast was deepening U.S. involvement in foreign affairs and a greatly intensified Cold War.

Heightened Cold War: The Marshall Plan and Germany

While the Truman Doctrine was under way, the administration turned toward resolving the massive economic problems in Europe left by World War II. Europe, Churchill lamented, was "a rubble heap, a charnel house, a breeding ground of pestilence and hate." Despite billions of dollars of U.S. assistance through the UN Relief and Rehabilitation Administration (UNRRA) and other organizations by mid-1947, Europe lay open to despair, revolution, and totalitarian exploitation, particularly in France and Italy where local Communist parties were strong and threatening to win national elections. Furthermore, the United States had withdrawn from UNRRA in 1946 because of charges that Communist East European nations were distributing food only to political allies. The last U.S. aid installments arrived the following year, forcing an end to UNRRA and highlighting the desire of Americans, in Acheson's words, to extend relief "in accordance with our judgment and supervised with American personnel." The central dilemma was clear: No recovery could take place in Europe without Germany playing an integral role in that recovery. And that entailed further alienation of the Soviet Union—as well as France.

In spring 1947, after a frustrating Council of Foreign Ministers' conference in Moscow, Secretary of State Marshall visited Western Europe and was visibly shaken by the devastation. Europeans were unable to buy American products, and the drought of 1946 had almost wiped out the grain crop. The ensuing winter of 1946–1947 had brought heavy snowstorms followed by spring floods that threatened the next year's yield and raised the distinct possibility of spreading a famine across Europe. The British were also in dire straits. Officials had reserved coal for emergency use only, and they had even ordered brief daily shutdowns of electricity to save the sharply diminishing supply. Communist party victories in the fast-approaching elections in France and Italy would mean that for a second time within the decade, Britain would stand alone against totalitarian aggression. In exchange for Britain's relaxation of commercial restrictions, the United States had approved a loan of $4.4 billion in July 1946, but even this huge sum was not enough to stave off impending disaster. Upon Marshall's return to Washington he instructed Kennan, now head of the state department's new Policy Planning Staff, to prepare a study of the European situation and recommend a policy promoting relief and recovery.

George C. Marshall
He eventually became President Truman's secretary of state and a proponent of the Marshall Plan in Europe. *U.S. Army.*

At Harvard University's commencement ceremony on June 5, 1947, the secretary of state delivered an address on European affairs that became the essence of the Marshall Plan. Partly basing his remarks on Kennan's report, Marshall warned that the widespread "economic, social, and political deterioration" of Europe was conducive to political instability, totalitarian exploitation, and the obstruction of peace. Kennan had earlier argued that "world communism is like a malignant parasite which feeds only on diseased tissue." Marshall now expressed this same thought, which had already become the prevailing view in the state department. Following the stand advocated by Undersecretary of State for Economic Affairs William L. Clayton, Marshall called on all European governments—East and West—to draw up a mutual aid program and inform the United States how it could contribute to their recovery. "The initiative," he emphasized, "must come from Europe."

To avoid antagonizing the Soviets, Marshall insisted, the United States must make no distinction between the forms of government receiving assistance. "Our policy is directed not against any country or doctrine but against hunger, poverty, desperation, and chaos." As Acheson noted in an earlier speech in Mississippi, these problems were common to all Europeans. Such a stance, however, raised fears that U.S. aid might go to Communist East Europe and even to the Soviet Union. This was unlikely, according to Kennan and Charles E. Bohlen, who had been with Kennan in witnessing Stalin's brutal purges of the 1930s and was the principal writer of Marshall's Harvard address and later ambassador to Moscow. The Soviets, Kennan believed, could not accept U.S. help, especially when the stipulations for doing so included U.S. participation in planning the recipient's economy and full disclosure of that government's files to verify need. Anxiety remained, however. If the Moscow government accepted the U.S. invitation and Congress refused to approve an aid bill, the United States would suffer a serious propaganda defeat.

Marshall's offer of economic assistance caused a flurry of activity in Europe that culminated in a tripartite conference in Paris. In late June, British Foreign Secretary Ernest Bevin met in that city with French Foreign Minister Georges Bidault and after considerable discussion decided to invite Soviet Foreign Commissar Molotov to join them. Molotov at first hesitated to attend, even though he doubtless realized that failure to do so would increase the chances of a Western alliance. Yet if the Soviet Union became part of that bloc, its allied states would be susceptible to Western penetration. U.S. assistance, Molotov feared, might draw Eastern Europe toward the West, revive Germany, and endanger Soviet military security. Although disgruntled by the situation, he finally accepted the invitation.

Accompanied by eighty-nine economic advisers and clerks, Molotov attended the meeting in Paris, where he blasted the aid proposal as a "new venture in American imperialism" and objected to nearly every aspect of the program. He opposed U.S. control over reconstruction and called for a decentralized approach to preserve the integrity of each participant. He wanted each government to compile its own list of needs and send it directly to the United States. Bevin and Bidault disagreed. "Debtors do not lay down conditions when seeking credits from potential creditors," Bevin remarked to Molotov. "If I went to go to Moscow with a blank check and ask you to sign it I wonder how far I would get at your end." The following day Molotov warned them not to act without Soviet approval. His arguments had no impact. Bevin and Bidault rejected these stipulations, and Molotov stalked out of the conference.

Molotov's decision greatly relieved the Truman administration. Harriman, now secretary of commerce, declared that "Bevin did a superb job of getting Molotov out of Paris—by careful maneuvering. Bidault claims to have had a part in it. But Bevin had the courage to invite Molotov and the bluntness to get rid of him. He could have killed the Marshall Plan by joining it." Kennan confessed to having no faith in Soviet cooperation in trying to establish trade between East and West. "So, in a sense, we put Russia over the barrel.... When the full horror of [their] alternatives dawned on them, they left suddenly in the middle of the night."

After Molotov's departure, France and Britain invited more than twenty European governments to Paris to draft a proposal for U.S. aid. Those governments under Soviet influence—Yugoslavia, Albania, Bulgaria, Poland, Rumania, Czechoslovakia, Hungary, and Finland—either did not attend or denounced the aid program as an "imperialist" conspiracy. By September, sixteen Western European governments requested a four-year allotment of $22 billion of assistance aimed at bringing economic stability to the continent by 1951.

Poland and Czechoslovakia had rejected the chance for U.S. aid only with great reluctance and because of Soviet intimidation. Both had initially shown interest in participating in the program but changed their minds because, they declared with more than a little trepidation, acceptance "might be construed as an action against the Soviet Union." A Czech delegation led by Foreign Minister Jan Masaryk had been in Moscow to negotiate a commercial treaty when a question arose about whether their government should accept U.S. assistance. Stalin bitterly attacked the program as an effort "to form a Western bloc and to isolate the Soviet Union." He continued in an icy tone: "We look upon this matter as a question of principle, on which our friendship with Czechoslovakia depends.... All the Slavic states have refused.... That is why, in our opinion, you ought to reverse your decision." To refuse to do so, Stalin pointedly warned, carried dangerous repercussions: "If you take part in the conference, you will prove by that act that you allow yourselves to be used as a tool against the Soviet Union." Neither the Czech nor the Polish governments sent representatives to Paris.

The Soviet Union tried several tactics to reduce the impact of the proposed Marshall

Plan. It negotiated defense pacts with Finland, Bulgaria, Hungary, and Rumania, which were additions to those agreements already signed with Poland, Czechoslovakia, and Yugoslavia. It rigged elections in Hungary to ensure Communist victory. In early October 1947 Molotov arranged the establishment of the Cominform in Belgrade, a nine-member organization that succeeded the now-defunct Comintern, which the Kremlin had dissolved four years earlier. The new Cominform now attempted to disrupt U.S. influence in Europe. Moscow also announced the Molotov Plan, a series of bilateral treaties promising Soviet economic assistance to Communist governments in Europe. Strikes broke out in Italy and France, which apparently were Communist efforts to undermine faith in those governments and prevent them from becoming recipients of Marshall Plan aid.

In January 1948, shortly after another abortive Council of Foreign Ministers' meeting in London, Truman sparked a lively debate over the European aid bill when he asked Congress to appropriate $6.8 billion for fifteen months, followed by more than $10 billion during the next three years. The purpose, he stated, was to "contribute to world peace and to its own security by assisting in the recovery of sixteen countries which, like the United States, are devoted to the preservation of the free institutions and enduring peace among nations." Economic and political stability in Europe meant greatly enhanced trade for the United States and a halt to the spread of communism. Wallace, already ousted from the administration after his speech in New York, termed the aid program a "Martial Plan," and Senator Taft denounced it as a "European T.V.A." Too much money had already gone overseas, many charged, and such a program might worsen U.S.-Soviet relations and further divide Europe into hostile camps.

Despite this vocal opposition, it quickly became evident that Congress would approve the aid program. Among its supporters were farmers, laborers, manufacturers, and the press. Also working in its favor was the Cold War

itself. In an action strikingly reminiscent of the Munich crisis of a decade before, the Communists overthrew the Czech republic in February 1948 and installed a regime tied to the Kremlin. Masaryk's sudden death, reported as suicide though attributed by Truman to "foul play," especially appalled the West and promoted the bill's passage. Other inducements to congressional support of the Marshall Plan were the forced Russo-Finnish alliance, the expected Communist victory in the impending elections in Italy, and rising tensions in Germany. General Clay in Berlin noted a "new tenseness in every Soviet individual with whom we have official relations." In an effort to convince Congress to allot more money to the military but which raised fear about the outcome in Germany, he warned that war "may come with dramatic suddenness." The Senate approved the aid bill by a wide margin (69 to 17), and as it went before the House, Truman delivered a speech to Congress calling for a universal military training program and resumption of the selective service.

In March 1948 the House of Representatives overwhelmingly approved the Economic Cooperation Act (ECA), or Marshall Plan (329 to 74), which became a prime example of the administration's containment policy. The act established the European Recovery Program, which eventually provided more than $12 billion of assistance by its termination date of 1952. Congress also restored selective service, and even though it rejected universal military training, it strengthened the air force. In the meantime the European governments, as members of the Organization of European Economic Cooperation (OEEC), prepared to receive U.S. aid.

The Marshall Plan, which the president signed into law on April 3, 1948, was the result of a combination of idealistic and realistic concerns. Although it attempted to help Europe for humanitarian reasons, it also sought to halt the spread of communism. By extending credits to Europeans to purchase American goods, the United States hoped to restore order to the continent, prevent Communist takeover, and enhance U.S. prestige. The United States also aimed to promote economic growth by expanding capitalism through the multilateral trade principles spelled out in the Bretton Woods agreements of 1944. To further ensure free commercial exchange, the United States that same year of 1948 joined twenty-two other nations in establishing the General Agreement on Tariffs and Trade (GATT), which rested on the most-favored-nation principle. Thus liberal trade agreements between two countries would extend automatically to the others as well. The key to economic recovery, however, was the integration of Europe and the reintegration of Germany into a system of multilateral world trade.

The Marshall Plan was a success in many ways. With U.S. assistance, the European economic recovery that was already under way picked up in intensity. In addition, the aid probably helped to undercut the Communist party in France while proving instrumental in that party's defeat in the elections in Italy. Europe did not become commercially interdependent: Cartels and other obstacles to trade remained. Yet the Marshall Plan made headway by following many principles underlying the New Deal. In meshing private capital interests with the government, it exemplified the new sense of cooperation between the public and the private sector that led to greater efficiency through planning and control, reduction of commercial barriers, and ready convertibility of currencies. The central objective was to build a multilateral, corporatist system that guaranteed global security by tying together economic, political, social, and strategic interests. Like the Truman Doctrine, however, the Marshall Plan became heavily military in character. When it ended in 1952, eighty percent of its assistance had become military, partly stemming from the outbreak of the Korean War in 1950 and partly because of the 1951 decision to merge the ECA with the Military Defense Aid Program. This broadened program then became the Mutual Security Administration in 1952 and continued to distribute military aid funds to Europe. In one sense, however, the accomplishments of the Marshall Plan bore mixed results: Although the aid program brought enormous benefits to its recipients, it drove the wedge deeper between East and West by helping to reconstruct Germany and thereby encouraged the Kremlin to clamp down even more on Eastern Europe.

The Berlin Crisis

The Marshall Plan contributed to the Soviets' ongoing fear of a reunified Germany and helped bring on a crisis in Berlin during the summer of 1948 that caused the Truman administration to discuss using the atomic bomb. The city lay almost one hundred miles within the Soviet zone of occupation, landlocked from the West though guaranteed access by air. Only under great pressure from the United States and Britain had France recently joined its occupation forces with

Postwar Germany
In the rubble of Essen, Germany, was a new citizen who benefited from American aid. *Harry S. Truman Library, Independence, Mo.*

theirs in creating "Trizonia," which they believed might save Germany's economy. The Soviets, however, feared that Trizonia would lead to the West's ultimate absorption of their economically weaker eastern zone. The entire German economy was in bad shape. The reichsmark was so inflated that American cigarettes had become a medium of exchange. Food supplies and steel production were down, relief costs were rising, and the Communist party was becoming stronger.

The Western governments had met in London that spring of 1948 and recommended that the Germans elect a constitutional convention to establish a government for the western section of Germany. They had also instituted changes in the currency system designed to ease the inflationary spiral and promote economic reunification under Western leadership. Indeed, the currency issue became a vital consideration. Not only would the new currency provide the financial base for economic restoration, but it would further encourage political unification under Western control. Such reforms, in combination with the Marshall Plan, would rehabilitate Germany, promote Europe's revival, and, as a matter of course, threaten the Soviet Union.

In early June the West established the West German Republic, while the Joint Chiefs of Staff in the United States urged the Truman administration to seek a military alliance with Western European countries that approved the use of German troops. Although the Council of Foreign Ministers had repeatedly failed to resolve the German unification question, the growing economic unity of the West's three zones increased the likelihood of a self-governing West Germany. In spring 1948 representatives of the United States, Britain, France, Belgium, Luxembourg, and the Netherlands gathered in London to establish a government in West Germany. The Ruhr industries would remain under their supervision, but in cooperation with the West Germans. Residents of West Germany would elect a parliament, which would draft a constitution for a federal government inviting East German membership. To alleviate fears of a rearmed Germany, the United States and others would maintain restrictions on West Germany's foreign activities, prevent rearmament, and terminate foreign occupation only when calm returned to Europe. The wisest approach for the time being was to secure a defense alignment with Western Europe that did not include Germany but which nonetheless sought to establish the independence of that country's western zones.

There were precedents in the Western Hemisphere for such collective defense arrangements. In August 1947 U.S. representatives had attended a conference in Rio de Janeiro that had established a regional defense agreement, encouraged multilateral status for the Monroe Doctrine, and assured help to any American republic undergoing armed assault until the UN Security Council could take action. The Inter-American Treaty of Mutual Assistance of September, or Rio Pact, fulfilled the intentions of Article 51 of the UN Charter by providing collective security in the hemisphere. In early 1948 Marshall sought a treaty against communism when he led a U.S. delegation to the Ninth International Conference of American States at Bogotá, Colombia. As a sweetener, he offered $500 million of assistance through the Export-Import Bank. But the recipients had expected considerably more than that. Street riots, rumored to be Communist-inspired but probably driven more by hunger and anger with the United States, temporarily disrupted the conference and underscored the Truman administration's perceived need for an agreement. More than one thousand people died in the violence that left large parts of the city in ruins.

After authorities restored order in Bogotá, the Latin American republics returned to the conference and signed the charter of the Organization of American States (OAS), which went into effect in 1951. The United States praised this regional defense pact as another triumph over communism; Latin Americans considered it a victory over U.S. interventionism. Over the Truman administration's strenuous objections, the Latin American delegations exacted a high price for allying with the United States: They inserted Article 15 of the OAS Charter, which declared that "no State or group of States has the right to intervene, directly or indirectly, for any reason whatever, in the internal or external affairs of any other State."

These agreements still did not satisfy Latin Americans, who demanded an aid program similar to that of the Marshall Plan in Europe. Despite the very real economic problems plaguing the Americas south of the United States, the Truman administration presented an argument that set policy until the early 1960s: The Cold War dictated greater emphasis on Europe. Moreover, Truman's advisers insisted, the development of markets abroad would help Latin America by absorbing its exports. But Latin Americans wanted greater access to U.S. markets and deeply resented White House priorities.

The United States had meanwhile continued to work toward a military pact in Europe. In March 1948 Britain, France, Belgium, Luxembourg, and the Netherlands signed the Brussels Treaty, which established a fifty-year collective defense system known as Western Union, and shortly afterward Truman called on Congress to support the pact. In June the Senate overwhelmingly approved the Vandenberg resolution, which called for U.S. cooperation "with such regional and other collective arrangements as are based on continuous and effective self-help and mutual aid, and as affect its national security." The United States, the resolution continued, should make known "its determination to exercise the right of individual or collective self-defense under article 51 [of the UN Charter] should any armed attack occur affecting its national security."

By the summer of 1948 the West's new measures appeared threatening to Moscow, driving its foreign policy into disarray. West European nations were banding together under the Marshall Plan and had moved closer to a military alliance with the United States. An independent West Germany necessarily meant its eventual incorporation into a military organization opposed to the Soviets. U.S. economic assistance had already gone to Yugoslavia, whose Communist regime under Tito had left the Communist bloc and exposed a deep crack in the alleged monolith. With Germany revived, Western Europe strengthened and unified, and Eastern Europe perhaps loosening its loyalties to Moscow, the security of the Soviet Union itself came into question.

That same June of 1948, doubtless sparked by the West's announcement that month of a fledgling West German Republic, the Soviets took drastic action. They imposed a blockade of all surface routes into West Berlin (rail, highway, and water) in an effort to intimidate and divide the Western alliance, halt the move toward a West German government, and undermine U.S. influence in Europe. In addition, they froze bank deposits in the city's central bank (located in the Soviet sector) and greatly reduced the flow of electricity into West Berlin from power plants also found in the eastern sector of the city. The diminished power carried enormous potential for trouble because it would hit everyone by slowing down the pumps handling sewage disposal and maintaining the water supply. The same day the blockade went into effect, the Soviets issued the Warsaw Declaration, which demanded a return to the four-power division of Germany stipulated at Potsdam.

The Soviets appeared to hold the upper hand. The West had no specific guarantee of any surface connections through Soviet-controlled eastern Germany, meaning that it would have to either pull out of Berlin and leave the Soviets in total control of East Germany or agree to negotiations that would restore the four-power wartime agreements on all Germany. The latter measure would assure the Soviets a major governing voice throughout the country because by an earlier agreement, every decision had to come from a unanimous vote. In either case, the Soviets would have achieved their chief objective of halting the creation of a West German government. Certainly, Stalin must have reasoned,

The Berlin Chess Game
After Stalin imposed a blockade on Germany on
June 24, 1948, Truman countered with the
Berlin Airlift. *Simon and Schuster, New York.*

the West would reject the use of force in opening the surface routes. He now held more
than two million Germans hostage in their
own country.

Stalin correctly assumed that the West
would not directly challenge the blockade.
The U.S. military governor in Berlin, General
Clay, called for a strong reaction that his superiors in Washington ultimately rejected. Clay
had warned the Pentagon in early April that
"when Berlin falls, Western Germany will be
next. If we mean . . . to hold Europe against
communism, we must not budge. . . . If we
withdraw, our position in Europe is threatened. If America does not understand this
now, then it never will and communism will
run rampant. I believe the future of democracy requires us to stay." The Soviet action
was a bluff, Clay believed; the United States
should test the Soviet will by ordering an
armed convoy into Berlin. But the army chief
of staff, General Omar Bradley, warned that

the Soviets could impede the passage of Allied
trucks without the use of force. They could
simply close the roads for repairs, or "a bridge
could go out just ahead of you and then
another bridge behind, and you'd be in a hell
of a fix." General Albert C. Wedemeyer, director of Army Plans and Operations in Washington, noted the Soviets' military superiority
in the region and warned that "our forces
would have been annihilated." Colonel Frank
Howley, chief of the military government in
the U.S. zone, put it even more bluntly: "We
would have got our *derrieres* shot off."

Truman searched for a response that would
be equivalent to the Soviet blockade without
raising the ante and increasing the chances for
war. He realized that the Red Army outnum-
bered Allied forces in Germany three to one,
and he knew that reopened negotiations over
Germany would endanger the establishment
of the new West German government. So he
adopted a suggestion posed earlier by the
British: a massive airlift, carried out in con-
junction with the British and designed to
deliver supplies into the western part of the
city. In addition, he supported a counterblockade—an embargo on selected industrial
items considered integral to Soviet needs in
East Germany (including chemicals and steel).
The West had to act, warned a British general
on the scene. Otherwise, it "might wake up
some fine morning to find the Hammer and
Sickle already on the Rhine." No questions
could arise about the legality of an airlift,
because the Allied Control Council had earlier
authorized the establishment of three air lanes
connecting West Germany with Berlin.

In the event that the airlift failed, however,
the United States seemed prepared to resort
to the atomic bomb—or at least to leave the
impression with the Soviets that it would use
that weapon. Although the United States at
that time had fewer than fifty bombs (and not
all of them usable) and only thirty B-29s capable of delivering them, the president sent a
threatening signal to the Kremlin by securing
Britain's permission to base sixty B-29 bombers
into the country and declaring to the press that

they were "atomic-capable." Indeed, he hinted that they carried nuclear warheads. Not until the 1970s did it become clear that the planes were not yet adaptable to a nuclear cargo. But Truman's intimidation tactics might succeed—as long as Stalin did not dismiss them as a mere bluff. The Soviet premier probably remained uncertain whether the United States would actually use the bomb, but he must have been well aware of the limited nature of its nuclear capacity. One of his top-level spies, Donald Maclean, was in Washington from 1946 to 1948, where, in his capacity as Britain's joint secretary of the Combined Policy Committee on Atomic Energy, he had full access to atomic stockpile information.

By spring 1949 the Anglo-American airlift, occasionally harassed but never attacked by Soviet planes, had provided over 13,000 tons of goods per day (more than three times the amount required), enough to meet the needs of Americans plus the city's other 2,500,000 residents. From the beginning of the airlift in late June 1948, each citizen in West Berlin received more than half a ton of supplies from planes arriving daily at three-minute intervals.

From Berlin to NATO

If Stalin's central purpose was to drive the Western powers apart and stop the founding of a West German government, his strategy failed. The ongoing Berlin crisis solidified the West and further stimulated the drive toward a self-governing West Germany tied to the West. It also served as an important impetus for the formation of the North Atlantic Treaty Organization (NATO) that might join the Truman Doctrine and Marshall Plan in bringing postwar order to the continent. On April 4, 1949, twelve nations assembled in Washington to sign the North Atlantic Treaty, which established a European defense pact that initially included the United States, Britain, Canada, France, Italy, Belgium, Luxembourg, Norway, Denmark, Iceland, Portugal, and the Netherlands. By the mid-1950s, however, NATO's membership grew to fifteen with the additions

of Greece, Turkey, and West Germany. Unlike the Rio Pact of 1947, NATO was a military alliance of permanent duration, uniting signatories "by means of continuous and effective self-help and mutual aid." Article Five of the treaty of 1949 declared that "an armed attack against one or more [signatory nations] . . . shall be considered an attack against them all" and promised "such action as it deems necessary, including the use of armed force." The United States alone possessed atomic weapons, and NATO had the Strategic Air Command (SAC) with its long-range bombers. Direction of the new organization would come through the North Atlantic Council, comprised of the foreign, defense, and finance ministers of member nations.

The ensuing debate over U.S. membership in NATO raised familiar arguments. Critics predicted involvement in European wars and ultimate bankruptcy caused by deepening foreign commitments. Taft warned that NATO would provoke an arms race and, in an argument remindful of the Lodge-Wilson fight over the League of Nations, declared that the pact would tie U.S. soldiers to Europe without constitutional sanction. NATO's advocates countered that the pact contained no provisions for mandatory military action, that the United States had vital interests in Europe's security, and that a Soviet attack was unlikely, largely because only the United States had the bomb. Acheson, now secretary of state after Marshall's resignation in January 1949, assured the Senate that membership in NATO did not require the United States to commit more ground forces to Europe; the new system constituted a warning to the Soviets that NATO and the U.S. presence would have a "tripwire" effect intended to generate even a nuclear response in an extreme case.

The success of the Berlin airlift, the pressures resulting from the Western counterblockade, and the tightened Western alliance provided by NATO forced the Soviets to call off their blockade in May 1949. The West had gained a major victory in the Cold War. Anxious moments had not led to a military confrontation, and the United States had acted calmly, legally, and with resolution. World public opinion had meanwhile judged the Soviet Union to be in the wrong. In exchange for the Soviet retreat, the United States agreed to discuss the German question at another Council of Foreign Ministers' meeting in Paris later that month. Although the conference led to no agreements on Germany, Soviet actions in Berlin had ensured the formation of the West German Republic and encouraged the United States to join the European defense system.

The Senate approved U.S. membership in NATO by a wide margin on July 21, 1949, and two days later the president signed the agreement. That same day he sent Congress the Mutual Defense Assistance Bill, which provided a one-year appropriation of $1.5 billion to revamp and expand Europe's military strength. Thus, NATO furnished a viable alternative to the bomb in deterring Soviet aggression. At the same time, the pledge to use the bomb secured the much-needed European bases for B-29 bombers. Vandenberg considered NATO "the most important step in American foreign policy since the promulgation of the Monroe Doctrine." The United States had joined its first entangling alliance in Europe since the treaty with France in 1778 and its first formal military alliance in peacetime. It had also become part of a military organization that hardened Cold War divisions and, almost paradoxically, helped to reduce the likelihood of all-out war.

Another objective of the Truman administration's European policy was to win Allied support for rearming West Germany and making it part of NATO's military force. The organization needed German human and industrial resources, although France and the Benelux nations remained concerned about the restoration of their long-time enemy. In September 1949 Trizonia became West Germany, or the Federal Republic of Germany (which included the three Western sectors of Berlin). Its capital was Bonn, and its chancellor Konrad Adenauer. The government was civilian in orientation, although Allied military occupation continued under a High Commission of three members, one each from the Western occupying powers. As noted earlier, the United States approved Marshall Plan assistance for the new republic and agreed to participate in the international administration of the Ruhr Valley. West Germany's 50 million people had not only begun the long process of economic and political recovery, but their new government now seemed on the verge of a major military buildup.

The movement for West German military integration into NATO received a sudden boost in late September 1949, when Truman stunned Americans by announcing that the Soviet Union had exploded an atomic device—ten years earlier than some experts had envisaged. While this development unsettled Americans at home, it also severely weakened the central bond of NATO: the United States's atomic monopoly. The following month the Soviets announced the formation of the German Democratic Republic of East Germany. Two Germanies and two Berlins—each trying to absorb the other—became symbols of the East-West struggle for Europe. Western Europe's hatred for Germany, the Truman administration was convinced, would have to give way to the immediate need of halting further Soviet advances across the European continent. NATO required the integration of West German soldiers to balance the strength of the Red Army.

Prevailing thought in Washington dictated that with the East and West in atomic deadlock, the United States would have to work even harder to block Soviet infiltration of potential new nations and their resources. In the president's inaugural address of the previous January of 1949, he had outlined his foreign policy objectives: support for the United Nations, Marshall Plan, and "freedom-loving nations," and "a bold new program for making the benefits of our scientific advances and industrial progress available for the improvement and growth of underdeveloped areas." The last, a Technical Assistance Program for

Latin America, Asia, and Africa, became known as Point Four. It aimed at combating "hunger, misery, and despair" and thus preventing the spread of communism into the southern half of the globe. Congress, however, reacted with little enthusiasm. It implemented Point Four in 1950 by allocating the modest sum of $35 million for technical aid and placing the program under the Technical Cooperation Administration. Despite the dearth of funds, the United States soon negotiated agreements with more than thirty countries and helped fight disease and famine while raising living standards through the building of facilities for hydroelectric power and irrigation. The Soviets responded quickly. Less than a week after the president called for Point Four, they established a Council for Mutual Economic Assistance, designed to help their fellow Communist states.

By 1950 the United States's emphasis in foreign aid had shifted dramatically from economic to military assistance. The Truman Doctrine had proved the State-War-Navy Coordinating Committee to be correct: Crushing the rebellion in Greece was the necessary prerequisite to the country's economic rehabilitation. Marshall Plan aid gradually became more military oriented, and soon afterward the United States implemented a global military aid program under the Mutual Defense Assistance Act of 1949. Within two years the West lifted the restraints from Italy, permitting it to rearm. U.S. priorities had also become unmistakably military with the establishment of NATO, because that organization's stated purpose was to maintain a ground force large enough to hold off Soviet attack until the United States could engage the Strategic Air Command.

Yet NATO's conventional land forces never became as large as hoped, primarily because France led the movement to integrate Germany's industrial might into a broadly based program of West European control that would, as a necessary by product, prevent a resurgence of the German military machine. French Foreign Minister Robert Schuman succeeded in

instituting the Schuman Plan of 1951, which established the European Coal and Steel Community and was composed of France, West Germany, Italy, and the three Benelux countries. The United States's European allies seemed satisfied to remain under free nuclear protection while continuing to block the use of West German troops.

The biggest impetus to a militarized U.S. foreign policy was nuclear development. The Soviets' challenge to the United States's atomic monopoly, combined with the Communist victory in China shortly afterward (discussed in the next chapter), seemed too close in time to be coincidental. In January 1950 the president ordered the development of a hydrogen bomb that would be hundreds of times more powerful than either atomic bomb used on Japan. Opposition to the hydrogen bomb (or "Super") came from a long list of scientists that included J. Robert Oppenheimer, who had supervised the building of the atomic bomb and now joined David Lilienthal (chair of the AEC) in calling the hydrogen bomb "a weapon of genocide." The result, they all warned, would be an arms race that could escalate into nuclear war. Truman, however, pushed for the new bomb, which the United States successfully tested in 1952. A year later the Soviets did the same.

Toward a Global Strategy: NSC-68

In late January 1950 Truman directed the state and defense departments "to make an overall review and reassessment of American foreign and defense policy in the light of the loss of China, the Soviet mastery of atomic energy and the prospect of the fusion [hydrogen] bomb." Kennan feared a massive arms buildup intended to establish what Acheson called "situations of strength" and resigned as head of the state department's Policy Planning Staff. His replacement was Paul Nitze, a hard-liner who supervised the preparation of this report, which reached the president's desk in April. There was no foreseeable end to the Communist threat, according to National

Security Council Study 68 (NSC-68); conflict was "endemic." As Acheson later noted, the top secret document "combined the ideology of communist doctrine and the power of the Russian state into an aggressive expansionist drive, which found its chief opponent, and, therefore, target in the antithetical ideas and power of our own country." The Free World faced danger from a "combination of ideological zeal and fighting power."

Kennan had been correct in his prognosis: NSC-68 urged the United States to "strike out on a bold and massive program of rebuilding the West's defensive potential to surpass that of the Soviet world, and of meeting each fresh challenge promptly and unequivocally." Americans were to defend the non-Communists from Soviet encroachments through a military-oriented, globalist, and activist policy of containment. Such an objective necessitated expenditures almost four times greater than the budgeted amounts for 1950. Not only did the United States have to develop more "atomic weapons," but it must implement a decision already made by the president to build the infinitely more powerful "thermonuclear" or hydrogen bomb.

NSC-68, not declassified until the mid-1970s (and even then by accident), had defined the world's problems in the broad ideological terms of communism versus democracy. It had called on the United States to take the lead in restoring world stability as the first step toward destroying communism. Once the United States had contained the Communists, it was to "foster the seeds of destruction within the Soviet system." Any distinction between vital and peripheral interests had blurred, meaning that strategic areas included every point along the Soviet perimeter. No longer was there a distinction between the security of the United States and that of the world; they had meshed into a global and offensive policy that condoned any policy necessary to victory. "The integrity of our system will not be jeopardized by any measures, covert or overt, violent or nonviolent, which serve the purposes of frustrating the Kremlin design."

But before the Truman administration could decide how to implement these recommendations, its justification for a huge military buildup fortuitously appeared in June 1950, when war suddenly broke out in Korea.

Selected Readings

Acheson, Dean. *Present at the Creation: My Years in the State Department.* 1969.

Alexander, George M. *The Prelude to the Truman Doctrine: British Policy in Greece, 1944–1947.* 1982.

Ambrose, Stephen E., and Brinkley, Douglas G. *Rise to Globalism: American Foreign Policy since 1938.* 8th ed., 1997.

Anderson, Irvine H. *Aramco, The United States, and Saudi Arabia: A Study of the Dynamics of Foreign Oil Policy, 1933–1950.* 1981.

Anderson, Sheldon. "Poland and the Marshall Plan, 1947–1949," *Diplomatic History* 15 (1991): 473–94.

Anderson, Terry H. *The United States, Great Britain, and the Cold War, 1944–1947.* 1981.

Arkes, Hadley. *Bureaucracy, the Marshall Plan, and the National Interest.* 1972.

Backer, John H. *The Decision to Divide Germany: American Foreign Policy in Transition.* 1978.

———. *Winds of History: The German Years of Lucius DuBignon Clay.* 1983.

Ball, S. J. *The Cold War: An International History, 1947–1991.* 1998.

Barker, Elisabeth. *The British Between the Superpowers, 1945–1950.* 1983.

Barnes, Trevor. "The Secret Cold War: The C.I.A. and American Foreign Policy in Europe, 1946–1956. Part I," *The Historical Journal* 24 (1981): 399–415.

———. "The Secret Cold War: The C.I.A. and American Foreign Policy in Europe, 1946–1956. Part II," *The Historical Journal* 25 (1982): 649–71.

Baylis, John. *The Diplomacy of Pragmatism: Britain and the Formation of NATO, 1942–1949.* 1993.

Bernstein, Barton J. "American Foreign Policy and the Origins of the Cold War," in Bernstein, Barton J., ed., *Politics and Policies of the Truman Administration,* 15–77. 1970.

Best, Richard A., Jr. *Co-operation with Like-Minded Peoples: British Influences on American Security Policy, 1945–1949.* 1986.

Bill, James A. *The Eagle and the Lion: The Tragedy of American-Iranian Relations.* 1988.

Black, Allida M. *Casting Her Own Shadow: Eleanor Roosevelt and the Shaping of Postwar Liberalism.* 1995.

Blum, Robert M. "Surprised by Tito: The Anatomy of an Intelligence Failure," *Diplomatic History* 12 (1988): 39–57.

Bohlen, Charles E. *Witness to History, 1929–1969.* 1973.

Boll, Michael M. *Cold War in the Balkans: American Foreign Policy and the Emergence of Communist Bulgaria, 1943–1947.* 1984.

Borowski, Harry R. *A Hollow Threat: Strategic Air Power and Containment before Korea.* 1982.

Boyer, Paul S. *By the Bomb's Early Light: American Thought and Culture at the Dawn of the Atomic Age.* 1985.

Brands, H. W. *Inside the Cold War: Loy Henderson and the Rise of the American Empire, 1918–1961.* 1991.

———. *The Devil We Knew: Americans and the Cold War.* 1993.

———. *The Specter of Neutralism: The United States and the Emergence of the Third World, 1947–1960.* 1989.

Brands, Henry W., Jr. "Redefining the Cold War: American Policy toward Yugoslavia, 1948–60," *Diplomatic History* 11 (1987): 41–53.

Browder, Robert P., and Smith, Thomas G. *Independent: A Biography of Lewis W. Douglas.* 1986.

Buhite, Russell D., and Hamel, William C. "War for Peace: The Question of an American Preventive War against the Soviet Union, 1945–1955," *Diplomatic History* 14 (1990): 367–84.

Byrnes, James F. *All in One Lifetime.* 1958.

———. *Speaking Frankly.* 1947.

Callahan, David. *Dangerous Capabilities: Paul Nitze and the Cold War.* 1990.

Campbell, Thomas M. *Masquerade Peace: America's UN Policy.* 1973.

Chace, James. *Acheson: The Secretary of State Who Created the American World.* 1998.

Cohen, Michael J. *Truman and Israel.* 1990.

Cohen, Warren I. *America in the Age of Soviet Power, 1945–1991.* 1993.

Conquest, Robert. *Stalin: Breaker of Nations.* 1991.

Costigliola, Frank. *France and the United States: The Cold Alliance since World War II.* 1992.

Couloumbis, Theodore A. *The United States, Greece and Turkey.* 1983.

Cronin, Audrey K. *Great Power Politics and the Struggle over Austria, 1945–1955.* 1986.

Davison, W. Phillips. *The Berlin Blockade: A Study in Cold War Politics.* 1958.

DePorte, A. W. *Europe Between the Superpowers: The Enduring Alliance.* 1979.

DeSantis, Hugh. *The Diplomacy of Silence: The American Foreign Service, the Soviet Union, and the Cold War, 1933–1947.* 1980.

Deutscher, Isaac. *Stalin: A Political Biography.* 2nd ed., 1967.

Doenecke, Justus D. *Not to the Swift: The Old Isolationists in the Cold War Era.* 1979.

Donovan, John C. *The Cold Warriors.* 1974.

Donovan, Robert J. *Conflict and Crisis: The Presidency of Harry S Truman, 1945–1948.* 1977.

———. *Tumultuous Years: The Presidency of Harry S Truman, 1949–1953.* 1982.

Dozer, Donald. *Are We Good Neighbors?* 1961.

Edmonds, Robin. *Setting the Mould: The United States and Britain, 1945–1950.* 1986.

Eisenberg, Carolyn. *Drawing the Line: The American Decision to Divide Germany, 1944–1949.* 1996.

Elliott, Mark R. *Pawns of Yalta: Soviet Refugees and America's Role in Their Repatriation.* 1982.

Ellwood, David W. *Rebuilding Europe: Western Europe, America, and Postwar Reconstruction.* 1992.

Evangelista, Matthew A. "Stalin's Postwar Army Reappraised," *International Security* 7 (1982–83): 110–38.

Evensen, Bruce J. *Truman, Palestine, and the Press: Shaping Conventional Wisdom at the Beginning of the Cold War.* 1992.

Fawcett, Louise L. *Iran and the Cold War: The Azerbaijan Crisis of 1946.* 1992.

Feis, Herbert. *From Trust to Terror: The Onset of the Cold War, 1945–1950.* 1970.

Ferrell, Robert H. *George Marshall.* 1966.

———. *Harry S. Truman: A Life.* 1994.

———. *Harry S. Truman and the Modern American Presidency.* 1983.

Fleming, D. F. *The Cold War and Its Origins, 1917–1960.* 2 vols., 1961.

Folly, Martin H. "Breaking the Vicious Circle: Britain, the United States, and the Genesis of the North Atlantic Treaty," *Diplomatic History* 12 (1988): 59–77.

Freeland, Richard. *The Truman Doctrine and the Origins of McCarthyism: Foreign Policy, Domestic Politics, and National Security, 1946–1948.* 1970.

Fried, Richard M. *Nightmare in Red: The McCarthy Era in Perspective.* 1990.

————. *The Russians Are Coming! The Russians Are Coming! Pageantry and Patriotism in Cold-War America.* 1998.

Gaddis, John L. "The Corporatist Synthesis: A Skeptical View," *Diplomatic History* 10 (1986): 357–62.

————. "The Emerging Post-Revisionist Synthesis on the Origins of the Cold War," *Diplomatic History* 7 (1983): 171–90.

————. "Intelligence, Espionage, and Cold War Origins," *Diplomatic History* 13 (1989): 191–212.

————. *The Long Peace: Inquiries into the History of the Cold War.* 1987.

————. "NSC-68 and the Problem of Ends and Means," *International Security* 4 (1980): 164–80.

————. *Russia, the Soviet Union, and the United States: An Interpretive History.* 2nd ed., 1990.

————. *Strategies of Containment: A Critical Appraisal of Postwar American National Security Policy.* 1982.

————. *The United States and the Origins of the Cold War, 1941–1947.* 1972.

————. *We Now Know: Rethinking Cold War History.* 1997.

Gardner, Lloyd C. *Architects of Illusion: Men and Ideas in American Foreign Policy, 1941–1949.* 1970.

Gimbel, John. *The American Occupation of Germany: Politics and the Military, 1945–1949.* 1968.

————. *The Origins of the Marshall Plan.* 1976.

Goldman, Eric F. *The Crucial Decade and After.* 1960.

Goode, James F. *The United States and Iran, 1946–51: The Diplomacy of Neglect.* 1989.

Gori, Francesca, and Pons, Silvio. *The Soviet Union and Europe in the Cold War, 1945–53.* 1996.

Gormly, James L. *The Collapse of the Grand Alliance, 1945–1948.* 1987.

————. *From Potsdam to the Cold War: Big Three Diplomacy, 1945–1947.* 1990.

Green, David. *The Containment of Latin America: A History of the Myths and Realities of the Good Neighbor Policy.* 1971.

Griffith, Robert. *The Politics of Fear: Joseph R. McCarthy and the Senate.* 1970.

Hahn, Peter L. *The United States, Great Britain, and Egypt, 1945–1956: Strategy and Diplomacy in the Early Cold War.* 1991.

Hamby, Alonzo L. *Man of the People: A Life of Harry S. Truman.* 1995.

Hanhimäki, Jussi M. *Containing Coexistence: America, Russia, and the "Finnish Solution."* 1997.

Harbutt, Fraser J. "American Challenge, Soviet Response: The Beginning of the Cold War, February–May, 1946," *Political Science Quarterly* 96 (1981–82): 623–39.

————. *The Iron Curtain: Churchill, America, and the Origins of the Cold War.* 1986.

Harper, John L. *America and the Reconstruction of Italy, 1945–1948.* 1986.

Harrington, Daniel F. "The Berlin Blockade Revisited," *International History Review* 6 (1984): 88–112.

————. "Kennan, Bohlen, and the Riga Axioms," *Diplomatic History* 2 (1978): 423–37.

————. "United States, United Nations and the Berlin Blockade," *Historian* 52 (1990): 262–85.

Hathaway, Robert M. *Ambiguous Partnership: Britain and America, 1944–1947.* 1981.

Haynes, John E. *Red Scare or Red Menace? American Communism and Anticommunism in the Cold War Era.* 1996.

Haynes, Richard F. *The Awesome Power: Harry S. Truman as Commander-in-Chief.* 1973.

Herken, Gregg. *Counsels of War.* 1985.

————. *The Winning Weapon: The Atomic Bomb in the Cold War, 1945–1950.* 1980.

Herring, George C. *Aid to Russia, 1941–1946: Strategy, Diplomacy, the Origins of the Cold War.* 1973.

Hershberg, James G. *James B. Conant: Harvard to Hiroshima and the Making of the Nuclear Age.* 1993.

Hess, Gary R. "The Iranian Crisis of 1945–46 and the Cold War," *Political Science Quarterly* 89 (1974): 117–46.

Hitchcock, William I. "France, the Western Alliance, and the Origins of the Schuman Plan, 1948–1950," *Diplomatic History* 21 (1997): 603–30.

Hixson, Walter L. *George F. Kennan: Cold War Iconoclast.* 1989.

Hogan, Michael J. "Corporatism: A Positive Appraisal," *Diplomatic History* 10 (1986): 363–72.

————. *A Cross of Iron: Harry S. Truman and the Origins of the National Security State. 1945–1954.* 1998.

————. *The Marshall Plan: America, Britain, and the Reconstruction of Western Europe, 1947–1952.* 1987.

————. "Revival and Reform: America's Twentieth-Century Search for a New Economic Order Abroad," *Diplomatic History* 8 (1984): 287–310.

———. "The Search for a 'Creative Peace': The United States, European Unity, and the Origins of the Marshall Plan," *Diplomatic History* 6 (1982): 267–85.

Hoopes, Townsend, and Brinkley, Douglas. *Driven Patriot: The Life and Times of James Forrestal.* 1992.

Iatrides, John O. *Revolt in Athens: The Greek Communist "Second Round," 1944–1945.* 1972.

Ireland, Timothy P. *Creating the Entangling Alliance: The Origins of the North Atlantic Treaty Organization.* 1981.

Isaacson, Walter, and Thomas, Evan. *The Wise Men: Six Friends and the World They Made: Acheson, Bohlen, Harriman, Kennan, Lovett, McCloy.* 1986.

Jackson, Scott. "Prologue to the Marshall Plan: The Origins of the American Commitment for a European Recovery Program," *Journal of American History* 65 (1979): 1043–68.

Jenkins, Roy, *Truman.* 1986.

Jessup, Philip C. "Park Avenue Diplomacy—Ending the Berlin Blockade," *Political Science Quarterly* 87 (1972): 377–400.

Johnson, Robert H. *Improbable Dangers: U.S. Conceptions of Threat in the Cold War and After.* 1994.

Jones, Howard. "The Diplomacy of Restraint: The United States' Efforts to Repatriate Greek Children Evacuated During the Civil War of 1946–49," *Journal of Modern Greek Studies* 3 (1985): 65–85.

———. *"A New Kind of War": America's Global Strategy and the Truman Doctrine in Greece.* 1989.

———, and Woods, Randall B. "Origins of the Cold War in Europe and the Near East: Recent Historiography and the National Security Imperative," *Diplomatic History* 17 (1993): 251–76.

Jones, Joseph. *The Fifteen Weeks (February 21–June 5, 1947).* 1955.

Kaplan, Lawrence S. *A Community of Interests: NATO and the Military Assistance Program, 1948–1951.* 1980.

———. *The Long Entanglement: NATO's First Fifty Years.* 1999.

———. *NATO and the United States: The Enduring Alliance.* 1988.

———. *The United States and NATO: The Formative Years.* 1984.

Kaufman, Burton I. *The Arab Middle East and the United States: Inter-Arab Rivalry and Superpower Diplomacy.* 1996.

Kennan, George F. *American Diplomacy.* Expanded ed. 1984. Originally published as *American Diplomacy, 1900–1950.* 1951.

———. *Memoirs, 1925–1950.* 1967.

———. ["X"], "The Sources of Soviet Conduct," *Foreign Affairs* 25 (1947): 566–82.

Kent, John. *British Imperial Strategy and the Origins of the Cold War, 1944–49.* 1993.

Kimball, Warren F. *Swords or Ploughshares? The Morgenthau Plan for Defeated Nazi Germany, 1943–1946.* 1976.

Klehr, Harvey, and Radosh, Ronald. *The Amerasia Spy Case: Prelude to McCarthyism.* 1996.

Kofas, Jon V. *Intervention and Underdevelopment: Greece during the Cold War.* 1989.

Kofsky, Frank. *Harry S. Truman and the War Scare of 1948: A Successful Campaign to Deceive the Nation.* 1993.

Kolko, Joyce, and Kolko, Gabriel. *The Limits of Power: The World and United States Foreign Policy, 1945–1954.* 1972.

Kuklick, Bruce. *American Policy and the Division of Germany: The Clash with Russia over Reparations.* 1972.

Kuniholm, Bruce R. *The Origins of the Cold War in the Near East: Great Power Conflict and Diplomacy in Iran, Turkey, and Greece.* 1980.

Kunz, Diane B. *Butter and Guns: America's Cold War Economic Diplomacy.* 1997.

LaFeber, Walter. *America, Russia, and the Cold War, 1945–1996.* 8th ed., 1997.

Laqueur, Walter. *Stalin: The Glasnost Revelations.* 1990.

Larson, Deborah W. *Anatomy of Mistrust: U.S.-Soviet Relations during the Cold War.* 1997.

———. *Origins of Containment: A Psychological Explanation.* 1985.

Lees, Lorraine M. "The American Decision to Assist Tito, 1948–1949," *Diplomatic History* 2 (1978): 407–22.

———. *Keeping Tito Afloat: The United States, Yugoslavia, and the Cold War.* 1997.

Leffler, Melvyn P. "The American Conception of National Security and the Beginnings of the Cold War, 1945–48," *American Historical Review* 89 (1984): 346–81.

———. *A Preponderance of Power: National Security, the Truman Administration, and the Cold War.* 1992.

———. *The Specter of Communism: The United States and the Origins of the Cold War, 1917–1953.* 1994.

———. "Strategy, Diplomacy, and the Cold War: The United States, Turkey, and NATO, 1945–1952," *Journal of American History* 71 (1985): 807–25.

———. "The United States and the Strategic Dimensions of the Marshall Plan," *Diplomatic History* 12 (1988): 277–306.

Leonard, Thomas M. *The United States and Central America, 1944–1949: Perceptions of Political Dynamics.* 1984.

Leslie, Stuart W. *The Cold War and American Science: The Military-Industrial-Academic Complex at MIT and Stanford.* 1993.

Levering, Ralph B. *The Cold War: A Post-Cold War History.* 1994.

Lieberman, Joseph I. *Scorpion and Tarantula: The Struggle to Control Atomic Weapons, 1945–1949.* 1970.

Liedtke, Boris N. *Embracing a Dictatorship: U.S. Relations with Spain, 1945–53.* 1998.

Lindee, M. Susan. *Suffering Made Real: American Science and the Survivors at Hiroshima.* 1994.

Loescher, Gil, and Scanlan, John A. *Calculated Kindness: Refugees and America's Half-Open Door, 1945 to the Present.* 1986.

Louis, William R. *The British Empire in the Middle East, 1945–1951: Arab Nationalism, the United States, and Postwar Imperialism.* 1984.

Lukas, Richard C. *Bitter Legacy: Polish-American Relations in the Wake of World War II.* 1982.

Lundestad, Geir. *America, Scandinavia, and the Cold War, 1945–1949.* 1980.

———. *The American Non-Policy towards Eastern Europe, 1943–1947: Universalism in an Area Not of Essential Interest to the United States.* 1975.

Lytle, Mark. *The Origins of the Iranian-American Alliance, 1941–1953.* 1987.

Maddox, Robert J. *The New Left and the Origins of the Cold War.* 1973.

Mark, Eduard. "American Policy toward Eastern Europe and the Origins of the Cold War, 1941–1946: An Alternative Interpretation," *Journal of American History* 68 (1981): 313–36.

Mastny, Vojtech. *The Cold War and Soviet Insecurity: The Stalin Years.* 1996.

———. *Russia's Road to the Cold War: Diplomacy, Warfare, and the Politics of Communism, 1941–1945.* 1979.

———. "Stalin and the Militarization of the Cold War," *International Security* 9 (1984–85): 109–29.

Max, Stanley M. *The United States, Great Britain, and the Sovietization of Hungary, 1945–1948.* 1985.

Mayers, David A. *Cracking the Monolith: U.S. Policy Against the Sino-Soviet Alliance, 1949–1955.* 1986.

———. *George Kennan and the Dilemmas of US Foreign Policy.* 1988.

Mazuzan, George T. *Warren R. Austin at the U.N., 1946–1953.* 1977.

McCormick, Thomas J. *America's Half-Century: United States Foreign Policy in the Cold War.* 1989.

McCoy, Donald R. *The Presidency of Harry S. Truman.* 1984.

McCullough, David. *Truman.* 1992.

McFarland, Stephen L. "A Peripheral View of the Origins of the Cold War: The Crises in Iran, 1941–47," *Diplomatic History* 4 (1980): 333–51.

McLellan, David S. *Dean Acheson: The State Department Years.* 1976.

McNeal, Robert H. *Stalin: Man and Ruler.* 1988.

Mee, Charles L., Jr. *The Marshall Plan: The Launching of the Pax Americana.* 1984.

Messer, Robert L. *The End of an Alliance: James F. Byrnes, Roosevelt, Truman, and the Origins of the Cold War.* 1982.

———. "Paths Not Taken: The United States Department of State and Alternatives to Containment, 1945–1946," *Diplomatic History* 1 (1977): 297–319.

Miller, Aaron D. *Search for Security: Saudi Arabian Oil and American Foreign Policy, 1939–1949.* 1980.

Miller, James E. *The United States and Italy, 1940–1950: The Politics and Diplomacy of Stabilization.* 1986.

Milward, Alan S. *The Reconstruction of Western Europe, 1945–1951.* 1984.

———. "Was the Marshall Plan Necessary?" *Diplomatic History* 13 (1989): 231–53.

Miscamble, Wilson D. *George F. Kennan and the Making of American Foreign Policy, 1947–1950.* 1992.

Morgan, Roger. *The United States and West Germany, 1945–1973: A Study in Alliance Politics.* 1974.

Naimark, Norman. *The Russians in Germany: A History of the Soviet Zone of Occupation, 1945–1949.* 1995.

Nelson, Anna K. "President Truman and the Evolution of the National Security Council," *Journal of American History* 72 (1985): 360–78.

Nelson, Daniel J. *Wartime Origins of the Berlin Dilemma.* 1978.

Newman, Robert P. *Truman and the Hiroshima Cult.* 1995.

Ninkovich, Frank. *The Diplomacy of Ideas: U.S. Foreign Policy and Cultural Relations, 1938–1950.* 1981.

———. *Modernity and Power: A History of the Domino Theory in the Twentieth Century.* 1994.

Osgood, Robert E. *NATO: The Entangling Alliance.* 1962.

Ovendale, Ritchie. *The English-Speaking Alliance: Britain and the United States, the Dominions and the Cold War, 1945–1951.* 1985.

Pach, Chester, Jr. *Arming the Free World: The Origins of the United States Military Assistance Program, 1945–1950.* 1991.

Painter, David S. *The Cold War: An International History.* 1999.

———. *Oil and the American Century: The Political Economy of U.S. Foreign Oil Policy, 1941–1954.* 1986.

Paterson, Thomas G. *On Every Front: The Making of the Cold War.* 1979.

———. *Soviet-American Confrontation: Postwar Reconstruction and the Origins of the Cold War.* 1973.

Patterson, James T. *Mr. Republican: A Biography of Robert Taft.* 1972.

Peterson, Edward N. *The American Occupation of Germany: Retreat to Victory.* 1977.

Pfau, Richard. "Containment in Iran, 1946: The Shift to an Active Policy," *Diplomatic History* 1 (1977): 359–72.

Pisani, Sallie. *The CIA and the Marshall Plan.* 1991.

Pogue, Forrest C. *George C. Marshall: Statesman, 1945–1949.* 1987.

Pollard, Robert A. *Economic Security and the Origins of the Cold War, 1945–1950.* 1985.

———. "Economic Security and the Origins of the Cold War: Bretton Woods, the Marshall Plan, and American Rearmament, 1944–50," *Diplomatic History* 9 (1985): 271–89.

Prados, John. *Presidents' Secret Wars: CIA Pentagon Covert Operations from World War II through the Persian Gulf.* 1996.

Rabel, Roberto G. *Between East and West: Trieste, the United States, and the Cold War, 1941–1954.* 1988.

Radzinskii, Edward. *Stalin: The First In-Depth Biography Based on Explosive New Documents from Russia's Secret Archives.* 1996.

Randall, Stephen J. *United States Foreign Oil Policy, 1919–1948: For Profits and Security.* 1985.

Ranelagh, John. *The Agency: The Rise and Fall of the CIA.* 1986.

Rappaport, Armin. "The United States and European Integration: The First Phase," *Diplomatic History* 5 (1981): 121–49.

Raucher, Alan R. *Paul G. Hoffman: Architect of Foreign Aid.* 1986.

Rearden, Steven L. *History of the Office of the Secretary of Defense. Vol. 1: The Formative Years, 1947–1950.* 1984.

Reid, Escott. *Time of Fear and Hope: The Making of the North Atlantic Treaty, 1947–1949.* 1977.

Resis, Albert. *Stalin, the Politburo, and the Onset of the Cold War, 1945–1946.* 1988.

Robertson, David. *Sly and Able: A Political Biography of James F. Byrnes.* 1994.

Rogers, Daniel E. *Politics After Hitler: The Western Allies and the German Party System.* 1995.

Roman, Eric. *Hungary and the Victor Powers, 1945–1950.* 1996.

Rose, Lisle A. *After Yalta.* 1973.

Rosenberg, David A. "American Atomic Strategy and the Hydrogen Bomb Decision," *Journal of American History* 66 (1979): 62–87.

Rubenberg, Cheryl. *Israel and the American National Interest.* 1986.

Rubin, Barry. *The Great Powers in the Middle East, 1941–1947: The Road to the Cold War.* 1980.

Ruddy, T. Michael. *The Cautious Diplomat: Charles E. Bohlen and the Soviet Union, 1929–1969.* 1986.

Ryan, Henry B. *The Vision of Anglo-America: The US-UK Alliance and the Emerging Cold War, 1943–1946.* 1987.

Schlaim, Avi. *The United States and the Berlin Blockade, 1948–1949: A Study in Crisis Decision-Making.* 1983.

Schlesinger, Arthur M., Jr. "Origins of the Cold War," *Foreign Affairs* 46 (1967): 22–52.

Schoenbaum, David. *The United States and the State of Israel.* 1993.

Schwartz, Thomas A. *America's Germany: John J. McCloy and the Federal Republic of Germany.* 1991.

Siracusa, Joseph M. *Rearming the Cold War: Paul H. Nitze, the H-Bomb and the Origins of a Soviet First Strike.* 1983.

Smith, E. Timothy. *The United States, Italy, and NATO, 1947–52.* 1991.

Smith, Gaddis. *Dean Acheson.* 1972.

Smith, Jean Edward. *The Defense of Berlin*. 1963.

———. "General Clay and the Russians: A Continuation of the Wartime Alliance in Germany, 1945–1948," *Virginia Quarterly Review* 64 (1988): 20–36.

Snetsinger, John. *Truman, the Jewish Vote, and the Creation of Israel*. 1974.

Spanier, John W. *American Foreign Policy since World War II*. 14th ed., 1998.

Stavrakis, Peter J. *Moscow and Greek Communism, 1944–1949*. 1989.

Steel, Ronald. *Walter Lippmann and the American Century*. 1980.

Steinitz, Mark S. "The U.S. Propaganda Effort in Czechoslovakia, 1945–48," *Diplomatic History* 6 (1982): 359–85.

Stephanson, Anders. *Kennan and the Art of Foreign Policy*. 1989.

Stivers, William. "The Incomplete Blockade: Soviet Zone Supply of West Berlin, 1948–49," *Diplomatic History* 21 (1997): 569–602.

Stoff, Michael B. *Oil, War, and American Security: The Search for a National Policy on Foreign Oil, 1941–1947*. 1980.

Stoler, Mark A. *George C. Marshall: Soldier-Statesman of the American Century*. 1989.

Taubman, William. *Stalin's American Policy: From Entente to Detente to Cold War*. 1982.

Theoharis, Athan G. *The Yalta Myths: An Issue in U.S. Politics, 1945–1955*. 1970.

Thomas, Evan. *The Very Best Men: Four Who Dared: The Early Years of the CIA*. 1995.

Thomas, Hugh. *Armed Truce: The Beginnings of the Cold War, 1945–46*. 1987.

Trachtenberg, Marc. *A Constructed Peace: The Making of the European Settlement, 1945–1963*. 1999.

———. "A 'Wasting Asset': American Strategy and the Shifting Nuclear Balance, 1949–1954," *International Security* 13 (1988–89): 5–49.

Troy, Thomas F. *Wild Bill and Intrepid: Donovan, Stephenson, and the Origin of CIA*. 1996.

Truman, Harry S. *Memoirs*. 2 vols., 1956.

Tusa, Ann, and Tusa, John. *The Berlin Airlift*. 1988.

Ulam, Adam B. *The Communists: The Story of Power and Lost Illusions, 1948–1991*. 1992.

———. *The Rivals: America and Russia since World War II*. 1971.

Ullmann, Walter. *The United States in Prague, 1945–1948*. 1978.

Wala, Michael. "Selling the Marshall Plan at Home: The Committee for the Marshall Plan to Aid European Recovery," *Diplomatic History* 10 (1986): 247–65.

Walker, J. Samuel. *Henry A. Wallace and American Foreign Policy*. 1976.

Wall, Irwin M. *The United States and the Making of Postwar France, 1945–1954*. 1991.

Walton, Richard J. *Henry Wallace, Harry Truman and the Cold War*. 1976.

Wandycz, Piotr S. *The United States and Poland*. 1980.

Ward, Patricia D. *The Threat of Peace: James F. Byrnes and the Council of Foreign Ministers, 1945–1946*. 1979.

Wells, Samuel F., Jr. "Sounding the Tocsin: NSC-68 and the Soviet Threat," *International Security* (1979): 116–58.

Wexler, Immanuel. *The Marshall Plan Revisited: The European Recovery Program in Economic Perspective*. 1983.

White, Graham, and Maze, John. *Henry A. Wallace: His Search for a New World Order*. 1995.

Whitnah, Donald R., and Erickson, Edgar L. *The American Occupation of Austria: Planning and Early Years*. 1985.

Williams, William A. *The Tragedy of American Diplomacy*. 1959. Rev. ed., 1972.

Williamson, Samuel R., and Rearden, Steven L. *The Origins of U.S. Nuclear Strategy, 1945–1953*. 1993.

Wittner, Lawrence S. *American Intervention in Greece, 1943–1949*. 1982.

———. "The Truman Doctrine and the Defense of Freedom," *Diplomatic History* 4 (1980): 161–87.

Woods, Randall B. *A Changing of the Guard: Anglo-American Relations, 1941–1946*. 1990.

———, and Jones, Howard. *Dawning of the Cold War: The United States' Quest for Order*. 1991, 1994.

Yergin, Daniel H. *Shattered Peace: The Origins of the Cold War and the National Security State*. Rev. ed., 1990.

Zubok, V. M., and Pleshakov, Constantine. *Inside the Kremlin's Cold War: From Stalin to Khrushchev*. 1996.

CHAPTER 10

Cold War and Containment in East Asia, 1950–1953

Outbreak of War in Korea

Early in the morning of June 25, 1950, more than 100,000 North Korean troops, using Soviet-made tanks and artillery, invaded the Republic of Korea along a 150-mile front and set off the first major military conflict of the Cold War. Succeeding events in East Asia became symbolic of the new military tactics necessitated by the dangers of atomic warfare. Indeed, the sudden and dramatic return to conventional conflict highlighted the irony confronting the United States: It possessed the bomb but could not use it. Americans believed they were fighting the Communists by proxy—that the Moscow government had manipulated the North Koreans into the attack and that the United States had to counter this new threat by any method short of all-out war. Kennan's theories seemed correct: The Soviets were determined to test Americans' will by probing soft spots throughout the world. The United States had shored up Western Europe and the Near East by the Truman Doctrine, Marshall Plan, and NATO; proponents of containment were convinced that the Soviets had now turned to East Asia.

Recent events in East Asia reinforced that belief. The United States's postwar occupation of Japan under General Douglas MacArthur

had implanted democratic reforms that provided a model of Western ideals in East Asia and thereby threatened Soviet interests in that part of the world. But then, in late 1949, Jiang Jieshi's Chinese Nationalist forces had collapsed before Mao Zedong's Communists and retreated to the island of Formosa. It appeared that a monolithic communism out of the Kremlin had brought the "fall" of China and now tried to counter U.S. successes in Japan as an attempt to restore Soviet influence in East Asia. Washington's leaders perceived the invasion of South Korea as, for practical purposes, a Soviet invasion, and sought to resist it by working through a UN force dominated by U.S. soldiers, money, and war materiel. To avoid the label of war, the conflict became officially known as a "police action."

U.S. policy toward East Asia rested on three assumptions, none of them sound. The first was that communism in Korea, China, and every place else in East Asia was a single movement directed from Moscow. In fact, there were many Communist movements, some more or less controlled by the Kremlin and others not; and thus the United States failed to exploit these differences to its own strategic advantage. The second assumption was that every revolutionary movement in East Asia was Communist-inspired or had communism as its goal. Actually, the most powerful force pushing for revolutionary change in East Asia was nationalism, not ideology, so despite an official (and usually sincere) U.S. policy of anticolonialism, discontented Easterners perceived the continued U.S. presence and intervention in East Asia as the same type of Western colonialism practiced earlier by France, Britain, and the Netherlands. The third misguided assumption was the belief that "limited war" furnished a viable method for deterring the spread of communism. In actuality Americans, accustomed to fighting through to victory, were unwilling to endure the frustrations that limited war entails; and thus, in 1952 they voted the Democrats out of power for the first time in twenty years.

Japan

The U.S. occupation of Japan lasted from 1945 through 1952 and left the defeated country with markedly changed features. In December 1945 the United States, Britain, and China met with the Soviet Union in Moscow and established an advisory group in Tokyo known as the Four-Power Allied Council for Japan. The United States rejected the Soviets' call for a share in the occupation of Japan and agreed to their participation only in an advisory role. Authority rested in the Supreme Commander for the Allied Powers (SCAP) in Japan, General Douglas MacArthur. He worked under the supervision of the Far Eastern Advisory Commission in Washington, which was composed of the eleven nations (later expanded to thirteen) that had fought Japan in the war. By a firm and businesslike disposition, MacArthur dominated policy in Japan. His stern, authoritarian, and military manner—along with his sunglasses and the ever-present corncob pipe jutting upward from his mouth—appealed to people accustomed to worshipping an emperor. In truth, however, the war's devastation left the Japanese no choice.

The United States's initial aims were to reduce Japan to lesser power status and to institute an ambitious democratic reform program. The first intention gradually changed as East Asia became a battleground of the Cold War and the grand hopes for making China into a major power sputtered and failed. The second goal, however, remained constant and soon became integral to restoring Japan to a position strong enough to balance off Soviet influence in East Asia. MacArthur drew up a constitution for Japan in May 1947, patterned after that of the United States. Under it, Japan "forever renounced war as a sovereign right of the nation and the threat or use of force as a means of settling international disputes." Japan also agreed to discard "land, sea, and air forces, as well as other war potential." Americans reformed the education system, barred warmakers from official positions in the country, sponsored war crimes trials that led to imprisonment and executions, stripped Japan of overseas possessions, and allowed it to retain only the four islands comprising the homeland. The monarchy remained only in form, because final power rested in delegates chosen by the people—including the votes of women (a revolution in itself). The United States also encouraged economic opportunity by breaking up industrial monopolies (the *zaibatsu*) and dividing huge land tracts among the peasants. As the Cold War intensified in East Asia by 1950, the U.S. occupation forces relaxed restrictions on industrial production and encouraged former Japanese leaders to reassume official responsibilities. Japan became a model of democratic reform in East Asia, a growing industrial ally with the United States, and a constant source of embarrassment to the Soviet Union.

China

The resumption of civil war in China after the end of World War II had threatened to cause the government's collapse under Communist attack. Such a possibility stunned Americans. Their long-time paternal policy toward China had expressed itself in continuing missionary and humanitarian interests, in the Open Door with its drive for the fabled "China market," and in Franklin D. Roosevelt's objective of establishing the huge country as a postwar world power. Yet these high trade expectations never materialized, and China did not become the reformed and progressive mammoth capable of bringing a balance of power to East Asia. In August 1945 the Soviets signed a treaty of "friendship" with the Nationalists that sent a signal to the Communists that they were on their own. Jiang's forces meanwhile received increased U.S. assistance in regaining control over the cities and the China coast. Communist forces meanwhile held on to the upper interior and advanced toward Manchuria, where they confiscated war materiel from the Japanese. Furthermore, Stalin violated his treaty with Jiang by extending secret aid to the Chinese Communists. Mao, however, refused to play a subordinate role to the Moscow government,

which led Stalin to remark that the Chinese Communists were "not real communists" but "'margarine' communists." Despite the crack in the alleged Communist monolith, Americans continued to believe that the movement, whether inspired by Stalin or Mao, could cause the collapse of Nationalist China and constitute a major defeat in the Cold War.

The U.S. ambassador to Nationalist China, General Patrick Hurley, thought that the Kremlin's August 1945 decision to help Jiang provided an opportunity to defeat Mao's Communist forces. Hurley first tried to persuade Jiang and Mao to settle their differences, but after six weeks of negotiations in Chongqing he failed, largely because Jiang demanded too much. Hurley resigned his post in November and accused the Foreign Service of supporting Mao (whom he disdainfully called "Mouse Dung"). Hurley's rebuke left an erroneous impression of the Foreign Service

Jiang Jieshi and Wife
He headed the Chinese Nationalists until defeated in the civil war with Mao Zedong's Communists and driven off the mainland to Formosa in October 1949. *Roger Viollet.*

Mao and Hurley
Arriving at Chongqing airport from Yenan for a conference with the chiefs of the
Central Chinese government in August 1945. *National Archives, Washington, D.C.*

officers. They had long emphasized that Mao would win the civil war because of the Nationalists' weaknesses and lack of popular support, but their reasoned assessment seemed to question the United States's traditional support for China, and for that they appeared to be Communist sympathizers.

After Hurley's resignation, President Truman appointed General George C. Marshall, retired army chief of staff and revered World War II figure, to head a special mission to resolve the problems in China. Like Stilwell and Hurley before him, Marshall was to arrange a cease-fire and build a coalition government, but with Jiang's regime standing as "the only legal government" and the "foundation of the new political structure." Marshall tried to bring the opposing groups together, but this objective showed that Washington had failed to recognize Mao's strength. Marshall did secure a truce in January 1946, and the Communists seemed interested in a coalition government—perhaps as a less costly route to victory. Under the truce terms, each side agreed to scale down its armies before combining them into a single force, which was to be trained by one thousand Americans in a Joint U.S. Military Advisory Group situated in Nanking. Both antagonists would then write a new constitution for China. But the Marshall mission failed because neither the new government nor the army came into being.

Stilwell and the Foreign Service officers in China had been correct: Jiang's army was incapable of winning the war and uniting the country. Peace lasted fitfully through 1946, but in the meantime the Communists had established control over nearly all of Manchuria. Marshall realized that war was imminent and returned to the United States. The following month he submitted a report attributing the dire situation in China to "extremist elements on both sides." Compromise between Jiang's conservative supporters and Mao's self-proclaimed

"Marxists" was out of the question. That same month, January 1947, Marshall became secretary of state.

Fear of a Communist takeover in China and pressure from the opposition Republican party to save the huge country led Truman to send another mission during the summer of 1947. General Albert C. Wedemeyer, the new appointee, recommended UN supervision of Manchuria, massive "moral, advisory, and material support" to the Nationalists, and a wide range of reforms in the army requiring the help of ten thousand U.S. military advisers. His proposals won no support from the Truman administration. In fact, Marshall prevented their release to the public—which doubtless added to the growing impression that the White House was doing little or nothing to save China from the Communists. Given the magnitude of U.S. commitments in Europe, the secretary of state opposed further involvement in China and warned that UN intervention in Manchuria could cause the Moscow government to call for a reciprocal arrangement in Greece. Past experience, he warned, demonstrated the futility in attempting to reform the Chinese Nationalist Army. The secretary was amenable to limited military and economic aid to the Nationalists, and he authorized a few advisers to upgrade Jiang's army. But this was as far as he would go. The United States's postwar priorities had become strikingly similar to those before 1941: an emphasis on Europe and a hope that problems in East Asia would take care of themselves.

Marshall's recommendations for China were not sufficient to prevent a Communist victory. In May 1948 Congress appropriated $400 million of military and economic aid under the Foreign Assistance Act. Whereas critics warned that this was not enough, Senator Vandenberg contended that no amount was enough: "China aid is like sticking your finger in the lake and looking for the hole." On August 5, 1949, a state department White Paper of more than a thousand pages of text and documents attributed China's impending collapse to the ineptitude of Jiang's National-

ists. In covering remarks, Dean Acheson, who had become secretary of state in January 1949, offered an accurate assessment of the situation. "Nothing that this country did or could have done within the reasonable limits of its capabilities could have changed that result," he wrote; "nothing that was left undone by this country has contributed to it. It was the product of internal Chinese forces." Acheson concluded that "a decision was arrived at within China, if only a decision by default." The first loyalty of the Chinese Communists, according to the White Paper, was to the Soviet Union.

Events in China took on momentum as the Communists tightened their hold on the country. At a September conference in Beijing (Peiping, but now changed back to the title and spelling of ancient days as Peking), they drew up a constitution for the "People's Republic of China," which had the outward markings of democracy but was clearly Communist. Mao declared the regime in effect on October 1, 1949, with himself as head and Zhou Enlai (Chou En-lai) as premier and foreign minister. The Soviet Union extended recognition the next day, leading Jiang's Nationalists to break relations with Moscow on October 3. Although Britain and other non-Communist countries eventually recognized Communist China, the United States again rejected *de facto* recognition policy and on October 4 affirmed support for the Nationalists as China's legitimate government. After a series of military retreats from Nanking, then from Canton, and finally from Chongqing, the Nationalists withdrew from the mainland for the island of Formosa (also known as Taiwan). In December they resumed governmental functions in the island's capital city of Taipei.

Several factors contributed to Jiang's failure, none of which the United States could have significantly altered. Americans did not lose China to communism; they never owned or controlled the country. Despite the unfortunate comparison of China to Greece, a proportionate economic and military aid program in China would have required enormous expenditures and countless more military advisers. Ambassador John L. Stuart, born in China and president of Yenching University in Beijing, probably offered the best explanation of China's collapse. In his memoirs, *Fifty Years in China,* he blamed the outcome on "a gigantic struggle between two political ideologies with the overtones of democratic idealism perverted by bureaucratic incompetence on the one side, succumbing to a dynamic socialized reform vitiated by Communist dogma, intolerance and ruthlessness on the other. And the great mass of suffering inarticulate victims cared for neither but were powerless to do anything about it." Neither antagonist, he asserted, had many avid party members. The Chinese people were "merely Chinese" who wanted "to live their own lives with a minimum of government interference or oppression."

The Communist success in China was attributable to a long history of internal troubles, to repeated instances of outside intervention, to the destruction of World War II, and to Jiang's disastrous rule. Group after group had vied for control in Beijing, and in the provinces numerous independent warlords competed for power. Jiang's early military triumphs had come to an abrupt end during the Sino-Japanese War of the 1930s, which itself meshed into the events of World War II. Billions of dollars of U.S. aid to Jiang disappeared in inflation, bureaucratic inefficiency, nepotism, corruption, and his decision to hoard war materiel for future use against Mao rather than against Japan in the present war. Moreover, he failed to win popular support because of the lack of land reforms, the chronic instability of the country, his own incapacities, and the devastation of the world war. Jiang's strength rested on the landlords, who opposed land reform, whereas the Communists gained widespread peasant support by promising agrarian reforms. Thus, the revolution swept the countryside while Jiang and his forces remained in the cities, insulated from the need for change and failing to grasp the realities of his rule collapsing all around him.

Washington's decision to withhold recognition of Communist China did not necessarily imply protection to Formosa, but the White House soon found that refusal to help the Nationalists left the appearance of tacitly favoring the Communists. In January 1950 Truman informed Jiang's advocates in the United States that he had no plans for furnishing "military aid or advice" to the Nationalists. Indeed, Acheson was quietly searching for steps toward establishing diplomatic relations with the new government in Beijing in view of firsthand reports by Foreign Service officers that Mao sought a policy independent of Stalin and would soon crush Jiang's ill-fated regime. But that realistic stance quickly changed. Members of the Republican party were already claiming that Communists in Washington had betrayed Nationalist China.

As shown in the previous chapter, the great publicity surrounding the Alger Hiss trial, followed by the sensational charges made by Republican Senator Joe McCarthy, left the impression that communism had infiltrated the very halls of the nation's government. Not long afterward, authorities arrested Julius Rosenberg (who had worked on the Manhattan Project) and his wife Ethel for espionage. The resulting wave of fear and suspicion aroused by "McCarthyism" thoroughly discredited Acheson, who had remained loyal to Hiss and whose tailored mustache, expensive Ivy League clothing, mincing manner, and arrogant bearing gave him the image of a dangerous intellectual—more European than American. The fallout did not stop with him. As part of the administration's 1947 security program, government employees had to take loyalty oaths. Indeed, anyone suspected of engaging in "radical" activity—including those in academia and Hollywood—was subject to being fired or blacklisted. Books allegedly professing the doctrine of communism were burned or banned from the libraries. In one remarkable instance, *Robin Hood* was pulled from the library shelves because the hero exemplified Communist principles by taking from the rich and giving to the poor. The national hysteria damaged the reputation of the Foreign Service, converted judgmental errors into a believed Communist conspiracy, and made the administration wary of admitting to any mistakes or failures in diplomatic policy that critics could label as treason, or at least as being "soft on communism."

In February 1950 the Soviet Union and the People's Republic of China further alarmed Americans by signing a thirty-year mutual defense pact. The treaty added to the fear in the United States that a single brand of communism, guided by the Kremlin, was spreading throughout the world. Americans became convinced that the Communist Chinese had come under the Soviet heel. Few realized that the agreement of 1950 resulted from mutual need and not from ideological ties. Mao wanted to stem the United States's deepening influence in East Asia; Stalin sought assurances for the Yalta guarantees and was leery of a strong and independent Communist China. The Soviets demanded that Mao's China replace Jiang's Nationalists in the UN Security Council. When this effort failed, the Soviet delegate walked out, signifying his government's boycott of that organization.

The Korean War

The situations in Japan and China constituted an important and related background to the conflict in Korea, a peninsula that became the hot spot of the Cold War by mid-1950. The ensuing problems quickly raised questions about U.S. resolve in Japan and the effectiveness of its policies in China. Korea became symbolic of the struggle between East and West.

The Soviet Union and the United States had temporarily divided Korea at the thirty-eighth parallel in 1945, with the understanding that the Soviets would wind down the war against Japanese invasion forces in the north and the United States would do the same in the south. Afterward full withdrawal would take place, in line with wartime agreements stipulating that Korea was to be "free and independent." The partition at the thirty-

eighth parallel was a military decision, even though it cut off the industrialized north from the agricultural south and left the north larger in area though smaller in population. At the time it was a sound decision in Washington's view because the United States was unable to transport soldiers there immediately, and the Soviet agreement to remain above that parallel would perhaps prevent the Red Army from occupying all of Korea.

But problems soon developed over the agreement's implementation. In December 1945 and again in March 1947, the Soviet and U.S. foreign ministers agreed in Moscow that the military commands in Korea should discuss the procedure for installing a government favorable to reuniting the north and south. But each time the talks failed to resolve the composition of that government. The United States referred the Korean issue to the UN General Assembly, which in November 1947 established a Temporary Commission on Korea to sponsor nationwide elections. The Soviets, however, refused to allow the commissioners above the thirty-eighth parallel. Elections took place in May 1948—but only in the south. Syngman Rhee, seventy-three years old and a long-time resident of the United States who held a doctorate degree in international law from Princeton, emerged as president of the Republic of Korea in Seoul. In September Kim Il-sung became president of a Soviet-supported regime in Pyongyang, capital of the Democratic People's Republic of Korea. The following December, Rhee signed an economic and military aid pact with the United States. When the question of South Korea's admission to the United Nations came before the Security Council, the Soviet delegate vetoed the measure. As in Germany, two Koreas became symbolic of the Cold War rivalry.

Meanwhile the North Korean government had surged ahead of the south in military power. Both Koreas had armies, but whereas the Soviets had provided heavy artillery and tanks to Kim, the Americans had refused to grant Rhee anything more than light defensive weaponry because of his dictatorial rule and

Syngman Rhee
Delivering an address to the Republic of Korea
troops in November 1956. *U.S. Army.*

undisguised intention to reunite the country. Only after great pressure from Washington did Rhee hold long-promised general elections, and when they did take place the negative results exposed his shaky control in South Korea. Yet the United States had no feasible alternative to Rhee. The Soviet Union withdrew its troops from Korea in December 1948 and the United States did the same in June 1949, but neither power's commitment had ceased. The Soviets left behind heavy artillery and tanks; the Americans maintained a considerable amount of light military equipment and four hundred technical and military advisers.

By early 1950 the United States appeared to have left the South Koreans on their own. The military withdrawal reinforced that impression, as did MacArthur's ill-timed announcement from Japan that he opposed a land war in Asia. The U.S. Army had ten poorly equipped and inadequately manned divisions, and the Joint Chiefs of Staff con-

sidered South Korea of only secondary military importance. On January 12, 1950, Acheson seemed to affirm his nation's retreat from East Asia. Before the National Press Club in Washington, he defined the "defense perimeter" of the United States in Asia as a line enveloping the Aleutians, Japan, the Ryukyus, and the Philippines, which implied that the United States felt no responsibilities toward either Formosa or the Chinese mainland. Should aggression occur, Acheson emphasized, "the initial reliance must be on the people attacked to resist it and then upon the commitments of the entire civilized world under the Charter of the United Nations which so far has not proved a weak reed to lean on by any people who are determined to protect their independence against outside aggression." The secretary was perhaps attempting to give subtle notification to the Communist Chinese that the United States wished to withdraw support from the Nationalists. Not inconsistent with this supposition, he wished to place emphasis on economic and administrative assistance to South Korea rather than military, exemplifying Washington's belief that sound economies and democratic governments provided the best insurance against communism. Whatever his intentions, the effect was not what he had anticipated. Observers were convinced that Acheson had removed both South Korea and Formosa from the U.S. defense system.

When in the summer of 1950 the North Korean forces launched their invasion of South Korea, they met little resistance. News of the attack reached Washington, which was thirteen hours behind Korean time, late in the evening of June 24. Acheson met with other state department officers in emergency session and decided that the United States would take action through the UN Security Council. Truman was at home in Independence, Missouri, and returned to Washington the following day. Meanwhile the state department worked all night drafting a resolution condemning the North Korean aggression, which the U.S. delegation would present to the Security

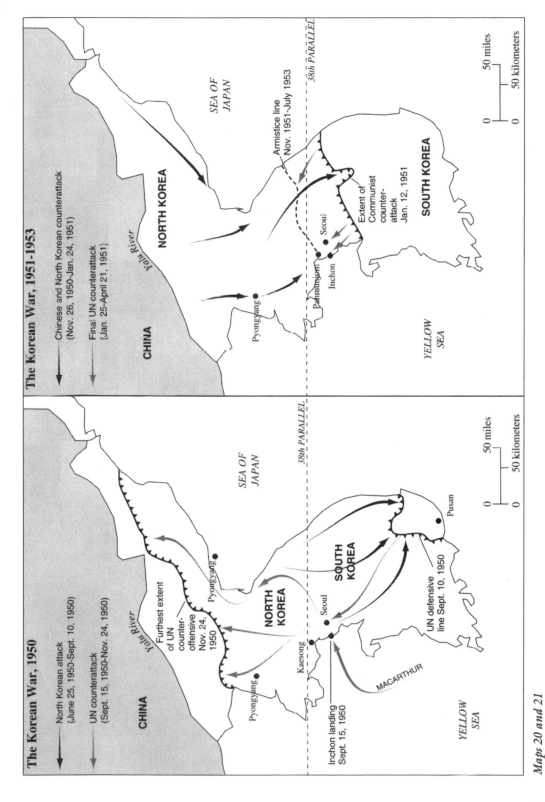

The Korean War, 1950

North Korean attack
(June 25, 1950-Sept. 10, 1950)

UN counterattack
(Sept. 15, 1950-Nov. 24, 1950)

CHINA

Yalu River

Furthest extent
of UN counter-
offensive
Nov. 24,
1950

Pyongyang

*SEA OF
JAPAN*

NORTH
KOREA

Pyongyang

38th PARALLEL

Kaesong

Seoul

SOUTH
KOREA

Inchon landing
Sept. 15, 1950

MACARTHUR

UN defensive
line Sept. 10, 1950

Pusan

*YELLOW
SEA*

0   50 miles

0   50 kilometers

The Korean War, 1951-1953

Chinese and North Korean counterattack
(Nov. 26, 1950-Jan. 24, 1951)

Final UN counterattack
(Jan. 25-April 21, 1951)

CHINA

Yalu River

Pyongyang

*SEA OF
JAPAN*

NORTH KOREA

Armistice line
Nov. 1951-July 1953

38th PARALLEL

Panmunjom

Seoul

Inchon

Extent of
Communist
counter-
attack
Jan. 12, 1951

SOUTH KOREA

*YELLOW
SEA*

0   50 miles

0   50 kilometers

Maps 20 and 21
Over three years of war resulted in a stalemate as the fighting came to a close in almost exactly the same area it began.

Council. The Truman administration ordered Americans in Seoul to evacuate at once.

No debate took place in Washington about the Soviet Union's role in the attack. Everyone held the Moscow government responsible and felt that the United States had to act. Washington's officials agreed that the Soviets had begun probing for weak areas susceptible to Communist takeover. Korea therefore loomed as a major test of the United States's will in East Asia. The state department alerted its foreign offices to this danger: "Possible that Korea is only the first of series of coordinated actions on part of Soviets. Maintain utmost vigilance."

Washington's assumption of Soviet complicity in the attack made it a test of the U.S. commitment to Asia. North Korea's effort to reunify the country by force caused the Truman administration to alter its Korean policy and adopt measures that were stronger than the mere extension of economic aid and military advice. One state department official, John Foster Dulles, publicly expressed the common belief that the North Koreans "did not do this purely on their own but as part of the world strategy of international communism." The successes of the United States's containment policy in Europe and the Near East had seemingly evoked this aggressive Soviet response.

Without Soviet, Chinese, and North Korean documentation, it is impossible to know whether the North Korean invasion surprised the Soviets as much as it did the West. Some certainties exist, however. Kim Il-sung and Syngman Rhee were bitter rivals, both fully capable of acting on their own. Border incidents had dramatically increased before June; since 1946 more than 100,000 Koreans had died in what had become by 1950 a bloody civil war. Indeed, the same morning of the attack, South Korean forces had raided a town above the thirty-eighth parallel. Had Moscow known of the impending North Korean attack, its delegate would surely have returned to the Security Council, where he could have vetoed UN military action and bought time for the North Koreans before the General

Assembly could act. It also made little sense for Stalin to move so clearly for peace in Europe, only to instigate a war in Asia. Admittedly, he had extended some help to North Korea but probably in an attempt to avert Communist Chinese accusations that he opposed revolutions in Asia. Conceivably, he calculated that even if the United States did nothing to protect the South Koreans, it would certainly continue its protection of Formosa and thereby undermine any chance of a U.S. settlement of that issue with the People's Republic of China. Mao would thus have no choice but to turn to Moscow for assistance.

Questions remain about the Kremlin's assumed role in these events. One theory is that the Soviets were unaware of the imminent North Korean attack and once aware even wanted to call it off until its surprising success suddenly offered the opportunity of accomplishing everything they sought in East Asia. Another, which is probably nearer the truth, holds that Kim had wanted to strike a posture more independent of Mao's Communists and therefore traveled to the Kremlin twice to talk with Stalin of a planned attack on the south without specifying its timing. The Soviet premier, it seems, approved Kim's intentions and assured him of materiel but made clear that he was on his own. Should Kim fail, Stalin could disclaim involvement; if successful, Kim would stand clear of China's influence and unite Korea under his direction. In either case, the Soviets could cite the success of the attack as further evidence of U.S. military weakness, already exemplified in China. Moreover, the North Koreans' actions threatened to diminish U.S. credibility in Japan. If U.S. prestige fell in Asia, only the Soviet Union would gain—as long as it quietly furnished military assistance to the North Koreans while publicly castigating the United States, the region's unmistakable outsider, as the interventionist aggressor. Whatever the background of the attack, the Soviet Union had apparently fallen into a winning situation.

Truman never doubted Soviet culpability and called for strong action. Here was an opportunity to regain flagging popular support at home, resulting largely from the Republicans' charges that the administration was "soft on communism." Truman regarded the North Korean attack as another test of the Free World's commitment to liberty. "Communism," he wrote in his *Memoirs,* "was acting in Korea just as Hitler, Mussolini, and the Japanese had acted ten, fifteen, and twenty years earlier." He assured an anxious senator that his administration would not give in to the Soviet Union and told reporters that Korea was "the Greece of the Far East." Acheson explained years afterward that "to back away from this challenge, in view of our capacity for meeting it, would be highly destructive of the power and prestige of the United States."

The perceived Soviet threat in Asia caused both the United States and its NATO allies to move with determination. By the afternoon following the attack, the Security Council had overwhelmingly approved the U.S. resolution (nine to zero, the Soviets absent and Yugoslavia abstaining) labeling the attack a "breach of the peace" and calling on the North Koreans to withdraw from below the thirty-eighth parallel. The Council then approved a second resolution urging member nations to "furnish such assistance to the Republic of Korea as may be necessary to repel the armed attack and to restore international peace and security." Truman warned the Communist Chinese not to exploit the Korean situation by attacking the Nationalists on Formosa. To emphasize the point he approved military assistance to the Philippines and to the French in Indochina. Communism, the president explained, "has passed beyond the use of subversion to conquer independent nations and will now use armed invasion and war." In a single day he had committed the United States to Nationalist China, the Philippines (just granted independence by the United States in July 1946), and Indochina, all of them experiencing severe internal problems believed to be Communist-inspired.

On June 27, 1950, Truman ordered the Seventh Fleet to the Chinese coast to "prevent any attack on Formosa" that would cause a resurgence of civil war. Whether to "leash" Jiang or to protect Formosa, Truman's actions angered Communist China because they constituted blatant interference in its domestic affairs. They also upset the UN members who had extended recognition to the Communist regime and believed it justified in wanting to absorb Formosa. But because the Republicans charged the administration with already having "lost" China, the White House had to adopt strong policies to prevent the loss of South Korea. To keep the war limited in nature, Truman emphasized that the United States sought only "to restore peace and . . . the border."

The shocking collapse of the capital city of Seoul to the North Koreans on June 28 exposed the weaknesses in the United States's containment effort and led to the decision to send U.S. troops to save South Korea. On June 29 Truman approved U.S. air strikes above the thirty-eighth parallel, and the following day in Tokyo MacArthur recommended that the United States send soldiers, blockade the coast, and bomb areas in North Korea "wherever militarily necessary." In a decision that Truman later called "the most important" of his presidency, he ordered U.S. combat forces into Korea as part of what would become a UN command. This term was misleading, however, because only sixteen of the sixty UN members eventually contributed manpower. Although South Korea furnished a considerable number of military forces, the United States provided more than one million members of the total armed forces (more than half) and the great bulk of planes, ships, goods, and money. The president did not ask Congress for a declaration of war because, he explained, the U.S. soldiers had undertaken a "police action." The situation was desperate. The North Koreans had pushed the South Koreans all the way down to Pusan at the bottom of the peninsula and were on the verge of driving them into the sea. MacArthur, as commander in chief in the Far East, received orders on June 30 to secure a port and air base in the Pusan area. Acheson later explained with some satisfaction that the decision to send soldiers to Korea "removed the recommendations of NSC-68 from the realm of theory and made them immediate budget issues." According to that document, the Soviet Union sought "domination of the Eurasian land mass," leaving the United States no alternative to pursuing a global military policy.

Great symbolic importance rested in the U.S. decision to commit troops to Korea. Bases in the peninsula were not vital in a strategic military sense. Soviet control of Korea could not have posed a greater threat to Japan than did Soviet bases in Manchuria or China. Moreover, the limited size of the U.S. military force in 1950 meant that the relocation of ground forces to East Asia would seriously weaken Europe. Yet the symbolism of the commitment was fast approaching the level of the U.S. national interest. The United States had found it necessary to demonstrate assurances to South Korea, Japan, and other nations subject to aggression—especially the Europeans. Failure to do so would constitute a major defeat in the propaganda war with the Communists and perhaps sacrifice all hopes of winning the allegiance of the emerging postwar nations. Furthermore, a weak will would raise doubts among the United States's NATO allies. The nation's credibility was on the line.

Truman repeatedly emphasized the global context of the war. The decision to use combat troops escalated Korean events into a conflict having international ramifications. On July 8 the Security Council chose MacArthur to head the UN forces in Korea (although all his orders came from Washington), and on August 1 the Soviet representative to the Council, Yakov Malik, returned to his seat. To calm nervous Europeans who were worried that U.S. priorities had shifted to Asia, Truman launched a military buildup on the continent. Acheson horrified the British and French by proposing that Germany contribute ten divisions to the European defense system. He overcame vehement protests by assuring them that the German forces would be integrated into a European army and that the United States would send four additional divisions to the continent. Finally, the president announced that General Eisenhower had agreed to take leave from the presidency of Columbia University and become NATO's Supreme Commander.

The UN forces now prepared to take the offensive. While South Korean units and a small number of U.S. forces were backed to the water's edge at Pusan, MacArthur made a daring move: On September 15 he launched an amphibious landing at Inchon on the western side of the peninsula, hundreds of miles behind the North Korean front. Most military experts had argued that such a landing could not work because of enormously high tides and rocky cliffs; MacArthur promised that "we shall land at Inchon, and I shall crush them." He succeeded magnificently and soon freed Seoul from the Communists. The counter-invasion broke the North Koreans' advance and drove them back above the thirty-eighth parallel. Meanwhile, South Korean and U.S. forces gained the initiative in Pusan and severed the enemy's supply line. And despite these successes, Americans noted one telling fact: Neither the Soviet Union nor Communist China had intervened.

MacArthur's landing at Inchon had an exhilarating effect in the United States that soon highlighted a major policy decision in Washington already made in early August: Invade the north and reunify Korea. Despite the claim by some critics that the general acted on his own, the truth is that the Truman administration had decided to convert the policy of containment into a liberating force through what became known as "rollback," and the new military situation afforded by MacArthur's success provided an excellent opportunity for its implementation. In late September, state department official H. Freeman Matthews wrote the Joint Chiefs of Staff that if the United States could reunify Korea, "the resultant defeat to the Soviet Union and to the Communist world" would be of

Inchon
Gen. MacArthur's UN forces launched an invasion at Inchon
on September 15, 1950. *National Archives, Washington, D.C.*

"momentous significance." Korea would join
Japan as a model of national self-determination
in East Asia and would at the same time mark
the successful culmination of the United
States's Korean policy established during
World War II. Over protests from Kennan,
who warned that the Soviets would never allow
MacArthur near the "gates of Vladivostok,"
the administration approved the military advance across the thirty-eighth parallel that
would set an example for the world by liberating all of Korea from Communist control.

The Communist Chinese meanwhile warned
the United States, through India's delegate
to the United Nations, that they would not
"sit back with folded hands and let the Americans come to the border." Washington's leaders ignored the warning. The long civil war in
China, they declared with certainty, had spent

that regime's sparse resources and would permit no such involvement. Moreover, Mao's
focus was on northern China, where Soviet
interests clashed with his and loomed as a far
more important danger than that in Korea.
Chinese intervention in the Korean War
would be "sheer madness," according to
Acheson. They had enough problems with the
Soviet Union and would certainly not want to
alienate "all the free nations of the world who
are inherently their friends." MacArthur was
also confident that the Chinese would stay out
of the conflict and had earlier given the president personal assurances at Wake Island. "We
are no longer fearful of their [Chinese] intervention," the general told Truman. "They
have no air force . . . [and] if the Chinese tried
to get down to Pyongyang there would be
the greatest slaughter. . . . We are the best."

To the president's advisers, MacArthur asserted that "the Oriental follows a winner. If we win, the Chinese will not follow the USSR [Union of Soviet Socialist Republics]."

With the Soviet delegate now back in the Security Council, the Truman administration pushed a proposal through the General Assembly that suddenly elevated that body's importance in international affairs. Acheson won support for a "Uniting for Peace" program that authorized General Assembly members to recommend force in maintaining collective security if the veto blocked action by the Security Council. On October 9, 1950, the same day that two U.S. jets mistakenly strafed a Soviet airstrip near the huge naval base at Vladivostok (a swift apology eased Soviet protests), the General Assembly resolved that MacArthur should push for "a unified, independent and democratic Korea."

The General Assembly's action in reality was pro forma. On September 29 MacArthur had learned that the White House was disgruntled with his apparent decision to stop at the thirty-eighth parallel and await UN approval before moving northward. Marshall, now secretary of defense, sent a cable to MacArthur: "We want you to feel unhampered tactically and strategically to proceed north of [the] thirty-eighth parallel. Announcement above referred to may precipitate embarrassment in the UN where evident desire is not to be confronted with necessity of a vote on passage, rather to find you have found it militarily necessary to do so." MacArthur replied that he had not declared any intention of halting his advance and that the parallel was "not a factor in the mil[itary] employment of our forces." He added that "unless and until the enemy capitulates, I regard all of Korea open for our mil[itary] operations." MacArthur promised reporters that "the war very definitely is coming to an end shortly."

The UN decision to cross the thirty-eighth parallel dramatically elevated the Cold War to a level just short of full conflict. In an effort to avert a wider war, President Truman rejected MacArthur's request to attack strategic spots in China itself and, in an inexplicable move, authorized UN forces to bomb only the southern half of the bridges connecting the Chinese banks of the Yalu River with those of North Korea. "How can we bomb half a bridge?" the general indignantly asked his staff.

The Truman administration seems not to have recognized that the UN invasion of North Korea was tantamount to a thrust toward China that would necessitate a strong counteraction. Mao had not been on good terms with the North Koreans and had not expected the original attack on South Korea. He could not have wanted to enter the Korean conflict after his own recent long and costly civil war. His philosophy of survival argued against military confrontation with a superior military force. But Mao recognized that failure to halt the UN drive toward the Yalu River would discredit his regime's claim to the mainland and endanger his own leadership. Furthermore, here was opportunity, perhaps too soon presented, for the Beijing government to come of age. Should it establish hegemony over that area, Mao would gain stature in East Asia approaching that of the Soviets. Pushed into action by the UN decision to move toward the Yalu, Communist China prepared to protect its vital interests in Asia.

The manner of Communist China's intervention in the Korean War suggested Mao's reluctance to act. On October 26, 1950, a large number of "Chinese volunteers" attacked the UN forces, thereby maintaining the fiction of no official involvement while halting their advance and driving them back. A week later the Chinese disappeared from the field. The message should have been clear: Mao had warned the United Nations to confine the fighting to South Korea. His priority, it seemed, was still Formosa, as evidenced by his agreement to send representatives to the United Nations to discuss the situation in Formosa. MacArthur did not see it that way. He called for an all-out attack and on November 24, the day of the Chinese delegates' arrival at the United Nations, proudly declared that his men had begun an "end-the-war offensive" that would have them "home by Christmas"—after they saw the Yalu. This news infuriated both the Communist Chinese and the Europeans, who accused MacArthur of trying to "wreck the negotiations" over Formosa. Two days later, as UN soldiers again clawed their way northward, the first large contingent of nearly 400,000 Communist Chinese soldiers suddenly swarmed into the seventy-five-mile-wide gap between MacArthur's two advancing and dangerously exposed flanks. Combined with the onset of a blizzard marked by temperatures of thirty degrees below zero, this attack drove the remnant of his vastly depleted 20,000 troops back below the thirty-eighth parallel within two weeks.

Communist China's second entry into the fighting drastically changed the tenor of the Korean conflict. MacArthur pronounced it "an entirely new war" and sought an air bombardment of China, and the UN General Assembly overwhelmingly condemned China for aggression. When Truman left the impression with reporters that use of the atomic bomb was under consideration, British Prime Minister Clement Attlee frantically rushed to Washington to urge a negotiated settlement of the conflict in Korea. Meanwhile, the president secured additional military appropriations from Congress to bolster Europe and other parts of the world. In a few weeks the Chinese again pushed the UN forces below the thirty-eighth parallel and once more took

China in the Korean War
Massive human wave assaults by the Chinese resulted in more than 400 casualties at the hands of the U.S. Marines wielding machine guns and rifles during one ten-hour battle in the spring of 1951. *U.S. Marine Corps.*

Seoul. The United Nations sought a cease-fire, but China refused until the following conditions were met: withdrawal of "foreign troops" from Korea, cessation of U.S. support to Formosa, and admission of Communist China to the UN Security Council as the legitimate Chinese government. The United States rejected all three demands.

The Chinese intervention sparked a major debate within the Truman administration over whether to return to the original objectives of containment. After a massive countereffort, MacArthur's forces stopped the Chinese assault and arduously began another offensive that took them back to the thirty-eighth parallel in March 1951. At that point Truman called for a negotiated settlement, but MacArthur unilaterally destroyed any chances for a cease-fire by crossing the border again and demanding an unconditional Chinese surrender. To achieve this objective, he asserted, the United States should blockade the Chinese coast, bomb the enemies' "privileged sanctuary" in Manchuria along with China's major industrial centers, permit the Nationalists to attack the mainland, and, as he later noted in his *Reminiscences,* "sever Korea from Manchuria by laying a field of radioactive wastes—the byproducts of atomic manufacture—across all the major lines of enemy supply." Truman staunchly objected. In accordance with the Joint Chiefs of Staff, he argued that MacArthur's strategy was militarily unsound. First, a blockade and bombings could cause Soviet intervention in accordance with its defensive pact with Communist China. Second, these tactics would not cut inland communication and supply lines. Third, Jiang had already proved his ineptitude on the battlefield. Fourth, the United States's European allies were not supportive. Finally, and most important, use of atomic materials could bring on World War III.

MacArthur rigidly opposed any restrictions on his military actions. Insisting that Asia would be the next major battleground between communism and the Free World, he argued that the United States should "go it

alone if necessary." He publicly implied that Truman was guilty of appeasement, and in a move raising questions about the constitutionality of civilian over military authority, he wrote a letter to the leading Republican in the House of Representatives, Joseph Martin, in which he asserted that "there is no substitute for victory." In Asia, MacArthur wrote, "the communist conspirators have elected to make their play for global conquest. Here we fight Europe's war with arms while the diplomats there still fight it with words." Martin dramatically read the letter before the House on April 5, 1951. MacArthur had earlier ignored the president's directive against issuing public statements concerning foreign policy without prior approval from the state department. He had then undermined his own credibility by assuring the president that the Chinese would not intervene in the war. Although many others had agreed with his assessment of the Chinese, it was MacArthur who as field commander engaged in histrionics and therefore attracted the most attention. Publication of the letter now challenged the president either to remove the seventy-one-year-old general from his East Asian duties on grounds of insubordination or to alter military policy to suit the commander in the field. Truman, with full support from the Joint Chiefs of Staff, chose to relieve MacArthur of his East Asian command. "The son of a bitch isn't going to resign on me," the president hotly told General Omar Bradley, chair of the joint chiefs. "*I want him fired.*"

The announcement on April 11 of the "firing" of MacArthur set off an immediate storm of protest in the United States that led some Americans to demand Truman's impeachment. The furor was attributable to several factors. Frustrations over the no-win nature of containment ("police actions" or "limited wars") headed the list, because this seemingly passive approach to war violated the U.S. military tradition of total victory and threatened to undermine the related illusion that the United States had "won" all of its wars. The rage over MacArthur's treatment also provided an outlet for some Americans' long-standing isolationist discontent with the nation's interventionist foreign policy and for Republican desperation over losing the White House again in 1948.

Suspicion of Communist infiltration of the government also drove numerous Americans, who regarded the Hiss case and McCarthy's sensational charges as only the surface of a dark and weblike conspiracy. Many events since the Democrats' victory in 1932 had suggested a pattern of un-Americanism: the socialistic nature of the New Deal; diplomatic recognition of the Soviet Union; Roosevelt's alleged "maneuverings" of the United States into World War II; the Yalta "betrayals"; the "fall" of China to communism; and now the Truman administration's decision to fire the only person brave enough to insist on victory. McCarthy's accusations took on greater credibility with MacArthur's removal. "How can we account for our present situation," asked the senator, "unless we believe that men high in this government are concerting to deliver us to disaster?" McCarthy's heated charge was a thinly veiled reference to General Marshall, who had long been offended by MacArthur's inordinate vanity and had recommended his dismissal. Marshall, according to McCarthy on the Senate floor, was an integral part "of a great conspiracy on a scale so immense as to dwarf any previous venture in the history of man."

Another reason for the public's wrath was the mistaken impression that all MacArthur wanted was a conventional assault on the Chinese mainland. Indeed, it was not until 1964, a few days after his death, that the general's earlier private and highly revealing conversations with two reporters finally became public. In 1951 MacArthur had wanted to drop atomic bombs on North Korea as a prelude to a land offensive led by Americans and Nationalist Chinese. These forces would have invaded North Korea from the west and east, he insisted, imposing a stranglehold on the Korean peninsula that would have resulted in total victory in less than two weeks. No reinforcements could have arrived from the north

because in the meantime the United Nations would have laid a five-mile-wide strip of cobalt along the Chinese-Korean border. For the lifetime of the cobalt—more than half a century—no one could have entered the zone. MacArthur had no fear of Soviet intervention. "It makes me laugh," he declared, "that Russia would commit its armies to a war in China's behalf at the end of an endless one-track railroad to a peninsular battleground that led only to the sea. Russia could not have engaged us," he continued. "She would not have fought for China. She is already unhappy and uncertain over the colossus she has encouraged." He concluded that "it was in our power to destroy the Communist Chinese army and Chinese military power. And probably for all time. My plan was a cinch."

MacArthur's popularity in the United States remained high for about six weeks before beginning to recede—in line with the president's prediction. In April the general received an impassioned public welcome upon his return to the United States for the first time since 1937. Congress invited him to speak before a joint session, which became a nationwide media event over radio and television. In his thirty-four-minute address, he called for a stepped-up war in Asia and included a moving peroration based on the lines of a popular song that "old soldiers never die; they just fade away." At the conclusion, he declared that "like the old soldier of that ballad, I now close my military career and just fade away—an old soldier who tried to do his duty as God gave him the light to see that duty." After a pause, he whispered, "good-bye" and left the podium. Not a dry eye remained in the chamber. Former President Herbert Hoover christened MacArthur as the "reincarnation of St. Paul into a great General of the Army who came out of the East." And Missouri Representative Dewey Short, a former preacher educated at Harvard, Oxford, and Heidelberg, told reporters: "We heard God speak here today, God in the flesh, the voice of God."

But soon the emotional reaction wore thin and reason took over. When MacArthur

Gen. MacArthur before Congress
In early April 1951, after President Truman dismissed MacArthur from his Far Eastern command, the general presented his case to Congress and the American people, concluding his remarks with the famous words, "Old soldiers never die; they just fade away." *National Archives, Washington, D.C.*

showed up late for a press conference, a reporter snidely remarked that the general's friends had probably experienced some difficulty in removing the nails holding him to the cross. In subsequent Senate inquiries, General Bradley, the highly respected chair of the Joint Chiefs of Staff, gave a persuasive defense of the administration that soon undermined MacArthur's strategy. "Taking on Red China," Bradley declared, would have created "a larger deadlock at greater expense" and without the support of the United States's allies. The Soviet Union was the "main antagonist" and Western Europe the "main prize." In the most telling words, he insisted that an assault on China would have involved the United States "in the wrong war at the wrong place at the wrong time and with the wrong enemy." Bradley's argument was calm, reasoned, and based on military and political realities, not on emotional charges of Communist subterfuge and U.S. cowardice and stupidity.

Truman meanwhile repeatedly reminded Americans that their European allies opposed MacArthur's attempt to widen the conflict. But perhaps just as important to the argument, the president emphasized that in the United States the civilian authority outranked that of the military. MacArthur's actions, he declared, were a violation of the Constitution. Faced with such unassailable arguments, the general's credibility began to dip.

Meanwhile, hopes for an end to the Korean conflict arose when the Communists agreed to enter truce talks in the summer of 1951. On June 23 the Soviet delegate to the Security Council called for a cease-fire. The Chinese Communists approved, but with the stipulation that foreign soldiers had to pull out of Korea. Armistice discussions began in early July at Kaesong near the thirty-eighth parallel, although the negotiators eventually moved to Panmunjom. In November the antagonists tentatively accepted an armistice line at the point where the fighting ended, but the United States steadfastly refused to approve a UN withdrawal from South Korea. The Communists then heightened their demands and accused the United States of using germ warfare, and violence broke out among the prisoners of war (POWs) in UN camps. The talks stalemated. Over the next year and a half the antagonists argued about the location of the cease-fire line, the steps necessary to implement an armistice agreement, and the repatriation of prisoners. By the spring of 1952 only the last question remained an issue. Whereas the Communists wanted all prisoners returned, the United Nations refused to repatriate those who did not want to go home. This was no small problem: Nearly one-half of the United Nations's 170,000 POWs opposed repatriation.

While the fighting continued under the leadership of MacArthur's replacement, General Matthew Ridgway of World War II valor, the United States moved toward establishing a tighter alliance with countries in East Asia. On August 30, 1951, it signed a security pact with the Philippines, and two days later it became party to the Tripartite Security Treaty (ANZUS) with Australia and New Zealand. Both pacts were intended to allay those countries' anxieties over the Truman administration's real objective of rebuilding Japan as a counterweight to Soviet influence in East Asia.

Thus, the Korean War catalyzed a move already under way in Tokyo to conclude a

Gen. Matthew Ridgway
Gen. Ridgway discusses strategy with Maj. Gen. Frank W. Milburn on December 27, 1950, just one day after Ridgway assumed command of the Eighth Army in Korea. *U.S. Army.*

peace treaty with Japan and make it an ally against communism. More than fifty nations gathered in San Francisco in early September 1951 to begin negotiations under the leadership of John Foster Dulles, adviser to the secretary of state. Four days later the United States secured the Peace of Reconciliation, which recognized Japan's sovereignty over its home islands, awarded the United States a military base on Okinawa, and referred reparations problems to individual negotiations between Japan and concerned countries. There were no longer any prohibitions against Japanese rearmaments, and the United States would continue to occupy the Ryukyu and Bonin islands. That same day, September 8, the United States and Japan signed a Security Treaty permitting U.S. soldiers to remain in Japan as long as necessary "to contribute to the maintenance of international peace and security in the Far East and to the security of Japan." On April 28, 1952, the two treaties with Japan went into effect, marking the close of the U.S. administration of the Tokyo government and officially ending World War II in the Pacific.

The fighting continued in Korea, however, arousing deeper concern about the imminence of a global conflict. U.S. planes bombed hydroelectric plants on the Yalu River in June 1952, and in early October Truman declared that "we are fighting in Korea so we won't have to fight in Wichita, or in Chicago, or in New Orleans, or in San Francisco Bay." Later that same year, in November, American scientists developed the hydrogen bomb, a thermonuclear device possessing a thousand times more destructive capacity than the atomic bombs dropped over Hiroshima and Nagasaki. Instead of comforting Americans, this news heightened their uneasiness over the military escalation in Korea and intensified demands to end the conflict.

Armistice in Korea

As the presidential election of 1952 approached, Americans became increasingly suspicious that Communist sympathizers in Washington were obstructing the war effort. The campaign tied these issues together when the Republicans used the symbol "K_1C_2" to refer to Korea, communism, and the several instances of corruption recently uncovered among administration officials. At the Republican convention, MacArthur delivered the keynote address, in which he denounced the Free World's "headlong retreat from victory." McCarthy followed with a speech blasting Acheson and others for their "abysmal stupidity and treason" and assured listeners that he would never fight communism "with a perfumed silk handkerchief." The party's choice for vice president was Richard M. Nixon, who had led the House committee attack on Alger Hiss and earlier in the campaign had labeled the Democratic candidate, Adlai Stevenson, as "a Ph.D. from Dean Acheson's cowardly college of Communist containment." Its candidate for the top office in the land, Dwight D. Eisenhower, aroused enormous support by promising that if victorious, "I shall go to Korea." His unquestioned honesty, disarmingly homespun personality, and numerous military successes in World War II won him the confidence of voters. Eisenhower rolled over the less colorful though highly eloquent Stevenson of Illinois with 55 percent of the popular vote. In December the president-elect kept his campaign promise and went to Korea for three days. There he mingled with the soldiers on the front and announced support for the UN decision not to return the POWs who refused to go home.

Shortly after his inauguration in January 1953, President Eisenhower moved toward ending the Korean conflict. His administration took on the image of boldness and resolution, partly because of the outspoken nature of his secretary of state, John Foster Dulles, a Wall Street attorney and chief negotiator of the peace and security treaties with Japan. Seemingly bred as a diplomat (his family had long experience in the state department), this son of a Presbyterian minister viewed the Cold War as a virtual religious conflict between the forces of good and evil. Dulles guaranteed an aggressive foreign policy and soon became identified with the terms "massive retaliation," "brinkmanship," "liberation," and the "New Look" in suggesting that the United States was willing to use military force and even atomic weaponry to free people from communism.

The Eisenhower-Dulles team left the implication that the United States was at last rejecting containment and returning to the time-honored drive for total victory. The president had earlier notified the North Koreans and Communist Chinese through private channels that he wanted an immediate ceasefire; should they fail to comply, he warned, the United States might retaliate "under circumstances of our choosing." In his first State of the Union Message, he announced that the Seventh Fleet would "no longer be employed to shield Communist China," implying that he had "unleashed" Jiang's Nationalist forces to attack the mainland. Eisenhower's resort to the "MacArthur strategy" sounded convincing—so much so that Dulles had to make a sudden trip to London and Paris to calm the United States's worried allies. Another factor also encouraged peace prospects: Stalin died in March 1953, opening the possibility of a softer line from Moscow. His successor, Georgi Malenkov, seemed moderate in tone and more interested in focusing on his country's internal problems.

In July 1953 armistice talks began in earnest at Panmunjom, and by the end of the month the negotiators had reached an agreement. The previous month Syngman Rhee had threatened to wreck the discussions by suddenly freeing 27,000 North Korean POWs who opposed communism, in an effort to abort a settlement that he knew would not unify the Koreas under his rule. Rhee was a "zealous, irrational, and illogical fanatic," according to a presidential envoy sent from Washington. But the Communists did not break off the talks, which suggested that they, too, wanted to end the war. The antagonists finally agreed to the establishment of a neutral commission to deal with prisoner exchanges. The armistice line was to be the present battle front, which meant that although the North Koreans lost some territory, the war would end at approximately the same place it had begun—the thirty-eighth parallel. A demilitarized zone would serve as a buffer between the Koreas. The United States won Rhee's acquiescence by assuring military and economic aid.

Domestic American politics also played a role in ending the war. As columnist Walter Lippmann astutely observed, President Truman "was not able to make peace, because politically he was too weak at home. He was not able to make war because the risks were too great. This dilemma of Truman's was resolved by the election of Eisenhower. . . . President Eisenhower signed an armistice which accepted the partition of Korea and a peace without victory because, being himself the victorious commander in World War II and a Republican, he could not be attacked as an appeaser."

The Impact of the Korean War

The Korean War had an enormous and yet mixed effect on international affairs. Unrest remained between the Koreas, which outside nations continued to exploit. If the conflict did little for Soviet prestige in Asia, it greatly enhanced that of the Communist Chinese. Their intervention assumed the appearance of a bold move in defense of the North Koreans and had a powerful impact on nations wanting to be neutral in the world's power struggles. The war also postponed any chance that the United States would extend recognition to Communist China: U.S. support for Nationalist China was stronger than ever. Indeed, it now appears that the Truman administration lost an opportunity to exploit the growing Sino-Soviet rift when it approved the UN advance across the thirty-eighth parallel and forced the Communist Chinese to intervene. Furthermore, the U.S. alienation of the Chinese continued for more than two decades,

creating perceptions of an even more harrow-
ing "yellow peril" than that of the Japanese
and converting what one contemporary called
"700 million potential customers" into "700
million dangerous adversaries."

The war stimulated the U.S. economy, but
even that came at great expense. The United
States furnished one-half of the ground forces
(with the South Koreans supplying most of
the rest), eighty percent of the naval assistance, and ninety percent of the air power in
the conflict. It expended more than $15 bil-
lion and incurred 138,000 casualties (four-
fifths attributable to the fighting above the
parallel), including 34,000 dead. South Korea
suffered more than one million casualties; the
Chinese and North Koreans counted more
than one million dead.

If the establishment of a truce at the point
of the war's origins constituted a victory for
containment, it also meant that no one had
won the conflict. Korea remained divided and
in an uneasy stalemate. World affairs became
more tense in August 1953 when the Soviet
Union likewise exploded a hydrogen bomb.
According to the physicist Robert Oppenheimer, the two superpowers were like "two
scorpions in a bottle, each capable of killing
the other, but only at the risk of his own life."
Yet the United Nations had gained in stature
by containing Communist aggression, and in
October 1953 the United States and South
Korea signed a mutual defense pact, which
the Senate overwhelmingly approved the following year. The most important legacy of the
Korean conflict, however, was its impetus to
containment. Despite the new foreign policy
labels associated with the Eisenhower administration, the United States had affirmed
its acceptance of the containment doctrine,
which meant continued military buildups, repeated refusals to compromise with the Communists, and the virtual guarantee of a long
Cold War. President Eisenhower offered the
most direct appraisal: "We have won an armistice on a single battleground, not peace in
the world. We may not now relax our guard
nor cease our quest."

Selected Readings

Acheson, Dean. *Present at the Creation: My Years in the State Department.* 1969.

Ambrose, Stephen E., and Brinkley, Douglas G. *Rise to Globalism: American Foreign Policy since 1938.* 8th ed., 1997.

Ball, George W., and Ball, Douglas B. *The Passionate Attachment: America's Involvement with Israel 1947 to the Present.* 1992.

Blum, Robert M. *Drawing the Line: The Origins of the American Containment Policy in East Asia.* 1982.

Borden, William S. *The Pacific Alliance: United States Foreign Economic Policy and Japanese Trade Recovery, 1947–1955.* 1984.

Brands, H. W. *The Devil We Knew: Americans and the Cold War.* 1993.

Buhite, Russell D. *Patrick J. Hurley and American Foreign Policy.* 1973.

———. *Soviet-American Relations in Asia, 1945–1954.* 1982.

Callahan, David. *Dangerous Capabilities: Paul Nitze and the Cold War.* 1990.

Caridi, Ronald J. *The Korean War and American Politics: The Republican Party as a Case Study.* 1968.

Carter, Carolle J. *Mission to Yenan: American Liaison with the Chinese Communists, 1944–1947.* 1997.

Chen, Jian. *China's Road to the Korean War: The Making of the Sino-American Confrontation.* 1994.

Christensen, Thomas J. *Useful Adversaries: Grand Strategy, Domestic Mobilization, and Sino-American Conflict, 1947–1958.* 1996.

Cohen, Warren I. *America's Response to China: An Interpretive History of Sino-American Relations.* 2000.

Cumings, Bruce, ed. *Child of Conflict: The Korean-American Relationship, 1943–1953.* 1983.

———. *Korea's Place in the Sun: A Modern History.* 1997.

———. *The Origins of the Korean War.* Vol. I: *Liberation and the Emergence of Separate Regimes, 1945–1947.* 1981.

———. *The Origins of the Korean War.* Vol. II: *The Roaring of the Cataract, 1947–1950.* 1990.

Dobbs, Charles M. *The Unwanted Symbol: American Foreign Policy, the Cold War, and Korea, 1945–1950.* 1981.

Donovan, Robert J. *Tumultuous Years: The Presidency of Harry S Truman, 1949–1953.* 1982.

Dower, John W. *Embracing Defeat: Japan in the Wake of World War II.* 1999.

Dulles, Foster R. *American Foreign Policy Toward Communist China.* 1972.

Feis, Herbert. *The China Tangle.* 1953.

———. *Contest Over Japan.* 1967.

Ferrell, Robert H. *Harry S. Truman and the Modern American Presidency.* 1983.

Finn, Richard B. *Winners in Peace: MacArthur, Yoshida, and Postwar Japan.* 1992.

Fish, M. Steven. "After Stalin's Death: The Anglo-American Debate Over a New Cold War," *Diplomatic History* 10 (1986): 333–55.

Foot, Rosemary. "Anglo-American Relations in the Korean Crisis: The British Effort to Avert an Expanded War, December 1950–January 1951," *Diplomatic History* 10 (1986): 43–57.

———. *The Practice of Power: U.S. Relations with China since 1949.* 1995.

———. *A Substitute for Victory: The Politics of Peacemaking at the Korean Armistice Talks.* 1990.

———. *The Wrong War: American Policy and the Dimensions of the Korean Conflict, 1950–1953.* 1985.

Gaddis, John L. *The Long Peace: Inquiries into the History of the Cold War.* 1987.

———. *Russia, the Soviet Union, and the United States: An Interpretive History.* 2nd ed., 1990.

———. *Strategies of Containment: A Critical Appraisal of Postwar American National Security Policy.* 1982.

Gallicchio, Marc S. *The Cold War Begins in Asia.* 1988.

George, Alexander L. *The Chinese Communist Army in Action: The Korean War and Its Aftermath.* 1967.

Goncharov, S. N., Lewis, John W., and Litai, Xue. *Uncertain Partners: Stalin, Mao, and the Korean War.* 1993.

Goode, James F. *The United States and Iran, 1946–51: The Diplomacy of Neglect.* 1989.

Goulden, Joseph C. *Korea: The Untold Story of the War.* 1982.

Grasso, June M. *Harry Truman's Two-China Policy, 1948–1950.* 1987.

Griffith, Robert. *The Politics of Fear: Joseph R. McCarthy and the Senate.* 1970.

Harries, Meirion and Susie. *Sheathing the Sword: The Demilitarization of Japan.* 1987.

Hart, Robert A. *The Eccentric Tradition: American Diplomacy in the Far East.* 1976.

Hastings, Max. *The Korean War.* 1987.

Herring, George C., Jr. *America's Longest War: The United States and Vietnam, 1950–1975.* 3rd ed., 1996.

———. *The United States' Emergence as a Southeast Asian Power, 1940–1950.* 1987.

Higgins, Trumbull. *Korea and the Fall of MacArthur.* 1960.

Hogan, Michael J. *The Marshall Plan: America, Britain, and the Reconstruction of Western Europe, 1947–1952.* 1987.

Hunt, Michael H. *The Genesis of Chinese Communist Foreign Policy.* 1996.

Iriye, Akira. *The Cold War in Asia: A Historical Introduction.* 1974.

James, D. Clayton. *Refighting the Last War: Command and Crisis in Korea, 1950–1953.* 1992.

———. *The Years of MacArthur.* Vol. 3: *Triumph and Disaster, 1945–1964.* 1985.

Kaufman, Burton I. *The Korean War: Challenges in Crisis, Credibility, and Command.* 1986.

Keefer, Edward C. "President Dwight D. Eisenhower and the End of the Korean War," *Diplomatic History* 10 (1986): 267–89.

Kusnitz, Leonard A. *Public Opinion and Foreign Policy: America's China Policy, 1949–1979.* 1984.

LaFeber, Walter. *America, Russia, and the Cold War, 1945–1996.* 8th ed., 1997.

———. *The Clash: A History of U.S.-Japanese Relations.* 1997.

Leckie, Robert. *Conflict: The History of the Korean War, 1950–1953.* 1962.

Lee, Chae-jin, ed. *The Korean War: 40-Year Perspectives.* 1991.

Leffler, Melvyn P. *A Preponderance of Power: National Security, the Truman Administration, and the Cold War.* 1992.

———. *The Specter of Communism: The United States and the Origins of the Cold War, 1917–1953.* 1994.

Levine, Steven I. "A New Look at American Mediation in the Chinese Civil War: The Marshall Mission and Manchuria," *Diplomatic History* 3 (1979): 349–75.

Lowe, Peter. *The Origins of the Korean War.* 1997.

MacDonald, Callum A. *Korea: The War before Vietnam.* 1987.

Martin, Edwin W. *Divided Counsel: The Anglo-American Response to Communist Victory in China.* 1986.

Matray, James I. *The Reluctant Crusade: American Foreign Policy in Korea, 1941–1950.* 1985.

———. "Truman's Plan for Victory: National Self-Determination and the Thirty-Eighth Parallel Decision in Korea," *Journal of American History* 66 (1979): 314–33.

May, Ernest R. *The Truman Administration and China, 1945–1949.* 1975.

May, Gary. *China Scapegoat: The Diplomatic Ordeal of John Carter Vincent.* 1979.

Mayers, David A. *Cracking the Monolith: U.S. Policy Against the Sino-Soviet Alliance, 1949–1955.* 1986.

McGeehan, Robert. *The German Rearmament Question.* 1971.

McLean, David. "American Nationalism, the China Myth, and the Truman Doctrine: The Question of Accommodation with Peking, 1949–50," *Diplomatic History* 10 (1986): 25–42.

McMahon, Robert J. *Colonialism and Cold War: The United States and the Struggle for Indonesian Independence, 1945–1949.* 1982.

Merrill, John. *Korea: The Peninsular Origins of the War.* 1989.

Oshinsky, David M. *A Conspiracy So Immense: The World of Joe McCarthy.* 1983.

Paige, Glenn D. *The Korean Decision, June 24–30, 1950.* 1968.

Petillo, Carol M. "The Cold War in Asia," in Carroll, John M., and Herring, George C., eds., *Modern American Diplomacy,* 127–46. 1986.

Prados, John. *Presidents' Secret Wars: CIA Pentagon Covert Operations from World War II through the Persian Gulf.* 1996.

Purifoy, Lewis M. *Truman's China Policy: McCarthyism and the Diplomacy of Hysteria.* 1976.

Rees, David. *Korea: The Limited War.* 1964.

Rose, Lisle A., *Roots of Tragedy: The United States and the Struggle for Asia, 1945–1953.* 1976.

Rovere, Richard H., and Schlesinger, Arthur M., Jr. *The MacArthur Controversy and American Foreign Policy.* 1965. Revised and expanded version of the authors' *The General and the President.* 1951.

Sandler, Stanley. *The Korean War: No Victors, No Vanquished.* 1999.

Schaller, Michael. *The American Occupation of Japan: The Origins of the Cold War in Asia.* 1985.

———. *Douglas MacArthur: The Far Eastern General.* 1989.

———. "MacArthur's Japan: The View from Washington," *Diplomatic History* 10 (1986): 1–23.

Schwartz, Thomas A. *America's Germany: John J. McCloy and the Federal Republic of Germany.* 1991.

Spanier, John W. *American Foreign Policy Since World War II.* 14th ed., 1998.

———. *The Truman-MacArthur Controversy and the Korean War.* 1959.

Spector, Ronald H. *Advice and Support: The Early Years of the U.S. Army in Vietnam: 1941–1960.* 1983.

Stueck, William. *The Korean War: An International History.* 1995.

———. "The Korean War as International History," *Diplomatic History* 10 (1986): 291–309.

———. *The Road to Confrontation: American Policy toward China and Korea, 1947–1950.* 1981.

———. *The Wedemeyer Mission: American Politics and Foreign Policy during the Cold War.* 1984.

Theoharis, Athan G. *Seeds of Repression: Harry S. Truman and the Origins of McCarthyism.* 1971.

———. *The Yalta Myths: An Issue in U.S. Politics, 1945–1955.* 1970.

Toland, John. *In Mortal Combat: Korea, 1950–1953.* 1991.

Truman, Harry S. *Memoirs.* 2 vols. 1956.

Tsou, Tang. *America's Failure in China, 1941–1950.* 1963.

Tucker, Nancy B. *Patterns in the Dust: Chinese-American Relations and the Recognition Controversy, 1949–1950.* 1983.

Ulam, Adam B. *The Communists: The Story of Power and Lost Illusions, 1948–1991.* 1992.

———. *The Rivals: America and Russia since World War II.* 1971.

Weintraub, Stanley. *MacArthur's War: Korea and the Undoing of an American Hero.* 2000.

Whelan, Richard. *Drawing the Line: The Korean War, 1950–1953.* 1990.

Whiting, Allen S. *China Crosses the Yalu: The Decision to Enter the Korean War.* 1960.

Williams, William J., ed. *A Revolutionary War: Korea and the Transformation of the Postwar World.* 1993.

Zhang, Shu Guang. *Deterrence and Strategic Culture: Chinese-American Confrontations, 1949–1958.* 1992.

———. *Mao's Military Romanticism: China and the Korean War, 1950–1953.* 1996.

CHAPTER 11

Containment Continued
THE EISENHOWER YEARS, 1953–1961

The Rhetoric of Cold War

Despite the Cold War rhetoric of the Eisenhower presidency, U.S. foreign policy remained essentially the same: that of containment. Secretary of State John Foster Dulles, son of a Presbyterian minister and relative of two other secretaries of state before him (John W. Foster and Robert Lansing), was stern and self-righteous in manner, sour in disposition, and less than exciting in demeanor (one contemporary spoke of him as "Dull, Duller, Dulles"). He was also a staunch anti-Communist who saw political value in suggesting that the administration had discarded containment for "liberation" when he called for a cutback in conventional forces and a heavy reliance on nuclear weapons. America's containment policy, Dulles warned in a *Life* magazine article in 1952, endangered civil liberties by necessitating excessive taxes and a refusal to seek victory. The United States needed "a policy of boldness" that enabled Americans "to retaliate instantly against open aggression by Red armies, so that if it occurred anywhere, we could and would strike back where it hurts, by means of our own choosing." Four years later he elaborated on these ideas in another article in *Life*. "The ability to get to the verge without getting into the war is the necessary art," he asserted. "If you cannot master it, you inevitably get into war. If you try to run away from it, if you are scared to go to the brink, you are lost." Yet the explosive events of the 1950s showed that President Eisenhower recognized the realities of the nuclear standoff and often restrained his secretary of state by implementing a cautious foreign policy that avoided challenges to Soviet spheres of influence. Nikita Khrushchev, who became premier in 1958, later reminisced that Dulles "knew how far he could push us, and he never pushed us too far." Despite the administration's emphasis on the "New Look" in diplomacy, it adhered to the principles of containment.

Eisenhower exercised a greater degree of leadership over his administration than usually acknowledged. He chaired the numerous meetings of the National Security Council and, despite all the public attention Dulles commanded, maintained tight control over foreign policy. Dulles's busy nervousness, along with his numerous trips to Europe and Latin America, left the impression that he alone made the decisions. Indeed, he once drew the comment, "Don't do something, Foster, just stand there!" But it was Eisenhower himself who made foreign policy, though remaining deliberately in the background. It was he who condoned covert action through the CIA (headed by Allen

John Foster Dulles
Holding a press conference upon his arrival in Taipei, Taiwan, in October 1958, just before conferring with Generalissimo Jiang Jieshi, president of Nationalist China. *U.S. Army.*

Dulles, brother of the secretary of state) and shepherded the expansion of the country's nuclear warheads eighteen times over their number of one thousand in 1953. He also approved the development of both the B-52, a jet bomber capable of carrying a nuclear payload, and the Polaris, a ballistic missile fired from a submarine while underwater. Eisenhower considered atomic weaponry to be a vital part of the nation's defense network, not a last resort. His image of do-nothingism (a "national sedative," some declared) fulfilled a much-needed role, however. Given the past crises caused by the Great Depression, World War II, McCarthyism, Korean War, and the ever heightening Cold War, Eisenhower's unquestioned honesty, disarming personality, and outwardly calm manner reassured anxious Americans that their nation was once again in safe hands.

The 1950s: An Age of International Turmoil

Several crises during the decade highlighted the growing Cold War and tested the ability of the Eisenhower-Dulles foreign policy team to contain the spread of Soviet communism. Korea (see the previous chapter), the Third World, Iran, Guatemala, Indochina, Communist China, Poland, Hungary, Suez, Berlin, the U-2 incident, Latin America—all problems appeared to be Communist in origin. Eisenhower recognized that a balance of nuclear terror had developed that rested precariously on mutual Soviet-American distrust, and he knew that the only way to keep peace lay in diplomacy using nuclear strength as leverage. While Dulles publicly advocated massive retaliation and maintained an apocalyptic approach to foreign affairs, Eisenhower quietly exercised restraints without abandoning the nuclear alternative. Yet the nation's driving force throughout the decade remained consistent with that of the Truman administration: a Cold War perception of the world that interpreted nearly every troublesome event as part of the epochal struggle with the Soviet Union.

The rising postwar Third World nations played a vital role in the Cold War. By 1960 nearly forty nations had emerged in Asia,

Africa, and the Middle East, many rich in natural resources though desperately poor in economic development. Americans and Soviets found these new nations increasingly important to the search for strategic bases in the steadily intensifying rivalry between East and West. The largely uncontrollable factor was the growing number of nationalist revolutions that erupted from the anticolonial sentiment of World War II. Leaders were often leftist, Marxist, and only ostensibly democratic, building a following among peoples who were economically and politically destitute and hence subject to the bidding of Moscow's assumed proxies all over the world. A further complication was that as these peoples were accorded national status, they often adopted neutralist postures, preferring to play one superpower against the other rather than taking sides and thereby becoming the flashpoints of nuclear war. Indeed, in April 1955, twenty-nine non-aligned Asian and African nations gathered at the Bandung Conference in Indonesia, where Communist China's Zhou Enlai and India's Prime Minister Jawaharlal Nehru expressed the delegates' chief concerns about staying out of Cold War battles, remaining free of Western colonialism, and calling for "peaceful coexistence."

Washington's policymakers found themselves in an unenviable position in relation to the Third World. One could never be sure which direction a social revolution would take, and rather than risk a Communist takeover, the simplest approach was to support those leaders who were anti-Communist and promised stability, even at the cost of personal freedoms. The stakes were too high to allow any revolution to run its course, and for that reason the Eisenhower administration continued and even broadened the Truman policy of interventionism. Arguing that the Soviet Union was meddling in nearly every hot spot in the world, the United States extended military, economic, and political assistance, manipulated governments by virtually establishing surrogates in positions of power, participated in coups through the CIA, and demanded loyalty in the United

Nations and other major concerns. Thus, the United States adopted many of the same measures that it criticized the Soviet Union for using. Rather than regarding Third World unrest as local in origin, the Eisenhower administration established a precedent for equating nationalism and neutralism with communism and assuming that the party line emanated solely from the Kremlin. In this respect, the president and his staff failed to come to terms with Third World nationalism and thereby left a dangerous legacy for their successors.

Eisenhower's foreign policy, like that of Truman's, sought to achieve order and stability in the Third World through economic and military measures. Some of the methods changed. The new administration considered reciprocal trade agreements (even with Eastern Europe) to be more important than foreign aid programs in curbing communism, and it depended more on the Export-Import Bank in combating economic problems overseas. U.S. exports doubled from 1952 to 1960, although military aid under the Mutual Security Program averaged more than $3 billion a year in expenditures abroad.

Conservative Republicans fought both reciprocal trade pacts and the use of executive agreements in foreign affairs. Allied with conservative Democrats, they came within a single vote of passing an amendment proposed by Senator John Bricker of Ohio, which would have changed the Constitution to allow congressional regulation of executive agreements with foreign countries. The White House maintained control over foreign policy, although it continued to operate within more stringent limitations imposed by a nearly chaotic brand of domestic politics. The irony is that during the remainder of the decade Eisenhower so cautiously phrased his requests to Congress in matters relating to foreign affairs that it granted him more authority than anyone could have expected.

The frenzied political atmosphere at home resulting from McCarthyism obstructed the formulation of a realistic policy to deal with another major development of the period: the growing diversity in the Communist world. The Kremlin's hold had begun to loosen as local Communist parties preferred national objectives to ideology and threatened to further diffuse the international power structure. The first signal came in mid-1948, when Yugoslavia and the Soviet Union broke relations. A more profound change occurred during the 1950s, when the Communist Chinese intervened in the Korean War, earning them a sudden surge of prestige in Asia at Soviet expense. A U.S. foreign policy built on caution and restraint seemed wise, and yet internal politics put pressure on the Washington government to pursue an activist policy braced with rhetoric and warning. Furthermore, the policy's anti-Communist thrust led the United States to support reactionary, repressive regimes, often putting it on the side of those leaders who opposed legitimate domestic reforms.

The nation's racial policies at home also hurt its international standing and promoted Communist propaganda. Race relations were tense. In December 1952 the U.S. attorney general urged the Supreme Court to rule against school segregation on the ground that "it is in the context of the present world struggle between freedom and tyranny that the problem of racial discrimination must be viewed." Two years later the Supreme Court struck down segregation in the landmark case of *Brown* v. *Board of Education,* although the ruling's actual implementation was delayed by ensuing events of the decade. In perhaps the most highly publicized incident threatening to cause racial violence, Eisenhower sent federal troops to Little Rock, Arkansas, in 1957 to protect black school children from angry white citizens. The state, according to the president, had performed a "tremendous disservice . . . to the nation in the eyes of the world." While the state department and Voice of America tried to fend off Soviet propaganda, the United States continually fought racial battles at home while competing for Third World support and trying to hold together a Western alliance composed of Britain, France, and other former colonial powers.

If Eisenhower's foreign policy followed many of the same patterns established by his predecessor, it nonetheless was distinctive in attempting to negotiate with the Soviet Union. In April 1953, before the resolution of the Korean War, the president delivered a speech entitled "The Chance for Peace" that pushed for improved relations with Stalin's more moderate successor, Georgi Malenkov. Eisenhower's subsequent proposals for disarmament had no immediate effect, because in June workers in East Berlin, dissatisfied with increased work loads, set off a crisis in Germany by walking off their jobs. When their bold action grew into protests against the Soviet Union, Red troops and tanks swarmed into the city and brutally crushed the upheaval in less than twenty-four hours. The message seemed clear: Disharmony in the Communist world had left the door ajar for easing relations between East and West. By the end of the year the Korean War had wound down and the Moscow government had established diplomatic relations with Yugoslavia and Greece, dropped territorial demands on Turkey, relaxed denunciations of the United States, and liberated the captives in Stalin's labor camps. Eisenhower went before the UN General Assembly in early December 1953 to recommend a slowdown in the nuclear arms race and to advocate international cooperation in industrial development.

The CIA in Iran and Guatemala

But before talks could begin, the Eisenhower administration had to turn to growing problems in Iran that many in Washington attributed to Communist infiltration. In 1953 it appeared that Premier Muhammad Musaddiq had edged too close to the Soviet Union through the Tudeh, the Communist party in Iran. Two years earlier Musaddiq had nationalized the Anglo-Iranian Oil Company and in 1953 had seized control of the government, forcing the young Muhammad Reza Shah (King) Pahlavi into exile. Although Musaddiq's nationalism was probably his greatest liability to the West, the United States viewed his actions as Communist-inspired and cut off aid in the autumn of that year. The administration worked through the CIA (the venture led by the grandson of Theodore Roosevelt and former member of the Office of Strategic Services during World War II, Kermit Roosevelt, and by General H. Norman Schwarzkopf, Sr., who had engineered the establishment of the shah's secret police following the war), the British Secret Intelligence Service, and Iranian royalists in secretly organizing mass demonstrations in Teheran that embarrassed Musaddiq's government and led to his overthrow and imprisonment.

The shah, supported by U.S. military aid, returned to the throne in August 1953 and soon granted oil concessions to the West. Not by coincidence did he agree to the establishment of a consortium that provided for an even division of profits between it and Iran. The arrangement awarded the country's oil production rights primarily to Britain (forty percent) and the United States (five U.S. companies received forty percent) and split the remainder between a French firm and a Dutch firm. In 1957 the CIA assisted the shah, who was anti-Communist and pro-American, in building a secret police network called SAVAK, which used torture, arbitrary imprisonment, and other repressive measures to guarantee loyalty to the throne. The Eisenhower administration proudly proclaimed that Iran was no longer in danger of a Communist takeover.

Growing unrest in Latin America also seemed to be Communist-induced. Latin Americans had long needed economic assistance, but their pleas for help had seldom attracted attention in Washington. Although the United States had extended aid to Europe and Asia by the end of the 1940s, trouble and resentment had continued to fester in Latin America as a result of declining prices on the world market, steadily increasing poverty, illiteracy, and disease, and mounting overpopulation and production problems. Latin Americans wanted low-term government loans or outright grants, and they needed help in stabilizing prices. Reaction in the United States was not enthu-

siastic. Washington's leaders favored industrial growth through private funds and tied these funds to Latin American guarantees against nationalizing foreign holdings. Many Latin Americans considered private investment akin to imperialist exploitation and reminded the White House that U.S. businesses had traditionally drained the region of natural resources.

The Eisenhower administration instituted changes in Latin American policy that, though having the appearance of humanitarian concern, actually reflected an overwhelming emphasis on ridding the hemisphere of communism. In 1953 the president's brother Milton, who was president of Johns Hopkins University, headed a special mission that visited ten South American states and proposed price stabilization, public loans, stimulation of private investment, and increased technical assistance under the Point Four program. But these measures were insufficient to meet the need. By the early 1950s swelling economic and political unrest in Latin America had combined with growing nationalist fervor to create a highly combustible situation.

Problems in Guatemala became the focal point of the Eisenhower administration's concern over Latin America, because the administration was convinced that Communists, led by leftist president Jacobo Arbenz Guzmán, had infiltrated the republic. The facts belied the suppositions. Arbenz and his closest advisers were not Communists; only four of fifty-six members of Congress were Communists; and neither the Catholic Church nor the army—the chief sources of power in the country—was Communist. Dulles himself admitted that he could not prove a link between the Guatemalan government and the Kremlin; but this sound observation had the perverse effect of proving the Communist influence by suggesting the devious and skillful nature of that clandestine relationship.

The Arbenz regime had aroused massive unrest by calling for land reforms in a country where two percent of its people owned seventy percent of the land. The largest landholder in Guatemala was a U.S. firm, United

Fruit Company of Boston, which had long enjoyed favored treatment by the government. That company now saw 400,000 acres of its holdings that were not then in use expropriated by the Arbenz regime in 1953 without what the company considered to be adequate compensation. To regain its land, United Fruit sought the assistance of the state department in Washington by warning that if Arbenz succeeded, communism would spread into all of Latin America. Guatemala lay within air-striking distance of the Panama Canal, the company's representatives pointedly reminded the Eisenhower administration, and Arbenz was moving close to the Soviet Union in the United Nations. U.S. Ambassador John Peurifoy, who had been in Greece during the civil war of the late 1940s, assured his superiors in Washington that Arbenz "thought like a Communist and talked like a Communist, and if not actually one, would do until one came along."

The White House at first employed diplomatic measures to bring about the fall of Arbenz. In March 1954, at the Tenth International Conference of American States in Caracas, Venezuela, Dulles secured a nearly unanimous vote (Guatemala was the lone dissenter) condemning "the domination or control of the political institutions of any American state by the international Communist movement." The statement was milder than Dulles wanted, and even then, several of those voting for the resolution complained that they had done so only under enormous U.S. pressure. Over the bitter protests of Guatemala's foreign minister that the declaration meant "the internationalization of McCarthyism," the United States cut off aid to his country.

But diplomatic efforts failed to undermine the Arbenz regime, and the White House resorted to surreptitious means. The CIA cooperated with Carlos Castillo Armas—an exiled Guatemalan army colonel and graduate of the U.S. Army's Command and General Staff College in Fort Leavenworth, Kansas—in building a mercenary army based both in Honduras

and on an island off Nicaragua. Arbenz appealed to the UN Security Council for help, but the United States blocked any substantive consideration of the issue. Believing that the Eisenhower administration was seeking his overthrow with the help of Nicaraguan dictator Anastasio Somoza, Arbenz requested military assistance from the Communist states and drew a favorable response from the Soviet Union. In May a Swedish vessel arrived in Guatemala carrying machine guns and rifles produced in Czechoslovakia and authorized for delivery by the Kremlin. The United States did not interfere with the unloading of the weapons, but the CIA prepared for an imminent coup by airlifting arms and other materials to spots near United Fruit possessions in Guatemala.

The fall of the Arbenz regime came surprisingly easy. In June 1954 Armas opened the military assault while CIA pilots in U.S. planes bombed Guatemala City. Arbenz's army quickly deserted, forcing him to flee the country. Armas took power, United Fruit got back its land, and the new regime honored its debt by moving close to the United States. Although Armas had hundreds executed, the Eisenhower administration hailed his demise as a victory over communism. Yet the social, economic, and political situation in Guatemala remained dismal, and the country turned into a virtual police state as perhaps 100,000 died over the next three decades under harsh military rule. The ill feeling generated by the intervention damaged U.S.-Latin American relations for years.

Southeast Asia

Meanwhile the Eisenhower administration faced another Third World problem: the ongoing insurgent war in Indochina against the French. During the 1860s France had imposed colonial rule onto the small S-shaped province, and in the early 1880s it established protectorates over Laos and Cambodia, soon incorporating them—with Vietnam's three colonies of Annam, Tonkin, and Cochin China—into

Indochina. The French meanwhile extracted vast quantities of rice, rubber, tin, oil, and tungsten from the area but did little to help its people, the great majority of whom were poverty-stricken country peasants. A staunch and learned Vietnamese nationalist, Ho Chi Minh, appeared as a self-appointed representative for Indochina at the Paris Peace Conference ending World War I, where he failed to win support for democratic reforms at home. Disillusioned, he joined the French Communist party and throughout the 1920s and 1930s lived and campaigned in China, the Soviet Union, Thailand, and Vietnam. During that time he established the Indochinese Communist party, which tried unsuccessfully to undermine French rule.

The onset of World War II had a profound effect on Indochina. After Japan seized the area in 1941, Indochinese nationalists formed an underground resistance organization called the Vietminh, which combined the various nationalist groups under Ho's Communist leadership and used China as its base of operations. Toward the end of the war the Vietminh cooperated with agents of the U.S. Office of Strategic Services against the Japanese, and Ho spoke of impending support from Washington in implanting U.S. ideals in an independent Indochina during the postwar period. In late August 1945 the Vietminh proclaimed the establishment of the Democratic Republic of Vietnam (DRV), with its capital in Hanoi. After the war, Ho reiterated his call for Indochinese independence based on the same principles found in the United States's famous Declaration of Independence in 1776.

But the Washington government had never looked favorably on Ho Chi Minh's Vietminh forces. Indeed, it was not until autumn 1944 that the state department recognized the growing importance of Southeast Asia to U.S. interests in the Philippines. President Roosevelt opposed the long-standing colonial system and instead tried to establish an international trusteeship over Indochina, but he encountered vehement opposition from Churchill, who feared that such an example would endanger the British Empire's colonial interests. When Roosevelt died, the state department convinced President Truman that the restoration of French hegemony in Southeast Asia was necessary to win that government's support against the growing Soviet threat in Europe. Consequently, in 1946, after the war wound down in Asia, Indochina returned to French control.

Vietminh resistance immediately formed against the French, leading to what would become known as the First Indochinese War. In March 1946 Ho Chi Minh and the French attempted to resolve their differences. Under agreements reached in Hanoi, Vietnam was to become a "free state" within the French Union, in return for joining Laos and Cambodia under a French protectorate called the "Associated States." But the French did not follow through on a promised plebiscite, and conflict broke out in November. The French bombarded Haiphong and seized the cities

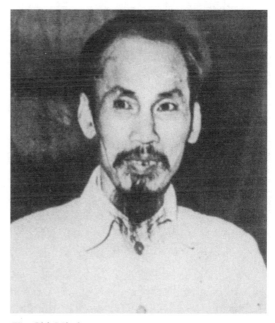

Ho Chi Minh
Leader of the Vietminh during World War II, who later fought for Vietnam's independence and reunification until his death in September 1969. *National Archives, Washington, D.C.*

while Vietminh guerrillas solidified control over the countryside. In 1949 the French installed the emperor of Annam, Bao Dai, as ruler of Vietnam and widened his domain to include Cochin China. Though genuinely concerned about his people, Bao Dai did not push for reforms primarily because he was too closely tied to his sponsors in Paris and to wealthy landholders within his regime. The Vietminh meanwhile attracted widespread popular support as the representatives of nationalism. They were also the "rebels," and the war continued.

U.S. interest in Indochina jumped dramatically during the early 1950s because of China's change to communism, the outbreak of the Korean War, and the Truman administration's realization that to win French support for its European policies, it had to back French interests in Indochina. Although Secretary of State Acheson termed this reciprocal arrangement with France "blackmail," the decision to comply with its demands came easier because the state department believed that the alternative was the spread of communism throughout Southeast Asia. Ho Chi Minh, according to the White House, was Moscow's Communist agent. Acheson, in fact, told the Senate in 1949 that Ho was an "outright Commie." In February 1950 the United States joined Britain in extending recognition to the French-sponsored government of Bao Dai. It also provided $150 million in military assistance that included planes, tanks, and napalm and dispatched a small number of U.S. military advisers to train Vietnamese soldiers loyal to the French. Indochina, declared Assistant Secretary of State Dean Rusk, had become "the most strategically important area of Southeast Asia."

As Southeast Asia became increasingly integral to the Cold War, the United States stepped up military aid to the French. By 1954 the number of U.S. military advisers had grown to more than three hundred, and its aid proportion now constituted eighty percent of France's war expenditures. Communist China and the Soviet Union countered by extending recognition to the Democratic Republic of Vietnam in the north and granting military assistance. The French commander in Indochina, General Henri Navarre, meanwhile called for a massive military buildup of the Vietnamese National Army and enough additional French soldiers to launch a major offensive against the Vietminh stronghold located in the far northern region of the Red River Delta. Although Dulles was confident that the Navarre Plan would "break the organized body of Communist aggression by the end of the 1955 fighting season," the general was not so sure. The best result, he told leaders in Paris, was a stalemate that might lead to a peace treaty with the Vietminh. Even as the United States began its aid program in 1950, the Vietminh controlled two-thirds of the countryside, counted hundreds of thousands within its ranks, and held the offensive in the war.

The showdown in the First Indochinese War came in March 1954 when the Vietminh, armed with Chinese artillery, surrounded a combined French and Vietnamese army of 20,000 in the northwest Vietnamese village of Dienbienphu, a remote valley fortress almost totally encircled by hills one thousand feet high. Navarre had intended to lure the Vietminh into an open engagement that would allow his superior weapons to take their toll. But the guerrillas surprised the French by first closing off air access to the fortress and then, in a superhuman effort, laboriously transporting heavy artillery to the high areas ringing the garrison. The French were isolated and appealed to the United States for an air strike and full-scale military intervention. The alternative, warned the Paris government, would be the fall of Indochina and the rest of Southeast Asia to communism.

The Eisenhower administration was divided in reaction to the French plea but appeared to lean toward intervention. Vice President Richard M. Nixon aroused stiff public opposition in April when he declared in an unauthorized remark that "if to avoid further Communist expansion in Asia and Indochina, we must take the risk now by putting our boys

French Indochina

Map 22
When Ho Chi Minh's Vietminh forces defeated the French at
Dienbienphu in 1954, they had won their independence only in the
north. After the Geneva Conference of that same year, the United
States engaged in a policy of "nation building" that was supportive
of Diem's government in the south.

in, I think the Executive has to take the politically unpopular decision and do it." Dulles
also wanted to send U.S. soldiers and bomb
the area, but Army Chief of Staff Matthew
Ridgway staunchly opposed direct military
involvement because it would lead to heavy
U.S. casualties and seriously undermine the
nation's military commitment to Europe
through NATO. At a press conference, Eisenhower spoke of the "domino theory," by
which he seemed to imply that U.S. military
intervention was necessary to prevent the fall
of Indochina and an ensuing chain reaction
that would cause the collapse of the entire

region. Yet he questioned the value of an air strike in guerrilla warfare and in densely forested topography. He also rigidly opposed the emotional argument of Air Force Chief of Staff Nathan Twining, who wanted to drop three atomic bombs on the Vietminh forces at Dienbienphu to "clean those Commies out of there."

In the end Eisenhower rejected the French request for intervention at Dienbienphu. An air strike, he asserted, was "just silly." Years later in a television interview with CBS news commentator Walter Cronkite, Eisenhower explained, "I couldn't think of anything probably less effective . . . unless you were willing to use weapons that could have destroyed the jungles all around the area for miles and that would have probably destroyed Dienbienphu

itself." There was no such thing as "partial involvement," Admiral A. C. Davis sharply warned. "One cannot go over Niagara Falls in a barrel only slightly."

Eisenhower refused to act unless he had other countries' assistance, popular support at home, and a French pledge of independence to Indochina. He had none of these. The United States's allies were not interested in Dulles's call for "United Action," and the British in particular refused to believe that the fall of Indochina would bring down all of Southeast Asia. A recent Gallup poll in the United States had shown ten to one opposition to the use of U.S. combat troops. Included among the congressional members resisting such a move were future presidents John F. Kennedy and Lyndon B. Johnson, the first declaring that

The Joint Chiefs of Staff
The debate over U.S. intervention at Dienbienphu in 1954. Admiral Arthur W. Radford (on left with back to camera) could convince only U.S. Air Force General Nathan Twining (to Radford's right) to favor intervention on behalf of the French. The other three joint chiefs (moving clockwise from Radford)—General Matthew Ridgway, U.S. Army Chief of Staff, General Lemuel Shepherd of the U.S. Marine Corps, and Admiral Robert Carney—opposed intervention. *National Archives, Washington, D.C.*

dispatching U.S. soldiers would be "dangerous, futile and self-destructive" and the second warning against "sending American GI's into the mud and muck of Indochina on a bloodletting spree." Finally, the French refused to guarantee independence to Indochina. Eisenhower privately criticized them for using "weasel words in promising independence" and disgustedly referred to France as "a hopeless, helpless mass of protoplasm." U.S. forces would not become "junior partners" to the French. Congress agreed with the president's reasoning.

On May 7, 1954, after a fifty-five-day horrendous siege, the French and Vietnamese forces surrendered at Dienbienphu. Although artillery was integral to the victory, the story grew to mythical proportions that a guerrilla army had proved the feasibility of defeating the superior conventional force of a major power.

There is an ominous note about the situation in Indochina: Had the Communist Chinese threatened to intervene, Eisenhower was prepared to use nuclear weapons as a deterrent. Communist China, he explained, was "the head instead of the tail of the snake," and its involvement would have necessitated a massive U.S. military response. In June, Dulles warned the Beijing government that its entry in the war "would be a deliberate threat to the United States itself." The early 1970s publication of *The Pentagon Papers,* a huge collection of top secret defense department documents pilfered from the files, shows that the president and his secretary of state were prepared to take these drastic actions. In late May 1954 Eisenhower approved proposals by the Joint Chiefs of Staff for "employing atomic weapons" if China intervened in Indochina. He added, however, that such a move would have taken place only after congressional approval and with the concurrence of the nation's allies. "Unilateral action by the United States in cases of this kind would destroy us," he told an aide. "If we intervened alone in this case we would be expected to intervene alone in other parts of the world."

A conference had meanwhile convened in Geneva to discuss Korea and Indochina, and by July the nineteen delegations present, including the Soviet Union, North Korea, Communist China, and the United States, had moved toward a series of agreements on Southeast Asia. Despite victory on the battlefield, however, the Vietminh failed in its quest to rid Vietnam of foreign influence. Indeed, the Communist Chinese opposed a total French withdrawal as a prelude to a deeper U.S. involvement. A divided Vietnam fitted Chinese security interests more than did an unfriendly neighbor unified and ready to expand into Laos and Cambodia. The Geneva Accords therefore did little for the Vietminh. They called for an armistice in Indochina, recognition of the independence of Laos and Cambodia, and, most important to the Chinese, the construction of a "provisional military demarcation line" at the seventeenth parallel in Vietnam, which would place thirteen million Vietnamese above the division and ten million below. The proposed agreements emphasized that this was a temporary partition, not "a political or territorial boundary." Although the Vietminh retained control over Hanoi and Haiphong in the north, Bao Dai was to remain emperor of the south. Free elections would take place in 1956 to unite the Vietnams, followed by elections in Laos and Cambodia. Neither region of Vietnam was to enter into military pacts or permit foreign occupation.

The United States refused to sign the Geneva agreements, even though it pledged not to interfere with their fulfillment and promised to support elections under UN supervision. The administration did not recognize Communist China and could enter no formal negotiations with its representatives, and it opposed any territorial awards to the Vietminh. The White House also disliked the prohibition against the introduction of new military forces and weaponry and the ruling against a move by either part of Vietnam to join a military pact. Eisenhower realized, however, that the Communists had won the war

Eisenhower, Dulles, and Diem
President Eisenhower and Secretary of State Dulles greet South Vietnamese
Premier Ngo Dinh Diem in Washington, D.C., in May 1957. *National Archives,
Washington, D.C.*

and agreed with the National Security Council's warning that Communist China would
now promote the spread of communism into
all of Southeast Asia. A two-year delay in
elections was advantageous, the president
believed, because he was certain that Ho Chi
Minh would easily win if elections took place
immediately.

To prevent a Communist takeover, the
Eisenhower administration prepared to aid the
non-Communists in the south. This arrangement seemed highly preferable because of the
recently installed premier in the south, Ngo
Dinh Diem. Even though a Catholic in a country overwhelmingly Buddhist, Diem was a fervent nationalist who steadfastly opposed the
French and the Communists. Furthermore, he
had lived in exile in the United States for years,
where he made many valuable contacts with
influential political and religious figures. The

State of Vietnam (South) joined the United
States in refusing to sign the Geneva Accords.

To protect Western interests, the United
States took the lead in establishing the South-
east Asia Treaty Organization (SEATO) to
safeguard South Vietnam, Laos, and Cambodia from communism. Toward that objective,
Dulles called a conference at Manila in September, which was attended by the United
States, Britain, France, Australia, New Zealand, the Philippines, Thailand, and Pakistan.
Other prominent governments in that region—
India, Indonesia, Burma, and Ceylon (now
Sri Lanka)—did not attend because they preferred remaining neutral to antagonizing the
Communist Chinese. Britain's refusal to recognize the Nationalists on Formosa barred that
government from the proceedings. On September 6, 1954, the delegates approved a recommendation by President Ramon Magsaysay

of the Philippines, which established a Pacific Charter ensuring support for "equal rights and self-determination of peoples."

Fear of an imminent Communist Chinese invasion of Formosa hurried the proceedings. Two days after approval of the Pacific Charter, the delegates signed the Southeast Asia Collective Defense Treaty, which asserted that in the event of attack, each signatory would "consult immediately" according to each member's "constitutional processes." Unlike NATO, the new organization contained no central armed force and depended almost exclusively on U.S. military support. In addition, it committed the United States to halt subversion coming from outside the Southeast Asian protected states. The ominous implication was the possibility of unilateral U.S. action if other signatories failed to regard communism as an international threat. Headquartered in Bangkok, SEATO went into effect in 1955.

By mid-decade the United States had adopted a highly precarious policy that rested on a firm commitment to Diem and to building an independent, non-Communist South Vietnam. The organization of SEATO raised questions about the sanctity of the Geneva Accords because it implied that the "temporary" demarcation line had taken on permanent status and had thereby left South Vietnam as a separate country. The United States also violated the Accords by stipulating that in exchange for Diem's assurances of social and economic reforms, it would send military and economic aid. But had Diem *wanted* to do so, he could not have implemented sweeping internal changes because his regime was elitist and nepotistic, overwhelmingly Catholic in a predominantly non-Catholic area, and primarily dependent on the landlords for support. Most important, Diem was a product of the privileged mandarin class and, accordingly, had never professed a belief in democracy. In fact, given Vietnam's devastation from the war, it is doubtful that the United States could have found a less likely place to engage in what Dulles would herald as a grand experiment in "nationbuilding."

While U.S. military advisers worked to improve Diem's army, the French remained in South Vietnam to carry out the promised elections. They only grudgingly assumed their new secondary status, however, and openly resented the United States's use of Diem to gain a foothold in Indochina. Indeed, from this time forward, the Eisenhower administration extended aid directly to South Vietnam and not through what Dulles called the French "protected preferential market." Diem faced the monumental task of trying to shore up a fragmented society, increasingly staggered by vast influxes of mostly Catholic northern refugees who were loyal to traditions and cultures vastly different from those already in the south. The south, in fact, soon became a haven for a variety of independent sects, each with its own beliefs and its own warlords and armies. At one point in 1955 Diem had to use brute force to put down a sect crisis led by the Mafia-like Binh Xuyen, which had seized control of the Saigon police force. Dulles had already begun hedging on the likelihood of an election in South Vietnam in 1956. He told reporters that the United States would recognize a government opposed to Diem only if "it seems to be expressive of the real will of the people and if it is truly representative." Dulles further expressed fear that the South Vietnamese did not understand that Ho Chi Minh was an advocate of international communism. In a statement that raised more questions than it answered, he emphasized that until the South Vietnamese recognized Diem's attractions, there could be no valid electoral process. The Communist Chinese, too, made clear their opposition to an election intended to unify Vietnam. By July 1955 most of the French had given up on the chances of an election and had gone home.

U.S. fear of communism in Southeast Asia led it to overlook many faults in Diem's regime. In October 1955 he held a plebiscite in South Vietnam, easily winning the presidency over Bao Dai in an obviously fixed proceeding. Massachusetts Senator John F. Kennedy nonetheless called Diem's Republic of Vietnam the "cornerstone of the Free World in Southeast Asia, the keystone in the arch, the finger in the dike." He continued, "It is our offspring, we cannot abandon it, we cannot ignore its needs." Although Diem worked closely with CIA operative Edward Lansdale in "psywar" (psychological warfare) programs against the Hanoi government, and although the Saigon regime instituted reform programs designed to undercut a growing insurgency by herding South Vietnamese peasantry into barbed wire encampments called "agrovilles," the situation in the south slowly and then rapidly deteriorated. Diem survived numerous domestic crises (including a coup attempt in November 1960) and consolidated his control only through increasingly repressive measures. The Vietminh in South Vietnam meanwhile followed Hanoi's secret directives in establishing the National Liberation Front (NLF) in December 1960. An anti-Diem organization led by Communists, the NLF attracted a significant following by calling for widespread reforms and the independence of a unified Vietnam. Diem's supporters derisively labeled the NLF as Vietcong, or Vietnamese Communists. Given North Vietnam's unyielding determination to drive out foreign intervention and incorporate the economically richer south, the forecast was a civil war that, to the United States, bore dire international ramifications that necessitated an expanded military and economic commitment.

Communist China and Formosa

In a move that the United States attributed to its deepening involvement in Asia, the Communist Chinese in autumn 1954 began bombarding the offshore Nationalist-controlled islands of Quemoy, Matsu, and the Tachens. Such action, Americans thought, marked the first step toward a Communist invasion of Formosa and an ultimate confrontation with the United States. Earlier, in August, Premier Zhou Enlai in Beijing had called for the liberation of Formosa because, he charged, it had become a U.S. military base. Jiang had

meanwhile heavily fortified Quemoy, and the Communist Chinese began shelling it on September 3, killing two U.S. military advisers. Eisenhower sternly warned that "any invasion of Formosa would have to run over the Seventh Fleet." Though willing to give up the Tachens (lying 200 miles north of Formosa), he refused to do the same with Quemoy and Matsu, which were much closer to Formosa and hence integral to its safety. The collapse of these two areas, the president later declared, would have endangered "the anti-Communist barrier" in the western Pacific of Japan, South Korea, Nationalist China, the Philippines, Thailand, and Vietnam and would have led to Communist triumphs in Burma, Cambodia, Indonesia, Laos, and Malaya.

In truth, however, the Eisenhower administration's fears were greatly exaggerated. Much of the tension during the 1950s, particularly in these offshore islands, stemmed from the preceding Chinese civil war, which suggests that the United States wrongfully interpreted these events as another salvo in the Cold War rather than as a continuation of internal troubles. The British government blamed the shelling on long-time animosities between Nationalists and Communists that had heated up during the previous summer. Indeed, the Nationalists had bombed the mainland and had long harassed the Communists by firing on their ships and launching commando expeditions ashore. But the United States regarded the shelling as a challenge to its deterrence policy, especially in light of the West's recent failures in Korea and Indochina. Chinese documentation, however, shows that the Beijing government ordered the shelling of Quemoy not as a prelude to an invasion of the island but as a political move warning against U.S. interference in Chinese domestic affairs. The Communists particularly feared an escalation in U.S. and Nationalist aggressions and the creation of a mutual defense pact between the two governments. The only islands under consideration for a Communist takeover were the Tachens, which were far to the north and under Nationalist control.

Mao considered the United States the aggressor and was unaware of U.S.-Nationalist tensions at the time brought on primarily by the White House's wish to restrict Jiang's assaults on the mainland and defuse tensions in the area.

Some members of the Eisenhower administration reacted strongly to these events, insisting that even though the islands were not vital to U.S. interests, they were symbolic of Free World resistance to communism. The Joint Chiefs of Staff recommended that the president instruct the Nationalists to bomb the Chinese mainland; if this measure led to a Communist attack on Quemoy, they continued, the United States should join in its defense. Nixon grimly declared that "we should stand ready to call international Communism's bluff on any pot, large or small. If we let them know that we will defend freedom when the stakes are small, the Soviets are not encouraged to threaten freedom where the stakes are higher." Quemoy and Matsu were important in "the poker game of world politics."

The president, however, agreed with General Ridgway, who warned that such a policy would cause war with China. "We're not talking now about a limited, brush-fire war," Eisenhower asserted to the National Security Council. "We're talking about going to the threshold of World War III. . . . Moreover, if we get into a general war, the logical enemy will be Russia, not China, and we'll have to strike there." Dulles had initially supported the joint chiefs' call for action but now had to change course. The president had already ordered him to Formosa to negotiate a treaty promising U.S. protection to Jiang but leaving the welfare of the offshore islands ambiguous. Dulles had wanted to specify them in the pact, but Eisenhower insisted on a vague authorization of a U.S. commitment to "such other territories as may be determined by mutual agreement." In December the United States and Formosa signed a mutual defense pact to prevent unilateral military action in exchange for a U.S. guarantee to keep forces "in and about" the island. The

following month, after the Communist Chinese seized one of the Tachens, Dulles solemnly warned the president of "at least an even chance that the United States will have to go to war."

But Eisenhower had laid the groundwork for a peaceful resolution of the crisis. The defense treaty had allowed him to satisfy Jiang's outspoken supporters within the Republican party and yet at the same time to place restraints on the Nationalists. In January 1955 Congress overwhelmingly approved the "Formosa Resolution," which authorized the president to use military force in defending Formosa and "such related positions and territories" as he considered necessary. Thus, Eisenhower's options remained open, leaving the Chinese uncertain about his intentions to protect Quemoy, Matsu, and the Tachens. In a letter to Churchill, the president expressed concern about his own ability to distinguish "between an attack that has only as its objective the capture of an off-shore island and one that is primarily a preliminary movement to an all-out attack on Formosa." U.S. policy depended on "circumstances as they might arise."

The artillery barrage continued, however, suggesting that the Beijing government had interpreted Eisenhower's inaction as an unwillingness to go to war over these islands. In response the White House issued a public warning that it was considering the use of nuclear weapons. In March, Dulles asserted in a speech that to stop the "aggressive fanaticism" of the Chinese, the United States was prepared to use "new and powerful weapons of precision which can utterly destroy military targets without endangering unrelated civilian centers." Although the CIA argued that a "clean" nuclear assault was an impossibility— that it would kill up to fourteen million Chinese civilians—Eisenhower alarmed reporters by declaring that Dulles was correct: Nuclear weapons could be used "as you use a bullet or anything else." He later wrote in his memoirs that his intention had been to convince the Chinese Communists that he *would* defend Formosa. According to his own assessment, his strategy of threatening preventive war worked because the shelling stopped in April. But the Beijing government had relented for reasons having little to do with Eisenhower's implied use of massive retaliation. Its decision makers had already decided to work toward peaceful coexistence with their country's neighbors just before the opening of the Bandung Conference of that month in Indonesia. One way to ensure harmony with fellow non-Western nations was to ease the pressure on the offshore islands.

The war scare had mixed results. On the one side, Communist China had succeeded in its political purpose of drawing worldwide attention to U.S. involvement in an internal affair, and it had achieved a long-time objective of opening direct talks with the United States. But the crisis had also hurt China's position by encouraging better U.S.-Nationalist relations through the Mutual Defense Treaty and the Formosa Resolution. On the other side, however, the United States could claim no victory for deterrence because the Communists had never intended to invade either Quemoy or Matsu. And even though the crisis encouraged the Washington government to push for peace through summit negotiations, it established a potentially dangerous precedent through the Formosa Resolution. The president now had authority to decide when to deploy U.S. forces in a troubled area, thereby chipping away at Congress's constitutional power to declare war. On yet another level, the mutual misinterpretation of each other's motives demonstrated the danger of an isolation policy that leaves ideological differences as the only guide for understanding each other. Brinkmanship and deterrence actually encouraged conflict.

The Spirit of Geneva and Europe

By early 1955 the situation had also stabilized in Europe, but at the cost of what appeared to be a permanently divided Germany within a permanently divided continent. The United States had earlier failed to persuade the French

to accept the integration of West German soldiers into an organization known as the European Defense Community, but in 1954 the European states had agreed to place West German forces under the control of a Western European Union. France accepted, but at the high price of a British commitment to send four divisions to Europe and a U.S. promise to retain troops already there since 1951. In turn, West German Chancellor Konrad Adenauer pledged not to produce long-range missiles and atomic, chemical, or bacteriological weapons without the consent of NATO's commander and a two-thirds approval of the WEU Council. The other members guaranteed that West Germany would not use force to reunify the country or modify its present boundaries. This plan went into effect in May 1955 and thereby brought to a close ten years of German occupation. The United States, Britain, and France proclaimed the Federal Republic of West Germany as the country's only legitimate government, effectively denying recognition to East Germany. West Germany also became part of NATO that year. A European standoff developed when the Soviets countered with the Warsaw Pact, a military organization of themselves, East Germany, and loyal East European Communist states.

The time for a Soviet-American agreement seemed auspicious. Premier Malenkov had resigned in February 1955, and his successor was Nikolai Bulganin, although the real power was Nikita Khrushchev, first secretary of the Communist party. The new Soviet regime seemed amenable to East-West cooperation. It approved a small number of visits by American tourists, and the United States allowed the entry of Soviet agriculturalists and journalists. In May the Soviet Union joined the United States, Britain, and France in signing the Austrian State Treaty, which ended ten years of joint occupation and established that country's independence and neutral status in international affairs. Although the Soviets simply preferred a neutral Austria to an Austria divided between East and West (like Germany), their withdrawal appeared altruistic and drew a favorable world reaction. On the very day of the treaty-signing ceremony, the Soviets agreed to the first summit since Potsdam, when they announced their willingness to meet in July with the United States, Britain, and France in Geneva.

The Geneva Conference of 1955 convened amid an air of optimism tempered by caution and uncertainty. The United States was confident in both its own strength and the Soviet Union's economic weaknesses. The United States's European allies were more concerned about stopping the race to war. NATO war games had recently indicated that if fighting broke out on the continent, Western Europe would become a fiery and radioactive holocaust as a result of hits from more than 170 atomic bombs.

Despite the widely heralded "spirit of Geneva," the Big Four reached no important agreements at the week-long conference. Both sides presented proposals virtually certain to fail. The Soviets called for an end to NATO, the withdrawal of U.S. soldiers from the continent, and a ban on the production and use of atomic weapons. The West pressed for Germany's unification through democratic elections. On arms control, Eisenhower made an "Open Skies" proposal, by which the United States and the Soviet Union would furnish maps of each other's military complexes to allow mutual aerial surveillance. The president was not naive. He knew that the Soviets were already aware of most U.S. military sites, and he therefore used this piece of drama to counter their earlier call for disarmament. "We knew the Soviets wouldn't accept it," he later recalled. Yet the president hoped that the proposal might ease international tension by opening the way to less comprehensive arms control measures. In a letter to General Alfred Gruenther, Eisenhower explained that his intention had been to secure "an immense gain in mutual confidence and trust." At Geneva the United States and the Soviet Union agreed only to encourage cultural exchanges; the other issues they forwarded to a meeting of the Big Four's foreign ministers.

The Geneva Conference nonetheless left the impression of a thaw in the Cold War. Eisenhower encouraged this feeling by highlighting the "new spirit of conciliation and cooperation." The Soviets likewise fostered this all-too-brief wave of euphoria by extending recognition to West Germany that same year. The optimism was misguided. Recognition of West Germany ensured a divided Germany and permitted the Soviets to build up the East German army. Moreover, it soon became evident that the conference was a mere publicity show in which photographers' pictures created the illusion of Soviet-American harmony. Khrushchev boasted that "we had established ourselves as able to hold our own in the international arena." Dulles warned against expecting an "era of good feelings," and W. Averell Harriman, former ambassador to Moscow and inveterate critic of its policies, expressed concern that the "free world was psychologically disarmed" by the "spirit of Geneva" and warned that it was a "smoke screen" for Soviet expansion. Khrushchev emphasized that no change had taken place in Soviet attitude. "If anybody thinks that for this reason we shall forget about Marx, Engels, and Lenin, he is mistaken. This will happen when shrimps learn to whistle."

Still, the image of improved relations continued into the new year, when in February 1956 Khrushchev shocked friends and foes alike by calling for peaceful coexistence and the de-Stalinization of Eastern Europe. Before the Twentieth Congress of the Communist party in Moscow, the first secretary delivered a speech in which he turned away from Lenin's assertion of the inevitability of war between Communists and capitalists, and called for a Communist victory through peaceful means. He then denounced Stalin's domestic crimes and urged party members to accept diversity in the Communist world. Khrushchev had several objectives, including an expansion of his power at home, a loosening of restraints on the country's economy to promote production, and a maintenance of domestic control short of outright repression. East European nations were bewildered and yet guardedly encouraged. There was little justification for the latter. Khrushchev had called for a new approach to the same goal: a Communist triumph by Soviet exploitation of the uncommitted nations of the world, whether or not they were Communist. The CIA soon secured a copy of his address and circulated copies in Eastern Europe and elsewhere. The state department published the speech in April.

The erosion of Communist unity had not gone unnoticed by the Eisenhower administration. Tito's defection, the growing division between the Soviets and the Communist Chinese, and now an admission to "national Communism"—all suggested that the United States needed to examine recent instances of unrest throughout the world to determine whether the Soviets were losing their grip on the Communist movement. Khrushchev's recognition of "Titoism" in 1955 was an important sign of change, as were the Soviets' decisions to disband the Cominform, arrange an exchange of visits between Tito and Khrushchev, and negotiate a pact with Yugoslavia that contained the surprising assertion that there were "different roads to socialism."

But before the United States could assess the potential impact of this new Soviet policy, thousands of dissidents in Poland and Hungary seized upon Khrushchev's speech as an invitation to self-determination and rose in revolt against Stalinist leaders in their countries. Americans interpreted the upheavals as fulfillments of Dulles's goal of "liberation" and supported the Voice of America and Radio Free Europe in encouraging further resistance in Eastern Europe. The dangerous implication was that the United States would assist anyone taking the first step toward breaking Soviet ties.

In June 1956 riotous demonstrations among workers in Poland soon developed into a widespread revolt against Soviet dominance in the country. The Soviets threatened to use force to put down the uprising, but in Octo-

ber Polish Communists led by Wladyslaw Gomulka met with Khrushchev and warned of full-scale armed resistance if the Soviets staged a coup. Khrushchev discreetly agreed to accept Gomulka (earlier rejected by Stalin as "Titoist") as chair of the Polish Communist party. Poland remained Communist and within the Warsaw Pact, even though its relationship with the Soviet Union was uneasy. Poland appeared to have won autonomy in October, when it elected Gomulka chair of the Communist party. As was the case with Yugoslavia in 1948, the United States extended economic aid to Poland.

The successes in Poland probably had a direct effect on Hungary, because in late October 1956 demonstrations in Budapest against Stalinism exploded in violence aimed at the Communist government and at the Soviet Union. The leader of the insurrection, Imre Nagy, feared Soviet military intervention and tried to restrain the extremism of his followers, but matters quickly got out of hand as the rebels demanded freedom, toppled the huge statue of Stalin in the city, and killed several Stalinist Communists. Nagy soon emerged as head of a new regime that included non-Communist members. It broke with the Warsaw Pact, demanded a Soviet troop withdrawal, and announced a neutralist position in international affairs. The new government then turned to the United States for aid based on the assurances of Eisenhower-Dulles "liberation."

The Eisenhower administration found itself in the uncomfortable position of wanting to see the Hungarians succeed but unable to do anything in an area deemed vital to Soviet interests. Dulles praised the revolution as proof of the "weakness of Soviet imperialism" and noted that these "captive peoples should never have reason to doubt that they have in us a sincere and dedicated friend who shares their aspirations." The secretary, however, was in ill health and would soon undergo emergency surgery for cancer; but even if Dulles had been healthy, the administration would not have intervened in Hungary. It is impossible to determine whether Eisenhower's foreign policy pronouncements influenced the outbreak of the Hungarian revolution, but they doubtless led the rebels to believe that U.S. aid would arrive after they took the initial step toward independence. The United States publicly expressed sympathy, introduced UN resolutions condemning Soviet actions and calling for withdrawal, and threw open its doors to thousands of Hungarian refugees. But that was the extent of U.S. involvement. The White House recognized that intervention could have led to war with the Soviet Union. Besides, troubles had meanwhile erupted in the Middle East, an area regarded as crucial to U.S. interests.

Events in Hungary threatened to establish a dangerous precedent for other Communist states interested in autonomy, and for that reason the Soviet Union had to act. It first installed a Communist regime in Budapest, which immediately requested Moscow's help in restoring order. On November 4, 1956, at the height of the concurrent crisis in the Middle East, Red tanks and troops stormed into Budapest to put down the revolution. Nagy sought refuge in the Yugoslav embassy, but came out after allegedly receiving assurances of a seat in the new government. (The Soviets sent him to Russia and executed him in 1957.) After weeks of street fighting, the Soviets squelched the rebellion at the horrendous cost of 30,000 Hungarian lives. "Poor fellows, poor fellows," Eisenhower lamented to a reporter. "I think about them all the time. I wish there were some way of helping them."

Several revealing aspects about U.S. and Soviet behavior emerged from the Hungarian crisis. Eisenhower "liberation" offered false hopes in areas considered vital to the Soviet Union. The Moscow government permitted nationalist uprisings only if they did not damage Soviet prestige or set precedents dangerous to international communism. The Soviets lost respect among Communists in other countries, because their troops had not performed well, their allies' military forces had defected in fairly large numbers, and Hungarian youths had not converted to commu-

nism. The revolution resulted in a severe propaganda defeat for the Kremlin, but Hungary remained within the Soviet bloc.

Suez

Toward the last stages of the Hungarian revolution, attention suddenly shifted to the Middle East, where a major power confrontation threatened to develop during the Suez crisis of 1956. Ancient issues in this region, combined with its growing military and strategic importance in the postwar era, created a situation highly conducive to war. Volatile ingredients were there: Arab-Israeli conflict, Anglo-Egyptian rivalry, French concern over the possible loss of Algeria, emerging nationalisms after World War II, big power interests in oil, suspicions between East and West, and divisiveness among the Western powers. As in other trouble spots in the world, the Eisenhower administration feared that continued disorder in the Middle East would invite Soviet involvement.

British policy lay at the root of many problems in the Middle East. During World War I Britain issued the Balfour Declaration, which offered renewed hope to the Zionist movement by guaranteeing "the establishment in Palestine of a National Home for the Jewish people." The year before, however, the British had assured the Arabs an independent state out of the remains of the old Ottoman Empire—including Palestine. The two promises were irreconcilable. At Versailles in 1919 the peacemakers assigned Britain the League of Nations mandate over Palestine and for years afterward attempted to resolve these conflicting policies. In more than one instance it earned the opprobrium of world opinion by turning away ships bearing Jewish refugees as they approached Palestine. Meanwhile, in September 1922, the U.S. Congress approved a joint resolution endorsing the Balfour Declaration. Two years later the United States negotiated a treaty recognizing the British mandate over Palestine and thereby set the direction of its own Palestinian policy.

Hitler's persecutions of the Jews during World War II revived Zionism and drove many European Jews toward their "homeland" in the postwar period. In 1947 Britain announced the termination of its Palestinian mandate the following year, leaving the question for the United Nations to resolve. In late November 1947 the General Assembly decided to partition Palestine into Arab and Jewish states and to establish international supervision of the ancient city of Jerusalem. But this plan aroused bitter Arab opposition. The Arabs had twice as many people in Palestine as did the Jews, and they claimed the right of possession by having resided there for centuries. Furthermore, the partition awarded the Jews the largest section of Palestine's farmland, along with most of its urban and railroad areas. The Arab delegation in the General Assembly stalked out in protest. On May 14, 1948, the day before Britain's mandate came to an end, the Jews proclaimed the independent state of Israel. Less than fifteen minutes later, President Truman rejected the advice of his diplomatic and military counselors and extended *de facto* recognition. Three days afterward the Soviet Union did the same.

In explaining the United States's rapid recognition of Israel, Truman emphasized humanitarian concern for the Jews, but he could not have been oblivious to domestic political considerations. He had earlier called on Britain to permit 100,000 Jews to enter Palestine. A few days afterward his probable Republican opponent in the presidential election of 1948, New York Governor Thomas Dewey, recommended raising the number to several hundred thousand. The election of 1948, everyone knew, would be close, and the Jewish vote in New York could award the White House to the Republicans for the first time since 1933. The state department had joined military advisers in opposing the UN partition plan because it would alienate the Arabs. The president supported the partition for humanitarian and political reasons.

Conflict erupted in May 1948 as the neighboring Arab states invaded Palestine, only to turn back in the face of the smaller yet better equipped Israeli forces—most of whose heavy weaponry came from Communist Czechoslovakia. Sentiment for Hitler's wartime victims and the need for the Jewish-American vote at home had generated a pro-Israel feeling in Washington. A serious complication became clear, however: Two-thirds of the world's oil reserves were in the Middle East, and its borders touched 3000 miles of the Soviet Union. Americans had more than enough oil for the present, but this situation could change with time. The United States had numerous ties with the Jews, but it also wanted to outmaneuver the Soviets for the Middle East's oil and secure strategic sites for military bases. In the interests of national security, the Washington government had to devise a policy that satisfied Jewish-Americans without driving the Arabs into the Soviet camp.

An armistice in February 1949 only temporarily wound down Arab-Israeli hostilities. Through UN mediation Israel received more land than the partition award had allowed, whereas Egypt and Jordan won control over the Arab section of Palestine. International supervision of Jerusalem never materialized, leaving the city divided between Israel and Jordan. The Arab states meanwhile boycotted Israel and cut off its land access to the outside. Egypt closed the Suez Canal to its use. Another problem had risen as well: The creation of Israel had displaced nearly 800,000 Palestinian Arabs, who now lived in poverty just outside the new state and were not welcomed by any of the Arab states. The UN Relief and Works Agency for Palestine Refugees tried to ease the situation, but some of the homeless Arabs had already organized terrorist bands to raid Israel.

The United States's Middle East policy remained uncertain because of its conflicting Jewish and Arab interests. Indeed, the White House found itself caught in a dilemma between the Zionists at home and in Israel and U.S. oil interests in that part of the world. To prevent further troubles believed conducive to Soviet intervention, the United States

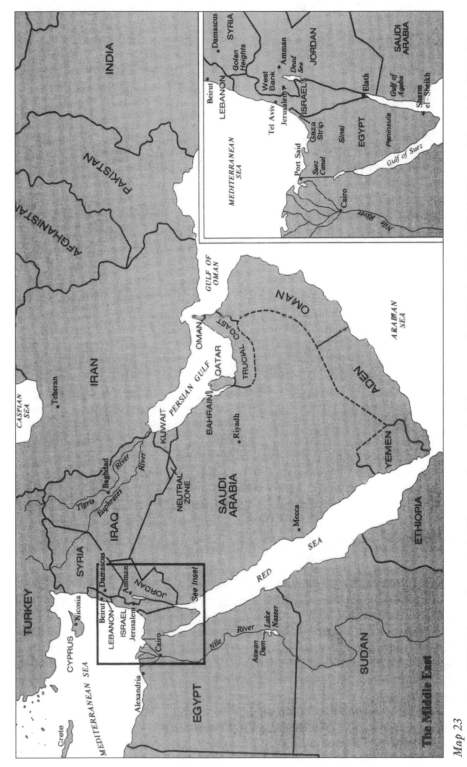

Map 23
The Suez crisis of 1956 almost shattered the Western alliance, raised the stature of the Russians in the Middle East, and forced the United States to take a more active part in that region's affairs.

worked closely with the UN Palestine Conciliation Commission. As a result, in May 1950 it joined Britain and France in the Tripartite Declaration, which ensured that if either the Israelis or Arabs violated the armistice in Palestine, the three powers would "immediately take action, both within and outside the United Nations." Finally, the state department devised a complicated financial arrangement with Saudi Arabia by which the United States acquired Arabian oil for a generous secret subsidy, while allowing the Truman administration to remain officially and publicly on the side of the Israelis. The United States meanwhile extended economic and technical aid to most governments of the Middle East, called for land and resettlement programs in Egypt and Iraq, and helped Saudi Arabia reform its tariff and customs laws. The problems persisted.

In 1952 dissidents in the Egyptian army rose in rebellion against the corrupt and incompetent regime of King Farouk, forcing him out of the country and within two years installing their leader, Colonel Gamal Abdel Nasser, as premier. Nasser gained widespread popular support by instituting a land reform program and promising to end Britain's control of the Suez Canal. That same year, 1954, the United States helped secure two agreements between Britain and Egypt, by which the British would gradually withdraw their military forces from the Suez Canal over the next twenty months. Britain's long-time involvement in Egypt would come to a close in 1956.

To preserve stability and Western influence in the Middle East, the United States supported but did not join the Baghdad Pact of 1955. Iraq had earlier that year pulled away from the Arab states in signing a Pact of Mutual Assistance with Turkey. Iran, Pakistan, and Britain later joined the agreement and set up headquarters in Baghdad (capital of Iraq) for the Middle East Treaty Organization (METO). The United States occasionally took part in the proceedings and extended military assistance on an individual basis. But it would

go no farther for fear of deepening Nasser's animosity toward the West, antagonizing Israel, or alienating the organization's opponents in Asia and Africa. The Baghdad Pact was part of Dulles's attempt to establish a defense line between Turkey and Pakistan and connect it with that already constructed around the Soviet Union by NATO and SEATO.

The effects were not all the secretary intended. METO united the Arabs against the West and virtually invited the Soviet Union to exploit Arab hostility toward the Jews. A decline in Western influence became plain by autumn 1955. The French were deeply involved in putting down an uprising in Algeria encouraged by Egypt, and British efforts to persuade Jordan to join the Baghdad Pact led to violent demonstrations in its capital of Amman.

In the meantime the situation worsened in the Suez area. The Israelis had retaliated against repeated border troubles by raiding Egypt's Gaza Strip along their common frontier in February 1955, and in late September Nasser mortgaged his country's entire year's cotton crop for an arms deal with Czechoslovakia, which was acting as a front for the Soviet Union. The following December the United States attempted to pull Nasser into the Western camp by agreeing to help finance a massive enlargement of the Aswan Dam (on the Nile River) to promote electricity and irrigation. More than one billion dollars was to come from the World Bank plus American and British funds. Jewish-Americans put pressure on the Eisenhower administration to cancel the deal, while southern congressional members complained that such a dam would hurt their own cotton manufacturers.

The Eisenhower administration failed to undercut the Soviets and win Egypt's support. The president and his secretary of state were already upset with Nasser for his recent decision to recognize Communist China, and they now feared that the arms deal was proof of his shift from neutralism to a pro-Soviet allegiance. Dulles put it simply: "Do nations which play both sides get better treatment than nations which are stalwart and work with us?" The administration's answer to Nasser's blackmail tactics came in July 1956, when Dulles suddenly and dramatically retracted the loan offer for the Aswan Dam. He had not consulted the British, who had agreed to share the financial burden, and he had chosen to make the announcement on the very day Nasser's foreign minister arrived in Washington to finalize the arrangement. Dulles was confident that the move would call the Soviet bluff and set a telling example for neutralists.

But the Soviets did not have time to act: Nasser nationalized the canal by taking over the British- and French-controlled Universal Suez Canal Company. The canal tolls, he announced, would finance the dam. To make the move legal, he promised to compensate the stockholders and pledged to keep the passage open. These assurances proved unsatisfactory. Nasser's action humiliated the British and infuriated the French, who already held him responsible for many of the arms used by their Algerian rebels. Dulles immediately flew to London to confer with British Prime Minister Anthony Eden and French Premier Guy Mollet, both of whom had discussed the use of force in regaining control over the canal. At a meeting of the twenty-four nations chiefly dependent on the canal, the vast majority supported the establishment of an international organization to administer the waterway. Nasser, however, rejected the plan because the organization would clearly be under British and French control. Dulles recommended forming a Suez Canal Users Association to collect the tolls and divide the funds between canal maintenance and payments to owners. Nasser likewise turned down this plan. In October the UN Security Council responded to the Anglo-French request for assistance by establishing guidelines for the canal's administration that included assurances of Egyptian sovereignty, no outside interference with the canal's operation, and "free and open transit through the Canal." Egypt accepted these terms, although Britain and France doubted

that Nasser would abide by them. Eden and Mollet decided to act on their own.

By late October 1956, at the same time as the upheavals in Poland and Hungary, the rapidly building crisis in the Middle East threatened to cause an East-West confrontation. In a move destined to have long-lasting ramifications, France, England, and Israel secretly collaborated to invade Egypt and bring about Nasser's collapse. Israel moved first. Its forces easily overran those of the Egyptians in the Gaza Strip and Sinai Peninsula, seizing nearly all of the Czech arms along with 6000 Egyptian soldiers and then heading toward the Suez Canal. The day after the invasion, Britain and France feigned surprise at Israel's actions and called for a cease-fire stipulating that both Egypt and Israel were to withdraw ten miles from the canal, thereby giving Israel a hundred miles of Egyptian territory. Thus, the British and French had violated the Tripartite Declaration of May 1950, which had guaranteed no border violations of either Israel or the Arab states.

The conflict then threatened to spread beyond the confines of the Middle East. Nasser angrily rejected the Anglo-French proposal and closed the canal by sinking ships in its passageway. Arab militants meanwhile sabotaged pumphouses that sent oil from the Persian Gulf to the Mediterranean, causing a shortage in Western Europe that necessitated a severe rationing program and underlined the importance of the Middle East. On the same day that Nasser turned down the Anglo-French demand, October 30, 1956, the United States and the Soviet Union sponsored cease-fire resolutions in the UN Security Council. Both Britain and France vetoed the measures and the next day, according to plan, used their combined forces in an offensive that culminated in the bombing of Egyptian air strips as the initial step toward seizing Port Said at the north end of the canal. The timing was not opportune, because the Anglo-French military action overshadowed and thereby blunted the United States's concurrent protests against Soviet attempts to put down the rebellion in Hungary.

Eisenhower, who was in the heat of a reelection campaign, became livid with the British and French when he learned of their actions in the Middle East. With Dulles hospitalized for stomach cancer, Eisenhower took the lead. He called Eden on the phone and gave his wartime friend a verbal lashing that brought the already distraught and physically ailing prime minister to tears. Eisenhower then blasted the British and French over radio and television on October 31 for endangering peace in the Middle East by pulling in the Soviet Union and blamed the two powers for turning the world's attention from Moscow's brutal suppression of Hungary. In early November the UN General Assembly overwhelmingly approved a U.S. resolution for cutting back Latin American oil to Britain and France as leverage to force them into a cease-fire and a withdrawal to the previous armistice line. Bulganin and Khrushchev meanwhile sought to exploit the widening rift in the Western alliance by suggesting joint military action with the United States. The Soviets, according to Khrushchev, were prepared to fire rockets onto London and Paris to halt the invasion and to send "volunteers" to evict the "aggressors." Eisenhower dismissed the Soviets' proposal as "unthinkable" but became increasingly disturbed about the possibility of a nuclear confrontation. The president assured the head of the CIA, Allen Dulles, that "if the Soviets should attack Britain and France directly, we would of course be in a major war." During this period of sharply escalating international tensions, the Hungarian and Suez crises rallied Americans around the president and helped sweep him to reelection that week.

The results in the Middle East were not surprising: Britain and France relented to the combined pressure of the United States, the United Nations, and the Soviet Union. On November 5 the General Assembly proposed the establishment of an Emergency Force for Palestine, and the next day Britain, France, and Israel agreed to a cease-fire. By Christmas, UNEF forces occupied the Gaza Strip and the Gulf of Aqaba, providing the Israelis with both protection from Egypt and a water link to the Red Sea through the port of Elath. But the Israelis had not secured use of the canal. In March 1957, under U.S. pressure, they withdrew behind the original armistice lines.

The Suez crisis furthered Soviet influence in the Middle East and thereby heightened U.S. involvement in the area. The United States had helped to save Nasser, but at the cost of British and French prestige, which put a severe strain on the Western alliance. Although he suffered a humiliating military defeat by the Israelis, Nasser held the canal and enjoyed great respect throughout the Arab world. The United States's retraction of money for the Aswan Dam drove Nasser closer to the Soviets, who had acquired stature in the Middle East and now furnished him arms and finances for improving the dam. The United States, however, had protected its oil interests and saw no choice but to assume the responsibilities for maintaining order in the Middle East, formerly undertaken by the British and the French.

The U.S. concern over Soviet penetration into the Middle East led to the announcement of the Eisenhower Doctrine in the spring of 1957. The Moscow government had negotiated economic and military agreements with Egypt and Syria, raising White House fear that with Syria's help Nasser might emerge as leader of the Arab world—and under Soviet influence. In January the president asked Congress for approval to issue a warning that the United States was prepared to defend the Middle East from outside encroachments. After lengthy debates, Congress in March approved a joint resolution that became known as the Eisenhower Doctrine. It empowered the president to use military force if any Middle Eastern government requested protection against "overt armed aggression from any nation controlled by International Communism." Congress also guaranteed economic and military aid for the Middle East. Dulles noted with satisfaction that "gradually, one part of the world after another is being brought into it [America's defense system] and perhaps we may end up with a, what you might call, universal doctrine reflected by multilateral treaties or multilateral worldwide authority from Congress." Although critics complained that Communist subversion was a greater danger than armed attack, the Eisenhower administration had dramatically assumed the long-time Anglo-French peacekeeping role in the Middle East. Furthermore, its policy marked a commitment to containment, though under a different name.

The Eisenhower Doctrine underwent immediate tests in Jordan and Lebanon, although in both cases Arab nationalism probably posed a greater threat to the Middle East's stability than did Soviet communism. When a leftist coup supported by Egypt and Syria threatened to overthrow Jordan's pro-Western King Hussein in spring 1957, the United States sent economic and military aid and moved the Sixth Fleet to the eastern Mediterranean. The situation eased. Early the following year Egypt, Syria, and Yemen established the United Arab Republic (U.A.R.), with Nasser as president. Jordan and Iraq countered with the Arab Union. In mid-July a military coup in Iraq led to the installation of a "republican" regime that moved close to the Soviet Union. The West erroneously assumed that Nasser was behind the revolution in Iraq and feared the same in Lebanon, located along the strategically important eastern Mediterranean. Lebanon's pro-Western and Maronite Christian president, Camille Chamoun, held the U.A.R. responsible for aiding a Muslim armed insurrection, and he joined Jordan in asking the United States and Britain for protection. The United States would confront no military problem in Lebanon, General Twining assured Dulles. The "Russians aren't going to jump us," and "if they do come in, they couldn't pick a better time, because we've got them by the whing whang and they know it." Eisenhower responded by dispatching 14,000 marines to Lebanon in July 1958 (who waded onto the beach through Lebanon sunbathers). Britain sent 3000 paratroopers to bolster Jordan's Hussein, again in danger of overthrow.

By autumn 1958 both the Jordanian and Lebanese crises had passed without incident. The UN Security Council was stymied, but because the Soviets were accusing the West of imperialism and demanding its withdrawal from the two countries, Arab leaders in the General Assembly took the lead toward peace. They proposed a resolution between the Western nations and the Soviets that pledged nonintervention in one another's domestic affairs, and they asked the UN secretary-general to guarantee its implementation in Jordan and Lebanon. The resolution prepared the way for military withdrawal. Meanwhile, U.S. diplomat Robert Murphy helped mediate an end to Lebanon's internal troubles, allowing the United States to pull out its forces in October. Britain left Jordan the following month. In March 1959 Eisenhower negotiated separate executive agreements with Turkey, Iran, and Pakistan, which guaranteed U.S. military assistance should they come under attack. These countries also set up headquarters in Ankara, Turkey, for a joint organization that became known as the Central Treaty Organization (CENTO). Its members were Turkey, Britain, Iran, and Pakistan. Iraq withdrew from the Baghdad Pact in March 1959 in favor of a neutralist position.

Berlin, Formosa (Again), and the Spirit of Camp David

Despite Eisenhower's easy reelection, Americans remained uneasy about the Democrats' continuing charges that the Soviet Union had surged ahead in the Cold War. The United States faced a paradoxical situation: Any move toward peace through disarmament could imply weakness, invite Soviet expansion, and lead to war. Early in 1957 Polish Foreign Minister Adam Rapacki recommended the establishment of a denuclearized zone in Central and Eastern Europe. The Soviets endorsed the plan, but the Eisenhower administration showed no interest. In June the Senate approved the Atoms-for-Peace Treaty, which Eisenhower had proposed four years earlier.

Similar to the abortive Baruch Plan of 1946, it called for the major powers to share atomic materials through an International Atomic Energy Agency. But the safeguards did not work, and the joint contributions of fissionable materials to the agency promoted a highly dangerous move toward nuclear proliferation. In late 1957 the Moscow government shocked Americans twice: first in late August by announcing the development of an intercontinental ballistic missile (ICBM), and then on October 4 by launching the Sputnik, the first space satellite of human origin.

The image of Soviet leadership in the space race deeply unsettled Americans. Ironically, the Eisenhower administration knew from secret U-2 reconnaissance planes flying high over the Soviet Union that Sputnik posed no threat to the United States, but the president could not say anything for fear of revealing the aerial operations. A second irony is that Khrushchev was aware of the reconnaissance flights but could also say nothing: The U-2s flew above Soviet firing range, and a protest would have constituted an admission to his nation's inability to defend itself against espionage. Furthermore, the Soviets would have lost ground in their growing rivalry with the Communist Chinese. The British ambassador in Washington noted that "the Russian success in launching the satellite has been something equivalent to Pearl Harbor. The American cocksureness is shaken." The following month the Soviets sent Sputnik II into orbit—carrying a canine passenger. Someone wittily remarked that the Soviets would probably send cows on the next flight, thus constituting "the herd shot 'round the world."

The Eisenhower administration quickly moved to regain the lead in the Cold War. The Gaither Report, a top-secret study by the Ford Foundation Commission that the American press uncovered and published, had enormous public impact because of its call for a huge armaments program to counter the Soviets' growing military and economic power. Although researchers were stepping up work on ballistic missiles, the president hesitated

to turn the nation into what he termed a "garrison state." And yet he dispatched SAC bombers to bolster the NATO alliance, agreed to furnish intermediate range ballistic missiles to NATO allies, and approved the continuation of U-2 flights. In January 1958 the United States launched Explorer I, the nation's first space satellite, and by July it had established the National Aeronautics and Space Administration (NASA) to promote aerospace research. The following September Congress passed the National Defense Education Act (NDEA) to provide federal aid for education in science, mathematics, and foreign languages.

As the military and missile buildup threatened to race out of control by late 1957, Soviet specialist George F. Kennan aroused great opposition when he called for a return to a less confrontational form of containment based on the "disengagement" of foreign military forces from Germany and Eastern Europe. In the prestigious BBC Reith Lectures over radio in London in autumn 1957, he urged the major powers to construct a unified, neutral Germany built around the "free city" of Berlin. If the United States could separate the German issue from NATO and the bitter rivalries of the Cold War, Kennan argued, the Soviets might withdraw their armies from Eastern Europe. Should the Eisenhower administration deemphasize NATO and turn to diplomacy, the Soviets might reciprocate by dismantling the Warsaw Pact. Then the much discussed European Common Market (or European Economic Community), established in June 1958, would have a chance to promote the economic integration of the continent through the elimination of tariffs and other obstacles to unity.

But the Washington government was not interested in disengagement. Former Secretary of State Dean Acheson expressed the feelings of many when he dismissed the idea as isolationist in thrust. Such a move, he warned, would undercut the Western alliance by encouraging the Red Army to take all of Europe and then negotiate a military agreement with an independent Germany. "Mr. Kennan has never, in my judgment," Acheson remarked, "grasped the realities of power relationships, but takes a rather mystical attitude toward them. To Mr. Kennan there is no Soviet military threat in Europe."

As the Western allies increasingly disagreed over European policy, the Soviets seized the moment in an attempt to win concessions in Berlin. The Western-held sector of the city had become a dangerous example for unhappy East Germans, who suffered severe economic and political hardships. The glaring contrasts in lifestyles between the two Germanies seemed to emphasize the superiority of capitalism over communism. West Berlin was not only prospering but also serving as an espionage and propaganda center for the West. Indeed, nearly three million East Germans had defected to West Berlin since 1949. Although the United States refused to recognize East Germany, it openly praised the courage of the East German people, sent armaments to West Germany to bolster the 11,000 U.S., British, and French soldiers occupying West Berlin, and repeatedly called for democratic elections to unite the Germans into a single state. West Berlin was a "bone in the throat," grumbled Khrushchev, now Soviet premier. The arming of West Germany, he charged, was a violation of wartime pledges to prevent the country from again becoming a military power. West Germany's imminent move to join France, Italy, Belgium, Luxembourg, and the Netherlands in the European Common Market finally pushed Khrushchev into action. Germany, he feared, was about to become irrevocably tied to the West.

In November 1958 Khrushchev delivered a blustery speech announcing abrogation of the wartime agreements relating to Germany and demanding an end to Western occupation of West Berlin. Unless negotiations began in six months, he warned, the Soviet Union would sign a separate peace treaty with the East Germans that terminated occupation and, as a matter of course, left West Berlin isolated more than a hundred miles inside a Communist nation. The Allies would then have to work out passage rights into Berlin through the East German government, which, he reminded them, they did not recognize. If they used force, the signatories of the Warsaw Pact stood ready to help East Germany. Berlin should be a "free city" within a confederation of East and West Germany, Khrushchev stated in notes to Washington, London, and Paris.

Khrushchev's ultimatum placed the United States in a bind. Recognition of East Germany would virtually turn it over to the Soviets and permanently divide the country. Kennan's disengagement plan was out of the question. Furthermore, if the United States pulled out of West Berlin, the Adenauer government's faith in NATO and the European Common Market would diminish, laying the groundwork for another Soviet-German arrangement only slightly less dangerous than the non-aggression pact they had negotiated on the eve of war in 1939. Some Americans, including Acheson and Army Chief of Staff Maxwell Taylor, recommended that the United States determine whether this was a Soviet bluff by sending more soldiers to West Berlin. Dulles told the press that "we are most solemnly committed to hold West Berlin, if need be by military force." General Twining, who had favored the use of atomic weapons during the Dienbienphu crisis and was now chair of the Joint Chiefs of Staff, assured the president that he was ready "to fight a general nuclear war." But Eisenhower was not. "Destruction is not a good police force," he declared. "You don't throw hand grenades around streets to police the streets so that people won't be molested by thugs." The outcome largely depended on the attitude of the Western allies, who had steadily drifted apart over numerous issues.

As in the Berlin crisis of 1948 and 1949, however, the West surprised the Soviets by uniting against their demands. At first the NATO allies disagreed over what action to take. President Charles de Gaulle of France did not favor German reunification, but he refused to retreat on Berlin. British Prime Minister Harold Macmillan, realizing that a Soviet nuclear attack would focus on England, seemed to support the conversion of West Berlin into a free city in line with Khrushchev's ultimatum. Eisenhower, however, refused to budge. "Any sign of Western weakness at this forward position," he warned, "could be misinterpreted with grievous consequences." Although he first wanted to "give peace forces a chance," Eisenhower made clear that if the East Germans stopped any U.S. vehicle after the six-month deadline, the United States would order a small armed convoy to Berlin. Should that convoy encounter interference, he would institute an airlift, sever relations with Moscow, take the matter before the United Nations, and prepare for war. The president privately remarked that "in this gamble, we are not going to be betting white chips, building up the pot gradually and fearfully. Khrushchev should know that when we decide to act, our whole stack will be in the pot."

After many anxious moments the Berlin crisis faded without incident. In December 1958 the foreign ministers of the United States, Britain, France, and West Germany met in Paris and decided not to capitulate, and two days later the NATO Council pledged support. The wartime victory over Germany had been a cooperative Allied effort, the West argued, and the Soviet Union had no right to alter the situation without common consent. Seeing the West unified, Khrushchev backed off from his ultimatum with the lame explanation that he had not meant six months in a literal sense. He agreed that the Big Four's foreign ministers should meet in Geneva to discuss Germany, Europe, and disarmament.

Perhaps because of the U.S. preoccupation with the Lebanon and Berlin crises, the Communist Chinese had in autumn 1958 resumed their bombardment of Quemoy, now fortified with 100,000 Nationalists, or a third of Jiang's army. Mao probably intended a resumption of the shelling to demonstrate again the growing U.S. presence in Chinese internal affairs and perhaps attract Soviet support. If so, the strategy appeared successful. Beijing radio threatened to "smash the American paper tiger and liberate Taiwan [Formosa]," and Khrushchev staunchly warned that "an attack on the Chinese People's Republic is an attack on the Soviet Union."

As in late 1954, the United States feared a Communist invasion of the islands and reacted strongly. Dulles was anxious to look strong without provoking a nuclear encounter and recommended mere "air bursts, so that there would be no appreciable fallout or large civilian casualties." The president seemed to agree. His purpose, as he recorded in his memoirs, was to convince the Chinese Communists that the United States would not retreat. Instead of using nuclear weaponry, Eisenhower approved airlifts of Jiang's troops, authorized the Seventh Fleet to convoy the Nationalists' supply ships, and, most ominous, dispatched marines into Quemoy bearing howitzers capable of delivering atomic shells. In September he asserted over television that the desertion of Quemoy would be a "Western Pacific Munich." Americans would not engage in "appeasement."

Despite the war threats, the second crisis over Formosa in less than five years again quickly dissipated. If the Communist Chinese agree to a cease-fire, Dulles proposed, the United States would seek a reduction of the Nationalist forces on Quemoy. He sweetened the offer by publicly declaring that the United States had "no commitment" to support Jiang's return to the mainland. The Communist Chinese responded by calling off the firing for a week. In return, Eisenhower ordered the Seventh Fleet to stop convoying Jiang's supply ships. Dulles traveled to Formosa in October and convinced Jiang to cut back on the number of soldiers on the islands and to renounce forceful attempts to take the mainland. The Beijing government nonetheless announced its intention to shell Quemoy on alternate days, a ploy that permitted Jiang to supply his troops on Quemoy and yet allowed the Communist Chinese to maintain a formal protest against the Nationalists' presence on the island. Eisenhower expressed bewilderment over this "Gilbert and Sullivan war."

Eisenhower and Khrushchev
Shortly after the Soviet leader arrived in the United States in 1959. *United Press International.*

Mao later declared with wonder, "Who would have thought when we fired a few shots at Quemoy and Matsu that it would stir up such an earth-shattering storm?"

After Dulles died of cancer in spring 1959, Eisenhower appointed a much less assertive secretary of state, Christian Herter, and assumed a more visible role in seeking better relations with Moscow. An encouraging sign was Vice President Nixon's visit to the Soviet Union in July, followed by Khrushchev's tour of the United States in September. Not all was harmonious. Nixon, who once characterized Khrushchev as a "bare knuckle slugger who had gouged, kneed, and kicked" his way to the top, took advantage of television cameras to score a Cold War victory in the famous "kitchen debate." Before a model kitchen at the American National Exhibition in Moscow, he and Khrushchev engaged in an animated discussion of capitalism and socialism in which Nixon shook his finger at Khrushchev, much to the delight of Americans. Eisenhower later welcomed Khrushchev to the United States, hoping to "soften up the Soviet leader even a little bit." Khrushchev was short-tempered and unpolished in manner and speech, yet Eisenhower considered him a "powerful, skillful, ruthless, and highly ambitious politician" who was "blinded by his dedication to the Marxist theory of world revolution and Communist domination." Khrushchev admitted that Eisenhower was "a good man, but he wasn't very tough."

Khrushchev's visit to the United States left the impression that Soviet-American relations had improved. But there were touchy moments. After touring an IBM plant, the premier visited a Hollywood set and concluded that the scant dress of actresses was proof of capitalism's decay. He also became upset that in the interest of security he was unable to see the recently opened amusement park at Disneyland. Yet Khrushchev toned down his belligerence by promising "peaceful coexistence" and explaining that his promise to "bury capitalism" did not constitute a military threat. "I say it again—I've almost worn my tongue thin repeating it—you may live under capitalism and we will live under socialism and build communism. The one whose system proves better will win. We will not bury you, nor will you bury us." Khrushchev called for total disarmament in a speech before the UN General Assembly in New York but would permit no inspection of Soviet arms.

After less than two weeks inside the United States, the Soviet premier accepted Eisenhower's invitation to discuss Berlin at his Camp David mountain retreat in Maryland. Although the two heads of state reached no settlement, they clarified their stands on major issues, expressed interest in negotiating on Berlin, renounced the use of force, and indicated support for disarmament. The "spirit of Camp David" seemed genuine when Eisenhower announced his intention to visit the Soviet Union in spring 1960.

The U-2 Incident

After the Camp David meeting, Britain and France joined the United States in calling for a summit conference; before it could take place, however, Soviet-American relations suddenly plummeted. On May 1, 1960, an American U-2 reconnaissance plane was soaring more than 1000 miles inside Soviet air space when engine trouble forced it below its normal flying range and a Soviet surface-to-air missile (SAM) shot it down. The U-2's pilot, Francis Gary Powers, parachuted safely from the plane. Soviet authorities seized both him and the wreckage.

The Soviets' heated protests over this intrusion of air space drew a confused and bungled U.S. reaction. On May 3 NASA announced that a weather "research airplane" operating over Turkey had apparently gone down; two days later Khrushchev coldly declared that Soviet missiles had shot down a U.S. plane over Soviet territory. To this charge, the state department supported the NASA cover by admitting that a "civilian" piloting a weather plane had mistakenly flown over Soviet air space. A spokesman for the agency declared emphatically on May 6 that "there was absolutely no—N-O, no—deliberate attempt to violate Soviet air space, and there never has been."

That same day Khrushchev exhibited photographs of Powers, the downed plane, and its reconnaissance instruments and followed these dramatic revelations with pictures of Soviet military plants taken by U-2 cameras. The state department then conceded that the U-2 had "probably" been on an intelligence mission, but on May 9 Secretary of State Herter admitted to full knowledge of the flights. When Khrushchev left Eisenhower a face-saving way out by expressing doubt that he was involved, the president infuriated him and shocked everyone else by accepting full responsibility for the missions and defending them on the basis of national security. Soviet secrecy, Eisenhower declared in his weekly press conference, had necessitated such measures to prevent "another Pearl Harbor."

The summit conference opened in Paris on May 16, 1960, in the midst of intense animosity over the U-2 episode. Khrushchev's rage far outweighed the magnitude of the incident. His fury undoubtedly was attributable to his desires to quiet critics at home who were starving for a Cold War victory and to subvert a conference in which his demands on Germany had no chance for success. While he was in Paris he bitterly attacked the United States and refused to discuss anything until Eisenhower apologized for the flight, punished those involved, and announced an end to U-2 activities over the Soviet Union. He also canceled the president's invitation to the Soviet Union. Eisenhower guaranteed only that no more U-2 flights would occur during his presidency. When de Gaulle and Macmillan tried to mediate, Khrushchev stormed out, ending the summit conference one day after it began.

The United States's actions during the U-2 affair helped to intensify the Cold War during the summer of 1960. Washington's clumsy handling of the incident had invited the verbal attack. Eisenhower's apparent ineptitude had damaged the nation's image abroad. Fur-

thermore, the episode forced accommodations in policy. After Khrushchev warned of a nuclear assault on those neutralist nations permitting U-2 bases, protesters in Japan demonstrated against the presence of three U-2s and opposed a mutual defense pact with the United States. The Washington administration removed the planes before the treaty went into effect in June 1960, but Eisenhower had to cancel a visit to Japan because of security risks. In September, Khrushchev arrived at the United Nations in New York and spent almost a month inside the United States without receiving an invitation to meet with Eisenhower. The Soviet premier bragged about his country's missile production, tried to shout down British Prime Minister Macmillan, called the United Nations a "spitoon," and at one point took off his shoe, shook it at the speaker, and pounded it on the table. Khrushchev's angry outbursts deepened the division between East and West and made a Berlin settlement even more remote.

U-2 Crisis
Khrushchev visiting exhibit of U-2 remains in 1960. *Library of Congress.*

Latin America

Meanwhile problems in Latin America had heated again. More than two years earlier, Vice President Nixon had made a goodwill visit to eight countries in South America, attempting to assure Latin Americans that they were "not only our neighbors but our best friends." But he encountered angry crowds at every stop, including riotous students at the University of the Republic in Montevideo, Uruguay, and at San Marcos University in Lima, Peru. Confronting what Nixon later called a "bunch of Communist thugs," he barely escaped rocks and eggs thrown by protesters yelling "Nixon get out!" In Caracas, Venezuela, a mob shouting "Death to Nixon!" surrounded his limousine, rocked it, kicked in its sides, and broke the windows before the driver could speed away. Eisenhower dispatched 1000 marines to U.S. bases in the Caribbean to prevent further incidents.

Nixon attributed these ill feelings primarily to Communists, an argument perhaps bolstered by the realization that by the mid-1950s nearly twenty Latin American republics had signed commercial agreements with either the Soviet Union or its allied states. The former president of Costa Rica, however, explained that Latin Americans hated the United States for backing dictators. In Venezuela, for example, the United States had long supported dictator Marcos Pérez Jiménez; even after his overthrow by a military junta in 1958 it awarded asylum to him and his police chief.

The Eisenhower administration encouraged reforms in Latin America, largely because it believed that the region's economic problems could lead to a Communist takeover. In 1958 a Brazilian diplomat in Washington complained that since 1946 the state department had followed "two patterns of action: the Marshall Plan dedicated to Europe and the John Foster Dulles Plan dedicated to Asia and the Middle East." To remedy the situation, the president's brother Milton made a second fact-finding visit to Latin America. The following year, 1959, the United States adopted several

measures to cure what the president called "the festering sore of underdevelopment." It established the Inter-American Development Bank to float loans, tried to stabilize coffee prices by restricting U.S. exports, and worked toward ending tariffs and establishing a common market among the Americas. In early 1960 the president visited South America, and the following August he requested $500 million in economic aid for the region. Congress quickly complied, albeit in a lukewarm manner. In September, twenty-one American states approved the Act of Bogotá, designed to implement the economic and social reform program.

Presidential Election of 1960 and Cold War Rhetoric

The heightened Cold War tensions carried over into the presidential election of 1960. Nixon, vice president for eight years, easily won the Republican nomination, and Senator John F. Kennedy of Massachusetts emerged as the Democrats' candidate. Both men tried to portray the image of youth, vitality, and strength of leadership against communism. Nixon reminded Americans of his long-time experience in the office closest to the presidency, his courage in standing up to Khrushchev in Moscow, and his resistance to the alleged Communists in Latin America. Kennedy, a naval war hero, member of the Senate Foreign Relations Committee, and author of *Why England Slept* and the Pulitzer Prize-winning *Profiles in Courage,* called for a hard-line approach to Soviet affairs and promised to support anyone willing to fight communism. Nixon defended Eisenhower's policies, but Kennedy accused the Republicans of permitting the United States to fall behind the Soviet Union in economic development and in the missile race. "I think it's time America started moving again," Kennedy declared at the close of his first television debate with Nixon. Pledging victory in the Cold War, Kennedy and the Democratic party won the election by a narrow margin.

President Kennedy inherited a world pulsating with Cold War tension. Berlin, Southeast Asia, Communist China, the Third World—all areas suggested the need for careful diplomacy rather than angry rhetoric. Indeed, in all these problem spots Eisenhower had kept the United States out of war by what many believe were the narrowest of margins. And yet, in the Formosa crisis and perhaps others as well, the White House had overreacted by casting all events within a Cold War context. The rhetoric had become more fevered as Dulles emphasized liberation and thereby missed chances to negotiate with the Soviet Union and the People's Republic of China. East-West divisions had hardened, covert actions had threatened to become the norm, and U.S. suspicions had grown that Third World nationalism was a mere front for the spread of communism. Kennedy used his inaugural address to assure Americans that his administration would not shrink from communism anywhere in the world. His challenging words guaranteed the continuation of a volatile international atmosphere.

Selected Readings

Accinelli, Robert. *Crisis and Commitment: United States Policy Toward Taiwan, 1950–1955.* 1996.

Adams, Sherman. *Firsthand Report: The Story of the Eisenhower Administration.* 1961.

Aguilar, Manuela. *Cultural Diplomacy and Foreign Policy: German-American Relations, 1955–1968.* 1996.

Alexander, Charles C. *Holding the Line: The Eisenhower Era, 1952–1961.* 1975.

Allen, Craig. *Eisenhower and the Mass Media: Peace, Prosperity, and Prime-Time TV.* 1993

Alteras, Isaac. *Eisenhower and Israel: U.S.-Israeli Relations, 1953–1960.* 1993.

Ambrose, Stephen E. *Eisenhower. Vol. 2: The President.* 1984.

———. *Ike's Spies: Eisenhower and the Espionage Establishment.* 1981.

———. *Nixon: The Education of a Politician, 1913–1962.* 1987.

———, and Brinkley, Douglas G. *Rise to Globalism: American Foreign Policy since 1938.* 8th ed., 1997.

Arnold, James R. *The First Domino: Eisenhower, the Military, and America's Intervention in Vietnam.* 1991.

Ashton, Nigel J. *Eisenhower, Macmillan, and the Problem of Nasser: Anglo-American Relations and Arab Nationalism, 1955–59.* 1996.

Ball, George W., and Ball, Douglas B. *The Passionate Attachment: America's Involvement with Israel 1947 to the Present.* 1992.

Ball, Howard. *Justice Downwind: America's Atomic Testing Program in the 1950s.* 1986.

Ben-Zvi, Abraham. *Decade of Transition: Eisenhower, Kennedy, and the Origins of the American-Israeli Alliance.* 1998.

Beschloss, Michael R. *Mayday: Eisenhower, Khrushchev and the U-2 Affair.* 1986.

Bill, James A. *The Eagle and the Lion: The Tragedy of American-Iranian Relations.* 1988.

Billings-Yan, Melanie. *Decision against War: Eisenhower and Dien Bien Phu, 1954.* 1988.

Botti, Timothy. *Ace in the Hole: Why the United States Did Not Use Nuclear Weapons in the Cold War, 1945–1965.* 1996.

Boyer, Paul S. *By the Bomb's Early Light: American Thought and Culture at the Dawn of the Atomic Age.* 1986.

Bradley, Mark Phillips. *Imagining Vietnam and America: The Making of Postcolonial Vietnam, 1919–1950.* 2000.

Brands, H. W. *The Devil We Knew: Americans and the Cold War.* 1993.

Brands, H. William, Jr. *Cold Warriors: Eisenhower's Generation and American Foreign Policy.* 1988.

Brinkley, Douglas. *Dean Acheson: The Cold War Years, 1953–71.* 1992.

Broadwater, Jeff. *Adlai Stevenson and American Politics: The Odyssey of a Cold War Liberal.* 1994.

———. *Eisenhower and the Anti-Communist Crusade.* 1992.

Buckley, Roger. *U.S.-Japan Alliance Diplomacy, 1945–1990.* 1992.

Bulkeley, Rip. *The Sputniks Crisis and Early United States Space Policy: A Critique of the Historiography of Space.* 1991.

Burns, William J. *Economic Aid and American Policy Toward Egypt, 1955–1981.* 1985.

Burr, William. "Avoiding the Slippery Slope: The Eisenhower Administration and the Berlin Crisis, November 1958–January 1959," *Diplomatic History* 18 (1994): 177–205.

Buzzanco, Robert. "Prologue to Tragedy: U.S. Military Opposition to Intervention in Vietnam,

1950–1954," *Diplomatic History* 17 (1993): 201–22.

Campbell, Craig. *Destroying the Village: Eisenhower and Thermonuclear War.* 1998.

Chang, Gordon H. *Friends and Enemies: The United States, China, and the Soviet Union, 1948–1972.* 1990.

———, and He Di. "The Absence of War in the U.S.-China Confrontation over Quemoy and Matsu in 1954–1955: Contingency, Luck, Deterrence?", *American Historical Review* 98 (Dec. 1993), 1500–24.

Christensen, Thomas J. *Useful Adversaries: Grand Strategy, Domestic Mobilization, and Sino-American Conflict, 1947–1958.* 1996.

Clark, Ian. *Nuclear Diplomacy and the Special Relationship: Britain's Deterrent and America, 1957–1962.* 1994.

Clark, Paul C., Jr. *The United States and Somoza, 1933–1956: A Revisionist Look.* 1992.

Clayton, Lawrence A. *Peru and the United States: The Condor and the Eagle.* 1999.

Clowse, Barbara B. *Brainpower for the Cold War: The Sputnik Crisis and the National Defense Education Act of 1958.* 1981.

Clymer, Kenton J. *Quest for Freedom: The United States and India's Independence.* 1995.

Cohen, Warren I. *America's Response to China: An Interpretive History of Sino-American Relations.* 2000.

———, and Iriye, Akira, eds. *The Great Powers in East Asia, 1953–1960.* 1990.

Cook, Blanche W. *The Declassified Eisenhower: A Divided Legacy.* 1981.

Cooper, Chester L. *The Lion's Last Roar: Suez, 1956.* 1978.

Costigliola, Frank. *France and the United States: The Cold Alliance since World War II.* 1992.

Cronin, Audrey K. *Great Power Politics and the Struggle over Austria, 1945–1955.* 1986.

Cullather, Nick. *Illusions of Influence: The Political Economy of United States-Philippines Relations, 1942–1960.* 1994.

———. *Secret History: The CIA's Classified Account of Its Operations in Guatemala, 1952–1954.* 1999.

Currey, Cecil B. *Edward Lansdale: The Unquiet American.* 1988.

Davidson, Phillip B. *Vietnam at War: The History, 1946–1975.* 1988.

Diamond, Sigmund. *Compromised Campus: The Collaboration of Universities with the Intelligence Community, 1945–1955.* 1992.

Divine, Robert A. *Blowing on the Wind: The Nuclear Test Ban Debate, 1954–1960.* 1978.

———. *Eisenhower and the Cold War.* 1981.

———. *The Sputnik Challenge: Eisenhower's Response to the Soviet Satellite.* 1993.

Dockrill, Saki. *Eisenhower's New-Look National Security Policy, 1953–61.* 1996.

Donovan, Robert J. *Eisenhower: The Inside Story.* 1956

Duiker, William J. *The Communist Road to Power in Vietnam.* 1981.

———. *Ho Chi Minh.* 2000.

Eisenhower, Dwight D. *The White House Years: Mandate for Change, 1953–1956.* 1963.

———. *The White House Years: Waging Peace, 1956–1961.* 1965.

Fall, Bernard B. *Hell in a Very Small Place: The Siege of Dien Bien Phu.* 1966.

———. *The Two Viet-Nams: A Political and Military Analysis.* 2nd rev. ed., 1967.

Finer, Herman. *Dulles over Suez: The Theory and Practice of His Diplomacy.* 1964.

Freiberger, Steven Z. *Dawn over Suez: The Rise of American Power in the Middle East, 1953–1957.* 1992.

Gaddis, John L. *The Long Peace: Inquiries into the History of the Cold War.* 1987.

———. *Russia, the Soviet Union, and the United States: An Interpretive History.* 2nd ed., 1990.

———. *Strategies of Containment: A Critical Appraisal of Postwar American National Security Policy.* 1982.

Gambone, Michael D. *Eisenhower, Somoza, and the Cold War in Nicaragua, 1953–1961.* 1997.

Gardner, Lloyd C. *Approaching Vietnam: From World War II Through Dienbienphu, 1941–1954.* 1988.

Gasiorowski, Mark J. *U.S. Foreign Policy and the Shah: Building a Client State in Iran.* 1991.

Gendzier, Irene L. *Notes from the Minefield: United States Intervention in Lebanon and the Middle East, 1945–1958.* 1997.

Gerson, Louis. *John Foster Dulles.* 1968.

Gordon, Leonard H. D. "United States Opposition to Use of Force in the Taiwan Strait, 1954–1962," *Journal of American History* 72 (1985): 637–60.

Graebner, Norman A. *The New Isolationism: A Study in Politics and Foreign Policy since 1950.* 1956.

Greene, Daniel P. O'C. "John Foster Dulles and the End of the Franco-American Entente in Indochina," *Diplomatic History* 16 (1992): 551–71.

Greenstein, Fred I. *The Hidden-Hand Presidency: Eisenhower as a Leader.* 1982.

Grose, Peter. *Gentleman Spy: The Life of Allen Dulles.* 1994.

Gurtov, Melvin. *The First Vietnam Crisis: Chinese Communist Strategy and United States Involvement, 1953–1954.* 1967.

Haddow, Robert H. *Pavilions of Plenty: Exhibiting American Culture Abroad in the 1950s.* 1997.

Hahn, Peter L. *The United States, Great Britain, and Egypt, 1945–1956: Strategy and Diplomacy in the Early Cold War.* 1991.

Hammer, Ellen J. *The Struggle for Indochina, 1940–1955.* 1966.

Harrison, James P. *The Endless War: Fifty Years of Struggle in Vietnam.* 1982.

Heale, M. J. *McCarthy's Americans: Red Scare Politics in State and Nation, 1935–1965.* 1998.

Heiss, Mary Ann. *Empire and Nationhood: The United States, Great Britain, and Iranian Oil, 1950–1954.* 1997.

Henriksen, Margot A. *Dr. Strangelove's America: Society and Culture in the Atomic Age.* 1997.

Herken, Gregg. *Counsels of War.* 1985.

Herring, George C. *America's Longest War: The United States and Vietnam, 1950–1975.* 3rd ed., 1986.

———. "'In the Lands of the Blind': Eisenhower's Commitment to South Vietnam, 1954," in Jones, Howard, ed., *The Foreign and Domestic Dimensions of Modern Warfare: Vietnam, Central America, and Nuclear Strategy*, 31–39. 1988.

———. ed. *The Pentagon Papers: Abridged Edition.* 1993.

———. "The Truman Administration and the Restoration of French Sovereignty in Indochina," *Diplomatic History* 1 (1977): 97–117.

———, and Immerman, Richard H. "Eisenhower, Dulles, and Dienbienphu: 'The Day We Didn't Go to War' Revisited," *Journal of American History* 71 (1984): 343–68.

Hess, Gary R. *America Encounters India, 1941–1947.* 1971.

———. "The First American Commitment in Indochina: The Acceptance of the 'Bao Dai Solution,' 1950," *Diplomatic History* 2 (1978): 331–50.

———. *The United States' Emergence as a Southeast Asian Power, 1940–1950.* 1987.

———. *Vietnam and the United States: Origins and Legacy of War.* 1998.

Hixson, Walter L. *Parting the Curtain: Propaganda, Culture, and the Cold War, 1945–1961.* 1997.

Hoopes, Townsend. *The Devil and John Foster Dulles.* 1973.

Hughes, Emmet J. *The Ordeal of Power: A Political Memoir of the Eisenhower Years.* 1963.

Immerman, Richard H. *The CIA in Guatemala: The Foreign Policy of Intervention.* 1982.

———. *John Foster Dulles: Piety, Pragmatism and Power in U.S. Foreign Policy.* 1999.

———. ed. *John Foster Dulles and the Diplomacy of the Cold War.* 1990.

———. "The United States and the Geneva Conference of 1954: A New Look," *Diplomatic History* 14 (1990): 43–66.

Irving, Ronald E. *The First Indochina War: French and American Policy, 1945–1954.* 1975.

Johnson, Loch K. *America's Secret Power: The CIA in a Democratic Society.* 1989.

Johnson, Robert H. *Improbable Dangers: U.S. Conceptions of Threat in the Cold War and After.* 1994.

Kahin, Audrey R., and Kahin, George McT. *Subversion as Foreign Policy: The Secret Eisenhower and Dulles Debacle in Indonesia.* 1995.

Kahin, George McT. *Intervention: How America Became Involved in Vietnam.* 1986.

———, and Lewis, John W. *The United States in Vietnam.* Rev. ed., 1969.

Kalb, Madeline. *The Congo Cables: The Cold War in Africa—From Eisenhower to Kennedy.* 1982.

Kaplan, Lawrence S., Artaud, Denise, and Rubin, Mark R., eds. *Dien Bien Phu and the Crisis of Franco-American Relations, 1954–1955.* 1990.

Karnow, Stanley. *Vietnam: A History.* Rev. ed., 1991.

Kattenburg, Paul. *The Vietnam Trauma in American Foreign Policy, 1945–1975.* 1980.

Kaufman, Burton I. *Trade and Aid: Eisenhower's Foreign Economic Policy, 1953–1961.* 1982.

Kendrick, Alexander. *The Wound Within: America in the Vietnam Years, 1945–1974.* 1974.

Killian, James R. *Sputnik, Scientists and Eisenhower.* 1978.

Kolko, Gabriel. *Anatomy of a War: Vietnam, the United States, and the Modern Historical Experience.* 1985.

Krenn, Michael L. *Black Diplomacy: African Americans and the State Department, 1945–1969.* 1998.

Kunz, Diane B. *The Economic Diplomacy of the Suez Crisis.* 1991.

LaFeber, Walter. *America, Russia, and the Cold War, 1945–1996.* 8th ed., 1997.

———. *Inevitable Revolutions: The United States in Central America.* 1984.

Langguth, A. J. *Our Vietnam: The War, 1954–1975.* 2000.

Latham, Earl. *The Communist Controversy in Washington.* 1969.

Ledeen, Michael, and Lewis, William. *Debacle: The American Failure in Iran.* 1980.

Leonard, Thomas M. *The United States and Central America, 1944–1949: Perceptions of Political Dynamics.* 1984.

Levey, Zach. *Israel and the Western Powers, 1952–1960.* 1998.

Lind, Michael. *Vietnam the Necessary War: A Reinterpretation of America's Most Disastrous Military Conflict.* 1999.

Little, Douglas. "His Finest Hour? Eisenhower, Lebanon, and the 1958 Middle East Crisis," *Diplomatic History* 20 (1996): 27–54.

Lloyd, Selwyn. *Suez, 1956.* 1978.

Louis, William R., and Owen, Roger, eds. *Suez 1956.* 1991.

Lowe, Peter. *Containing the Cold War in East Asia: British Policies Towards Japan, China and Korea, 1948–53.* 1997.

Lytle, Mark H. *The Origins of the Iranian-American Alliance, 1941–1953.* 1987.

Maclear, Michael. *The Ten Thousand Day War, Vietnam: 1945–1975.* 1981.

Maldonado, A. W. *Teodoro Moscoso and Puerto Rico's Operation Bootstrap.* 1997.

Manor, Robert. *A Grand Illusion: America's Descent into Vietnam.* 2001.

Marks, Frederick W. "The CIA and Castillo Armas in Guatemala, 1954: New Clues to an Old Puzzle," *Diplomatic History* 14 (1990): 67–86.

———. *Power and Peace: The Diplomacy of John Foster Dulles.* 1993.

Mayers, David A. *Cracking the Monolith: U.S. Policy Against the Sino-Soviet Alliance, 1949–1955.* 1986.

Mazuzan, George T. "American Nuclear Policy," in Carroll, John M., and Herring, George C., eds., *Modern American Diplomacy*, 147–63. 1986.

McMahon, Robert J. *The Cold War on the Periphery: The United States, India, and Pakistan.* 1994.

———. *Colonialism and Cold War: The United States and the Struggle for Indonesian Independence, 1945–49.* 1981.

———. "Eisenhower and Third World Nationalism: A Critique of the Revisionists," *Political Science Quarterly* 101 (1986): 453–73.

———. *The Limits of Empire: The United States and Southeast Asia since World War II.* 1999.

Meers, Sharon I. "The British Connection: How the United States Covered Its Tracks in the 1954 Coup in Guatemala," *Diplomatic History* 16 (1992): 409–28.

Melanson, Richard A., and Mayers, David, eds. *Reevaluating Eisenhower: American Foreign Policy in the Fifties.* 1987.

Merrill, Dennis. *Bread and the Ballot: The United States and India's Economic Development, 1947–1963.* 1990.

Montague, Ludwell L. *General Walter Bedell Smith as Director of Central Intelligence, October 1950–February 1953.* 1992.

Montgomery, Gayle B., and Johnson, James W. *One Step from the White House: The Rise and Fall of Senator William F. Knowland.* 1998.

Morgan, Joseph G. *The Vietnam Lobby: The American Friends of Vietnam, 1955–1975.* 1997.

Neff, Donald. *Warriors at Suez: Eisenhower Takes America into the Middle East.* 1981.

Nelson, Anna K. "The 'Top of Policy Hill': President Eisenhower and the National Security Council," *Diplomatic History* 7 (1983): 307–26.

Noer, Thomas J. *Cold War and Black Liberation: The United States and White Rule in Africa, 1948–1968.* 1985.

Olson, James S., and Roberts, Randy. *Where the Domino Fell: America and Vietnam, 1945–1995.* 3rd ed., 1995.

Oren, Michael. *Origins of the Second Arab-Israeli War: Egypt, Israel, and the Great Powers, 1952–56.* 1992.

Pach, Chester J., Jr., and Richardson, Elmo. *The Presidency of Dwight D. Eisenhower.* Rev. ed., 1991.

Palmer, Dave R. *Summons of the Trumpet: A History of the Vietnam War from a Military Man's Viewpoint.* 1978.

Parmet, Herbert S. *Eisenhower and the American Crusades.* 1972.

Paterson, Thomas G. *Contesting Castro: The United States and the Triumph of the Cuban Revolution.* 1994.

Patterson, James T. *Mr. Republican: A Biography of Robert A. Taft.* 1972.

Patti, Archimedes L. A. *Why Viet Nam? Prelude to America's Albatross.* 1980.

Pickett, William B. *Dwight David Eisenhower and American Power.* 1995.

Plummer, Brenda G. *Rising Wind: Black Americans and U.S. Foreign Affairs, 1935–1960.* 1996.

Poole, Peter. *The United States and Indochina from FDR to Nixon.* 1973.

Prados, John. *The Blood Road: The Ho Chi Minh Trail and the Vietnam War.* 1999.

———. *Presidents' Secret Wars: CIA Pentagon Covert Operations from World War II through the Persian Gulf.* 1996.

Pruessen, Ronald W. *John Foster Dulles: The Road to Power.* 1982.

Rabe, Stephen G. "The Clues Didn't Check Out: Commentary on 'The CIA and Castillo Armas,'" *Diplomatic History* 14 (1990): 87–95.

———. *Eisenhower and Latin America: The Foreign Policy of Anticommunism.* 1988.

Randle, Robert R. *Geneva 1954: The Settlement of the Indochina War.* 1969.

Ranelagh, John. *The Agency: The Rise and Decline of the CIA.* 1986.

Richardson, Elmo. *The Presidency of Dwight D. Eisenhower.* 1979.

Risse-Kappen, Thomas. *Cooperation Among Democracies. The European Influence on U.S. Foreign Policy.* 1995.

Roman, Peter J. *Eisenhower and the Missile Gap.* 1995.

Roosevelt, Kermit. *Countercoup: Struggle for the Control of Iran.* 1979.

Rubin, Barry. *The Arab States and the Palestine Conflict.* 1981.

———. *Paved with Good Intentions: The American Experience and Iran.* 1980.

Samii, Kuross A. *Involvement by Invitation: American Strategies of Containment in Iran.* 1987.

Saunders, Bonnie F. *The United States and Arab Nationalism: The Syrian Case, 1953–1960.* 1996.

Schick, Jack M. *The Berlin Crisis, 1958–1962.* 1971.

Schlesinger, Stephen, and Kinzer, Stephen. *Bitter Fruit: The Untold Story of the American Coup in Guatemala.* 1982.

Schmitz, David F. *Thank God They're on Our Side: The United States and Right-Wing Dictatorships, 1921–1965.* 1999.

Schoenbaum, David. *The United States and the State of Israel.* 1993.

Schoutz, Lars. *Beneath the United States: A History of U.S. Policy Toward Latin America.* 1998.

Schraeder, Peter J. *United States Foreign Policy Toward Africa: Incrementalism, Crisis, and Change.* 1994.

Schulzinger, Robert D. *A Time for War: The United States and Vietnam, 1941–1975.* 1997.

Shaplen, Robert. *The Lost Revolution: The U.S. in Vietnam, 1946–1966.* 1966.

Sheehan, Michael K. *Iran: The Impact of U.S. Interests and Policies, 1941–1954.* 1968.

Sheehan, Neil, et al., eds. *New York Times, The Pentagon Papers.* 1971.

Sick, Gary. *All Fall Down: America's Tragic Encounter with Iran.* 1985.

Singh, Anita I. *The Limits of British Influence: South Asia and the Anglo-American Relationship, 1947–56.* 1993.

Smith, Gaddis. *The Last Years of the Monroe Doctrine.* 1994.

Smith, Peter H. *Talons of the Eagle: Dynamics of U.S.-Latin American Relations.* 2nd ed., 2000.

Smith, R. B. *An International History of the Vietnam War. Vol. 1: Revolution versus Containment, 1955–1961.* 1983.

Snead, David L. *The Gaither Committee, Eisenhower, and the Cold War.* 1999.

Snetsinger, John. *Truman, the Jewish Vote, and the Creation of Israel.* 1979.

Spanier, John W. *American Foreign Policy since World War II.* 14th ed., 1998.

Spector, Ronald H. *Advice and Support: The Early Years of the U. S. Army in Vietnam: 1941–1960.* 1983.

Spiegel, Steven L. *The Other Arab-Israeli Conflict: Making America's Middle East Policy, from Truman to Reagan.* 1985.

Stevenson, Richard W. *The Rise and Fall of Detente: Relaxations of Tensions in U.S.-Soviet Relations, 1953–1984.* 1985.

Stookey, Robert W. *America and the Arab States: An Uneasy Encounter.* 1975.

Tananbaum, Duane A. "The Bricker Amendment Controversy: Its Origins and Eisenhower's Role," *Diplomatic History* 9 (1985): 73–93.

Thomas, Evan. *The Very Best Men: Four Who Dared: The Early Years of the CIA.* 1995.

Thomas, Hugh. *The Suez Affair.* 1967.

Tomes, Robert R. *Apocalypse Then: American Intellectuals and the Vietnam War, 1954–1975.* 1998.

Truong Nhu Tang. *A Vietcong Memoir.* 1985.

Tucker, Nancy B. *Taiwan, Hong Kong, and the United States, 1945–1992: Uncertain Friendships.* 1994.

Tucker, Spencer C. *Vietnam.* 1999.

Turley, William S. *The Second Indochina War: A Short Political and Military History, 1954–1975.* 1986.

Ulam, Adam B. *The Communists: The Story of Power and Lost Illusions, 1948–1991.* 1992.

———. *The Rivals: America and Russia since World War II.* 1971.

Von Eschen, Penny M. *Race Against Empire: Black Americans and Anticolonialism, 1937–1957.* 1998.

Wells, Samuel F., Jr. "The Origins of Massive Retaliation," *Political Science Quarterly* 96 (1981): 31–52.

Wenger, Andreas. *Living with Peril: Eisenhower, Kennedy, and Nuclear Weapons.* 1997.

Winks, Robin W. *Cloak and Gown: Scholars in the Secret War, 1939–1961.* 1987.

Wise, David, and Ross, Thomas B. *The U-2 Affair.* 1962.

Wittner, Lawrence S. *The Struggle Against the Bomb.* 1997.

Wolpert, Stanley A. *Nehru: A Tryst with Destiny.* 1996.

Wood, Bryce. *The Dismantling of the Good Neighbor Policy.* 1985.

Young, Marilyn B. *The Vietnam Wars, 1945–1990.* 1991.

Zhai, Qiang. *China and the Vietnam Wars, 1950–1975.* 2000.

———. *The Dragon, the Lion, and the Eagle: Chinese-British-American Relations, 1949–1958.* 1994.

Zhang, Shu Guang. *Deterrence and Strategic Culture: Chinese-American Confrontations, 1949–1958.* 1992.

CHAPTER 12

Containment at the Brink
KENNEDY AND CUBA, 1961–1963

A Global Commitment to Freedom

When sworn in on January 20, 1961, President John F. Kennedy called on Americans to resolve the world's problems. "Let every nation know that we shall pay any price, bear any burden, meet any hardship, support any friend or oppose any foe in order to assure the survival and success of liberty." Containment to its fullest extent was the promise of the new administration, because Kennedy intended that the doctrine encompass the globe with military force, economic pressure, or both. Staunchly anti-Communist, he was a product of the eras of appeasement and McCarthyism. Kennedy also symbolized a changing of the order, much as Franklin D. Roosevelt did to many Americans almost three decades before. As the youngest elected president—age forty-three—Kennedy replaced the oldest person ever to occupy that office up to that time—Eisenhower, at age seventy.

Kennedy's campaign program likewise suggested an abrupt change from that of the previous administration: His "New Frontier" assured Americans of a return to government activism in both domestic and foreign affairs. Although a bipartisan "conservative coalition" in Congress blocked much of the new president's domestic program, his foreign policy aroused considerable support because it coincided with the basic premise of Americans—that a monolithic communism emanating from the Kremlin threatened to absorb all vulnerable nations. Kennedy's concern was more sophisticated, however, in that he recognized the growing fragmentation among the Communists and regarded Communist China to be as dangerous as the Soviet Union. Yet he believed it the responsibility of the United States to guarantee each people's right to choose their own form of government. In addition to foreign military aid, the administration established a division in the defense department that focused on the sale of weapons to non-Communist governments. To expand U.S. trade and investment opportunities while winning allies against communism, Congress in 1962 authorized the president to lower tariffs fifty percent for nations buying American products. Finally, Kennedy came to realize soon after taking office that no "missile gap" existed; indeed, Eisenhower's administration had kept the United States well ahead of the Soviets in nuclear capacity. But to maintain this lead and to win the struggle against communism, the White House guaranteed a deepening involvement in world affairs, which, in turn, ensured confrontation with the Soviet Union.

White House Meeting
Left to right: Vice President Lyndon B. Johnson, Attorney General Robert F.
Kennedy, and President John F. Kennedy. *White House.*

Kennedy's Foreign Policy

Kennedy's brief tenure in the White House
emphasized image over reality. His presidency
ended abruptly in November 1963 with an
assassin's bullet in Dallas, leaving behind an
image of greatness born of martyrdom. And
yet even before these tragic events set him
firmly in their hearts, Americans spoke of the
"Kennedy style," which was characterized by
numerous attributes. Kennedy had personal
charm, affluence, and a Hollywood aura fostered by his father's investments in the business, and he showed the same grace under
pressure that he found in the historical figures
described in his Pulitzer Prize-winning *Profiles
in Courage.* The nation loved the sound of
children and the flair of a youthful and athletic
family living in the Executive Mansion, playing touch football with relatives and reporters
on the White House lawn. He brought the re-

vival of intellectual leadership, reinforced by the
appointment of a historian as special assistant
to the president (Arthur M. Schlesinger, Jr.,
who wrote a Pulitzer Prize-winning study of
Kennedy's 1000 days in office), and his beau-
tiful wife Jacqueline cultivated interest in the
arts and music. The president also showed wit
and humor, especially during his many press
conferences. Furthermore, Americans could
claim still another military hero in the White
House; during World War II Kennedy had
overcome lifelong back problems to rescue
sailors under his command after the Japanese
destroyed his torpedo boat, the PT-109. After
his assassination, his most avid followers used
the utopian musical stage play "Camelot" to
idealize Kennedy and his cohort as veritable
knights of King Arthur's mythical Round
Table who possessed all wisdom, knowledge,
and courage, while exuding genuine humanitarian concern.

Only decades after the assassination have observers been able to view the Kennedy administration with some degree of objectivity. As with most images, the Kennedy stories suffer when confronted with reality. Increasing numbers of historians have charged that both of Kennedy's major academic endeavors, *Why England Slept* (his senior thesis at Harvard, which criticized England for failing to use force against the aggressions of the 1930s) and *Profiles in Courage,* could not have been published without the extraordinary assistance of others. The image of "family" has also faded in light of the revelations of Kennedy's numerous sexual ventures (including those with Hollywood starlets), which continued throughout his presidency and were among Washington's best-known secrets. Still, the Kennedy "mystique" has endured. Although the adjectives of youth and vigor suggested advantages in leadership, they carried with them distinct disadvantages in international relations when the fledgling president faced the hardened and gruff Soviet premier, Nikita Khrushchev. In promising to close the alleged missile gap, Kennedy exemplified his belief that only a display of firm resolution and superior strength could discard his image of immaturity and inexperience in office and earn the respect of Moscow's leader. During a staff discussion of a planned summit meeting with Khrushchev, Kennedy declared, "I have to show him that we can be as tough as he is. . . . I'll have to sit down with him, and let him see who he's dealing with."

Supported by a "brain trust" of advisers, Kennedy appeared capable of turning the irrationality of the Cold War into the paths of reason. Secretary of Defense Robert McNamara, for whom Kennedy had the greatest admiration, was a Republican and a fast-rising business executive from Ford Motor Company who had a well-deserved reputation for quickness of mind and expertise in numbers. Secretary of State Dean Rusk (called "Buddha" by his critics because of his self-effacing personality and near baldness) was the son of a Presbyterian minister and had risen from the poorest confines of Georgia to become a Rhodes Scholar, career officer in the state department, and head of the Rockefeller Foundation. Intensely loyal to the White House, he was a Cold Warrior who viewed the world in 1940s terms and, while secretary of state for eight years, obeyed orders in a quiet, unassuming manner. McGeorge Bundy and Walt Rostow, college professors turned presidential advisers, were hard-line anti-Communists. Kennedy also relied heavily on his younger brother, Attorney General Robert F. Kennedy, and on his chief speechwriter Theodore Sorensen, even though in the opening days of the administration he adhered more closely to diplomatic, military, and intelligence experts. The president's campaign promise to close the missile gap encouraged a huge arms buildup, although U-2 flights soon substantiated U.S. military superiority and confirmed that the Soviets were not engaged in a large missile expansion program.

The Kennedy administration advocated a foreign policy program of "flexible response," which permitted the United States to defend itself against all types of threats. From 1961 to 1963 the defense budget increased dramatically, allowing American ICBMs (Intercontinental Ballistic Missiles) to grow almost sevenfold in number and giving the United States a three-to-one advantage over the Soviet Union. A group of Special Forces in the army, known as the Green Berets, became the object of Kennedy's special admiration—to the extent that he personally supervised their equipment and dress. Highly romanticized in the gloriously patriotic days of the early 1960s, the Green Berets employed the latest technical advances in developing counterinsurgency measures against guerrilla uprisings believed to be Communist-inspired. Kennedy's discovery that there was no missile gap encouraged him to support the maintenance of sufficient conventional strength to deal with limited conflicts, but he nonetheless worked to add to the nation's nuclear stockpile as a deterrence to all-out war. In the meantime, civil defense programs provided protection against radioactive fallout in the unlikely event of nuclear war.

Finally, the administration intended to work closely with the United Nations in keeping peace through collective security. *New York Times* writer David Halberstam characterized these young Kennedy people as the "best and the brightest," who truly believed themselves capable of changing the course of history.

In a special address to Congress in May 1961, the president declared that "the great battleground for the defense and expansion of freedom today is . . . Asia, Latin America, Africa and the Middle East, the lands of the rising peoples." To prevent the spread of communism into the Third World, the administration's foreign aid program encouraged the development of democratic nations through economic progress. Like his predecessor in the White House, Kennedy intended to channel the nationalist fervor of emerging nations into orderly societies capable of resisting leftist revolutions inspired by Communists. Modernization through U.S. aid became the means for converting potential revolutionary situations into evolutionary developments that would bring the domestic stability vital to elections and economic advance. Mao Zedong's explanation of his success in China struck Kennedy as correct: "Guerrillas are like fish, and the people are the water in which fish swim. If the temperature of the water is right, the fish will thrive and multiply."

The 1960s were a turbulent era at home and abroad, because events were intricately intertwined. Kennedy's activist foreign policy and his concern for halting communism carried his administration into an ill-fated venture in Cuba that colored his remaining days in office. In a tragic sense, the president tended to base his assessment of nearly every hot spot in the Cold War—Berlin, the Third World, and Southeast Asia, and particularly Vietnam—on his bitter experiences with Fidel Castro's Cuba beginning in early 1961.

Cuba and the Bay of Pigs

Kennedy's problems with Cuba were under way even before he became president. During the 1950s the United States, interested in maintaining economic and political stability in the Caribbean as conducive to trade and security, sold arms to Cuba's long-time dictatorial ruler Fulgencio Batista and furnished military advisers through the Mutual Security Program. But whereas the image of Cuba highlighted gambling casinos, tourism, and a general nightclub atmosphere, the reality was rampant corruption, Mafia domination, and unbridled prostitution. The overwhelming majority of islanders were poverty-stricken. The best lands belonged to American businesses, and the Havana government callously ignored the need for reform. Cuba was ready for revolution.

Fidel Castro, a young middle-class law school graduate, called for far-reaching reforms and with eighty followers initiated guerrilla operations against the government in 1956. Within two years his cohort had grown in number and strength, armed with weapons provided by Cubans in the United States. A coup seemed imminent, causing the United States to begin pulling away from Batista by cutting off his arms supply. In the ensuing popular revolution that became known as the "26th of July Movement," Castro forced Batista into exile the following January 1959. Within a week the Washington government extended recognition to the new regime, which had ensured democratic elections and freedom of speech and press. To many Americans, Castro became a highly romanticized revolutionary figure who had risen from the people to institute reform.

But by spring 1959 the enchantment had worn off as many suspected that Castro had been a Communist from the start. Their suppositions were probably wrong. It seems likely that Castro only used the weak Communist party on the island to further his own interests and that he might have converted to Marxist principles sometime after autumn 1960. The cardinal objective of the new regime was to push out the United States before making an effort to revive the Cuban economy. To bring changes to the island, Castro instituted an agrarian reform program and expropriated more than $1 billion worth of American holdings. Should there be doubt about his intentions, Castro boasted that "we will take and take, until not even the nails of their shoes are left." In the meantime thousands of Cubans fled to the United States: Democratic freedoms had not materialized in Cuba, and mock trials led to mass executions of Batista's followers. By summer 1959 Castro's need for a broader political base had driven him closer to the Communists on the island. CIA Director Allen Dulles warned President Eisenhower that "communists and other extreme radicals appear to have penetrated the Castro movement." Indeed, two Communists had joined his regime: Ernesto (Ché) Guevara and Raúl Castro, Fidel's brother. Washington could not shake the impression that Cuba threatened to become a propaganda center and training ground for promoting Communist revolutions throughout Latin America.

The United States became Castro's particular object of scorn because it had exploited the island for so long and because it protested the executions and granted asylum to refugees. The Washington administration responded by placing an embargo on nearly all of Cuba's goods and appealing for collective defensive action under the Rio Pact of 1947. But in August 1959, when the American foreign ministers met in Santiago, Chile, the United States failed to arouse full Latin American support against the alleged threat of communism in Cuba. Many leftists favored Castro, and numerous other Latin Americans simply enjoyed seeing the United States in an uncomfortable position. The meeting resulted in only a vague pronouncement against totalitarian rule that made no reference to Cuba.

Castro soon consorted openly with the Soviets, while intensifying his radio and television attacks on the United States. He demanded U.S. withdrawal from Guantánamo and gave the U.S. embassy in Havana forty-eight hours to reduce its three hundred-member staff to eleven. He called Eisenhower a "gangster" and a "senile White House golfer," extended

recognition to Communist China, and in February 1960 concluded a treaty with the Soviets by which Cuba agreed to exchange five million tons of sugar over the next five years for arms, oil, machinery, and technical advisers. In less than two years Cuba's trade with Soviet-controlled countries grew from two percent to eighty percent of its total commerce. Khrushchev bragged of his new Communist brother and warned that he would rain rockets on the United States if it interfered in Cuban affairs. Although he later claimed that the warning was only "symbolic," he pronounced the Monroe Doctrine dead and urged the United States to "bury it, just as you bury anything dead, so it will not poison the air."

By the end of the Eisenhower presidency, the United States had devised plans for Castro's overthrow. In March 1960 Eisenhower had approved a secret $13 million fund for the preparation of a small group of Cuban refugees to invade their homeland and stage a coup. The CIA, in accordance with the plan, began training 1400 Cuban exiles in Guatemala and Nicaragua. In August the American foreign ministers met in San José, Costa Rica, and criticized "extracontinental" intervention in the hemisphere, although they again did not refer to Cuba or suggest remedial measures. On January 3, 1961, the United States and Cuba broke diplomatic relations, leaving a legacy of trouble for the new president.

By the time Kennedy assumed office, Castro's regime had become synonymous with communism. The U.S. ambassador to Cuba, Philip Bonsal, attempted to downplay this fear. Although he opposed Castro, Bonsal attributed the dictator's Soviet leanings to the United States's unbending policies, not to communism. Castro's purpose, Bonsal later declared, "was radically and exclusively nationalistic; it became oriented toward dependence on the Soviet Union only when the United States, by its actions in the spring of 1960, gave the Russians no choice other than to come to Castro's rescue." Bonsal's reasoned assessment did not convince Washington. Kennedy had chastised the Republicans during

Castro and Khrushchev
A warm embrace at the UN in New York in late 1960.
Wide World Photos, New York.

the presidential campaign for allowing a "communist satellite" at "our very doorstep." Americans, he defiantly declared, would not be "pushed around any longer."

Kennedy had virtually announced his intention to rid the hemisphere of Castro's communism. Arkansas Senator J. William Fulbright, influential chair of the Foreign Relations Committee, assured Kennedy that the Castro regime was "a thorn in the flesh" and "not a dagger in the heart." Yet the new administration continued to treat the regime as a dire threat to U.S. prestige and security. Shortly after Kennedy's arrival in the White House, the CIA informed him of its invasion plans and insisted that the landing of Cuban exiles would set off a full-scale insurrection against Castro, just as an earlier coup had succeeded in Guatemala and erased another Communist menace. The CIA had already helped to establish a Cuban Revolutionary Council to take over the government after Castro's overthrow. The invasion point, Kennedy learned, was to be Cochinos Bay (Bay of Pigs), located on the southwest side of the island. D day was to be April 17, 1961.

At first Kennedy appeared hesitant about the invasion plan and approved it only as a "contingency" operation, subject to cancellation at any time. Such blatant interventionism bothered him: Not only would it raise widespread criticism both inside and outside the United States, but it might fail. And there would be no way, Kennedy realized, to deny complicity, whether direct or indirect in nature. Yet if the plan were successful, his administration would score an early victory in the Cold War and force the Soviets to sense the determination of the new leaders in Washington. Besides, the young president had become an advocate of the CIA as a result of his admiration for the fictional James Bond of Ian Fleming's best-selling spy thrillers. Had not the CIA in 1954 performed masterfully in Guatemala? asked Allen Dulles—without also noting that it had failed miserably four years later in Indonesia, when it attempted to bring down the suspected leftist-leaning regime of President Achmed Sukarno. Kennedy instructed Schlesinger to draft a White Paper justifying the U.S. decision to intervene in Cuba. The state department meanwhile published a pamphlet entitled "Cuba," which outlined Castro's broken promises and labeled his alleged Communist regime "a fateful challenge to the inter-American system." Without attempting to open negotiations with Castro and without consulting Congress, the Kennedy administration embarked on a dangerously uncharted course that had little assurance of success.

The secret plan was anything but secret. Rumors had spread that U.S. Marines were preparing Cuban exiles in Guatemala for an invasion of Cuba. Details were so widely known that two American reporters, working independently of each other, had written stories for national publication that were amazingly accurate. Their journals refrained from releasing them only after direct appeals from the White House. At a press conference less than a week before the invasion, Kennedy assured journalists of "no intervention in Cuba by United States armed forces."

Kennedy had told the truth, if only in a purely technical sense and to erect a basis for plausible denial: *U.S. armed forces did not intervene in Cuba.* About 1400 Cuban exiles, sixteen to sixty-one in age, poorly equipped, and largely inexperienced and untrained in military matters, set out by trucks from Guatemala to Nicaragua, where they boarded boats headed for the Bay of Pigs. Everything went wrong. A U.S. air strike on Cuba's air force two days before had not had the softening effect claimed by the CIA, and Kennedy's doubts about the expedition had become so deep that he called off the second air strike scheduled for the day of the invasion. When the landing party hit the beaches, 300 fell victim to Castro's tanks and soldiers, leaving the 1100 survivors no choice but to surrender. No general uprising had welcomed their arrival and, contrary to the CIA's earlier assurances, there were no mountains nearby for

refuge: The rag tag army had landed in a swamp. In an effort to save the remainder of the invasion force, the president authorized an airborne expedition that likewise failed because, incredibly, no one took into account the change in time zones when arranging the rendezvous of the rescue units. Most of the captives won their freedom nearly two years later, but, in a further humiliation, the United States had to pay more than $50 million in food and medicine as ransom. Castro's agents among the rebels had forewarned him of the attack, awarding his regime a phenomenal propaganda triumph at Kennedy's expense.

With his nation's prestige reeling badly, Kennedy accepted full blame for the Cuban disaster, recognizing that his greatest task now was to convince the Soviet Union that the Bay of Pigs episode was not a barometer of U.S. weakness. "How could I have been so stupid, to let them go ahead?" he moaned afterward. "All my life I've known better than to depend on the experts." Kennedy held the CIA and the Joint Chiefs of Staff responsible because of their careless planning and clumsy implementation of the operation. One can perhaps attribute part of the blame to his newness in office, and yet the fact remains that the idea of such an invasion was not alien to Kennedy's world view. The rub was the plan's inept execution by so-called intellectuals, exposing the youthful president to charges not only of failure but also of stupidity and weakness. In the biting words of Cyrus Sulzberger in the *New York Times,* "We looked like fools to our friends, rascals to our enemies, and incompetents to the rest." Latin Americans denounced Yankee imperialism and raised uncomfortable questions about whether this infamous action was consistent with the UN Charter and the principles of the OAS. "Fair Play for Cuba" rallies in the United States drew numerous Americans who blasted the administration for participating in such a zany scheme and sarcastically denounced the CIA as the "Cuban Invasion Authority." Most embarrassed was UN Ambassador Adlai Stevenson, who had not known of the impending attack and just

             Chapter 12

two days before had gone before member nations to deny rumors of an invasion.

The Kennedy administration was especially concerned about image. Even though the Soviets had in reality gained nothing on the United States, they publicly warned the White House to stay out of Cuban affairs, leaving the appearance that a dramatic shift was under way in the world balance of power. Attorney General Robert F. Kennedy recognized the danger. "We just could not sit and take it," he warned; the Soviets would consider Americans to be "paper tigers." White House adviser Walt Rostow tried to console the distraught president that "we would have ample opportunity to prove we were not paper tigers in Berlin, Southeast Asia, and elsewhere." In the minds of administration members, the Communist danger loomed larger than ever.

To restore faith in the United States, the president asserted that the nation's "restraint" was "not inexhaustible" and that it would continue to fight communism "in every corner of the globe." Responding to Khrushchev's warnings of war if the United States invaded Cuba, Kennedy insisted that *Americans* would determine the business of the hemisphere. "In the event of any military intervention by outside force we will immediately honor our obligations under the inter-American system to protect this hemisphere against external aggression." A few days later he told the American Society of Newspaper Editors that the United States's patience had limitations. "Should it ever appear that the inter-American doctrine of noninterference merely conceals or excuses a policy of non-action—if the nations of this hemisphere should fail to meet their commitments against outside Communist penetration—then I want it clearly understood that this Government will not hesitate in meeting its primary obligations, which are to the security of our Nation."

Cuba remained a major irritant to the Washington administration, because Castro used the Bay of Pigs fiasco as propaganda against the United States and swore to spread communism throughout the hemisphere. The White House tightened its economic restrictions on the island, continued to withhold recognition, criticized Castro through the U.S. Information Agency and other means, assisted his opponents in Miami, and, in a striking move, supported the CIA's plans for his assassination. Castro meanwhile proclaimed Cuba a "socialist" state under single-party control of the Popular Socialist (Communist) party. "I am a Marxist-Leninist and will be one until the day I die," he insisted over radio and television. Castro's professed socialism caused Colombia and Peru to assemble the American foreign ministers at Punta del Este, Uruguay, in late January 1962, where all delegations except Cuba's pronounced communism alien to the hemisphere and barred Cuba from the Inter-American Defense Board. Also by a large margin, the ministers halted the arms trade with Cuba and secured its ouster from the OAS by the minimum two-thirds majority. Even then, these measures had little effect because they drew no support from the larger, more populated Latin American states of Argentina, Bolivia, Brazil, Chile, Ecuador, and Mexico. Chastised but not leashed, Castro continued to accept Soviet aid and repeated his promise to spread communism into all of Latin America.

The Third World

Kennedy's ordeal with Cuba deeply affected his administration's policies toward the Third World. To prevent other Castrolike revolutions, the president deemed it necessary to control the nationalist energies of these emerging peoples by emphasizing calm, orderly development through U.S. aid and advice. Washington's policymakers continued to believe that the Third World's peculiar susceptibility to revolution furnished an invitation to communism. The remedy was an evolutionary nation-building process aimed at spreading democracy.

To bring stability to the new postwar nations, Kennedy had issued an executive order in March 1961 establishing the Peace Corps, which sent Americans to Latin America and Africa to aid in social and economic development. In the autumn, after the Bay of Pigs episode, Congress approved a bill giving the organization permanent standing. Within two years nearly 5000 Americans had joined the Peace Corps, working as teachers, doctors, and agricultural and technical advisers to bring about flood control, irrigation, and general community development. The goal was to alleviate poverty through economic and social uplift and thereby reduce the attraction of communism, although few recipients converted to U.S. ideals in return.

In an even more ambitious attempt to combat growing unrest in Latin America, the Kennedy administration pushed through a social and economic program known as the Alliance for Progress. Based on the Act of Bogotá of 1960, the idea of a new aid program first appeared in the president's inaugural address. To Latin American diplomats meeting in the White House, Kennedy praised the hemisphere's revolutions for independence and then asserted that the work was not over: "For one unfulfilled task is to demonstrate to the entire world that man's unsatisfied aspiration for economic progress and social justice can best be achieved by free men working within a framework of democratic institutions." In August 1961, Secretary of the Treasury Douglas Dillon told an Inter-American Economic and Social Conference at Punta del Este that nearly $20 billion of assistance was necessary over the next decade. The money would come from the United States, Europe, and Japan, although his government agreed to provide a major share of the funds. The resulting Charter of Punta del Este established the Alliance for Progress, whose purpose, according to the accompanying Declaration to the Peoples of America, was "to bring a better life to all the peoples of the Continent."

Despite high hopes and considerable publicity, the Alliance for Progress never fulfilled expectations. Within two years the United States had furnished nearly $2 billion for improvements, and yet the program did not

achieve the desired economic changes in Latin America. Several considerations account for this failure. Private investors in the United States were afraid of the certain disorder emanating from a program that encouraged such sweeping social and economic changes. Latin American landowners held authority and resisted land reforms, and the rest of the people resented U.S. intervention under any name. The region lacked the skilled workers needed to carry out the program, and the Alliance funds never reached those in need because of bureaucratic inertia in Washington and the overweening tendency of Latin Americans in power to keep the money for themselves. In addition, few Roman Catholics in Latin America were willing to adopt birth-control practices; indeed, they were encouraged to promote large families by exorbitant infant mortality rates and by leaders who insisted that the United States sought a reduction in family size as part of its devious effort to maintain control over the region. Within the decade of its mandated existence, the Alliance for Progress had virtually died out as military coups continued and political democracy remained elusive.

The Congo (now Zaire) in central Africa also raised apprehension in the Kennedy administration that the region was a potential breeding ground for communism. As the largest African state, the Congo's political direction would undoubtedly influence others on the continent. Under the threat of racial violence, Belgium had granted independence to the colony in June 1960, but civil war had broken out, and Moise Tshombe, an anti-Communist backed by Belgian mining interests, led the mineral-rich southern province of Katanga (gold, diamonds, uranium) in a separatist movement. The United States supported a UN Security Council decision to send peacekeeping forces to the Congo, but it did not favor Katanga's return to the central government. The Congo's premier, the staunchly nationalist Patrice Lumumba, bitterly opposed the UN action as a conspiracy against him and appealed to the Soviet Union for help. CIA Director Allen Dulles disgustedly referred to Lumumba as "a Castro, or worse" and won White House approval to engineer Lumumba's demise. In September 1960 Congolese President Joseph Kasavubu, regarded as conservative and pro-American, overthrew Lumumba and ordered the Soviets out of the country.

When Kennedy became president, he infuriated the Belgians by calling for a "middle-of-the-road government" in the Congo. To avert a Soviet-American confrontation, he added, the United Nations must maintain order through a trusteeship until the Congolese could administer the government. In January 1961 Lumumba was assassinated by Katangan authorities who were, according to some writers, encouraged by CIA operatives acting under past orders of former President Eisenhower. Less than six months later a moderate was elected premier and received U.S. support in his attempt to reunify the country. When continued efforts failed, the United Nations reversed its stance and authorized its forces to put down the government's opposition. They succeeded and in 1963 restored Katanga (now Shaba) to the Congo. Although problems persisted for two more years, Americans interpreted the Congo's reunification as a victory over communism, ignoring the probability that supporters of nationalism were the chief victims of their actions. The results of such alienation threatened to have serious ramifications in the United Nations, where by spring 1963 the Afro-Asian nations comprised the majority.

Berlin

The reverberations from the Bay of Pigs failure became evident during the first summit meeting between Kennedy and Khrushchev, held at Vienna in June 1961. The announced purposes of the tense two-day gathering were to discuss a nuclear test ban treaty and growing problems in Berlin and Laos, but the conference provided a grim opportunity for each leader to exchange caustic remarks designed to assess the will of the other. Except for Khrushchev's agreement to seek a negotiated set-

tlement in Laos, neither man retreated on any issue. After the Soviet premier suggested that the United States had exposed a basic weakness by refusing to launch a military invasion of Cuba, he suddenly announced an ultimatum on Berlin that resurrected the crisis of 1958. Berlin should be a "free city," Khrushchev declared. If Western occupation did not terminate within six months, his government would sign a separate peace with the East Germans, forcing the West to negotiate with them for continued access to West Berlin. Kennedy was determined to show strength, although newsreels and cameras revealed a nervousness that stood in sharp contrast to Khrushchev's calm and paternalistic bearing. The president realized that he had lost the battle at Vienna, but he made clear that he was not about to lose the war. "If Khrushchev wants to rub my nose in the dirt," Kennedy angrily declared, "it's all over."

By mid-July the Berlin issue had stirred up a war scare in the United States as the Kennedy administration took a hard-line position that outdid the measured response of his predecessor in 1958. The president insisted that his country, along with Britain and France, had "a fundamental political and moral obligation" to West Berlin. Any action endangering the city "would have the gravest effects upon international peace and security and endanger the lives and well-being of millions of people." Over television he proclaimed that "we cannot and will not permit the Communists to drive us out of Berlin, either gradually or by force." Americans "do not want to fight, but we have fought before."

Whereas Eisenhower had rejected any thought of expanding U.S. military strength in preparation for a ground war in Europe, Kennedy seemed willing to take such a hard step. He activated 250,000 reserves, asked Congress to expand the country's military forces by twenty-five percent, and aroused fears of a nuclear holocaust by calling for a nationwide civil defense program based on fallout shelters in case of attack. Congress approved the president's requests and added 45,000 troops for assignment to Europe. Meanwhile France and West Germany bolstered their numbers in NATO. "If we don't meet our commitments in Berlin," Kennedy warned, "it will mean the destruction of NATO and a dangerous situation for the whole world. All Europe is at stake in West Berlin."

As escalation fed escalation during that tense summer of 1961, the Soviets in the nighttime hours of August 13 erected a twenty-eight-mile long barricade of barbed wire (later reinforced with concrete slabs) between East and West Berlin to stop the vast and ongoing exodus of East Berliners into the free section of the city. The effort succeeded. The influx of refugees into West Berlin came to a sudden halt, but for the first time the Cold War had a visible symbol of totalitarianism that the United States could advertise to the world. Whereas the "iron curtain" was abstract and arguable in terms of actual existence, the Berlin Wall was physical and irrefutable. In a real sense, the United States could claim a victory in the Cold War: The very construction of the wall signified the Soviets' admission to Western control over West Berlin. The city, it appeared, would follow the path of Germany itself by becoming permanently divided. During the first trying moments of this new crisis in Germany, the United States ordered more soldiers through the East German passageway that led into West Berlin.

At the end of August, Khrushchev raised the ante by announcing an end to the three-year moratorium on nuclear tests in the atmosphere, a decision that ultimately led to the Soviets' explosion of a weapon 3000 times more powerful than the bomb dropped over Hiroshima. Although the United States still had a far superior delivery capability, the impression was that the Soviets had surged ahead in nuclear capacity. Kennedy, under enormous pressure to resume testing, finally agreed to underground tests in September 1961 and in the following April extended them to the atmosphere.

Berlin Wall
Construction of the Berlin Wall around the Brandenburg Gate, November 20, 1961.
U.S. Army.

As in 1958, however, neither nation wanted war, and the problems over Berlin did not graduate beyond mere rhetoric and shows of force. According to some reports, the president had learned from a spy, Soviet Colonel Oleg Penkovsky, that the Soviets lacked the nuclear strength claimed by Khrushchev, allowing the White House to take a strong stand on Berlin without fear of a holocaust. If so, the crisis nonetheless conjured up widespread apprehension of such a terrible outcome. The wall's construction had caused a war scare, even though neither antagonist sought a conflict. The United States was reluctant to fight over East Berlin, particularly when the wall constituted a visible Soviet manifestation of repressive tactics that furnished the Free World a superb source of propaganda. Kennedy defused the taut situation by asking for a negotiated settlement, which in turn suggested his willingness to forgo serious efforts to reunify Germany. Although the tension eased, Kennedy's offer to negotiate over Berlin further weakened NATO's unity by upsetting both Charles de Gaulle in France and Konrad Adenauer in West Germany. As for the Soviets, the December deadline set by Khrushchev (as during the Eisenhower administration) came and passed without incident.

The Cuban Missile Crisis

The long-feared Soviet-American showdown came not in Berlin but in Kennedy's own personal nemesis of Cuba. In 1962 Khrushchev made a stunning move: He arranged the construction of missile sites to test the Kennedy administration's resolve while protecting the island against an expected U.S. invasion. Doubtless encouraged by the president's apparent lack of fortitude in the Bay of Pigs, Vienna, and Berlin, the Soviet premier calculated that any leverage gained in Cuba could set examples for allies of both the United States and Soviet Union, force concessions in Berlin and elsewhere, and salvage his own tenuous position in Moscow. Khrushchev was under fire at

home because of his failing economic programs and his calls for "peaceful coexistence," which seemed to abdicate Communist leadership to the Chinese. Indeed, he could achieve the impression of nuclear parity with the United States (although the United States had a 17 to 1 advantage in atomic weaponry) by placing missiles within the Western Hemisphere. The United States had missiles in Turkey, he groused, and the presence of Soviet missiles in Cuba would now show Americans "what it feels like to have enemy missiles pointing at you." Even though Khrushchev later insisted that his paramount purpose had been to defend his Cuban ally against an imminent U.S. assault, this objective was probably only part of a broader program designed to regain prestige at home while establishing a strategic balance of power in foreign affairs that would permit a favorable settlement in Germany and encourage a move toward a nuclear test ban treaty.

Khrushchev's concern about the welfare of his Caribbean comrade was not groundless: The president seemed obsessed with toppling the Cuban dictator. Kennedy had condoned a trade embargo early in 1962 and had secured Cuba's ban from the OAS. U.S. Marines were on secret maneuvers in the Caribbean that April, training to free an island from a mythical ruler called "Ortsac"—Castro spelled backward. But even more far-reaching in purpose and ramifications was the president's earlier approval of "Operation Mongoose," a CIA-sponsored covert operation supported by a $50 million annual budget. Guided by his brother, the attorney general, Operation Mongoose sought to bring down Castro by spreading propaganda, running paramilitary operations, sabotaging the economy by burning cane fields and blowing up department stores, oil tanks, and factories, contaminating Cuban sugar headed for the Soviet Union, and, finally, assassinating Castro. Indeed, the CIA attempted five times to work with the criminal underworld in securing a "hit" on the Cuban leader. Failing that unorthodox effort, the CIA concocted several other wild

U-2 Photo of Cuban Missile Site
One of the aerial surveillance pictures that helped to set off the "thirteen days" of the Cuban missile crisis that threatened nuclear war between the United States and the Soviet Union. *CIA.*

schemes that included using poison pens, pills, cigars, and needles, implanting explosives in Castro's cigars, placing an ingredient in his shoes that would make his beard fall out, and, using Edward Lansdale of "psywar" fame in Vietnam, convincing the Cuban peasants of the imminent Second Coming of Christ by lighting up the night sky from incendiaries launched by submarines while driving home the allegation that the Lord was not pleased with their leader in Havana and wanted his immediate overthrow.

The Cuban missile crisis had its origins in July 1962, when American U-2 flights detected a growing number of Soviet ships in the island's waters. Refugees from Cuba and secret agents from the United States had also noted what might have been missile sites under construction. Furthermore, an extraordinary Soviet

troop buildup seemed to be under way on the island, which was years later determined to have included 42,000 troops and a number of armed short-range nuclear missiles. In August, U-2 reconnaissance discovered the construction of a missile site, but the director of the CIA, John McCone, was out of touch on a French Riviera honeymoon and could not authenticate the findings. Finally, someone in the CIA leaked the information to a reporter for the *Buffalo Evening News,* who failed to convert disbelievers with his published account of late August. The following month the president, who was then more concerned about problems in Europe and Southeast Asia, repeatedly assured the press that there was no evidence that the Soviets were establishing offensive military installations in Cuba. But in early October, U-2 commanders were under orders to photograph western Cuba, and by the middle of the month they had located missile sites close to San Cristóbal. The pictures revealed over forty IL-28 [Ilyshin-28] light bombers (capable of carrying nuclear payloads), the same number of strategic missiles, and nine missile sites in preparation. There was no sign of nuclear warheads, although evidence later showed that twenty of the planned forty warheads were already on the island and that the balance was en route by sea. The United States's early warning systems against air attacks lay in the distant Arctic north, leaving the southern part of North America dangerously exposed. The crucial point was that missiles fired from Cuba could reach Washington within eight minutes, considerably faster than the near half hour required when launched from the Soviet Union.

President Kennedy, then on the campaign trail, learned of these startling developments on October 16. Within the next few days he raised the matter of the Soviet military buildup in Cuba (but not the missiles) in meetings with Soviet Foreign Minister Andrei Gromyko and Soviet Ambassador Anatoly Dobrynin. Neither man, however, knew of the Kremlin's missile plans on the island and assured the president that the military additions were for defensive purposes only. Kennedy had not yet settled on a course of action regarding the missiles and decided against confronting either Soviet official with the photographs.

Thus, the most serious legacy of the Bay of Pigs fiasco became the supreme test of will during the ensuing Cuban missile crisis of October 1962. To deal with the problem, Kennedy established an Executive Committee of the National Security Council ("Ex Comm"), which met in an adjunct office of the state department to avoid press detection. Ex Comm included current administration figures along with some from the Truman presidency. Rusk chaired the proceedings, although he encouraged free discussion. President Kennedy avoided the meetings as much as possible to promote an open interchange of ideas among a varied group of individuals that included his brother, McNamara, national security affairs adviser McGeorge Bundy, the chair of the Joint Chiefs of Staff, General Maxwell Taylor, Air Force Chief Curtis LeMay, speechwriter Theodore Sorensen, former Secretary of State Dean Acheson, and, intermittently, UN Ambassador Adlai Stevenson.

During an emotion-packed week in October, Ex Comm met almost continuously to discuss Soviet motives for placing the missiles in Cuba and to decide how to resolve the crisis. Khrushchev, the committee members surmised, could not have expected to keep the weapons installation a secret. He was surely aware of the U-2 flights over Cuba, and yet he made no effort to conceal the arrival of Soviet ships and soldiers, along with the construction of missile sites. The placement of missiles in Cuba might not have actually changed the world power balance, Sorensen noted, but they would have forced an alteration "*in appearance;* and in matters of national will and world leadership, as the President [himself] said later, such appearances contribute to reality." The Soviets would leave the impression that they were supporting an ally against invasion, blunting the Communist Chinese claim that Khrushchev was reluctant to support "liberation" movements. At the same time, the missiles' presence in Cuba would damage U.S. prestige by raising questions about the nation's military power. One truth was certain: The United States could not allow the missiles to remain in Cuba. "The 1930s," President Kennedy observed, "taught us a clear lesson: aggressive conduct, if allowed to go unchecked and unchallenged, ultimately leads to war."

Ex Comm's discussions of the missile crisis were free and open, as Robert F. Kennedy's memoir *The Thirteen Days* dramatically attests. Its members were uncertain about Soviet motives but considered them dangerously provocative. Some believed that Khrushchev sought leverage to force the West out of Berlin; others thought he wanted the United States to remove its Jupiter missiles from Turkey. The latter suggestion brought a sharp reaction from the president. Kennedy recog-

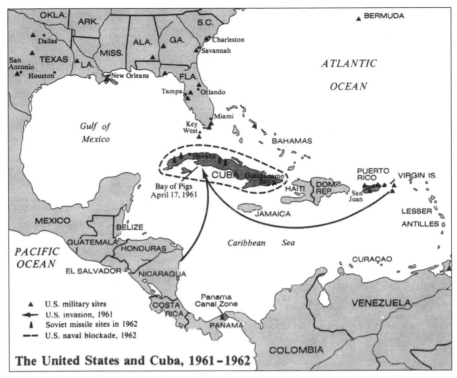

Map 24
Cuba became the center of the Cold War early in the Kennedy administration. After
the United States failed to achieve the overthrow of Castro, it went to the brink of
nuclear war after the Soviet Union implanted missile sites on the island.

nized that those missiles were outmoded and
had earlier called for their removal, but he
now realized that his directive had not yet
been implemented and that keeping them in
place was now more important to Turkey's
morale than to its defense. Furthermore,
under the 1959 agreement that authorized
the missiles' installation, the Turks owned the
missiles and the Americans, the nuclear warheads. Any attempt to remove the missiles
would inflict domestic political damage on the
Turkish government while drawing negative
reactions from other NATO members. And
now, the president could not remove the missiles without some suitable trade because to do
so would take on the appearance of capitulation. Khrushchev, several Ex Comm members
believed, did not seek a nuclear showdown,
but as the president and his brother realized

late one night, war could come through whim
or miscalculation.

After considerable debate, Ex Comm finally
focused on two options for the president: to
prevent the arrival of nuclear warheads by ordering an immediate air strike against the missile sites (promoted by Acheson and the Joint
Chiefs of Staff) or to prevent their arrival by
establishing a blockade of the island (advocated by Undersecretary of State George Ball).
At one point the joint chiefs called for an all-
out invasion to rid the hemisphere of both the
missiles and Castro. Opponents countered that
this measure would lead to a lengthy and costly
war with Cuba, leaving the Soviets free to take
Berlin. Suggestions for arranging private talks
with Castro or turning over the matter to the
United Nations led to staunch opposition,
as did Stevenson's recommendation that in

exchange for withdrawing the missiles, the United States should pull its missiles from Turkey and Italy and give up its naval base in Guantánamo. General LeMay argued that the Soviets would do nothing if the United States bombed their missile sites in Cuba. The president strongly disagreed. To a friend he tersely remarked, "Can you imagine LeMay saying a thing like that? These brass hats have one great advantage in their favor. If we listen to them, and do what they want us to do, none of us will be alive to tell them later they were wrong." The U.S. Air Force admitted that it could not ensure total destruction through air strikes and warned that the missiles left undamaged would be capable of hitting the United States. The air force also allowed that bombings might kill Soviet nationals and lead to full-scale war. Ball was leery of the air force's ability to carry out a "surgical air strike." Its questionable performance in World War II, he observed, suggested that the outcome in Cuba might be similar to that of a surgeon who intended to remove an appendix but took out the kidneys and lungs instead. "My brother is not going to be the Tojo of the 1960s," the attorney general asserted in clinching the argument for a blockade.

Ex Comm actually decided on a "quarantine" of Cuba, which would deny the island arms and supplies while, as McNamara argued, leaving the administration some flexibility either to escalate or mitigate the situation. Robert F. Kennedy and others had recommended using the term "quarantine" rather than "blockade" to avoid the international language of war, although some warned that in either case the Soviets could retaliate by shutting off Berlin without removing the missiles from Cuba. Proponents of the quarantine pointed out that Article 51 of the UN Charter permitted the use of force in "self-defense if an armed attack occurs" and argued that the installation of missiles was tantamount to an attack. The United States had to move quickly and alone. Attempts to work through either the United Nations or the OAS would lead to interminable delays, although the United States kept its allies informed and won their support along with that of the OAS and the Third World. De Gaulle was disgruntled about being informed rather than consulted, but he joined others in realizing that missiles aimed at the United States could also be turned toward Western Europe.

While U.S. air, land, and naval forces prepared for action, President Kennedy appeared over nationwide television on the evening of October 22, 1962, to deliver a chilling address on the crisis in Cuba. Kennedy's knowledge of the Soviets' nuclear capabilities rested heavily on pilfered information provided by the spy Penkovsky, who was in Soviet military intelligence and was soon thereafter arrested and executed. Indeed, Richard Helms of the CIA declared that Penkovsky's microfilmed materials from the Soviet Defense Ministry allowed the president to resist the pressure for an air strike because the CIA was able to tell him that "this is what we've got here and it will take them X days to be ready to fire." Thus assured of a few days of maneuverability, Kennedy first outlined to Americans the revelations of the past few days and declared that the Soviet Union's purpose in planting missiles in Cuba was "none other than to provide a nuclear strike capability against the Western Hemisphere." The missiles already there could hit Washington, Cape Canaveral, and the Panama Canal, and others under construction could reach as far north as Hudson's Bay and as far south as Lima, Peru. Such aggressive Soviet action came under the "cloak of secrecy and deception" and constituted "an explicit threat to the peace and security of the Americas." The United States therefore would "regard any nuclear missile launched from Cuba against any nation in the Western Hemisphere as an attack by the Soviet Union on the United States requiring a full retaliatory response upon the Soviet Union." He called on Khrushchev to "halt and eliminate this clandestine, reckless and provocative threat to world peace and to stable relations between our two nations." To encourage the premier to reverse his dangerous policy, the United States would establish "a strict quarantine on all offensive military equipment under shipment to Cuba," effective on the morning of October 24.

The United States adopted other measures as well. It reinforced Guantánamo, evacuated dependents of military personnel, and requested public declarations of support from the OAS and the United Nations. President Kennedy meanwhile approved the state department's plans to draw up a blueprint for civil rule over the island in the event of occupation. In the United Nations, Stevenson dramatically confronted Soviet Ambassador Valerian Zorin (who, like Dobrynin, knew nothing of the missiles) with giant photographs of the missile sites, challenging him to work toward a settlement before nuclear war developed. While nearly two hundred U.S. ships in the Caribbean prepared to enforce the quarantine, 7000 additional U.S. Marines went to Guantánamo, and the Strategic Air Command for the first time went into full-war readiness. Hundreds of huge B-52s were airborne, each carrying nuclear bombs.

The greatest concern, of course, was whether the Soviets already had nuclear warheads in Cuba and, if so, that some officer on the island could order their use. To the press shortly after the president's speech, McNamara somberly noted that nuclear warheads were "of such a size that it is extremely unlikely we would ever be able to observe them by the intelligence means open to us." But he thought it "almost inconceivable" that the Soviets would send missiles without warheads. The following day the CIA told Kennedy that even though it could not confirm the presence of warheads, U-2 photos had detected the construction of buildings near the missile sites that probably were meant for nuclear storage. One day later the CIA noted that the Soviets were building such storage sites at the rate of one per missile regiment. There was another, more immediate danger that the White House recognized. The missiles, it now seems clear, had no "permissive-action-link" (PAL) device, a safety measure instituted by the United States to guarantee that only the president could authorize the firing of nuclear warheads. Years afterward McNamara remembered his concern in 1962 that "some second lieutenant could start a nuclear war."

The minutes ticked by loudly during the following days. The day after the president's television appearance, the OAS Council met with Rusk and voted nearly unanimous support for a resolution urging "the immediate dismantling and withdrawal from Cuba of all missiles and other weapons with any offensive capability." It also called on member states to use any means necessary to stop a further missile buildup; the Rio Treaty of 1947, the Council pointed out, permitted assistance to any American state threatened by aggression. That same day the White House received a letter from Khrushchev asserting that the blockade was illegal. "The actions of [the] U.S.A. with regard to Cuba," he alleged, "are outright banditry or, if you like, the folly of degenerate imperialism." Kennedy, he charged, was pushing the nations into nuclear war.

October 24 loomed as the day of reckoning: Two Soviet ships, with a submarine between them, were approaching U.S. naval patrols in the Caribbean, only an hour away from Cuba. The U.S. aircraft carrier *Essex* prepared to contact the submarine by sonar and ask it to surface; upon refusal the U.S. captain was to employ small-scale depth charges to force it up. Robert F. Kennedy described his brother's tense waiting:

> His hand went up to his face and covered his mouth. He opened and closed his fist. His face seemed drawn, his eyes pained, almost gray. We stared at each other across the table. For a few fleeting seconds, it was almost as though no one else was there and he was no longer the President. Inexplicably, I thought of when he was ill and almost died; when he lost his child; when we learned that our oldest brother had been killed; of personal times of strain and hurt. The voices droned on.

The Soviet vessels suddenly stopped just shy of the quarantine line and turned back, a last-minute preemption of Khrushchev's order to run the blockade that resulted from the intervention of Anastas Mikoyan, the Soviet first deputy premier and second in command to the premier himself. Whether Mikoyan reversed the original decision on his own or somehow convinced Khrushchev to do so remains unclear. But either way, the October 24 confrontation at sea brought the two superpowers close to war.

Still the tension persisted, even while signs of an impending Soviet retreat became evident. UN Secretary-General U Thant called for negotiations, and Khrushchev sought a summit conference to resolve the question, but President Kennedy insisted that removal of the missiles had to come first. On October 26 Washington received encouraging news. A high official in the Soviet embassy informed the administration through ABC news correspondent John Scali that the Soviet Union would remove the missiles under UN auspices if the United States lifted the quarantine and guaranteed not to invade Cuba. That same Friday night Khrushchev sent a long, rambling letter offering similar conditions. "If you have not lost your self-control," he wrote the president, "we and you ought not to pull on the ends of the rope in which you have tied the knot of war." Insisting that he did not want war, Khrushchev appealed to Kennedy to "let us not only relax the forces pulling on the ends of the rope, let us take measures to untie that knot. We are ready for this."

Yet the conciliatory tone of these developments was puzzling because it did not coincide with other events. The FBI discovered the day afterward (October 27) that Soviet officials in New York City were destroying sensitive papers (a move signifying the possibility of war). A Soviet surface-to-air missile (SAM) shot down a U-2 over Cuba (later found to have resulted from a Soviet general in Cuba who violated orders), and no slowdown had occurred in the construction of the missile sites. Most ominous, a second note had arrived from Khrushchev, more belligerent than the first. The Soviets, asserted the premier, would pull their missiles from Cuba only if the United States withdrew its missiles from Turkey.

Khrushchev's second note threatened to heighten the crisis, because the White House responded with a virtual ultimatum to the Soviets. President Kennedy of course could not agree to Khrushchev's new proposal, but his brother and Sorensen followed the advice of others in suggesting a way out: Disregard the second letter and reply to the first with an ultimatum. On October 27 the president notified Khrushchev that in return for removing the missiles from Cuba, the United States would promise not to invade the island. The implication was clear: If the Soviets refused this offer, the United States would itself take out the missiles (and thousands of Soviet soldiers) with an air strike that would, in turn, have forced a military retaliation by the Kremlin. That same night, Robert F. Kennedy met privately with Dobrynin and assured him (a pledge approved beforehand by the president and several close advisers but unknown to many members of Ex Comm until publication of the attorney general's memoirs in 1969) that even though the president could not immediately remove the missiles from Turkey and Italy, he would do so shortly after the Cuban crisis had passed. If Khrushchev publicly divulged this offer, it would become null and void.

Another pivotal moment had presented itself. Would a Soviet refusal to accept this arrangement result in a nuclear confrontation? First, it seems clear now (although not clear then) that even though Khrushchev often engaged in adventurism, he certainly would not go to war when the opposition held an overwhelming logistic and atomic superiority. Second, evidence now suggests that had Dobrynin rejected the administration's terms, the president was prepared to make a concession designed to avert war: He would ask the United Nations to propose a withdrawal of the U.S. missiles from Turkey in exchange for the Soviet withdrawal of missiles from Cuba. Thus could the White House argue that the United Nations, not the United States, had made the explicit link between the missiles in Turkey and those in Cuba. But this step never became necessary. Dobrynin expressed satisfaction with the original terms and the next day made clear that the Soviet missiles would be withdrawn.

Thus, on Sunday, October 28, thirteen days after the first confirmation of missiles in Cuba, the crisis was over. Just two days before the United States would have launched an air strike, Khrushchev accepted Kennedy's assurance against an invasion of Cuba in exchange for the United Nations's on-site inspection of the withdrawal of Soviet missiles. As events would show, this verification never took place because of Castro's angry opposition, a stand that, in turn, released the United States from the pledge against invasion. Indeed, U.S. military forces remained on alert until November 20, when Castro at last approved the departure of the Soviet IL-28 bombers. Furthermore, Kennedy had conditioned his promise against invasion on the removal of "all offensive weapons" from Cuba and on Cuba's own pledge against committing "aggressive acts" in the hemisphere. Finally, recent documentation shows that the Soviets had nine short-range nuclear missiles specifically intended to stop a U.S. invasion of the island. Had the United States attempted such an operation, according to McNamara years afterward, there would have been "a ninety-nine percent probability" of nuclear war.

But these considerations now seem academic: The United States and the Soviet Union had narrowly averted the most serious threat to global peace since the period prior to World War II. Rusk later reminded Scali to "remember when you report this—that eyeball to eyeball, they blinked first." Rostow pointedly remarked that Khrushchev had relented only when "he felt the knife on his skin."

President Kennedy has received praise for courage under fire; and yet many critics have raised searching questions about whether he might have averted the Cuban missile crisis through careful diplomacy. Castro incisively remarked that "if the United States had not been bent on liquidating the Cuban revolution, there would not have been an October crisis." The Kennedy administration made no

effort to open discussions with the Castro regime before approving the disastrous course leading to the Bay of Pigs. Even had the invasion succeeded, it is doubtful that the certain unfavorable publicity surrounding U.S. involvement would have been worth the victory. Succeeding events do not substantiate the fear that Castro was spreading communism throughout Latin America. In fact, the critics insist, the aggressive actions of the Kennedy administration were largely responsible for the new wave of anti-Americanism in the southern half of the hemisphere. Kennedy's critics also note other diplomatic breakdowns in autumn 1962. Washington's leaders made no attempt to talk privately with Cuba before the October confrontation, despite this repeated suggestion during the Ex Comm meetings by two former ambassadors to the Soviet Union, Charles E. Bohlen and Llewellyn Thompson. As early as October 25 columnist Walter Lippmann wondered why the president, in his private meetings the week before with Gromyko and Dobrynin, did not reveal the U-2 photos and warn of public disclosure should the Soviets refuse to withdraw the missiles. Finally, the president's televised ultimatum virtually ruled out the chances for compromise.

The irony is that a presidential administration composed of what writer Theodore H. White termed "action intellectuals" was determined to change the course of events, and yet its members became themselves captives of those very events. The central force clouding the administration's foreign policy was the Bay of Pigs disaster: President Kennedy refused to sustain another loss of prestige. If he relied on Penkovsky's stolen information about the Soviets' weaknesses in nuclear capability, his decision to do so nevertheless rested on a risk-filled gamble that the information was accurate and up to date. Kennedy thus engaged in a policy of brinkmanship much more dangerous than that pursued by the Eisenhower administration during the 1950s. Khrushchev, too, had pursued the same hard-line tactics and had failed either to redress the nuclear balance of power or to break the stalemate over Berlin. Fortunately he chose to retreat. Economist John Kenneth Galbraith wrote afterward, "We were in luck, but success in a lottery is no argument for lotteries."

The Cuban missile crisis constituted the most dangerous series of events in the Cold War, and for that reason both powers took steps designed to avoid another direct confrontation. To reduce the chances of miscalculation, President Kennedy installed a "hot line," which was a private teletype directly connecting the White House and the Kremlin. He also worked toward an arms limitations agreement with the Soviet Union. To weaken Castro's rule, the United States banned travel to Cuba and prohibited international monetary exchange; the Soviets countered these efforts by increasing aid to Cuba. Despite Kennedy's directive against boasting of a U.S. victory in the missile crisis, the fact remained that the Soviet Union had suffered a heavy blow to its prestige. Khrushchev had foolishly challenged the United States in an area vital to its security and where it held conventional military superiority. One Soviet official eerily commented, "Never will we be caught like this again."

The missile crisis had severe repercussions. It exposed the Soviet Union's nuclear inferiority and led to a program of Soviet military expansion, contributed to a change in its leadership that saw Khrushchev ousted from power in 1964, and encouraged the governments in both Moscow and Washington to turn toward indirect and less dangerous policies in the Third World. The Communist Chinese ridiculed Khrushchev's capitulation on Cuba, leading the Soviet premier to retort that if the United States was a "paper tiger" it had "nuclear teeth." The new premier, Alexei Kosygin, was less belligerent than his predecessor, making this an opportune moment for the United States to pursue détente, or a reduction of tensions, and at the same time exploit the growing Sino-Soviet rift. Cuba meanwhile remained a Soviet protectorate as nearly 17,000 Soviet soldiers and technicians stayed on the island. If the Monroe Doctrine

was not dead as Khrushchev had earlier remarked, it had suffered a near lethal blow.

Southeast Asia

While Cuba monopolized the attention of the Kennedy administration, concurrent problems in Laos and Vietnam continued to grow. Laos, a landlocked agricultural country, had become independent under the Geneva Accords of 1954 and soon assumed a neutral position in international affairs. Three years later, under Prince Souvanna Phouma, the nationalists had established a coalition regime composed of neutralists and a former wartime resistance group, now Communist, known as the Pathet Lao ("Lao nation"). The Eisenhower administration countered with military assistance to the rightist Laotian army, which was concentrated in the towns, but the money did little to improve its performance in the field and in fact contributed to the country's inflated economy and widespread graft. Yet there had seemed no choice. Eisenhower wrote in his memoirs, "the fall of Laos to Communism would mean the subsequent fall—like a tumbling row of dominoes—of its still-free neighbors, Cambodia and South Vietnam and, in all probability, Thailand and Burma. Such a chain of events would open the way to Communist seizure of all Southeast Asia." Eisenhower had considered the Laotian problem so serious that he did not even mention Vietnam to President-elect Kennedy during the transition briefing of January 19, 1961.

Subterfuge and intrigue permeated the troubles in Laos. In 1958 the CIA worked with rightists in bringing down Phouma and installing a pro-American government clear of Pathet Lao representation. U.S. military advisers soon arrived to stabilize the new government, but trouble continued. The Laotian government asked the United Nations for help, and the situation calmed when the Security Council sent a team of inquiry. In August 1960 Phouma and the Pathet Lao regained control and soon received Soviet and North Vietnamese aid. But Phouma's regime collapsed again, forcing him to flee to Cambodia. Phouma later lamented, "The Americans say I am a Communist. All this is heartbreaking. How can they think I am a Communist? I am looking for a way to keep Laos non-Communist."

The Kennedy administration was also concerned that problems in Laos would spill into surrounding countries and spread communism throughout Southeast Asia. Guerrilla activities had intensified in both Laos and Vietnam by spring 1961, causing White House adviser Walt Rostow to urge the president to use counterinsurgency measures in restoring stability. In line with previous policy, Kennedy attributed Laos's problems to the Communists and supported the rightist regime as the basis of "a neutral and independent Laos." He stationed the Seventh Fleet in the South China Sea, had five hundred U.S. Marines helicoptered into Thailand, and ordered U.S. soldiers to Okinawa to be ready for action.

The Cuban fiasco had influenced the president's thinking on Southeast Asia, making him more cautious than he might otherwise have been about intervening in Laos. "I just don't think we ought to get involved," Kennedy told Nixon, "particularly where we might find ourselves fighting millions of Chinese troops in the jungles." Furthermore, he could not justify taking action in Laos, which was thousands of miles away, when he had not done so in Cuba, only ninety miles from American shores. The president, however, could not appear weak in Laos while undergoing the bitter criticisms arising from the Bay of Pigs episode. He made a show of force by ordering several hundred U.S. military advisers in Laos to don military uniforms. That same month of April, the Soviet Union supported the president's call for a cease-fire. But the Pathet Lao refused to follow the Soviet lead. Kennedy asked the Joint Chiefs of Staff if U.S. combat soldiers could deliver a victory in Laos. Although most of the commanders were skeptical, the chair, General Lyman Lemnitzer, argued that "if we are given the right to use nuclear weapons, we can guarantee victory." When

Ngo Dinh Diem
South Vietnamese President Diem reviews Air Force officers shortly after two pilots assaulted the presidential palace in February 1962.
National Archives, Washington, D.C.

someone asked what that "victory" would entail, Kennedy called the meeting to a close.

In May 1961 fourteen governments gathered in Geneva to devise a solution to the Laotian problem. Arguments focused on the guidelines for a coalition government composed of the three dissident groups—the neutralists, rightists, and leftists. The conference took place against a background of trouble, because the Pathet Lao was close to forcing the rightists out of Laos and into the neighboring country of Thailand. A believed Communist drive in Thailand prompted the United States to dispatch the first contingent of 5000 marines. They joined combat troops from Britain, Australia, and New Zealand, all under the auspices of the SEATO Treaty of 1954.

The rising tensions encouraged the delegations in Geneva to reach an agreement in June 1962, more than a year after they had convened. According to terms, Laos would be neutral and could enter no military pacts and house no foreign military bases. Its government would be a coalition of neutralists, rightists, and leftists, with Phouma as premier. The situation was not auspicious. The Pathet Lao held two-thirds of the country and was armed with Soviet weapons; the Kennedy administration continued to send military materiel to the rightists, justifying the aid on the basis of a believed North Vietnamese infiltration of upper Laos.

Then a strange mixture of events took place: The Kennedy administration's decision to negotiate over Laos seemed to combine with the embarrassment of the Bay of Pigs fiasco to transform Vietnam into a symbol of the U.S. stand against communism. "At this point we are like the Harlem Globetrotters," Bundy remarked, "passing forward, behind, sidewise, and underneath. But nobody has made a basket yet." Elections had not taken place in Vietnam in 1956, as stipulated in the Geneva Accords of 1954, partly because the Eisenhower administration had been reluctant, but also because, as the North Vietnamese Communists later asserted, Communist China had been willing to accept a divided Vietnam and had cut off military aid to the Hanoi government to ensure compliance. In either case, a succession of terrorist activities had transpired in the south during the late 1950s that Americans thought Communist-instigated. The United States, it appeared, was about to undergo another test of will.

Controversy still exists over the ensuing troubles in Vietnam. Were they due more to Diem's repressive regime than to alleged North Vietnamese aggression? Part of the confusion was attributable to the Kennedy administration's inconsistent policies. The state department implied that South Vietnam was a separate nation (contrary to the Geneva Accords of 1954) when it recommended U.S. aid to counter the believed threat from outside forces (in line with the same Geneva agreements). Several French and U.S. writers, however, called it a local rebellion against

Diem that the Hanoi government indeed aided by 1960, but only after Ho Chi Minh's former Vietminh forces in the south sought his assistance against U.S. intervention in Vietnamese domestic affairs.

The U.S. interpretation of the conflict in Vietnam was vital in justifying assistance to the south, because under the SEATO Treaty the White House had guaranteed the Senate that it would not become involved in the domestic troubles of Southeast Asian nations. If the North Vietnamese had intervened in the south as either Beijing's or Moscow's agent, of course, such action would have constituted a threat from the outside. Rusk was convinced of this. Reflecting the Munich mentality and acknowledging the dangers of appeasement, he argued that Communist China had incited the war in Vietnam as part of its effort to control all of Asia. Thus, according to this stance, Diem's Army of the Republic of Vietnam (ARVN) had become locked in a guerrilla war with the Chinese-assisted Vietcong (Vietnamese Communists), who in December 1960 became the military arm of the National Liberation Front (NLF) in South Vietnam and had gained control over nearly all rural areas. The primary threat was therefore external, requiring the United States to honor its assumed SEATO obligations. A recently published history of the war by the People's Army of Vietnam tends to support the administration's case. It asserts that Hanoi's leaders played an earlier and important part in promoting the Vietcong's military development in the south. Even then, the Hanoi government claimed that it was helping fellow Vietnamese in a civil war that did not concern the United States. This was the heightened military activity in the south that Kennedy faced when he became president in 1961.

By early 1961 the Kennedy administration was well under way toward making Vietnam a testing ground of the United States's will to combat communism. In May the president sent Vice President Lyndon B. Johnson on a fact-finding tour of Southeast Asia that focused on assuring Diem that negotiations over Laos did not imply the same approach to South Vietnam. If communism penetrated that region of the world, Johnson later reported to Kennedy, the United States would have to "surrender the Pacific and take up our defenses on our own shores." The United States had to protect "the forces of freedom in the area," even at the cost of deep commitment and great personal sacrifice. In fact, such involvement could lead to "the further decision of whether we commit major United States forces to the area or cut our losses and withdraw should our efforts fail." Johnson urged "a clear-cut and strong program of action" in behalf of Diem—whom the vice president praised in his effusive Texas manner as the "George Washington of Vietnam" and the "Winston Churchill of Southeast Asia." Though never explaining how Diem's collapse would automatically strip the United States of its Pacific bases and threaten national security, Johnson exuded a veritable Alamo mentality in warning of encirclement and insisting that the choice was either to "help these countries . . . or throw in the towel in the area and pull back our defenses to San Francisco and a 'Fortress America.'"

In response to Johnson's inquiry, Diem sought neither U.S. combat troops nor a bilateral treaty with the United States. Diem wanted more technical advisers and more U.S. aid, but not U.S. soldiers. He already felt too closely identified with Americans. North Vietnamese propaganda continually berated him for consorting with the United States and fostering what Hanoi derided as "American-Diem imperialism." That same month Kennedy sent another hundred military advisers and four hundred Green Berets to train the Vietnamese in counterinsurgency warfare. "If we can save Vietnam," Bundy declared, "we shall have demonstrated that the communist technique of guerrilla warfare can be dealt with."

Over the next few months, conflicting reports from Vietnam led the president to inquire deeper into the situation. Although Rusk and others argued that the south was in danger from the outside, U.S. intelligence agents in October 1961 claimed that nearly ninety percent of the 17,000 Vietcong in the south had come from South Vietnam itself. As the Joint Chiefs of Staff and the National Security Council considered sending combat troops, Kennedy dispatched two of his advisers to South Vietnam: Walt Rostow and General Maxwell Taylor. They returned with a dismal report. Although the South Vietnamese Army seemed incapable of taking the offensive, Diem still intended to maintain control over the grim military situation. Rostow called for U.S. bombings of North Vietnam and joined Taylor in recommending an 8000-person "logistic task force" of engineers, medical personnel, and infantry to assist the ARVN in closing North Vietnam's supply lines to the Vietcong in the south. The introduction of this thinly disguised combat unit, Taylor believed, would raise South Vietnamese morale by standing as a "visible symbol of the seriousness of American intentions." Indeed, these U.S. forces would provide an important source of military assistance if needed. To conceal their purpose, the Americans could arrive under the euphemistic title of a "flood control unit."

Kennedy, however, decided against sending combat forces to Vietnam, no matter what garb or title they wore. Such a provocative move, he feared, would jeopardize the negotiations over Laos and dangerously escalate the war in Vietnam. Besides, as Kennedy trenchantly remarked, "The troops will march in; the bands will play; the crowds will cheer; and in four days everyone will have forgotten. Then we will be told we have to send in more troops. It's like taking a drink," he declared. "The effect wears off, and you have to take another." Instead, Kennedy compromised between negotiations and combat troops by approving Diem's call for more advisers. Yet he realized that a further escalation might be necessary to save South Vietnam. By the end of 1961 over 3000 U.S. military advisers were in South Vietnam, more than triple the number there a year before.

In December 1961 the U.S. military presence in Vietnam became increasingly visible. A U.S. carrier brought in four single-engine training planes, more than thirty helicopters, and four hundred operations and maintenance personnel. Eventually minesweepers and reconnaissance planes would arrive. Meanwhile, the Green Berets trained the South Vietnamese in guerrilla warfare and worked with Diem in establishing a "strategic hamlet" program designed to undermine the Vietcong's war effort. According to its proponents, the purpose of the program (similar to the agrovilles tried during the 1950s) was to isolate the peasants by relocating them in bamboo stake encampments encircled by moats and soldiers, therefore denying the Vietcong any assistance, recruits, and places of refuge. Its greatest effects, however, were negative: The program failed to provide security along with promised medical, educational, and land reform benefits, and it tore peasants from their revered ancestral grounds and thereby allowed the Vietcong to assume the role of "liberators." The strategic hamlets nonetheless remained the heart of the counterinsurgency effort. Kennedy emphasized to Diem that "the campaign of force and terror now being waged against your people and your Government is supported and directed from the outside by the authorities at Hanoi." North Vietnam's actions had violated the Geneva Accords of 1954, the president explained, and the United States felt compelled to increase help to South Vietnam.

Despite optimistic reports, the Vietnamese situation continued to deteriorate. McNamara visited Vietnam in the summer of 1962 and declared that "every quantitative measurement we have shows we're winning this war." A few months later Rusk proclaimed that the war was coming to an end. Yet a Senate subcommittee had visited Southeast Asia and warned that a cut in U.S. aid would lead to domestic upheaval and the establishment of Chinese influence. The South Vietnamese, it appeared, could not win the war by themselves, although the subcommittee cautioned the administration against converting the conflict into "an American war, to be fought primarily with American lives." The United States, under

"present circumstances," had no interests in Vietnam that could justify such involvement.

In spring 1963 Diem's long-standing problems with the Buddhists erupted in a crisis that drew the United States ever deeper into South Vietnamese affairs. His Catholicism had long been a focal point of growing opposition from the Buddhists, who comprised more than eighty percent of the country's population. But then Diem stirred up a wave of angry protests by prohibiting the Buddhists from flying their religious flags in commemorating Buddha's birth, and in May the government's forces, armed with clubs and guns, turned on 10,000 protesters in the city of Hué, killing nine in the melee. The following month an elderly Buddhist monk protested the government's actions by having himself doused in gasoline and, as an American photographer and television crew recorded the grisly event (alerted beforehand by Buddhists), setting himself afire before horrified crowds in downtown Saigon. Madame Nhu, Diem's vitriolic sister-in-law, coldly dismissed such actions as "Buddhist barbecues." Her husband and Diem's closest confidant, Ngo Dinh Nhu, callously remarked that if more Buddhists wanted to immolate themselves he would gladly furnish the gasoline and matches. "Let them burn," Madame Nhu added, "and we shall clap our hands." Nationwide raids on Buddhist pagodas followed, engineered by Nhu, whose own private and U.S.-trained Special Forces (Can Lao, or Vietnamese Bureau of Investigation) disguised themselves in army apparel and destroyed religious shrines, ransacked the pagodas, killed anyone who resisted, and arrested more than 1400 Buddhists, including numerous children of Diem's own civil and military officials. Diem, as advised by Nhu, attributed the Buddhist unrest to the Vietcong. The United States, however, was already disenchanted with Diem's domestic failures and began to cut back assistance in an effort to force him into reform programs.

The Kennedy administration still opposed a direct military involvement in South Vietnam, but it had come to realize that Diem

The Buddhist Crisis
The self-immolation of a Buddhist monk in Saigon in June 1963
brought worldwide focus to Diem's problems and moved the United
States closer to government opposition elements in South Vietnam.
Wide World Photos, New York.

was not the solution to the problem but the problem itself. The president told CBS newsman Walter Cronkite: "In the final analysis, it is their war. They are the ones who have to win or lose it. We can help them, give them equipment, send our men out there as advisers, but they have to win it." On another occasion, Kennedy explained that "strongly in our mind is what happened in the case of China at the end of World War II, where China was lost. . . . We don't want that." Diem had not instituted democratic reforms in South Vietnam, as Americans had hoped. Indeed, nothing in his background suggested that he supported democracy. The "revolution" Diem envisioned called for the restoration of an imperial Vietnam that rested on his Chinese mandarin philosophy of personalist rule by a privileged and educated elite. Introverted, stubborn, cold, self-righteous, unlistening, unwilling to compromise, and devoid of charisma, Diem had aroused deep resentment by ending long-time elections in the villages, brutally repressing his opposition, exploiting the

strategic hamlet program to establish greater control over the peasants, engaging in rampant nepotism, and rejecting U.S. advice as interference in domestic affairs. "No wonder the Vietcong looked like Robin Hoods when they began to hit the hamlets," a U.S. civilian official commented.

The U.S. commitment became nearly irreversible in autumn 1963, when the Kennedy administration became identified with a conspiracy against Diem led by South Vietnamese Army generals. Dissatisfied officers, headed by General Duong Van Minh, notified the CIA in late August that Nhu intended to have them executed and then to negotiate away South Vietnam's independence by working out some sort of arrangement with Hanoi. They intended to overthrow Diem and wanted to know what the U.S. reaction would be. In a cable cleared with Kennedy, the state department instructed its newly arrived ambassador to Saigon, Henry Cabot Lodge, to persuade Diem to dismiss his brother Nhu from the regime. Should Diem refuse, the United States had to "face the possibility that Diem himself cannot be preserved." In that event, Lodge was to inform the generals that Diem no longer could count on U.S. aid and that they would receive "direct support in any interim period of breakdown of central government mechanism." Lodge was not to engage in the "active promotion of [a] coup" but "to identify and build contacts with possible alternative leadership as and when it appears." The cable found a receptive reader. Lodge had been appalled by the pagoda raids, and when Diem did not remove Nhu, the U.S. embassy dispatched a CIA agent to assure the generals of White House support if their scheme succeeded, but no assistance if it failed. The generals became uncertain about their prospects and called off the coup.

The next month was a confusing period for the Kennedy administration. McNamara wanted to investigate Diem's chances for winning the war and sent a mission of inquiry to South Vietnam led by General Victor Krulak of the defense department and state department official Joseph Mendenhall. But this effort only underlined the administration's dilemma. Krulak was optimistic about the war, Mendenhall was disenchanted with Diem, and Kennedy was frustrated with both emissaries. "You two did visit the same country, didn't you?" he asked with exasperation.

By late October the generals had revived their plot to overthrow Diem, and this time they went through with it. On November 1, 1963, again with the tacit approval of the Kennedy administration, they staged their coup, afterward killing both Diem and his brother Nhu. Suddenly the reality of the Vietnamese situation hit the White House. Upon learning of the murders of Diem and Nhu, Kennedy, according to Taylor, "leaped to his feet and rushed from the room with a look of shock and dismay on his face which I had never seen before."

After the coup the United States's promise of support now made it directly responsible for the welfare of the South Vietnamese government. The new regime in Saigon was civilian in form only. Power remained in the military, but the leaders promised elections and a free press, released political prisoners, and made much-needed changes in the war effort. When the United States extended recognition to the new government and restored full trade relations, the impression grew that it had been involved in the assassinations. The presence of nearly 17,000 U.S. military advisers and 8000 other Americans in South Vietnam seemed proof of a deepening commitment. Shortly after Diem's death the NLF in North Vietnam proposed negotiations with Saigon aimed at a cease-fire, to be followed by "free general elections" designed to establish a "national coalition government composed of representatives of all forces, parties, tendencies, and strata of the South Vietnamese people." Although some ARVN officials seemed interested, the United States opposed the offer. By November 1963 U.S. prestige was on the line: Both the successes and the failures of the South Vietnamese government now belonged to the United States.

Questions remain about the potential direction of the United States's Vietnam policy, had Kennedy not been assassinated that same November of 1963. Several signs suggest that he had matured in office because of the Cuban and Berlin war scares and would have worked for a more cooperative relationship with the Soviet Union that might have allowed a greatly reduced U.S. involvement in Vietnam. Indeed, the president had authorized the drafting of a plan that called for a phased withdrawal beginning in December 1963 and resulting by the end of 1965 in a return to the U.S. military levels of January 1961. He never advocated a total withdrawal, however. In one of his last press conferences, Kennedy asserted that "for us to withdraw from that effort would mean a collapse not only of South Vietnam but Southeast Asia. So we are going to stay there." Rusk, one of the president's most trusted confidants, insisted that during their many conversations Kennedy never discussed a withdrawal from Vietnam. Evidence suggests that the president was prepared to reduce the U.S. commitment to numbers that complied with the Geneva Accords of 1954 while training the ARVN to deal with the situation. He repeatedly resisted pressure from within his administration to send U.S. combat troops.

Whatever the outcome might have been, the fact was that the U.S. commitment had greatly expanded by the end of November 1963. Eisenhower's less than 1000 so-called advisers in Vietnam had grown to nearly 17,000 under Kennedy and included a large number of special forces who were steadily enlarging their role in the war while maintaining the fiction that they were only advising. Indeed, seventy-five Americans had died in combat by the end of 1963. Furthermore, the ARVN now had napalm and defoliants to go with all other types of war materiel coming regularly from the United States. And, most of all, the major share of the blame for the Diem coup had fallen on the White House, despite its insistence that the regime had self-destructed. The U.S. involvement in Vietnam was now much more extensive and volatile than when Kennedy came into office.

A Mixed Verdict

It remains unclear whether by late 1963 Kennedy had moved away from his initial foreign policy—built on challenge and response—and toward one emphasizing diplomacy and restraint. In June he delivered an address at American University, asserting that all peoples could live together peacefully and calling for disarmament and an end to the Cold War. And yet the nation's military arsenal had increased dramatically at every level during his brief presidency. Shortly after his June speech, in fact, the president tried to revive support for NATO, which had entered a state of decline largely because of Europe's fears brought on by the two superpowers' near clash over Cuba. Kennedy was especially worried that France would assert leadership on the continent, a concern justified by its recently developed nuclear device and an alliance with West Germany. De Gaulle had already blocked Britain's membership in the European Common Market because, he declared, "it would appear as a colossal Atlantic community under Ameri-

can domination and direction." West Germany's decision to remain closely aligned with the United States was due partly to Kennedy's efforts. In June 1963 he appeared before the Berlin Wall and defiantly challenged defenders of communism to "come to Berlin." To a wildly enthusiastic audience, he concluded with these famous words: "All free men, wherever they may live, are citizens of Berlin, and, therefore, as a free man, I take pride in the words 'Ich bin ein Berliner' (I am a Berliner)."

Even while Kennedy made provocative statements in Berlin that sent a clear warning to the Kremlin, he softened their impact by supporting negotiations over other important matters. The following August the United States, Britain, and the Soviet Union signed the Nuclear Test Ban Treaty, bringing a close to testing under water and in the atmosphere and outer space. Although its prohibitions did not apply to underground testing because of continued opposition to on-site inspection, this ban was the first arms limitations agreement between the nations after nearly two decades of attempts. Despite Kennedy's declaration that the pact was a great step forward on "the path of peace," the Joint Chiefs of Staff agreed to it only after McNamara assured them of a big program of underground tests and presented them a written promise to begin nuclear tests anew in the atmosphere "should they be deemed essential to our national security." In October the United States sold $250 million of surplus wheat and flour to the Soviet Union and Eastern Europe. Tensions seemed to have eased by the end of 1963.

The rhetoric had receded, and yet it still seems doubtful that Kennedy would have taken the monumental step of fully withdrawing from Vietnam. It would have been a sharp reversal indeed for him to have shed the past in such a bold manner. Had not President Truman prevailed over Communist forces in both Greece and South Korea? Kennedy's administration had already paid the price of hesitation at the Bay of Pigs. It had then compromised in Laos. He could not abandon Vietnam, although he leaned toward a phased withdrawal that would have greatly alleviated tensions in

Southeast Asia. The hard truth is that much of Kennedy's Vietnam policy resulted from his feelings of failure in Cuba and Laos. His sense of U.S. righteousness remained, and this necessitated the establishment of world order and stability in preventing the spread of totalitarian rule by either the Soviets or the Communist Chinese. Kennedy, like others before and after him, remained a hostage of the Cold War. If his administration never developed a plan for winning the war in Vietnam, it certainly refused to be the one to lose that war.

Selected Readings

Abel, Elie. *The Missile Crisis.* 1968.

Allison, Graham T. *Essence of Decision: Explaining the Cuban Missile Crisis.* 1971.

Ambrose, Stephen E. *Nixon: The Education of a Politician, 1913–1962.* 1987.

———, and Brinkley, Douglas G. *Rise to Globalism: American Foreign Policy since 1938.* 8th ed., 1997.

Ball, George W., and Ball, Douglas B. *The Passionate Attachment: America's Involvement with Israel 1947 to the Present.* 1992.

Baritz, Loren. *Backfire: A History of How American Culture Led Us into Vietnam and Made Us Fight the Way We Did.* 1985.

Ben-Zvi, Abraham. *Decade of Transition: Eisenhower, Kennedy, and the Origins of the American-Israeli Alliance.* 1998.

Beschloss, Michael R. *The Crisis Years: Kennedy and Khrushchev, 1960–1963.* 1991.

Bill, James A. *George Ball: Behind the Scenes in U.S. Foreign Policy.* 1997.

Bird, Kai. *The Color of Truth: McGeorge Bundy and William Bundy, Brothers in Arms: A Biography.* 1998.

Blair, Anne E. *Lodge in Vietnam: A Patriot Abroad.* 1995.

Blight, James G., and Welch, David A. *On the Brink: Americans and Soviets Reexamine the Cuban Missile Crisis.* 1989.

Brands, H. W. *The Devil We Knew: Americans and the Cold War.* 1993.

Brigham, Robert K. *Guerrilla Diplomacy: The NLF's Foreign Relations and the Viet Nam War.* 1999.

Brinkley, Douglas. *Dean Acheson: The Cold War Years, 1953–71.* 1992.

Brugioni, Dino A. *Eyeball to Eyeball.* 1992.

Burchett, Wilfred. *Catapult to Freedom: The Survival of the Vietnamese People.* 1978.

Buttinger, Joseph. *Vietnam: A Dragon Embattled.* 2 vols., 1967.

Buzzanco, Robert. *Vietnam and the Transformation of American Life.* 1999.

Cate, Curtis. *The Ides of August: The Berlin Wall Crisis, 1961.* 1978.

Catudal, Honor, M. *Kennedy and the Berlin Wall Crisis: A Case Study in U.S. Decision Making.* 1980.

Chayes, Abram. *The Cuban Missile Crisis: International Crises and the Role of Law.* 1974.

Cobbs, Elizabeth H. *All You Need Is Love: The Peace Corps and the Spirit of the 1960s.* 1998.

Cohen, Warren I. *America's Response to China: An Interpretive History of Sino-American Relations.* 2000.

———. *Dean Rusk.* 1980.

Conboy, Kenneth, and Andradé, Dale. *Spies and Commandos: How America Lost the Secret War in North Vietnam.* 2000.

Costigliola, Frank. "The Failed Design: Kennedy, deGaulle, and the Struggle for Europe," *Diplomatic History* 8 (1984): 227–51.

———. *France and the United States: The Cold Alliance since World War II.* 1992.

Currey, Cecil B. *Edward Lansdale: The Unquiet American.* 1988.

Davidson, Phillip B. *Vietnam at War: The History, 1946–1975.* 1988.

Detzer, David. *The Brink: Cuban Missile Crisis, 1962.* 1979.

DiLeo, David L. *George Ball, Vietnam, and the Rethinking of Containment.* 1991.

Dinerstein, Herbert S. *The Making of a Missile Crisis: October 1962.* 1976.

Duiker, William J. *The Communist Road to Power in Vietnam.* 1981.

———. *Ho Chi Minh.* 2000.

———. *U.S. Containment Policy and the Conflict in Indochina.* 1994.

Ernst, John. *Forging a Fateful Alliance: Michigan State University and the Vietnam War.* 1998.

Evans, John W. *The Kennedy Round in American Trade Policy.* 1973.

Fairlie, Henry B. *The Kennedy Promise.* 1973.

Fall, Bernard B. *Anatomy of a Crisis: The Laotian Crisis of 1960–1961.* 1969.

Ferrell, Robert H. *Ill-Advised: Presidential Health and Public Trust.* 1992.

Firestone, Bernard J. *The Quest for Nuclear Stability: John F. Kennedy and the Soviet Union.* 1982.

Fischer, Fritz. *Making Them Like Us: Peace Corps Volunteers in the 1960s.* 1998.

FitzGerald, Frances. *Fire in the Lake: The Vietnamese and the Americans in Vietnam.* 1972.

FitzSimons, Louise. *The Kennedy Doctrine.* 1972.

Freedman, Lawrence. *Kennedy's Wars: Berlin, Cuba, Laos, and Vietnam.* 2000.

Fursenko, Aleksandr, and Naftali, Timothy. *"One Hell of a Gamble": Khrushchev, Castro, and Kennedy, 1958–1964.* 1997.

Gaddis, John L. *The Long Peace: Inquiries into the History of the Cold War.* 1987.

———. *Russia, the Soviet Union, and the United States: An Interpretive History.* 2nd ed., 1990.

———. *Strategies of Containment: A Critical Appraisal of Postwar American National Security Policy.* 1982.

Gaiduk, Ilya V. *The Soviet Union and the Vietnam War.* 1996.

Garthoff, Raymond L. *Reflections on the Cuban Missile Crisis.* 1987.

———, Bernstein, Barton J., Trachtenberg, Marc, and Paterson, Thomas G. "Commentaries on 'An Interview with Sergo Mikoyan,'" in "The Cuban Missile Crisis Reconsidered," *Diplomatic History* 14 (1990): 223–56.

Gelb, Leslie H., and Betts, Richard K. *The Irony of Vietnam: The System Worked.* 1979.

Giglio, James N. *The Presidency of John F. Kennedy.* 1991.

Goodman, Allan E. *The Lost Peace: America's Search for a Negotiated Settlement of the Vietnam War.* 1978.

Greenstein, Fred I., and Immerman, Richard H. "What Did Eisenhower Tell Kennedy about Indochina? The Politics of Misperception," *Journal of American History* 79 (1992): 568–87.

Greiner, Bernd. "The Soviet View: An Interview with Sergo Mikoyan," in "The Cuban Missile Crisis Reconsidered," *Diplomatic History* 14 (1990): 205–21.

Gurtov, Melvin. *The United States against the Third World.* 1974.

Halberstam, David. *The Best and the Brightest.* 1972.

———. *The Making of a Quagmire: America and Vietnam during the Kennedy Era.* Rev. ed., 1984.

Hallin, Daniel C. *The "Uncensored War": The Media and Vietnam.* 1986.

Hammer, Ellen J. *A Death in November: America in Vietnam, 1963.* 1987.

Hammond, William H. *Reporting Vietnam: Media and Military at War.* 1998.

Harrison, James P. *The Endless War: Fifty Years of Struggle in Vietnam.* 1982.

Heath, Jim F. *Decade of Disillusionment: The Kennedy-Johnson Years.* 1975.

Hendrickson, Paul. *The Living and the Dead: Robert McNamara and Five Lives of a Lost War.* 1996.

Herring, George C., Jr. *America's Longest War: The United States and Vietnam, 1950–1975.* 3rd ed., 1996.

———, ed. *The Pentagon Papers: Abridged Edition.* 1993.

———. "The Vietnam War," in Carroll, John M., and Herring, George C., eds., *Modern American Diplomacy,* 165–81. 1986.

Hersh, Seymour M. *The Dark Side of Camelot.* 1997.

Hershberg, James G. "Before 'The Missiles of October': Did Kennedy Plan a Military Strike against Cuba?", *Diplomatic History* 14 (1990): 163–98.

Hess, Gary R. *Vietnam and the United States: Origins and Legacy of War.* 1998.

Higgins, Trumbull. *The Perfect Failure: Kennedy, Eisenhower, and the CIA at the Bay of Pigs.* 1987.

Hilsman, Roger. *To Move a Nation: The Politics of Foreign Policy in the Administration of John F. Kennedy.* 1967.

Kahin, George McT. *Intervention: How America Became Involved in Vietnam.* 1986.

———, and Lewis, John W. *The United States in Vietnam.* Rev. ed., 1969.

Kaiser, David E. *American Tragedy: Kennedy, Johnson, and the Origins of the Vietnam War.* 2000.

Kalb, Madeleine G. *The Congo Cables: The Cold War in Africa—From Eisenhower to Kennedy.* 1982.

Kaplowitz, Donna R. *Anatomy of a Failed Embargo: U.S. Sanctions Against Cuba.* 1998.

Karnow, Stanley. *Vietnam: A History.* Rev. ed., 1991.

Kattenburg, Paul M. *The Vietnam Trauma in American Foreign Policy, 1945–1975.* 1980.

Kendrick, Alexander. *The Wound Within: America in the Vietnam Years, 1945–1974.* 1974.

Kennedy, Robert F. *The Thirteen Days: A Memoir of the Cuban Missile Crisis.* 1969.

Kern, Montague, Levering, Patricia W., and Levering, Ralph B. *The Kennedy Crisis: The Press, the Presidency, and Foreign Policy.* 1983.

Kolko, Gabriel. *Anatomy of a War: Vietnam, the United States, and the Modern Historical Experience.* 1985.

Krepinevich, Andrew F., Jr. *The Army and Vietnam.* 1986.

LaFeber, Walter. *America, Russia, and the Cold War, 1945–1996.* 8th ed., 1997.

Langguth, A. J. *Our Vietnam: The War, 1954–1975.* 2000.

Langley, Lester D. "Latin America from Cuba to El Salvador," in Carroll, John M., and Herring, George C., eds. *Modern American Diplomacy,* 183–200. 1986.

Latham, Michael E. "Ideology, Social Science, and Destiny: Modernization and the Kennedy-Era Alliance for Progress," *Diplomatic History* 22 (1998): 199–229.

———. *Modernization as Ideology: American Social Science and "Nation Building" in the Kennedy Era.* 2000.

Levinson, Jerome, and Onís, Juan de. *The Alliance That Lost Its Way.* 1970.

Lewy, Guenter. *America in Vietnam.* 1978.

Lind, Michael. *Vietnam the Necessary War: A Reinterpretation of America's Most Disastrous Military Conflict.* 1999.

Logevall, Fredrik. *Choosing War: The Lost Chance for Peace and the Escalation of War in Vietnam.* 1999.

Maclear, Michael. *The Ten Thousand Day War, Vietnam: 1945–1975.* 1981.

Maga, Timothy P. *John F. Kennedy and New Frontier Diplomacy, 1961–1963.* 1994.

———. *John F. Kennedy and the New Pacific Community, 1961–63.* 1990.

Mahoney, Richard D. *JFK: Ordeal in Africa.* 1983.

Mangold, Tom, and Penygate, John. *The Tunnels of Cu Chi: The Untold Story of Vietnam.* 1985.

Mann, Robert. *A Grand Illusion: America's Descent into Vietnam.* 2001.

May, Ernest R., and Zelikow, Philip D., eds. *The Kennedy Tapes: Inside the White House During the Cuban Missile Crisis.* 1997.

McMahon, Robert J. *The Cold War on the Periphery: The United States, India, and Pakistan.* 1994.

———. *The Limits of Empire: The United States and Southeast Asia since World War II.* 1999.

McNamara, Robert S. *In Retrospect: The Tragedy and Lessons of Vietnam.* 1995.

Merrill, Dennis. *Bread and the Ballot: The United States and India's Economic Development, 1947–1963.* 1990.

Miroff, Bruce. *Pragmatic Illusions: The Presidential Politics of John F. Kennedy.* 1976.

Morgan, Joseph G. *The Vietnam Lobby: The American Friends of Vietnam, 1955–1975.* 1997.

Morley, Morris. *Imperial State and Revolution: The United States and Cuba, 1952–1985.* 1987.

Nash, Philip. *The Other Missiles of October: Eisenhower, Kennedy, and the Jupiters, 1957–1963.* 1997.

Neese, Harvey, and O'Donnell, John, eds. *Prelude to Tragedy: Vietnam, 1960–1965.* 2001.

Newman, John M. *JFK and Vietnam: Deception, Intrigue, and the Struggle for Power.* 1992.

Noer, Thomas J. *Cold War and Black Liberation: The United States and White Rule in Africa, 1948–1968.* 1985.

Oliver, Kendrick. *Kennedy, Macmillan, and the Nuclear Test-Ban Debate, 1961–1963.* 1998.

Olson, James S., and Roberts, Randy. *Where the Domino Fell: America and Vietnam, 1945–1995.* 3rd ed., 1995.

Palmer, Dave R. *Summons of the Trumpet: A History of the Vietnam War from a Military Man's Viewpoint.* 1978.

Parmet, Herbert S. *JFK: The Presidency of John F. Kennedy.* 1983.

Paterson, Thomas G., ed. *Kennedy's Quest for Victory: American Foreign Policy, 1961–1963.* 1989.

Pérez, Louis A., Jr. *Cuba and the United States: Ties of Singular Intimacy.* 1997.

Poole, Peter. *The United States and Indochina from FDR to Nixon.* 1973.

Prados, John. *The Blood Road: The Ho Chi Minh Trail and the Vietnam War.* 1999.

———. *Presidents' Secret Wars: CIA Pentagon Covert Operations from World War II through the Persian Gulf.* 1996.

Prochnau, William. *Once Upon a Distant War: David Halberstam, Neil Sheehan, Peter Arnett—Young War Correspondents and Their Early Vietnam Battles.* 1995.

Rabe, Stephen G. *The Most Dangerous Area in the World: John F. Kennedy Confronts Communist Revolution in Latin America.* 1999.

Reeves, Richard. *President Kennedy: Profile of Power.* 1993.

Reeves, Thomas C. *A Question of Character: A Life of John F. Kennedy.* 1991.

Rice, Gerald T. *The Bold Experiment: JFK's Peace Corps.* 1985.

Risse-Kappen, Thomas. *Cooperation Among Democracies: The European Influence on U.S. Foreign Policy.* 1995.

Rusk, Dean. *As I Saw It.* Papp, Daniel S., ed., 1990.

Rust, William J. *Kennedy in Vietnam.* 1985.

Schaffer, Howard B. *Chester Bowles—New Dealer in the Cold War.* 1993.

Schecter, Jerrold L., and Deriabin, Peter S. *The Spy Who Saved the World: How a Soviet Colonel Changed the Course of the Cold War.* 1992.

Schick, Jack M. *The Berlin Crisis, 1958–1962.* 1971.

Schlesinger, Arthur M., Jr. *A Thousand Days: John F. Kennedy in the White House.* 1965.

Schoenbaum, David. *The United States and the State of Israel.* 1993.

Schoenbaum, Thomas J. *Waging Peace and War: Dean Rusk in the Truman, Kennedy, and Johnson Years.* 1988.

Schoutz, Lars. *Beneath the United States: A History of U.S. Policy Toward Latin America.* 1998.

Schulzinger, Robert D. *A Time for War: The United States and Vietnam, 1941–1975.* 1997.

Schwab, Orrin. *Defending the Free World: John F. Kennedy, Lyndon Johnson, and the Vietnam War, 1961–1965.* 1998.

Seaborg, Glenn T., and Loeb, Benjamin S. *Kennedy, Khrushchev, and the Test Ban.* 1981.

Shaplen, Robert. *The Lost Revolution: The U.S. in Vietnam, 1946–1966.* 1966.

Shapley, Deborah. *Promise and Power: The Life and Times of Robert McNamara.* 1993.

Sheehan, Neil. *A Bright Shining Lie. John Paul Vann and America in Vietnam.* 1988.

———, et al., eds. *New York Times, The Pentagon Papers.* 1971.

Shultz, Richard H., Jr. *The Secret War Against Hanoi: Kennedy's and Johnson's Use of Spies, Saboteurs, and Covert Warriors in North Vietnam.* 1999.

Slusser, Robert M. *The Berlin Crisis of 1961: Soviet-American Relations and the Struggle in the Kremlin, June–November 1961.* 1973.

Smith, R. B. *An International History of the Vietnam War. Vol. 2: The Kennedy Strategy.* 1985.

Sorensen, Theodore C. *Kennedy.* 1965.

Spanier, John W. *American Foreign Policy since World War II.* 14th ed., 1998.

Stevenson, Richard W. *The Rise and Fall of Détente: Relaxations of Tensions in U.S.-Soviet Relations, 1953–1984.* 1985.

Summers, Harry G., Jr. *On Strategy: A Critical Analysis of the Vietnam War.* 1982.

Szulc, Tad, and Meyer, Karl E. *The Cuban Invasion: The Chronicle of a Disaster.* 1962.

Taylor, Sandra C. *Vietnamese Women at War: Fighting for Ho Chi Minh and the Revolution.* 1999.

Tomes, Robert R. *Apocalypse Then: American Intellectuals and the Vietnam War, 1954–1975.* 1998.

Truong Nhu Tang. *A Vietcong Memoir.* 1985.

Tucker, Spencer C. *Vietnam.* 1999.

Turley, William S. *The Second Indochina War: A Short Political and Military History, 1954–1975.* 1986.

Turner, Karen G. *Even the Women Must Fight: Memories of War from North Vietnam.* 1998.

Ulam, Adam B. *The Communists: The Story of Power and Lost Illusions, 1948–1991.* 1992.

———. *The Rivals: America and Russia since World War II.* 1971.

U.S. Information Agency, "Back from the Brink: The Correspondence Between President John F. Kennedy and Chairman Nikita S. Khrushchev on the Cuban Missile Crisis of Autumn 1962," in *Problems of Communism* 41 (1992). Special issue.

Vandenbroucke, Lucien S. *Perilous Options: Special Operations as an Instrument of U.S. Foreign Policy.* 1993.

Walton, Richard J. *Cold War and Counterrevolution: The Foreign Policy of John F. Kennedy.* 1972.

Weissman, Stephen. *American Foreign Policy in the Congo, 1960–1964.* 1974.

Welch, Richard E., Jr. *Response to Revolution: The United States and the Cuban Revolution, 1959–1961.* 1985.

Wenger, Andreas. *Living with Peril: Eisenhower, Kennedy, and Nuclear Weapons.* 1997.

White, Mark J. *The Cuban Missile Crisis.* 1996.

———, ed. *Kennedy: The New Frontier Revisited.* 1998.

———. *Missiles in Cuba: Kennedy, Khrushchev, Castro, and the 1962 Crisis.* 1997.

Winters, Francis X. *The Year of the Hare: America in Vietnam, January 25, 1963–February 15, 1964.* 1997.

Wyatt, Clarence R. *Paper Soldiers: The American Press and the Vietnam War.* 1993.

Wyden, Peter. *Bay of Pigs: The Untold Story.* 1979.

———. *Wall: The Inside Story of Divided Berlin.* 1989.

Young, Marilyn B. *The Vietnam Wars, 1945–1990.* 1991.

Zeiler, Thomas W. *Dean Rusk: Defending the American Mission Abroad.* 2000.

Zhai, Qiang. *China and the Vietnam Wars, 1950–1975.* 2000.

CHAPTER 13

Containment in Collapse
JOHNSON AND VIETNAM, 1963–1969

The Tragedy of LBJ

"Let us continue," the tall and robust Lyndon B. Johnson declared, as he assumed his new duties as president in November 1963. In an attempt to retain the Kennedy effect, Johnson promised to work toward his predecessor's domestic and foreign programs and persuaded several members of his staff to remain. McNamara, Rusk, Bundy, Rostow, and others stayed until many of them could no longer support the policies of the Johnson administration. But try as he did, the new president could not capture the "magic" that so many of Kennedy's distraught followers now perceived as the essence of his administration. Part of the reason was personal. Johnson was a boisterous and often ill-mannered Texan from the barren and poor south central sector of the state. Whereas Kennedy had gone to Harvard and engaged in numerous extracurricular activities that did not include politics, Johnson attended a local teachers' college and, while there, developed an inordinate skill in campus politics that he carried throughout his life. Kennedy was glamorous; Johnson was political.

As president, Johnson lived in the shadow of the wealthy and cultured Massachusetts-bred Kennedy, never managing to throw off the image of wheeler-dealer politician and riverboat gambler, the result of his domineering decades in Congress. The new president was grounded in the humanitarian principles of Franklin D. Roosevelt's New Deal program and implemented an ambitious range of domestic reforms under the label of the "Great Society." Johnson was hardworking, demanding, stubborn, egotistic, self-righteous, crude, and exceedingly sensitive to criticism. He expected total loyalty and used his famous "Johnson treatment" to achieve that objective. According to a fellow Texan, "Lyndon got me by the lapels and put his face on top of mine and he talked and talked and talked. I figured it was either getting drowned or joining." Benjamin Bradlee of the *Washington Post* once declared that when administered the "Johnson treatment, you really felt as if a St. Bernard had licked your face for an hour, had pawed you all over."

Johnson's central tragedy was his acceptance of unrestrained assumptions about containment that led him relentlessly deeper into Vietnam. Meanwhile he tried to maintain the costly Great Society—and not by taking the politically unpopular route of raising taxes but by borrowing huge sums of money that ultimately led to rampant inflation. Like Truman, Eisenhower, and Kennedy, Johnson was

President Johnson and Advisers on Vietnam
Left to right: Ambassador Henry Cabot Lodge, Secretary of State
Dean Rusk, President Johnson, Secretary of Defense Robert
McNamara, and Under Secretary of State George Ball. *White House
Photo Office, Lyndon B. Johnson Presidential Library, Austin, Texas.*

virtually the captive of appeasement and McCarthyism, and like them he was convinced that communism posed a threat in nearly every trouble spot in the world. Most social revolutions in the Third World, Johnson believed, were Communist-tinged if not inspired, necessitating a rigid U.S. stand for order and stability. Thus, he accepted the fundamental precept of the global containment policy: The nation's vital interests lay wherever there was a threat of communism.

As Cuba had been the supreme test of Kennedy's will, Vietnam became that of Johnson's. "I want to leave the footprints of America there," he declared. "We're going to turn the Mekong [River delta] into a Tennessee Valley" and democratize the surrounding area. In fact, however, he gave the United States's Vietnam policy a greater military orientation than Kennedy had conceived. By mid-1965 the United States found itself locked in a major land war in Southeast Asia that escalated into a bloody stalemate and eventually counted the hope for democracy in that area of the world

as one of the war's primary casualties. Johnson meanwhile encountered other issues that often became intertwined with the Vietnam involvement and starkly showed the dangers in overcommitment: problems in the Dominican Republic; secret attempts to reestablish diplomatic relations with Cuba; de Gaulle's challenges to U.S. influence in Southeast Asia and Europe; riots in Panama over the U.S. presence; the timeless Arab-Israeli struggle in the Middle East; the effort to promote détente or a reduction of tensions with the Soviet Union, built on nuclear proliferation treaties and other measures; and Soviet repression of an uprising in Czechoslovakia similar to that in Hungary both in causes and results. Yet it was the United States's war in Vietnam that continuously interfered with many of these matters. Indeed, Vietnam brought down Johnson's presidency in 1968 and ushered in the Republican party and Richard M. Nixon. Johnson's rigid adherence to global containment climaxed in failure and necessitated a search for new directions in foreign policy.

"Americanizing" the War in Vietnam, 1963–1965

The United States's deepening involvement in Vietnam ultimately consumed the Johnson presidency. Although the president considered Vietnam a "raggedy-ass fourth-rate country," he feared that if the United States failed to "stop the Reds in South Vietnam, tomorrow they will be in Hawaii, and next they will be in San Francisco." Along with former Kennedy advisers, he was convinced that Communist China sought to control Southeast Asia and that North Vietnam's aggressions were part of that objective. "I am not going to lose Vietnam," Johnson promised soon after becoming chief executive. "I am not going to be the president who saw Southeast Asia go the way

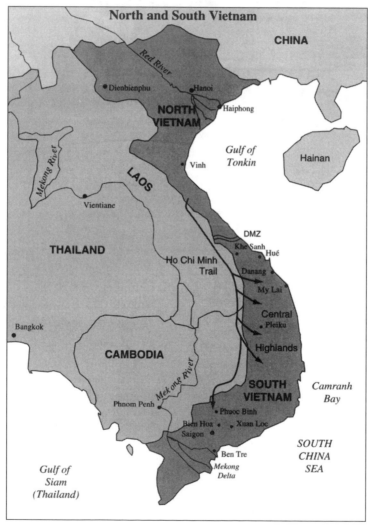

North and South Vietnam

Map 25
America's involvement in Indochina began in 1950 during the Korean War, escalated into troop involvement in 1965, and officially ended with a cease-fire agreement in 1973 that the Nixon administration termed "peace with honor."

China went." As was the case with the Kennedy administration, Johnson seemed to have no strategy for victory, except to escalate involvement while avoiding defeat.

Johnson firmly believed that U.S. military strength would resolve the problems in Vietnam, but he failed to recognize that since its peak year of power in 1945, the United States had been steadily losing its capacity to influence global events. The world's power structure was becoming increasingly diffused as the Soviet Union grew in military strength, as NATO members acted more independently, and as the Third World stepped up demands for a greater voice in international affairs. But the most baffling dilemma, which the administration never resolved, was how the small country of North Vietnam could handcuff the mighty United States, denying it a military victory ensured by every resource statistic available. After Diem's assassination in November 1963, the pressure had grown for the establishment of a coalition government and a neutral stance for Vietnam in international affairs. But Johnson insisted on victory. The "neutralization of South Vietnam," he declared in a statement that forecasted the aggressive direction of his administration, "would only be another name for a Communist takeover." To the new South Vietnamese leader, General Duong Van Minh, he wrote, "The United States will continue to furnish you and your people with the fullest measure of support in this bitter fight."

Despite U.S. aid, the situation in Vietnam continued to unravel in early 1964. General Minh's fall in a military coup in January resulted in a long period of political uncertainty complicated by repeated changes in leadership and rapid intensification of the war. The South Vietnamese raided North Vietnam and hit its sources of supplies in Laos, but by April the Vietcong had gained control of most Vietnamese villages in the south and had taken the offensive. Indeed, the Vietcong had established a checkpoint a bare fifty miles outside Saigon, forcing the city to become a veritable armed fortress, complete with barbed wire and concrete sentry barricades bolstered by sand bags and heavily armed soldiers. In retrospect, it seems clear that the most crucial ingredient in achieving victory was not the field of battle but popular political support gained by satisfying the legitimate needs of the peasantry. The Washington government, however, emphasized the use of superior firepower to stop a Communist threat believed to originate from Hanoi—an approach that had the adverse impact of alienating the surrounding peoples, whose support the South Vietnamese government could least afford to lose.

In autumn 1964 the Johnson administration encountered a series of incidents in the Gulf of Tonkin off North Vietnam that led to a more direct involvement in the war. The U.S. destroyer *Maddox* was engaged in a top secret program of electronic espionage (a "DeSoto Mission" that was part of "Operation 34-A," actually developed under Kennedy in 1962 though not approved until January 1964) in the Gulf of Tonkin when, on the morning of August 1, it underwent fire by several North Vietnamese torpedo boats in an area close to the offshore islands but nonetheless in international waters. U.S. air fire drove away the assailants, but Johnson was outraged and ordered the *Maddox* to return to those waters, accompanied by another destroyer, the *C. Turner Joy*. On the evening of August 4, according to U.S. accounts, North Vietnamese torpedo boats fired on both vessels, then cruising sixty miles at sea, but failed to hit either one.

Considerable doubt exists about the authenticity of a second attack. The Hanoi government had admitted to the first assault on the *Maddox* as retaliation for U.S. collaboration with recent South Vietnamese commando raids, but it vehemently denied the second incident. Indeed, U.S. commanders were probably mistaken about whether an attack had actually occurred. The fog was thick and the night so black that one sailor termed it "darker than the hubs of Hell." Star shells had failed to light up the sky because they exploded above the low and extremely dense cloud cover. One pilot flying directly overhead, James B.

Gen. Nguyen Khanh
In the summer of 1964, South Vietnamese General Khanh alarmed the White House
by calling for attacks on North Vietnam. *National Archives, Washington, D.C.*

Stockdale, held what he called "the best seat in the house from which to detect boats" and saw "no boat wakes, no ricochets, no torpedo wakes—nothing but the black sea and American firepower." The Americans had fired into the blackness for several hours, during which time the "enemy" had appeared only on sonar and radar, and the captain of the *Maddox* later admitted that both detection systems were unreliable in such bad weather. Because there had been no "visual sightings," he strongly urged a "complete evaluation" before taking action. Each U.S. vessel could have been firing at the wakes of the other. Johnson later put it more directly to an aide: "Hell, those dumb stupid sailors were just shooting at flying fish."

But the truth became academic because the Johnson administration had already decided to upgrade its involvement in the war and take it north, as later shown in *The Pentagon Papers,* a pillaged collection of secret defense department documents on Vietnam that the *New*

York Times published in 1971. This material suggests that the president and his advisers had been frustrated with South Vietnam's war effort and were looking for an opportunity to justify direct U.S. action. In a matter of hours the Washington administration, without launching an investigation, authorized a "firm, swift retaliatory [air] attack" on North Vietnamese torpedo boat bases. U.S. planes thus took the war into the north for the first time by bombing North Vietnamese torpedo boat bases and oil supply depots at Vinh, which lay well above South Vietnam's upper border at the seventeenth parallel. Johnson appeared on television that same evening—August 4, 1964—to inform Americans of recent events in the Gulf of Tonkin and accuse North Vietnam of "open aggression on the high seas." Although the SEATO Treaty pledged only *consultation* about military aid, the president asserted that it was the duty of the United States to help any member "requesting assistance in defense of its freedom." Johnson relied on his old friend Senator J. William Fulbright, chair of the Foreign Relations Committee, to steer a resolution through Congress asking for authorization to use military force. But the president did not reveal to either Fulbright or Congress that the *Maddox* had been involved in espionage and raiding expeditions, pointing instead to official reports that the vessel had been on patrol in international waters and had not provoked an attack.

After virtually no debate in either chamber, Congress took the first major step toward "Americanizing" the conflict when it approved the Gulf of Tonkin Resolution on August 7—three days following the U.S. assault on Vinh. By a unanimous vote in the House and the wide margin of eighty-eight to two in the Senate (the only negative votes coming from Ernest Gruening of Alaska and Wayne Morse of Oregon), Congress empowered the president to "take all necessary measures to repel any armed attacks against the forces of the United States and to prevent further aggression." A high-ranking official in the state department called the resolution "a functional equivalent of a declaration of war." Johnson, however, had no intention of broadening the war effort. He still thought it possible to achieve success in Vietnam through what his advisers called "graduated overt pressures."

The administration believed that the Tonkin Resolution would accomplish both foreign and domestic objectives. It would show the North Vietnamese that Americans were determined to uphold their commitments in Southeast Asia. The White House would also appear resolute and in control, which would help Johnson fend off his challenger in the presidential contest of 1964, conservative Republican Barry Goldwater of Arizona. In the heat of the campaign, Johnson attacked Goldwater for wanting to escalate the war by authorizing air strikes on North Vietnam and reviving MacArthur's claim that there was no substitute for victory. In response to the Republican campaign slogan, "In your heart, you know he's right," the Democrats coun-

tered with, "In your heart, you know he might." Such an unreasoned approach, the president warned, could lead to the use of U.S. fighting forces. He pledged against sending Americans "nine or ten thousand miles away from home to do what Asian boys ought to be doing for themselves."

Perhaps out of fear of a Goldwater victory or because of the Tonkin Resolution, the Hanoi government had secretly offered to negotiate, but the president refused. As a former White House aide later explained, "the very word *negotiations* was anathema in the Administration." National security affairs adviser Walt Rostow belligerently insisted that "it is on this spot that we have to break the liberation war—Chinese type. If we don't break it here, we shall have to face it again in Thailand, Venezuela, elsewhere." In a statement that expressed the administration's central feeling, Rostow declared that "Vietnam is a clear testing ground for our policy in the world." There were other considerations. The country's strategic location, some believed, was vital to the United States's position in Southeast Asia. Neither the Johnson administration nor the ARVN leaders in Saigon were interested in the establishment of a coalition government. Nor would Johnson subject himself to charges of appeasement and the possible loss of Vietnam—especially on election eve.

Johnson won a massive victory in November, and soon afterward his administration made a highly secretive decision to use air power in Vietnam. The objectives were mixed. Some officials thought that bombings would raise morale in South Vietnam; others hoped that aerial attacks would reduce suspected North Vietnamese Army infiltration from the north and perhaps even cause the Hanoi regime to suspend its aid to the Vietcong. Even though administration critics disagreed, the truth is that the Gulf of Tonkin episode helped to push the North Vietnamese into sending army regulars into the south. During the early 1980s, Communist leaders in Vietnam attested to the escalated infiltration in the period, thereby confirming the validity of

Johnson's advisers' suspicions. No one in Washington seemed to realize that the Tonkin Resolution had perhaps encouraged a North Vietnamese troop involvement.

The decision to bomb did not come without opposition. Undersecretary of State George Ball strongly objected to such tactics as pointless in dealing with a primitive industrial country and useless in trying to close the infinite number of infiltration routes into the south that wound through the dense jungles of Laos and Cambodia as the "Ho Chi Minh Trail." It was certain, Ball said, to unite *all* Vietnamese on the ground against the intruder from the sky. Intelligence reports likewise warned that air assaults would have minimal effect on the fighting in South Vietnam. The Vietcong were an insurgency group with no air force, he reminded his colleagues, and bombings aimed at their believed whereabouts on the ground would alienate the area's inhabitants and result in political calamity. Some observers pointed out that if the Vietcong's tools were primarily nonmilitary—propaganda, terror, political subversion—then the key to victory lay in winning the people's support. Bombings lacked that potential. One U.S. artilleryman noted that in World War II, "there were real targets to aim at—enemy artillery or fortresses or fortified positions or massed enemy-troop formations or even bridges." But in Vietnam such targets did not exist. Artillery fire "did nothing but kill a lot of innocents and alienate us from those we were supposedly trying to help." By implication, bombing would have the same effect—except on a wider scale. Ball warned that the United States would find it impossible to control events in the midst of military escalation. "Once on the tiger's back," he prophetically declared, "we cannot be sure of picking the place to dismount."

But these counterarguments did not change the direction of the Johnson administration, and by the end of the month it had secretly adopted a bombing program that lay midway between all-out assaults and nothing at all—what one adviser proudly called a "carefully orchestrated bombing attack" on North Viet-

nam. Proponents of the new strategy countered the fears of a dramatically widened war with the assertion that restrained bombing raids would not endanger North Vietnam's existence and thus would furnish no grounds for a Chinese intervention. Air assaults would also allow the South Vietnamese government a "breathing spell and opportunity to improve." Communist China's recent development of a nuclear device seemingly made it imperative to protect South Vietnam and, according to a telling argument presented by some in the White House, the use of air power would greatly diminish the chances of having to send U.S. combat troops. Although the bombing decision turned out to be one of the most monumental moves in the war, presidential adviser William Bundy clearly failed to grasp its dangerous implications. Bombing, he admitted, might not have much effect on the war, but it offered "at least a faint hope of really improving the Vietnamese situation."

On the night of February 6, 1965, Vietcong forces provided the Johnson administration with a reason for implementing its bombing program when they attacked the huge U.S. army barracks and air base at Pleiku in central South Vietnam, inflicting more than one hundred U.S. casualties that included nine dead. National security affairs adviser McGeorge Bundy, then on an investigative mission in Saigon, rushed to the scene. He joined two others there—the U.S. ambassador to South Vietnam, General Maxwell Taylor, and the commander of U.S. forces, General William Westmoreland of the Military Assistance Command, Vietnam (MACV)—in calling for instant retaliation. As fate would have it, Johnson authorized air strikes on North Vietnam at precisely the time that the new Soviet premier after Khrushchev's ouster, Alexei Kosygin, was in Hanoi—perhaps discussing whether to increase military aid. The president's need for a show of force, however, overrode the risk of creating a confrontation with the Soviets. "We have kept our guns over the mantel and our shells in the cupboard for a long time now," Johnson declared. "I can't ask our American soldiers out there to continue to fight with one hand behind their backs."

The attack on Pleiku had thus provided the pretext, rather than the cause, for U.S. bombing operations. Indeed, McGeorge Bundy later remarked that "Pleikus are like streetcars," suggesting that if that incident had not occurred, another one would have come along soon. Within twelve hours of the Vietcong attack, the first of nearly fifty U.S. jets penetrated North Vietnamese air space and raided military installations above the seventeenth parallel. First known as "Flaming Dart," the air raids graduated from individual retaliatory missions to a sustained bombing campaign by the summer of 1965. The campaign, later known as "Rolling Thunder," lasted until the end of the U.S. involvement in the war in 1973. In the course of eight years, the United States dropped eight million tons of bombs on the whole of Vietnam—four times the amount used in World War II. Besides hitting key military targets, the bombs eventually struck Hanoi, Haiphong (with Soviet vessels in the harbor), and the railroad from Hanoi to China, inflicting some damage a bare ten miles outside China's borders. Furthermore, recently declassified documents suggest that the U.S. decision to bomb above the seventeenth parallel made the administration's charge of North Vietnamese interference in the south a self-fulfilling prophecy: Rolling Thunder proved integral to the first military involvement of North Vietnamese Army regulars (People's Army of Vietnam, or PAVN) in May 1965. The PAVN quickly numbered 6500 and fought with the Vietcong guerrillas in the war. The attack on Pleiku had provided the rationale for bombing the north, which in turn had brought about an unforeseen escalation of the war.

Despite the pilots' claims that they hit military targets with "surgical" accuracy, the bombings ultimately became indiscriminate and inadvertently included civilian centers. Still, this was not enough for hard-liners such as Air Force Chief of Staff General Curtis LeMay. "We are swatting flies," he indignantly protested, "when we should be going after

the manure pile." Hanoi's leaders held on. To counter the effects of the bombings, the North Vietnamese moved urban civilians to the countryside, spread out industrial and storage centers, often placing them in caves or underground, and dug thousands of miles of tunnels (many there since the Vietminh's war against the French) for transportation and living purposes. UN Secretary General U Thant urged an end to the bombing, and French President Charles de Gaulle ignored his own country's past pillaging of Vietnam in calling it "detestable" for "a great nation to ravage a small one." The United States became subject to the charge of atrocity as up to 1000 Vietnamese civilians a week were added to growing casualty lists. Within the United States, Americans were shocked by the apparent suddenness of the decision to bomb North Vietnam. Some wondered whether the United States might not be the aggressor.

The growing emphasis on bombing had another unforeseen and bitterly ironic effect: Whereas the Johnson administration had counted on the new strategy to rule out the need for ground forces, U.S. soldiers now became necessary to protect air bases from Vietcong assaults. Thus did the administration find itself in the anomalous position of needing to send troops to protect an air offensive intended to avoid the use of troops. General Taylor understood the necessity of defending such air bases, but he warned about the dire implications of such a move. "Once we brought any troops in," he declared, "that was the nose of the camel." Never would we know how many were enough. Furthermore, the troop introduction raised another danger: Americans could not be sure which Vietnamese were Vietcong, whereas the Vietcong would have no trouble identifying their enemy.

In February 1965 the president gave in to Westmoreland's requests for protection of the air base at Danang and ordered two battalions of marines, accompanied by tanks and eight-inch howitzers, to South Vietnam. The highly publicized arrival of 3500 marines near Danang on March 8 (Westmoreland had wanted a

America at War
U.S. marine engaged in counterinsurgency action near Danang in March 1965.
National Archives, Washington, D.C.

dramatic "re-enactment of Iwo Jima") further Americanized the conflict. "When we marched into the rice paddies on that damp March afternoon," according to Marine Lieutenant Philip Caputo in his highly acclaimed autobiographical account *A Rumor of War,* "we carried, along with our packs and rifles, the implicit convictions that the Viet Cong would be quickly beaten and that we were doing something altogether noble and good." Less than a week after their landing, an equally ebullient Johnson spoke to an assistant about the United States's offer of economic aid to the Mekong. Patting his knee, the president declared that "Old Ho can't turn that down."

Although the U.S. forces were at first restricted to patrol duty, Westmoreland soon enlarged their role and ultimately completed the job of Americanizing the war. "The first troops were invited in to protect our air bases," he declared. "Now once those troops were at those bases, it made no sense at all to have them dig in and go strictly on the defensive." They soon engaged in "search and destroy" missions that more deeply alienated the populace and paradoxically diminished chances for winning the war, almost in direct relation to their military success. Taylor supported the use of U.S. combat troops, but he warned of the inherent danger of taking the war away from the ARVN. "There was every tendency," he asserted, "to push the little brown men to one side" and proclaim, "Let us go do it."

Surprisingly, the Johnson administration thought it could succeed in its efforts to conceal the steady escalation of the war from Americans and others outside the country. Its goal of an imperceptible widening of the war rested on a policy of gradualness intended to avoid a confrontation with either Communist China or the Soviet Union. Johnson also wanted to prevent a vicious debate in Congress over Vietnam that would, in the president's words, destroy "the woman I really loved—the Great Society." The White House efforts were largely unsuccessful. A growing chorus of protests against the war came from the *New York Times,* numerous university students, and leading Democratic senators such as Frank Church of Idaho, Mike Mansfield of Massachusetts, and George McGovern of South Dakota. Outside the United States, UN Secretary General U Thant of Burma called for a negotiated end to the war, as did Britain, Canada, and seventeen neutralist nations.

The United States's expanded involvement in Vietnam developed out of a strange mixture of the olive branch and the sword. In early April 1965 Johnson delivered a speech at Johns Hopkins University in which he warned that "the appetite of aggression is never satisfied" and declared that the United States had a "promise to keep." The nation's primary stipulation for peace was "an independent South Vietnam—securely guaranteed and able to shape its own relationships to all others—free from outside interference—tied to no alliance—a military base for no other country." Once peace was restored, he added, the United States

would provide $1 billion for the economic development of the Mekong Delta. "We want nothing for ourselves—only that the people of South Vietnam be allowed to guide their own country in their own way." Johnson warned of "the deepening shadow of Communist China" and reaffirmed the U.S. commitment. Failure to take action would lead to a "Red Asia" and a dangerous shift in the global balance of power. "Let no one think for a moment that retreat from Vietnam would bring an end to the conflict. The battle would be renewed in one country and then another. . . . We must say in southeast Asia—as we did in Europe—in the words of the Bible: 'Hitherto shalt thou come, but no further.' "

The next day a reply came from Hanoi that both mystified and angered the White House. The North Vietnamese government demanded that the United States sever military ties with Saigon, withdraw from South Vietnam and allow it to become neutralized, guarantee no "foreign interference" in the reunification of the Vietnams, and accept the establishment of a coalition government based on the National

U.S. Soldiers on Search-and-Destroy Mission
U.S. marines in rice paddies looking for Vietcong. *National Archives, Washington, D.C.*

Liberation Front's social, political, and economic reform program. Furthermore, the United States had to end the bombing before peace talks could begin. With the United States committed to an independent, non-Communist South Vietnam, and with the North Vietnamese determined to unify the country under their lead, the differences between the two antagonists in the war were nonnegotiable.

Revolution in the Dominican Republic

While the bombing went on, another problem suddenly interjected itself into the concerns of the Johnson administration, the successful resolution of which doubtless contributed to its decision to adopt even stronger military measures in Vietnam. The crisis grew out of a leftist revolution in the Dominican Republic. The United States's goals and methods were the same there as in Vietnam: Halt the spread of communism by intervening with military force to uphold domestic stability. After a brutal and murderous dictatorship of more than thirty years, Dominican President Rafael Trujillo (trained by U.S. Marines) was assassinated by military figures in 1961, and the following year the islanders elected liberal reformer Dr. Juan Bosch as president. Although a military coup forced Bosch into exile less than a year later, his leftist supporters mounted an insurrection against the military regime in April 1965 that brought on civil war. "Men and women like this," warned the U.S. ambassador to the Dominican Republic, John Bartlow Martin, "have nowhere to go except to the Communists." Military action by Washington seemed necessary to prevent the establishment of another Castro-like regime in the Caribbean.

Johnson quickly dispatched over 20,000 troops to support a conservative government and thereby safeguard U.S. interests on the island. Having decided against first consulting either the United Nations or the OAS, he spoke on television on April 28 to defend his decision. The soldiers were not only to restore order and bring citizens home, the president explained, but to deal with a new menace. The Dominican revolution had taken a Communist turn, an argument he buttressed with a dubious list of over fifty "identified and prominent Communist and Castroite leaders" among the rebels. Another Cuba seemed likely. "We don't intend to sit here in our rocking chair with our hands folded and let the Communists set up any governments in the Western Hemisphere." Lest there be doubt about his determination, he reiterated his stand in May in a statement later referred to as the "Johnson Doctrine": "American nations cannot, must not, and will not permit the establishment of another Communist government in the Western Hemisphere."

Despite bitter opposition in the United States and Latin America, the U.S. soldiers remained and predictably became enmeshed in the Dominican conflict. Many critics claimed that the U.S. action violated the OAS Charter, which stipulated that "no State or group of States had the right to intervene, directly or indirectly, for any reason whatever, in the internal or external affairs of any other State." Johnson countered with an argument that had a highly questionable foundation in fact: "People trained outside the Dominican Republic are seeking to gain control." Senator Fulbright doubted that the Communist danger was real and denounced the intervention as the work of hard-line anti-Communists who had seized control of U.S. foreign policy. In an observation that perhaps applied to numerous instances outside the hemisphere, the influential chair of the Foreign Relations Committee declared that Americans had become "the prisoners of the Latin American oligarchs who are engaged in a vain attempt to preserve the status quo—reactionaries who habitually use the term *communist* very loosely, in part . . . in a calculated effort to scare the United States into supporting their selfish and discredited aims."

The United States finally turned to the OAS as a way out of the imbroglio. In early

May the American foreign ministers' deputies met in Washington, where after a week of debate the United States narrowly won the two-thirds support needed (despite the opposition of the larger states) to establish a five-nation OAS Inter-American Peace Force. Most U.S. soldiers could now leave, although some stayed with the force as it tried to build a new regime composed of military and civilian leaders.

Although the Dominican intervention had been costly in credibility and prestige, the Johnson administration claimed a victory in blocking the installation of a leftist president. The United States's unilateral action, however, had violated a number of assurances given to Latin America as early as Franklin D. Roosevelt's Good Neighbor policy and as late as John F. Kennedy's Alliance for Progress. In June 1966 moderate rightists, led by Joaquín Balaguer, defeated Bosch for the presidency. The following month Balaguer took office and accepted a few of Bosch's followers into the cabinet. Bosch bitterly asserted that his had been "a democratic revolution smashed by the leading democracy of the world." Johnson, however, remained convinced that his forceful actions had prevented a Communist takeover in the Dominican Republic and that the same resolute action in Vietnam could achieve similar results.

Continued Escalation in Vietnam

Meanwhile, the war in Southeast Asia threatened to escalate again as the governments in both Saigon and Washington adopted harder positions. For nearly a week in May 1965 the United States called off the bombing to encourage negotiations, but with no results. In June, Saigon's government came under the control of the flamboyant and dashingly attired Air Marshal Nguyen Cao Ky, who had fought with the French against the Vietminh during the First Indochinese War. Ky became premier and his cohort, the ruggedly capable and less pretentious General Nguyen Van Thieu, became commander in chief of the armed forces. Although Americans attested to Thieu's abilities, they could not do the same with Ky. The CIA simply dismissed Ky as grossly irresponsible and concerned only about "drinking, gambling and chasing women." It was "the bottom of the barrel, absolutely the bottom of the barrel," one of Johnson's advisers recalled. Less than a week before Ky took over, the war took another dramatic turn upward: U.S. soldiers received authority to engage in full combat duty.

In the pivotal month of July, Johnson, without congressional approval, made an open-ended commitment to a ground war in Asia by assuring Westmoreland of as many troops as he needed. By the end of the year U.S. combat troops in Vietnam numbered more than 184,000, a figure that more than doubled a year later and continued growing. The U.S. economy could support a guns-and-butter policy, he declared. In justifying the momentous decision to inject so many more Americans, McNamara first admitted that such a heavy troop presence would make it more difficult to withdraw later on; and yet, in a statement that revealed the administration's failure to develop a cohesive strategy for conducting the war, he added that the move might "stave off defeat in the short run and offer a good chance of producing a favorable settlement in the longer run."

Thus had the administration thoroughly Americanized the war. The effort had become an all-out war of attrition that sought to pass the "enemy's threshold of pain" by the graduated use of superior manpower and resources. Not the least among the considerations underlying this objective was the widespread belief that the Vietnamese were racially and materially inferior rather than cunning, wily, and amazingly resilient. In retrospect, however, such a monumental decision conjures up the dark words of British writer Rudyard Kipling, which were openly displayed in U.S. clubs and bars in South Vietnam during the war. In his famous piece entitled "The Ballad of East and West," Kipling included these piercing lines:

McNamara and Westmoreland
Secretary of Defense McNamara in South Vietnam to discuss General Westmoreland's call for more than 100,000 U.S. troops. *National Archives, Washington, D.C.*

Now it is not good for the Christian's health
   to hustle the Aryan [Asian in Vietnam] brown
For the Christian riles, and the [Asian] smiles
   and weareth the Christian down;
And the end of the fight is a tombstone white
   with the name of the late deceased
And the epitaph drear: "A fool lies here
   who tried to hustle the East."

That same month of July several key Great Society programs had reached critical junctures in the legislative process, leading some writers to believe that Johnson feared he would lose South Vietnam at precisely the time he needed leverage to force through his reform program at home. Therefore, the argument goes, the president raised the level of involvement in Vietnam out of both domestic and foreign considerations. Whatever the truth, it appears that Johnson lacked a coherent military strategy and simply followed the day-to-day developments, with the central emphasis of wearing down the enemy while avoiding defeat. Johnson's decision to approve the escalation in Vietnam further transformed

the conflict into an American war, narrowing succeeding options and making his nation's commitment virtually unlimited.

As the fighting in Vietnam intensified in 1965, the United States defended its involvement on several grounds. First and foremost, it sought to halt outside "aggression" through military action while shoring up a rapidly deteriorating South Vietnam. The state department argued that the Tonkin Resolution was a natural extension of the SEATO Treaty, by which signatory nations agreed to aid members whose "peace and safety" were in jeopardy. The Johnson administration, like Kennedy's, believed that North Vietnam had infiltrated South Vietnam, thereby constituting an armed attack requiring protection by SEATO's members. In addition, Article 51 of the UN Charter allowed "collective self-defense" and justified U.S. action. Furthermore, a failure to protect South Vietnam would breach a moral duty, setting an example injurious to U.S. prestige and security throughout the world. There was "light at the end of the tunnel" and victory "just around the corner," according to an outwardly optimistic McNamara after visits to Vietnam in 1965 and 1966. Conflicting reports came from Hanoi's Premier Pham Van Dong, who solemnly warned, "There's no light at the end of the tunnel." Washington's most dangerous assumption was that a mere show of U.S. military strength would shatter the Vietcong and end the war.

Growing numbers of Americans questioned the wisdom of widening the nation's commitment to South Vietnam. In view of the widening rift between Moscow and Beijing (as best shown by the rising number of border clashes between Soviet and Chinese troops in early 1966), the traditional argument of halting a Kremlin-directed Communist monolith suddenly rang hollow. Questions arose about containment's open-ended premise that vital U.S. interests encompassed every area of the world threatened by communism—which meant that the United States was in danger of overextending itself. The United States had assumed the uncomfortable position of opposing all social revolutions simply because they opened the door for Communist subversion; the only safe situation seemed to be the status quo, which meant upholding stability even at the price of reform. By the mid-1960s the justification for U.S. involvement in Vietnam, begun by the Truman administration in 1950, had to come from other sources. The United States could not pull out of Vietnam without losing prestige and honor. The first intervention necessitated a deeper commitment, which in turn grew because of the first involvement: The longer the United States remained in Vietnam the longer it had to stay.

Seeds of "Vietnamization," 1966–1969

Continuation of the bombings had serious repercussions inside the United States because it tended to divide Americans into two broadly defined camps: the "doves," a mixed group of liberals and others who wanted a negotiated withdrawal, and the "hawks," primarily right-wing Republicans and conservative Democrats who advocated victory through increased military force. Protest demonstrations grew into a firestorm as the escalated involvement drained the dollar and fed inflation, threw the nation's budget into disarray, forced major cutbacks in foreign aid, and badly damaged the attention and support given to the Great Society's domestic reform programs. "Teach-ins" began in 1965 at the University of Michigan and spread to other places of learning, as faculty members opposed to the war held informal classes that analyzed the reasons for U.S. involvement. Many youths either burned their draft cards and chanted "Hell no, we won't go" or avoided the draft by going to Canada or to jail. "Hey, hey, LBJ, how many kids have you killed today?" chanted demonstrators around the White House, as they called the United States immoral, racist, and imperialist. The U.S. government, they bitterly complained, was killing reform at home and innocents abroad. The presidency was becoming imperial in callously ignoring the wishes of Congress and the people. Involvement in Vietnam, the doves argued, was wrecking the Western alliance and undercutting U.S. authority and prestige. Furthermore, it was unconstitutional because Congress had not declared war. Withdrawal from Vietnam was the only solution.

Although the hawks accused the doves of being led by Communists, criticism of the administration's Vietnam policies came from all parts of the nation and were attributable to factors beyond mere propaganda. The most vocal opponents of the war included Senators Fulbright, Mansfield, and Morse, containment architect George F. Kennan, journalist Walter Lippmann, civil rights leader Dr. Martin Luther King, Jr., numerous other notables from both major political parties, and leading newspapers such as the *New York Times* and the *Washington Post*. Others who emphasized the immoral nature of the war included "New Left" writers already critical of the country's alleged capitalist and exploitative "ruling class," long-time pacifist A. J. Muste and radical Tom Hayden, writer Norman Mailer, pediatrician Benjamin

Spock, heavyweight boxer Muhammad Ali, popular rock singers Joan Baez and Bob Dylan, Hollywood actress Jane Fonda, and a great number of college students. The United States, they claimed, was guilty of aggression in a civil war that had no relation to the SEATO charter.

The war's opponents presented many arguments that were difficult to refute. They charged that the United States was the only SEATO member that felt a responsibility to South Vietnam and that it was doing so by helping a repressive government crush a movement of the people. Furthermore, the United States had not supported the elections called for by the Geneva Accords of 1954, and Diem and his successors had released the United States from its commitments by failing to implement reforms. Johnson, they argued, had broken his word in sending soldiers to an Asian war. Moreover, they concluded, "victory" could come only at the cost of annihilating Vietnam: The United States could not win the war through conventional means, and the bombings would devastate the land in the name of peace. The most fundamental failure, some argued, was that the village pacification program had alienated the vast majority of peasants, encouraging the Vietnamese people to hate Americans. The bombings had now underlined the problem by thoroughly antagonizing the victims below. U.S. "globalism" was the root of the problem, many asserted, a feeling of superiority based on what Fulbright denounced as an "arrogance of power."

Defeat, the doves admitted, might allow Vietnam to become Communist, but that did not mean the country would automatically become Communist China's puppet. The Chinese confronted many problems at home and abroad that hampered their involvement in Southeast Asia. Serious foreign policy reverses had helped set off widespread domestic upheaval, causing Mao to begin a "cultural revolution" that necessitated a less active foreign policy while he worked to squelch his opposition at home. Furthermore, ancient hatreds between Vietnam and China blocked their cooperation—an argument the Johnson ad-

ministration could not refute with any degree of certitude because of its continued refusal to recognize the Beijing government and its resultant inability to gain firsthand information pertaining to that Communist regime's real feelings about the war.

In any case, the very multiplicity of arguments against the war guaranteed division among the doves, preventing unified resistance and helping the hawks stay in command. The hawks' defense of the war was formidable because they based their arguments on the fear of global communism and on Americans' fictional belief that they had won all their wars. Americans insisted that withdrawal from Vietnam would constitute their first military defeat, and Johnson refused to be the first chief executive to lose a war. Furthermore, the hawks declared, the president as commander in chief could send U.S. soldiers anywhere, a power confirmed by the Tonkin Resolution. On the charge of immorality, the hawks declared that the Vietcong were the aggressors and that South Vietnam had asked for U.S. help. It was not a civil war any longer—if indeed it ever had been—because the North Vietnamese depended on Chinese and Soviet assistance. The hawks insisted that Johnson's pledge against using U.S. combat forces was no longer applicable, because conditions had deteriorated so rapidly that South Vietnam needed direct assistance. Containment of communism was vital to U.S. security because failure in Southeast Asia would have a "domino" effect that would ultimately reach Pacific shores. Appeasement in Vietnam, the hawks concluded, would show a lack of U.S. will, inviting direct intervention by the Soviet Union and Communist China.

Unrest over the war continued to grow throughout 1966 and 1967. In early 1966 Fulbright chaired a series of televised hearings by the Senate Foreign Relations Committee regarding U.S. involvement in Vietnam. Asking probing questions of administration supporters, he could get no satisfactory answer regarding which country's communism the United States was trying to contain in Southeast Asia. The major spokesman for the ad-

The Anguish of America's Longest War
A U.S. infantryman buries his head in his hands after reading a letter from home. *Associated Press.*

ministration, Secretary of State Rusk, argued that the United States was fighting the spread of Chinese communism, ignoring growing reports that by the mid-1960s China's domestic and foreign troubles had permitted the Soviet Union to assume a major burden of aid for North Vietnam. In a move that struck many listeners as utterly anachronistic, he quoted from the Truman Doctrine of 1947 in justifying the U.S. presence in Southeast Asia: "I believe it must be the policy of the United States to support free peoples who are resisting attempted subjugation by armed minorities or by outside pressures."

Criticisms of the administration's Vietnam policies were steadily intensifying. Kennan asserted that he never intended the containment doctrine to entail the use of military force at virtually any point in the world. There was "no reason why we should wish to become so involved" in Vietnam. The United States should begin a phased withdrawal, he declared; containment was not the solution to Asian problems as it had been to Europe's crises of the 1940s. Communism was too diverse and the world's problems too monumental for the United States alone to resolve. Even McNamara, one of Johnson's closest supporters, changed his stance. In 1967 he resigned as head of defense in protest over the administration's policies in Vietnam, joining McGeorge Bundy, George Ball, and the president's political adviser and friend Bill Moyers, all of whom had already left Washington.

While the arguments drummed on, the United States slowly sank into what writers later called the "quagmire" of Vietnam. By 1967, after three years of direct military involvement, the situation in South Vietnam had not improved and the United States had sustained great losses, including the downing of $6 billion worth of aircraft in North Vietnam. But General Westmoreland was calling for more soldiers. Johnson was reluctant. "When we add divisions," he asked in April, "can't the enemy add divisions? If so, where does it all end?" The "search and destroy" missions had led to heavy loss of life and property but had failed to root out villagers suspected of helping the Vietcong. On television news programs, Americans heard grisly accounts of skyrocketing "body counts" of enemy dead that allegedly proved the imminence of a victory that never came. And they watched with shock and dismay as their soldiers cleared the Vietcong from villages and countryside (many areas declared "Free Fire Zones" and hence subject to all-out assault) by using napalm, tear gas, flame throwers, saturation bombing, chemical defoliants that included "Agent Orange," and firepower of all kinds.

The United States's prospects in Vietnam were dismal at best. "Pacification" centers (the once heralded strategic hamlets erected to guarantee peasant security) were filled and failing, and increasing numbers of U.S. soldiers had fallen victim to mines and booby traps (packed with shrapnel called "American spaghetti," which consisted of short strips of barbed wire chopped off posts) set by peasants and by the ghostlike enemy referred to as "Charlie" (the "Orwellian unperson," as French news correspondent and author Bernard Fall called him). Corruption and governmental incompetence in Saigon continued its relentless upward spiral; the Vietcong found sustenance and sanctuary in Laos and Cambodia; and the Ho Chi Minh Trail, according to one special forces soldier, reminded him of the "Long Island expressway—during rush hour." The number of refugees by the beginning of 1968 had soared to four million, or one-quarter of the country's population. Even the environment worked to the advantage of the Vietcong. To Americans, Vietnam was an unfamiliar and foreboding land called "Apache country"—a dense tropical jungle characterized by insufferable heat and humidity, countless legions of leeches and fire ants, towering elephant grass that made passage extremely difficult, deadly diseases that included malaria and jungle fever, and monsoons and heavy fog cover that severely hampered both ground and air operations. All the while, the fiercely determined enemy countered the United States's superior artillery and air power by engaging in what one U.S. officer called "violent, close-quarters combat." Thus did the Americans as outsiders wage a war of attrition that almost inevitably alienated the great masses of people, whose support was critical to success.

As General Taylor had warned, the Americanization of the war carried the seeds of its own destruction. The move had indeed reduced the role of the ARVN and made it less effective, and Ky's Saigon government had further embarrassed the United States by imprisoning thousands of political enemies because of another Buddhist upheaval. In the meantime, the political battle over the people's support was being lost as mounting numbers of peasants, including refugees, flocked into the ranks of the Vietcong, thereby disproving the theory of Westmoreland's advisers that the number of enemy killings would eventually reach that highly coveted "crossover point" at which more died than the Hanoi government could replenish. Ironically, as the United States's firepower became more effective, its chances for gaining popular support and winning the war seemed to decline correspondingly. Johnson claimed he felt like a hitch-hiker on a road in a Texas hailstorm: "I can't run. I can't hide. And I can't make it stop."

U.S. relations with most other Asian countries also steadily deteriorated in almost direct proportion to its military escalation in Vietnam. The United States accused Cambodia of providing sanctuary for the Vietcong, leading that government to break relations with Washington in 1965. Americans meanwhile bombed supply lines in neutral Laos (a top secret operation code-named "Steel Tiger") to close the Ho Chi Minh Trail. Japan increasingly questioned U.S. involvement in Southeast Asia, especially after Okinawa became the headquarters for launching aerial attacks on North Vietnam. Thailand was an exception to the region's growing anti-American feeling: It feared Communist guerrillas in the east and permitted the establishment of U.S. military plants and bombing bases. As in the Korean War, Americans comprised the great bulk of fighting forces in Vietnam, although 50,000 soldiers from South Korea joined the few contributed by Thailand, Australia, New Zealand, and the Philippines. SEATO, as many feared, had become a transparent cover for what was fast becoming a unilateral U.S. involvement.

Johnson continued his call for peace (more than 2000 attempts between 1965 and 1967) while refusing to condone any appearance of capitulation to aggression. But the administration insisted on an independent, non-Communist South Vietnam, whereas the North Vietnamese demanded an end to the bombing, a total U.S. withdrawal, and the ultimate unification of the entire country "in accordance with the program of the National Liberation Front." The opposing stands were irreconcilable. The United Nations, the Vatican, and Poland offered to mediate an end to the war, and several times the United States authorized bombing pauses to encourage negotiations. During a month-long bombing halt that began on Christmas Eve of 1965, Johnson sent a much publicized peace mission to forty foreign capitals to explain the U.S. stand and to seek these governments' help in ending the war. The delegation's membership was impressive—Vice President Hubert Humphrey, UN Ambassador Arthur Goldberg, and Ambassador-at-Large W. Averell Harriman—and its program sounded irresistibly Wilsonian and morally principled in carrying the name of the "Fourteen Points." Rusk boasted, "We put everything into the basket but the surrender of South Vietnam."

But to Hanoi, this was everything. The effort failed, and the bombings resumed. Under no conditions would the United States permit the Vietcong into the government. That would be like "putting the fox in a chicken coop," Humphrey publicly scoffed. The president then instructed Goldberg to take the issue before the UN Security Council, but that body took no action.

The United States stood virtually alone in Vietnam, and yet the Johnson administration still refused to relent. In an interview, the president explained his position in Rooseveltian language: "I deeply believe we are quarantining aggression over there, just like the smallpox. Just like FDR and Hitler, just like Wilson and the Kaiser. . . . What I learned as a boy in my teens and in college about World War I was that it was our lack of strength and failure to show stamina that got us into that war."

The Six Day War in the Middle East

In spring 1967, the danger of a U.S. over-commitment in Vietnam became evident when in the Middle East, Israeli forces again grappled with those of Egypt in a fierce but abbreviated conflict known as the Six Day War. The region had remained unstable after the Suez crisis of 1956. The United States had continued its dual policy toward the Israelis and Arabs, including the sale of arms to both sides to maintain a power balance, but Nasser had also received Soviet planes and tanks, worked with other Arab leaders in 1964 in establishing the Palestine Liberation Organization (PLO) to tear Palestine from Israel, and demanded that the UN peacekeeping force withdraw from the Egyptian-Israeli border. When the United Nations complied with his wishes in May 1967, the two age-old antagonists directly confronted each other again for the first time since Britain's departure in 1956. Shortly afterward Nasser moved his forces into the Sinai Peninsula and seized Sharm el-Sheikh, a camp strategically overlooking the entrance into the

Gulf of Aqaba. His actions effectively closed the gulf and denied Israel its only port.

Nasser seemed to be preparing for an invasion of Israel. His seizure of Sharm el-Sheikh had brought the United States into the matter because in 1956 the Eisenhower administration had secured Israel's withdrawal from the area with a promise to support its access to the Gulf of Aqaba. Meanwhile, PLO terrorist groups from Syria and Jordan began guerrilla raids on Israel that drew immediate reprisals and threatened to engulf the entire region in war.

As Egyptian, Syrian, and Jordanian troops massed along Israel's borders, the Israelis decided to repeat their strategy of 1956 by striking first. On the morning of June 5, 1967, Israeli planes, evading Egyptian radar by approaching over the Mediterranean rather than the Sinai, launched a series of devastating raids on Nasser's air force, which was still on the ground. They then did the same with those of Jordan, Syria, and Iraq. Israeli tanks and soldiers meanwhile crossed the Sinai desert and within six days had blocked the Suez Canal and controlled Sharm el-Sheikh, the old city of Jerusalem, the West Bank of the Jordan River, the Golan Heights along Syria's border, and parts of Jordan and Syria. Neither the Soviet Union nor the United States intervened, although their use of the "hot line" between Moscow and Washington perhaps reduced the chances of a misunderstanding that could have widened the war. With the Arabs defeated, the Soviets recommended a cease-fire, and on June 11 the UN Security Council accepted it. The fighting was over.

The United Nations managed a shaky agreement in late November 1967. The vaguely worded document, Security Council Resolution 242, stipulated that in exchange for the Israelis' withdrawal from recently occupied Arab territories, they would receive guarantees of border security and free use of regional waterways. To ensure peace, the resolution called for the establishment of "demilitarized zones," the nondiscriminatory use of inter-

national waters in the area (the Suez Canal was closed again, because as in 1956 Nasser sank ships at its entrance), and "a just settlement of the refugee problem," which the Palestinians interpreted as the establishment of a homeland. Resumption of the age-old conflict seemed predictable—particularly when the antagonists did not implement the terms of the resolution.

In the aftermath of the Six Day War the Middle East remained unstable, further revealing the incapacity of the United States to keep peace all over the world. U.S. relations with the Arabs plummeted. Nasser broke relations after making erroneous charges that U.S. and British planes had aided the Israeli offensive, and several Arab nations responded by instituting a short-lived oil embargo against the West. Meanwhile the Israelis argued that Security Council Resolution 242 meant that satisfactory security treaties must *precede* their withdrawal from the newly occupied lands and continued to hold the Sinai Peninsula (part of Egypt for more than 5000 years), the Gaza Strip, and the east bank of the Suez Canal. Furthermore, they barred access to the waterway until it was open to everyone. The Soviet Union finally broke relations with Israel after warning it to return all Arab lands before negotiations could begin. Although the United States refused to recognize the Israelis' occupation of the old sector of Jerusalem, it understood their need for security and tried to persuade them to return the lands taken, in exchange for guaranteed access to the canal and Gulf of Aqaba. But neither the Soviets nor the Americans were able to arouse enough support for their program, and Israel steadfastly refused to return territories taken during the Six Day War.

While several mediation attempts failed, sporadic border incidents and increasing terrorist acts by the rapidly growing PLO underlined the need for a permanent settlement. Peace continued to elude the region throughout Johnson's tenure in office, further draining the energy his administration needed to deal with the ongoing war in Vietnam.

Attempted Negotiations With Hanoi and the *Pueblo* Incident

By the end of 1967 the imminence of hostilities in the Middle East had highlighted the dangers of the United States's growing global commitments and provided renewed impetus to the search for an honorable way out of Vietnam. Indeed, peace prospects had improved. Earlier that year in June the president had met with Soviet Premier Kosygin at Glassboro State College in New Jersey, and even though the two leaders had failed to reach agreements on either Vietnam or the ongoing Middle East crisis, they left the image of a friendly atmosphere conducive to détente. In autumn, opinion polls showed that a majority of Americans considered intervention in Vietnam to have been a mistake.

That September in San Antonio, Texas, Johnson set out a plan for peace that became known as the "San Antonio formula." The United States, he declared, was "willing to stop all aerial and naval bombing of North Vietnam when this will lead promptly to productive discussions. We, of course, assume that while discussions proceed, North Vietnam would not take advantage of the bombing cessation or limitation." The White House now demanded only an end to new infiltration as a prerequisite to negotiations and, in a remarkable turnaround, dropped its rigid opposition to Vietcong participation in the political process. Two months later the United States withdrew its opposition to negotiating with the National Liberation Front as a separate organization. North Vietnam, in turn, also retreated from some of its stringent conditions for talks. No longer did it demand a total U.S. military withdrawal, although it still insisted on a bombing halt before any discussions could begin. The Hanoi government also seemed willing to accept a long-range reunification plan.

Yet neither side was willing to concede anything on the premier issue of South Vietnam's future, and that bitter standoff dictated a prolongation of the war. The United States reiterated its call for an independent non-Communist South Vietnam, and North Vietnam repeated its demand for a reunited country free from foreign influence. The U.S. ambassador to South Vietnam, Ellsworth Bunker, nonetheless assured superiors in Washington that the pacification program was working. That same year of 1967, the CIA station chief in Saigon, William Colby, had helped to create the "Phoenix Program," which allegedly promoted pacification by undermining the "Vietcong Infrastructure" in South Vietnam through mass arrests and trials of civilians accused of helping the enemy. But all too quickly "Phoenix" became synonymous with assassinations: Due process was discarded, and thousands of suspected Vietcong and their sympathizers were "neutralized" every month as part of the "Accelerated Pacification Campaign." On the surface, however, the prognosis looked good. "We are winning a war of attrition," Westmoreland declared. Figures compiled by MACV suggested that the U.S. military effort was about to reach the magical "crossover point," because American and ARVN armies were close to killing more North Vietnamese regulars than the Hanoi government could replace. Although the CIA argued that MACV's calculations were misleading and that North Vietnam's military force included many not in uniform, Westmoreland chose to accept MACV's findings and thereby offered the president an optimistic assessment of the war's progress. Within two years, the general asserted, the United States could begin a gradual withdrawal that would allow South Vietnam to take over the war. But even though the United States's chief diplomatic and military representatives in South Vietnam had finally discerned a timetable for withdrawal, two more years of fighting seemed interminable to those who wanted out immediately.

Several events in early 1968 suddenly complicated the U.S. involvement in Vietnam. An American B-52 disappeared in Greenland carrying four H-bombs; Democratic Senator Eugene McCarthy from Minnesota had entered the presidential race on an antiwar platform and gained a surprising amount of support;

U.S. Embassy in Saigon
With their dead comrades lying nearby, these American soldiers held out against the
Vietcong attacking the embassy during the Tet Offensive. *Wide World Photos, New York.*

and new troubles developed in Berlin that perhaps necessitated more U.S. troops. But most
exasperating was the incident involving the
U.S. intelligence vessel *Pueblo*. On January 23
North Korean forces seized the *Pueblo* in the
Sea of Japan, charging it with invading their
territorial waters and imprisoning the ship's
eighty-two officers and sailors. Though Americans demanded prompt military action, the
Johnson administration could not risk a war
in Korea while immersed in one in Vietnam.
After nearly a year of negotiations the U.S.
sailors, clearly under duress, admitted to violating North Korean waters and signed an
apology. In a bizarre twist the U.S. commander had permission from his captors to
renounce the confession before and after
signing it. The men were freed, although the
Communists kept the ship and won a major
propaganda victory that further underlined
the finite nature of the United States's superpower status.

Tet—and After

A week after the *Pueblo* incident, on January 30, 1968, Vietcong and North Vietnamese forces violated the long-honored truce
during Tet, or the lunar new year holiday, by
launching a massive surprise offensive against
the cities and provinces of South Vietnam that
the Hanoi regime expected would cause a
popular uprising against the Americans and
the ARVN. At 2:45 A.M., nineteen Vietcong
exploded a hole in the thick-walled, eight-
foot-tall barricade around the U.S. embassy in
Saigon, killing two military policemen on duty
at the time. Using antitank guns and rockets
that had been brought surreptitiously into
the city weeks earlier, the Vietcong entered
the courtyard but never managed to seize the
embassy building, which at the time housed
only a few CIA and Foreign Service officers.
U.S. soldiers retaliated at daybreak. Marines
and paratroopers landed by helicopter on the

embassy roof and regained control of the grounds a little after 9 A.M. Five Americans died in the heated exchange; all nineteen Vietcong were either killed or seriously wounded.

The greatest casualty of the Tet Offensive was the Johnson administration's credibility at home. Americans were shocked to see televised coverage of their embassy grounds overrun by Vietcong and of U.S. soldiers and civilians frantically running through the carnage and gunfire, searching out other assailants. The timing of the assault was particularly traumatic. Westmoreland had just returned to the United States in late 1967 to report imminent victory, and the president himself had declared just two weeks before Tet in his State of the Union message that South Vietnam was nearly all "secure." In surveying the damage on the embassy grounds (which one journalist called "a butcher shop in Eden"), Westmoreland presented a coldly formal statement

over television, during which he asserted that the Communists had "very deceitfully" exploited the holiday truce "to create maximum consternation." He then drew groans of disbelief among reporters by dismissing the assault as the Vietcong's "last gasp" and claiming that the enemy's "well-laid plans" had met a crushing defeat.

The urban offensive had completely surprised the United States and South Vietnam, primarily because both had thought the central North Vietnamese assault would be an ongoing siege on the huge marine garrison at Khe Sanh. Located in the far northwest section of South Vietnam and close to the Laotian border, the military fortress was an imposing part of the continuing effort to end infiltration through the Ho Chi Minh Trail. Indeed, some observers considered Khe Sanh to be the chief object of North Vietnam's offensive, another Dienbienphu—which was what North

General William Westmoreland
The leader of American forces in Vietnam (second from left) talks to military personnel in the U.S. embassy in Saigon after the Vietcong siege during Tet, January 31, 1968. *U.S. Army.*

Battle of Khe Sanh
U.S. Marines under siege by the North Vietnamese at Khe Sanh in 1968. *National Archives, Washington, D.C.*

Vietnamese military chieftain and strategist Vo Nguyen Giap later claimed he had intended. The North Vietnamese Army's offensive against Khe Sanh was a diversionary move, he argued, designed to draw Americans' attention from the plan's central thrust: a massive Vietcong assault on South Vietnam's major urban areas, which would set off the revolution that ultimately liberated the south by bringing down the Saigon government and sending the Americans home. As is the goal of any sound military strategist, Giap attempted to strike at his antagonist's most vulnerable point. Tactically, he knew he could not prevail over the United States's vastly superior firepower; but psychologically and politically he could win a crucial battle by convincing Americans at home that the war was not winnable. The Johnson administration's continued optimism in the face of such adversity would then open a credibility gap that the president could not close. With the decline of

domestic support for the war, Giap reasoned, the United States would have no choice but to withdraw.

Westmoreland was correct in terming the outcome of Tet a military victory for the United States, but he missed the point: Americans refused to believe him. Renowned CBS newsman and staunch administration supporter Walter Cronkite stormed, "What the hell is going on? I thought we were winning the war!" He soon called the war a stalemate and urged the White House to negotiate "as an honorable people who lived up to their pledge to defend democracy, and did the best they could." Although Johnson agreed with his field commander that the assault was a "complete failure," he quietly admitted that the Vietcong had won a "psychological victory." Nor was Westmoreland naïve. Privately he conceded that Tet was a "severe blow" to South Vietnam. And yet, the U.S.–South Vietnamese counterassault also dealt the Vietcong a near lethal blow. No revolution occurred, and local television accounts of the stacks of Vietcong bodies in Saigon sent a horrifying message to many villagers in South Vietnam that it would be wiser to send their young males into the local defense units rather than have them forced into the Vietcong.

But despite the unquestioned success in the field, most talk of victory in the war came to an abrupt end as U.S. leaders took the first important turn toward a negotiated peace based on the reality of a stalemate. Perhaps the critics were correct: The United States could not win the war because the Hanoi government adamantly refused to negotiate until the Americans left the Vietnamese to resolve their own problems. Yet the presence of U.S. troops upheld the Saigon government and thereby denied the North Vietnamese a victory. Most important, the Tet Offensive raised the question that many Americans had been silently asking for some time: If the war was going so well, why was it lasting so long?

Although the furious U.S.-ARVN counter-offensive was enormously successful, it further highlighted the ghastly nature of the fighting and, almost paradoxically, increased opposition to U.S. involvement in the war. Using rockets and gas, the combined armies regained control of the city of Hué, but only at the heavy cost of three weeks of vicious street-to-street fighting that led to 4000 civilian deaths and added more than 100,000 refugees to the already bloated list. "Nothing I had seen during the Second World War in the Pacific, during the Korean War, and in Vietnam," journalist Robert Shaplen wrote, could compare to the "destruction and despair" in Hué. By the middle of March, according to perhaps inflated estimates, more than 40,000 Vietcong, or half of their forces, lay dead throughout the country. The American dead numbered 1000, and the ARVN's was twice that amount. The war seemed to have reached a new level of atrocity. Mass graves uncovered in Hué yielded close to 3000 bodies of civilian men,

The Totality of War
South Vietnamese civilians evacuating the village of My Tho in Dinh Tuong province during the Tet Offensive of 1968. *National Archives, Washington, D.C.*

The TV War in Vietnam
A Vietcong guerrilla executed by South Vietnamese national police
chief, Brigadier General Nguyen Ngoc Loan, in Saigon on February 1,
1968. Associated Press photographer Eddie Adams took the picture
that brought the war home to Americans and others around the
world. *Wide World Photos, New York.*

women, and children, all executed by the North Vietnamese and Vietcong and many buried alive. Another 2000 of Hué's citizens were missing and probably murdered. But even more shocking was an NBC news program in February that showed footage of Saigon's police chief executing a handcuffed Vietcong prisoner in the street by a pistol shot to the head. In the provincial capital of Ben Tre, U.S. and ARVN troops killed 1000 civilians while rooting out the Vietcong, causing one U.S. officer to capsulize the new nightmarish direction of the war in these words: "We had to destroy the town to save it."

By March, North Vietnamese Army units had resumed their earlier attack on Khe Sanh, but even though the Americans held on to the garrison, people in the United States were convinced that their soldiers were on the defensive. In fact, it now appears that the U.S. and ARVN counterattack was so successful that North Vietnamese regulars had to fill the Vietcong's sharply diminished ranks, finally converting the fighting into a conventional war between North and South Vietnam.

By early 1968 skepticism about the U.S. involvement in Vietnam had permeated the top echelons of the Johnson administration. In late February the president asked his new secretary of defense, Clark Clifford, to assess the nation's Vietnam policy. Westmoreland had just called for 206,000 more soldiers to join the 535,000 already there, in preparation for a major offensive. To send such a large military contingent, Johnson realized, required mobilizing the reserves and enlarging the draft. Indeed, he had already dismissed the idea of a massive troop buildup, only to see that someone in the administration had leaked the request to the press and thereby set off another barrage of criticism. In March, Rusk suggested a cease-fire based on a bombing halt, and presidential hopeful Eugene McCarthy, calling for an immediate U.S. withdrawal, made a strong showing in the New Hampshire Democratic primary. His success may have been due to the votes of unhappy hawks rather than doves, but it nonetheless showed Americans' mounting displeasure with the administration.

Meanwhile, even the strongly supportive foreign policy "establishment" had changed its views on the war. Former Secretary of State Dean Acheson assured the president that "the Joint Chiefs of Staff don't know what they're talking about" in asking for more men, and Clifford bolstered this charge by reporting that the generals could give him no specific answers regarding when and how victory would come or at what cost. In early March, Clifford recommended the addition of only 22,000 more U.S. soldiers, the call-up of an undetermined number of reserves, and a "highly forceful approach" to Ky and Thieu to take over more of the fighting. Support for the "gradual disengagement" of Americans from the war (later called "Vietnamization") came from the Senior Informal Advisory Group on Vietnam (the "Wise Men"), a collection of fourteen diplomatic and military figures of the Truman years who stunned the president by expressing doubt about the nation's ability to win the war.

Thus, by 1968 serious misgivings about the U.S. role in Vietnam had reached the White House, where the lack of progress in the war and its tremendous expense soon forced a change both in tactics in Vietnam and leadership in Washington. The ARVN's surprising recovery from the Tet Offensive upheld the argument that scaling down U.S. involvement to its pre-1965 level might be the most feasible way out of the war. Johnson, believing that his generals had misled him in Vietnam, decided against sending even the 22,000 men Clifford had recommended and then ordered Westmoreland home and promoted him to Army Chief of Staff to spare him the blame for the United States's failure to win the war. Finally, in view of marked domestic unrest over the war, the president announced in a televised broadcast on March 31, 1968, that he would call off much of the bombing of North Vietnam to encourage peace talks. Lest his plea appear to be a cheap political effort to ensure reelection, he surprised the nation and most of his advisers by adding that he would neither seek

McNamara and Clifford
McNamara was secretary of defense from 1961 to 1968, when he resigned and Clifford took his place and worked toward America's withdrawal from the war in Vietnam. *U.S. Army.*

nor accept his party's nomination for the presidency.

Within a week of the president's withdrawal from the 1968 campaign, the North Vietnamese surprised the White House by agreeing to peace talks, which began in Paris on May 13. But high hopes just as suddenly dissipated as snags immediately developed. The U.S. delegation, headed by veteran diplomat W. Averell Harriman, encountered resistance from the North Vietnamese, who refused to discuss terms until the United States stopped *all* bombing. The Johnson administration declined on the same ground as earlier: The North Vietnamese might exploit the truce to strengthen their forces and therefore endanger U.S. soldiers. With neither side willing to retreat, the United States and South Vietnam intensified their pacification and de-Americanization programs, apparently leaving the peace talks as the legacy for a new presidential administration in Washington.

The Presidential Election of 1968

With Vietnam as the major issue of the 1968 presidential election, the Republicans met in Miami Beach in early August and nominated the staunch anti-Communist Richard M. Nixon for the office. Trying to walk down the political middle, the former vice president offered experience in office and a hard-nosed tenacity in seeking his objectives. Had he not risen from the political grave after his presidential defeat in 1960 followed just two years later by a gubernatorial defeat in California? Most important, he promised reductions in government spending and no retreat in Vietnam. In a reminder of the Eisenhower strategy of 1952, Nixon assured Americans that he had a "secret plan" designed to "end the war and win the peace." When pressed to reveal the plan, Nixon explained that secrecy was essential because of the ongoing Paris negotiations.

The Democrats prepared for battle. With Johnson out of the race, Vice President Humphrey declared his intention to run, as did Senator Robert F. Kennedy of New York, who announced his candidacy on an antiwar platform and took most of McCarthy's supporters. Kennedy won the June primary in California but, like his brother five and a half years earlier, was assassinated that very evening. His death shocked the nation and left the antiwar campaign in disarray. Had the United States become a nation of violence? asked many Americans, who had just witnessed the riots and burning cities (including Washington) in the aftermath of the murder of civil rights leader Martin Luther King, Jr., in Memphis the previous April. Kennedy's followers had no choice but to shun the campaign in frustration or fall back with McCarthy: Humphrey was locked into administration policies that called for continued bombing until concessions from North Vietnam allowed peace with honor.

Later that August the Democratic party gathered in Chicago, where a siegelike atmosphere prevailed, both inside and outside the convention hall. Inside, an extremely bitter political battle developed over the Democratic platform on Vietnam. McCarthy's followers demanded an end to the bombing, immediate negotiations, and withdrawal of U.S. forces. Humphrey's supporters countered with the administration's hard-line argument and after a bitter three-hour debate defeated the peace plank. In celebration of their victory, Democratic hard-liners on Vietnam tactlessly arranged film coverage on the wide auditorium screen of air force action footage while the band struck up the tune "Up We Go, Into the Wild, Blue Yonder." Outside the hall, antiwar protesters carrying Vietcong flags called the police "pigs," sang the popular song "I Ain't Marchin' Anymore," and chanted "Ho, Ho, Ho Chi Minh," "Sieg Heil, Sieg Heil, Sieg," and "The Whole World Is Watching." In what an investigative commission afterward termed a "police riot," violence broke out in Chicago's streets as thousands of troops and hundreds of club-wielding policemen swarmed into the crowd, injuring hundreds of demonstrators, bystanders, and reporters, and taking many to jail. Out of concern for personal safety, President Johnson did not attend the nomination proceedings. In an instance in which symbolism took center stage, NBC-TV interjected clips of the violence on the streets just as Humphrey's nomination was to receive a second, thus adding an appropriate bloody context for the chaos and disorder reigning all around him.

The political sides had not yet been fully drawn, because a third party entered the contest. The American Independence Party (AIP) nominated Alabama Governor George Wallace for the presidency on a "law and order" campaign, which many called a euphemism for a "white backlash" against the civil rights movement. The AIP demanded continued racial segregation and a crackdown on all protesters. Wallace insisted on victory in Vietnam, and his vice presidential running mate, General Curtis LeMay, lamented the United States's "phobia" over nuclear weapons and told observers that he favored bombing North Vietnam "[back] into the stone age." One wag labeled the AIP candidates as "the bombsy twins."

Nixon's "hawkish" candidacy suddenly received a big boost when on the night of August 20–21, Soviet tanks and troops stormed into Czechoslovakia to put down an uprising similar to that of the late 1940s. To justify this action, Soviet General Secretary Leonid Brezhnev asserted in what became known as the "Brezhnev Doctrine" that the Soviets had the right to intervene in any allied country to defend "proletarian internationalism." Although Johnson protested, he found it difficult to fend off the strongly indignant counterattacks pointing to the United States's recent military intervention in the Dominican Republic and its ongoing war in Vietnam. The Soviet intervention in Czechoslovakia seemed to have undermined hopes for détente. It heightened the Cold War by dredging up the black memories of Stalinism, stimulated a missile and arms buildup that threatened to interfere with the Senate's approval of the nuclear nonproliferation agreement, drew the NATO alliance closer together again, and underscored the United States's inability to determine world events. The hawks in the United States cited the Czech crisis as evidence of the need to stand up to the Communists in Vietnam, and many Americans became convinced that Nixon's long record of fighting communism made him the best choice in 1968.

With Nixon running ahead in the polls, Johnson announced late in the campaign, on October 31, that all bombing would end the following day. His move suddenly lifted Humphrey's chances for winning and offered new hope for the staggering peace talks in Paris. But the change of course came too late. On November 5 Nixon won a narrow victory despite Humphrey's rapid surge following the bombing halt. With 302 electoral votes but only 43.4 percent of the popular vote, and with Democratic majorities in both Houses of Congress, Nixon prepared to assume the presidency and "win the peace" in Vietnam. Prospects looked good: On January 16, 1969, four days before the inauguration, the Paris conferees agreed to sit at a round table, resolving a long and bitter dispute by awarding all participants equal status, and the three delegations from South Vietnam, North Vietnam, and the National Liberation Front agreed with the Americans to turn to substantive matters.

Containment in Free Fall

The containment policy followed since the Truman era had virtually collapsed during the Johnson presidency. All of its assumptions had come into question: that a huge Communist monolith existed under Moscow's direction; that the United States had to defend "vital interests" in whatever area in the world the Communists sought (never seeming to doubt, for example, South Vietnam's strategic importance, its viability as a nation-state, or the popularity of its government); that the instability resulting from social revolutions was an automatic breeding ground for communism and had to be resisted with either military or economic means; that the American sense of mission necessitated the exportation of democracy into every nation in the world; and, above all, that the United States could leave no indications of a weakened will. The Vietnam crisis had gone on for so long that the future of the world appeared to rest in that small country, which dictated a total commitment that forced the collapse of containment. Fighting without the ideological belief in containment proved devastating to Americans' morale, moral fiber, and sense of righteousness. The consolation was that the new presidential administration seemed to offer a different direction in foreign policy.

Selected Readings

Ambrose, Stephen E., and Brinkley, Douglas G. *Rise to Globalism: American Foreign Policy since 1938.* 8th ed., 1997.

Anderson David L., ed. *Facing My Lai: Moving Beyond the Massacre.* 1998.

Ashby, LeRoy, and Gramer, Rod. *Fighting the Odds: The Life of Senator Frank Church.* 1994.

Ball, George W., and Ball, Douglas B. *The Passionate Attachment: America's Involvement with Israel 1947 to the Present.* 1992.

Baritz, Loren. *Backfire: A History of How American Culture Led Us into Vietnam and Made Us Fight the Way We Did.* 1985.

Barrett, David M. *Uncertain Warriors: Lyndon Johnson and His Vietnam Advisers.* 1993.

Ben-Zvi, Abraham. *Decade of Transition: Eisenhower, Kennedy, and the Origins of the American-Israeli Alliance.* 1998.

Berman, Larry. *Lyndon Johnson's War: The Road to Stalemate in Vietnam.* 1989.

———. *Planning a Tragedy: The Americanization of the War in Vietnam.* 1982.

———. *William Fulbright and the Vietnam War.* 1988.

Bernstein, Irving. *Guns or Butter: The Presidency of Lyndon Johnson.* 1996.

Bill, James A. *George Ball: Behind the Scenes in U.S. Foreign Policy.* 1997.

Bird, Kai. *The Color of Truth: McGeorge Bundy and William Bundy, Brothers in Arms: A Biography.* 1998.

Blair, Anne E. *Lodge in Vietnam: A Patriot Abroad.* 1995.

Bornet, Vaughn Davis. *The Presidency of Lyndon B. Johnson.* 1983.

Brands, H.W. *The Devil We Knew: Americans and the Cold War.* 1993.

———. *The Wages of Globalism: Lyndon Johnson and the Limits of American Power.* 1995.

Brigham, Robert K. *Guerrilla Diplomacy: The NLF's Foreign Relations and the Viet Nam War.* 1999.

Brinkley, Douglas. *Dean Acheson: The Cold War Years, 1953–71.* 1992.

Burchett, Wilfred. *Catapult to Freedom: The Survival of the Vietnamese People.* 1978.

Buttinger, Joseph. *Vietnam: A Dragon Embattled.* 2 vols., 1967.

———. *Vietnam: A Political History.* 1968.

Buzzanco, Robert. *Masters of War: Military Dissent and Politics in the Vietnam Era.* 1996.

———. *Vietnam and the Transformation of American Life.* 1999.

Cable, Larry. *Unholy Grail: The US and the Wars in Vietnam, 1965–8.* 1991.

Caputo, Philip. *A Rumor of War.* 1977.

Cincinnatus [pseudonym for Currey, Cecil B.], *Self-Destruction: The Disintegration and Decay of the United States Army during the Vietnam Era.* 1981.

Clifford, Clark. *Counsel to the President: A Memoir (with Richard Holbrooke).* 1991.

Clodfelter, Mark. *The Limits of Air Power: The American Bombing of North Vietnam.* 1989.

Cohen, Warren I. *America's Response to China: An Interpretive History of Sino-American Relations.* 2000.

———. *Dean Rusk.* 1980.

Conboy, Kenneth, and Andradé, Dale. *Spies and Commandos: How America Lost the Secret War in North Vietnam.* 2000.

Cooper, Chester L. *The Lost Crusade: America in Vietnam.* 1970.

Costigliola, Frank. *France and the United States: The Cold Alliance since World War II.* 1992.

Currey, Cecil B. *Edward Lansdale: The Unquiet American.* 1988.

Dallek, Robert. *Flawed Giant: Lyndon Johnson and His Times, 1961–1973.* 1998.

Davidson, Phillip B. *Vietnam at War: The History, 1946–1975.* 1988.

DeBenedetti, Charles. "The Antiwar Movement in America, 1955–1965," in Jones, Howard, ed., *The Foreign and Domestic Dimensions of Modern Warfare: Vietnam, Central America, and Nuclear Strategy,* 76–93. 1988.

———. *The Peace Reform in American History.* 1980.

DiLeo, David L. *George Ball, Vietnam, and the Rethinking of Containment.* 1991.

Draper, Theodore. *The Dominican Revolt*. 1968.

Duiker, William J. *The Communist Road to Power in Vietnam*. 1981.

———. *Ho Chi Minh*. 2000.

———. *U.S. Containment Policy and the Conflict in Indochina*. 1994.

Fall, Bernard B. *Last Reflections on a War*. 1967.

———. *The Two Vietnams: A Political and Military Analysis*. 2nd ed., 1967.

FitzGerald, Frances. *Fire in the Lake: The Vietnamese and the Americans in Vietnam*. 1972.

Gaddis, John L. *The Long Peace: Inquiries into the History of the Cold War*. 1987.

———. *Russia, The Soviet Union, and the United States: An Interpretive History*. 2nd ed., 1990.

———. *Strategies of Containment: A Critical Appraisal of Postwar American National Security Policy*. 1982.

Gaiduk, Ilya V. *The Soviet Union and the Vietnam War*. 1996.

Gardner, Lloyd C. *Pay Any Price: Lyndon Johnson and the Wars for Vietnam*. 1995.

Gelb, Leslie H., and Betts, Richard K. *The Irony of Vietnam: The System Worked*. 1979.

Geyelin, Philip. *Lyndon B. Johnson and the World*. 1966.

Gleijeses, Piero. *The Dominican Crisis*. 1978.

Goldman, Eric F. *The Tragedy of Lyndon Johnson*. 1968.

Goodman, Allan E. *The Lost Peace: America's Search for a Negotiated Settlement of the Vietnam War*. 1978.

Gurtov, Melvin. *The United States against the Third World*. 1974.

Halberstam, David. *The Best and the Brightest*. 1972.

Hallin, Daniel C. *The "Uncensored War": The Media and Vietnam*. 1986.

Hammond, Paul Y. *LBJ and the Presidential Management of Foreign Relations*. 1992.

Hammond, William H. *Reporting Vietnam: Media and Military at War*. 1998.

Harrison, James P. *The Endless War: Fifty Years of Struggle in Vietnam*. 1982.

Havens, Thomas R. H. *Fire Across the Sea: The Vietnam War and Japan, 1965–1975*. 1987.

Heath, Jim F. *Decade of Disillusionment: The Kennedy-Johnson Years*. 1975.

Hendrickson, Paul. *The Living and the Dead: Robert McNamara and Five Lives of a Lost War*. 1996.

Herring, George C., Jr. *America's Longest War: The United States and Vietnam, 1950–1975*. 3rd ed., 1996.

———. *LBJ and Vietnam: A Different Kind of War*. 1994.

———, ed. *The Pentagon Papers: Abridged Edition*. 1993.

———, ed. *The Secret Diplomacy of the Vietnam War: The Negotiating Volumes of the Pentagon Papers*. 1983.

———. "The Vietnam War," in Carroll, John M., and Herring, George C., eds. *Modern American Diplomacy*, 165–81. 1986.

Hess, Gary R. *Vietnam and the United States: Origins and Legacy of War*. 1998.

Hoopes, Townsend. *The Limits of Intervention: An Inside Account of How the Johnson Policy of Escalation in Vietnam Was Reversed*. Rev. ed., 1987.

Hunt, Michael H. *Lyndon Johnson's War: America's Cold War Crusade in Vietnam, 1945–1968*. 1996.

Johnson, Robert D. *Ernest Gruening and the American Dissenting Tradition*. 1998.

Kahin, George McT. *Intervention: How America Became Involved in Vietnam*. 1986.

———, and Lewis, John W. *The United States in Vietnam*. Rev. ed., 1969.

Kaiser, David E. *American Tragedy: Kennedy, Johnson, and the Origins of the Vietnam War*. 2000.

Kalb, Marvin, and Abel, Elie. *Roots of Involvement*. 1971.

Karnow, Stanley. *Vietnam: A History*. Rev. ed., 1991.

Kattenburg, Paul M. *The Vietnam Trauma in American Foreign Policy, 1945–1975*. 1980.

Kearns, Doris. *Lyndon Johnson and the American Dream*. 1976.

Kendrick, Alexander. *The Wound Within: America in the Vietnam Years, 1945–1974*. 1974.

Kolko, Gabriel. *Anatomy of a War: Vietnam, the United States, and the Modern Historical Experience*. 1985.

Krepinevich, Andrew F., Jr. *The Army and Vietnam*. 1986.

LaFeber, Walter. *America, Russia, and the Cold War, 1945–1996*. 8th ed., 1997.

Langguth, A. J. *Our Vietnam: The War, 1954–1975*. 2000.

Lanning, Michael L., and Cragg, Dan. *Inside the VC and the NVA: The Real Story of North Vietnam's Armed Forces*. 1992.

Lewy, Guenter. *America in Vietnam*. 1978.

Lind, Michael. *Vietnam the Necessary War: A Reinterpretation of America's Most Disastrous Military Conflict*. 1999.

Logevall, Fredrik. *Choosing War: The Lost Chance for Peace and the Escalation of War in Vietnam.* 1999.

Lowenthal, Abraham F. *The Dominican Intervention.* 1972.

Maclear, Michael. *The Ten Thousand Day War, Vietnam: 1945–1975.* 1981.

Mangold, Tom, and Penygate, John. *The Tunnels of Cu Chi: The Untold Story of Vietnam.* 1985.

Mann, Robert. *A Grand Illusion: America's Descent into Vietnam.* 2001.

McMahon, Robert J. *The Cold War on the Periphery: The United States, India, and Pakistan.* 1994.

———. *The Limits of Empire: The United States and Southeast Asia since World War II.* 1999.

McMaster, H. R. *Dereliction of Duty: Lyndon Johnson, Robert McNamara, the Joint Chiefs of Staff, and the Lies That Led to Vietnam.* 1997.

McNamara, Robert S. *In Retrospect: The Tragedy and Lessons of Vietnam.* 1995.

Moise, Edwin E. *Tonkin Gulf and the Escalation of the Vietnam War.* 1996.

Moore, Harold G., and Galloway, Joseph L. *We Were Soldiers Once … And Young: Ia Drang: The Battle That Changed the War in Vietnam.* 1992.

Morgan, Joseph G. *The Vietnam Lobby: The American Friends of Vietnam, 1955–1975.* 1997.

Neese, Harvey, and O'Donnell, John, eds. *Prelude to Tragedy: Vietnam, 1960–1965.* 2001.

Oberdorfer, Don. *Tet!* 1971.

Olson, James S., and Roberts, Randy. *Where the Domino Fell: America and Vietnam, 1945–1995.* 1995.

Page, Caroline. *U.S. Official Propaganda During the Vietnam War, 1965–1973: The Limits of Persuasion.* 1996.

Palmer, Bruce, Jr. *Intervention in the Caribbean: The Dominican Crisis of 1965.* 1989.

Palmer, Dave R. *Summons of the Trumpet: A History of the Vietnam War from a Military Man's Viewpoint.* 1978.

Pérez, Louis A., Jr. *Cuba and the United States: Ties of Singular Intimacy.* 1997.

Pike, Douglas. *PAVN: People's Army of Vietnam.* 1986.

———. *Viet Cong: the Organization and Techniques of the National Liberation Front of South Vietnam.* 1966.

Pisor, Robert L. *The End of the Line: The Siege of Khe Sanh.* 1982.

Poole, Peter. *The United States and Indochina from FDR to Nixon.* 1973.

Prados, John. *The Blood Road: The Ho Chi Minh Trail and the Vietnam War.* 1999.

———. *Presidents' Secret Wars: CIA Pentagon Covert Operations from World War II through the Persian Gulf.* 1996.

Prochnau, William. *Once Upon a Distant War: David Halberstam, Neil Sheehan, Peter Arnett—Young War Correspondents and Their Early Vietnam Battles.* 1995.

Race, Jeffrey. *War Comes to Long An: Revolutionary Conflict in a Vietnamese Province.* 1972.

Redford, Emmette S., and McCulley, Richard T. *White House Operations: The Johnson Presidency.* 1986.

Risse-Kappen, Thomas. *Cooperation Among Democracies: The European Influence on U.S. Foreign Policy.* 1995.

Rusk, Dean. *As I Saw It.* Papp, Daniel S., ed. 1990.

Rystad, Göran. *Prisoners of the Past?: The Munich Syndrome and Makers of American Foreign Policy in the Cold War Era.* 1982.

Schaffer, Howard B. *Chester Bowles—New Dealer in the Cold War.* 1993.

Schandler, Herbert Y. *The Unmaking of a President: Lyndon Johnson and Vietnam.* 1977.

Schlesinger, Arthur M., Jr. *The Imperial Presidency.* 1973.

Schoenbaum, David. *The United States and the State of Israel.* 1993.

Schoenbaum, Thomas J. *Waging Peace and War: Dean Rusk in the Truman, Kennedy, and Johnson Years.* 1988.

Schoutz, Lars. *Beneath the United States: A History of U.S. Policy Toward Latin America.* 1998.

Schulzinger, Robert D. *A Time for War: The United States and Vietnam, 1941–1975.* 1997.

Schwab, Orrin. *Defending the Free World: John F. Kennedy, Lyndon Johnson, and the Vietnam War, 1961–1965.* 1998.

Seaborg, Glenn T., and Loeb, Benjamin S. *Stemming the Tide: Arms Control in the Johnson Years.* 1987.

Shaplen, Robert. *The Lost Revolution: The U.S. in Vietnam, 1946–1966.* 1966.

———. *The Road from War: Vietnam, 1965–1970.* 1970.

———. *Time Out of Hand: Revolution and Reaction in Southeast Asia.* Rev. ed., 1970.

Shapley, Deborah. *Promise and Power: The Life and Times of Robert McNamara.* 1993.

Sheehan, Neil. *A Bright Shining Lie: John Paul Vann and America in Vietnam.* 1988.

———, et al., eds. *New York Times, The Pentagon Papers.* 1971.

Shultz, Richard H., Jr. *The Secret War Against Hanoi: Kennedy's and Johnson's Use of Spies, Saboteurs, and Covert Warriors in North Vietnam.* 1999.

Slater, Jerome. *Intervention and Negotiation: The United States and the Dominican Revolution.* 1970.

Small, Melvin. *Covering Dissent: The Media and the Anti-Vietnam War Movement.* 1994.

———. *Johnson, Nixon, and the Doves.* 1988.

Spanier, John W. *American Foreign Policy Since World War II.* 14th ed., 1998.

Spector, Ronald H. *After Tet: The Bloodiest Year in Vietnam.* 1993.

Spiegel, Steven L. *The Other Arab-Israeli Conflict: Making America's Middle East Policy, from Truman to Reagan.* 1985.

Stevenson, Richard W. *The Rise and Fall of Detente: Relaxations of Tensions in US-Soviet Relations, 1953–1984.* 1985.

Summers, Harry G., Jr. *On Strategy: A Critical Analysis of the Vietnam War.* 1982.

Taylor, Sandra C. *Vietnamese Women at War: Fighting for Ho Chi Minh and the Revolution.* 1999.

Thies, Wallace J. *When Governments Collide: Coercion and Diplomacy in the Vietnam Conflict, 1964–1968.* 1980.

Thompson, James C. *Rolling Thunder: Understanding Policy and Program Failure.* 1980.

Tomes, Robert R. *Apocalypse Then: American Intellectuals and the Vietnam War, 1954–1975.* 1998.

Truong Nhu Tang. *A Vietcong Memoir.* 1985.

Tucker, Spencer C. *Vietnam.* 1999.

Turner, Karen G. *Even the Women Must Fight: Memories of War from North Vietnam.* 1998.

Turner, Kathleen J. *Lyndon Johnson's Dual War: Vietnam and the Press.* 1985.

Ulam, Adam B. *The Communists: The Story of Power and Lost Illusions, 1948–1991.* 1992.

———. *The Rivals: America and Russia Since World War II.* 1971.

Valentine, Douglas. *The Phoenix Program.* 1990.

VanDeMark, Brian. *Into the Quagmire: Lyndon Johnson and the Escalation of the Vietnam War.* 1991.

Vandenbroucke, Lucien S. *Perilous Options: Special Operations as an Instrument of U.S. Foreign Policy.* 1993.

Vandiver, Frank E. *Shadows of Vietnam: Lyndon Johnson's Wars.* 1997.

Weis, W. Michael. *Cold Warriors & Coups D'Etat: Brazilian-American Relations, 1945–1964.* 1993.

Wells, Tom. *The War Within: America's Battle Over Vietnam.* 1994.

Westmoreland, William C. *A Soldier Reports.* 1976.

Winters, Francis X. *The Year of the Hare: America in Vietnam, January 25, 1963–February 15, 1964.* 1997.

Wirtz, James J. *The Tet Offensive: Intelligence Failures in War.* 1991.

Woods, Randall B. *Fulbright: A Biography.* 1995.

———. *J. William Fulbright, Vietnam, and the Search for a Cold War Foreign Policy.* 1998.

Wyatt, Clarence R. *Paper Soldiers: The American Press and the Vietnam War.* 1993.

Young, Marilyn B. *The Vietnam Wars, 1945–1990.* 1991.

Zaroulis, Nancy, and Sullivan, Gerald Sullivan. *Who Spoke Up? American Protest Against the War in Vietnam, 1963–1975.* 1984.

Zeiler, Thomas W. *Dean Rusk: Defending the American Mission Abroad.* 2000.

Zhai, Qiang. *China and the Vietnam Wars, 1950–1975.* 2000.

CHAPTER 14

Vietnamization through Détente
A NEW CONTAINMENT, 1969–1977

Détente: A Structure of Peace

The primary objective of the Nixon administration was to build what the president called a "structure of peace" through détente, which would allow the United States to end its involvement in Vietnam and turn to other problems, both at home and abroad. The task would not be easy. The new Republican administration faced a Democratic Congress, a shattered consensus of popular support for the White House, and an American people thoroughly disenchanted with containment. Détente's supporters heralded its ideas as the basis of a new foreign policy, but this was not the case. Actually begun during the 1960s, détente aimed to reduce tensions with both the Soviet Union and Communist China by avoiding confrontations, supporting nuclear nonproliferation, and calling for an end to the struggle against monolithic communism. But there was more. To the United States, détente offered an honorable way out of Vietnam. The growth of a multipolar world order helped to promote détente, because the forces of nationalism that encouraged neutralism among numerous Third World countries also created a polycentric system within the Soviet bloc that reduced dependence on the Kremlin. If the United States could establish good relations

with the Soviet Union and Communist China, even by playing one against the other, it might be able to wind down involvement in Asia. "I'm not going to end up like LBJ," Nixon proclaimed, "holed up in the White House afraid to show my face in the street. I'm going to stop that war. Fast."

The president's closest adviser in foreign affairs was Henry Kissinger, who rigidly adhered to *realpolitik* in foreign relations and became the chief architect of détente. Basing his philosophy of foreign policy in part upon his doctoral studies in political science at Harvard, Kissinger sought to erect a balance of power patterned after the Congress of Vienna of 1815. All states had legitimate rights, he admitted, but no state could have "absolute security" because such a situation necessitated "absolute insecurity for all the others." He understood, as did the continental powers after the Napoleonic Wars, that peace could come only through a world order based on recognition of shared interests and the determination of the major powers to defuse international troubles. Rather than reconstruct a traditional balance of power system, however, Kissinger wanted to replace ideology with an emphasis on geopolitical considerations designed to achieve what he termed an "equilibrium of strength" conducive to world peace.

His plan did not rest on specific, unyielding commitments and treaty terms but on a general frame of mind or attitude that repeatedly adjusted to constantly shifting power realities. Détente constituted an ongoing attempt to find new grounds for agreements that promoted a general peace. As he told a congressional committee in 1974, it was "a process of managing relations with a potentially hostile country in order to preserve peace while maintaining our vital interests." The underlying stipulation was clear: The major powers had to renounce the use of nuclear weapons in achieving their objectives.

As national security affairs adviser until September 1973, when he took on the additional duties of secretary of state, Kissinger initially enjoyed an independence in foreign affairs that someone tied to the state department could not have. This arrangement suited the White House, because as the president remarked, "No Secretary of State is really important. The President makes foreign policy." New York attorney William Rogers headed the state department but was continually upstaged by Kissinger and therefore had little impact on foreign affairs. Nixon privately assessed the situation in these words: "Henry thinks Bill [Rogers] isn't very deep and Bill thinks that Henry is power crazy. In a sense they are both right."

For a time Kissinger seemed to dominate foreign affairs. Critics considered the German-born and heavily accented adviser to be arrogant and intensely loyal to "the Establishment," and yet they admitted that his individualism, wit, charm, and personal style of diplomacy allowed him to avert the entrapments of state department bureaucracy and get things done. Those same critics warned, however, that Kissinger did not formalize many of his agreements and that his word was good only as long as he was in a position of power. Because he held no formal office during the first four years of the Nixon administration, Kissinger took advantage of "executive privilege" to engage in secret diplomacy, approve wiretappings of underlings and journalists, avoid congressional hearings (leaving an uninformed Rogers to testify), and answer only to the president. In fact, he seldom consulted his own staff. An observer remarked that "Henry's chief lieutenants are like mushrooms. They're kept in the dark, get a lot of manure piled on them, and then get canned."

Nixon and Kissinger favored détente for several reasons, the most fundamental being to halt a dangerously escalating arms race. They were aware of certain realities: the United States's declining prestige, brought on primarily by the war in Vietnam; the Cold War's constant drain on human and material resources; the Soviet Union's rapid military expansion after the Cuban missile crisis; the rising importance of the Third World; the fruitlessness of refusing to recognize Communist China; the steady descent of the dollar; and the growing economic and political strength of Western Europe and Japan. A number of agreements with the Soviet Union had pointed to better relations, and yet the all-important element of trust was still missing. In the mid-1960s the United States found that the Soviet Union supported the development of antiballistic missiles (ABMs), which if successful would undermine the United States's deterrence capacity by permitting the destruction of approaching intercontinental ballistic missiles (ICBMs). The Soviet Union's ABMs would raise the chances of a nuclear confrontation by reducing the level of its own "assured destruction" to an "acceptable" casualty figure of a few million. In 1969 the Nixon administration pushed for an improved ABM system, called "Safeguard," to protect U.S. missile sites. More alarming, both superpowers were trying to develop a greater offensive capability through the multiple independently targeted reentry vehicle (MIRV), a first-strike ICBM carrying up to ten independently fired nuclear warheads and thus able to counteract ABMs by its sheer number and diversified direction of projectiles. Although each side had a satellite reconnaissance system, neither could determine the number of warheads in a MIRV and therefore could not know the other's nuclear capability. With the two nations approaching strategic parity, détente was not a choice but a necessity.

Détente carried both advantages and disadvantages. First and foremost, it offered a lessening of international tensions as a major step toward a way out of Vietnam. If instituted as policy, the United States could lower arms expenditures and encourage negotiations over cutbacks, reduce the need for combat forces and end the draft, curtail the assumed necessity for intervening in other countries, and build a greater international trade system leading to world order. Kissinger explained that the world consisted of five major areas of power—the United States, the Soviet Union, China, Japan, and Western Europe—and that each should have hegemony in its own locale. None would interfere in another's region, and all would cooperate in preventing neutralist nations from manipulating the superpowers. Détente called for a continuously shifting global balance of power in which the leading nations discouraged aggressions within their own spheres. As Nixon put it in 1971, the "five great economic superpowers will determine the economic future" as well as "the future of the world in other ways in the last of this century."

Détente worked better in theory than in application. The Third World preferred diplomatic nonalignment, increasingly resisting efforts by either the Soviets or the Americans to dictate its policies. Thus, emerging nationalist movements in Asia, the Middle East, and Africa continued to cause major problems for the big powers. Indeed, the developing nations of the "South" put pressure on the more advanced nations of the "North" to forgo huge profits in the interests of helping the less fortunate peoples close the gap between them and the wealthy. Economic troubles stemmed from many sources—including competition from Europe and Japan, the balance of payments deficit, devaluation of the dollar in 1971 and 1973, and recurring inflation. But the most immediate problem emanated from the Organization of Petroleum Exporting Countries (OPEC), whose oil-producing members

aggravated an energy crisis during the early 1970s by raising prices for consumer nations. At the same time, terrorists and hijackers repeatedly posed dilemmas seemingly incapable of resolution. Especially alarming were the massive hunger problems that took millions of lives in the economically destitute and poverty-stricken "Fourth World." Critics in the United States complained that détente was only a new form of globalism that would again overextend the nation's foreign involvement in economic, political, and military affairs. Others wondered what would happen if the Communist Chinese tried to play off the Soviets against the Americans or if the Soviets attempted the same with the Americans and the Chinese. Yet despite the pitfalls of détente, there seemed to be no viable alternative.

Kissinger used the idea of "linkage" in trying to reduce his country's tensions with the Soviet Union and Communist China. By exerting economic pressure on the Moscow and Beijing governments, the United States might convince them to halt their arms supply to North Vietnam and force Ho Chi Minh into a compromise settlement of the war. Despite the apparent new direction in foreign policy, this approach actually looked backward because it assumed that the North Vietnamese lacked a will of their own and that the United States could manipulate and control history. Another premise of linkage was the indivisibility of peace—that an act of aggression in any part of the world constituted a threat to the overall network of peace. Kissinger hoped that the three major powers might tie all facets together in one magnificent design for peace. According to theory, the United States would furnish economic assistance to the Soviets in exchange for helping to wind down the war in Vietnam and accepting arms limitations. The Washington government would then open negotiations with Beijing's leaders to guarantee peace. By linking economic aid to military events in Southeast Asia, the United States would lay the basis for détente by improving relations with the Soviet Union and inaugurating a new era with the People's Republic of China. Military withdrawal from Vietnam would also unite Americans at home and allow the United States to negotiate from a position of strength. Détente and linkage sought to alleviate tensions; distrust and rivalry would remain.

Linkage came laden with questionable premises that offered little assurance of success. Policymakers during the Franklin D. Roosevelt presidency had had minimal effect on achieving world order when they tried to tie together seemingly unrelated issues. Furthermore, the amount of war materiel that the Soviets and Communist Chinese furnished to the North Vietnamese was small compared to the help that the Americans gave the ARVN. In truth, linkage was little different from containment in that both rested on the highly dubious assumption that world events depended primarily on the decisions of the major powers. The Nixon administration nonetheless sought a Soviet-American arms control agreement and expanded commercial relations, which it claimed would end the war in Vietnam and ease world unrest. Washington's policymakers still ignored the central truth repeatedly hammered home by the nation's ongoing experience in Vietnam: The United States was unable to determine the world's events. Although its destructive capacity was greater than it had been in 1945, its leverage over global affairs had steadily declined since the war because of the world's constantly shifting balance of power. Détente and linkage were attempts to deal with these developments, but the central objective of U.S. foreign policy remained the same—to contain communism.

Vietnam and Détente

Meanwhile the war in Vietnam continued. Nixon's alleged "secret" plan turned out to be more of the same—"Vietnamization" of the war, a term created by Secretary of Defense Melvin Laird but reflecting a process of de-Americanization of the conflict first sought by Kennedy but which did not begin until the Johnson administration. Vietnamization ensured

a scaled withdrawal in proportion to expanded aid to Saigon or, as one U.S. official cynically put it, "changing the color of the corpses." The scheme rested on the improved fighting skills of the ARVN, which so far had displayed little evidence of such prowess. There was no longer any debate about *whether* the United States was going to pull out of Vietnam; the question was how to do so without marring U.S. respect throughout the world. If the United States appeared weak in Vietnam, détente had little chance for success. President Nixon therefore adopted an unyielding stance in the Paris peace talks and at the same time sought leverage by resuming the bombing. Both measures, he assured Americans, would promote Vietnamization. Privately, however, he had already observed to Laird that "there's no way to win the war. But we can't say that, of course." Like Kennedy and Johnson, Nixon refused to allow the appearance of defeat to cloud his administration, and like those before him, his central goal remained an independent, non-Communist South Vietnam. Above all, he could not condone a coalition government because it would eventually come under Communist control. Impatient critics, however, soon charged that the administration sought only a "decent interval" between the time the United States withdrew its combat forces and when South Vietnam collapsed to the Communists—presumably two to three years.

Nixon tried to promote the peace process by exerting more military pressure on the battlefield. Little hope came out of Paris, where the talks had bogged down over several issues that included procedural matters, whether the Vietcong and the Saigon government should have representatives at the proceedings, the timing of U.S. and North Vietnamese withdrawals, and Vietnam's postwar political framework. The president feared that a premature U.S. withdrawal meant immediate Communist victory and decided to exploit his hard-line anti-Communist image as a critical bargaining point with the North Vietnamese. As he told an adviser, "They'll believe any threat of force Nixon makes because it's Nixon. We'll just slip the word to them that 'for God's sake, you know Nixon's obsessed about Communism . . . and he has his hand on the nuclear button.'" Yet he realized that the use of nuclear weapons would arouse worldwide condemnation, foment opposition among Americans, and create a situation that could lead to total war. The only alternative was Vietnamization, because it would leave the impression that the United States had fulfilled its objectives in Vietnam while reserving the option of escalating the war.

The North Vietnamese did not make the problem easy for the United States: In February 1969, a month after Nixon's inauguration, they launched a massive offensive across the demilitarized zone (DMZ) that took a heavy toll on Americans. The war's end seemed nowhere in sight. Television reporters pointed out that U.S. forces in Vietnam numbered nearly 542,000, the most there during the entire war, and that its death totals were now more than 40,000, a figure higher than that of the Korean War. Nixon emphasized that U.S. withdrawal depended on success in Paris and on the behavior of North Vietnamese forces in the field. Yet just as the Hanoi regime had earlier baffled Washington's leaders by standing up to expanding U.S. military strength, it now refused to reduce military actions in proportion to the assumed enticement of U.S. withdrawal. The reason was simple though totally unacceptable to the White House: Any termination of the war short of a reunified Vietnam under Hanoi's leadership constituted a defeat.

The North Vietnamese assault in February evoked a strong response from the Nixon administration, both on the battlefield and at the peace table. The United States began bombing North Vietnam's supply routes out of Cambodia (Operation MENU), an action kept secret from Congress and the American people for four years. When the *New York Times* published a story on the campaign, the White House plugged the leaks by ordering FBI wiretaps on reporters and government officials. As in the earlier phases of the war, the B-52s were unable to stop the transportation of goods by humans and bicycles over count-

less winding and largely hidden jungle trails. In mid-May of 1969 Nixon presented what he termed a "comprehensive peace plan" that called for the reestablishment of the DMZ between the antagonists and the mutual withdrawal of U.S. and North Vietnamese forces from South Vietnam within a year of a cease-fire agreement. Internationally supervised elections would follow, although South Vietnam's military president, Nguyen Van Thieu, would remain in office during the interim.

But Nixon's proposals had no effect. North Vietnam angrily rejected them as a "farce" and warned that it was prepared to stay in Paris "until the chairs rot." The Hanoi government remained firm in its demands for a total U.S. withdrawal, the establishment of a provisional coalition regime that would *not* include Thieu, and the final disposition of Vietnam to be settled by the "Vietnamese parties among themselves." There was still no basis for a settlement, which meant that Vietnamization would take longer than expected.

In summer 1969 the White House announced the first of several reductions in U.S. forces in Vietnam and called for a program of greater assumption of international responsibility by the allies that eventually became known as the "Nixon Doctrine." The president met with Thieu at Midway Island in June, where Nixon declared that as of August 1, 1969, 25,000 combat forces would pull out of Vietnam, followed by more in relation to the ARVN's improved battle performance. Shortly after the announcement, on July 20, the nation's prestige received a huge lift when worldwide television covered two U.S. astronauts from the Apollo 11 mission who became the first human beings to land on the moon. Two days later Nixon was en route to Asia and Europe, stopping at Guam and delivering an address on July 25 that called for a new direction in foreign policy. Speaking within the context of Vietnam, the president asserted that in the future the United States would avoid heavy military involvement in Asian affairs; but he added that the principles he expounded would apply "to all our international relationships." Lest some worry about a return to isolationism, Nixon promised to honor treaty obligations, provide military and economic aid in combating aggression, and furnish a nuclear shield to any ally or nation deemed vital to U.S. security. The key point in the Nixon Doctrine was the president's pledge to "look to the nation directly threatened to assume the primary responsibility of providing the manpower for its defense." His administration called for partnerships based on "shared burdens and shared responsibilities."

The Nixon Doctrine did not signal an end to the United States's global commitments; but it marked another step toward détente and a withdrawal from Vietnam, because it constituted an admission of power limitations and an invitation to antagonists to wind down the Cold War. Laird explained that "America will no longer try to play policeman to the world. Instead, we will expect other nations to provide more cops on the beat in their own neighborhood." The United States would rely more on Japan in Asia, Iran in the Middle East, and Zaire (formerly the Belgian Congo), Angola, and South Africa in Africa.

The Nixon administration's program also encompassed massive arms sales—with nearly predictable repercussions. The arms influx encouraged the use of military force in the Middle East, Latin America, and Africa, tied the Nixon administration to white regimes in Africa and to the shah in Iran, hurt other nations financially, and endangered relations with Japan, which refused to accept the upgraded role the United States wanted it to assume in Asia. The inflated prices charged by arms producers, in fact, encouraged Iran, a U.S. ally, to raise oil prices to facilitate the purchase of war materiel. At these heavy costs the United States struggled toward an honorable withdrawal from Vietnam.

While the Nixon administration maintained a strong public position in the war, Kissinger secretly opened new peace talks in Paris with North Vietnam's representative, Xuan Thuy. Virtually ignoring South Vietnam, Kissinger in August 1969 called for a cease-fire, the return

of American POWs, and Thieu's retention as president in Saigon. In exchange the United States would withdraw, implicitly recognizing Communist control over much of South Vietnam. The offer aroused no interest. North Vietnam wanted both the United States and Thieu out of the country, and it was in the strong military position to demand all of the south. Still another problem appeared: Thieu felt betrayed by Washington's attempt to get out of Vietnam "with honor."

As the secret talks went on, so did the war. Ho Chi Minh died in September 1969, causing great mourning throughout North Vietnam and turning over leadership to long-time nationalists Pham Van Dong (premier), Vo Nguyen Giap (general), and Le Duan (leader of the Lao Dong or Communist Workers' party, in North Vietnam). Nixon continued to defend his policies to Americans becoming increasingly impatient with the pace of Vietnamization. Antiwar demonstrations spread during October and November, attracting thousands of participants to "The Vietnam Moratorium" in Boston and Washington. In a television appearance on November 3, Nixon repeated that the United States would pull out "on an orderly scheduled timetable" that depended on progress in Paris, "the level of enemy activity," and the speed with which the South Vietnamese assumed responsibilities. Should North Vietnam step up resistance, he promised, the United States would adopt "strong and effective measures." At the end of his speech, Nixon asserted that "North Vietnam cannot humiliate the United States. Only Americans can do that." The establishment of a draft lottery system that month helped to take the fire out of the protest movements by making the system fairer in application.

Nixon cited several reasons for repeatedly insisting that the United States would remain in Vietnam as long as necessary. Moving out too quickly would endanger the lives of U.S. troops and supporters in Saigon. Defeat in South Vietnam would threaten other U.S. interests in Asia. The United States had treaty obligations and moral commitments to honor.

It had to ensure the return of the POWs. To Congress in January 1970, Nixon proclaimed that "when we assumed the burden of helping South Vietnam, millions of South Vietnamese men and women placed their trust in us. To abandon them would risk a massacre that would shock and dismay everyone in the world who values human life."

Suddenly the war seemed to take a turn in South Vietnam's favor. Faced with U.S. troop withdrawals, Thieu had announced a general mobilization that called in all men eighteen to thirty-eight years of age, placing more than half of South Vietnam's male population in military service and raising the army's rolls from 700,000 to more than one million. Refugees flocked into the cities, where they worked in the ARVN or for Americans and added to the outward appearance that the metropolitan centers were thriving. The truth was otherwise. Saigon was only a façade of industrial growth, because the peasants had fled there for safety from the "Free-Fire Zones" in which the U.S. armed forces were trying to root out pockets of help for the Vietcong. U.S. dollars were the country's sole financial base, and the only bustling industry was the war machine underwritten almost entirely by the United States. If the soldiers pulled out now, the South Vietnamese economy would collapse.

The irony was that whereas the United States had not intended to make South Vietnam a colony, its very existence had come to depend almost totally on the United States. Americans had not drained the country's wealth as had the French, but they had established a widespread network of services for themselves that the Vietnamese had filled through the armed forces as well as through household duties, office work, and other menial tasks. The United States had also failed to encourage the production of rice and other commodities, handing Thieu a government without an economic base. As long as the Americans required services, the Vietnamese people remained in a state of dependency that had nothing to do with patriotism or ideals. In 1969 and 1970 the United States cited

statistics allegedly proving Vietnamization a success—climbing Vietcong body counts, an expanded ARVN, and increasing supplies of weapons. But the new South Vietnamese soldiers were poor fighters because they were there without choice and lacked morale and a cause. The essential ingredient of U.S. victory—"winning the hearts and minds of the people"—had little chance in this uncertain atmosphere.

Hopes for détente seemed to brighten with the Strategic Arms Limitations Talks (SALT) with the Soviet Union, which began in Helsinki, Finland, in November 1969 and shifted back and forth between there and Vienna for the next two and a half years. Although the United States's triad strategic force had ICBMs, submarine-launched ballistic missiles (SLBMs), and long-range bombers, the Soviet Union had made rapid advances, passing the United States in ICBMs though remaining behind in the other two categories. Rather than seek superiority in strategic weapons, Nixon appeared to have become satisfied with parity. Kissinger emphasized that "an attempt to gain a unilateral advantage in the strategic field" was "self-defeating." Yet the policy seemed inconsistent. Nixon had campaigned in 1968 on dealing only "from a position of superiority" and had secured the Senate's narrow passage of the Safeguard ABM system in August, just before he notified the Moscow regime of the United States's readiness to discuss issues. To ensure leverage in the SALT talks, he approved the development of the MIRV. The president nonetheless reaffirmed to Congress in February 1970 that his administration sought a partnership in maintaining world peace. "America cannot—and will not—conceive *all* the plans, design *all* the programs, execute *all* the decisions and undertake *all* the defense of the free nations of the world." Détente was the only way out of Vietnam, and that process began with arms limitations agreements.

But before the SALT talks could make headway, attention dramatically returned to the war in Southeast Asia. On April 30, 1970,

Nixon shocked the nation by declaring that the United States and South Vietnam had expanded the military effort into Cambodia to destroy the enemy's bases of operation. The United States had known of the Cambodian sanctuary for some time, he explained over television, but had done little for fear of pushing the neutralist Cambodian regime of Prince Norodom Sihanouk into the Communist camp. Sihanouk, however, had fallen in a coup assisted by the United States and led by a pro-Western general named Lon Nol, who now sought U.S. help against a possible military takeover by the thousands of North Vietnamese forces inside his country.

Nixon's speech was filled with misleading statements and, according to some critics, deceptions and falsehoods. Should the North Vietnamese overthrow the Lon Nol regime, Nixon warned, "Cambodia would become a vast enemy staging area and springboard for attacks on South Vietnam along 600 miles of frontier." Lon Nol had asked for assistance, and the United States intended to "go to the heart of the trouble" by destroying the enemy's military "nerve center"—the Central Office for South Vietnam (COSVN)—which was "the headquarters for the entire Communist military operation in South Vietnam." There was no choice. "We will not be humiliated. We will not be defeated." In true Cold War language, complete with allusions to Armaggedon, he warned Americans that, "if when the chips are down, the world's most powerful nation . . . acts like a pitiful helpless giant, the forces of totalitarianism and anarchy will threaten free nations and free institutions throughout the world." This was not an invasion of Cambodia, he insisted; the assault force would concentrate only on locations "completely occupied and controlled by North Vietnamese forces. . . . Once enemy forces are driven out of these sanctuaries and their military supplies destroyed, we will withdraw." The military operation in Cambodia, Nixon assured, would further promote a U.S. withdrawal from Vietnam.

Nixon's speech drew such a furious reaction inside the United States that he felt compelled to impose limits on the new military campaign. Americans were enraged that the administration's way out of Vietnam seemed to lie in taking the war into Cambodia. Demonstrations broke out in hundreds of colleges and universities across the United States, and in the Senate a move began toward prohibiting funds for the military effort in Cambodia after June 30. On May 4 an explosive atmosphere at Kent State University in Ohio caused National Guardsmen to fire into a group of students, killing four and injuring nine. As legions of protesters stormed the streets of Washington, U.S. soldiers moved into the White House basement, ready to defend it from a feared attack by fellow Americans. The day following the events at Kent State, Nixon attempted to defuse the national anger by promising that U.S. combat forces would go no farther than twenty-two miles into Cambodia without congressional approval and that troops and their advisers would pull out of the country by June 30. In addition, he assured Americans that there would be no secret deals with the Lon Nol regime and asserted that U.S. assistance to Cambodia would consist only of war materiel and air cover. At the same time, however, Nixon was furious at the growing protests at home and directed the FBI and CIA to intensify their search for connections between radical organizations in the United States and those abroad. "Don't worry about divisiveness," he told aides. "Having drawn the sword, don't take it out—stick it in hard."

After June 30, and with the U.S. troops withdrawn as promised, Nixon proclaimed the Cambodian mission a huge success. South Vietnamese forces had killed or taken prisoner thousands of North Vietnamese and Vietcong, confiscated or destroyed great amounts of war materiel, and cleared the enemy from miles of jungle. Yet he did not mention that U.S. and allied units had failed either to close the supply route or locate the alleged COSVN. In fact, the defense department in Washington was unsure whether such a nerve center actually existed. The North Vietnamese and Vietcong, it now seems clear, never operated out of a central command headquarters comparable to anything in the West. Nor did the president point out that the campaign had set off widespread unrest in Cambodia, providing cause for a brutal Communist insurgency movement led by the Khmer Rouge and thus breathing life into the domino theory. The invasion widened the war in Southeast Asia by committing the United States to another weak regime, this one in Cambodia.

In the meantime the Senate infuriated Nixon by acting to curb the war-making activities of the White House. On June 24 it had overwhelmingly voted to repeal both the Eisenhower Doctrine of 1957 and the Tonkin Resolution of 1964 and had forwarded the bill to the House. Nixon had not fought these moves because, he argued, his policies in Vietnam and Cambodia were justified by his constitutional duty to safeguard members of the armed forces. But evidence was growing that the Executive Office was becoming isolated from the rest of the country and increasingly suspicious of any calls for change. One of Nixon's aides later recalled that during the summer of 1970 a "siege mentality" was developing "quite unknowingly" inside the White House. "It was now 'us' against 'them.' Gradually, as we drew the circle closer around us, the ranks of 'them' began to swell."

In autumn 1970 Nixon asserted that the Cambodian venture had opened new peace avenues in Vietnam. Both North Vietnam and the National Liberation Front (NLF) had boycotted the Paris proceedings because of the invasion, but in mid-September the North Vietnamese returned to the talks with repeated demands for an unconditional U.S. military withdrawal from Vietnam and the assurance of Vietcong participation in a political settlement. Nixon countered with a "major new initiative for peace" that drew bitter reactions in Hanoi and Moscow and among the Vietcong. On television on October 7, he called for a "standstill" cease-fire and the immediate exchange of POWs; inclusion of Cambodia and Laos in the peace talks, thereby establishing the war in

Vietnam as an Indochinese conflict and not a civil war; total U.S. military withdrawal according to a determined schedule; and assurances that Thieu would remain in control until elections took place. Thus, neither side would make concessions. Nixon's effort had attracted no interest. The Hanoi government joined the Vietcong in refusing to consider the proposals and spokespersons in Moscow called them "a great fraud."

A month later the war in Vietnam intensified again as the United States began bombing the DMZ and the Hanoi-Haiphong region in an extensive campaign that Nixon termed "protective reaction strikes." According to the White House, the bombings would continue until the North Vietnamese stopped firing at U.S. reconnaissance planes over North Vietnam. This announcement drew a sharp reaction from Hanoi's defense minister and long-time military strategist Vo Nguyen Giap, who indignantly declared that North Vietnam was "a sovereign independent country, and no sovereign independent country will allow its enemy to spy freely upon it." Congress also opposed the bombings. The House had meanwhile approved the Senate's bill repealing the Tonkin Resolution (a move that Nixon dismissed as unnecessary to his continuing the war) but would not repeal the Eisenhower Doctrine. The modified measure became law in January 1971. Although Congress refused to deny funds to U.S. soldiers, it prohibited the use of money to broaden the war in Vietnam and barred the deployment of U.S. troops in either Cambodia or Laos. Congress did not prohibit the use of planes, however, and when in February 1971 the ARVN invaded Laos to close the Ho Chi Minh Trail, Nixon authorized air cover. But South Vietnam's field performance was disastrous. In less than two months the North Vietnamese inflicted fifty percent casualties and drove the ARVN out of Laos—with some of the retreating soldiers perilously hanging onto the skids of the escaping helicopters.

By spring 1971 Americans at home had again mobilized against the war. Nearly

200,000 antiwar activists, including Vietnam War veterans, demonstrated in Washington, only to draw Nixon's cutting remark that they were "mobs" who did not speak for "the great silent majority." But a Gallup poll in May suggested that the president was wrong. According to the survey, six of ten Americans thought the United States should not be in Vietnam, which was an exact reversal of the opinion expressed in autumn 1965. Furthermore, the opposition was bipartisan. Later studies revealed that contrary to popular belief, the war's greatest critics by the early 1970s were not the country's youths but were older Americans, women, lower-class Americans, and blacks. The black population argued with considerable justification that a disproportionate share of black soldiers were fighting and dying in Vietnam.

Other revelations had meanwhile deepened Americans' resentment of the war and, in some cases, of the actions of their soldiers. In early 1971 a court-martial had found Lieutenant William Calley guilty of "at least twenty-two murders" of men, women, and children in the South Vietnamese village of My Lai in 1968. The village, Calley alleged, had been Vietcong-infested and was therefore a legitimate military target. Nixon soon added to the widespread indignation over the massacre and seeming army coverup by ordering Calley's release while the decision came under review and by ultimately extending him a full pardon. The image of the U.S. fighting man received another severe blow when CBS News reported that large numbers of U.S. soldiers in Vietnam used drugs and that nearly 15,000 were heroin addicts. Furthermore, the advent of Vietnamization meant a winding down of the war, which had the unexpected result of making U.S. soldiers increasingly reluctant to engage in combat. No one wanted to be the last American killed in Vietnam.

Still other issues soured the U.S. experience in Vietnam. The American economy was hurting from recession, inflation, a steady outflow of dollars from the country, and an unfavorable balance of trade that found the United

States for the first time since the 1890s importing more than it exported. Finally, in June 1971 the *New York Times* published *The Pentagon Papers,* selections from a long series of classified documents that government employee Daniel Ellsberg had illegally removed from the defense department in an effort to halt the war in Vietnam. The Pentagon materials supported the long-time allegations that Kennedy and Johnson had been less than truthful about their nation's involvement in Southeast Asia. When the Supreme Court decided against preventing publication of the documents, the White House used its special task force called the "plumbers" to halt further leaks and to discredit Ellsberg. Ultimately a federal judge dismissed charges against him when it became clear that the justice department, with CIA help, had illegally wiretapped his phone and burglarized the files of his psychiatrist to "find some dirt" about Ellsberg.

High Tide of Détente: Communist China, the Soviet Union, Salt I, and Vietnamization

To encourage détente, President Nixon made a stunning announcement in July 1971: He had accepted an invitation from Beijing to visit China to "seek the normalization of relations," which were in total disarray following the Communist triumph of 1949. Considerable quiet preparation had taken place for this pathbreaking decision. In early 1969 Nixon had directed Kissinger to reassess the situation with China for the purpose of restoring relations. That same year the United States eased commercial and travel restrictions with China, pointedly referred to its regime as the People's Republic of China, and terminated the Seventh Fleet's regular patrol of the Taiwan Strait. The following year the United States resumed talks with China in Warsaw, adjourned since early 1968 as a result of friction over Vietnam. When war broke out in 1971 between India (supported by the Soviet Union) and Pakistan (which received help from China), the Nixon administration leaned toward Pakistan. That same year, in April, American table tennis players then in Japan accepted an invitation to China, where they played a match and lost to the world champions. Their trip to China, however, popularized the term "Ping-Pong diplomacy" as a breakthrough to détente. Shortly afterward the United States ended its trade embargo on China. Kissinger had secretly traveled to Beijing less than a week before Nixon's announcement, where he made arrangements with Zhou Enlai, second only to Mao Zedong in the Chinese Communist party. "What we are doing now with China," Kissinger later declared, perhaps too effusively, "is so great, so historic, the word *Vietnam* will be only a footnote when it is written in history." In August the state department announced support for Communist China's admission into the United Nations with the simultaneous membership of the Republic of China. This "Two-Chinas policy" lasted until October, when the UN General Assembly approved the admission of Communist China and expelled Taiwan.

Numerous factors account for this revolution in U.S. foreign policy, but as in all reciprocal arrangements, the basic consideration was mutual need. Since 1969 both nations had given subtle indications of interest in establishing relations, based on the common grounds of halting Soviet expansion and promoting trade. China was alarmed over recent clashes with Soviet troops stationed along the nations' common border. It was also concerned about Japan, fearing that the establishment of relations with the United States might either reduce the Tokyo government's belligerence or perhaps even promote a foundation for Sino-Japanese relations—still bro-

Henry Kissinger at the Great Wall of China, October 1971
In preparation for President Nixon's visit, the national security affairs adviser went to China with orders to avoid any publicity that would upstage his superior's place in history. The president was enraged when this picture appeared worldwide—as was UN Ambassador George Bush, who, at the time, was trying to save Taiwan's seat in the organization. *National Archives, Washington, D.C.*

ken since the two sides went to war in 1937. The United States's prime objective, however, was to widen the rift in Sino-Soviet relations and develop a power balance conducive to détente and world peace. The resulting stimulus to trade might also revive the ailing U.S. economy by securing it a greater share of the China market before Japan established a monopoly. As the *New York Times* declared, "The President is in the position of the lovely maiden courted by two ardent swains, each of whom is aware of the other but each of whom is uncertain of what happens when the young lady is alone with his rival."

Nixon also had personal reasons for wanting to normalize relations with China. Such a dramatic move would award him a place in history that only he could occupy because of his staunch anti-Communist reputation. The presidential election of 1972 was another factor. Nixon had still not extricated the United States from Vietnam, and peace-minded Democrats led by Senator George McGovern seemed to be making gains, as evidenced by their strong showing in the New Hampshire primary of the previous March. Nixon, however, remained in a sound political position. Right-wing Republicans could not accuse him of being "soft on communism," and liberal Democrats could not be critical because many of them had been advocating recognition of China for some time. Although the powerful China lobby and much of the U.S. labor lobby favored the Chinese in Taiwan, Nixon realized that Americans' emotions over that issue had calmed considerably. Indeed, during the mid-1960s about one-quarter of Americans had not even known that the mainland Chinese government was Communist.

But the most immediate goal in Nixon's China decision was to promote détente and allow a U.S. withdrawal from Vietnam. Relations with Beijing might force the Moscow government to ease its anti-American stance and cause both the Soviets and China to cut aid to North Vietnam and the Vietcong, thereby permitting the United States to complete the Vietnamization of the war and turn

to other matters. If handled correctly, détente would heighten concern within the Soviet Union about the consequences of a U.S. alliance with China. The basic goal was to leave the Thieu regime intact and permit U.S. withdrawal from Vietnam.

Nixon's trip to China in February 1972 received worldwide attention. According to the president as he left the United States, his visit would "signal the end of a sterile and barren interlude in the relationship between two great peoples." Accompanying him on the 20,000-mile journey were nearly ninety journalists plus almost forty members of the mission, including Secretary of State Rogers, who remained conspicuously subordinate to Kissinger in discussing foreign policy.

Nixon's landing in China on February 21 aroused little outward enthusiasm, although the Chinese had probably staged this quiet reception to suggest that the United States was more eager to establish relations than were the Chinese. Premier Zhou Enlai greeted Nixon with a formal handshake and then warmly welcomed Kissinger as his "old friend." No ceremony took place, although the band played America's National Anthem, followed by China's "The March of the Volunteers." That same day Nixon and Kissinger met with Mao and Zhou for nearly an hour, and later that evening they attended a huge banquet in the Great Hall of the People, where numerous toasts to good relations set the tone of succeeding discussions. "What we do here," Nixon proclaimed, "can change the world."

The image fostered by the White House and the news media was that Nixon's visit to China was monumental in importance. As the presidential party stood before the Great Wall, Nixon made the inane remark before television cameras that "I think that you would have to conclude that this is a great wall. . . . As we look at this wall, we do not want walls of any kind between peoples." On February 27 in Shanghai the two nations signed a vaguely worded joint communiqué that offered assurances of normal relations. The United States declared that its goal was peace in Asia with

Nixon and Zhou Enlai
The president called his visit to the People's Republic of China "the
week that changed the world." *Wide World Photos, New York.*

"social progress for all peoples . . . [and] free of outside pressure or intervention." After reiterating the desire to withdraw from Vietnam, the United States affirmed that its "ultimate" goal was "the withdrawal of all U.S. forces and military installations from Taiwan" to promote "a peaceful settlement of the Taiwan question by the Chinese themselves." China approved, emphasizing that Taiwan was the "crucial question obstructing the normalization of relations." The two nations probably aimed this statement at the Soviet Union: "Neither should seek hegemony in the Asia-Pacific region and each is opposed to efforts by any other country or group of countries to establish such hegemony." The United States and China concluded the Shanghai communiqué with a call for expanded commerce and cultural interchange. Formal recognition seemed imminent. As Nixon departed for home the next day, he triumphantly pronounced this "the week that changed the world."

Nixon's China visit had mixed consequences for détente. Japan was stunned about the imminent establishment of Sino-American diplomatic relations, particularly because it remained technically at war with China (since 1937). But the time had come to break with the past. In autumn 1972 the Japanese premier traveled to Beijing to repair relations and soon afterward severed ties with Taiwan. Both Vietnams felt threatened by the new accord between China and the United States—the north because it depended upon Beijing for arms and the south because the Chinese were its avowed enemy. The Chinese action, in fact, aroused considerable suspicion among numerous Third World peoples who were undecided about whom to trust. But if the central purpose of Nixon's China trip was to promote détente by placing pressure on Moscow, it was successful. Shortly after he had announced his intention to travel to China, the Soviets invited him to Moscow. The president decided to go in May 1972, just three months after the trip to Beijing.

If the Nixon administration felt confident that détente's success had established a firm grasp on the direction of events, it soon found out that lesser powers can exert considerable influence as well. In late March 1972 North Vietnam challenged both the claimed accomplishments of Vietnamization and the new U.S.-China arrangement by launching the mammoth "Easter Offensive" against the south. In an assault that approximated the Tet Offensive in ferocity and posed a severe test to détente, nearly 200,000 North Vietnamese forces, with Soviet tanks and heavy artillery, hit South Vietnam across the DMZ, into the Central Highlands, and out of Cambodia just northwest of Saigon. The invaders came within sixty miles of the capital, convincing many observers that the Saigon government was on the verge of collapse. To counter the widespread offensive, Nixon approved the largest bombing campaigns of the war— later called "Linebacker I," a reflection of his avid love of football—which lasted from May through October and included the use of computer-guided "smart bombs" to hit railway lines to China. As American B-52s struck Hanoi and Haiphong for the first time since 1968, Nixon ignored fears of involving Communist China and the Soviet Union and authorized the mining of the port of Haiphong and the imposition of a naval blockade of the north. "The bastards have never been bombed like they're going to be bombed this time," he asserted. If the United States lost in Vietnam because of failure to use the power it possessed, "there would have been no respect for the American President. . . . We must be credible."

Like Johnson, Nixon coupled the stick with the carrot and, like Johnson, Nixon succeeded in safeguarding the Saigon regime but at the heavy cost of escalating the destructive level of the war. Nixon prohibited the bombing of civilian targets and held out the possibility of peace by assuring the Hanoi government that if it agreed to return all American POWs and accept an internationally supervised cease-fire, the United States would pull out of Vietnam within four months. For the first time the White House had set a timetable for withdrawal, and for the first time it had made no demand that the North Vietnamese leave the south. Furthermore, the long-standing stipulation of Thieu's survival was noticeably missing. But North Vietnam, perhaps testing détente's resilience, turned down the offer. In the meantime, even though the Soviets lost four merchant vessels during the bombardment of Haiphong, they raised no objections—doubtless because of ongoing border problems with China and their desire for détente with the United States. China publicly criticized the Nixon administration, but it likewise took no action in behalf of North Vietnam. The reluctance of either Communist power to intervene must have put Hanoi's leaders into a quandary. Although the new fighting again resulted in a stalemate, the North Vietnamese undoubtedly had become more amenable to a cease-fire. Pummeled and exhausted by the bombs and the fighting, they now found themselves alone: Neither the Chinese nor the Soviets had come to their side during the U.S. offensive.

The Soviets' restraint over the escalated U.S. military actions in the Vietnam War demonstrated that they attached great importance to Nixon's impending arrival in May. Soviet General Secretary Leonid Brezhnev had signaled his readiness for détente a year before, when at the Twenty-Fourth Party Congress he spoke of peace measures for the 1970s. The Soviet economy was in dire shape, because the recent failure of a Five-Year Plan had underlined his people's need for grain and technological assistance. Revolutionaries in several Communist states were still bitter over the Red Army's heavy-handed tactics in putting down the 1968 uprising in Czechoslovakia. Poland and Rumania, for example, increasingly leaned toward the West for trade. In August 1970 the Moscow government had signed a nonaggression pact with West German Chancellor Willy Brandt that smoothed the path toward détente with the United States and also allowed the dispatch of additional Soviet troops to the tense Chinese frontier. The treaty terms relieved Soviet fears of a revived, powerful Germany by conceding the reality of two Berlins and two Germanies. Three months later West Germany signed a nonaggression agreement with Poland that recognized the Oder-Neisse River as the common border, a move restoring Polish control over territories lost in 1945. Finally, in September 1971, Brezhnev signed a pact pledging Western access to Berlin in exchange for West Germany's recognition of the East European borders established by the Red Army in 1945. Fear of encirclement was a major Soviet concern, especially after China began negotiations with the United States and Japan.

Nixon's visit to the Soviet Union in May led to agreements more substantial than any reached with China. The atmosphere in Moscow was more cordial than in Beijing, and Nixon was even allowed to speak to the Soviet people over radio and television. He and Brezhnev agreed to cooperate in space exploration, environmental protection, medical and scientific research, and other matters of common concern. They also discussed Vietnam but would only state that small nations should not stand in the way of détente. The major accords related to arms limitations. On May 26 Nixon and Brezhnev signed a document proclaiming their goal of "peaceful coexistence" and then reached an agreement based on more than two years of SALT talks. Known as SALT I (Strategic Arms Limitations Treaty), it included two pacts: the Treaty of Anti-Ballistic Missiles Systems and the Interim Agreement on Limitation of Strategic Offensive Arms. The first agreement, aimed at those systems designed to intercept and neutralize approaching nuclear warheads, initially restricted each party to no more than two ABM systems, but later cut them to one. According to the theory that appropriately became known as MAD (Mutual Assured Destruction), both sides' major cities would be vulnerable to attack, ensuring that neither would choose to begin war. The sec-

ond—the Interim Agreement—attempted to establish a five-year ceiling on the construction of offensive missiles. Bombers were not part of these agreements, however, leaving the United States at a distinct advantage. By September 1972 both agreements had received formal U.S. approval by wide margins. The following month the two nations negotiated a commercial pact that included the sale of U.S. grain and the Soviet Union's agreement to pay back its Lend-Lease debt of World War II by the year 2001.

The appearance of compromise in Moscow was deceptive, however, because the SALT I agreements had actually encouraged an arms race in new weapons—the United States in cruise missiles and the Soviet Union in "Backfire" supersonic bombers. The ABMs were costly and yet ineffective, thus constituting no concession by either side. The United States seemed to have maintained the upper hand in technology, because the agreements had no bearing on the multiple-headed MIRVs. A single U.S. submarine (of which the United States had thirty) could carry MIRVs capable of delivering the impact of Hiroshima 160 times over. Within a year the United States had 6000 nuclear warheads to the Soviets' 2500, and by the time the SALT I agreements expired as scheduled in 1977, the Americans' weapons doubled those of the Soviets.

Thus, the SALT discussions in Moscow paradoxically stimulated an arms race by placing limitations on older models and diverting attention from the ongoing development of newer, more sophisticated weapons. To prevent interference with the MIRVs, Nixon prohibited his negotiating team from discussing them during the SALT talks in Helsinki. In addition, each side was capable of "overkill" numerous times, and both possessed satellite surveillance systems that made secret testing a phenomenon of the past. The terms of agreement were forwarded to Helsinki, where the intent of SALT II was to convert the interim agreement into a permanent pact.

And yet, the SALT I agreements in Moscow encouraged the image of détente, which in

May 1972: High Point of Détente
Just three months after his visit to China, President Nixon was in Moscow drinking a toast to the SALT 1 agreement with Premier Alexei Kosygin and Chairman Leonid Brezhnev. *Wide World Photos, New York.*

turn had favorable repercussions in Europe. The improvement of Soviet-American relations offered the opportunity to resolve problems in Germany remaining from World War II. In June 1972 the Quadripartite Treaty, or Berlin Agreement, went into effect when the four occupying powers—the United States, Soviet Union, Britain, and France—extended recognition to East Germany. Two years later the United States established formal diplomatic relations, making divided Germany a fact and ending the wartime goal of reunification. Détente also furthered the Helsinki Accords of 1972, which called for recognition of boundaries in East European Communist states in exchange for the signatory nations' pledge of respect for human rights. These agreements likewise endorsed the results of World War II in Eastern Europe by admitting to Soviet domination of the area, a fact resisted since the Truman years.

Détente also affected events in the Pacific, because by the 1970s Japan had stepped up

demands that the United States relinquish Okinawa, held by the Americans as a military base since 1945. In addition to the Tokyo government's wish to reestablish control over one million of its people on the island, the return of Okinawa would remove the last reminders of defeat in World War II while reducing the chances of being drawn into an Asian conflict. In November 1969 the Nixon administration had agreed to return Okinawa and the other Ryukyu Islands sometime in 1972, thereby completing the process begun by President Johnson, when he had given up the Bonin Islands. The official transfer of the Ryukyus took place in May 1972.

Despite these concessions by the United States, détente had not yet freed it from Vietnam, and as the presidential election of 1972 approached, Nixon stepped up the pressure by approving an air offensive against North Vietnam, Cambodia, and Laos. The use of ground forces was out of the question, because by autumn 1972 the Vietnamization program had left only 70,000 U.S. troops in the country, and the overwhelming majority of them were in noncombat roles. The outlook still seemed promising. Nixon was a certain winner in the election, the Soviets and Chinese were following détente, and the North Vietnamese were reeling badly from the new assault. The Hanoi government decided to negotiate. It apparently thought that the Washington administration might permit better terms before the election than afterward.

Cease-Fire in Vietnam

Kissinger had meanwhile continued peace talks in Paris with North Vietnam's chief negotiator, Le Duc Tho, and finally, in October, a break seemed imminent. The Hanoi government expressed willingness to turn over the POWs simultaneously with a U.S. withdrawal sixty days after a cease-fire. An international commission was to supervise elections and implement treaty terms. The North Vietnamese had dropped their demands for Thieu's immediate removal from office, and the Americans had not insisted on North Vietnam's withdrawal from the south. Nixon accepted a cease-fire at the points of present military occupation and approved an electoral commission, both major concessions from his previous stance.

On October 26, less than two weeks before the election, Kissinger returned from Paris and triumphantly proclaimed that "peace is at hand." At almost the same time, North Vietnam published the terms worked out in the talks, probably to prevent leaders in Washington and Saigon from making private arrangements. North Vietnam set a deadline of October 31 for signing an agreement, a move designed to place pressure on Nixon before the election, but which also had the unintended effect of further undercutting his Democratic opponent, Senator George McGovern, who had promised to end the war as soon as he took office. The president assured Americans that he would accept only "peace with honor."

But South Vietnam sensed a sellout to the Communists and blocked the settlement. Thieu vehemently opposed any arrangement that approved U.S. withdrawal while permitting North Vietnamese forces to remain in the south during the cease-fire period. He also complained that an electoral commission was tantamount to a coalition government that the Communists would ruthlessly seek to dominate. Restoration of the DMZ between the Vietnams, he declared, was vital. Although Kissinger was furious with Thieu, Nixon worried that the South Vietnamese premier might complain of a betrayal and wreck the Republicans' promise of "peace with honor." The president, however, sought more than extrication from Vietnam. He considered Thieu's objections defensible and, based on that stand, would permit a delay in the negotiations until after the election had provided a mandate to press for additional concessions from the Hanoi regime. In the meantime the United States could send more aid to Saigon, eliminate the undesirable parts of the treaty, and further impair North Vietnam's capacity to break the peace. To save face, Nixon announced his refusal to bend to North Vietnam's pressure tactics. The deadline came and passed, and on November 2 he declared that he would sign "only when the agreement is right."

Nixon overwhelmingly won reelection and then, to revive the Paris peace talks, sharply escalated the war by what Kissinger termed "jugular diplomacy"—a series of air assaults that became known as "Linebacker II," or the "Christmas bombings." After the election in the United States, each side in Vietnam had moved quickly to expand its holdings before a cease-fire in place went into effect. On December 15 Le Duc Tho walked out of the Paris discussions in disgust. Three days later Nixon explained that to promote the release of the POWs he had ordered immediate large-scale bombings on North Vietnamese cities (attempting to avoid populated areas by the use of smart bombs) and military points— including Hanoi and Haiphong. To the chair of the Joint Chiefs of Staff, Admiral Thomas

Moorer, Nixon sternly declared, "I don't want any more of this crap about the fact that we couldn't hit this target or that one. This is your chance to use military power to win this war, and if you don't, I'll consider you responsible." For nearly two weeks (except for Christmas Day) American B-52s, carrying huge bomb loads and possessing all-weather flying ability, thundered around the clock more than 30,000 feet over North Vietnam. They unloaded more than 36,000 tons of bombs (more than the amount dropped from 1969 to 1971), killed close to 2000 civilians, and damaged or destroyed numerous military and nonmilitary sites. All the while Air Force F-4s used smart bombs in attacking the Hanoi Rail Yard and destroying its surface-to-air missile assembly plant. During the bombing, nearly thirty B-52s and fighter-bombers were shot down, adding almost one hundred to the POW list and supporting the arguments of the generals in Washington who had warned the administration that the Soviets had effectively safeguarded the North Vietnamese capital against an air attack.

The Christmas bombings drew bitter protests from all over the world. According to critics, Nixon was a "madman" who waged "war by tantrum." Tom Wicker of the *New York Times* expressed the feelings of the international press in calling the air offensive "Shame on Earth," and Senate Democratic Majority Leader Mike Mansfield denounced what he termed "a Stone Age tactic." Admiral Moorer later denied that the U.S. planes had engaged in blanket bombing and insisted that the pilots had specific strategic targets in mind that were located primarily on Hanoi's periphery. But he could say nothing during the bombing campaign for fear of alerting the North Vietnamese as to which areas to protect with their limited number of surface-to-air missiles. A journalist noted that Nixon privately declared that he "did not care if the whole world thought he was crazy for resuming the bombing." The Soviets and Chinese "might think they were dealing with a madman and so better force North Vietnam into

a settlement before the world was consumed into a larger war."

Nixon's brutal tactics had seemingly worked: The day after Christmas, Kissinger was in Washington when he received a call from Hanoi asking for a resumption of his talks with Le Duc Tho. Kissinger observed that "we had not heard such a polite tone from the North Vietnamese since the middle of October." The bombings above the twentieth parallel ceased on December 30.

For several reasons the Nixon administration was also ready to talk. U.S. generals warned that North Vietnam's air defenses were inflicting long-range damages on the strategic strength of the United States; worldwide revulsion had developed for the bombings; the Hanoi government's peace conditions seemed the best possible; and the Democrats now controlled Congress and in January would doubtless cut off funds for future bombings. Nixon boasted that the Christmas assault had brought peace, although one of his administration officials disagreed. "We were in an embarrassing situation. Could we suddenly say we'll sign in January what we wouldn't in October? We had to do something," he declared. "So the bombings began, to try to create the image of a defeated enemy crawling back to the peace table to accept terms demanded by the United States." Whatever the truth, the terms were strikingly similar to those of the previous October.

The question of whether Linebacker was instrumental in bringing the peace remains unclear. Nixon's credibility certainly soared in view of the massive air assault, and not purely by coincidence, of course, did the Hanoi government consent to resuming the Paris talks during the aerial bombardment. Kissinger noted that Le Duc Tho repeatedly insisted that what brought him back to the peace table was "the President's firmness and the North Vietnamese belief that he will not be affected by either congressional or public pressures." The North Vietnamese no longer had enough food to survive a prolonged attack, and by the end of December they had used all their surface-to-air missiles and, with no defenses left, were totally vulnerable to destruction. Also important was the diplomatic and military isolation that North Vietnam experienced while under siege. Linebacker I had destroyed rail access from China, and even though the North Vietnamese had restored the lines and managed to stockpile large amounts of Soviet materiel before December, Linebacker II had quickly destroyed those supplies and, with bombing and mining, cut off Hanoi and Haiphong from the rest of the world. Just as important, however, was North Vietnam's feeling that a settlement with the United States might lead to its withdrawal, thereby permitting the Vietnamese to settle their problem by themselves. Nixon was convinced that soon after Linebacker II, North Vietnam had learned of his ultimatum to Thieu as a result of their infiltration of the Saigon government. The bombing campaign bought more time for Vietnamization to work and more likely complemented other realities in the war rather than demonstrating that, by itself, it brought the peace.

On January 27, 1973, the Paris negotiators signed a cease-fire agreement in the old Hotel Majestic in Paris, twenty-three years after the initial U.S. commitment in Vietnam and eight years following its first assignment of combat troops. In the pact signed by Kissinger, the foreign ministers of North and South Vietnam and the "South Vietnamese Provisional Revolutionary Government," or PRG (formerly the National Liberation Front), accepted the following terms: an immediate cease-fire in place; U.S. withdrawal of its final 27,000 troops from South Vietnam and the return of all American POWs (nearly 600), both within sixty days; enforcement of treaty provisions through an international commission; general elections carried out through the establishment of a National Council of Reconciliation and Concord; an international conference on Vietnam to convene within thirty days; and authorization for the United States to replace South Vietnam's damaged or worn-out military equipment, but not to add to existing

stores. In an unofficial, semisecret arrangement that was not part of the pact, the United States agreed to furnish Hanoi $4.75 billion of reconstruction assistance. To secure Thieu's compliance with the treaty, the United States threatened to withdraw all aid.

The agreement came with mixed blessings. The atmosphere in Paris was so bitter that the South Vietnamese and the PRG refused to sign the same copy of the treaty. Although the Nixon administration had assured Americans of open agreements in Paris, the president had earlier made a private pledge of military aid to Thieu if North Vietnam violated the cease-fire. To the South Vietnamese premier, Nixon wrote that if you will "go with us, you have my assurance of continued assistance in the post-settlement period and that we will respond with full force should the settlement be violated by North Vietnam." The alternative was equally clear: A little over a week later Nixon assured Thieu that the United States would sign the pact by itself if necessary. "In that case," Nixon declared, "I shall have to explain publicly that your Government obstructs peace. The result will be an inevitable and immediate termination of U.S. economic and military assistance which cannot be forestalled by a change of personnel in your government." Just one week before the treaty-signing session, Thieu sent his foreign minister to take part in the Paris negotiations, thereby indicating acquiescence to the president's pressure tactics. With Thieu in line, Nixon sent him additional arms that same year.

Even the peacemakers recognized that the cease-fire they had crafted bore no relation to honor, and thus did they turn their backs on the praise that some accorded to them. Kissinger and Le Duc Tho received the Nobel Peace Prize in 1973 for their roles in the Vietnam agreement. Le Duc Tho rejected the award, and Kissinger declined to attend the awards proceedings at the University of Oslo and then gave the $65,000 cash prize to a scholarship designed to aid children of U.S. soldiers killed in Vietnam. Long-time critic of the war and former Undersecretary of State

Kissinger and Le Duc Tho
Kissinger received the Nobel Peace Prize in 1973 for his efforts in arranging the cease-fire of January that year. *Wide World Photos, New York.*

George Ball cynically remarked that "the Norwegians must have a sense of humor."

The Nixon administration hailed the events of January 1973 as a victory for détente, although it quickly became clear that the United States had won neither "peace" nor "honor." Conflict went on in Vietnam, even while people all over the world praised the cease-fire. The treaty had left North Vietnamese forces in the south, without specifying which areas belonged to whom, and Hanoi's leaders were more determined than ever to seize control of the entire country. In March 1973 twelve nations met in Paris—including the United States, China, and the Soviet Union—and formally approved the cease-fire agreement. The U.S. presence in Vietnam was still visible, though altered: Numerous U.S. military advisers remained in South Vietnam, albeit hurriedly discharged from the service and no longer in uniform as part of a poorly disguised effort to circumvent the Paris terms, and rather than dismantle its military installations as required, the White House transferred the titles to the South Viet-

namese. The United States also continued sending military goods but designated them as nonmilitary, and the U.S. Air Force maintained its bombing of Cambodia to protect the Lon Nol regime from the Communist Khmer Rouge. Resentment for Linebacker II continued to grow in the United States, despite the revelations that in comparison with the damage caused, the civilian casualties were remarkably low. These findings affirmed not only successful evacuation proceedings by the North Vietnamese, but also the Nixon administration's directives to avoid nonmilitary targets. A journalist toured Hanoi in March 1973 and declared that "pictures and some press reports had given a visitor the impression Hanoi had suffered badly in the war—but in fact the city is hardly touched." When Congress cut off funds for the bombing, Nixon angrily vetoed the measure in late June, but he soon had no choice other than to sign a bill requiring an end to all U.S. combat in Indochina by August 15.

Congress's attempt to reassert itself in foreign affairs contributed to the nation's subdued global presence in the period following its direct involvement in Vietnam. Impeachment proceedings then under way for the president's role in Watergate may have pushed him into a retreat. But another development was also important. That November of 1973, Congress narrowly overrode Nixon's veto in passing the War Powers Act, which marked an effort to make any armed venture by the United States a joint responsibility of Congress and the Executive Office. It asserted that "in every possible instance" the president was to consult Congress before sending soldiers into situations "where imminent involvement in hostilities is clearly indicated by circumstances." Should he intervene outside the country without a formal declaration of war, he must "report" his actions to Congress within forty-eight hours. Unless that body endorsed the intervention, the military forces would have to pull out within sixty days—extended to ninety days if the president certified "unavoidable necessity." In effect, however, the president could still react immediately to a crisis and wage war for sixty to ninety days without congressional approval—a period so long, critics warned, that the United States might find extrication difficult if not impossible. But this was not the real problem, Kissinger warned. Congress was too closely tied to public opinion to formulate meaningful, long-range foreign policies. Though severely criticized by Nixon and Kissinger, the War Powers Act illustrated the inseparability of domestic and foreign policy and therefore provided an appropriate epitaph for the United States's military experience in Southeast Asia.

Disintegration of Détente, 1973–1977

The new peace seemingly ushered in by détente was paradoxically eroding from within because of problems with the Western alliance, among Third World nations, and within both the Western Hemisphere and the United States. France and other West European governments were hurting economically and had become unhappy with the United States's emphasis on non-European affairs and with its insistence on dictating their policies in line with Cold War strategy. West Europeans joined the Japanese in complaining about the decline of the dollar, Washington's high balance-of-payments deficits, and U.S. accusations that they were guilty of commercial discrimination. Nixon and Kissinger hoped that détente's umbrella effect would bring peace to countries outside the major power blocs. Freed of Vietnam, they sought to patch relations with their continental allies by heralding 1973 as "The Year of Europe." Yet Italy was becoming Communist in orientation, Portugal was angry over criticisms of its African policies, and Greece and Turkey were bitter rivals over the Mediterranean island of Cyprus. In the Middle East, Latin America, and Africa, pressures for social reforms were likewise creating explosive situations that the White House stubbornly attributed to Communist influence. Furthermore, the United States faced deepening recession and spiraling inflation, and the seemingly endless unraveling of the Watergate scandals (explained later) undermined the Nixon administration's credibility at home, dividing Americans and further undercutting the nation's foreign policy.

The most immediate threat to détente came in the Middle East. As discussed earlier, the center of controversy was the Arab-Israeli feud, kept under control only by a series of fragile agreements. Three times—in 1948, 1956, and 1967—the Arabs had attempted to destroy Israel, and in every instance they had failed disastrously. After the Six Day War of 1967, Jews inside the United States had exerted pressure on Washington to approve the sale of fifty F-4 Phantom jets to Israel. A number of Arab states had responded by severing relations with the United States and opening their ports to Soviet ships. The growing crisis in the Middle East endangered détente because of competing Soviet-American economic and strategic interests in the area, along with the persistent U.S. fear of Communist infiltration.

Conflict again loomed in the Middle East as the Nixon administration moved into the White House in early 1969. Israel refused to withdraw from areas occupied during the war of June 1967, and in spring 1969 Suez again became the troublespot because of Arab actions. Nasser brought in heavy weapons, and the newly created Palestine Liberation Organization (PLO) promised death to any Arab leader who called for a peaceful settlement of the Israeli dispute. Under the leadership of Yasir Arafat, the PLO intensified demands for a homeland in Palestine and, using Syria and Jordan as bases, launched a series of raids on Israel. The Israelis retaliated against neighboring states helping the PLO: Some of their bombing strikes even touched the outskirts of Cairo. The Moscow government sent troops and antiaircraft materiel to Egypt, including SAM-3 (surface-to-air) missiles operated by Soviets to counter Phantom jet attacks and Soviet pilots to fly MIGs earlier furnished to Nasser. As the problems escalated, the Israelis appealed to the United States for help, and in July 1970 President Nixon responded with 125 Phantom and Skyhawk jets. "We will do what is necessary to maintain Israel's strength," he declared over television. "Not because we want Israel to be in a position to wage war— that isn't it—but because that is what will deter its neighbors from attacking it."

By autumn 1970 the Arabs and Israelis had managed another cease-fire that was again quickly violated. Nasser had visited Moscow in July and had afterward agreed to the U.S. proposal for a UN-supervised, ninety-day armistice. The Israelis accepted, but only after the United States guaranteed their security. Ensuing peace discussions then broke down over charges that Nasser, with Soviet help, had moved missiles into the cease-fire area west of the Suez Canal, exposing Israel to attack along the east bank. The Israelis withdrew from the talks until the Egyptian leader removed the missiles.

The same day that the Israelis left the negotiations, September 6, Palestinian guerrillas began a new wave of terrorism that was followed by the outbreak of civil war in Jordan. The PLO hijacked four commercial airliners, including a Pan American 747 jumbo jet, and after evacuating all passengers, destroyed the planes. Nearly sixty people, including Americans, Israelis, British, Swiss, and West Germans, were held hostage to secure the freedom of imprisoned Arab terrorists. Negotiations quickly began with the help of the International Red Cross, but these talks were hampered by the conflict in Jordan between government forces and Palestinians living in the country. As Syrian tanks roared into Jordan to help the guerrillas, the Nixon administration reinforced the Sixth Fleet in the Mediterranean and readied its airborne forces at home and in West Germany. But the Syrians, perhaps as a result of Soviet pressure, suddenly pulled out of Jordan, leaving the Palestinians to defeat and exile to Lebanon, where they became a continuing source of instability in the region. After a cease-fire in Cairo on September 25, the Red Cross soon won the freedom of the hostages in exchange for the release of the Arab terrorists.

The end of both the Jordanian civil war and the hostage crisis once again temporarily eased the situation in the Middle East. But during that same month of September Nasser died, leaving the office of premier to Anwar el-Sadat, who promised to continue Egypt's hard-line policies toward Israel. With Soviet backing, he refused to remove the missiles from the cease-fire zone; Israel subsequently built up defenses along the east bank and secured a promise of U.S. military assistance. Israel then returned to the peace negotiations after the United States guaranteed support against excessive Arab demands. Sadat intended to open a new offensive against Israel, but he was unable to persuade the Soviets to furnish more arms because of their desire for détente with the United States. Exasperated with the Moscow government, he ordered the "expulsion" of thousands of Soviet military advisers and technicians from Egypt in the summer of 1972. Although the PLO continued its terrorist acts—including killing Israeli athletes at the Munich Olympics that same year—Sadat's move again relieved the situation in the Middle East.

The peace was not to last, because on October 6, 1973, the Arabs invaded Israel for the fourth time. The invasion took place on Yom Kippur (the Jews' holy day, the Day of Atonement) in an attempt to regain lands lost in the 1967 war and thereby set off what became known as the Yom Kippur War. Egypt, aided by Jordan, Iraq, Morocco, and Saudi Arabia, relied heavily on Soviet materiel and advice to surprise both Israel and the United States by attacking Israeli armies in the Sinai and at the Golan Heights. With Israel nearly split in two by the assault, Prime Minister Golda Meir appealed for U.S. military assistance and debated whether to use her country's atomic bomb against the Arabs. The Nixon administration called for an immediate meeting of the UN Security Council, but a series of unfriendly sessions on October 8 and 9 brought no results. Forgetting their differences of the past, the Soviets sent military aid to Egypt and prepared to airlift a ground force into the combat zone. Although the Nixon administration was reeling from Watergate and other domestic scandals, it approved an airlift of planes, tanks, and war materiel, enabling Israel to hold its ground.

The Arabs only briefly enjoyed their military successes, because the Israelis once again quickly reversed the fortunes of the war. Soviet Premier Alexei Kosygin traveled to Cairo, hoping to convince Sadat to accept a cease-fire, but instead aroused U.S. fears by giving increased visibility to Soviet sympathies in the war. Meanwhile, Arab forces had overrun the east bank and swept toward Israel across the Sinai desert, where between October 14 and 19 they engaged in the fiercest tank battles since World War II. At the same time, Syrian ground troops aided by tanks advanced across the Golan Heights and toward Israel. The Israelis, however, soon turned back the assault both at the canal and along the Syrian front. Israeli forces won a stretch of land along the western side of the canal, positioning them

within seventy miles of Cairo. In doing so, the Israelis surrounded 20,000 Egyptian soldiers on the east bank, cutting them off from the main force and putting them in danger of mass destruction.

The Israelis' reversal of the war's direction forced new peace talks. Sadat appealed to Brezhnev for help, and on October 20 the Soviet general secretary met with Kissinger in Moscow to draft a peace proposal for presentation to the Security Council. En route home, Kissinger stopped in Israel to assure its leaders that the plan was fair. But the only way Kissinger could secure an Israeli cease-fire was to threaten a cutoff in military aid. The following evening the Security Council met in emergency session, and early the next morning it approved the peace resolution. It called for an immediate cease-fire at present military positions, for the implementation of UN Resolution 242, which in 1967 called for Israeli withdrawal from lands occupied in the Six Day War in exchange for defensible borders, for the assignment of a large peacekeeping force comprising soldiers from non-Security Council member nations, and for the promise of negotiations aimed at a permanent peace.

Although Egypt and Israel accepted the truce, the Israelis provided an excuse for direct Soviet intervention when they violated the cease-fire lines, seizing more territory and threatening to crush the Egyptian army. Israel's minister of defense, General Moshe Dayan, later explained to the *New York Times* that if he had captured several thousand Egyptian soldiers, "Sadat would have had to admit it to his people. We might only have held them for a day and let them walk out without their arms, but it would have changed the whole Egyptian attitude about whether they had won or lost the war." Kissinger was irate because such a humiliation would upset the delicate balance between Arabs and Israelis and abort a negotiated peace. Furthermore, Brezhnev and Sadat proposed a joint Soviet-American military contingent to supervise the cease-fire, which the Nixon administration flatly rejected as a thinly disguised excuse for full-scale Soviet intervention. That evening a Soviet note jolted the White House, because it declared that if the United States did not join, "we may be obliged to consider acting alone." Israel, the note insisted in a menacing tone, "cannot be permitted to get away with the violations." The White House feared a Soviet push into Suez and, without informing NATO allies, placed U.S. armed forces and nuclear strike commands on "precautionary alert." The United States, Nixon asserted, "would not accept any unilateral move" by the Soviets. Two days later, on October 24, 1973, the Security Council approved a second peace resolution. Under threat of a U.S. arms embargo, the Israelis honored this resolution.

As in the earlier Arab-Israeli wars, no one was satisfied with the outcome. The Arabs had not regained territories lost in 1967, and the Israelis did not feel secure. Most Arab nations in OPEC were angry with the United States for aiding Israel and with the West European nations for allowing the Americans to use NATO bases on the continent. Acting without Iran, the OPEC nations stunned the United States with an oil embargo that lasted until March 1974 and raised prices dramatically for U.S. allies in Japan and Europe. OPEC's oil embargo of 1973–1974 led to gasoline shortages in the United States (which had recently begun to import most of its oil and thus felt the crunch) but caused a severe strain on the Western alliance. Whereas the United States was committed to Israel and received only twelve percent of its oil from the Middle East, Western Europe and Japan were almost totally dependent on the Arabs. When allies chose not to support the United States in the Middle East, Kissinger called them "contemptible."

Kissinger meanwhile tried to arrange a permanent peace in the Middle East by flying back and forth between Egypt and Israel in a series of visits that became known as "shuttle diplomacy." For two years he attempted to secure a pact that would exclude Soviet and Palestinian participation and end the Arab oil embargo. In November 1973, Kissinger left for Egypt, where he arranged the restoration of diplomatic relations with the United States (broken in 1967). A few days later he helped bring about an Egyptian-Israeli cease-fire, and in May 1974 he managed the same between Israel and Syria. In September 1975, after repeated travels between Cairo and Tel Aviv, Kissinger persuaded the two antagonists to initial an agreement. Israel was to evacuate part of the Sinai to enable it to become a UN-guaranteed buffer area. A detachment of two hundred U.S. "civilian technicians" would be assigned to "early warning" stations to watch for the beginnings of trouble. The United States also made general assurances of military assistance to Israel and Egypt, to maintain a balance. Finally, the oil flow was to resume—at quadrupled prices.

Kissinger's diplomacy had mixed results. Boundaries remained uncertain, because the Israelis remained in the Sinai, the Golan Heights, and the West Bank of the Jordan. The PLO's demands for a homeland were still unfulfilled, and both the Soviets and Palestinians were unhappy over being shut out of negotiations affecting their interests in the Middle East. Kissinger's efforts also widened the gulf between Arab moderates and extremists. Yet there was a saving factor: Sadat was disenchanted with the Soviets and had turned to the United States for help. The Washington government now assumed the role of chief mediator in the Middle East, a move that improved the prospects for peace.

Lack of unity within the Western Hemisphere also threatened détente. Canada began to follow policies that opposed those of the United States. It opened trade with China and the Soviet Union, established rigid controls on foreign investments, and raised its export prices for oil and natural gas sold to the United States while retaining enough at home to ensure cheaper energy for Canadians. The situation in Latin America was more serious. Anti-American feeling remained strong, as exemplified by the unfriendly reception accorded New York Governor Nelson Rockefeller during his fact-finding tour of 1969.

Although he recommended more economic help by the United States, the Alliance for Progress was virtually dead and the Nixon administration had shown little interest in reviving it. Mexico was upset over the United States's economic blockade of Cuba and its intervention in the Dominican Republic in 1965, and Venezuela sought to use its OPEC membership and rich oil deposits to win economic independence from the United States. The Panamanians still demanded a renegotiation of the canal treaty of 1903, and discussions were under way toward formalizing an agreement arranged by Kissinger in 1974. Terrorists and guerrillas meanwhile exploited Latin America's dire economic and political situation, and new regimes increasingly expropriated U.S. holdings without providing suitable compensation. Washington's leaders responded to the alleged Communist threat by selling arms to friendly governments.

Cuba remained a special obstruction to détente. Pressure had grown in the United States for lifting the trade embargo and reestablishing diplomatic relations, despite Castro's continued refusal to compensate Americans whose properties had fallen victim to expropriation. "Skyjacking" incidents grew in number because Castro permitted hijacked planes to return to the United States but granted refuge to perpetrators on the basis of the U.S. failure to return Cubans who had hijacked boats and escaped to the United States. In the early 1970s, however, the United States agreed to block attempts by Cuban exiles in the United States to invade the island if Cuba would extradite or punish hijackers and return victimized properties and people. Two years later, with representatives of the Castro regime, Kissinger began secret talks in the United States that were aimed at settling differences between the countries. But in 1975 a Senate committee inquiring about CIA activities in Cuba found evidence of "at least eight" plots in the past to kill Castro—including a box of poisoned cigars—and some wondered if Castro had not countered by arranging the assassination of President Kennedy. In Decem-

ber, Castro sent nearly 20,000 soldiers and military advisers to aid a leftist insurrection in Angola, and the United States later found that he had sent thousands more to Ethiopia. Cuba, it appeared, had become a base for spreading communism overseas as well as throughout the hemisphere.

The Nixon administration's greatest concern in Latin America was Chile, where in autumn 1970 Salvador Allende, a Marxist and a founder of the Socialist party, overcame CIA interference to win election as president on the Popular Unity party ticket. Allende's coalition government, which included Communists and soon leaned toward Moscow for help against the Americans, promised constitutional amendments barring totalitarian rule and instituted a reform program designed to free the country from the control of large landowners and the United States's multinational corporations. In so doing, Allende nationalized $1 billion of U.S. holdings, although with assurances of compensation. International Telephone and Telegraph (ITT) and other business corporations nonetheless put pressure on the Nixon administration to take action against Allende.

Both Nixon and Kissinger regarded Allende as another Castro and hence a potential ally of the Soviet Union. While the White House maintained what it called a "cool but correct" stance toward Allende, it worked surreptitiously to destabilize his government. The U.S. government persuaded the World Bank and Inter-American Bank to deny funds to Chile, and the CIA collaborated with American businesses to take action against Chile. Together they halted the flow of credit and other materials, secretly paid the Chilean press and opposing political parties to criticize Allende's rule, sent arms to the military, and then cooperated with its leaders in staging a coup. In September 1973 the Chilean army overthrew the government, resulting, according to the U.S. ambassador, in Allende's death by suicide. A brutally repressive but staunchly anti-Communist and rightist military regime under General Augusto Pinochet came to power. When the U.S. ambassador complained about the new government's use of torture, Kissinger abruptly told him "to cut out the political science lectures." There was no "right for people to vote in Communists," he coldly asserted; once in office, they refused to leave. The United States must not "let a country go Marxist just because its people are irresponsible." The following year Americans learned that the CIA had participated in the coup that led to Allende's death. Two major investigations into the organization's conduct led to revelations in 1975 that mobilized Congress to restrict CIA activities overseas.

Another serious threat to détente had come from within the United States, because by late 1973 the Watergate scandal was full-blown. It had greatly weakened the Nixon administration's effectiveness in foreign affairs and soon led to a change in national leadership. During the presidential campaign of 1972, veteran CIA operative E. Howard Hunt (who had helped engineer both the Guatemalan invasion of 1954 and the Bay of Pigs disaster seven years later) led the White House "plumbers" in breaking into the Democratic National Committee's headquarters at the Watergate Hotel in Washington, apparently intending to pilfer political plans. Public knowledge of the break-in fostered the perception of a presidential pattern of abuse of power that led to demands for Nixon's impeachment or resignation. To turn the nation's attention from Watergate as well as to revive détente, the president appointed Kissinger secretary of state (while maintaining him as national security affairs adviser) in the autumn of 1973 and soon attended another well-publicized summit meeting in Moscow. But the political scandals had irrevocably undermined presidential authority, leading to a virtual abdication of domestic and foreign policy formation to Congress. Faced with certain impeachment, Nixon resigned the presidency in August 1974, leaving as chief executive Vice President Gerald Ford (who had just assumed this position after Spiro Agnew resigned because of revelations that he had accepted bribes while governor of Maryland).

Ford and Kissinger continued the struggle for détente, but in the wake of Watergate and Vietnam, their actions were severely curtailed. As previously mentioned, Congress had restricted the president's authority with the War Powers Act. Furthermore, the Senate had tied his hands even tighter by stipulating that in exchange for U.S. trade, the Soviets had to respect the human rights of all dissidents—including Jews. The Senate also tried to establish a maximum amount on loans the United States could authorize for the Soviet Union. But these attempts at linkage did not work. The Soviets resented the United States's intervention in their domestic affairs and, instead of relaxing their treatment of Jews, sharply reduced the number allowed to leave the country. The Senate's conditions ultimately blocked Soviet approval of the commercial treaty. To avoid further offense to the Soviet Union, President Ford even refused a White House visit to Alexander Solzhenitsyn, a famous Soviet writer who had been exiled for exposing widespread brutality inside his homeland.

In late 1974 Ford and Kissinger tried to revive détente by accepting guidelines for SALT II, begun in Geneva two years earlier. The president met with Brezhnev in Vladivostok in November and tentatively agreed to a ten-year limit of 2400 each on the total number of ICBMs, SLBMs, and big bombers. Of the 2400 on each side, a maximum of 1320 could have multiple warheads. In effect, SALT II blanketed the arms race with legal issues, ensuring drawn-out discussions over what kinds of weapons fell within the boundaries.

Meanwhile in Vietnam, the most damaging blow to détente came as the Thieu regime approached its final days in early 1975. The Third Indochina War had begun in late 1973 with the ARVN's surprisingly successful attacks on North Vietnam's holdings in the south, but the optimism was unfounded: The Hanoi government had restricted its military response until it was sure the Americans were gone. In January 1975 the North Vietnamese felt free of a U.S. threat and launched a crushing offensive that succeeded primarily because of the rapid disintegration of the ARVN owing to poor leadership and widespread corruption, but also because of the huge cutbacks in U.S. assistance, South Vietnam's excessive dependence on the United States, and, according to Communist accounts, the popular support given the advancing forces. Thieu appealed to Ford to deliver the "full force" promised him by Nixon two years before. But the letter Thieu alluded to had not been made public, and Kissinger had earlier told the press that such a pledge did not exist. In the meantime Phuoc Binh, the capital of Phuoc Long Province, collapsed in January, confirming North Vietnam's suspicions that the United States would not reenter the war. Thieu then ordered a retrenchment that turned into a full-fledged rout as terrified ARVN soldiers and panicky civilians fled what they feared as certain death. The U.S. decision not to intervene in the new fighting meant that the Vietnamese would settle the matter among themselves.

The ensuing collapse of South Vietnam was so sudden that it surprised the Hanoi regime and aroused suspicions of a trap. On March 26, 1975, Hué fell, followed by Danang within a week, and on April 21 Thieu resigned, bitterly charging over radio and television that the United States was responsible for the debacle. After he escaped with friends and relatives to Taiwan, the Saigon government eventually fell into the hands of Duong Van Minh, who had been instrumental in the Diem coup of 1963. The ARVN soon pulled out of Xuan Loc, forty miles east of Saigon, and on April 28 Ford approved emergency helicopter evacuations of Americans in Saigon. Meanwhile, Bien Hoa air base fell to the Vietcong, who were now only fifteen miles outside the city and still advancing. Nearly 150,000 Vietnamese managed to escape the country, many of them by boats or U.S. planes in the days just before the fall of Saigon. But not enough transportation was available to save everyone from a predicted bloodbath. U.S. Marines used rifle butts to fight off frantic Vietnamese outside the gates of the U.S. embassy in Saigon, as Americans and Vietnamese pushed and shoved their way into the helicopters taking off from the embassy roof. The final spectacle was that of angry ARVN soldiers shooting at Americans as they left the country.

On April 30, 1975, Saigon fell and the Third Indochina War was over. The expected bloodbath had not occurred, largely because Duong Van Minh had approved the unconditional surrender of South Vietnam. In their elation, the Vietcong renamed the South Vietnamese capital Ho Chi Minh City. Twenty-one years after the Geneva Accords of 1954, Vietnam was reunited in an epochal victory for the government in Hanoi. Almost simultaneously, the domino theory appeared to become a fact. The Lon Nol regime in Cambodia fell to the Communist Khmer Rouge, and soon afterward Laos also came under Communist control. The fall of these three Southeast Asian countries to communism sounded the death knell of an already mortally wounded SEATO and ended the United States's long ordeal in Asia by the spring of 1975.

The United States's Asian policy lay in shambles. At tremendous costs, successive administrations in Washington had fought to preserve the Saigon regime as a symbol of the Free World's resistance to Communist takeover. And yet South Vietnam had collapsed. North Vietnam seized $5 billion in U.S. military goods to become the leading military regime in Southeast Asia, although its government, like that of the Khmer Rouge in Cambodia, became repressive and caused thousands to flee the country. Although Cambodia and Laos had also changed leadership, there was little unity among the new Communist regimes. Less than a year after the fall of Saigon, Communist Vietnam was at war with Communist Cambodia, and in 1978 it was at war with Communist China. Vietnam's invasion of Cambodia led to the collapse of the Khmer Rouge as well as the onset of a famine that threatened to decimate the population. Japan, South Korea, and Taiwan were stunned by the U.S. withdrawal from Vietnam and feared that it might pull out of South Korea and expose Japan to Communist assault.

Thailand told Americans stationed in the country to leave, because it now had to deal regularly with other Asian nations.

The Vietnam War left numerous legacies, most of which were bitter and long lasting. First and foremost, the United States had not emerged victorious, exploding the myth that it had never lost a war and never would. Second, the cost of the war had been heavy in U.S. armed forces and materiel, immeasurable in national spirit, and nearly devastating to the nation's image abroad. More than 58,000 Americans had died (more than 20,000 during the Nixon years of Vietnamization), 300,000 had been wounded, and at least 1400 (including civilians) were missing. The United States had spent more than $150 billion, much of it in support of corrupt regimes. Third, U.S. involvement dealt a serious blow to the presidency, which, combined with the emerging Watergate scandals, gave a corresponding impetus to the power of Congress. And yet at the same time, the Vietnam experience aroused widespread distrust for public officials and severely restricted the performance of both branches of government. Fourth, the war encouraged the continued shift in

U.S. foreign policy from its dominating role in containing communism to one calling for partnerships and détente. The Vietnam experience had shaken Americans' confidence in containment, because the war showed the danger of defining every problem as Communist in origin and then trying to resolve it, whether or not the region was vital to U.S. interests. On another level, some critics wanted the United States to distinguish between areas capable of being defended and those that were not; others discerned danger in the development of a national security state that was impervious to public opinion and overly military in character.

The nation's long involvement in Vietnam has raised questions of blame, which, in view of most policymakers' Cold War mindset, suggests that everyone involved contributed to the outcome. By itself, the status of Vietnam presented no problems that endangered vital U.S. interests. But placed within the context of the Cold War, Vietnam had assumed a perceived importance far beyond reason. U.S. credibility before the world had seemed to be at stake, and thus to the list of considerations deemed vital to national interests had been added an

Fall of Saigon, April 1975
A U.S. embassy building in Saigon served as the launching pad for Americans and South Vietnamese soldiers. The helicopters carried the evacuees to U.S. aircraft carriers waiting off the coast. *United Press International.*

intangible—credibility—that was both difficult to measure and impossible to control. The United States's failure to win the war did not affect security at home, nor did the outcome set off a string of Communist conquests throughout Asia, except for Laos and Cambodia. Perhaps long-time presidential adviser Clark Clifford said it best: "What we thought was the spread of Communist aggression in my opinion now seems very clearly to have been a civil war in Vietnam. The domino theory proved to be erroneous." Tragically, he observed, the United States made an "honest mistake."

In the face of growing lack of respect for the United States, the Ford administration took advantage of an incident involving an American merchant vessel, the *Mayaguez,* to make a show of force. In May 1975 Cambodian patrol boats seized the *Mayaguez,* then in the Gulf of Siam, for allegedly violating their country's territorial waters. Occurring barely a month after the fall of Vietnam, the episode afforded the president a chance to restore the military credibility of his government. Without allowing time for either a full investigation or a Cambodian response to his demand for the return of ship and crew, he denounced the act as piracy and approved military action. Not realizing that the captors had already freed the thirty-nine Americans aboard, Ford ordered marines to the islands off Cambodia's coast. U.S. warships sank three Cambodian gunboats, and planes bombed an air base and oil depot. At the cost of forty-one Americans' lives (soldiers killed in an accidental explosion during a raid), the Ford administration proudly announced that it had saved both the *Mayaguez* and its men. The American public, as frustrated as the White House over the Vietnam War and other foreign policy failures, praised the president's use of force.

There were other attempts to bolster the staggering policy of détente. In July 1975 Ford joined the representatives of more than thirty nations in Helsinki at the Conference on Security and Cooperation in Europe to tie together the loose ends of World War II. In exchange for Soviet pledges to respect human rights and allow cultural interchange between East and West, the signatories approved the wartime borders of the Baltic States, Poland, and Eastern Europe. The following September the SEATO Council met in New York and voted to phase out the organization; its central reason for existence, South Vietnam, was gone. Before the United Nations in September 1976, Kissinger called for "coexistence with the Soviet Union" and for "reciprocal [restraint], not just in bilateral relations but around the globe." Finally, the death of Mao Zedong that same year preceded the installation of a moderate government in Beijing, which was more receptive to establishing formal Sino-American relations.

Another threat to détente came in Africa, where the United States became convinced that the Soviet Union intended to spread communism among the new postwar nations. Angola's recently won independence from Portugal had led to a civil war in which the United States worked with China and South Africa in covertly aiding the rightists. The Soviet Union helped the leftist MPLA—the Popular Movement for the Liberation of Angola—by sending thousands of Cuban soldiers to Angola in late 1975. Kissinger angrily condemned this new Soviet action as expansion by proxy and asked Congress to appropriate aid. Africa's rich mineral resources, he explained to a Senate committee, made the continent important to the United States. But Congress feared another Vietnam, and the public was indignant over new revelations that its government had already become secretly involved in Angola. Even though some representatives and senators had earlier known of the intervention and privately concurred, Congress responded to the growing public anger by cutting off funds for military assistance. Ford reverted to Cold War language in chiding that body for failing to perceive that "resistance to Soviet expansion by military means must be a fundamental element of United States foreign policy."

The MPLA emerged victorious in early 1976 and then surprised Washington by seeking technological assistance from Americans in developing Angola's oil resources. Instead of recognizing a fundamental reality—that the Angolans were concerned more about their own welfare than about communism and the Cold War—the Ford administration ill-advisedly rebuked the Soviet Union for the outcome of the civil war and ceased talking about détente.

The U.S. experience in Angola promoted a reassessment of its policies toward Africa. Americans had invested nearly $4 billion in the huge continent, but about forty percent of the money had gone to the white government of South Africa, which was strategically located at the Cape and was rich in gold and uranium. South Africa, however, posed an embarrassing liability: Its government in Pretoria had created a police state atmosphere by pursuing the racial segregationist policies of apartheid (apartness) against the black people, who outnumbered whites by almost four to one. The United States had alienated most black regimes in Africa, especially by its decision to trade with Rhodesia for its chrome ore (to avoid dependence on the other chief source of the product, the Soviet Union) despite the United Nations's economic boycott of that country's white minority regime. In early 1976 Kissinger visited South Africa, although violence had broken out in Rhodesia, and won concessions for South African blacks. The United States, he explained, had reversed its African policies to "avoid a race war" and "to prevent foreign intervention." But the Washington administration's central objective remained that of preventing Soviet exploitation of what Kissinger called "the radicalization of Africa."

Toward a New Foreign Policy

Détente seemed even more remote by late 1976 as Ford lost his bid for election to a newcomer on the national political scene, a successful peanut farmer, former governor of Georgia, and born-again Baptist—James Earl Carter, Jr. During the campaign, right-wing Republicans denounced détente so vehemently that Kissinger referred to it as "a word I would like to forget." Ford had dropped it from his speeches in preference for the phrase "peace through strength." His administration's strong showing in the *Mayaguez* affair had only temporarily soothed the national frustration over Vietnam. Furthermore, Ford had alienated many Americans by pardoning Nixon for his role in Watergate and by making the surprising assertion during his television debates with Carter that "there is no Soviet domination of Eastern Europe, and there never will be under a Ford administration." When Carter challenged this misguided observation, Ford refused to retreat, citing his recent visit to Eastern Europe as proof of his claim. Carter also took advantage of Watergate and U.S. foreign policy failures to promise to run an honest administration, freed from Washington's bureaucracy, that would restore the nation's domestic and foreign credibility.

Some of Carter's charges were not consistent, but they were effective. He attacked Kissinger's secret diplomacy, his support for repressive regimes, and the Republicans' exorbitant defense spending. Yet at the same time he criticized the Ford administration for conceding too much during arms discussions and for the failure of the Helsinki Agreements to guarantee civil liberties within the Soviet Union. The Soviets, he asserted, had exploited détente to the disadvantage of the United States. Carter's strategy was nonetheless successful. He won a little more than half of the popular vote, defeating Ford by about a two percent margin. The effects of Watergate and Vietnam doubtless influenced Americans to choose Jimmy Carter—a president determined to revive faith in the country by expounding Wilsonian idealism and appeals to respect human rights.

Selected Readings

Alexander, Robert J. *The Tragedy of Chile.* 1978.

Ambrose, Stephen E., and Brinkley, Douglas G. *Rise to Globalism: American Foreign Policy since 1938.* 8th ed., 1997.

Ball, George W., and Ball, Douglas B. *The Passionate Attachment: America's Involvement with Israel 1947 to the Present*. 1992.

Baritz, Loren. *Backfire: A History of How American Culture Led Us into Vietnam and Made Us Fight the Way We Did*. 1985.

Baskir, Lawrence M., and Strauss, William A. *Chance and Circumstance: The Draft, the War and the Vietnam Generation*. 1978.

Bell, Coral. *The Diplomacy of Détente: The Kissinger Era*. 1977.

Bill, James A. *The Eagle and the Lion: The Tragedy of American-Iranian Relations*. 1988.

Bilton, Michael, and Sim, Kevin. *Four Hours in My Lai*. 1992.

Brandon, Henry. *The Retreat of American Power*. 1972.

Brands, H. W. *The Devil We Knew: Americans and the Cold War*. 1993.

Brigham, Robert K. *Guerrilla Diplomacy: The NLF's Foreign Relations and the Viet Nam War*. 1999.

Brown, Seyom. *The Crises of Power: Foreign Policy in the Kissinger Years*. 1979.

Burchett, Wilfred. *Catapult to Freedom: The Survival of the Vietnamese People*. 1978.

———. *Grasshoppers & Elephants: Why Vietnam Fell*. 1977.

Butler, David. *The Fall of Saigon: Scenes from the Sudden End of a Long War*. 1985.

Cahn, Anne H. *Killing Détente: The Right Attacks the CIA*. 1998.

Campagna, Anthony S. *The Economic Consequences of the Vietnam War*. 1991.

Cannon, James M. *Time and Chance: Gerald Ford's Appointment with History*. 1994.

Clodfelter, Mark. *The Limits of Air Power: The American Bombing of North Vietnam*. 1989.

Cohen, Warren I. *America's Response to China: An Interpretive History of Sino-American Relations*. 2000.

Coker, Christopher. *The United States and South Africa, 1968–1985*. 1986.

Conboy, Kenneth, and Andradé, Dale. *Spies and Commandos: How America Lost the Secret War in North Vietnam*. 2000.

Costigliola, Frank. *France and the United States: The Cold Alliance since World War II*. 1992.

Davidson, Phillip B. *Vietnam at War: The History, 1946–1975*. 1988.

DeBenedetti, Charles, and Chatfield, Charles. *An American Ordeal: The Antiwar Movement of the Vietnam Era*. 1990.

DeForest, Orrin, and Chanoff, David. *Slow Burn: The Rise and Bitter Fall of American Intelligence in Vietnam*. 1990.

Duiker, William J. *The Communist Road to Power in Vietnam*. 1981.

———. *U.S. Containment Policy and the Conflict in Indochina*. 1994.

DuPuy, Trevor N. *Elusive Victory: The Arab-Israeli Wars, 1947–1974*. 1978.

Ely, John H. *War and Responsibility: Constitutional Lessons of Vietnam and Its Aftermath*. 1993.

Engelmann, Larry. *Tears Before the Rain: An Oral History of the Fall of South Vietnam*. 1990.

FitzGerald, Frances. *Fire in the Lake: The Vietnamese and the Americans in Vietnam*. 1972.

Foot, Rosemary. *The Practice of Power: U.S. Relations with China since 1949*. 1995.

Ford, Gerald R. *A Time to Heal: The Autobiography of Gerald R. Ford*. 1979.

Franck, Thomas M., and Weisband, Edward. *Foreign Policy by Congress*. 1979.

Freedman, Robert O. *Soviet Policy toward the Middle East Since 1970*. 1978.

Froman, Michael B. *The Development of the Idea of Détente: Coming to Terms*. 1991.

Gaddis, John L. *The Long Peace: Inquiries into the History of the Cold War*. 1987.

———. *Russia, the Soviet Union, and the United States: An Interpretive History*. 2nd ed., 1990.

———. *Strategies of Containment: A Critical Appraisal of Postwar American National Security Policy*. 1982.

Gaiduk, Ilya V. *The Soviet Union and the Vietnam War*. 1996.

Garthoff, Raymond L. *Détente and Confrontation: American-Soviet Relations from Nixon to Reagan*. 1994.

Gelb, Leslie H., and Betts, Richard K. *The Irony of Vietnam: The System Worked*. 1979.

Glassman, Jon D. *Arms for the Arabs: The Soviet Union and War in the Middle East*. 1975.

Goldman, Marshall I. *Détente and Dollars: Doing Business with the Soviets*. 1975.

Goode, James F. *The United States and Iran: In the Shadow of Musaddiq*. 1997.

Goodman, Allan E. *The Lost Peace: America's Search for a Negotiated Settlement of the Vietnam War*. 1978.

Gottlieb, Sherry G. *Hell No, We Won't Go! Resisting the Draft During the Vietnam War*. 1991.

Greene, John R. *The Limits of Power: The Nixon and Ford Administrations*. 1995.

———. *The Presidency of Gerald R. Ford*. 1995.

Guimarês, Fernando A. *The Origins of the Angolan Civil War: Foreign Intervention and Domestic Political Conflict*. 1998.

Hallin, Daniel C. *The "Uncensored War": The Media and Vietnam*. 1986.

Hammond, William H. *Reporting Vietnam: Media and Military at War*. 1998.

Harding, Harry. *A Fragile Relationship: The United States and China since 1972*. 1992.

Harrison, James P. *The Endless War: Fifty Years of Struggle in Vietnam*. 1982.

Harrison, Michael M. *The Reluctant Ally: France and Atlantic Security*. 1981.

Haslam, Jonathan. *The Soviet Union and the Politics of Nuclear Weapons in Europe, 1969–87*. 1990.

Havens, Thomas R. H. *Fire Across the Sea: The Vietnam War and Japan, 1965–1975*. 1987.

Hellmann, John. *American Myth and the Legacy of Vietnam*. 1986.

Herring, George C., Jr. *America's Longest War: The United States and Vietnam, 1950–1975*. 3rd ed., 1996.

———, ed. *The Pentagon Papers: Abridged Edition*. 1993.

Hersh, Seymour M. *The Price of Power: Kissinger in the Nixon White House*. 1983.

Hess, Gary R. *Vietnam and the United States: Origins and Legacy of War*. 1998.

Hoff-Wilson, Joan. *Nixon Reconsidered*. 1994.

Holloway, David. *The Soviet Union and the Arms Race*. 1983.

Hyland, William. *Mortal Rivals: Superpower Relations from Nixon to Reagan*. 1987.

Isaacs, Arnold R. *Without Honor: Defeat in Vietnam and Cambodia*. 1983.

Isaacson, Walter. *Kissinger: A Biography*. 1992.

Jeffreys-Jones, Rhodri. *Peace Now! American Society and the Ending of the Vietnam War*. 1999.

Jiang, Arnold X./Chiang, Hsiang-tse. *The United States and China*. 1988.

Joiner, Harry M. *American Foreign Policy: The Kissinger Era*. 1977.

Kalb, Bernard, and Kalb, Marvin. *Kissinger*. 1974.

Kaplan, Robert D. *The Arabists: The Romance of an American Elite*. 1993.

Karnow, Stanley. *Vietnam: A History*. Rev. ed., 1991.

Kattenburg, Paul M. *The Vietnam Trauma in American Foreign Policy, 1945–1975*. 1980.

Keith, Ronald C. *The Diplomacy of Zhou Enlai*. 1989.

Kendrick, Alexander. *The Wound Within: America in the Vietnam Years, 1945–1974*. 1974.

Kimball, Jeffrey. *Nixon's Vietnam War*. 1998.

Kissinger, Henry. *White House Years*. 1979.

———. *Years of Upheaval*. 1982.

Kolko, Gabriel. *Anatomy of a War: Vietnam, the United States, and the Modern Historical Experience*. 1985.

Kunz, Diane B. *Butter and Guns: America's Cold War Economic Diplomacy*. 1997.

Krepinevich, Andrew F., Jr. *The Army and Vietnam*. 1986.

LaFeber, Walter. *America, Russia, and the Cold War, 1945–1996*. 8th ed., 1997.

———. *The Clash: A History of U.S.-Japan Relations*. 1997.

———. *The Panama Canal: The Crisis in Historical Perspective*. Updated ed. (with Scott LaFeber), 1989.

Lake, Anthony. *The "Tar Baby" Option: American Policy Toward Southern Rhodesia*. 1976.

Landau, David. *Kissinger: The Uses of Power*. 1972.

Langguth, A. J. *Our Vietnam: The War, 1954–1975*. 2000.

Lanning, Michael L., and Cragg, Dan. *Inside the VC and the NVA: The Real Story of North Vietnam's Armed Forces*. 1992.

Larson, Thomas B. *Soviet-American Rivalry*. 1978.

Lewy, Guenter. *America in Vietnam*. 1978.

Lind, Michael. *Vietnam the Necessary War: A Reinterpretation of America's Most Disastrous Military Conflict*. 1999.

Litwak, Robert S. *Détente and the Nixon Doctrine*. 1984.

Lomperis, Timothy J. *From People's War to People's War: Insurgency, Intervention, and the Lessons of Vietnam*. 1996.

———. *The War Everyone Lost—And Won: America's Intervention in Vietnam's Twin Struggles*. 1984.

Lukas, J. Anthony. *Nightmare: The Underside of the Nixon Administration*. 1976.

Maclear, Michael. *The Ten Thousand Day War, Vietnam: 1945–1975*. 1981.

Mandelbaum, Michael. *The Nuclear Question: The United States & Nuclear Weapons, 1946–1976*. 1979.

Mangold, Tom, and Penygate, John. *The Tunnels of Cu Chi: The Untold Story of Vietnam*. 1985.

Mann, Jim. *About Face: A History of America's Curious Relationship with China from Nixon to Clinton*. 1999.

Mann, Robert. *A Grand Illusion: America's Descent into Vietnam.* 2001.

Matusow, Allen J. *Nixon's Economy: Booms, Busts, Dollars, and Votes.* 1998.

McMahon, Robert J. *The Cold War on the Periphery: The United States, India, and Pakistan.* 1994.

———. *The Limits of Empire: The United States and Southeast Asia since World War II.* 1999.

Melanson, Richard A. *American Foreign Policy Since the Vietnam War: The Search for Consensus from Nixon to Clinton.* 2000.

Moran, Theodore H. *Multinational Corporations and the Politics of Dependence: Copper in Chile.* 1974.

Morgan, Joseph G. *The Vietnam Lobby: The American Friends of Vietnam, 1955–1975.* 1997.

Morley, Morris H. *Washington, Somoza, and the Sandinistas: State and Regime in U.S. Policy Toward Nicaragua, 1969–1981.* 1994.

Morris, Roger. *Uncertain Greatness: Henry Kissinger and American Foreign Policy.* 1977.

Nelson, Keith L. *The Making of Détente: Soviet-American Relations in the Shadow of Vietnam.* 1995.

Newhouse, John. *Cold Dawn: The Story of SALT.* 1973.

Nixon, Richard. *No More Vietnams.* 1985.

———. *RN: The Memoirs of Richard Nixon.* 1978.

Olmsted, Kathryn. *Challenging the Secret Government: The Post-Watergate Investigations of the CIA and FBI.* 1996.

Olson, James S., and Roberts, Randy. *My Lai: A Brief History with Documents.* 1998.

———, and ———. *Where the Domino Fell: America and Vietnam, 1945–1990.* 1991.

Page, Caroline. *U.S. Official Propaganda During the Vietnam War, 1965–1973: The Limits of Persuasion.* 1996.

Palmer, Dave R. *Summons of the Trumpet: A History of the Vietnam War from a Military Man's Viewpoint.* 1978.

Pérez, Louis A., Jr. *Cuba and the United States: Ties of Singular Intimacy.* 1997.

Petras, James, and Morley, Morris. *The United States and Chile: Imperialism and the Overthrow of the Allende Government.* 1975.

Pike, Douglas. *PAVN: People's Army of Vietnam.* 1986.

Pipes, Richard. *U.S.-Soviet Relations in the Era of Détente: A Tragedy of Errors.* 1981.

Podhoretz, Norman. *Why We Were in Vietnam.* 1982.

Polk, William R. *The Arab World Today.* 5th ed., 1991.

Poole, Peter. *The United States and Indochina from FDR to Nixon.* 1973.

Porter, Gareth. *A Peace Denied: The United States, Vietnam, and the Paris Agreement.* 1975.

Powers, Thomas. *The Man Who Kept the Secrets: Richard Helms and the CIA.* 1979.

Prados, John. *The Blood Road: The Ho Chi Minh Trail and the Vietnam War.* 1999.

———. *Presidents' Secret Wars: CIA Pentagon Covert Operations from World War II through the Persian Gulf.* 1996.

Quandt, William B. *Decade of Decisions: American Policy Toward the Arab-Israeli Conflict, 1967–1976.* 1977.

Rabe, Stephen G. *The Road to OPEC: United States Relations with Venezuela.* 1982.

Reich, Bernard. *Quest for Peace: United States-Israeli Relations and the Arab-Israeli Conflict.* 1977.

Risse-Kappen, Thomas. *Cooperation Among Democracies: The European Influence on U.S. Foreign Policy.* 1995.

Ross, Robert S. *Negotiating Cooperation: The United States and China, 1969–1989.* 1995.

Rubin, Barry. *Paved with Good Intentions: The American Experience and Iran.* 1980.

Safran, Nadav. *Israel.* 1978.

Sayigh, Yezid. *Armed Struggle and the Search for State: The Palestinian National Movement, 1949–1993.* 1997.

Schaller, Michael. *Altered States: The United States and Japan since the Occupation.* 1997.

———. *The United States and China in the Twentieth Century.* 2nd ed., 1990.

Schell, Jonathan. *The Time of Illusion.* 1976.

Schlesinger, Arthur M., Jr. *The Imperial Presidency.* 1973.

Schoenbaum, David. *The United States and the State of Israel.* 1993.

Schoutz, Lars. *Beneath the United States: A History of U.S. Policy Toward Latin America.* 1998.

Schulzinger, Robert D. *Henry Kissinger: Doctor of Diplomacy.* 1989.

———. *A Time for War: The United States and Vietnam, 1941–1975.* 1997.

Schurmann, Franz. *The Foreign Politics of Richard Nixon: The Grand Design.* 1987.

Searles, P. David. *The Peace Corps Experience: Challenge and Change, 1969–1976.* 1997.

Shaplen, Robert. *Bitter Victory.* 1986.

Shawcross, William. *Sideshow: Kissinger, Nixon and the Destruction of Cambodia.* 1979.

Sheehan, Edward R. F. *The Arabs, Israelis, and Kissinger.* 1976.

Sheehan, Neil, et al., eds. *New York Times, The Pentagon Papers.* 1971.

Sigmund, Paul E. *The Overthrow of Allende and the Politics of Chile, 1964–1976.* 1977.

———. *The United States and Democracy in Chile.* 1993.

Small, Melvin. *Covering Dissent: The Media and the Anti-Vietnam War Movement.* 1994.

———. *Johnson, Nixon, and the Doves.* 1988.

Smith, Gerard. *Doubletalk: The Story of the First Strategic Arms Limitation Talks.* 1980.

Smith, Peter H. *Talons of the Eagle: Dynamics of U.S.-Latin American Relations.* 2nd ed., 2000.

Snepp, Frank. *Decent Interval: An Insider's Account of Saigon's Indecent End Told by the CIA's Chief Strategy Analyst in Vietnam.* 1978.

Sorley, Lewis. *A Better War: The Unexamined Victories and Final Tragedy of America's Last Years in Vietnam.* 1999.

———. *Arms Transfers Under Nixon: A Policy Analysis.* 1983.

Spanier, John W. *American Foreign Policy Since World War II.* 14th ed., 1998.

Spiegel, Steven L. *The Other Arab-Israeli Conflict: Making America's Middle East Policy, from Truman to Reagan.* 1985.

Stares, Paul B. *The Militarization of Space: U.S. Policy, 1945–1984.* 1985.

Stevenson, Richard W. *The Rise and Fall of Détente: Relaxations of Tensions in US-Soviet Relations, 1953–84.* 1985.

Stockwell, John. *In Search of Enemies: A CIA Story.* 1979.

Stookey, Robert W. *America and the Arab States.* 1975.

Sulzberger, C. L. *The World and Richard Nixon.* 1987.

Szulc, Tad. *The Illusion of Peace: Foreign Policy in the Nixon Years.* 1978.

Taylor, Sandra C. *Vietnamese Women at War: Fighting for Ho Chi Minh and the Revolution.* 1999.

Terriff, Terry. *The Nixon Administration and the Making of U.S. Nuclear Strategy.* 1995.

Todd, Olivier. *Cruel April: The Fall of Saigon.* 1987.

Tomes, Robert R. *Apocalypse Then: American Intellectuals and the Vietnam War, 1954–1975.* 1998.

Truong Nhu Tang. *A Vietcong Memoir.* 1985.

Tucker, Nancy B. *Taiwan, Hong Kong, and the United States, 1945–1992: Uncertain Friendships.* 1994.

Tucker, Spenser C. *Vietnam.* 1999.

Turley, William S. *The Second Indochina War: A Short Political and Military History, 1954–1975.* 1986.

Turner, Karen G. *Even the Women Must Fight: Memories of War from North Vietnam.* 1998.

Ulam, Adam B. *The Communists: The Story of Power and Lost Illusions, 1948–1991.* 1992.

Valentine, Douglas. *The Phoenix Program.* 1990.

Wells, Tom. *The War Within: America's Battle Over Vietnam.* 1994.

Whitaker, Arthur P. *The United States and the Southern Core: Argentina, Chile, and Uruguay.* 1976.

Wills, Garry. *Nixon Agonistes: The Crisis of the Self-Made Man.* 1970.

Wyatt, Clarence R. *Paper Soldiers: The American Press and the Vietnam War.* 1993.

Young, Marilyn B. *The Vietnam Wars, 1945–1990.* 1991.

Zaroulis, Nancy, and Sullivan, Gerald. *Who Spoke Up? American Protest Against the War in Vietnam, 1963–1975.* 1984.

Zhai, Qiang. *China and the Vietnam Wars, 1950–1975.* 2000.

CHAPTER 15

The New World Order
JIMMY CARTER AND THE DIPLOMACY OF HUMAN RIGHTS, 1977–1981

Carter and the New World Order

The Carter administration's foreign policy was more vocal about a world order based on human rights than any presidency since that of Woodrow Wilson, even though the underlying objective remained the containment of Soviet expansion. Human rights, the new executive declared, was "the soul of our foreign policy." Indeed, he called on the United States to repent of its past sins by exercising leadership through example rather than through domination. The change in public emphasis partly resulted from the limitations on U.S. power imposed by the recent military growth of other nations, particularly that of the Soviet Union. But the human rights emphasis was also consistent with ideas growing during the last four decades, most notably those highlighted in Franklin D. Roosevelt's Four Freedoms of 1941, the UN Charter of 1945, the Universal Declaration of Human Rights of 1948, and the Helsinki Agreements of 1975. To guarantee "no more Vietnams," Carter asserted, the United States would no longer be directed by "an inordinate fear of communism." His administration would concentrate on tying the world together by economic and social means, including the establishment of a law of the seas. It would seek to "replace bal-

ance of power politics with world order politics." The ultimate objective was to reduce the chances for nuclear war by achieving success in the SALT talks and halting arms sales to other countries.

Problems plagued the administration from the outset because of conflicts between the goals of Soviet containment and the support of human rights. First, containment of the Soviet Union dictated the development of new weapons, the recognition of China, and aid to non-Communist regimes, whereas the drive for human rights led to the encouragement of nationalism, the establishment of a North-South economic relationship between advanced countries and the Third World, public denunciations of the Soviets' policies toward dissidents at home, and support for the SALT talks. Second, morality rarely fit with the government's strategic and economic interests, often exposing the administration to charges of hypocrisy. Carter attacked the repressive tactics of Fidel Castro in Cuba and Idi Amin in Uganda, and he angered Leonid Brezhnev by criticizing his civil liberties policies. But the president ignored similarly harsh practices in countries important to U.S. interests, such as Iran, Nicaragua, the Philippines, South Korea, and Zaire (formerly the Congo). Although the U.S. ambassador to the United Nations, Andrew

Young, asserted that the human rights program was never "thought out and planned," the administration actually spent an enormous amount of time formulating these policies. Finally, the administration never succeeded in establishing a law of the seas that regulated their use and created a sense of interdependence among users of the waterways.

The Vietnam experience encouraged the new executive to adopt a diplomacy of restraint. The war in Southeast Asia and the Watergate scandals had destroyed the nation's political consensus, allowing the emergence of numerous special interest groups that often operated independently of Washington. The declining global influence of the United States since World War II added to its inability to steer events. Disillusionment and a sense of national guilt over the war in Vietnam meanwhile fostered a greater disengagement in foreign affairs and bred skepticism over the reality of a Communist danger. The new attitude manifested itself in an aversion to foreign intervention and in a call for cooperation in furthering human rights and helping poverty-stricken peoples, especially those in the so-called Fourth World countries having few resources. Indeed, Americans temporarily seemed to develop a sense of collective amnesia about the war in Vietnam, preferring to focus on almost any issue other than their nation's longest war. The Washington government was confident that the Kremlin would have to relax its offensive because of the growing aspirations of China, NATO, and the Third World. The United States, it appeared, had finally accepted the limits of power.

The Carter administration encountered numerous problems in its foreign policy. The new president was a novice in national politics and was unable to work effectively with Congress. Many Democrats in Congress had won their seats by greater margins than Carter had, and they did not feel bound to him. The domestic political structure was in constant flux because of shifting alliances, which obstructed the formation of a new national consensus. The economy continued to suffer from recession and skyrocketing inflation, a predicament exacerbated by OPEC's periodic raising of oil prices. The nation's allies meanwhile distanced themselves because Washington's leaders seemed unable to manage their own political and economic situation. Carter's emphasis on human rights hurt détente, because a return to idealism in foreign affairs not only disrupted Soviet relations but also caused trouble in Latin America and Europe. Moreover, a call for human rights could lead to policies similar to those of President Wilson: self-righteous interference in other countries' internal affairs. As Carter's policies eventually floundered in indirection and indecisiveness, his performance ratings plunged.

Carter at first leaned toward the views of Secretary of State Cyrus Vance, who preferred an orderly, behind-the-scenes formulation of policy through the state department. U.S. foreign policy underwent a marked change from Kissinger's independent, flashy style of diplomacy to that of patient and quiet negotiations led by experienced career diplomats. Vance had been deputy secretary of defense from 1964 to 1967 and had participated in the Paris peace talks of 1968–1969 relating to Vietnam. A wealthy New York attorney from West Virginia, he opposed military interventionist policies, refused to hold the Soviets responsible for all the world's problems, urged disarmament measures, emphasized the need for dealing with change in developing nations outside the competitive context of the Cold War, and believed that the Vietnamese War had demonstrated the principle that Americans could not "prop up a series of regimes that lacked popular support." With the United States's diminished role in world politics, he declared publicly, "there can be no going back to a time when we thought there could be American solutions to every problem." Peace could come only through negotiations and the establishment of economic ties. SALT II became his premier objective.

Vance relied heavily on his chief adviser for Soviet affairs, Marshall Shulman, who was on leave from his position as professor of Russian studies at Columbia University. Shulman argued that the United States should emphasize "soft linkage"—discreet suggestions to Moscow that U.S. economic aid would be forthcoming only if the Soviets respected human rights at home and allowed international matters to calm. He hoped that "within-the-system-modernizers" inside the Soviet Union—youthful and middle-aged professionals and technicians—would bring internal changes conducive to cooperation with the West. But time and patience were required. He and Vance agreed that troubles in emerging nations were attributable more to nationalist tendencies than to Soviet instigation. Change in Eastern Europe, they continued, had to come slowly. Otherwise, the Soviets would use military force to settle questions as they had done in Hungary in 1956 and Czechoslovakia in 1968.

But the president's national security adviser, Zbigniew Brzezinski, sharply disagreed with Vance, eventually prompting a division in the administration's foreign policy. A political science professor from Columbia University who specialized in Soviet affairs, Brzezinski was born in Poland and held hard-line anti-Communist views. He saw the world as bipolar and regarded the Soviet Union as the central threat to peace. An early critic of détente, Brzezinski was skeptical about SALT, especially if the Soviets did not change their aggressive policies in Africa and the Middle East. Furthermore, he did not believe "that the use of nuclear weapons would be the end of the human race. . . . That's egocentric," Brzezinski declared.

Carter seldom found a common ground between these opposing viewpoints and therefore failed to institute a firm and consistent foreign policy. He promised peaceful resolutions of world problems, cooperation with Congress, restraints on the CIA, a more open foreign policy, restrictions on arms sales, gradual military withdrawal from South Korea, and curtailment of foreign aid to nations refusing to respect human rights. Past experiences suggested that these objectives were impractical. But for Carter they seemed attainable on an individual basis. One official noted that the president looked at problems "like an engineering student thinking you can cram for the exam and get an A." To Carter, a graduate of the Annapolis Naval Academy and a nuclear engineer, long hours of studying and mastering details left him with a comfortable feeling of understanding the issues. But his approach was virtually meaningless without a corresponding understanding of how the issues were interrelated, and that to deal with them required knowledge of both general strategy and history. In 1979 Carter tried to correct the latter deficiency when he admitted to having read more history since becoming president than at any time in his life. Yet the president's fundamentalist religious views influenced him to adopt a simplified world outlook that led him to regard morality as the primary determinant in foreign policy. Thus, those nations not professing idealism rejected Carter's calls for human rights as unwarranted attempts to meddle in their domestic affairs. The president sincerely believed in his pleas for human decency, but he was hampered by practical global politics, by his country's diminished world prestige, and by the conflicts between his advisers. The gap between idealistic objectives and realistic policies proved too wide to close.

Perhaps Carter's central difficulty was a lack of vision and direction. A former speechwriter noted that the president "holds explicit, thorough positions on every issue under the sun . . . but he has no large view of the relations between them." Carter "fails to project a vision larger than the problem he is tackling at the moment." The president was doubtless correct in arguing that a "national malaise" had caused a "crisis of the American spirit," but he never seemed to grasp the importance of laying out a general course of action designed to combat the problem.

The Carter administration sought to counter Soviet military expansion in Eastern Europe by tightening the Western alliance and furthering the SALT talks. The Moscow government had apparently matched that of

Washington in nuclear power, necessitating a greater U.S. reliance on its allies and on arms limitations programs. In January 1977 Carter attempted to draw the allies closer together by calling for a program of "trilateralism"—social and economic cooperation among North America, Western Europe, and Japan that would also help the Third World. Less than a week after the inauguration, Vice President Walter Mondale promoted the idea during his goodwill visit to Western Europe and Japan. This program was no surprise; during the early 1970s Carter and Vance had been members of the Trilateral Commission, a private group of Americans, West Europeans, and Japanese brought together by Brzezinski and U.S. banker David Rockefeller to rebuild economic and political ties hurt by the Nixon administration's willingness to deal with enemy nations. But the commission rarely agreed on anything. In spring 1977 President Carter attended an economic conference in London of seven industrial nations—the United States, Britain, Canada, France, Italy, West Germany, and Japan—that agreed to work toward halting inflation, promoting trade, creating employment, and helping underdeveloped nations. Afterward, he reaffirmed ties with NATO as a core of U.S. foreign policy.

The Carter administration spent most of 1977 trying to advance the SALT negotiations in Moscow. Vance led the delegation in late March as it tried to advance the principles of November 1974, worked out by Ford and Brezhnev in Vladivostok. Vance offered a well-publicized plan containing several proposals: formal approval of the Vladivostok principles, a specific program calling for a joint cutback in missile launchers and multiple warheads, cessation of the development of new weapons, and a freeze on ICBMs at their present level of about 550. Vance also recommended an end to mobile missiles, limits on the scope of cruise missiles, and restrictions against the Soviets' new supersonic "Backfire" bomber. His proposals unleashed a furious reaction in Moscow, because they reversed the Ford-Brezhnev understandings by calling for mas-sive reductions in the exact areas of Soviet strengths. Vance's plan was preposterous, Soviet Foreign Minister Andrei Gromyko announced in a televised news conference, because it required the Soviets to phase out their largest missiles. Although the two nations agreed to continue studying the problems relating to nuclear materials, they abruptly terminated the SALT talks. SALT I was due to expire in October 1977, but the governments in Washington and Moscow agreed to extend its life until SALT II became effective. Soviet-American relations had taken a sharp downward turn.

In an effort to defuse the East-West division, Carter relied on UN Ambassador Andrew Young to build a meaningful North-South relationship. Young, a black minister, civil rights leader, and former congressman from Georgia, promoted closer relations with the Third World by advancing the Vance-Shulman position that new nations could seek help from the United States as long as Cold War issues did not intervene. But Young had to leave office in 1979 in the wake of revelations that he had secretly initiated unauthorized communications with the PLO (not recognized by the United States) to arrange its participation in settling the Middle East crisis.

The administration's human rights stance toward the Third World necessitated understandings with the Soviet Union. There seemed little choice by the late 1970s: Americans were weary of foreign policy commitments and had supported recent attacks on the so-called "imperial presidency." According to this argument, the nation's presidents had for too long operated independently of the people's wishes and needed both restraints through the War Powers Act and controls over the CIA. The Cold War was over, many wanted to believe. Détente was crucial to the success of the new world order.

The United States thus prepared to deal with the realities of a multipolar political and economic system. Should it oppose international cooperation in resolving global problems, growing instability would lead to more political unrest injurious to trade and invest-ment. The world's economy was in a down-spin, and Fourth World peoples needed massive assistance to combat droughts, famines, and other natural disasters. Thousands of "boat people" from Vietnam, Laos, and Cambodia sought refuge in the United States from re-pressive Communist governments; at the same time, however, Third World nations controlled valuable natural resources such as oil and demonstrated a strong desire to use their eco-nomic leverage against the great powers. The new postwar nations had become a majority in the United Nations by the 1970s, and the con-tinued proliferation of nuclear weapons was alarming. The Western alliance was shaky, and Latin Americans were increasingly resentful of Washington's exploitative policies. Finally, Watergate, Vietnam, and the manipulative ac-tivities of the CIA and multinational corpora-tions caused an erosion of respect for the United States. Carter appeared to recognize these realities, but his rhetorical and often inconsistent appeals to human rights so badly interfered with his positions on events that even the nation's allies viewed his administration as devious, self-righteous, and undependable.

The Third World:
Africa and Latin America

The Carter administration made noteworthy strides toward establishing good relations with Third World countries. Vance, Young, and others in the administration tried to deal with the troubles of the underdeveloped nations on their own merits; not every problem, they argued, was Soviet-inspired. Nationalist up-heavals could be indigenous and thus have no relation to great power rivalries. During the first half of his presidency Carter was receptive to these arguments, even restraining those advisers who called for interventionist policies designed to curb believed Soviet expansion-ism. Economic assistance programs, tied to as-surances of human rights reforms, became the central thrust of the administration's policies toward the Third World.

Africa was a major concern of the United States. Politically, the representation in the United Nations was already one-third African, and inside the United States blacks pressed for a policy recognizing African nationalism. Economically, the continent was rich in min-erals and an excellent source of trade and in-vestment. Nigeria, in fact, had become the second largest supplier of oil for the United States. Strategically, Africa offered airstrips and ports at key points interconnecting the world. Should the Washington administration con-tinue to support white regimes, however, the Soviets would be in the position to exploit black nationalism and become a major force in Africa.

Young ultimately convinced the president that Africans should resolve their own prob-lems. Both the Kennedy and Johnson admin-istrations had told the United Nations that they disliked white minority rule in Rhodesia (Zimbabwe after 1980) and South Africa. But despite Johnson's opposition, Congress had permitted Americans to purchase Rhodesia's chrome, violating a UN embargo that the United States itself had helped to institute. The Nixon administration had then refrained from criticizing white rule in Africa because it believed that whites would remain dominant for years. But a shift in policy had begun under Kissinger in 1976, which Carter continued. After Young visited black regimes in Africa, Carter denounced the racist policy of apart-heid and argued that an independent Africa bolstered by U.S. aid would pose a strong obstacle to Soviet infiltration. Congress, under immense White House pressure, restored the embargo on Rhodesian chrome. In the mean-time the Carter administration worked with the British government to persuade Rhode-sia's prime minister, Ian Smith, to approve a gradual change to majority rule. As a result, British and American negotiations led to an election in April 1980 that installed a gov-ernment in Rhodesia headed by a black insur-gent and Marxist, Robert Mugabe. In South Africa, however, the Washington government failed to persuade the white regime to change its policies toward blacks, who comprised eighty-five percent of the population.

A conflict between the Marxist regimes of Somalia and Ethiopia dramatically exposed Soviet-American differences over Africa. In 1977 Somalia, the Kremlin's closest ally in Africa since 1969, sent soldiers to fight with the insurgent Western Somali Liberation Front in the Ogaden area of Ethiopia, then populated by a number of Somalis. The Soviets had to choose between the antagonists. Although Somalia had a naval base and air facilities along the Indian Ocean, the Soviets leaned toward Ethiopia because it was much larger than Somalia and its location would facilitate Soviet access to the strategically important Horn of Africa on the central eastern coast of the continent. In November, Somalia's president abrogated his country's friendship with the Soviet Union. The Moscow government promptly sent Ethiopia $1 billion in military assistance, 1000 advisers, and 20,000 Cuban soldiers to put down the Ogaden insurrection. By March 1978 they had succeeded, forcing Somali regulars out of Ogaden. The Carter administration now feared that if the Soviet Union won greater influence in Ethiopia and went on to seize the southern end of the Red Sea, it would endanger the Suez Canal and Israel and cut off the oil flow from the Persian Gulf to the West.

Growing division within the Carter administration led to a confused reaction to events in Africa. Brzezinski and the defense department wanted to send military assistance to Somalia, whereas Vance and the state department argued that Africa's problems were internal and that U.S. intervention would alienate the entire continent. Although Ethiopia had invited Moscow's help, Vance and Young argued that Somalia was the aggressor. Carter therefore wavered before lashing out at the Soviet Union and Cuba, hurting détente by warning that if the Soviets did not withdraw the Cuban forces from Africa, SALT II was in danger. The United States did not intervene but urged a moderate policy in Ogaden and a peaceful settlement of Somali-Ethiopian diffi-

culties. Somalia meanwhile eased the situation by agreeing to keep its soldiers out of Ogaden. But the Soviets entered a twenty-year pact with Ethiopia that condoned their involvement and that of the Cubans.

Despite Young's unceremonious departure from the administration in 1979, U.S. relations with Africa had improved. Commercial ties were growing, and the United States soon secured port and airfield rights in Somalia. In another part of the continent, the Carter administration airlifted supplies to Belgian and French forces in Zaire (the United States's chief source of cobalt) during May 1978, after Soviet- and Cuban-aided Katangans had invaded the province through Angola, but that was the extent of U.S. military action. The restraint paid off. Numerous African regimes voted with the United States in matters before the UN General Assembly, and although the Soviets and Cubans remained influential in Angola and Ethiopia, the Angolans showed signs of wanting to deal with the West. Africans, the Carter administration seemed to realize, had one overriding objective: never again to become colonials.

Latin America likewise continued to be a major source of U.S. concern. Persisting problems of poverty and overpopulation had stimulated drives for nationalism that were, in turn, repeatedly squelched by harsh military regimes whose power was often maintained by U.S. arms and materiel. Brazil, Cuba, and Mexico had become more independent, although the majority of Latin Americans still sought U.S. help in securing technological assistance, reduced tariffs, higher prices for their goods, and more controls over multinational corporations. Like Africa, Latin America commanded votes in the United Nations and was an important source of trade and investment. The United States could no longer ignore the problem.

The Carter administration sought to relieve Latin America's problems by using economic pressures to force right-wing regimes to respect human rights. In a speech before the Permanent Council of the Organization of

American States in April 1977, the president called for greater consultation among the American states that rested on three principles: "a high regard for the individuality and sovereignty of each Latin American and Caribbean nation"; "respect for human rights"; and the intention to resolve "the great issues which affect the relations between the developed and developing nations." Carter urged commercial cooperation in stabilizing prices and building a sound economy and promised that the United States would stimulate lending through the American Development Bank. These efforts, however, were contingent on a firm Latin American commitment to human rights.

Carter's first diplomatic offensive in Latin America—his attempt to reestablish formal relations with Cuba—was a failure. As prerequisites for U.S. recognition, Castro first had to guarantee respect for human rights, and second, he had to cease sending troops to Africa. In Havana from April through June of 1977, U.S. and Cuban delegates discussed their countries' difficulties. A short time earlier the Carter administration had lifted the ban on travel to Cuba, and Castro had promised to continue efforts to discourage airplane hijacking. But by the close of the Havana negotiations in mid-1977, the two delegations had succeeded only in creating "diplomatic interest sections" in the nations' capitals. The U.S. trade embargo was still in effect, Cuban troops remained in Angola and Ethiopia, and Soviet military and economic influence was conspicuous in Cuba. In fact, more than $20 million of economic aid arrived in Havana every week. Although secret U.S.-Cuban discussions continued through 1980, they neither lifted the commercial embargo nor restored diplomatic relations.

The Carter administration's most ambitious effort to build a better relationship with Latin America was a success: the termination of the United States's control over the Panama Canal established by the Hay–Bunau-Varilla Treaty of 1903. A long-time source of resentment, the pact had been the subject of nego-

tiations during both the Johnson and Nixon presidencies. By mid-century, controversy had focused on a local disagreement over the flying of Panamanian and U.S. flags on high school grounds. In January 1964 U.S. high school students in Panama had torn down and allegedly desecrated the Panamanian flag. Angry Panamanians stormed the Canal Zone, where U.S. soldiers had driven them back at the cost of twenty-six lives, including those of three Americans. The Panamanian government had then broken relations with the United States and turned for help to the United Nations and the OAS. An OAS committee tried to mediate the dispute, but Johnson refused the Panamanian government's demand to renegotiate the old Panama Treaty. After his election victory in November, he announced his country's intention to build a sea-level canal through either Panama, Nicaragua, or Colombia. The Panama Canal, he explained, was susceptible to sabotage, unable to service the huge volume of ships passing through daily, and not equipped to accommodate America's large aircraft carriers. But Panamanians objected to America's insistence on controlling the canal and retaining its bases in the area, and the issue remained unsettled. The Nixon administration had pledged support for a new treaty, and now Carter as president promised an agreement combining "Panama's legitimate needs as a sovereign nation" with America's "interests in the efficient operations of a neutral canal, open on a nondiscriminatory basis to all users." His administration had a chance to improve relations with Latin America with one bold stroke: turning over the canal to Panama.

The resulting treaties between the United States and Panama were the work of many people, most notably Sol Linowitz as head of the U.S. delegation, Secretary of State Vance, and two senators, Democrat Robert Byrd of West Virginia and Republican Howard Baker of Tennessee. The two pacts, drawn in 1977 and approved in Panama by a two-to-one margin in October of that same year, would abrogate the 1903 treaty, raise Panama's share of the canal tolls, and grant the United States the perpetual right to protect the canal's "neutrality." By the first treaty, the "Panama Canal Treaty," the United States would retain central responsibility for the canal until the year 2000, at which time Panama was to assume all duties associated with the Canal Zone but with the guarantee that Americans already employed would keep their jobs. The second pact, the "Treaty Concerning the Permanent Neutrality and Operation of the Panama Canal," authorized the United States to ensure the permanent "neutrality of the waterway" and promised "no discrimination" against any country wishing to use the canal. An attached statement provided that after the year 2000, the United States could use the canal to move warships as well as "defend the canal against any threat to the regime of neutrality."

U.S. resistance to the canal treaties was nationwide and highly emotional. Opponents denounced the agreements as another retreat similar to that in Vietnam; the treaties would become monuments to appeasement. The United States owned the canal, others proclaimed. One senator bluntly stated that "we stole it fair and square." Republican Ronald Reagan of California, presidential hopeful in the 1980 election, showed no awareness of the historical record in asserting that the Canal Zone was "sovereign United States territory just the same as Alaska . . . and the states that were carved out of the Louisiana Purchase." Loss of the canal, critics charged, would hurt the U.S. economy, undercut the nation's defense, and invite Soviet involvement in the regime of Panamanian President Omar Torrijos, which already seemed to be leaning toward communism.

With public opinion polls showing nearly eighty percent of Americans against giving up the canal, the Carter administration faced an imposing uphill battle. Proponents of the treaties concurred with Carter that their handiwork would establish goodwill throughout Latin America. They also argued that the canal's economic advantages were no longer substantial and that the United States had a moral obligation to relinquish an area belonging to Panama. Less than ten percent of U.S. trade, in fact, depended on the canal. It offered even less in strategic advantages, asserted the Joint Chiefs of Staff. The canal was subject to sabotage, aircraft carriers and tankers were too large for the waterway, and nuclear submarines wishing to use it would have to surface and reveal their location. To one critic who questioned what the United States would do if Panama declared the canal "closed for repairs," Brzezinski pointedly replied that, "according to the provisions of the Neutrality Treaty, we will move in and close down the Panamanian government for repairs."

Arguments over canal ownership lay at the heart of the controversy. The head of the North American negotiating team in 1976, Ellsworth Bunker, correctly argued that "we bought Louisiana; we bought Alaska. In Panama, we bought not territory, but rights. . . . It is clear that under law we do not have sovereignty in Panama." Carter underlined this point in a "fireside chat," when he asserted that "we do not own the Panama Canal Zone. We have never had sovereignty over it. We have only had the right to use it." Defenders of the treaties rallied behind the Committee of Americans for the Canal Treaties, which numbered among its membership the noted diplomat, W. Averell Harriman, and a former director of the CIA, William Colby. Indeed, actor John Wayne helped to ease the fears expressed by fellow conservative Ronald Reagan by supporting the treaty and offering assurances about the trustworthy nature of his new acquaintance General Torrijos. Even more impressive, leading Republicans, including former President Ford and Secretary of State Kissinger, joined the nation's big businesses in favoring the treaties.

During spring 1978 the two Panama Canal treaties won narrow approval in the Senate. On March 16 that body approved the neutrality treaty by a margin of sixty-eight to thirty-two, a scant one vote more than the two-thirds majority needed. To secure its passage, however, supporters attached a statement reserving the United States's right to keep the canal open, "including the use of military force *in* the Republic of Panama." Despite this blatant violation of Panamanian sovereignty, Torrijos accepted this reservation after a special appeal from Carter. In a "Statement of Understanding" in October that became part of the neutrality treaty, Torrijos agreed to the United States's right after the year 2000 to halt "any aggression or threat directed against the Canal or against the peaceful transit of vessels through the Canal." In addition, he assured the United States that in times of trouble its vessels could "go to the head of the line." Carter in turn guaranteed against any claimed U.S. right to intervene in Panama's internal affairs. By the same thin margin, on April 18, the Senate approved the other treaty, turning over the canal to Panama in 2000. Had the United States rejected the treaties, Torrijos later declared, he would have had the canal destroyed.

Thus, after three-quarters of a century of disagreement with Panama, the United States had accepted the abrogation of the treaty of 1903. In a single move the Carter administration had taken a major step toward establishing U.S. credibility in the southern half of the hemisphere. But succeeding events would show that more than one agreement was necessary to remove the ill will engrained among Latin Americans by the United States's long history of interventionism.

In the same part of the hemisphere, the Central American state of Nicaragua, the Carter administration's diplomatic efforts were likewise a mixture of idealism and realism that for only a brief time seemed to approximate an effective foreign policy. Since 1936 the United States had supported the anti-Communist dictatorship established by General Anastasio Somoza Garcia. Over the years, Americans had ignored the Somoza dynasty's repressive practices and sold it arms, in return receiving Nicaragua's cooperation in interventionist actions in Guatemala in 1954, Cuba in 1961, and the Dominican Republic in 1965. But while the Somozas thrived, the oppressed Nicaraguan people suffered from this exceptionally tyrannical regime, which had alienated the Catholic Church, middle class, and peasants by its systematic plunder and its ruthless National Guard. Finally, in 1978, a leftist organization known as the Sandinista National Liberation Front (FSLN) rose in rebellion. Named after César Augusto Sandino, who had led insurgents against U.S. forces from the 1920s until his death at the hands of General Somoza in 1934, the Sandinistas picked up widespread support from the people, the Catholic Church, and business interests. The Carter administration at first tried to mediate the dispute, but it was unsuccessful. The Sandinistas launched a major offensive in 1979 and soon captured control of the government. In mid-July, Anastasio Somoza Debayle, a West Point graduate and son of the original patriarch, Anastasio Somoza Garcia, fled the country, only to be assassinated in Paraguay.

To persuade the Sandinistas to promote reform, Carter asked Congress to appropriate $75 million for economic aid to Nicaragua. In July 1980 that body approved his request over numerous heated protests that Sandinista leader Daniel Ortega was Communist. The Sandinistas, however, promised open political and economic affairs and continued to receive assistance from the United States until early 1981. Despite inconclusive CIA findings, the Washington government cut off aid after accusing them of arming anti-American insurgents in El Salvador.

The problems in El Salvador, as in other desperately poor Latin American states, had developed over a long period. Five million people were jammed into the tiny country, mostly in poverty-stricken areas characterized by a high birth rate and rampant disease. Calls for reform had gone unheeded by rightist regimes, which were comprised of a small minority of landowners allied with the army and relying on repressive measures to stay in power. But in October 1979 young, reformist, middle-grade officers in the army won control. They installed an anti-Communist regime headed by a civilian president who had been educated at the University of Notre Dame, José Napoleón Duarte of the Christian Democratic party (PDC). The Carter administration sent economic and military assistance to Duarte, who had himself undergone torture years earlier at the hands of the military and now promised land reform and other social and political changes. A brutal reaction by the former ruling minority led to a wave of assassinations by right-wing terrorists known as "death squads," which prevented Duarte from establishing control over the internal security groups within the government and forced him to rely on the military to stay in power. Finally, the death squads assassinated the archbishop of El Salvador during Mass in March 1980 and in December raped and killed four American Catholic missionaries (all women, including three nuns). Carter angrily stopped further assistance to Duarte when his regime failed to punish those responsible.

But Carter soon had to reverse this decision: Civil war had broken out after the leftists joined other dissatisfied groups in forming the Democratic Revolutionary Front (FDR) in April 1980 to oppose the regime. According to some estimates, in trying to put down the uprising, government security forces killed 13,000 Salvadorans by the end of that year, and there was no end in sight. The military in El Salvador, complained U.S. Ambassador Robert E. White in the *New York Times,* was "one of the most out-of-control, violent, bloodthirsty groups of men in the world."

Mexican-U.S. relations also remained uneasy. Millions of illegal aliens had entered the United States by 1980, many of them young men in search of temporary jobs. Americans complained that Mexicans either took the few jobs available and drove down wages or failed to find employment and went on welfare. In August 1977 Carter took action. He recommended that Congress grant amnesty to illegal aliens already in the United States and then upgrade border patrols and fine American businesses that hired illegal aliens. Congress established a study commission.

Economic problems also interfered with U.S. relations with Mexico. Nationalists in Mexico sought to break U.S. domination over trade and investment in their country by persuading the United States either to lower tariffs or to place more restrictions on foreign investment. Mexico had won bargaining power during the late 1970s as a result of its vast holdings of oil and natural gas. Although it was not a member of OPEC and Americans expected to buy these resources at low prices, the Mexican government charged higher prices than did Saudi Arabia. After several disputes the United States agreed to Mexico's prices in late 1979. Within a year, oil and natural gas comprised half of Mexico's exports to the United States.

Despite the Panama Canal treaties, Latin Americans continued to regard the United States with suspicion. One act could not erase nearly 160 years of resentment stemming from the United States's assumed role as guardian of the hemisphere. Whether or not the charges of imperialism were just, its southern neighbors believed they were. For too many years the United States had appeared callous, arrogant, and exploitative, ignoring the plight of Latin Americans while extending massive aid programs to other parts of the world. Critics had warned that if communism was indeed a threat in the Western Hemisphere, that situation was in large part the result of the United States's own longtime neglect of its neighbors. Rather than interpret every insurrection as Communist-inspired, they argued, it seemed wiser to recognize that dire economic problems may have led to desperate political and military actions that the United States might have alleviated through astute diplomacy. It needed to extend economic assistance—not increase arms sales to military regimes that assured only a repressive form of internal order justified by their opposition to communism. The Panama Canal treaties suggested that the United States had altered its policies toward Latin America; only time and additional bold actions could provide proof.

The Middle East

The Carter administration meanwhile worked toward a second breakthrough in foreign policy, this time in the Middle East. There the president personally intervened and apparently achieved the first major move toward peace. The region was beset with numerous troubles and increasing troubles by the late 1970s. Besides the ancient Arab-Israeli feud, civil conflict had escalated in Lebanon, PLO terrorist acts had grown in number and ferocity, widespread unrest had developed in Iran, and the West's needs for oil from the Persian Gulf had escalated. Even Israel's military successes in 1967 came at unexpected expense. The "annexation" of the West Bank imposed severe strains on Israel. Not only did the military occupation program involve heavy financial obligations, but it entailed restrictions on fundamental freedoms that violated Israel's cherished democratic principles. In addition, a refugee problem continued to grow that was both Palestinian and Israeli in scope. About 900,000 Palestinians had been displaced after the war of 1948–1949, leading the United Nations to establish refugee camps primarily in Egypt, Jordan, Syria, and Lebanon. The Six Day War of 1967 had complicated the refugee problem, because more than 800,000 Palestinian Arabs inhabited the areas occupied by Israeli forces—the West Bank and the Old City of Jerusalem. By the late 1970s displaced Palestinians numbered perhaps four million, a large mass of dissatisfied people who provided a rich source for PLO recruitment. The Israelis noted another side to the refugee issue: Nearly one million Jewish refugees had left the Arab states, many forced into Israel after the war of 1948–1949, and were still holding legitimate claims against Arab governments. There were too many issues to resolve in the Middle East, according to one European observer. It is "something like playing billiards on a small boat in a rough sea—and each ball with a shifting center of gravity."

President Carter was convinced that the key to a comprehensive peace in the Middle East was an Arab-Israeli settlement, and in March 1977 he told reporters that the United States sought a general agreement based on the establishment of fair boundaries and a "homeland" for the Palestinians. Although he insisted that such a homeland did not entail a separate Palestinian state, the Israelis feared that the White House would enter negotiations with the PLO, which they regarded as a fanatical revolutionary group dedicated to their violent overthrow. Two months later the chances for peace seemed to diminish when the Israelis elected a new government—a coalition regime led by Menachem Begin as prime minister. Begin was himself a former terrorist who had long resisted concessions to the Arabs. In the meantime the Carter administration joined the Soviet Union in a statement of October 1977 admitting to the "legitimate rights of the Palestinian people." Carter believed that Kissinger's decision to leave out the Soviets in a Middle East settlement was a mistake because of their influence with the PLO and the Syrians. But Carter's new line of action with the Moscow regime did not interest either Israel or Egypt.

In November 1977, peace prospects suddenly brightened when Egyptian President Anwar el-Sadat courageously took an unprecedented step toward peace: He risked assassination (which did occur at the hands of his own soldiers in October 1981) by visiting Jerusalem and actually appearing before the Israeli Knesset, or Parliament. There he delivered a worldwide televised speech in which he made the surprising concession that "Israel has become an established fact." Optimism seemed justified, because the Israelis had earlier proclaimed that if the Arabs dealt with them directly, which constituted recognition, Israel would return the territories occupied during the Six Day War of 1967. Sadat proposed Israeli withdrawal from these lands, followed by the establishment of a Palestinian state derived from the West Bank and Gaza. In exchange, Egypt would sign a peace treaty ensuring Israel's security and legitimacy as a nation. But there was an ominous sign: Only one other Arab nation showed interest in Sadat's proposal—Saudi Arabia, an ally of the United States.

The initial optimism faded as Begin announced that he did not favor the terms. Although willing to withdraw from the Sinai desert, he refused to concede self-determination to the Palestinians on the West Bank and in the Gaza Strip. The Israeli army would remain in the West Bank, Gaza, and the Golan Heights. Begin did not consider the West Bank (which he called by its Hebrew names Judea and Samaria) to be occupied. The West Bank was a liberated area, he proclaimed, now part of Israel along with Gaza. Begin agreed only to postpone the issue for five years and then negotiate the final status of the disputed areas, but many believed that in the meantime he intended to enlarge Israel's control over them by establishing new settlements.

Not surprisingly, the talks stalemated. Sadat complained that Begin's proposal would prolong Israeli occupation of the West Bank and Gaza. There could be no separate peace with Israel unless the Palestinians received self-rule and the Israelis withdrew from all Arab areas. In March 1978 the situation worsened when Israeli forces attacked the PLO in Lebanon, killing more than 1000 noncombatants in response to a recent PLO terrorist act that killed thirty-five Israeli civilians. In this heated atmosphere, Sadat realized that to approve Israel's demands would make him a traitor, adding to the widespread condemnation of him in the Arab world caused by his visit to Jerusalem. Already the leader of Libya, Colonel Muammar al-Qaddafi, had demanded Sadat's assassination.

When the negotiations broke down, Carter intervened. He had hesitated because of diverging U.S. interests in Israeli security and Arab oil. But fear of Soviet infiltration became decisive. U.S. involvement in the matter, however, carried a built-in danger: It exposed the Washington government's differences with Israel on how to achieve peace. Carter argued that Sadat had offered security to Israel and warned Begin that failure to accept would

worsen matters. West Europeans, the president noted, had long called for Arab recognition of Israel in exchange for the evacuation of lands taken in 1967. After reminding the Israelis that only the United States supported them, he called for the implementation of UN Resolution 242 of 1967, which had stipulated their withdrawal from areas occupied in the Six Day War. To Carter this meant the return of most Arab territories taken in 1967 (with some adjustments for security reasons), the creation of a Palestinian homeland, and the establishment of diplomatic relations between Israel and the Arab states. Begin, however, interpreted the UN resolution to mean that for security reasons Israel had to retain the West Bank and Gaza and could not permit the establishment of a Palestinian homeland. As for the Old City of Jerusalem, that too must remain in Israeli hands. With the eastern sector occupied in 1967 and now inhabited by 43,000 Israelis, it was, according to Israeli decree, "one city indivisible, the capital of the State of Israel."

The settlements issue underlined the differences between Israel and the United States. Since 1967 the Washington government had considered it illegal for Israel to establish settlements in wartime-occupied lands. Carter now criticized the Israelis' efforts to add to them while negotiations were under way. Although Vance denounced the new settlements as an "obstacle to peace," the Israelis refused to halt the practice, leading the Carter administration to suspect Begin of using the security argument as a guise for annexation. To show dissatisfaction with the Israelis, the White House approved the sale of fighter planes to Israel but also, for the first time, did the same for Egypt and the Saudis. There was still no break in the situation.

Carter, his prestige already low, took a high political risk and arranged a meeting between Begin and Sadat at the presidential retreat in Camp David, Maryland. After nearly two weeks of discussions in which Carter worked as a full partner, the negotiators emerged with a compromise on September 17, 1978. Their general program aimed at completing a formal treaty before Christmas and Israeli withdrawal from Arab territory within three years.

The president had mediated two path-breaking settlements: "A Framework for Peace in the Middle East" and a "Framework for the Conclusion of a Peace Treaty between Egypt and Israel." According to the agreements, there would be "transitional arrangements for the West Bank and Gaza for a period not exceeding five years." To implement "full autonomy to the inhabitants," Israel was to withdraw "as soon as a self-governing authority has been freely elected by the inhabitants of these areas." Thus, the full autonomy question was to become the subject of negotiations *after* Egypt and Israel had signed a peace treaty. But the accords contained no resolution to the two most explosive issues between the antagonists: the status of Jerusalem and Palestinian self-rule. Furthermore, the wording of the agreements stood open to competing interpretations that would block a meaningful settlement. What were the "legitimate security concerns" of the parties involved? The "legitimate rights" of the Palestinians? Was Israeli security compatible with Palestinian autonomy?

It was clear that the PLO issue was the basis of most Arab-Israeli troubles. If that organization dominated a Palestinian state in the West Bank and Gaza, it would be in a prime position to launch terrorist attacks on Israeli families. Begin refused to approve PLO participation in either the negotiations or the establishment of a homeland; Sadat hoped that the Israelis would withdraw from the West Bank and Gaza and that the Palestinians there would win a governing voice. The first step, Sadat believed, was Israeli withdrawal from the Sinai settlements; the second was a peace treaty between Israel and Egypt; the third was Israeli withdrawal from the Sinai Peninsula. Sadat counted on Jordan to enter the negotiations concerning the West Bank, and he hoped that the Saudis would remain supportive. Most of all, he relied on the United States to persuade Israel to accept the terms.

But the Arab states bitterly opposed the settlement because Israel, they believed, would gain too much. A separate peace with the strongest Arab state, Egypt, would ensure Israeli security by reducing the likelihood of attack by other Arabs. Israel would retain the West Bank, Gaza, and the Golan Heights, and the Palestinians would never gain self-rule. The Saudis, unwilling to stand alone among their Arab neighbors, banded together with Algeria, Iraq, Jordan, Libya, and Syria in denouncing Sadat, virtually isolating him and paradoxically making Israel's position even stronger.

At this crucial point Carter again intervened, this time to visit Egypt and Israel and make a personal appeal for the treaty. His bold strategy worked. Less than a month later, on March 26, 1979, Sadat and Begin signed an agreement at the White House. Anxious moments had developed during the intervening days. Sadat had repeated his demands for Palestinian autonomy in the West Bank, and Begin had declared before his country's parliament that Israel would not retreat to the 1967 borders, that Jerusalem was Israel's "eternal capital," and that the Palestinians would never establish a state in the West Bank or Gaza. Although Begin's provocative speech nearly scuttled the treaty proceedings, Carter convinced the two leaders to sign.

The Egyptian-Israeli Peace Treaty was an important first step toward a general settlement. According to terms there would be a scaled Israeli withdrawal from the Sinai Peninsula, to be completed in 1982. UN forces were to supervise the boundary, assisted by U.S. air surveillance. Diplomatic and economic relations were established between the countries and there was to be free passage through international waterways. Israel could buy oil from the Sinai after the region was returned to Egypt, and negotiations were to begin on Palestinian rights in the West Bank and Gaza. To smooth potential difficulties the United States repeated its pledges to defend Israel and then furnished $5 billion in economic and military aid to the two countries. Critics complained that the United States had bribed the

Signing Egyptian-Israeli Peace Treaty
Left to right: Cyrus Vance, Anwar Sadat, Jimmy Carter, and Menachem Begin. *Wide World Photos, New York.*

antagonists; proponents countered that any peace was better than continued fighting. Although Carter hailed the pact as "the first step of peace," it only indirectly touched on Jerusalem, the Golan Heights, and the PLO. He had earlier hoped for a sweeping settlement, and yet his recent approach had adopted Kissinger's call for piecemeal procedures. If the antagonists could first settle the less inflammatory issues, Carter hoped, they might build a momentum leading to resolution of the other matters and end three decades of bitter unrest.

The Arab states, however, immediately condemned the Egyptian-Israeli Peace Treaty. Jordan's King Hussein denounced the pact as a "dead horse" because it did not guarantee a Palestinian homeland. Israel's policies, the Arabs contended, were baldly annexationist. The Arab League expelled Egypt and imposed an economic boycott, and most of the Arab states severed diplomatic relations with Egypt. Israel's

actions did not ease the precarious situation. Although it withdrew from the Sinai in early 1982, it announced the establishment of new settlements in the West Bank, incorporated the Golan Heights into Israel in 1982, prepared to take additional land from the large number of Arabs in the region, staunchly refused self-determination to the Palestinians, and intensified military measures against the PLO.

The United States praised the treaty, even though two of its friends in the Middle East, Saudi Arabia and Jordan, had moved deeper into the Arab camp. The Saudis held a quarter of the world's known oil reserves and were pro-West and anti-Communist, but they could not support the treaty because it contained no Israeli concessions on the Old City of Jerusalem and failed to provide political autonomy for Palestinians. The Saudis were small in population and depended on an outside labor force to modernize their country, and the result was that numerous foreigners lived in Saudi Arabia, many of them Palestinians or other Arabs. The Saudis did not want to break with Egypt, nor did they seek to loosen ties with the United States. But they had to avoid charges of treason by fellow Arab states. King Hussein joined King Khalid of Saudi Arabia in emphasizing to the White House that Israel was their chief antagonist, not the Soviet Union. The Egyptian-Israeli Peace Treaty shook the Saudis' faith in U.S. policies, but it nonetheless edged the principal antagonists toward some solution short of war.

Declining Soviet-American Relations

For several reasons, Soviet-American relations markedly deteriorated throughout 1979. Economically, the Soviets were in deep trouble. Although leading the United States in the production of cement, coal, oil, and steel, they had added to their own problems by investing too much in Cuba and Vietnam and in vast military improvements, none of which brought profitable returns. Much of the Soviets' land was suited for agriculture, but the ongoing process of collectivization had not yielded sufficient food. In fact, nearly one-half of the Soviet Union's farm products came from privately owned concerns that comprised only three percent of the country's agricultural area. Soviet industry meanwhile demonstrated little innovation, and in technology it lagged behind the United States, West Germany, and Japan. The Soviets also suffered from an inefficient and poorly managed labor force as well as from ethnic divisions obstructing the integration of workers outside Greater Russia. Furthermore, a drop in the birth rate during the 1950s and 1960s had caused a dip in the size of the labor force by the 1980s. Finally, economists projected that the Soviets might have to import oil before the decade was over. Outside the country, problems with China threatened to worsen because of the change in leadership in Beijing, the closer ties between China and Japan, and the imminent establishment of formal diplomatic relations between the United States and China. The Carter administration

tried to exploit the Kremlin's troubles. After the early setbacks in the SALT talks in Moscow, the White House criticized Soviet activities in Africa, implied that it would consider arms sales to China, and warned that Soviet military actions in Eastern Europe would encourage a buildup of NATO.

The Soviets' central concern was the establishment of Sino-American relations. Shortly after Carter's inauguration, the United States moved toward completing the recognition process begun by Nixon's visit to China in 1972. Liaison officers had been established soon after the initial contact, and Carter now sought to remove final obstacles. In April 1977 a congressional delegation traveled to China accompanied by one of the president's sons, and in late August Vance visited Beijing to talk with Vice-Premier Deng Xiaoping. More than a year later President Carter announced in a televised speech that the two nations would establish diplomatic relations on January 1, 1979. According to the joint communiqué of December 15, 1978, the United States severed relations with Taiwan, agreed to withdraw "its remaining military personnel [about 700 soldiers] from Taiwan within four months," and served the required one-year notice of terminating the Mutual Defense Treaty of 1954 with Taiwan. Although the communiqué asserted that Taiwan was "part of China," the United States maintained "cultural, commercial, and other official relations with the people of Taiwan." The Taiwanese accused the United States of breaking commitments, and right-wing Americans joined a few congressional members in expressing anger over the move, but on January 1, 1979, the United States and the People's Republic of China exchanged ambassadors and announced formal relations.

Carter emphasized that the establishment of Sino-American relations offered commercial possibilities and the potential of easing the tense situation in East Asia. There already seemed to be proof of the latter claim. In December 1978 Vietnamese Communist forces invaded Kampuchea (formerly Cambodia) to depose Pol Pot, leader of a repressive Communist regime that favored China. The following February, Chinese forces invaded upper Vietnam, and even though the Pentagon and other Americans wanted the United States to act, Carter refused. After the Chinese administered what they called "punishment" to the Vietnamese, they withdrew. In the meantime the Soviets had signed an amity treaty with the Vietnamese, demanded an earlier Chinese pullout, and threatened to take military action. The crisis passed without a confrontation, but the Soviet threats aroused more U.S. skepticism about the SALT talks and increased the call for an arms buildup.

The establishment of Sino-American diplomatic relations, along with the Soviet desire to avoid a costly arms race and curb the United States's development of new weapons, promoted the signing of SALT II in Vienna in June 1979. The treaty aimed to establish equality in the total number of strategic nuclear delivery missiles by permitting each nation to have 2400 long-range missiles and bombers, to be lowered to 2250 by 1981. It also set MIRVed ballistic missiles (ICBMs and SLBMs) at a ceiling of 1200, established maximum warhead figures for other launchers, drew up verification procedures, and made clear that SALT III would focus on reducing nuclear stockpiles.

Like most agreements, both sides could claim advantages. On the U.S. side, the Soviets would have to cut back on 250 delivery vehicles already in existence, whereas the United States could add to its supply of 2060. Furthermore, the Soviets failed to halt the United States's development of the intercontinental MX (missile experimental), a mobile missile capable of carrying ten MIRVs and designed to move ICBMs through a maze of underground tunnels, in an effort to confuse Moscow on their location. Despite Carter's campaign assurances of arms cutbacks, he approved the MX—at nearly $30 billion in cost. SALT II also placed no restrictions on several missile types: the cruise missile, which carried a single warhead and was capable of striking the Soviet Union; the Pershing II ballistic missile, guided by radar to evade obstacles in hitting targets more than 1000 miles away with great accuracy; and the Trident-II SLBM, which could carry fourteen warheads. The Americans, however, were unable to halt Soviet development of either the Backfire supersonic bomber or the SS-20 intermediate-range nuclear missile, the latter carrying three warheads and able to reach Western Europe.

Widespread disagreement was evident inside the United States over the wisdom of SALT II. Some Americans warned that the maximum limits were too high and sought to link the pact with Soviet behavior elsewhere. Many did not trust the Moscow government and argued that verification was impossible. Others supported the arguments of the "Committee on the Present Danger," which was led by veteran hard-line policymaker Paul Nitze (who helped write NSC-68) and which accused Carter of appeasement and endangering U.S. security. Still others wondered whether the MX might not cause an arms race. At tremendous costs in dollars and in environmental damage, they declared, the MX would not even be ready until 1990. It seemed wise to continue negotiations aimed at establishing more controls. The president countered that SALT II would stem the Soviets' buildup and benefit the United States because restrictions on its own program were less prohibitive. He added that the United States's ICBMs were not highly susceptible to destruction because the Soviets were unlikely to achieve the extreme accuracy and timing vital to attack. Besides, the United States would have a twenty minute warning that enabled it to move the ICBMs from their silos to places of safety. Other than land-based ICBMs, Carter noted, the remaining seventy percent of the triad strategic system—the SLBMs and big bombers—would be intact and ready for a counterstrike.

While the national debate went on over SALT II, its approval seemed ever more unlikely when the Carter administration announced in summer 1979 that U.S. intelligence sources had discovered a Soviet brigade of 2500 combat troops in Cuba. White House spokesmen asserted that until the Soviet soldiers withdrew from the island, ratification of SALT II was out of the question. The "status quo was not acceptable," the president insisted. The Moscow government argued that the soldiers had been on the island for years solely to train Cubans. Furthermore, it accused Carter of choosing to publicize the matter at a particularly opportune time—when his reelection possibilities were down and he needed an issue to rally Americans around him.

Whether or not the president had acted too hastily in an effort to rebuild his image, the outcome proved damaging both to his prestige and to SALT II. The Democratic chair of the Senate Foreign Relations Committee, Frank Church, postponed hearings on SALT II and noted that approval was doubtful until the Soviet troops left Cuba. It soon became evident, however, that the Soviet forces had indeed been there for years and were not about to leave, and Carter had no choice but to accept the status quo that he had earlier found objectionable. In a vain attempt to save SALT II, he told the American people that "I have concluded that the brigade issue is certainly no reason for a return to the Cold War." In January 1980 the president admitted defeat by withdrawing the treaty from the Senate.

The arms rivalry continued to escalate as Europe increasingly became the focal point of concern. In the previous December, NATO had made a "two-track" decision calling for the deployment of 572 Pershing IIs in Western Europe (track one) that would proceed until their readiness in 1983 unless the United States and the Soviet Union meanwhile reached an arms control agreement (track two) that secured the continent by requiring the removal of the hundreds of Soviet SS-20s recently installed in Eastern Europe. As this issue intensified, so did antinuclear demonstrations spread across the continent and into the United States.

In the meantime the Cuban episode and the arms controversy suddenly fell from Americans' attention as the focus of trouble dramatically shifted again to the Middle East.

The Hostage Crisis in Iran

On November 4, 1979, four hundred student militants in Iran stormed into the U.S. embassy in Teheran, seizing sixty-six U.S. diplomats and military personnel as hostages and causing a crisis that staggered and finally brought down the Carter presidency. Americans' frustrations over recent foreign policy failures seemed to culminate in this national humiliation, which the *New York Times* called "a metaphor for American decline." Although most Americans were shocked that their longtime Iranian ally had permitted such an act, the truth was that relations between the countries had been in serious trouble for years.

By the time Carter became president, Iran had become vital to the United States's strategic and economic interests in the Middle East. Besides offering the advantage of lying just south of the Soviet Union, Iran was second only to the Saudis in oil production among non-Communist countries. Over the years the CIA had installed listening devices along the Iranian-Soviet border, designed to detect Soviet nuclear and military activity. To solidify U.S. ties with Iran, Carter visited Teheran in late 1977 and on New Year's Eve had toasted the country as "an island of stability." He then had praised Mohammed Riza Shah Pahlavi as deserving "the respect and the admiration and love which your people give to you." The Iranian people, however, had developed an intense hatred for the shah that was magnified by the U.S. aid he continued to receive after the CIA facilitated his return to power in the early 1950s. Fundamentalist Shi'ite Muslims (ninety percent of the population) were appalled by the shah's efforts to improve the place of women in society and to import Western lifestyles into Iran. Youths detested the absence of civil liberties and wanted a constitutional government to replace the shah's corrupt regime. Merchants, landowners, and young laborers opposed his "white revolution," which had allegedly modernized the economy by instituting land reform, profit sharing in industry, women's right to vote, and other measures; and all groups resented the 50,000 Americans in Iran who trained the military, constructed industries, and ran the rich oil reserves. Ethnic rivalries, severe economic problems, increasingly crowded and slum-ridden urban areas, and heightening terrorist actions by the secret police (called SAVAK) added to the growing resentment, which was exacerbated by foreigners' monopoly on the few good jobs in Iran and the government's spending on weaponry from the United States that militarized the country at the expense of helping the Iranian people. Some observers argued that the shah's arms purchases alienated more of his subjects than any other single act.

Despite Carter's glowing praise for the shah, U.S. relations with his regime were dangerously uneasy. The shah complained that he was not receiving enough military aid, leading him to buy a nuclear reactor from France after the United States turned him down. By the mid-1970s Americans were unhappy that Iran had joined other OPEC nations in raising the price of oil, and in 1976 Congress had protested when the Ford administration sold fighter planes to the shah. Carter's public adulation for the shah had been the result of poor U.S. intelligence sources that were grossly out of touch with reality. By late 1978 SAVAK was hated, the shah was despised, and Iran stood on the verge of a revolution instigated by both the leftist "Fedayeen," which had close ties to the PLO, and the rightist Islamic clergy or Mullahs, who sought a return to traditional customs and lifestyles. What animated this strange alliance was a mutual hatred of the shah and the United States.

In 1978 violence had finally erupted in Iran, causing the shah to impose martial law and further feed the revolutionary fervor. Striking

The Shah and Nixon
American assistance in Iran greatly increased during the Nixon administration. Here, President Nixon and the shah shake hands in the Rose Garden by the South Lawn of the White House. Secretary of State William Rogers stands to the president's left.
U.S. Army.

groups halted oil production, which hurt the United States, and Carter whipped up more anger among Iranians by following Brzezinski's advice to send military assistance to the regime. By the end of the year, Americans in Iran had feared for their lives as the shah, now stricken with cancer and increasingly unable to take strong action, steadily lost ground to his rapidly growing political and religious opposition. The anti-shah forces had become too powerful to contain, and U.S. diplomats in Iran urged him to abdicate the throne.

In January 1979 the revolutionaries forced the shah to flee the country, leaving Iran to the victorious Muslims. The Muslims' chief religious leader, the Ayatollah Ruhollah Khomeini, was eighty-one years old, with black eyes glowing above his long white beard. Even at that moment in January he was still in France as part of sixteen years of exile. For years Khomeini had been directing his fanatical followers to use any destructive means to bring down the throne, and he now announced the formation of the Islamic Republic. These events shook Americans' confidence in the Carter administration, because the unexpectedness of the revolution had raised serious questions about both the abilities of intelligence sources in Iran and the failure of the White House to heed warnings. The U.S. ambassador in Iran, William Sullivan, recommended a meeting with Khomeini, but the White House had already come to suspect its emissary of disloyalty to its policies and ignored the suggestion. Instead, the administration infuriated Sullivan by considering Brzezinski's call for a military coup intended to restore the shah.

On February 1 Khomeini returned triumphantly to Iran as the informal head of state and promptly declared that the new regime would cleanse the country of the Westernizing and secular influences stemming from the shah's "white revolution." Despite public outcries against the United States, it was evident that the Muslims hated the Communists' atheism as much as the West's capitalism and that Sullivan's proposed meeting with the ayatollah

had perhaps been worth pursuing. But if an opportune time for negotiations had existed, its moment had passed. The new Iranian regime, a theocracy, lacked governing experience, and the country quickly moved to the edge of administrative disintegration. The United States faced the unhappy prospect of having to intervene to safeguard Iranian oil, which Khomeini prepared to cut off from Americans while selling it to Japan and Western Europe. Worse, Marxists were among the anti-shah groups, causing anxiety in Washington that the Soviets had gained an opening into the Persian Gulf and oil-rich Middle East.

The shah meanwhile moved from one country to another, looking for refuge but finding none: Any government welcoming him would surely alienate Iran or other Arab states and lose access to the region's oil. Carter had at first invited the shah to the United States, but Vance convinced him to withdraw the offer as it became plain that the United States was the chief source of resentment in Iran. In October 1979, however, the shah was in Mexico, dying of cancer and in need of medical attention. Even though the embassy in Teheran warned that moving the shah to the United States would endanger the lives of Americans in Iran, Carter yielded to the pressure of Brzezinski, David Rockefeller of Chase Manhattan Bank in New York (which had monetary connections with Iran), and Kissinger, who had personal and financial ties with the Rockefeller family and whose support the White House valued in securing passage of SALT II. Carter's decision to admit the shah into the country, where he entered a New York hospital, "threw a burning branch into a bucket full of kerosene," according to an embassy worker in Teheran. Khomeini angrily told his people that the shah would now conspire firsthand with the hated Americans. Two weeks later, on the Sunday morning of November 4, Iranian students seized the U.S. embassy in Teheran.

The reasons cited for the break-in were many and varied. Khomeini called the embassy a "nest of spies" and denounced the "Great

Satan Carter." The militants, who refused to believe that the shah was ill, demanded his wealth and announced that they would free the Americans in exchange for his return to Iran to stand trial for alleged past crimes. Iranian custody of the shah would also prevent his collaboration with the United States in a counterrevolutionary move to regain the throne. Furthermore, taking hostages promoted a diplomatic break with Washington that freed Iran from U.S. domination. Khomeini would be able to exploit anti-American feeling and establish control over the moderates and clerics who had opposed him in the revolution.

Whatever the reasons for taking the embassy, it was the first time that diplomats had not received immunity in times of trouble. Americans were shocked to see televised coverage of huge crowds of angry Iranians denouncing the United States as the "Great Satan" and yelling "Death to America." They were more appalled to see American hostages blindfolded and apparently undergoing unspeakable treatment by their captors. In television interviews Khomeini and others condemned the United States's long-time support for the shah and criticized the U.S. naval presence in the Indian Ocean. The ayatollah even accused the United States of planning an assault on the ancient Muslim religious city of Mecca, an unfounded charge that set off anti-American demonstrations in Muslim areas stretching from the Middle East to the Philippines and which resulted in the deaths of two Americans in Pakistan.

The Carter administration's reaction to the hostage crisis was a confused mixture of shock and dismay that critics considered symbolic of the United States's declining position in the world. No nation expecting to command the respect of others could permit such a dastardly act to occur, Americans indignantly complained. Yet as Carter later lamented so incisively, the seizure revealed "the same kind of impotence that a powerful person feels when his child is kidnapped." U.S. honor, commitment, and the certainty of the shah's execution dictated that the president could not send the shah home. Besides, the shah had entered the United States

Ayatollah
The Muslims' religious leader who, after the shah's departure, came home from exile in 1979 to proclaim the Islamic Republic of Iran. *Wide World Photos, New York.*

legally, and Carter had no legal right either to deport him or to confiscate his wealth. Nor would the United States apologize for past policies toward the Iranians and allow a UN investigation of its conduct in those matters. Although many Americans demanded military action to free the hostages, the White House realized that such a course could lead to their deaths, stir up more Muslim violence against Americans throughout the Middle East, and cause a war that benefited only the Soviets.

The United States initially responded with a series of steadily escalating pressures on Iran that nonetheless failed to force its government (under various prime ministers of only nominal power) to intervene and secure the release of the hostages. First, the visas of 50,000 Iranian students in the United States would undergo examination; those not enrolled in school would be sent home. This approach, however, necessitated deliberation through the courts, which not only proved slow and cumbersome but ultimately resulted in decisions supporting the students' rights. Second, the United States froze nearly $8 billion of Iranian assets inside the country. Third, the Carter administration suspended the sale of arms to Iran, which had no impact because its government no longer sought them. Fourth, the White House covertly enlisted the aid of PLO leader Yasir Arafat, who convinced the Iranian regime to free thirteen of the hostages, mostly female and black Americans. Fifth, the United States sought the assistance of other nations and private individuals in securing the freedom of the remaining fifty-three hostages. Sixth, it worked through the United Nations and the International Court of Justice in calling for the hostages' release. None of these measures succeeded in securing the hostages' freedom.

On April 7, 1980, in seeming desperation, the United States broke diplomatic relations with Iran and imposed an economic embargo. These steps likewise had no effect. Western Europe and Japan needed Iranian oil and refused to join the embargo, and by the spring of that year the Iranian cutoff of oil to the United States (at least in part the result of the government's inability to produce enough oil for its own use) had already led to a 130 percent price rise that heightened U.S. inflation and unemployment. In the meantime the shah had left the United States for Panama in late 1979, and negotiations with the Iranians never got under way. A stable government did not emerge from the revolution, as the Carter administration had hoped, and Khomeini, whether he outright refused to free the hostages or had no choice in view of his supporters' fervor, did not intervene on their behalf.

On April 24 the Carter administration authorized a daring rescue attempt that ended in a humiliating failure and further underlined the helplessness of the United States. Vance

Iranian Hostage Crisis
The U.S. Embassy compound in Teheran as Iranians release some American hostages.
Wide World Photos, New York.

had objected to the idea. Not only had he assured European allies against the use of force, but he warned of certain casualties. Even if successful, he noted, the Iranians could seize other Americans. The president nonetheless directed the Joint Chiefs of Staff to organize a rescue mission code-named "Eagle Claw." Eight helicopters embarked from the USS *Nimitz,* a carrier then based in the Arabian Sea, while six C-130 Hercules transports left their Middle East base, both military teams eluding radar detection and heading for a rendezvous in the Iranian desert south of Teheran. The plan called for marine commandos to burst into the embassy, kill all the Iranian guards, and free the hostages. But everything went wrong. Three helicopters threatened to break down in a swirling dust storm before reaching the desert and turned back, one of them colliding with a C-130 and killing eight Americans. By now frustrated and disappointed with the initial stages of the operation, Carter called it off. In a final tragic embarrassment the C-130s left so hurriedly in the night that they abandoned helicopters, weapons, maps, and a batch of secret documents. A few days afterward, Americans watched TV coverage of Iranians exhibiting the charred remains of the Americans who had died in the midair collision.

Over television the following morning Carter informed the American people of the abortive rescue expedition, his somber tone suggesting the administration's concession that the hostage crisis would last until the Iranians themselves brought it to an end. The hostages were now separated and relocated in different hiding places, making it nearly impossible to consider another rescue attempt, and Khomeini darkly warned that the cost of another such operation would be the hostages' deaths. In the meantime Vance quietly resigned from the administration, partly because of the rescue fiasco but also because of growing dissatisfaction over steadily worsening relations with the Soviet Union. SALT II seemed dead, and the United States and its allies were drifting farther apart. The Carter administration, mired in a crisis over which it had no control, underwent criticism from Americans who believed it had gone too far in a rescue effort that could have led to the deaths of the hostages, as well as from Americans who were exasperated that the president seemed too squeamish to take the hard military actions called for in such a situation.

While the Carter administration stood helpless in the hostage crisis, another issue took over the front pages of U.S. newspapers: Soviet military forces had invaded neighboring Afghanistan in late December of 1979 in an effort to support a tottering leftist regime, and by the following spring were locked in battle with Afghan resistance groups.

Last Days: Crisis in Afghanistan and the Resurgence of the Cold War

The Soviets' military invasion of Afghanistan had its roots in a coup of 1978, when they established a Marxist regime that soon began to cave in because of assaults from Muslim rebels unhappy with its antireligious emphasis. Islamic teachings in Iran and Pakistan might sweep across Afghanistan and into the Soviet Union, the Moscow government seemed to fear. The growing crisis attracted U.S. attention because Afghanistan bordered China, Iran, and Pakistan, the last of which fluctuated in and out of Washington's graces. Although Afghan revolutionary forces became stronger in 1979, the Soviets at first hesitated to make a military move. One factor was the imminent possibility of a successor problem in Moscow: Brezhnev was seventy-three years of age and in ill health. Another was Soviet concern about the effect that military intervention would have on SALT II. But the Muslim insurgency in Iran and now in Afghanistan raised fears in Moscow that a similar uprising would develop among the millions of Muslims inside the Soviet Union.

Thus, during the Christmas holidays of 1979, nearly 85,000 Red Army troops rolled into Afghanistan to put down the mounting unrest. Soviet authorities immediately executed the failing Marxist leader and within six months established an occupation force of more than 100,000 troops. The result was a lengthy guerrilla war with Muslim rebels and a brutal clampdown on resistance at home to the Kremlin's new policies. Numerous Soviet dissidents were imprisoned, including Andrei Sakharov, the Nobel Prize-winning physicist who led the human rights movement inside the Soviet Union. Soon the Moscow regime resurrected the Brezhnev Doctrine, announced after the Soviet military invasion of Czechoslovakia in 1968, which defended the use of force in halting any "deviation from socialism" in Marxist states. The Soviets had used similar tactics in Hungary, but this was the first time they had done so outside Eastern Europe.

The Soviet invasion of Afghanistan shattered the Carter administration's illusions about détente. In response the White House adopted stringent measures that erroneously raised the specter of imminent Soviet troop expansion into the entire Middle East and succeeded only in again calling attention to the United States's diminished influence on world events. The act, Carter admitted, had "made a more dramatic change in my opinion of what the Soviets' ultimate goals are than anything they've done in the previous time I've been in office." The Afghanistan invasion appeared to be a "steppingstone to their possible control over much of the world's oil supplies"—including those of Iran. Brzezinski's hard-line, anti-Soviet stance won instant credibility in the White House as Vance lost influence and departed the administration. Carter meanwhile took several courses of action that were more shadow than substance but which the American people at first favored because of the impression of a resolute response. His approach had seven parts: (1) He withdrew the almost defunct SALT II treaty from the Senate and broadened commercial, financial, and military ties with China; (2) he cut off sales of grain (which hurt U.S. farmers) and high technology items to the Soviet Union; (3) he restricted Soviet fishing rights in U.S. waters and temporarily suspended the opening of new consulates in the United States; (4) he sent more arms to Pakistan and approved covert CIA help to the Afghan rebels; (5) he supported the establishment of a Rapid Deployment Force to be ready for immediate action in time of crisis; (6) he asked Congress to require registration of both men and women for a possible draft; and (7) in one of the most controversial moves of the time, he called for a boycott of the Olympic Games scheduled in Moscow that summer of 1980.

The president's most provocative action was his proclamation of the Carter Doctrine, which revived memories of the early Cold War by warning the Soviets to halt their expansionist activities in the Middle East. In his State of the Union address of January 24, 1980, the president warned that "an attempt by any outside force to gain control of the Persian Gulf region will be regarded as an assault on the vital interests of the United States of America, and such an assault will be repelled by use of any means necessary, including military force." Carter declared that the Soviet invasion of Afghanistan threatened the Persian Gulf-Indian Ocean oil supply line and asserted that the United States would act alone if necessary to protect Middle East oil from Soviet takeover. Thus, the administration broke with the Nixon Doctrine, which had called for partnership (albeit with the United States as senior partner), in preference for a return to the unilateral approach inherent in the Truman and Eisenhower doctrines. The United States appeared ready to contain the Soviets by establishing military strongholds in the Indian Ocean, East Africa, and the Middle East.

The Soviet Union must have expected that its invasion of Afghanistan would end hopes for SALT II. Carter warned Brezhnev over the hot line that the Soviet action constituted the most serious threat to world peace since 1945. About one-third of U.S. oil came from the Persian Gulf, but even more important, Western Europe and Japan received the overwhelming bulk of their supplies from that region. The Soviet move, according to Washington officials in a statement dramatically reminiscent of the Cold War 1940s, was part of a concerted effort to take over the whole region. Regional and national issues again threatened to become pawns of big power confrontation.

The Carter administration's reaction to the Afghan crisis was undercut by resistance from U.S. allies, who refused to support either an economic embargo on the Soviet Union or the Olympic boycott. West Germany and Japan had heavy trade with Moscow and Eastern Europe, and they argued that Soviet military action had been predictable because no country could permit trouble along its borders. The Afghan invasion was a localized matter, they insisted. West German Chancellor Helmut Schmidt told the *New York Times* that he opposed "nervousness, war cries, or excited or provocative speeches." The reaction by allies in Western Europe was understandable: They stood vulnerable to military retaliation by having agreed to allow the United States to deploy nearly six hundred intermediate-range ballistic missiles (IRBMs) aimed at the Soviet Union. Despite U.S. pressures, European defense allotments had remained distressingly low. Inflation and economic problems were also important considerations, but the fact was that, above all, the Europeans sought to avert a confrontation with the Soviets.

The Carter administration encountered other obstacles. The president had not consulted Congress before announcing his "doctrine." Many Americans chastised him for resurrecting the domino theory and insisted that the Soviets were merely trying to bolster a friendly regime. Others warned that Carter had needlessly revived the Cold War by attempting to force the Persian Gulf states to choose between East and West. Some wanted the White House to pull back and allow the Kremlin to expend itself in a guerrilla war in Afghanistan that they termed "Russia's Vietnam." Argentina and Brazil took advantage of the U.S. grain embargo to increase their sales to the Soviet Union. Pakistan complained that the United States's military aid offer was too low, and Saudi Arabia turned down a U.S. request for

bases. Furthermore, numerous countries ignored Carter's call for an Olympic boycott and prepared to participate in the games, and the director of the international committee, Lord Killanin, publicly denounced the United States for using athletes "as pawns in political problems that politicians cannot solve themselves." One White House official admitted that the Carter Doctrine had resulted from demands for a presidential statement on the matter, not from a careful assessment of the Middle East situation.

While Carter's policies toward the Afghan crisis settled into grim failure, numerous signs in the United States pointed to a Republican victory in the presidential race of 1980. Many Americans had attributed the country's decline in prestige to the Carter administration. Four years of international embarrassment now capitalized by the hostage crisis, they lamented, had underlined the world's lack of respect for the United States. In fairness to Carter, most Americans were unaware of the unalterable changes forcing the United States out of its 1945 position of unquestioned unilateral world leadership into that of increased cooperation with allies. But whereas the Nixon and Ford administrations had acted in accordance with the new forced guidelines in foreign policy, Carter only briefly adhered to them before wandering into threatening policies that were virtually incapable of enforcement. After initially accepting the new limitations on U.S. policies, he wavered back and forth between the polarized stances advocated by Vance and Brzezinski until chronic internal division led to frustration and finally the declaration of a hardline position that had little chance for success.

During spring 1980 the president's human rights efforts aroused anger among Americans, particularly in Florida, when he welcomed Cuban refugees into the country. Castro had permitted dissident Cubans to leave the island if they secured visas from Peru, and as thousands pushed into the Peruvian embassy and Carter threw open the doors to the United States, Castro announced that Cubans could leave the island by boat. Soon a "freedom flotilla" of 100,000 Cubans flocked into the United States, creating havoc and riots at processing and detention centers and posing economic problems to a country already burdened with inflation, unemployment, and lengthening welfare rolls. As Castro emptied Cuba's jails, Miami's mayor moaned that "Fidel has flushed his toilet on us."

The Republican presidential candidate, Ronald Reagan of California, exploited Carter's plummeting popularity by pointing to contradictions and inconsistencies in policy. Despite Carter's campaign assurances in 1976, he did not scale down military expenditures, reduce foreign arms sales, or abide by nuclear nonproliferation. Neither did he cut back on U.S. forces overseas nor order military withdrawal from South Korea—the latter decision in part attributable to dramatic revelations of South Koreans' attempted bribes of congressional members. On the human rights issue, the administration was not uniformly critical of allies along with the Soviet Union, and it sold arms to repressive regimes. While welcoming Cubans into the United States, the White House ran afoul of the state department in attempting to deport thousands of Haitians who had fled the oppressive rule of Jean-Claude ("Baby Doc") Duvalier. The Haitian regime, state department advisers warned the president, was a friend of the United States.

Carter, Reagan insisted, had contributed to the waning respect for the United States. Inflation and the faltering economy were the results of Democratic fiscal and bureaucratic mismanagement. The United States, Reagan declared, had to adopt a hard-nosed, consistent policy toward the Soviet Union. It was time to expand U.S. military forces to counter the Soviet Union's global "game of dominoes." Although Carter's popularity had briefly surged upward after his initial Iranian and Afghan policies, it lasted only long enough to contribute to victories in the primaries.

These lingering difficulties led Americans to elect Reagan to the presidency by a wide margin and award the Senate to the Republicans for the first time since 1952. Carter's

defeat, in a bitter twist of fate, took place on November 4, the first anniversary of the hostage crisis.

Epitaph to a Presidency: Release of the Hostages

Several events had combined to force a resolution of the Iranian hostage question. First, in July 1980 the shah died in Egypt after having moved there from Panama, thus eliminating the most inflammatory issue between the United States and Iran. Second, Khomeini's Islamic followers won control over the Iranian Parliament, making the hostages irrelevant to his political fortunes. Third, war had broken out between Iraq and Iran in September 1980, leaving Iran with sparse outside help, little money, and virtually no income from oil sales after saboteurs wrecked the pipeline. In addition, Iran fought with U.S.-made planes and tanks and no longer had a source for replacement parts. For the first time U.S. economic pressures were having a positive effect, particularly the freeze on Iranian funds in U.S. banks. Fourth, Reagan was a hard-liner who had blasted the Iranians as "barbarians" and "kidnappers." Military force to free the hostages, it seemed, was likely after Reagan's inauguration on January 20, 1981.

As a final epitaph, the Carter administration was not even able to claim fair credit for gaining the release of the hostages in Iran. On January 19, just one day before Reagan's inauguration, Algerian mediators finally secured an agreement freeing the Americans in exchange for the release of the $8 billion of frozen Iranian assets in the United States (but with $5 billion of the amount earmarked to pay Iran's debts to U.S. and European banks). The United States met none of the other Iranian demands: an apology for past interference in their affairs during the 1950s and a promise not to engage in such activity again; an international investigation of alleged U.S. violations in Iran; and a return of the shah's vast holdings. As a calculated final insult to Carter, the following day, just moments after

Reagan took the presidential oath, the Iranians freed the final fifty-two hostages (one had already been released for health reasons) after 444 days in captivity.

In retrospect, Carter perhaps should have downplayed the hostage issue at its beginning and dealt with it through quiet diplomatic channels. This was not feasible, however. Continuous television and newspaper publicity, along with Carter's own sense of compassion and Kissinger's repeated condemnations of U.S. failures in foreign policy, stirred up a national sense of outrage and indignation requiring an immediate resolution that the administration found impossible to achieve. Suspicions of permanent physical injury to the hostages or sexual violations by the Iranian captors proved unfounded, but the hostages had suffered lengthy denials of personal freedom underlined by mock executions, some instances of solitary confinement, and more than a few cases of physical abuse. The Iranian mobs' daily insults to the United States, combined with the continued affronts to the Carter administration, added to the mood of national insult and frustration that helped sweep out the Democrats in 1980.

Selected Readings

Allin, Dana H. *Cold War Illusions: America, Europe, and Soviet Power, 1969–1989.* 1995.

Ambrose, Stephen E., and Brinkley, Douglas G. *Rise to Globalism: American Foreign Policy since 1938.* 8th ed., 1997.

Armony, Ariel C. *Argentina, the United States, and the Anti-Communist Crusade in Central America, 1977–1984.* 1997.

Arnson, Cynthia. *Crossroads: Congress, the President, and Central America, 1976–1993.* 1994.

Berman, William C. *America's Right Turn: From Nixon to Clinton.* 2nd ed., 1998.

Bermann, Karl. *Under the Big Stick: Nicaragua and the United States Since 1848.* 1986.

Bill, James A. *The Eagle and the Lion: The Tragedy of American-Iranian Relations.* 1988.

Bradsher, Henry S. *Afghanistan: Soviet Invasion and U.S. Response.* 1981.

Brands, H. W. *The Devil We Knew: Americans and the Cold War.* 1993.

Brinkley, Douglas. *The Unfinished Presidency: Jimmy Carter's Journey Beyond the White House.* 1998.

Brzezinski, Zbigniew. *Power and Principle: Memoirs of the National Security Adviser, 1977–1981.* 1983.

Buckley, Roger. *U.S.-Japan Alliance Diplomacy, 1945–1990.* 1992.

Carter, Jimmy. *Keeping Faith: Memoirs of a President.* 1982.

Christopher, Warren, Saunders, Harold H., Sick, Gary, et al. *American Hostages in Iran: The Conduct of a Crisis.* 1985.

Clark, Paul C., Jr. *The United States and Somoza, 1933–1956: A Revisionist Look.* 1992.

Cohen, Warren I. *America's Response to China: An Interpretive History of Sino-American Relations.* 2000.

Coker, Christopher. *The United States and South Africa, 1968–1985.* 1986.

Coleman, Kenneth M., and Herring, George C., eds. *The Central American Crisis: Sources of Conflict and the Failure of U.S. Policy.* 1985.

Cornelius, Wayne. *Building the Cactus Curtain.* 1980.

Cottam, Richard W. *Iran and the United States: A Cold War Case Study.* 1988.

Diederich, Bernard. *Somoza and the Legacy of U.S. Involvement in Central America.* 1981.

Dumbrell, John. *The Carter Presidency: A Re-Evaluation.* 1995.

Dupree, Louis. *Afghanistan.* 1978.

Engstrom, David W. *Presidential Decision Making Adrift: The Carter Administration and the Mariel Boatlift.* 1997.

Erb, Richard D., and Ross, Stanley R. *United States Relations with Mexico.* 1981.

Furlong, William L., and Scranton, Margaret E. *The Dynamics of Foreign Policymaking: The President, the Congress, and the Panama Canal Treaties.* 1984.

Gaddis, John L. *The Long Peace: Inquiries into the History of the Cold War.* 1987.

———. *Russia, the Soviet Union, and the United States: An Interpretive History.* 2nd ed., 1990.

———. *Strategies of Containment: A Critical Appraisal of Postwar United States National Security Policy.* 1982.

Garthoff, Raymond L. *Détente and Confrontation: American-Soviet Relations from Nixon to Reagan.* 1994.

Gasiorowski, Mark J. *U.S. Foreign Policy and the Shah: Building a Client State in Iran.* 1991.

Gaushon, Arthur. *Crisis in Africa.* 1981.

Glad, Betty. *Jimmy Carter: In Search of the Great White House.* 1980.

Goode, James E. *The United States and Iran: In the Shadow of Musaddiq.* 1997.

Grayson, George W. *The Politics of Mexican Oil.* 1981.

Halliday, Fred. *Iran: Dictatorship and Development.* 1979.

Hansen, Roger D. *Beyond the North-South Stalemate.* 1979.

Harding, Harry. *A Fragile Relationship: The United States and China since 1972.* 1992.

Hargrove, Edwin C. *Jimmy Carter as President.* 1989.

Harrison, Michael M. *The Reluctant Ally: France and Atlantic Security.* 1981.

Hellmann, John. *American Myth and the Legacy of Vietnam.* 1986.

Hogan, Michael J. *The Panama Canal in American Politics: Domestic Advocacy and the Evolution of Policy.* 1986.

Hull, Richard W. *American Enterprise in South Africa: Historical Dimensions of Engagement and Disengagement.* 1990.

Hyland, William. *Mortal Rivals: Superpower Relations from Nixon to Reagan.* 1987.

Ismael, Tareq Y. *Iraq and Iran: Roots of Conflict.* 1982.

Jabber, Paul. *Not By War Alone: Security and Arms Control in the Middle East.* 1981.

Jordan, Hamilton. *Crisis: The Last Year of the Carter Presidency.* 1982.

Jorden, William J. *Panama Odyssey.* 1984.

Kaufman, Burton I. *The Presidency of James Earl Carter, Jr.* 1993.

Kennedy, Paul. *The Rise and Fall of the Great Powers: Economic Change and Military Conflict from 1500 to 2000.* 1987.

Khalid, Walid. *Conflict and Violence in Lebanon.* 1980.

Korn, David A. *Ethiopia, the United States, and the Soviet Union.* 1986.

LaFeber, Walter. *America, Russia, and the Cold War, 1945–1996.* 8th ed., 1997.

———. *The Clash: A History of U.S.-Japan Relations.* 1997.

———. *Inevitable Revolutions: The United States in Central America.* 1984.

———. *The Panama Canal: The Crisis in Historical Perspective.* Updated ed. (with Scott LaFeber), 1989.

Lake, Anthony. *Somoza Falling, The Nicaraguan Dilemma: A Portrait of Washington at Work.* 1989.

Ledeen, Michael, and Lewis, William. *Débacle: The American Failure in Iran.* 1981.

Lenczowski, George. *The Middle East in World Affairs.* 1980.

LeoGrande, William M. *Our Own Backyard: The United States in Central America, 1977–1992.* 1998.

Litwak, Robert S. *Détente and the Nixon Doctrine.* 1984.

Love, Janice. *The U.S. Anti-Apartheid Movement: Local Activism in Global Politics.* 1985.

Major, John. *Prize Possession: The United States and the Panama Canal, 1903–1979.* 1993.

Mann, Jim. *About Face: A History of America's Curious Relationship with China from Nixon to Clinton.* 1999.

Massie, Robert. *Loosing the Bonds: The United States and South Africa in the Apartheid Years.* 1997.

McLellan, David S. *Cyrus Vance.* 1985.

Melanson, Richard A. *American Foreign Policy Since the Vietnam War: The Search for Consensus from Nixon to Clinton.* 2000.

Meredith, Martin. *In the Name of Apartheid: South Africa in the Postwar Period.* 1988.

Moffett, George D., III. *The Limits of Victory: The Ratification of the Panama Treaties.* 1985.

Morley, Morris H. *Washington, Somoza, and the Sandinistas: State and Regime in U.S. Policy Toward Nicaragua, 1969–1981.* 1994.

Morris, Kenneth E. *Jimmy Carter, American Moralist.* 1996.

Moses, Russell L. *Freeing the Hostages: Reexamining U.S.-Iranian Negotiations and Soviet Policy, 1979–1981.* 1996.

Mower, A. Glenn. *Human Rights and American Foreign Policy: The Carter and Reagan Experiences.* 1987.

Newell, Nancy P., and Newell, Richard S. *The Struggle for Afghanistan.* 1981.

Pastor, Robert. *Condemned to Repetition: The United States and Nicaragua.* 1987.

Payne, Samuel, Jr. *The Soviet Union and SALT.* 1980.

Pérez, Louis A., Jr. *Cuba and the United States: Ties of Singular Intimacy.* 1997.

Pierre, Andrew J. *The Global Politics of Arms Sales.* 1982.

Pipes, Richard. *U.S.-Soviet Relations in the Era of Détente: A Tragedy of Errors.* 1981.

Prados, John. *Presidents' Secret Wars: CIA Pentagon Covert Operations from World War II through the Persian Gulf.* 1996.

Quandt, William B. *Camp David: Peacemaking and Politics.* 1986.

Raat, W. Dirk. *Mexico and the United States: Ambivalent Vistas.* 1996.

Ramazani, Rouhollah K. *Revolutionary Iran: Challenge and Response in the Middle East.* 1986.

Reimers, David. *Still the Golden Door: The Third World Comes to America.* 1985.

Rosati, Jerel A. *The Carter Administration's Quest for Global Community.* 1987.

Rotberg, Robert I. *Suffer the Future: Policy Choices in Southern Africa.* 1980.

Rubin, Barry. *Paved with Good Intentions: The American Experience and Iran.* 1980.

Ryan, Paul B. *The Iranian Rescue Mission: Why It Failed.* 1985.

———. *The Panama Canal Controversy.* 1977.

Saikal, Amin. *The Rise and Fall of the Shah.* 1980.

Sayigh, Yezid. *Armed Struggle and the Search for State: The Palestinian National Movement, 1949–1993.* 1997.

Schoutz, Lars. *Beneath the United States: A History of U.S. Policy Toward Latin America.* 1998.

———. *Human Rights and United States Policy toward Latin America.* 1981.

———. *National Security and U.S. Policy toward Latin America.* 1987.

Shawcross, William. *The Shah's Last Ride: The Fate of an Ally.* 1988.

Sick, Gary. *All Fall Down: America's Tragic Encounter with Iran.* 1985.

———. *October Surprise: America's Hostages in Iran and the Election of Ronald Reagan.* 1991.

Skidmore, David. *Reversing Course: Carter's Foreign Policy, Domestic Politics, and the Failure of Reform.* 1996.

Smith, Gaddis. *The Last Years of the Monroe Doctrine, 1945–1993.* 1994.

———. *Morality, Reason, and Power: American Diplomacy in the Carter Years.* 1986.

Smith, Peter H. *Mexico: The Quest for a U.S. Policy.* 1980.

Spanier, John W. *American Foreign Policy Since World War II.* 14th ed., 1998.

Spiegel, Steven L. *The Other Arab-Israeli Conflict: Making America's Middle East Policy, from Truman to Reagan.* 1985.

Stares, Paul B. *The Militarization of Space: U.S. Policy, 1945–1984.* 1985.

Stempel, John D. *Inside the Iranian Revolution.* 1981.

Stevenson, Richard W. *The Rise and Fall of Détente: Relaxations of Tensions in US-Soviet Relations, 1953–84.* 1985.

Sullivan, William H. *Mission to Iran: The Last U.S. Ambassador.* 1981.

Talbott, Strobe. *Endgame: The Inside Story of SALT II.* 1979.

Ulam, Adam B. *The Communists: The Story of Power and Lost Illusions, 1948–1991.* 1992.

———. *Dangerous Relations: The Soviet Union in World Politics, 1970–1982.* 1983.

Vance, Cyrus. *Hard Choices: Critical Years in America's Foreign Policy.* 1983.

Vogelgesang, Sandy. *American Dream, Global Nightmare: The Dilemma of U.S. Human Rights Policy.* 1980.

Walker, Thomas W. *Nicaragua: The Land of Sandino.* 1982.

———. *Revolution and Counterrevolution in Nicaragua, 1977–1989.* 1990.

Wesson, Robert. *Communism in Central America and the Caribbean.* 1982.

Wolfe, Thomas W. *The SALT Experience.* 1979.

Wolpert, Stanley. *Roots of Confrontation in South Asia: Afghanistan, Pakistan, India, and the Superpowers.* 1982.

Zonis, Marvin. *Majestic Failure: The Fall of the Shah.* 1991.

CHAPTER 16

Cold War II
REAGAN AND THE REVIVAL OF
CONTAINMENT, 1981–1989

The Return of the United States

As Ronald Reagan assumed the presidency on January 20, 1981, the nearly seventy-year-old former Hollywood movie actor and California governor dramatically pronounced an end to the "era of self-doubt" and called on Americans to counter the growing Soviet menace by reasserting their nation's "ideals and interests" throughout the world. In a provocative speech strikingly reminiscent of Kennedy's 1961 inaugural call for a New Frontier, President Reagan warned of a missile gap, emphasized the hardening lines of bipolarity, and revived the combative rhetoric of containment. The Soviets, he had earlier declared, were the basis of "all the unrest going on." At his first press conference in the Oval Office, he charged that they were "prepared to commit any crime, to lie, to cheat." The Soviet Union, he proclaimed before various public groups, was "an evil empire."

Thus did Reagan draw the battle lines immediately upon becoming president. Early in his administration, his focus on countering the Kremlin even led him to put great strains on the Western alliance by blocking an effort to build a Soviet pipeline intended to provide Western Europe with Soviet natural gas. The pipeline, he feared, would make the United

States's continental allies so economically dependent on the Soviet Union that NATO would lose its force. In addition, opposition to the pipeline was part of the administration's strategy to isolate the Soviets economically and surpass them technologically. Although the pipeline opened anyway in January 1984, it ran only from Siberia to France and was much smaller than hoped. White House relations with the Kremlin became so bitter that Reagan reversed his initial opposition to dealing with the Chinese and visited Beijing in 1984 in an effort to restore the ties cultivated by Nixon and Carter. U.S. disillusionment with Soviet détente, Reagan made clear, was complete.

Some writers have argued that the president's real intention in this heightened assault on the Soviet Union was to drive its government into a ruinous arms race that would destroy its already struggling economy and end the Cold War. If so, this brinkmanship strategy was extremely risky. The Reagan administration's anti-Communist, anti-Soviet thrusts ensured a startling upsurge of Cold War tensions, making negotiations secondary to a major buildup of the United States's strategic and conventional military forces. To restore faith in the United States, the president insisted that its democratic aims were just

Reagan at Desk in Oval Office
Calling the war in Vietnam a "noble cause," he attempted to heal
divisiveness by restoring faith in America at home and respect for
the nation abroad. *Wide World Photos, New York.*

and that "Marxism-Leninism" would ultimately take its place on "the ashheap of history." Americans, he declared, had to discard
their "no more Vietnams" syndrome and recognize that the war in Southeast Asia had
been "a noble cause." If Reagan intended his
aggressive foreign policy to force the Soviet
Union to spend itself into submission, his
approach came at the heavy price of creating
an intense adversary relationship with the
Moscow government that contemporaries
soon termed Cold War II.

The new president's call for a military
buildup to halt Soviet expansion did not come
without opposition. Numerous critics agreed
with Soviet specialist George F. Kennan that
the president's assessment of the Kremlin's
behavior was a sign of "intellectual primi-
tivism." But Reagan pointed out that the Soviets had surpassed the United States in ICBMs,
SLBMs, and megatonnage (total explosive
force carried as warheads) and argued that
they could soon forge ahead in numbers and
size of warheads. Skeptics insisted that his sta-

tistics were misleading and insisted that a
general nuclear balance existed between the
superpowers. Soviet production costs were
higher than those of the United States, leaving the erroneous impression that the Kremlin's greater military expenditures meant
military superiority. Moreover, they added,
Reagan's prognosis did not take into account
either the contributions of NATO's defense
expenditures or the proportion of Soviet
strength directed at China.

Reagan nonetheless called for the largest
peacetime defense budget in the country's history. The nation's priority, he asserted, was to
safeguard its Minuteman land-based ICBMs
and B-52 bombers. He also directed the production of the B-1 bomber, thus revoking
Carter's cancellation of the project, and went
ahead with plans made by NATO in December 1979 to install Pershing IIs (single-warhead
missiles capable of striking the Soviet Union)
and ground-launched cruise missiles in Western Europe, reaffirming Europeans' fears that
the superpowers had decided to make Europe

Vietnam Memorial
On May 28, 1984, veterans form an unofficial color guard at the Vietnam Memorial
on the day of the State funeral for the Unknown Serviceman of the Vietnam Era.
U.S. Army.

the battleground in a nuclear Armageddon. Finally, he approved massive arms sales around the world that virtually ensured a rash of regional conflicts.

But the Reagan White House, despite a whopping forty percent boost in military spending during its first three years in office, fully realized that in areas vital to the Soviet Union all the sophisticated weaponry in the world could have little impact on undermining Communist control. Consequently, the administration resorted to covert operations to stir up reform movements in Czechoslovakia, Hungary, and Poland. It made financial aid available to Warsaw Pact countries willing to protect human rights and move toward political and economic changes based on democracy and a free-market system. It also relied on Radio Free Europe to show Western support. Increasing signs of discontent behind the Iron Curtain dictated some sort of encouragement from the outside.

Poland provides the most striking example of heightening problems within the Soviet bloc. In 1980 long-time unrest had peaked in a workers' upheaval that soon included demands for civil liberties and thereby threatened the ruling Communist party. Polish workers had wanted an independent trade union, and after a series of strikes threatened to upend the government, that body recognized the legitimacy of the Solidarity workers' union led by Lech Walesa. But as the Communist regime in Poland conceded some of its economic and political power, Solidarity increased its demands and attracted support from Catholics and nationalists who hated the Soviets. The organization soon counted ten million members, or about one-third of the Polish population, which raised questions about whether the Communist party would have to use force to remain in control.

In a series of events markedly similar to those in Hungary a quarter of a century earlier, Solidarity risked a Soviet military crackdown by pushing for a national referendum on the present government in Warsaw and its military ties with the Soviet Union. The Kremlin must have considered the use of force. Poland bordered the Soviet Union and had served as a well-trodden roadway in numerous past invasions. It was more vital to Soviet interests than either Hungary or Czechoslovakia, and certainly more so than Afghanistan. In December 1981 Polish military and police forces, perhaps reacting to Moscow's pressure, imposed martial law and imprisoned Walesa and other labor leaders. The Polish government then outlawed Solidarity and adopted other stringent measures to break the movement. Solidarity, Soviet leaders realized, was not a mere trade union; it was a broadly based and well-run organization attempting to take Poland toward a socialist form of democracy. Solidarity's success could set a dangerous example for workers in other East European countries or in the Soviet Union itself.

Despite the widespread U.S. support for Solidarity, the Reagan administration could do nothing on its behalf except to place mild economic sanctions on Poland and the Soviet Union. Neither the United States nor the other Western nations took steps that would have comprised more than a token protest: They did not call in more than $25 billion of late debts, and the White House did not impose a grain embargo—because such a measure would have hurt U.S. farmers. White House criticisms of the Kremlin's policies in Poland had won little support from the NATO countries, which refused to take any action that might encourage full-scale Soviet intervention in Poland or damage their own trade with the Soviets and their allies. After the Polish military relaxed some of its restrictions, the Reagan administration revoked most of its economic sanctions in August 1984. The new administration realized what both President Truman and President Eisenhower had understood in Cold War I: The United States was unable to implement any effective mili-

tary strategy toward Eastern Europe because the region lay within the Soviet sphere of influence.

Internal division in the Reagan administration, like that of his predecessors, also impeded the president's intention to restore a firm foreign policy. Reagan's secretary of state, General Alexander Haig, was the most outspoken member of the cabinet and soon found himself at odds with many of his colleagues, including Secretary of Defense Caspar Weinberger, who like Haig had served in the Nixon presidency and was likewise vocal. Haig competed for control of foreign policy with national security affairs adviser Richard Allen, who also was a staunch anti-Soviet but soon left the White House under charges of having used his office for personal gain.

Haig was almost obsessed with the Soviets' recent military buildup and growing first-strike capability, and he sought to enhance the United States's deterrent strength by greatly expanding its strategic and conventional forces. The Kremlin, he claimed, sought influence in the Third World by using proxies such as the Vietnamese in Kampuchea (Cambodia) and the Cubans in Africa and by supporting a growing band of international terrorists who were state sponsored by Iran and other nations having PLO connections. In an argument consistent with Kennan's analysis of Soviet behavior during the Cold War 1940s, Haig attributed the Soviets' aggressive foreign policy to rising internal problems. But in a stance opposing Kennan's, Haig insisted that the United States had to contain the Soviets through a major military buildup. He concluded that "there are more important things than peace. . . . There are things which we Americans must be willing to fight for."

By summer 1982 Haig had resigned as secretary of state, and the office had gone to George Shultz, whose "team player" reputation and calm demeanor exemplified a White House effort to close the breach in its foreign policymaking apparatus. Haig, mercurial in temperament and accused of being a power seeker (critics tagged him CINCWORLD, or

"Commander in Chief of the World"), had failed in a widely publicized effort to mediate a dispute between the United Kingdom and Argentina over the sovereignty of the Falkland Islands in the South Atlantic. After several clashes with other administration members, he departed in June following a disagreement with the president over policies in Europe and the Middle East.

The change in secretaries of state did not ensure harmony in the administration. Shultz had a background in business and economics and a Ph.D. from the Massachusetts Institute of Technology, and although he was also concerned about Soviet expansion, he was not as brusque and impatient as Haig. And yet, like Haig, Shultz soon found himself in bitter disagreement with Weinberger over the nation's defense system. Whereas Shultz sought arms reduction talks that would quietly wind down the Cold War, Weinberger insisted that the United States win the contest by engaging in a massive nuclear expansion program that would far surpass that of the Soviets while driving them into bankruptcy. For most of Reagan's two terms in office, U.S. foreign policy was torn between these two conflicting themes of arms reduction and nuclear expansion.

But even bigger issues confronted the new administration. On Reagan's ascension to the presidency in 1981, the United States faced a new and far more challenging international situation. His harsh Cold War rhetoric belied the fact that bipolarity had receded, only to be replaced by the unpredictable and uncontrollable tensions caused by a multipolar world. Both the United States and the Soviet Union encountered serious difficulties at home, as well as in areas previously considered part of their spheres of influence. Furthermore, many formerly subjugated nations exemplified strong feelings of nationalism that encouraged a long pent-up drive for independence. Americans' confidence in their government and culture had been shaken by Watergate and Vietnam, by expanding economic problems at home, and by declining worldwide respect for their nation. The Reagan administration intended to overcome these realities by implementing a strongly militant foreign policy.

The central problem was that U.S. global dominance, so evident in 1945, was less evident in the post-Vietnam years. Part of the explanation rested in the Soviet Union's great advances since World War II; another element was the increasing leverage in world affairs held by Western Europe, Japan, and the Third World countries, particularly members of OPEC. Soviet military growth, stimulated especially by the outcome of the Cuban missile crisis of 1962, had brought a precarious balance of power in the world that necessitated arms limitations talks and overtures to Third World nations. The horrors of nuclear war left no alternative to drawn-out negotiations and big power competition for Third World support. The courted nations, however, found nonalignment more advantageous to their interests and in that way managed to dictate much of the superpowers' policy.

The Reagan administration proved reluctant to accept either the need for arms limitations talks or the growing prominence of the Third World. The White House chose instead to expand its nuclear arsenal and deemphasize Carter's attempts to establish North-South relationships based on U.S. economic assistance. It aimed to swell trade and investment through private enterprise and hard work, and it looked with little interest on the SALT talks or the recent call for a New International Economic Order (NIEO), which amounted to the Third World's claim for compensation for its long history of exploitation by the West. Within the Western Hemisphere the Reagan administration in early 1982 called for the Caribbean Basin Initiative, which promoted private trade in an effort to help non-Communist governments in the Caribbean and Central America. Globalism again dominated White House policy, intensifying the rivalry between the superpowers for Third World allegiance and paradoxically allowing the smaller nations to continue to wield inordinate influence on world events.

President Reagan's attempt to restore pride in the United States raised high hopes about reestablishing a global leadership role that proved impossible to fulfill. Escalating the arms race, whether or not to undermine the Soviet economy, constituted a high-risk approach that, even if successful, could likewise exhaust the United States while leaving its people under the illusion of having regained sole global leadership. In truth, this policy offered false hopes of total victory in the Cold War and a wishful look back to the days when the United States could claim a solitary superpower status. The multipolar nature of the world meant that the United States could no longer intervene anywhere it chose and expect to dictate the outcome. Failure to win the war in Vietnam had demonstrated the need to limit commitments to areas that were indisputably vital to U.S. security. But this fundamental truth got lost in the evangelical revival of patriotism that the new president so successfully engendered with his eloquent speech and confident manner.

The Search for a Soviet-American Arms Agreement

To enhance its position in the Cold War struggle, the Reagan administration postponed the SALT talks and made several proposals designed to expand the nation's strategic force. Rejecting an arms freeze, the president called for the development of the MX, as Carter had done. Some of the new missiles, Reagan declared, would be located in old Minuteman ICBM silos in Wyoming and Nebraska; the others would await further decision. Congress, however, rejected this plan as making the MX as vulnerable as the Minuteman. Reagan proposed the "dense pack plan," which called for deploying a hundred MIRVed MX missiles in a fifteen-square-mile area in Wyoming, on the theory that onrushing Soviet attack missiles would enter the small air space above the MXs and destroy each other. Not surprisingly, Congress likewise rejected this plan. As an option to the controversial MX, Reagan supported

the development of a new single-warhead mobile missile dubbed "Midgetman," which would be distributed over a wide area to ensure its safety against attack. He also ordered one hundred B-1 bombers to be ready by 1986, even though experts thought the B-1 expensive and the projected "Stealth" bomber more effective because it was not as susceptible to radar detection. Finally, Reagan insisted on the production of cruise missiles, despite warnings that their capacity to avoid verification would escalate the arms race by encouraging the Soviets to develop them too.

Arms control attempts during the 1970s, the president thought, had endangered national security. He argued that their purpose had been to slow the Soviets' growth in numbers while the United States developed more sophisticated strategic weapons—better MIRVs, longer-range SLBMs, and highly mobile air launched cruise missiles (ALCMs). But this approach had not worked, and the Soviet Union had surged dangerously ahead. It was now time to revamp the U.S. military program. Thus, the Reagan administration adopted a time-consuming course of action that would likely encourage a sharp rise in the arms race before it had any effect on curbing the Cold War by undermining the Soviet economy.

To mollify growing popular concern about the arms buildup, the Reagan administration in the spring of 1982 replaced SALT with the Strategic Arms Reduction Talks (START). In actuality, this new program aimed at quieting public criticisms while introducing an idea that the Soviets would have to reject: reducing the stockpile of U.S. and Soviet ICBMs and missile warheads. Such an approach would serve as excellent propaganda while buying time for the United States to expand its nuclear arsenal. But the White House did not seem to take into account that while the START discussions were under way, the Soviet Union could join the United States in a military buildup. Although both superpowers had for years sought to avert nuclear war by maintaining a strategic balance based on the concept of MAD, or mutual assured destruction, the danger now was that each power would strive for superiority and thereby escalate the arms race. The Reagan administration's insistence on greater military security and additional limitations on Soviet strategic growth raised Moscow's fears about U.S. motives and added to the tension. But the president countered that the only way to achieve arms reductions was through a U.S. military buildup intended first to regain Soviet respect.

In an effort to resolve one of Reagan's greatest problems—keeping the NATO alliance intact—his administration presented a plan known as the "zero option." Called for in late 1981 at the Geneva Conference on Intermediate-Range Nuclear Forces (INF), the plan proposed that the United States deploy none of its planned 572 Pershing II and cruise missiles in Western Europe *if* the Soviets agreed to dismantle all their 613 INFs aimed at Europe. The Kremlin rejected the plan on the grounds that its missiles lacked the range to strike the United States, whereas the new NATO missiles (Euromissiles) *could* reach the Soviet Union. The United States's NATO allies meanwhile hotly complained that the president's proposal would leave them unprotected.

To ward off a dangerous division between the United States and its allies, the president urged an interim solution requiring the Soviet Union to withdraw a large number of its 351 triple-warhead missiles, in exchange for which the United States would scale down the number of missiles scheduled to go into Western Europe in December 1983. The United States would put in enough to match the Soviets, warhead for warhead. In mid-April, West German Chancellor Helmut Kohl offered some hope for European support when he commented that the president's interim solution provided "a basis for flexible and dynamic negotiations."

Not surprisingly, Reagan's interim solution met bitter opposition from the Soviet Union, which sought to promote a NATO split and prolong arms discussions while the growing antinuclear movement in Europe gained more momentum. Foreign Minister Andrei Gromyko called a rare news conference in Moscow to denounce the president's proposal. Reagan's interim solution was "absurd," Gromyko declared. If the United States insisted on such a plan, there was "no chance of an agreement" at the INF proceedings in Geneva. Furthermore, it was ridiculous for Reagan to repeat his earlier argument that French and British missiles should not be counted in any attempt to limit warheads in Europe. If an attack took place on the Soviet Union, "Will a French missile have a stamp on it, 'I am French. I was not to be taken into account?'" Should the United States deploy its missiles in Europe, Gromyko darkly warned, the Soviet Union would "take the necessary measures in order to defend its legitimate interests."

In late March 1983 Reagan unveiled a new and much more ambitious defense plan that critics soon derided as "Star Wars." To erase the Soviet Union's "margin of superiority," he declared, the United States would give up deterrence through MAD in favor of a defensive strategy known as SDI, or the strategic defense initiative. SDI, he explained, offered a highly effective "layered defense" that depended on satellites to "intercept and destroy" enemy missile attacks by lasers or particle beams in the initial stage—*before* the warheads separated from the missiles and headed for an array of targets. As for the warheads that made it through the nuclear shield, the ABM (anti-ballistic missile) defense system on the ground would provide the final safeguard. Most U.S. scientists claimed that the plan necessitated such sophisticated technology that it would not work. Even if SDI destroyed nearly all the missiles, the few that got through could render enormous destruction—particularly as the Soviets countered the new U.S. defense program by simply increasing their number of missiles and warheads. Over these objections, Reagan asserted that confrontations in space offered the attractive prospect of sparing the earth from a nuclear holocaust.

The Soviet reaction to SDI was sharply negative. Yuri Andropov, a former head of the

Soviet state security committee or secret police (KGB), had recently become leader of the Communist party after Brezhnev's death and now warned that Reagan's highly touted plan "would actually open the floodgates of a runaway race of all types of strategic arms, both offensive and defensive." A push for a major missile defense system could undermine the basis of peace—the mutual fear of instant retaliation in the event of attack. Even if SDI were impractical, Andropov declared, research into its development could yield other technological advances that would place his nation farther behind in the arms race. Indeed, if SDI was not foolproof, the Americans might be tempted to launch a first strike and then rely on SDI as a defense against any shrunken counterstrike ability that the Soviet Union had left after sustaining the initial assault.

The United States's European allies likewise opposed the plan, despite Reagan's insistence that the new emphasis on defense would result in a reduction in offensive weapons. Critics warned that the opposite would occur. Should either the United States or the Soviet Union appear ready to deploy an ABM system, the very danger of that occurring would encourage a frantic search for new offensive weaponry by the other superpower and increase the likelihood of war. West Europeans denounced what the *Times* of London called "one of the most fundamental switches in American policy since the Second World War." A British colonel complained that the president's plan would lead to "Fortress America," leaving Europeans "out in the cold" because they would no longer pose a nuclear threat to the Soviet Union. The president's message was alarming because it called for replacing MAD with an "anti-ballistic missile umbrella." Devised to prevent nuclear attack, the new plan actually threatened to cause such an attack by setting off a greatly intensified arms race in space that would dangerously upset the present balance of nuclear power.

The arms control situation remained uncertain and explosive. SALT II was still not ratified, and the ABM Treaty of 1972, the only binding arms-control agreement in existence, now stood in jeopardy because of the president's new defense recommendations. The ABM Treaty, based on the fear that defensive systems could disturb the nuclear balance, ensured that "each party undertakes not to develop, test, or deploy ABM systems or components which are sea-based, air-based, space-based, or mobile-land-based." When critics charged that Reagan's plan for a defensive buildup would violate the above provision against space-based ABMs, the White House countered that mere research into such a project did not constitute a treaty violation. In mid-1983 the president and Congress tried to ease growing concerns about a nuclear war by showing interest in a "build-down" strategy, which guaranteed the destruction of a certain number of nuclear weapons for every new one developed. Reagan also leaned toward the recommendation of a bipartisan commission, which warned against the production of MIRVs because their destructive capacity would alarm the Soviets and make the United States increasingly subject to a first strike. Some observers argued that a proposed reduction in the number of warheads, rather than in the number of missiles, would move the United States closer to the Soviet Union in the START talks.

Relations between the United States and the Soviet Union continued their uneven and dangerous course. In September 1983 Soviet planes shot down a South Korean jumbo jet (KAL 007), killing all 269 aboard—including a member of Congress among sixty Americans. When the United States and other nations bitterly denounced the act, the Moscow government refused to apologize because, it charged (without justification), the civilian plane was fitted with spy equipment and had purposely violated Soviet air space over military installations on Sakhalin Island. In November, when the United States began installing the promised Pershing II and cruise missiles in Britain and West Germany, the Soviets broke off the START discussions in Geneva after angrily declaring that the missile placement left them only ten minutes' warning time in the event of an attack. By the end of the year, relations between the superpowers were, according to a Soviet high government official, "white hot, thoroughly white hot."

As the U.S. defense budget grew, many observers questioned whether the Reagan administration had developed a comprehensive strategy to deal with the Soviets, other than to build more arms and insist that in a "protracted" nuclear war, the United States would somehow emerge the victor. A high-ranking Pentagon official promised safety if Americans would "dig a hole, cover it with a couple of doors, and then throw three feet of dirt on top." Another administration official assured Congress that in the aftermath of nuclear war, mail would go through "even if the survivors ran out of stamps." He was not taken aback by a congressional member who cynically noted the difficulty in delivering mail where there were "no addresses, no streets, no blocks, no houses." A large group of doctors warned that nuclear war would bring the "last epidemic," and scientific studies supported that terrifying view by showing that a nuclear holocaust would cause countless deaths and lead to a "nuclear winter." During that bleak period, scientists somberly predicted, a contagion of fires and smoke resulting from the nuclear blasts could destroy the chain of life on earth by blackening the skies for a year, causing a global freeze, and disrupting the sun's capacity to provide the basis for food. Despite these dire forecasts, an escalated arms race seemed likely as the United States continued to push for SDI as an alternative to deterrence theory and as the Soviets made greater efforts at building offensive missiles to outdistance the massive U.S. defense buildup.

More than a few observers hoped that a recent change in Soviet leadership would enhance the possibility of arms reductions. Andropov died after a long illness in early 1984 and was succeeded by Konstantin Chernenko. But Chernenko was also elderly and ill and continued the party's rigid control at home and hard-line policies abroad. Upon Chernenko's death in March 1985, Mikhail Gorbachev became the Soviet General Secretary of the Communist party. He was considerably younger than his predecessors (in his early fifties), warm and charismatic, and well educated in Western philosophy, law, and agriculture. Gorbachev was a Christian whose wife, Raisa, held a doctorate in philosophy. Furthermore, he was experienced in dealing with the West in foreign affairs and sought reform in both Soviet domestic and foreign policy. Most important, he recognized that his country faced serious internal and external problems that required immediate rectification. Such objectives necessitated an end to the debilitating arms race and a winding down of the Cold War.

Gorbachev's major goal was to maintain socialism by the two interlocking goals of restructuring the Soviet economy (*perestroika*) and liberalizing the country's political system through a policy of openness (*glasnost*). Although the Communist party would maintain its dominant position, it would undergo changes through democratization and an emphasis on persuasion rather than force. The centralized economy and administrative network would become decentralized and market oriented. Such an ambitious program required an easing of tensions with the United States that permitted a greater focus on economic and political reforms inside the Soviet Union.

Toward these ends, Gorbachev adopted several measures designed to prove his sincerity. He stopped nuclear testing and called for on-site verification, unilaterally halted the ongoing installation of Soviet intermediate-range missiles trained on Western Europe, and sought technological assistance from Japan and West Germany. He removed the Cold War hard-liner, Andrei Gromyko, from his twenty-eight-year-long post as foreign minister, replacing him with the much more accommodating Eduard Shevardnadze of Georgia. Gorbachev then went on a goodwill trip to Europe, Latin America, and the United States, everywhere impressing his counterparts with his compassion and earning high praise from even the staunch anti-Soviet British Prime Minister Margaret Thatcher, who hailed him as a "friend."

But Gorbachev's announced objectives encountered great skepticism in the United States. In November 1985 he and Reagan (reelected a year earlier by a wide margin) attended a summit meeting in Geneva, the first since 1979. Although the two leaders reached no agreements, they developed a warm, personal relationship that only their wives sullied by finding each other insufferable. During the negotiations, Gorbachev displayed a superior deftness and familiarity with detail that proved embarrassing to the less agile and not equally knowledgeable president. They failed to find common ground on either SDI or SALT II, even though careful observers found hope in the remarkable lack of hostilities between the chief diplomats.

With the nuclear deadlock remaining a growing danger, Reagan and Gorbachev agreed to try again—this time at Reykjavik in Iceland—where they developed a general framework of understanding that might yield specific agreements at later meetings. Gorbachev had publicly declared his intention to work toward the eradication of all nuclear weapons by the turn of the century, thereby providing a challenging backdrop to his meeting with Reagan in October 1986. At one point they seemed close to an agreement that would remove all intermediate-range missiles from Europe and phase out ballistic missiles over the next ten years. Although such a pact would not actually eliminate nuclear weapons, it would constitute a first step toward a meaningful arms reduction. But then Gorbachev offered what became known in White House circles as the "grand compromise"—a halt in research toward SDI in exchange for major reductions in strategic arms. Reagan, however, refused to consider any proposal endangering the development of SDI and thereby curtailed all progress toward a meaningful settlement. Still, the two heads of state had further cultivated their cordial personal relationship and in so doing had gone home convinced of a mutually sincere interest in peacefully ending the nuclear standoff.

To most observers, however, the outlook for nuclear arms reductions seemed as dismal as ever. Critics on the left denounced the president for holding on to a defense system that was astronomically expensive and eminently unworkable; those on the right found it difficult to believe that he was willing to give up the nation's nuclear arsenal when its conventional weapons lagged so far behind those of its chief rival. Many wondered about the administration's growing ineffectiveness—especially as the worn and obviously disappointed Secretary of State Shultz informed the press of the failed negotiations and the White House followed with several muddled and contradictory statements about the results. The chilling prophecy made by Winston Churchill some years earlier still seemed valid: "Safety will be the sturdy child of terror, and survival the twin brother of annihilation."

Despite the shattered hopes at Reykjavik, the reality was that the utter necessity of détente led the superpowers back to the peace table. Both leaders endorsed a statement that provided a guide for their talks: "A nuclear war cannot be won and must never be fought." At still another summit meeting, in Washington in December 1987, the two leaders managed to agree on less ambitious terms contained in what became known as the Intermediate-Range Nuclear Forces (INF) Treaty. Rather than call for the elimination of all missiles, it stipulated the disbandment of only those U.S. and Soviet INF missiles in Europe and then, in an epochal move, authorized on-site inspections to verify their destruction. Gorbachev had taken the first real step toward this historic agreement by accepting the president's "zero option" and then convincing him of the Soviets' sincere desire for arms reduction. The two superpowers had taken the initial step toward that grand objective and thereby eased tensions in Europe. With Shultz's strong support and Weinberger's earlier resignation from the defense post, the INF Treaty went into effect on June 1, 1988, after sailing through the

Toward the End of the Cold War
Soviet leader Mikhail Gorbachev and wife Raisa visit President Reagan
and wife Nancy in Washington during the ceremonial signing of the
INF Treaty in December 1987. *White House Photo Office, Ronald
Reagan Presidential Library, Simi Valley, California.*

Senate by the overwhelming margin of ninety-three to five.

Gorbachev undertook other changes, all promoting his aim of easing the Cold War. In April 1988 he agreed to a UN mediation proposal calling for a Soviet troop withdrawal from Afghanistan by the beginning of the new year. Although they left behind military advisers and a friendly government, the Soviets had clearly experienced their own Vietnam, complete with soldiers' addictions to drugs and alcohol, a casualty list of more than 40,000, and a defeat that was partly attributable to another country's intervention—the introduction of U.S. "Stinger" antiaircraft missiles sent by the Reagan administration to the Afghan rebels (*mujahedeen* or "holy warriors"). In May the president met again with Gorbachev, this time in Moscow, where in a scene eerily suggestive of an impending Armaggedon, the two men walked through Red Square and talked with people on the street while each leader's military aide lagged not far behind, carrying the codes required to order a nuclear attack.

But in an astounding about-face, Reagan returned to Washington with the glowing report that his cohort was a "friend" and that the Soviets had "changed." Gorbachev meanwhile reinforced Reagan's revelation by cutting aid to the Sandinistas in Nicaragua and working with Castro to pull his troops from Angola. In December 1988 Gorbachev visited the United States, where he became the first Soviet premier since 1960 (when Khrushchev engaged in his shoe-pounding tirade at the United Nations) to speak before the UN General Assembly in New York. Gorbachev used that august occasion to announce a huge reduction in the Soviet military establishment of one-half million ground troops and 10,000 tanks. That same day a devastating earthquake took the lives of 25,000 Soviet Armenians, drawing a phenomenal outpouring of sympathy and assistance from the United States and other countries in the West.

The whirlwind of events was mind boggling, suggesting that Thatcher was correct in asserting that "the cold war is over." In the brief span of eight years, the Soviet Union and the United States, primarily because of Gorbachev's courageous initiatives, had moved from a dangerously revived Cold War to perhaps its demise. More than forty years earlier, Kennan had argued that the U.S. containment policy would eventually force a mellowed atmosphere in the Soviet Union. Gorbachev's sweeping reforms had already gone too far to be reversed; indeed, they were moving openly at home away from communism and even socialism and toward democracy and a free-market system. Kennan's prediction appeared to be correct, because the Cold War seemed to be drawing to an end. If so, this was indeed a watershed period in history.

Central America and the Caribbean

Even as the two chief rivals in the world worked toward settling their differences, the Reagan administration regarded the ongoing civil war in the small Central American country of El Salvador as Communist-inspired and hence an integral part of the Cold War. The Salvadoran conflict raised many of the most hotly debated issues during the Cold War years, particularly during the latter period of the U.S. involvement in Vietnam. El Salvador was desperately poor and the most densely populated country in Central America. Its government, Reagan warned, was threatened by a Communist insurgent movement aided by Soviet and Cuban weapons filtered into the country through neighboring Nicaragua. In retrospect, it is clear that internal economic and political problems threatened El Salvador more than did alleged Communist infiltration. But in the heightened atmosphere of Cold War II, realities gave way once again to perceptions.

To counter this claimed Communist menace in the hemisphere, the Reagan administration engaged in several policies. It ignored Castro's interest in restoring relations and continued an economic embargo on Cuba in an effort to stop him from harboring Soviet troops and exporting revolutionary principles throughout the hemisphere. In 1981 the United States agreed to support a land reform

program started by Salvadoran President José Napoleón Duarte and sent fifty-five military advisers to help his army put down resistance from Marxist and Social Democratic insurgents. Finally, the White House reversed the Carter administration's policy by cutting off economic assistance to the leftist Sandinista government in Nicaragua—although Mexico and France lightened the impact of that measure by offering aid.

El Salvador had emerged as a vital ingredient in the United States's global considerations. Should El Salvador fall to communism, the president explained to reporters and others gazing at a huge map of Central America, the neighboring American states would collapse, one by one, until the entire region became Communist and endangered the United States. The Soviets must not achieve a victory in the Western Hemisphere, he emphasized to Congress. Although offering assurances that no U.S. combat soldiers would go to El Salvador, Reagan unsettled listeners by warning that everything was at stake: "We are the last domino."

Skeptics countered that the administration was taking the same treacherous path that had earlier led to disaster in Vietnam: a steady escalation of U.S. economic and military aid, the assignment of advisers (referred to as "trainers" by the Reagan administration in an effort to dispel the Vietnam analogy) and administrators, and the ultimate dispatch of combat troops. The Salvadorans' problems were internal in origin, critics insisted, and the United States was again helping an unpopular elitist regime that opposed reforms. Americans could not accomplish a "victory" for democracy by repeatedly seeking military solutions to social, political, and economic problems. In fact, administration opponents pointed out, Western Europe and many Latin American countries, particularly Mexico, believed that the guerrillas themselves offered more hope for an improved society. Whether a Soviet threat existed in El Salvador or, as some White House officials privately admitted, the United States wanted to use the issue to exemplify a

War in Central America—El Salvador
U.S. Army officer demonstrating map reading to Salvadoran soldiers during field
training exercise. *U.S. Army.*

strong course against Communist aggression, the Reagan administration found that its chief obstacle to assuming a greater role in El Salvador was the cry of "No more Vietnams."

The White House further altered Carter's policy regarding El Salvador by sending more military aid and shifting the emphasis from land reform to victory in the war. The state department justified this harder stance by proclaiming the situation a "textbook case of indirect armed aggression by Communist powers." The present regime in El Salvador, the Reagan administration insisted, would lead the way to reform, whereas the left-wing guerrillas were simply Soviet proxies. This was an example of "international terrorism" emanating from the Soviet Union: encouragement to radical groups promoting political changes through violence. Reagan insisted that the United States wanted to help the Salvadoran government because it sought peaceful reforms and was under siege by leftists.

The Reagan administration attempted to make a distinction between "authoritarian" and "totalitarian" regimes in justifying its assistance to El Salvador. The president drew from the earlier writings of now UN Ambassador Jeane

Kirkpatrick, who argued that even though authoritarian governments prohibited political freedoms, they offered stability and the chance of becoming democratic while welcoming foreign investments and most often favoring the United States. Totalitarian governments, she noted, were usually Communist and therefore opposed to democracy, capitalism, and the United States. Acting on these premises, Reagan conceded that authoritarian regimes, such as that in El Salvador, had to stamp out criticisms in civil wars; but, he continued, they were not totalitarian in the sense of seeking to squelch all dissent and close their doors on outside involvement. Religious beliefs, family matters, cultural pursuits, economic concerns—much latitude remained for individual development in authoritarian countries as long as these activities did not grow into a dangerous form of political instability that hampered the eventual development of democracy and markets for investment and trade. Thus could the Reagan administration support governments on the right and oppose those on the left.

The United States, according to the White House, had no choice but to support the military government of El Salvador. Whereas

Map 26
Whether caused by internal problems or by outside interference—or both—the fighting in Central America deeply divided the United States over what remedies to offer.

authoritarian regimes exercised varying degrees of repression and therefore had the leeway to become more democratic, those of a totalitarian nature could not change. The best proof was Nicaragua, Reagan asserted. The Carter administration had erred in supporting the Sandinistas over the Somozan government. Once the Sandinistas had gained power, they had suppressed civil liberties and moved close to the Soviet Union and Cuba. Congress gave in to the president and agreed to send economic and military assistance along with advisers, but it added one stipulation: Such aid depended on improvements in human rights.

Although Kirkpatrick's ideas provided a seemingly clear guideline to foreign assistance programs, they did not work in practice as well as in theory. Any emphasis on human rights, of course, fell victim to the higher priority of quietly encouraging authoritarian regimes to permit evolutionary democratic changes. According to theory, the tenure of such regimes constituted an unavoidable step in a long transition period leading to democracy. It followed that Americans must ignore human rights abuses and sham elections as only temporary detours on the road to democracy. And, as in all imperfect theories, the administration at times had to engage in contradictory actions that raised questions about its direction. In 1982 the United States supported Britain's efforts to hold on to its Falkland Island possessions when they came under attack from the "authoritarian" government of Argentina. Furthermore, sharply deteriorating relations with the Soviet Union led the White House to reestablish ties with the "totalitarian" regime in China. Most important, however, a strict adherence to Kirkpatrick's dictum ensured continued embarrassment for the administration because it required an endorsement of authoritarian and hence repressive regimes all over the world.

For a time, however, the theory seemed sound. Secure in its logic, the Reagan administration asked Congress during spring 1983 to approve more military aid to El Salvador as part of a global effort to combat communism. The year before, Americans had met with Mexican emissaries, and a short time afterward, in March 1982, elections had taken place in El Salvador. Although the insurgents refused to take part, Duarte's moderate Christian Democrats lost control of the National Assembly to a coalition of right-wing leaders, and the land reform program came to a halt. The problems, according to the Reagan administration's greatly distorted assessment, were attributable to the Communists. The Soviets had infiltrated Nicaragua and now El Salvador and soon would concentrate on Honduras and Guatemala. This threatening activity had global implications, Reagan warned: "Soviet military theorists want to destroy our capacity to resupply Western Europe in case of an emergency." They intend "to tie down our attention and forces on our own southern border and so limit our capacity to act in more distant places such as Europe, the Persian Gulf, the Indian Ocean, the Sea of Japan." Central America was "simply too close and the strategic stakes . . . too high, for us to ignore the danger of governments seizing power there with ideological and military ties to the Soviet Union." U.S. assistance was necessary.

Central America had become an integral part of White House foreign policy. To placate those Americans who feared "another Vietnam," Reagan explained in March 1983 that he was willing to have Salvadoran troops trained inside the United States so they could conduct the war themselves. Though repeating his pledge against sending U.S. combat troops to the troubled country, he warned that he would increase the number of advisers if Congress failed to comply with his requests for more military aid. "Two-thirds of all our foreign trade and petroleum pass through the Panama Canal and the Caribbean," the president explained in May. Should a crisis develop in Europe, "at least half of our supplies for NATO would go through these areas by sea." The Caribbean basin was a "magnet for adventurism."

Despite the heavy influx of U.S. aid, the situation in Central America continued to deteriorate, leading the White House to adopt stern measures. Charges grew that the United States was secretly aiding the contras (an anti-Sandinista force of perhaps 2000 soldiers based in Honduras) in an attempt to overthrow the regime in Nicaragua and ease the alleged Communist pressures on El Salvador. The White House denied the accusation as a "myth," claiming instead that the new fighting was indigenous. U.S. aid to the anti-Sandinistas, the administration continued, was aimed only at "interdicting" or prohibiting further military assistance to the Sandinistas' cohort in El Salvador, the Communist insurgents. "The United States isn't invading anybody," UN Ambassador Kirkpatrick declared. But actually in November 1981 the president had secretly authorized the expenditure of close to $20 million by the CIA to prepare the contras for action against a government in Nicaragua that the United States, strange to say, officially recognized as legitimate. Some of the contras' military leaders had received their training in Florida.

The White House noted an increasingly dangerous situation in El Salvador that necessitated even more active U.S. intervention. A state department representative warned congressional committees that the United States might have to escalate its military and political involvement in Nicaragua because of the possible introduction into Central America of either Soviet or Cuban "modern fighter aircraft" or "even Cuban combat troops." Should Soviet and Cuban intervention take place, he asserted, the Reagan administration was prepared to launch air strikes, increase aid to friendly nations, and invoke the Rio Treaty of 1947, which authorized U.S. participation in the collective defense of Latin America. The president declared, however, that "we do not view security assistance as an end in itself, but as a shield for democratization, economic development and diplomacy." Shortly afterward the White House announced that one hundred military advisers had left for Honduras to train Salvadoran troops.

Tensions rose in summer 1983 when a U.S. military adviser was assassinated in El Salvador, but the United States continued to act with outward restraint. The Reagan administration adopted a strategy called "symmetry," which sought to buy time for democratic development in the Central American country. According to theory, the United States would treat the Sandinista regime in Nicaragua in the same way it treated the U.S.-supported government of President Alvaro Magaña in El Salvador: Because the Sandinistas sought Magaña's overthrow, the United States would help the guerrilla group in Nicaragua (that is, the contras) seeking to oust the Sandinistas. In late July, Reagan appointed former secretary of state Henry Kissinger as head of a twelve-member bipartisan commission instructed to develop a long-range policy on Central America. The president also made a show of force by sending an aircraft carrier battle group to engage in military maneuvers along Nicaragua's Pacific coast. Perhaps these demonstrations of U.S. interest in Central American affairs would convince the governments and rebels in both Nicaragua and El Salvador to consider a cease-fire, negotiations, and democratic elections.

At least in part to send a message to the Sandinistas, the Reagan administration in

War in Central America—Nicaragua
Contras standing guard in Matagalpa in eastern Nicaragua in September 1985. *Wide World Photos, New York.*

October 1983 took military action in nearby Grenada to thwart what it claimed was a threatened Communist takeover on that tiny island in the British Commonwealth. Four years earlier, in March 1979, leftists led by Maurice Bishop had overthrown the repressive and corrupt but anti-Communist government in a bloodless coup. In less than a week a Cuban ship had arrived carrying Soviet arms and ammunition. The following November, Bishop had announced that Castro would help Grenada build an "international airport." After beginning construction of the airstrip, Bishop had signed a treaty with the Moscow government that allowed the Soviets to land long-range reconnaissance planes. Although the Reagan administration had complained that these moves endangered peace in the hemisphere, Bishop had visited Moscow in July 1982 and declared that he had received assurances of long-term financial assistance. Over national television in March 1983, Reagan displayed a photograph of the Cuban barracks and airstrip on the island. Grenada had no air force, he asserted. "The Soviet-Cuban militarization of Grenada can only be seen as power projection into the region."

An outbreak of violence on the island provided the opportunity for the United States to act. White House pressure on Bishop had forced him to ease his criticisms of the United States; but Cuba's insistence on a hard-line policy encouraged dissidents on Grenada to seize control in mid-October and place Bishop under house arrest. Bishop's followers soon stormed the building and freed him, whereupon he spoke before a huge rally in the capital city of St. George's. But so-called revolutionary armed forces fired into the crowd, killing several before capturing and executing Bishop. As the militants imposed martial law, the White House declared that close to 1000 Americans on the island, more than half of them students at St. George's University School of Medicine, were in mortal danger.

With the approval of an obscure group of six member nations, the Organization of Eastern Caribbean States, Reagan resorted to military force—*without* consulting the British government. Probably spurred by news from Lebanon just two days earlier of a terrorist bombing in Beirut that took the lives of 241 U.S. soldiers (discussed later), the president defiantly declared: "We cannot let an act of terrorism determine whether we aid or assist our allies in the region. If we do that," he asked, "who will ever trust us again?" On October 25, 1983, a naval task force of 1900 marines en route for Lebanon was diverted to Grenada. There they encountered brief and surprisingly strong resistance at the airstrip from Grenadan troops and nearly eight hundred Cuban construction workers. The Americans soon secured the island, but only after the injection of 4000 additional troops and six hard days of fighting that resulted in 134 U.S. casualties, including 18 dead, along with 396 Cuban and Grenadan casualties that included 69 dead.

Reagan then capitalized on the success to issue a warning to those who interfered in the Western Hemisphere. Documents and weapons captured in the assault, he claimed, proved that the Marxist government had become increasingly reliant on Cuba, the Soviet Union, and North Korea—particularly for arms. The White House believed that Castro had intended to use Grenada as a staging ground for spreading communism into the entire region. Most important, however, the president hoped that the use of force would demonstrate to the Sandinistas that Nicaragua itself was not immune to such harsh treatment. The "rescue mission," as Reagan called it, was necessary to save the Americans and liberate the island from the threat of communism.

Searching questions remained about the Grenada expedition, even though the administration's supporters hailed the outcome as a victory for Reagan's foreign policy and simply ignored the complaints. Democratic Speaker of the House Thomas P. O'Neill accused the president of violating the War Powers Act of 1973 by not consulting with Congress. New York Senator Daniel P. Moynihan, also a Democrat, denounced the assumed right of the United States to invade another sovereign nation. While seven members of the House prepared a resolution of impeachment against the president (which failed to win sufficient support), other observers wondered if the White House had too readily resorted to the military option. They remained dubious about the danger to the hemisphere and asked embarrassing questions about the efficiency level of U.S. military forces. Many disputed Reagan's argument that the new airfield would primarily serve Cuban and Soviet military forces, claiming instead (and probably correctly) that its chief purpose was to support tourism. Still others remained skeptical about the president's defense of the invasion as vital to the safety of Americans on the island. British Prime Minister Thatcher had opposed the military action as a violation of Grenada's sovereignty and urged economic sanctions, and numerous Latin American governments denounced the move as a revival of nineteenth-century "gunboat diplomacy." The UN Security

Council had opposed the action, only to have the United States veto the measure. The Grenada expedition nonetheless won widespread public approval in the United States—especially when television cameras showed American medical students arriving home and falling on their knees at the airport to kiss the ground.

With a pro-American group in charge, the troops cleansed the island of all dangerous intruders. They sent the Cubans home and then shut down the Soviet embassy. In late December the Americans began their departure from the island, following seven weeks of occupation and a total cost of nearly $80 million.

Shortly afterward, in early 1984, the Kissinger Commission presented conclusions that indirectly lent credence to the Reagan administration's assessment of the danger in Grenada. The United States, according to the findings, had vital interests in Central America and had to expand its economic and military commitment in an effort to curtail the Soviets' "gradualist" policy. The commission recommended that Congress authorize $8 billion in economic aid to Central America over a five-year period. Most members of the commission took exception to the president's emphasis on the role of private business and urged the United States to condition *all* aid on changes in human rights. Kissinger warned, however, that the United States must not emphasize the "conditionality" of aid "in a manner that leads to a Marxist-Leninist victory." It would be "absurd," he told reporters, to cut off military assistance to El Salvador in defense of human rights if the move ensured a Communist victory that led to more killing. Reagan approved the report but spoke favorably of Kissinger's warning. Congress responded by approving an aid package of less than half the amount recommended but urged continued assistance to the Salvadoran military and contras in Nicaragua.

The situation in El Salvador meanwhile showed signs of easing in intensity. In May 1984, with the United States supervising election proceedings and the CIA providing monies in strategic places, Duarte emerged victorious as president. The following year his Christian Democratic party won control over the National Assembly, and the military appeared receptive to his moderate policies and assurances of reforms. The death squads decreased their activity, and Duarte seemingly surprised the White House by meeting with the rebels to explore the possibilities of a negotiated settlement that included their participation in government. The discussions failed, however, and the United States expanded its assistance to Duarte's military forces—which had the unforeseen effect of weakening his appeal to the country's moderates and encouraging the civil war to continue throughout the remainder of the Reagan administration.

The White House meanwhile continued to help the contras in Nicaragua as part of the overall effort to bring down the Sandinistas and ease the pressure on El Salvador. It sent aid, worked to train the army, and urged land reform. In mid-August 1983 the first of nearly 6000 army and marine troops landed in Honduras to begin "training exercises." Despite a congressional act of 1982 banning the use of classified funds in trying to undermine the Nicaraguan government (the Boland Amendment, presented by Democrat Edward Boland of the House Intelligence Committee), the White House continued its efforts in Central America by relying on the other part of the Boland Amendment that permitted overt help to any government in the region endangered by insurgents receiving military assistance from Cuba or Nicaragua. Consequently, the CIA actively but clandestinely participated in the fighting by directing assaults into Nicaragua, flying air missions, sabotaging oil depots, plotting assassinations of Sandinista leaders, and cooperating with the contras in mining the country's harbors.

But in late 1983 the secret war waged by the Reagan administration became public and threatened to come to an end. The mines damaged several neutral vessels and injured ten sailors, exposing the CIA's covert operations and leading an outraged Congress to take preventive measures. The Sandinista government took the matter to the World Court, where it accused the United States of violating Nicaragua's sovereignty. The Reagan administration, however, ignored international law and simply rejected the right of the Court to deal with such matters. Without U.S. involvement in the ensuing judicial process, the World Court in June 1986 found the United States in violation of international law by aiding the contras and mining the harbors and ordered it to make compensation to Nicaragua. The president refused to comply. An irate Congress responded with a second Boland Amendment, however, which prohibited the use of *any* government funds to undermine the Nicaraguan government and by late 1984 effectively stopped all aid to the contras.

The White House, however, insisted that the Boland Amendment did not apply to the work of the National Security Council (which Congress hotly disputed) and continued to maintain pressure on the Sandinistas in Nicaragua. The president carefully circumvented the wording of the Boland Amendment by calling for an end to arms shipments to insurgents in El Salvador while no longer mentioning the overthrow of the Nicaraguan government. Congress remained adamantly opposed to Reagan's transparent maneuverings. Although agreeing to assist Duarte and El Salvador, it repeatedly turned down the president's requests to aid the contras. Not to be denied, members of the Reagan administration appealed to private groups of Americans, who donated $5 million of supplies to the contras in 1984 and 1985. The president meanwhile solicited contributions from Texas oil magnates, wealthy widows (both groups able to claim tax writeoffs), and Arab leaders, including the king of Saudi Arabia.

The situation in Central America continued to deteriorate. The Sandinistas held an election in late 1984 that solidified their control over Nicaragua by putting their leader, Daniel Ortega, into the presidency, even though they lost a few seats in the government to opposition groups. The following year, Ortega took measures that substantiated the Reagan administration's worst fears. Ortega imposed martial law, imprisoned many members of his opposition, and shut down media criticism. When the Sandinistas then edged closer to Cuba and the Communist bloc, Reagan warned that Nicaragua had become "a Communist totalitarian state" and declared that the United States must help the contras, who were, he insisted, the "moral equal of our Founding Fathers."

The president authorized several actions intended to undermine the Sandinistas. He ordered the contras based in Honduras into maneuvers and stationed U.S. warships off the Nicaraguan coasts. He instituted an economic embargo on Nicaragua in May 1985. Soon afterward the administration blocked Nicaragua's effort to secure funds from the World Bank and Inter-American Development Bank. Under the International Emergency Economic Powers Act of 1977, the president explained, he could impose sanctions without congressional approval if he declared a "national emergency." Reagan announced that Nicaragua's "aggressive activities" were clear in its "continuing efforts to subvert its neighbors, its rapid and destabilizing military buildup, its close military and security ties to Cuba and the Soviet Union and its imposition of Communist totalitarian internal rule." In the summer of 1985, Congress still refused to open its military coffers to the contras, although it agreed to extend $27 million in "humanitarian" aid.

In his December State of the Union address, the president kept the heat on Congress by announcing what became known as the "Reagan Doctrine." His administration, he proclaimed, would support anti-Communist "freedom fighters" as part of the nation's "self-defense." Reagan's pronouncements resurrected memories of the Eisenhower fifties, when Secretary of State John Foster Dulles called for the "rollback" of communism and its replacement with Wilsonian ideals of freedom aimed at liberating oppressed peoples everywhere. "Our mission," Reagan declared, "is to nourish and defend freedom and democracy." Covert assistance to counterinsurgents (in what some were now calling "low intensity conflict") would ultimately unseat dangerous regimes and allow the growth of democracy. To facilitate this moral and ideological process, Reagan seemed to imply, the CIA could use congressional funds to assist the contras in Nicaragua and insurgents anywhere else who were resisting totalitarian rule.

Meanwhile, Soviet ties with Nicaragua seemed to grow tighter. Two days before the United States announced the economic sanctions, Ortega visited Gorbachev in the Kremlin and, before television cameras, openly displayed their alleged friendship. In this visit, Ortega's fourth since the Sandinista takeover in July 1979, he clearly sought new economic assistance. The Soviet Union had delayed news of the planned visit until after Reagan's recent contra aid defeat in Congress. Soviet news agency TASS confirmed the president's suspicions by announcing the establishment of a Soviet-Nicaraguan commission on economic, commercial, and scientific-technical cooperation.

In March 1986 Reagan again appealed for congressional money for arms to the contras. Three months later Congress (doubtless in reaction to Ortega's visit to Moscow) approved $100 million but restricted the package to "nonlethal" aid. For only a brief time the problems in Central America dropped from the headlines.

The Middle East

Despite the enormous difficulties arising in U.S.-Soviet relations and the immediacy of the alleged Soviet connection with Central America, the most perplexing problem facing the United States continued to be the Middle East. The Egyptian-Israeli Treaty of 1979 had not resolved the region's difficulties; indeed, it added still more complications to a list that was already long. The pact negotiated by the Carter administration had actually strengthened Israel's

stature in the Middle East by alienating Egypt from the other Arab nations, and at the same time it kept the United States in the awkward position of having to honor commitments to the Israelis while trying to maintain ties with the oil-rich Saudis and other Arabs. If the treaty constituted a first step toward peace, it also brought even more focus to the numerous problems that stood in the way.

As in the 1970s, the Reagan administration followed what seemed to be the only feasible approach: to extend military and economic aid to both major antagonists (the Israelis and the Arabs), hoping somehow to maintain a balance of power designed to avert conflict. In an effort to counter long-time military aid to Israel, the White House permitted the Saudis to buy U.S. tanks and air-to-air missiles for their F-15 fighter planes, which took away Israel's control of the skies. The new sale angered Congress, because the administration had earlier offered pledges against such an act to win congressional support for the original sale of the F-15s. Furthermore, in response to the Saudis' fear of an assault by Iran during its ongoing war with the Saudis' political ally Iraq, the Reagan administration prepared to sell them Sidewinder missiles and five Airborne Warning and Control System planes (AWACS), which were highly effective Boeing 707s equipped with huge disk-shaped radar antennas capable of tracking up to four hundred aircraft within a 350-mile radius. The White House pushed through the hotly debated AWACS sale by a slim four-vote margin in the Senate.

The Reagan administration's arms sales to Saudi Arabia greatly exacerbated the already precarious Middle East situation. Israel was angry with the United States over the AWACS deal, which further undercut the hopes of the treaty with Egypt. Although Israel reaffirmed its intention to withdraw from the Sinai in April 1982, uncertainty remained. Then, in October 1981, matters became even more complicated: Sadat was assassinated by Muslim extremists in the Egyptian army, forcing his successor, Hosni Mubarek, to seek credibility at home by affirming that his loyalties to Egypt were more important than the treaty with Israel. This objective necessitated an effort by his new regime to restore relations with moderate Arab states.

When Begin visited Washington shortly after the AWACS deal, Reagan recommended a policy called "strategic collaboration," which sought to revive the Camp David accords by offering more security assurances to Israel. The Washington administration hoped that such a move would make Begin more open to compromise on the Palestinian issue and relax his resistance to the AWACS agreement. But this effort failed. Begin remained determined to annex the West Bank, and in December he ordered the virtual annexation of the Syrian portion of the Golan Heights by integrating the area into the Israeli administrative and judicial system. When the Reagan administration reacted by suspending the discussions over strategic collaboration, Begin angrily denounced the United States as anti-Semitic and accused it of treating Israel as a "banana republic." Instead of returning to pre-1967 borders in exchange for promises of security, he intended to win the war by strengthening his country's hold on East Jerusalem, the Golan Heights, the West Bank, and Gaza.

Although the central issue in the Middle East remained the Arab-Israeli conflict, the Reagan administration tried to draw the two peoples together by emphasizing the Soviet threat to the entire region and calling for a "strategic consensus" against Moscow. If the United States could convince the ancient antagonists that the Soviet menace superseded their own difficulties, it might be able to maintain relations with both the Arabs and the Israelis and keep peace in the region. The Reagan administration therefore undertook the formidable tasks of deemphasizing Arab-Israeli differences and postponing the Palestinian issue, in hope of shifting the focus to containing the Soviet Union. Success would bring greater security to the region's pro-Western nations, in turn ensuring peace in the Middle East and a continued oil supply for the West.

The policy of strategic consensus proved a dismal failure. Not even the Soviet-American rivalry could overshadow Arab-Israeli hostilities. Israel's major concerns, Reagan's critics argued, were the Palestinians and U.S. arms sales to the Arabs. The Arab states declared that only the establishment of a Palestinian state would ease anti-American sentiment in the Middle East and improve economic and military ties with the United States. Despite the Reagan administration's efforts to ignore history and inject the Cold War as a sedative for easing the Middle East's problems, it could not diminish the overwhelming centrality of Arab-Israeli strife.

Lebanon soon became the focal point of another Middle East crisis. Located north of Israel on the eastern side of the Mediterranean, Lebanon had recently been rocked by an intensely bitter civil war between Christians and Muslims. The Christians, more powerful and wealthy than their hated enemy, had demanded restrictions on the Palestinians in south Lebanon, who had grown in number after their forced departure from Jordan during the early 1970s. The Palestinians now posed a threat to Lebanon because they were armed and therefore attractive to left-wing Muslim militants who sought PLO help against the Christians. Should war develop between Israel and a Muslim-controlled Lebanon, neighboring Syria would have to become involved. Syria considered it imperative to keep Lebanon intact, first by mediation and then, failing that, by military force.

The United States made a major effort to mediate the growing dispute—especially after Israeli forces raided southern Lebanon to destroy the PLO centers and then armed the Christians as a step toward creating a friendly buffer state between Israel and the PLO. Israel had just complied with the Camp David accords in withdrawing from the Sinai in April 1982, and Begin now felt free to turn toward the festering problem in Lebanon. Internal conflict erupted on an even wider scale: The Syrians emplaced ground-to-air missiles in Lebanon, and the Israelis countered by destroying the missiles in a preemptive strike. War between Israel and Syria, the Reagan administration knew, would drive the Arab states into Syria's arms and leave the United States alone with Israel, thus alienating the Saudis. The Soviet Union, which had recently entered an amity pact with Syria, would then align with the other Arab states and gain a major inroad into the Middle East.

Heightening tensions finally exploded into conflict in mid-1982, when PLO agents assassinated the Israeli ambassador in London and the Israelis retaliated in June by launching a massive invasion of Lebanon. Israeli forces had entered Lebanon for the ostensible reason of crippling the PLO's ability to endanger Jewish settlements in the north; in reality, however, the Israelis sought to destroy the PLO in West Beirut, undermine the hopes of Palestinian nationalists on the West Bank, force the Syrians out of Lebanon, and put the beleaguered country under the control of the Christians, whose close ties with Israel could guarantee some measure of security along their common frontier. At the same time, the Israelis further shocked the White House by bombing the nuclear reactor that Iraq had recently acquired from France to prevent Iraqi production of nuclear bombs capable of destroying Israel.

The timing of the Israeli attack on Lebanon thoroughly embarrassed the United States. President Reagan was on a goodwill visit in Europe, and his administration was involved in the Middle East peace talks. The widespread impression was that the United States either had been unable to restrain Israel or, even worse, had tacitly approved the invasion. The Israeli offensive violated the recent fragile and unwritten cease-fire with the PLO secured after long and delicate negotiations by U.S. Special Envoy Philip Habib. Now more problems lay ahead. A state department spokesman insisted that "Israel will have to withdraw its forces from Lebanon, and the Palestinians will have to stop using Lebanon as a launching pad for attacks on Israel." A British diplomat was blunt: Israel was "acting as recruiter in chief for the PLO."

The Israeli military offensive in Lebanon threatened to wreck U.S. hopes for peace in the Middle East. World condemnation of the siege developed as nightly news programs televised the Israeli air and ground assaults, which, to most observers, appeared to be unprovoked aggression. Israel once more stood alone against the Arab world, restricting Reagan's attempts to build a sweeping consensus against the Soviet Union. The Israeli actions added weight to the charge that Egypt's earlier treaty had been a betrayal of fellow Arab states. It made U.S. mediation of the Lebanese dispute more remote and, by raising the possibility of war with Syria, virtually invited Soviet intervention in the region.

Israel's behavior also threw American domestic politics into turmoil. White House support of Israel would alienate the Arabs and stop the oil flow, but lack of support would alienate the powerful Jewish lobby at home and cost votes. A compromise of sorts was the result. Inside the United Nations the United States joined Iraq in condemning Israel; but the White House did not support sanctions, except for a delayed delivery of seventy-five promised F-16 fighter planes. Even then, this mild rebuke had no effect because the planes were not due to arrive until 1985.

The Reagan administration meanwhile hoped for a Labor party victory in the 1982 elections in Israel, because that group had adopted a moderate position toward peace; but the Labor party lost to the hard-line Likud party and Begin continued as prime minister. To his cabinet he appointed a foreign minister who had resisted the treaty of 1979 with Egypt and a defense minister who, as minister of agriculture, had earlier pushed for rapid Israeli settlement of the West Bank. Begin also placed the minister of the interior in charge of the Palestinian autonomy discussions, which implied that the issue was internal in nature and annexation of the West Bank imminent. Begin's renewal in office elevated the Arab-Israeli problem to prominence again and further damaged the Reagan administration's declining hopes for the anti-Soviet strategic consensus in the

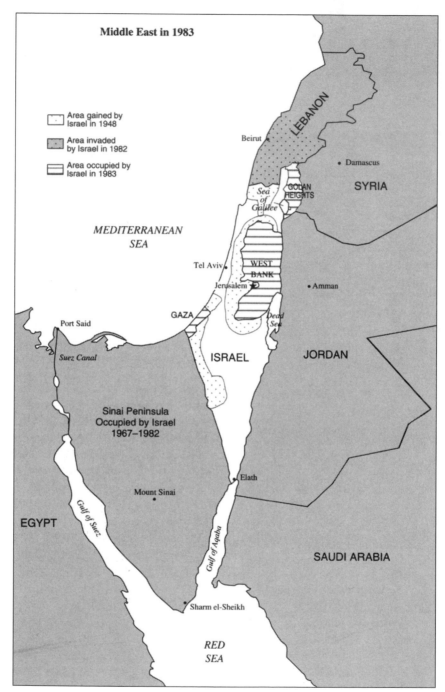

Middle East in 1983

Area gained by
Israel in 1948

Area invaded
by Israel in 1982

Area occupied by
Israel in 1983

LEBANON

Beirut

• Damascus

GOLAN
HEIGHTS

SYRIA

*Sea
of
Galilee*

*MEDITERRANEAN
SEA*

Tel Aviv

WEST
BANK

Jerusalem

• Amman

*Dead
Sea*

Port Said

GAZA

JORDAN

Suez Canal

ISRAEL

Sinai Peninsula
Occupied by Israel
1967–1982

Elath

Mount Sinai
•

Gulf of Suez

Gulf of Aqaba

EGYPT

SAUDI ARABIA

•
Sharm el-Sheikh

*RED
SEA*

Map 27
From ancient times to the present, the Middle East has remained almost
impervious to a peaceful resolution of its many problems.

Middle East. The Arab radicals' position was confirmed, the Palestinians in the West Bank became even more embittered, and the Soviet standing in the Middle East seemed to become stronger in proportion to the United States's diminishing position.

The Middle East remained a steaming cauldron of trouble. The Israelis' attack on the PLO in West Beirut had already led to the deaths of numerous civilians, and when Israel began a steady shelling of the city's PLO camps in August, many Americans demanded that their government renounce the action. The public's mood helped lead to the resignation of Secretary of State Haig, who was openly pro-Israel. Habib meanwhile arranged a compromise in September by which the Israelis ended the barrage in exchange for a PLO evacuation from Beirut to Jordan and Tunisia under American, British, French, and Italian troop protection. PLO leader Yasir Arafat warned that the Israeli army would seize control of Beirut as soon as the PLO and the international force were gone—and he was correct. On September 14, 1982, Muslim terrorists assassinated the recently elected pro-Israel president of Lebanon, Bashir Gemayel of the Christian, or Phalangist, militia. The following day, under the guise of protecting the Muslims from Christian retaliation, Israeli forces violated the truce and occupied the Muslim sector of West Beirut. On September 17 Gemeyel's Christian militia adhered to Israel's urgings to clear out PLO terrorists from the refugee camps and, in a brutal act of vengeance, machine-gunned nearly 800 Palestinian civilians in what became known as the "Sabra-Shatila Massacres." The episode led to the return of U.S. Marines as part of another multinational peacekeeping force.

Suspicion grew that the Begin ministry had been involved in the slaughter. The main responsibility for the massacres, many argued, lay with the extremist Lebanese Christian Phalangists; but these same observers noted that the killings could not have occurred without Israeli connivance. They had taken place in an area under Israel's military control and with

Israeli observation posts nearby. Furthermore, the critics declared, Israeli army officers and government ministers knew about the impending act some thirty-six hours beforehand and had done nothing to stop it. A stormy session followed in the Israeli government, after which a commission of inquiry eventually called for the resignation of the country's fiery defense minister, Ariel Sharon, long-time veteran of Israeli-Arab clashes. Sharon admitted to having permitted Lebanese militia into the camps to clear out Palestinian guerrillas—but, he insisted, only after securing their promise not to harm civilians. Even if Sharon had not actually condoned the killings, he had certainly recognized the danger in sending the Phalangists into the PLO camps in the direct aftermath of Gemayel's death. After a bitter fight inside Israel's highest governing circles, Begin reluctantly accepted an inquiry into the massacres. The judicial commission found Israel "indirectly responsible."

Supported by an angry Jewish community in the United States, the White House stepped up its efforts toward peace by first securing the withdrawal of Israeli military forces from Lebanon. Reagan proposed that the 720,000 Palestinians in the West Bank and Gaza receive self-rule under Jordanian supervision. Begin argued instead for a neutralized Lebanon free of PLO and Syrian involvement, a government dominated by the Christian Phalangists, a Lebanese special force to patrol the country's southern border, the establishment of a buffer zone policed by an international peacekeeping unit, and the right of Israeli forces to enter Lebanon at any time for searches and arrests. The United States joined Lebanon, which was now under shaky Christian control and fearful of alienating its large Arab population, in rejecting Begin's proposals. The White House then attempted to persuade Jordan's King Hussein to represent the Palestinians in the talks. This plan likewise proved unsuccessful. Besides the PLO's opposition to this arrangement, Hussein refused to act without the support of other Arab leaders. In any case his prior stipulations had not been fulfilled: The United States had not convinced Begin either to withdraw his military forces from Lebanon or to halt the spread of Jewish settlements on the West Bank. "If the U.S. cannot push the Israelis out of Lebanon," a baffled Jordanian politician asked, "why should anyone believe it can get them out of the West Bank?"

Time was not on the side of the peace-makers. The West Bank Palestinians warned that further delay would promote Begin's long-range goal of settling 100,000 Jews in the area, effectively annexing Jordan and all of the West Bank. As a Jordanian official warned, "If we do not force the Israelis to negotiate about the West Bank now, they will force us to negotiate over the East Bank later." The Reagan administration called for a freeze on new Israeli settlements in the West Bank, which had already raised the number of Jewish inhabitants in the area from 5000 in 1977 to nearly 30,000 by the summer of 1983. Begin dismissed Reagan's proposal with the remark that "it is as impossible to freeze the settlements as it is to freeze life." The Arabs held President Carter responsible for their troubles because he had failed to insist on a settlements freeze in the Camp David accords. As an Israeli admitted, "Begin started the rapid expansion after Camp David because nowhere does the treaty rule settlements out." With the Middle East talks stalemated, Begin felt no pressure to halt the settlements.

Meanwhile, the situation in Lebanon continued to deteriorate. In mid-April 1983, terrorists blew up a large sector of the U.S. embassy in Beirut, killing more than sixty people (including seventeen Americans) and injuring more than one hundred others also in the building. Although the White House assured the participants that this terrorist act would not interrupt the peace talks over Lebanon, there was little progress, if any. The Israelis and the Lebanese concurred on the need for a security zone in south Lebanon that would be free of Palestinian guerrillas and would safeguard northern Israel from attack. The Israelis, however, wanted their soldiers to

accompany Lebanese patrols and to have military or police powers, whereas the Lebanese approved Israeli participation only in "joint supervisory teams" having no such powers. The Syrians opposed any form of Israeli-Lebanese agreement as an obstruction to their aim of regaining the Golan Heights, taken by Israel in the Six Day War of 1967 and formally annexed in 1981. The Reagan administration feared that the Christian and pro-Israeli Lebanese government would collapse and give way to one having close ties to Iran, Libya, and the Soviet Union. By mid-1983 there remained in Lebanon a dangerous combination of 38,000 Israeli troops and 50,000 Syrian troops, along with perhaps 15,000 PLO commandos—a situation hardly amenable to the control of a small peacekeeping contingent of U.S., British, French, and Italian soldiers.

The multinational force in Lebanon soon became involved in another terrorist crisis. Arab dissidents regarded the Americans as the chief enemy and began pummeling the U.S. quarters at Beirut International Airport. On the Sunday morning of October 23, 1983, a Muslim suicide mission drove a truck laden with dynamite through the barricade and into the U.S. Marines' command center, blowing up the main military barracks and killing 241 sleeping marines. Two miles from the U.S. compound, another explosion a few minutes later killed more than fifty French paratroopers. The president refused to evacuate the remaining military personnel: Their presence, he declared, was "central to our credibility on a global scale." To pull out now would make "others feel confident they can intimidate us and our allies in Lebanon" and encourage the terrorists to "become more bold elsewhere."

But Reagan's hard talk brought no results: The government in Lebanon fell, wiping out its treaty with Israel and leaving Beirut in utter disarray. As the violence intensified among warring factions, the 1600 marines still there found themselves isolated, trapped, and virtually defenseless in the garrison, and in February 1984 the president ordered their withdrawal to nearby U.S. naval vessels. The U.S. retreat sent an alarming message to friends in the region. With the Americans' departure, Lebanese groups joined Syria in expressing interest in peace talks. The following September a more moderate government took over in Israel and directed the withdrawal of its own soldiers from southern Lebanon.

On December 6, 1987, the Palestinians revolted against the Israelis occupying the West Bank and Gaza Strip in an uprising by Arab young men called the "intifada," which had far-reaching effects. The following July, as the Israelis escalated their response to the intifada with a brutal military force that repelled many of the world's observers, Jordan's King Hussein made a surprising move: He withdrew all claims to the West Bank, effectively turning over the disputed area to the Palestinians for a homeland.

Jordan's action placed the initiative in PLO hands. Arafat came under enormous pressure to accept the offer: A refusal would alienate leaders of the intifada in the West Bank and, with Syrian assistance, allow the more extreme wing of the Palestinians to gain control of the PLO. Consequently, in November 1988 he went before the Palestine National Council (PNC) in Algiers and proclaimed the establishment of an independent Palestinian state, a move resting on the UN General Assembly's partition plan of 1947. On the surface, Arafat's two-state plan proved attractive in that it grounded the legitimacy of Palestine in the same UN resolution that had legitimized Israel. But it also meant that he was speaking of the Israel of 1947, which was only one-third of its present size. The resulting "Political Communiqué" (approved overwhelmingly by the PNC) reiterated this point by calling for an international peace conference as provided by UN Security Council Resolution 242, which in 1967 had stipulated Israeli withdrawal from lands occupied in the Six Day War in exchange for secure borders.

Only at first did the Reagan administration staunchly reject the seemingly imminent creation of a Palestinian state. Israel, of course, adamantly refused to negotiate with the PLO

Beirut Rescue, October 23, 1983
A rescue mission at work after a dynamite-filled truck driven by Muslims blew up the main military barracks in Beirut, killing 241 sleeping U.S. Marines. *National Archives, Washington, D.C.*

or to accept boundaries defined before 1967. As the violence spread, Secretary of State Shultz offered a plan in 1988 that rested on the principle of "land for peace" but, not surprisingly, aroused no interest from either Israel or the PLO. When Arafat requested a chance to present his own peace plan before the UN General Assembly in New York, Shultz in late November refused to grant him a visa. Other members of the United Nations, however, were infuriated with Shultz's action and agreed to meet with Arafat in Geneva. There, on December 7, 1988, Arafat renounced terrorism and any intention to interfere with Israel. But critics noted that his apparent change in policy had come with two distinct qualifications: His renunciation of terrorism did not include Palestinian actions inside Israel, and he meant the Israel *before* the Six Day War. Shultz nonetheless regarded these concessions as potentially pathbreaking, and in a move that shocked the world and enraged the Israelis, he agreed to negotiate with the PLO. Talks began in Tunis in mid-December 1988, shortly before Reagan completed his second term in office, and therefore carried over into the administration of his successor.

The ongoing war between Iran and Iraq meanwhile complicated the already tangled situation in the Middle East by threatening to drag in other nations. Long-standing differences between these two Arab states had exploded in an incredibly bloody conflict in 1980 that had imperiled passage through the Persian Gulf and thus affected oil interests all over the world. The Soviets had tried to play both sides by providing Iraq with planes and ammunition while approving Syria's delivery of Soviet arms to Iran. As a result, neither antagonist trusted the Soviet Union. The United States claimed to be neutral, although its relations with Iraq had improved when the state department took that government off the list of countries supporting terrorism and thus permitted the extension of export credits.

Arms sales to the antagonists caused the greatest furor. Although the White House publicly refused to approve the sale of weapons to Iraq, evidence now shows that huge supplies of U.S. arms went to Iraq's military ruler, Saddam Hussein. Indeed, for a time in 1985 and 1986 the Reagan administration also secretly sent arms to Iran until exposure of this policy (the Iran-contra affair, discussed later) unleashed a furious reaction. Americans still resented the hostage crisis of the Carter years, and Iranian-supported terrorists had stirred up more hard feelings by recently kidnapping other Americans in the Middle East, including news correspondents and state department and CIA employees. As the Iranian-Iraqi fighting settled into a bitter war of attrition, the chances for a negotiated settlement became increasingly elusive. The president of Iran during the early part of the Khomeini regime, Abolhassan Banisadr, put it bluntly when he declared from outside Paris that "for us, the war will only end with a gen-

eral embargo on arms deliveries to both belligerents [Iran and Iraq]."

Tensions in the Gulf mounted, however, as the Reagan administration became more deeply involved in the fighting and showed an unmistakable tilt toward Iraq. In May 1987 the United States tried to maintain the flow of commerce by flying its flag on Kuwaiti tankers carrying oil to Japan. U.S. planes then strafed two Iranian oil decks in retaliation for the Iranians' firing missiles at one of these tankers. That same month, however, an Iraqi plane hit the U.S. destroyer *Stark* with two French missiles, killing thirty-seven and drawing vehement White House protests. The Baghdad government responded with an apology and reparations. U.S. assistance to Iraq continued even while the president directed minesweepers and helicopters to protect U.S. vessels in the troubled waters. The following July of 1988 the commander of the USS *Vincennes* erroneously thought he was under attack and fired on what turned out to be a civilian Iranian airliner. All 290 aboard died in the fiery blast. The Reagan administration accepted blame for the mistake and, in a move that did not appeal to an American public still bitter over the long hostage crisis, awarded compensation to the victims.

The heightening threat of a widened war in the Gulf hurried the United Nations's ongoing efforts to secure a cease-fire. In August, barely one month after the *Vincennes* tragedy, the two totally exhausted warring nations laid down their arms, effectually admitting to the existence of a long and ghastly stalemate that had consumed two million lives and inestimable treasure. Iraq had gained a small piece of territory from the fighting, but even that had not changed the fundamental reality: The war had not yielded a victor and thereby intensified the bitterness in the region.

Other problems had surfaced over Libya, which, though not part of the Middle East, bordered Egypt and compounded the region's difficulties by supporting terrorism. In spring 1981 the Reagan administration had accused Libyan ruler Muammar Qaddafi of engineering international terrorism with the help of Soviet money. In May it had ordered his diplomats out of Washington in retaliation for the burning of the U.S. embassy in 1980 and for the dismissal of the U.S. diplomats. The following August 1981, Qaddafi accused U.S. forces on maneuvers in the Mediterranean off Libya's shores of violating his country's territorial waters, and in an ensuing aerial exchange, U.S. jets downed two Libyan planes. Relations worsened by the end of the year when the White House announced that Qaddafi had ordered Libyan terrorists in the United States to assassinate Reagan (a charge never confirmed). In early 1982 the administration (without European allied support) stopped Libyan oil imports into the country and placed an embargo on all goods to Libya. "We have to put Qaddafi in a box and close the lid," Shultz told reporters.

Problems intensified between the United States and Libya. In December 1985 terrorist attacks at the Rome and Vienna airports killed nineteen (including five Americans and one Israeli) and injured 112 others. Responsibility seemed to belong to a Palestinian group based in Libya and openly supported by Qaddafi. Sensing an imminent U.S. attack, he warned that government and Israel that a strike against his country would cause Libyans to take action against Americans "in their own streets" and would lead to the spread of terrorism throughout the Mediterranean area. In early 1986 U.S. naval vessels in the Mediterranean made another show of force off Libya's coast. When Libyan patrol boats approached the Americans, U.S. planes fired on the boats as well as on Libyan military positions ashore.

Then, in April 1986, relations between the countries reached the breaking point. An explosion rocked a West Berlin discotheque, killing one U.S. soldier and a Turkish woman and injuring 230, including dozens of off-duty U.S. soldiers. Suspicions of Libya's involvement in the bombing grew, encouraged by electronic eavesdropping by the United States that revealed Qaddafi's intentions to launch more terrorist attacks. At a news conference

President Reagan denounced the Libyan ruler as the "mad dog of the Middle East."

That same April, the White House (with the support of Britain, Canada, and Israel) retaliated against Libya's alleged complicity in the West Berlin killings by approving a surprise air raid on its capital of Tripoli. Using bases in Britain, thirteen F-111s began a 5600-mile round trip (lengthened by 2400 miles because France and Spain refused to allow the planes to use their air space) and bombed Qaddafi's living quarters and his command and communications center. In less than twelve minutes the planes destroyed several military targets, but they also hit some nonmilitary areas and killed a number of civilians, including one of Qaddafi's children. Although the Arabs and many Europeans denounced the assault, the United States's allies on the continent soon exerted diplomatic pressure on the Libyans, and the terrorist threat eased for a few months. The sense of satisfaction was misplaced, however, because evidence later showed that the Syrians, not Qadaffi, were responsible for the violence in West Berlin.

Time had appeared to stand still in the Middle East. All its problems seemed to be as unsolvable during the 1980s as in the immediate period after World War II. Ancient issues remained, complicated by Cold War rivalries, international terrorism, and the endemic lack of trust.

The Iran-Contra Affair

In an ironic twist, the issues in the Middle East and Central America merged in the 1980s in a zany scheme freighted with illegalities and soon called the Iran-contra affair. Public exposure of the escapade began in October 1986, when the Sandinistas shot down a plane flown by three Americans and carrying materiel to the contras. Curiously, the sole survivor admitted to being a CIA agent. A month afterward, a Lebanese newspaper revealed a White House attempt to secure the freedom of six American hostages in Lebanon taken by Iranian-supported terrorists after 1983 by arranging the sale of arms to Iran through the Israelis. As the story unwound, suspicions grew that the president had become as obsessed with the hostages' fate as had Carter—particularly when news arrived of the torture of the captured CIA station chief in Beirut, William Buckley. Later, when the president asked for Buckley's release in accordance with the delivery of arms to Iran, it became clear that he had died from the torture. Indeed, only a single American won his freedom as a result of all the intricate work put into the Iran-contra plan—clergyman Benjamin Weir.

The president decided to admit to the basics of the plan. To win the freedom of Iran's U.S. hostages in Lebanon, he told shocked Americans, his administration had sent a small number of "defensive weapons" to Iran in an effort to establish contact with "moderates" in Teheran (never named) who might serve as intermediaries in negotiations. He had also wanted to help Iraq win its war with Iran, whose Islamic fundamentalists threatened to spread their anti-American and revolutionary doctrines throughout the Middle East. The White House, he insisted, had broken no laws, agreed to no "ransom" payments, and remained steadfast in its determination not to deal with terrorists. And yet as the secret process unfolded, it became clear that the terrorists had intended to free the hostages one at a time rather than all at once and then had kidnapped three others to replenish their leverage for additional arms. Less than one month later, the White House added a bizarre twist to the story by announcing that money from the arms sales had been deposited in a Swiss bank account earmarked for the contras in Nicaragua. Accusations flew as numerous groups wondered about presidential involvement and drew comparisons with the Watergate scandal. A conspiracy seemed evident—one involving the CIA, nameless arms dealers, and perhaps the White House itself.

By the end of the year, Reagan's foreign policy team was in deep trouble. The previous May 1986, it became clear that national security adviser Robert McFarlane had secretly traveled to Iran to offer military hardware in exchange for assistance in freeing the U.S. hostages in Lebanon. Soon, like the Watergate scandal, the entire story began to unravel, threatening to leave the administration's foreign policy in shambles. The White House had blatantly violated the Boland Amendments in attempting to undermine the Nicaraguan government. McFarlane's successor in December 1985, Admiral John Poindexter, had to resign under presidential pressure: Without congressional knowledge, he had authorized a National Security Council staff member, Vietnam veteran Marine Lieutenant Colonel Oliver North, to oversee the illegal covert operation.

North soon became the focal point of nationwide interest. Not only had he worked with Israel and private arms dealers in sending missiles and other kinds of military materiel to Iran in 1985 and 1986, but he had also collaborated with Panama General Manuel Noriega (later convicted of international drug trafficking) in illegally funneling up to $30 million of war materiel directly to the contras. In addition, North had raised millions of dollars from conservatives at home and had supervised an elaborate system of air and water communications with Central America while arranging the construction of a huge airfield in Costa Rica. Indeed, he had worked under the close supervision of the president's long-time friend, CIA Director William Casey, who had taken the Reagan Doctrine to heart and, with a greatly escalated budget, had carried out all these clandestine Iran-contra actions in willing contravention of the law. Giving in to growing public pressure, Reagan also called for North's resignation, even while heralding him as a "national hero" who deserved to be the subject of a Hollywood movie.

Was the president directly involved in this singular episode? Reagan admitted to knowledge of the arms-for-hostages negotiations but appeared befuddled in declaring that he could not recall when he had made a decision on the matter. Furthermore, he professed surprise at the alleged Iran-contra connection. If not skirting the truth, he at least promoted the growing image of ineptness in office. Secret aid to the contras, of course, was a violation of the congressional prohibition on trafficking in military goods, and assistance in this highly unorthodox piece of foreign policy would have broken his own repeated assurances against dealing with Iranian terrorists. Critics declared that the arms-for-hostages deal was tantamount to blackmail. Numerous observers complained that the hard-nosed Reagan administration had reversed its position on terrorism and negotiated with, of all nations, the detested Iran. Had he not called that government an "outlaw state" dominated by "misfits, Looney Tunes, and squalid criminals"? Still others wondered why White House Chief of Staff Donald Regan, Secretary of Defense Weinberger, and Secretary of State Shultz, who all knew about the arrangement before its public exposure and roundly condemned it, did not stop it. How much did Vice President (and former CIA head) George Bush know? North's diaries and an independent investigation, it later became clear, suggested Bush's awareness of the Iran arms sale. But the big question related to the president himself. Could he have been oblivious to such a far-fetched scheme?

Various investigations turned up many fascinating details about the operation, but nothing that could lead to an indictment of the president for criminal behavior. A Senate Intelligence Committee in December 1986 summoned Poindexter and North, who appealed to the Fifth Amendment in declining to answer questions. The following February a special commission appointed by the president and chaired by former Republican Senator John Tower of Texas reported that the plan had emanated from the machinations of McFarlane, Casey, North, some Israelis, and a single Iranian. The Tower Commission found "no direct evidence" that the president knew of the illegal diversion of funds to the Nicaraguan rebels. In remarkably obtuse language, the commission concluded that Rea-

gan had "a concept of the initiative that was not accurately reflected in the reality of the operation." But its members questioned his defense argument that the weapons transactions were mere diplomatic ventures intended to encourage ties with moderates in the Iranian government. The Tower Commission left nearly all key questions unanswered, thereby turning national attention to a congressional inquiry over television from May through July 1987 that proved reminiscent of the captivating Watergate hearings. The tangled web of intrigue pointed to the White House and was akin to the worst sort of dime novel.

For a brief moment, however, the lengthy congressional testimony seemed to confirm the president's pronouncement of a real hero— Lieutenant Colonel Oliver North—who testified for four days that in the name of justice he had participated in the Iran-contra deal. But North's flirtation with stardom quickly burned out when he admitted to having lied to Congress and to shredding evidence just before justice department agents arrived to seize the obviously incriminating materials. It was later discovered that much of the alleged grassroots support expressed for North through an avalanche of telegrams had been manufactured by deep-pocketed Republicans who used Western Union to advantage.

The Iran-contra scandal thus moved to some still-unknown end without lifting the cloud of suspicion over the president. To avoid criminal prosecution, North suddenly turned on his superiors and unveiled his close ties with Casey and Poindexter. Shortly afterward, Poindexter effectively stifled any further inquiry into the president's role when he informed the committee that he had destroyed the findings of a presidential investigation into the matter. Poindexter then told the congressional committee that he had not shared the plan with the president and took full blame for the operation. The committee agreed with the Tower Commission that McFarlane (who tried to commit suicide under the strain) had received verbal approval from the president to make the arms arrangements with the Israelis and Iran. But no one could establish a contra connection. As for Casey, he died of a brain tumor before the testimonies began. Without hard evidence, the congressional investigation into the executive's role came to a close.

The U.S. judicial system ultimately took over the case. In March 1988 McFarlane pleaded guilty to withholding information from Congress, a misdemeanor, and was sentenced to two years' probation. North was convicted in mid-1989 of giving false information to Congress, a felony, and received a three-year suspended sentence. The following year Poindexter was found guilty of five felonious charges of conspiracy, obstructing congressional inquiries, and lying to Congress. The judge ordered him to prison for six months, making Poindexter the only Iran-contra participant to receive a jail sentence.

While the Iran-contra controversy dominated the news headlines in the United States, the crisis in Central America began to ease as the Latin American states themselves developed a plan of settlement between El Salvador and Nicaragua. In January 1983 Colombia, Mexico, Panama, and Venezuela (the "Contadora group") had met on the island of Contadora off Panama and agreed to work toward convincing the five Central American republics to oppose the further involvement of outside powers and to develop a peace resting on democratic principles. Negotiations between Nicaragua and El Salvador, according to the mediators, were the key to a far-reaching regional settlement. After four years of deliberation, the president of Costa Rica, Oscar Arias Sánchez, offered a settlement in 1987 based on a cease-fire and a general amnesty. Even though Sánchez won the Nobel Peace Prize for his attempt, the White House did not actively support the plan because it provided for continued Sandinista control in Nicaragua while requiring the contras to disband.

Although the crisis had eased, peace in Central America still seemed unattainable. In March 1988 El Salvador and Nicaragua agreed to a truce followed by negotiations aimed at implementing a democratic political process in both countries. The following year, the cancer-stricken Duarte lost the presidential election to the extreme right, making a permanent peace as elusive as ever. The fighting was under way again as Reagan left the presidency.

Other Global Troublespots

In other regions of the world, the Reagan administration attempted to exercise U.S. influence, only to encounter obstacles that were often insurmountable. The problems in the Philippines, Africa, Japan, Haiti, and South Korea all lay beyond U.S. control.

Growing popular unrest in the Philippines provides a striking illustration of the Reagan administration's entanglements in foreign affairs. Hesitating to accept the reality of widespread discontent with long-time ally Ferdinand Marcos, the White House continued to support him out of Cold War considerations. In August 1983 Marcos's chief opponent, Benigno Aquino, was assassinated in the Manila airport as he returned from exile in the United States. That event, carried out by Marcos's supporters, became known to the Filipinos primarily through U.S. and Japanese newscasts recorded on VCRs smuggled into the islands, and it quickly set off a wave of bitter protests against his dictatorial, corrupt, and inept rule. The White House recognized that U.S. economic and strategic interests were in danger. Not only were commercial and financial investments heavy in the islands, but strategic considerations required the United States to hold on to Clark Air Base and the Subic Bay Naval Station—leased from Marcos under terms scheduled to expire in autumn 1991. The White House advised Marcos to institute badly needed reforms in the Philippines; Marcos instead continued his despotic policies and thereby stimulated more protests—including the revival of a Communist insurgency under the label of the Nationalist People's Army.

Facing a now thoroughly alienated public, Marcos sought to regain U.S. faith in his rule by permitting elections in February 1986 that he intended to orchestrate. But the opposition put up the widow of the martyred Aquino, Corazon Aquino, who drew widespread popular support in calling for democratic reforms. Marcos's henchmen engaged in massive and unquestioned fraud to salvage his victory, but the Reagan administration blandly affirmed the fairness and honesty of the outcome as proof of "a strong two-party system now in the islands." It soon had to reverse this ill-advised stance when numerous U.S. observers, including the media, easily exposed the wrongdoing in the midst of ever heightening demonstrations and defections by Marcos's top military leaders. Marcos's refusal to accept the verdict of the elections, it became clear, would doubtless result in a long and bloody civil war injurious to U.S. interests on the islands. His long dictatorial reign had to end.

Reagan found this reality difficult to accept. He had liked Marcos since their first meeting in 1969 and had believed his fabricated story that he and Filipino guerrillas had heroically helped Americans against the Japanese in World War II. Now, in a remarkable turn of events, Reagan relented to the urgings of Shultz and other advisers in asking Marcos by phone to resign and leave the country. By the end of the month, Marcos gave in to U.S. pressure and, transported on a U.S. Air Force plane with his wife Imelda and a cargo of wealth illegally amassed by racketeering and other such activities, arrived in Hawaii to live in exile. The new president of the Philippines was Corazon Aquino.

The Philippines remained a serious concern for the White House that it could not resolve because of its economically driven retrenchment policy in foreign affairs. Aquino received an enthusiastic welcome in the United States when she addressed Congress in September 1986, but she proved unable to stem either the rampant corruption or the Communist insurgency that had spread into almost every one of the country's provinces. In 1990 the Communists even forced the Peace Corps to withdraw after threatening to kidnap its workers. As one Aquino supporter quipped, "Ali Baba Marcos fled, leaving behind the forty thieves." U.S. aid

funds all but dried up, primarily because of its own economic troubles at home. Natural calamities then struck the islands, further obstructing the chances for real change.

There was reason for hope, however. Aquino managed to introduce some political and economic reforms, and in the next election she cast her support for its winner, General Fidel Ramos, who had been one of the early defectors from Marcos. Under Marcos's rule, the Philippines had been a democracy in name only, forcing the White House to break with an ally having no popular base of support. In 1992 the United States went even farther in placing the Philippines more on their own: It implemented a huge reduction in military commitment to Asia that included giving up its two bases in the Philippines after almost a century of control.

Africa posed another major problem that the Reagan administration found impossible to manage. Not only did famine and civil wars threaten to devastate large parts of the huge continent, but Soviet and Cuban soldiers continued to influence events in Angola and Ethiopia while apartheid lay at the heart of increasing racial violence in South Africa. With regard to South Africa, many Americans criticized President Reagan for failing to react strongly enough against the white government's segregationist policies. Instead of calling on American business leaders to "divest" their holdings in South Africa, Reagan argued that the United States lacked sufficient leverage to force a rapid change and supported a calm and business-oriented approach called "constructive engagement." Under this program, he intended to build better diplomatic and economic ties in an effort to influence leaders to alter their racial policies over an extended period of time. In all instances, however, the Reagan administration found itself unable to exert real leadership, largely because these matters lay beyond its control.

Reagan's policies toward Africa were a failure. As most of the 350 American businesses in South Africa rejected divestiture, Congress reacted to public pressure and imposed economic sanctions on that nation in mid-1986—but only after overriding the president's veto. The measure proved effective. Soon more than half of the American firms had pulled out of South Africa. Two and a half years later, in December 1988, pressure eased in Africa when Angola, Cuba, and South Africa agreed to a UN plan supported by both the United States and Soviet Union. Within the next two years, according to terms, Cuban troops would withdraw from Angola, and the last colony in Africa, uranium-rich Namibia (Southwest Africa), would finally become independent of South African rule. Apartheid remained in South Africa, but the white government in Pretoria under President F. W. de Klerk showed signs in early 1990 of relenting to the constant pressure. It ended a thirty-year ban on the highly influential black organization, the African National Congress, and, over worldwide television, released its leader, Nelson Mandela, who had been in prison for twenty-seven years and immediately resumed his political battle against apartheid.

Still another problem raised questions about the effectiveness of Reagan's foreign policy: the ever-growing trade deficit with Japan. The United States maintained military bases in the possessions of its former foe in World War II and considered Japan a valuable ally against Soviet influence in Asia. But Japan had expanded its commercial arm so rapidly that the United States soon confronted the fact that a powerful Cold War supporter had become an even more powerful commercial rival. The reason was simple: The Japanese offered better products at lower prices, which created a highly unfavorable balance of trade for the United States and resulted in a slowed U.S. economy and the loss of jobs.

As the ranks of the unemployed increased in the United States, Americans blamed Japan for much of their troubles. In truth, numerous other factors contributed to this dire economic situation: the higher cost of U.S. goods in foreign markets along with the lower cost of foreign goods in the U.S. market; foreign ownership or control of U.S. industrial and financial assets as well as foreign claims on the national debt; the greatly restricted capacity of Third World peoples to buy U.S. goods because of their own governments' heavy debts, which endangered the Western banking system by putting billions of dollars into possible default. But it was *Japan* that drew the brunt of Americans' anger.

Again, the Reagan administration found itself groping for a policy. As increasing numbers of Americans (many of them speaking for special interest groups) placed pressure on Congress to pass high protective tariffs to keep out Japanese goods, the Tokyo government tried to stem this move in 1985 by announcing limits on certain key exports to the United States (including automobiles) and ensuring reductions in its own tariff barriers. President Reagan did not regard these actions as enough, however, and in 1987 he barred the further entry of selected Japanese goods. The following year Congress passed the Omnibus Trade and Competitiveness Act, which allowed retaliatory tariffs against countries pursuing a program of commercial restrictions. U.S.-Japanese commercial animosity remained a major sore spot as Reagan left the presidency.

The Reagan administration could claim some credit in early 1986 for the demise of other long-time dictators considered "friendly" to the United States. To Congress in March, the president suggested a new direction in foreign policy when he broke from the Kirkpatrick dictum favoring authoritarian over totalitarian regimes and proclaimed that "the American people believe in human rights and oppose tyranny in whatever form, whether of the left or the right." In Haiti, the White House warned Jean-Claude ("Baby Doc") Duvalier not to use force on Haitians demonstrating against his rule, and when it became evident that he had lost control, it facilitated his departure to France. The following year the White House applied the new principles to South Korea, where the military regime was encountering violent protests and, under U.S. pressure, agreed to democratic elections for the presidency. Reagan denied having taken the

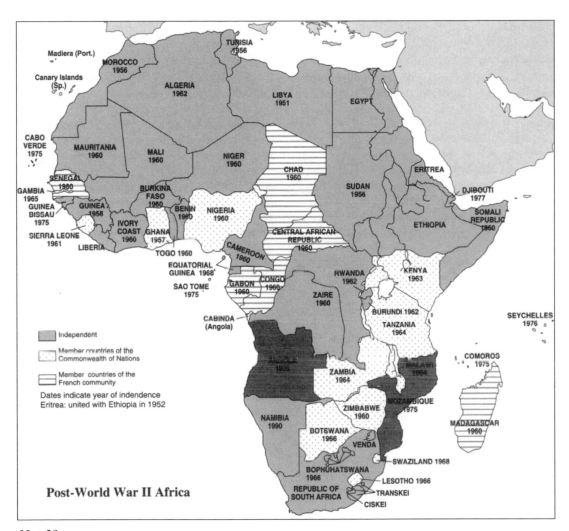

Map 28

Post-World War II Africa

Legend:
- Independent
- Member countries of the Commonwealth of Nations
- Member countries of the French community
- Dates indicate year of indendence
- Eritrea: united with Ethiopia in 1952

Map 28
The emerging war nations in post-colonial Africa made that huge continent a vital part of the new world order.

approach advocated by Carter in Iran and Nicaragua—that of undermining rightist regimes favorably inclined to the United States. The changes in government, Reagan insisted, had emanated from domestic pressures that his administration regarded as too strong to resist.

The White House had found it exceedingly difficult to influence other countries' policies. In the Philippines, the president had at first insisted on maintaining ties with Marcos but had finally relented after popular resistance to his rule had become impossible to contain.

And, in 1986 and 1987, Reagan had no choice but to support popular demands for changes in Haiti and South Korea that led to the ousting of regimes long supported by the White House. Problems in Africa were also beyond the United States's capacity to control or guide. Indeed, the Reagan administration's reluctance to support divestiture in South Africa placed it on the opposite side of a black majority that continued to move ever closer to a dominant leadership role. Finally, the administration failed to accept Japan's growing economic prominence and made no concerted effort to establish a reciprocal trade relationship. The increasingly diffused power structure in the world dictated that no single nation had the resources to determine all events.

Reagan in Perspective

Although the Reagan White House made military and economic efforts to restore the United States's global status and keep the Western alliance intact, it too quickly relegated diplomacy to a military-oriented foreign policy. Indeed, the military-industrial complex was vital to the president's political coalition and guided most of his decision making. Early in his first administration, Reagan publicly and unnecessarily whipped up bitter animosity toward the Soviet Union. He then tied Central America's long-time troubles to the Cold War, globalizing what was essentially a local or regional issue and further intensifying his problems with the Soviet Union and with Congress. His aid to the contras actually prolonged the bloody conflict in Central America. The Middle East remained a tinderbox, also made worse by Reagan's ill-advised attempt to inject the Cold War into ancient indigenous issues by his tragic misjudgment in sending U.S. troops to Lebanon and by his involvement (whether total or partial) in the shadowy Iran-contra affair. Indeed, his administration managed to link two failing policies into one: that in Central America with that in the Middle East.

As Reagan's second term came to a close, the Cold War appeared to be winding down, but even that monumental result was attributable primarily to the efforts of Soviet Leader Mikhail Gorbachev. If Reagan's supporters were correct in declaring that the United States's arms buildup had put such severe strains on the Soviet Union that it had to withdraw from the Cold War and give priority to domestic affairs, they could not deny that such an approach had proved enormously costly: The United States had stirred up nightmarish fears of nuclear destruction and had likewise diminished its own power by lowering taxes

while raising military defense expenditures and thereby tripling the national debt to $3 trillion in 1989 (a third of which was run up in the Reagan years alone). In just four years, the United States had undergone a revolutionary change in position from the world's number one creditor nation in 1981 to the world's largest debtor nation in 1985. Not since World War I had the United States been in debt.

Two years later, in October 1987, fears of another Great Depression developed when the stock market collapsed in response to global financial problems encouraged by Reagan's economic policies. Even as the Soviet Union's drive for *perestroika* and *glasnost* had unleashed powerful nationalist forces both at home and abroad that required diplomatic rather than military solutions, the United States found itself shackled by enormous domestic and foreign problems that necessitated the same sort of reasoned diplomatic response. Gorbachev confronted these issues by looking ahead to a new world order; Reagan looked backward in trying to restore the old.

Still unlearned was the central truth resulting from the nation's Vietnam experience and now underlined by the dramatic thawing of the Cold War: The United States was no longer the chief determinant in international affairs. Among the entities vying for the top role was the revitalized United Nations, which was composed of many peoples and which had slowly but steadily grown in prominence by mediating settlements in numerous troublespots in the world. Perhaps the grand hope of 1945—that the United Nations would become the supreme arbiter of world difficulties—was about to transpire. All these problems and more awaited Reagan's successor, former Vice President George Bush.

Selected Readings

Allin, Dana H. *Cold War Illusions: America, Europe, and Soviet Power, 1969–1989.* 1995.

Ambrose, Stephen E., and Brinkley, Douglas G. *Rise to Globalism: American Foreign Policy since 1938.* 8th ed., 1997.

Armony, Ariel C. *Argentina, the United States, and the Anti-Communist Crusade in Central America, 1977–1984.* 1997.

Armstrong, R., and Shenk, J. *El Salvador: The Face of Revolution.* 1982.

Arnson, Cynthia. *Crossroads: Congress, the President, and Central America, 1976–1993.* 1994.

———. *El Salvador: A Revolution Confronts the United States.* 1982.

Baker, Pauline H. *The United States and South Africa: The Reagan Years.* 1989.

Ball, George W. *Error and Betrayal in Lebanon.* 1984.

Barrett, Lawrence I. *Gambling with History: Ronald Reagan in the White House.* 1983.

Bell, Coral. *The Reagan Paradox: American Foreign Policy in the 1980s.* 1989.

Berman, Larry, ed. *Looking Back on the Reagan Presidency.* 1990.

Berman, William C. *America's Right Turn: From Nixon to Clinton.* 2nd ed., 1998.

Bermann, Karl. *Under the Big Stick: Nicaragua and the United States Since 1848.* 1986.

Bialer, Seweryn, and Mandelbaum, Michael, eds. *Gorbachev's Russia and American Foreign Policy.* 1988.

Bill, James A. *The Eagle and the Lion: The Tragedy of American-Iranian Relations.* 1988.

Blacker, Coit D. *Reluctant Warriors: The United States, the Soviet Union and Arms Control.* 1987.

Bonner, Raymond. *Waltzing with a Dictator: The Marcoses and the Making of American Policy.* 1987.

Bradlee, Ben, Jr. *Guts and Glory: The Rise and Fall of Oliver North.* 1988.

Brands, H. W. *Bound to Empire: The United States and the Philippines.* 1992.

———. *The Devil We Knew: Americans and the Cold War.* 1993.

Buckley, Roger. *U.S.-Japan Alliance Diplomacy, 1945–1990.* 1992.

Burns, E. Bradford. *At War in Nicaragua.* 1987.

Burton, Sandra. *Impossible Dream: The Marcoses, the Aquinos, and the Unfinished Revolution.* 1989.

Cannon, Lou. *President Reagan: The Role of a Lifetime.* 1991.

Chace, James. *Endless War: How We Got Involved in Central America.* 1984.

Cimbala, Stephen J. *The Reagan Defense Program.* 1986.

Cockburn, Leslie. *Out of Control: The Story of the Reagan Administration's Secret War in Nicaragua, the Illegal Arms Pipeline, and the Contra Drug Connection.* 1988.

Cohen, Warren I. *America's Response to China: An Interpretive History of Sino-American Relations.* 2000.

Coker, Christopher. *The United States and South Africa, 1968–1985.* 1986.

Coleman, Kenneth M., and Herring, George C., eds. *The Central American Crisis: Sources of Conflict and the Failure of U.S. Policy.* 1985.

Dallek, Robert. *The American Style of Foreign Policy.* 1983.

———. *Ronald Reagan: The Politics of Symbolism.* 1984.

Dallin, Alexander. *Black Box: KAL 007 and the Superpowers.* 1985.

Didion, Joan. *Salvador.* 1983.

Diederich, Bernard. *Somoza and the Legacy of U.S. Involvement in Central America.* 1981.

Drell, Sidney, et al. *The Reagan Strategic Defense Initiative.* 1985.

Drew, Elizabeth. *Portrait of an Election: The 1980 Presidential Campaign.* 1981.

Duignan, Peter, and Gann, Lewis H. *The United States and Africa: A History.* 1984.

Ehrman, John. *The Rise of Neoconservatism: Intellectuals and Foreign Affairs, 1945–1994.* 1995.

Emerson, Steve. *Secret Warriors: Inside the Covert Military Operations of the Reagan Era.* 1988.

Ewell, Judith. "Barely in the Inner Circle: Jeane Kirkpatrick," in Crapol, Edward P., ed. *Women and American Foreign Policy: Lobbyists, Critics, and Insiders,* pp. 153–71. 1987; 2nd ed., 1992.

Falcoff, Mark, and Royal, Robert. *Crisis and Opportunity: U.S. Policy in Central America and the Caribbean.* 1984.

Fisk, Robert. *Pity the Nation: The Abduction of Lebanon.* 1990.

Friedman, Thomas L. *From Beirut to Jerusalem.* 1989.

Gaddis, John L. *The Long Peace: Inquiries into the History of the Cold War.* 1987.

———. *Russia, the Soviet Union, and the United States: An Interpretive History.* 2nd ed., 1990.

Gardner, Lloyd C. *A Covenant with Power: America and World Order from Wilson to Reagan.* 1984.

Garthoff, Raymond L. *Détente and Confrontation: American-Soviet Relations from Nixon to Reagan.* 1994.

————. *The Great Transition: American-Soviet Relations and the End of the Cold War.* 1994.

Gettleman, Marvin E., et al., eds. *El Salvador: Central America in the New Cold War.* 1981.

Goode, James E. *The United States and Iran: In the Shadow of Musaddiq.* 1997.

Gorbachev, Mikhail. *Perestroika: New Thinking for Our Country and the World.* 1987.

Greenstein, Fred I., ed. *The Reagan Presidency: An Early Assessment.* 1983.

Gutman, Roy. *Banana Diplomacy: The Making of American Policy in Nicaragua, 1981–1987.* 1988.

Haig, Alexander M., Jr. *Caveat: Realism, Reagan, and Foreign Policy.* 1984.

Harding, Harry. *A Fragile Relationship: The United States and China since 1972.* 1992.

Haslam, Jonathan. *The Soviet Union and the Politics of Nuclear Weapons in Europe, 1969–87.* 1990.

Hersh, Seymour M. *"The Target Is Destroyed": What Really Happened to Flight 007 and What America Knew About It.* 1986.

Hull, Richard W. *American Enterprise in South Africa: Historical Dimensions of Engagement and Disengagement.* 1990.

Hunt, Michael H. *Ideology and U.S. Foreign Policy.* 1987.

Hyland, William. *Mortal Rivals: Superpower Relations from Nixon to Reagan.* 1987.

Jabber, Paul. *Not By War Alone: Security and Arms Control in the Middle East.* 1981.

Jentleson, Bruce. *Pipeline Politics.* 1986.

Johnson, Haynes. *Sleepwalking Through History: America in the Reagan Years.* 1991.

Karnow, Staley. *In Our Image: America's Empire in the Philippines.* 1989.

Kenworthy, Eldon. *America/Américas: Myth in the Making of U.S. Policy Toward Latin America.* 1995.

Kirkpatrick, Jeane J. *Dictatorship and Double Standards.* 1982.

Klare, Michael T., and Arnson, Cynthia. *Supplying Suppression: U.S. Support for Authoritarian Regimes Abroad.* 1981.

Kolko, Gabriel. *Confronting the Third World.* 1988.

LaFeber, Walter. *America, Russia, and the Cold War, 1945–1996.* 8th ed., 1997.

————. *The Clash: A History of U.S.-Japan Relations.* 1997.

————. *Inevitable Revolutions: The United States in Central America.* 1989.

Lake, Anthony. *Somoza Falling, The Nicaraguan Dilemma: A Portrait of Washington at Work.* 1989.

Laqueur, Walter. *The Age of Terrorism.* 1987.

Ledeen, Michael A. *Perilous Statecraft: An Insider's Account of the Iran-Contra Affair.* 1988.

LeoGrande, William M. *Our Own Backyard: The United States in Central America, 1977–1992.* 1998.

Love, Janice. *The U.S. Anti-Apartheid Movement: Local Activism in Global Politics.* 1985.

Lowenthal, Abraham F. *Partners in Conflict: The U.S. and Latin America.* 1987.

Mann, Jim. *About Face: A History of America's Curious Relationship with China from Nixon to Clinton.* 1999.

Martin, David C., and Walcott, John. *Best Laid Plans: The Inside Story of America's War Against Terrorism.* 1988.

Massie, Robert. *Loosing the Bonds: The United States and South Africa in the Apartheid Years.* 1997.

Mayer, Jane, and McManus, Doyle. *Landslide: The Unmaking of the President, 1984–1988.* 1988.

Melanson, Richard A. *American Foreign Policy Since the Vietnam War: The Search for Consensus from Nixon to Clinton.* 2000.

————, ed. *Neither Cold War nor Détente? Soviet-American Relations in the 1980s.* 1982.

Menges, Constantine C. *Inside the National Security Council: The True Story of the Making and Unmaking of Reagan's Foreign Policy.* 1988.

Meredith, Martin. *In the Name of Apartheid: South Africa in the Postwar Period.* 1988.

Montgomery, Tommie S. *Revolution in El Salvador.* 1982.

Morley, Morris. *Imperial State and Revolution.* 1987.

Morris, Roger. *Haig: The General's Progress.* 1982.

Mower, A. Glenn. *Human Rights and American Foreign Policy: The Carter and Reagan Experiences.* 1987.

Oberdorfer, Don. *From the Cold War to a New Era: The United States and the Soviet Union, 1983–1991.* 1998.

————. *The Turn: From the Cold War to a New Era. The United States and the Soviet Union, 1983–1990.* 1991.

Olson, Robert. *U.S. Foreign Policy and the New International Economic Order.* 1981.

Oye, Kenneth A., Lieber, Robert J., and Rothchild, Donald, eds. *Eagle Resurgent? The Reagan Era in American Foreign Policy.* 1987.

Pastor, Robert A. *Condemned to Repetition.* 1987.

Peretz, Don. *Intifada: The Palestinian Uprising.* 1990.

Pérez, Louis A., Jr. *Cuba and the United States: Ties of Singular Intimacy.* 1997.

Pierre, Andrew J. *The Global Politics of Arms Sales.* 1982.

Prados, John. *Presidents' Secret Wars: CIA Pentagon Covert Operations from World War II through the Persian Gulf.* 1996.

Prestowitz, Clyde V., Jr. *Trading Places: How We Are Giving Our Future to Japan and How to Reclaim It.* 1989.

Pryce-Jones, David. *The Closed Circle: An Interpretation of the Arabs.* 1989.

Raat, W. Dirk. *Mexico and the United States: Ambivalent Vistas.* 1996.

Reagan, Ronald. *Speaking My Mind.* 1989.

Rubin, Barry. *Secrets of State: The State Department and the Struggle over U.S. Foreign Policy.* 1985.

Sayigh, Yezid. *Armed Struggle and the Search for State: The Palestinian National Movement, 1949–1993.* 1997.

Schell, Jonathan. *The Fate of the Earth.* 1982.

Schoutz, Lars. *Beneath the United States: A History of U.S. Policy Toward Latin America.* 1998.

———. *National Security and U.S. Policy toward Latin America.* 1987.

Schulzinger, Robert D. *The Wise Men of Foreign Affairs: The History of the Council on Foreign Relations.* 1984.

Scranton, Margaret E. *The Noriega Years: U.S.-Panamanian Relations, 1981–1990.* 1991.

Shafer, Michael D. *Deadly Paradigms: The Failure of U.S. Counterinsurgency Policy.* 1988.

Shipler, David K. *Arab and Jew: Wounded Spirits in a Promised Land.* 1986.

Shultz, George P. *Turmoil and Triumph: My Years as Secretary of State.* 1993.

Sick, Gary. *October Surprise: America's Hostages in Iran and the Election of Ronald Reagan.* 1991.

Sklar, Holly. *Washington's War on Nicaragua.* 1988.

Smith, Gaddis. *The Last Years of the Monroe Doctrine, 1945–1993.* 1994.

Spanier, John W. *American Foreign Policy Since World War II.* 14th ed., 1998.

Spiegel, Steven L. *The Other Arab-Israeli Conflict: Making America's Middle East Policy, from Truman to Reagan.* 1985.

Stares, Paul B. *The Militarization of Space: U.S. Policy, 1945–1984.* 1985.

———. *Space and National Security.* 1987.

Stevenson, Richard W. *The Rise and Fall of Détente: Relaxations of Tensions in US-Soviet Relations, 1953–84.* 1985.

Talbott, Strobe. *Deadly Gambits: The Reagan Administration and the Stalemate in Nuclear Arms Control.* 1984.

———. *The Master of the Game: Paul Nitze and the Nuclear Peace.* 1988.

———. *The Russians and Reagan.* 1984.

Ulam, Adam B. *The Communists: The Story of Power and Lost Illusions, 1948–1991.* 1992.

Van Crefeld, Martin. *Nuclear Proliferation and the Future of Conflict.* 1993.

Vanderlaan, Mary B. *Revolution and Foreign Policy in Nicaragua.* 1986.

Walker, Thomas W. *Nicaragua: The Land of Sandino.* 1982.

———. *Revolution and Counterrevolution in Nicaragua, 1977–1989.* 1990.

———, ed. *Reagan versus the Sandinistas.* 1987.

Weinberger, Caspar. *Fighting for Peace: Seven Critical Years in the Pentagon.* 1990.

Wills, Garry. *Reagan's America: Innocents at Home.* 1987.

Woodward, Bob. *Veil: The Secret Wars of the CIA, 1981–1987.* 1987.

CHAPTER 17

The End of the Cold War...
and Afterward, 1989–

Overview

When Vice President George Bush became president in January 1989, he showed little understanding of the ongoing revolutionary events that finally brought the Cold War to a close. A staunch Cold Warrior, he had served as a naval pilot in World War II before becoming involved in Texas oil and politics and then arriving in Washington as a congressional representative in 1968. After losing a bid for the Senate, his fortunes changed during the 1970s as he served as ambassador to the United Nations, U.S. representative to China, and director of the CIA before becoming vice president in 1981. Enormous changes in the Cold War atmosphere had begun during the latter half of the Reagan presidency when Mikhail Gorbachev launched his reform programs of *perestroika* and *glasnost* while pursuing massive arms reductions, drastic cutbacks in his own conventional forces, and surprising withdrawals from foreign commitments. But skeptics wondered if this were not another Soviet trick designed to relax the United States's guard, or, if true, whether Gorbachev's successors would (or could) continue such a liberal program. The Bush strategy emerged from an internal policy review following the Malta Summit of December 1989. In the words of U.S. Ambassador to the Soviet Union Jack Matlock, "Our marching orders are clear: Don't do something, stand there!" The Soviets dubbed it the *pauza*—the pause.

Given the long and bitter history of the Cold War, the new president initially adopted a standoffish policy toward these dramatic events. Whether he simply failed to fathom their importance or shrewdly pursued a careful if not dubious reaction, he continued the Reagan administration's emphasis on national defense and chose not to encourage or exploit these world-shaking events by taking any diplomatic or economic initiative. Still, an unmistakable pattern in executive leadership soon emerged. Even as the United States sank deeper into a major economic recession, Bush preferred to let problems take care of themselves while often denying that they existed. In one of the most momentous events of the twentieth century—the approaching end of the Cold War—Bush sat quietly by as Gorbachev almost single-handedly wound down international tensions in a desperate effort to save the remnants of a once proud Soviet empire.

The rapidly changing global situation dictated a flexible U.S. approach to foreign affairs, but Bush continued his predecessor's rigid Cold War policy, leaving little room for adjustments to changing realities. Longtime friend

James Baker became secretary of state. A master politician, Baker knew little about foreign policy, which meant that Bush would take the lead. Most important, Bush intended to seek a Soviet détente while supporting the U.S. military buildup and the Strategic Defense Initiative. He planned to tighten the NATO alliance, continue the fight against communism in Central America, press for peace in the Middle East, maintain the gradualist approach in dealing with apartheid in South Africa, seek commercial accommodations with Japan, strive for better relations with China, and wage war on the escalating international drug trade. Despite a vastly changing world, the Bush administration intended to perpetuate a military-oriented foreign policy that aimed at stemming a shrinking Soviet influence. Through military dominance the United States would take its accustomed place as the world's leader.

The Bush administration thus stood as a passive observer of nearly all the epochal developments that ended the Cold War era. Despite landmark changes in the Soviet Union and Eastern Europe, the president formulated no comprehensive strategy for dealing with a nascent post–Cold War period. Instead, he exercised a cautious wait-and-see policy that reflected the weakened U.S. economic situation as much as an effort to restrict his country's involvement in these historic events. The United States was the world's leading debtor nation, and the new president had pledged throughout the campaign that he and his Republican party would never raise taxes. He also had prided himself as unemotional and extremely cautious, hesitant to take any action until events had assumed a meaningful form. As the world stumbled toward a new order, the United States failed to exert effective leadership.

Disintegration of the Soviet Union and the End of the Cold War

Developments inside the Soviet Union continued to assume world-shattering proportions. Shortly after Bush became president, democratic elections took place in the Soviet Union

for the first time since the Russian Revolution of 1917. Most surprising to Gorbachev and outside observers, the Communist party lost a large number of seats in the national assembly. Gorbachev's call for *perestroika* had not revived the economy and had thoroughly discredited his cohort. Despite his confidence that the Soviet people would work with his party in instituting economic reform, they broke with the long-hated and increasingly impotent Communist regime and moved toward a decentralized government and a free-market economy.

The fallout from *perestroika* thus went farther than Gorbachev could have anticipated. It unleashed powerful forces of nationalism inside the sprawling Soviet empire that threatened to tear it apart and leave behind a multitude of ethnic, racial, and religious disputes. In the far northwest, the three Baltic States of Estonia, Latvia, and Lithuania sought to regain their independence, lost a half-century before; and in the oil-rich area lying south between the Black and Caspian seas, ancient animosities between Muslims in Azerbaijan and Christians in Armenia exploded in a bitter conflict. Gorbachev reacted only mildly to events along the Baltic, but when Azerbaijan threatened to secede from the Soviet Union and fall under the control of the popular front, he sent 30,000 soldiers to restore order.

In truth, President Bush could have done little to affect these epoch-making events. The dire economic situation in the United States precluded substantial assistance to the great masses of people seeking change. Besides, these unstable areas lay within the Soviet sphere of influence. Bush and his advisers studied the developments inside the Soviet Union and declared months afterward that the United States had adopted a "status-quo plus" approach. Whatever the administration's policymakers meant by that innocuous term, they intended primarily to watch. In the meantime, the president claimed victory in the Cold War and attributed that success to the containment strategy. Gorbachev, Bush asserted, must now cut back Soviet influence in Eastern Europe and the Third World as well.

To the president's surprise, Gorbachev abandoned his country's interventionist policy. The tottering Communist regime in Poland received no military assistance from Moscow and had to legalize Solidarity under Lech Walesa's leadership. Soon afterward, Solidarity demanded and received a primary leadership role in Warsaw, adding more weight to the Nobel Peace Prize won by Walesa in 1981 for bringing peaceful reform to his country. Then, in an astonishing move, Gorbachev in July 1989 renounced the right of any nation to interfere with the sovereignty of another, thus laying to rest the roundly despised Brezhnev Doctrine that had led to the military subjugation of Czechoslovakia and other East European countries.

Gorbachev's restraint astounded observers in both East and West. The Hungarian government, long regarded as the most liberal of those behind the Iron Curtain, tore down the 150 miles of barbed wire that had comprised its border with Austria. Almost immediately, thousands of East Germans looking for family and loved ones flocked into Hungary and then into Austria before relocating in West Germany. Soon afterward, a massive popular uprising in Czechoslovakia (with participants chanting "We are not like them" in the streets of Prague) likewise brought an end to Communist control and culminated in the election of playwright Vaclav Havel as president. For a time the Communist parties in Bulgaria and Rumania held on to power only by changing their names in the first democratic elections after the Soviet collapse and assuring their reform-minded people that they too had reformed. Only in Rumania did violence erupt. The aged tyrant Nicolae Ceaucescu was the only Communist ruler in Eastern Europe to resist the reformers with military force; the effort failed, albeit just barely, and he and his wife were both executed following a quick trial.

On November 9, 1989, the East German government set off the most dramatic series of events of all when it admitted to the reality of the mass exodus already under way by announcing the right of its people to leave the country. Within a week, on November 15, East German workers began tearing down the Berlin Wall, the ugly twelve-foot-tall concrete and barbed wire barrier that had been the ultimate symbol of Soviet oppression for twenty-eight years. More than any single act, the human demolition of this tangible reminder of the dark past marked the end of the Cold War.

In the face of such great changes, Bush maintained a course of what he termed "prudence," which his detractors derisively called "timidity." Critics argued that he should have seized the moment to work closely with Gorbachev in establishing good post–Cold War relations by extending economic aid to the crumbling Soviet empire. At the least, many declared, he could have granted most-favored-nation status to the Soviet Union and thereby given its commerce an advantage in the U.S. market. Did not the administration permit this same privilege to China, even after its Communist regime had brutally unleashed tanks and soldiers against students in Beijing (discussed later) who had peacefully demonstrated for freedom that previous June? The president was correct in declaring that the nation's containment policy had encouraged the Soviet demise, but, unfortunately for the White House in 1989, the architect of that policy, George F. Kennan, had not provided guidelines for a U.S. response should those sweeping changes actually occur.

Bush realized that any sort of aid package to the Soviet Union would have been problematic. The United States had its own economic troubles, and Americans would be reluctant to help a longtime distrusted empire that still adhered to Communist principles. Moreover, Bush could not have known whether the Soviet Union would survive the rapidly spreading political assault at home. Even if a decentralized and much-weakened Soviet Union remained in the aftermath, its deep structural changes would have international repercussions that did not necessarily benefit the United States. The imminent collapse of the Soviet threat to European security meant that NATO would lose its chief reason for being; indeed, the European nations had already begun to work out their own problems. They had established the European Community to advance economic development through a single market, and they had turned more to an organization founded in Helsinki in 1975 to deal with political and human rights issues, the Conference on Security and Cooperation in Europe (CSCE). The United States was only one of thirty-five CSCE participants and did not wield a deciding influence.

If the times had changed, the Bush administration refused to change with them. In a crucial period that required new approaches to a world no longer burdened by the Cold War, Bush continued Ronald Reagan's example of working with Gorbachev toward a greater nuclear arms reduction. On December 2 and 4, 1989, the two heads of state met on an informal basis off Malta in the Mediterranean, where they agreed to work toward limitations on both their nuclear stores and conventional weaponry and to integrate the Soviet Union into the global economy. But the president, on his return to Washington, rejected proposals to reduce the long-standing twenty-four-hour airborne defense system and to cut the defense budget for 1990. Furthermore, he intended to maintain the United States's heavy military presence in Germany. When the White House should have been establishing good relations with the Soviet Union, according to Kennan's testimony before the Senate Foreign Relations Committee in 1989, it was instead maintaining the U.S. military arsenal for a possible confrontation with a Red Army that was beating a fast retreat in Eastern Europe.

The chief European issue throughout the Cold War—the status of Germany—now emerged as the chief point of divisiveness between Bush and Gorbachev. Bush was at first hesitant to support reunification until it became clear that he could do nothing to stop it. He then did an about-face to argue that failing to support Germany's unification could force it to become neutral in the East-West struggle, thereby endangering continental stability. A

unified Germany must be part of both NATO and the European Community. Gorbachev, however, joined France and Britain in staunchly opposing German reunification. If his efforts failed, Gorbachev preferred a neutral Germany rather than one allied with NATO. He also sought limitations on the size of Germany's army, a ban on its acquisition of nuclear arms, its acceptance of the boundary fronting Poland that the victorious powers had drawn in 1945 (farther west of the Soviet Union), and a continued U.S. military presence in Europe that would prevent the rise of another militarized German nation. In all these aspects, however, neither superpower had the capacity to determine the outcome. Gorbachev finally accepted a reunited Germany in NATO—a decision facilitated by Germany's extending $8 billion of credit to the Soviet Union.

In February 1990 the revolutionary changes inside the Soviet Union brought the most stunning news of all: The Communist party lost control of the government that it had held since 1917. Opposition parties won a series of elections in the spring that included the installation of Gorbachev's onetime protégé turned bitter political rival, Boris Yeltsin, as the leader of the Russian Federation. As the largest Soviet republic, Russia made up two-thirds of the former Soviet Union in size and nearly one-half of its people and was rich in oil and other natural resources. Gorbachev had regarded Yeltsin, who had risen from abject poverty, as too strongly reformist and had effectively undermined his influence in the Communist party by a Stalinist-type purge just three years earlier. But Yeltsin had bounced back as a virtual martyr of *perestroika*, demanding a complete restructuring of the country and openly brandishing a popular mandate that Gorbachev himself could not claim: Gorbachev's presidential position had resulted primarily from the closed-door maneuverings of Communist party leaders in the Supreme Soviet. Gorbachev now stood in the unenviable position of having to balance the demands of reformers and embittered Communist party members. As the hard-liners used military force to prevent Lithuania from leaving the Soviet Union, he realized that further moves toward reform could spark even stronger actions against dissidents.

Bush continued to support Gorbachev, even while Yeltsin's steadily growing influence became evident. The president felt a personal tie with the Soviet leader that was matched only by his equally strong personal distaste for Yeltsin. More important, Yeltsin's reformist ideas tended to encourage the further breakup of the Soviet Union, which ensured uncertainty and confusion. Gorbachev was a known quantity, popular with Americans and a recipient of the Nobel Peace Prize in 1990 for his work in ending the Cold War. White House stories at first sharply criticized Yeltsin and then, in another remarkable reversal of tactics, the president hosted the Russian challenger in an effort to convince him of the wisdom of developing close ties with Gorbachev. To enhance Gorbachev's image, Bush cut back on the United States's nuclear expenditures and placements of its arsenal and then cooperated with him in a mutual reduction of nuclear and conventional weaponry on the European continent in 1991.

Bush's decision to stay with Gorbachev turned out to be a mistake. While the United States was deeply involved in peace negotiations ending its Gulf War with Iraq in 1991 (discussed later), Soviet hard-liners rose in rebellion against Gorbachev, placing him under house arrest and clamping down on the country's people and news media. Military officers had long been angry at Gorbachev for doing nothing to deter the surrender of Eastern Europe and reunification of Germany and thereby giving up all they had won in World War II. Then, in the Gulf War, Gorbachev had infuriated Soviet military officers by working closely with Bush against an Iraqi force that they had advised and supplied. Their disgust with the recent turn of events even grew into a suspicion that their leader intended to tie the Soviet Union to the United States. When Gorbachev agreed with nine of the fifteen Soviet republics to establish a confederation

that decentralized authority by guaranteeing sovereignty to each member, eight disgruntled civilian and military leaders decided to take over the government on the day before the treaty-signing proceedings, which were scheduled for August 20, 1991.

The August 19 coup only at first appeared to be a huge success. After seizing Gorbachev, the military turned on Yeltsin and his Russian colleagues, who were in a building close to the Kremlin. But Yeltsin's group proclaimed support for Gorbachev's legitimacy and refused to capitulate to the old guard. By that time thousands of Yeltsin's supporters had gathered outside the building, forcing the military into making the hard decision of whether to launch an assault. The army decided not to do so. At that point the coup attempt fell apart, the victim not only of diminishing numbers and aging ideas but also of liquor: Several leaders were intoxicated. Gorbachev, however, paid a heavy price for clinging to office. Shortly after arriving on the scene, he declared victory over the coup when he found that seven of its leaders were under arrest and that the eighth had committed suicide. But the crisis only *seemed* to have passed. Observers now questioned Gorbachev's judgment. It was he, after all, who had placed these same traitorous men in top-level positions. More important, Gorbachev faced a country that had taken on a radically different political complexion—one no longer supportive of the Communist party and ideology.

Yeltsin suddenly emerged as the stronger of the two men and drew widespread support as he purged the country of Communist influence. Down came statues of Lenin and other Communist patriarchs, and up went a new name for Leningrad—once again St. Petersburg, in honor of Czar Peter the Great of pre-Revolutionary days. In a dramatic move that came too late to stop Yeltsin's acquisition of power, Gorbachev resigned from the Communist party and worked toward abolishing its once dominant Central Committee. In December, however, Yeltsin led the creation of the Commonwealth of Independent States (CIS), which allied his Russian Federation with the Ukraine and Belarus (formerly Byelorussia). Before the month was over, the CIS counted eleven former Soviet republics among its membership, leaving outside the new organization only the three Baltic States (who remained insistent on their own independence) and Georgia (dominated by hard-liners and beset by civil war).

On Christmas Day 1991, the red flag with hammer and sickle came down from the Kremlin, signaling the death of the Soviet Union. Gorbachev was president of a once-powerful nation that no longer existed. That same day he presided over its interment when he resigned his position over nationwide television. As a final stamp of legitimacy, Russia replaced the Soviet Union as one of the five permanent members of the UN Security Council. The revolution set off by Gorbachev's reform programs had taken the path of so many other upheavals in the past: It consumed its founder en route to greater changes than the founder had originally envisioned.

By now, in early 1992, the direction of European events had become clearer, but the Bush administration still failed to exert leadership. Yeltsin visited the White House in February, where he joined the president in pronouncing an end to the Cold War and promising to work toward more arms reductions. But when the Russian leader asked for economic assistance, Bush offered no encouragement to what many analysts hailed as burgeoning liberal and democratic tendencies. He did not suggest either high-profile help in the form of technical assistance and advice or an exchange program for training Russians in the many skills needed to establish a democratic political system and free-market economy. Yeltsin went away empty-handed but nonetheless pushed for liberal market reforms at home. The Russian economy, however, continued to stumble in the face of resistance from conservatives, national and ethnic divisions within the CIS, an endemic poverty that pervaded one-third of the Russian people, and threats of massive starvation during the exceptionally brutal winter of 1991–1992 that only a U.S.–West European airlift prevented. As Bush completed his term in office, he remained determined to establish his country's primacy in what a classified document secured from the Pentagon called a "one-superpower world."

East Asia

As these events were under way in Europe, Bush had to deal with a host of issues regarding East Asia. While attending the funeral of the aged Emperor Hirohito in January 1989 the new president urged Japan's leaders to work toward improving commercial relations with the United States. Almost half of the U.S. trade deficit came from a trade imbalance with Japan, which had enabled its businesses to accumulate huge stocks of American dollars and buy all types of holdings in the United States. The Bush administration had to handle the growing economic problems with Japan with great care: The United States considered it vital to maintain more than 50,000 military personnel in Japan; the Japanese had assumed a larger share of defense expenditures and needed encouragement to continue doing so; and they were extending welcome aid to needy countries. In South Korea, where nationalist feeling had focused on reducing the U.S. military presence, Bush intended to maintain the 40,000 American personnel while working with the Seoul government to establish a better commercial relationship that had tipped heavily in South Korea's favor. And in North Korea, the White House became especially concerned that the Communist regime there would develop nuclear weaponry and threaten Japan and the entire region.

Rapidly escalating unrest inside China likewise caused serious concern for the Bush administration. The president had once served as the U.S. diplomat to that country and still had warm relations with its leaders. During a visit to Beijing in early 1989, he emphasized the need to expand commercial relations and came back to assure Americans that an approaching Sino-Soviet summit would not endanger U.S. interests. But the ruling Communist regime in

Beijing had recently countered a Tibetan move for independence by imposing martial law in an effort to halt the growing violence. When the Senate in Washington passed a resolution condemning this crackdown, the Chinese snapped back that their internal affairs were not subject to U.S. scrutiny.

Then, in the spring of 1989, students' demands for an open and democratic society in China led to huge demonstrations in Beijing's Tiananmen Square that even drew the support of numerous Communist party leaders. At first the government outlawed the public protests, but when the students ignored the edict and boycotted classes, police swarmed into the square to break up the crowd. The move succeeded only in swelling the number of participants to more than 200,000. By the time Gorbachev arrived on May 15 to begin a scheduled summit meeting with Communist leader Deng Xiaoping, the students counted among their supporters a large contingent of workers, intellectuals, and government employees that skyrocketed the total to well over one million. As the demonstrators chanted and marched within sight of the huge picture of Mao Zedong, they carried signs hailing Gorbachev as a pioneer of reform whose example might convert Communist China to democracy.

But conservative Chinese leaders staunchly opposed democracy—particularly when an outsider, Gorbachev, loomed as inspirational leader. Had he not termed the uprising a necessary part of a "painful but healthy" process pointing to democracy? Furthermore, the timing of the protests proved embarrassing: Television crews from all over the world were on hand to cover the summit and were conveniently in place to broadcast the demonstrations. Deng had witnessed the national chaos caused by the Cultural Revolution just two decades earlier and regarded the students' demands as injurious to governmental order. On May 19 his regime imposed martial law and attempted to halt live telecasts of the protests. That move stirred up more resistance. The next day, soldiers and tanks moved into Tiananmen Square to seize control, but the demonstrators

had clogged the streets and refused to move. Deng did not hesitate. On June 3 his military forces fired machine guns into the crowd, inflicting thousands of casualties. The Communist regime then attempted to cover up the number hurt and killed while engaging in a round of arrests and executions, authorizing government purges of those seeking reform, and holding indoctrination sessions for students who had supported what Deng harshly denounced as "bourgeois liberalization."

Television coverage, however, had exposed the Beijing government's oppressive policies and inflamed world opinion. The United States joined other nations, both Communist and non-Communist, in condemning China's brutal actions. President Bush publicly criticized the use of force against what television cameras showed as nonviolent demonstrations for democracy. Two days later, on June 5, he stopped the sale of military goods to China and within a week declared that the United States would not consider reestablishing good relations until Beijing's leaders acknowledged "the validity of the prodemocracy movement." On June 20 the White House effectually broke relations with China by ordering a halt to governmental contacts.

In a short time, however, the priorities of power politics overruled human rights considerations and Bush retracted his punitive actions. That July, he secretly directed his national security adviser, Brent Scowcroft, to meet with China's leaders in Beijing and, in effect, restore relations. When this surreptitious move was exposed months afterward, Americans in both political parties became infuriated. Bush then vetoed a congressional bill that would have extended the visas for about 40,000 Chinese students who had supported the prodemocracy movement and now feared punishment on their return to China. Soon afterward, Bush lifted the ban on weapons sales and approved loans to businesses dealing with China, thereby canceling a congressional prohibition against such practices. In that December of 1989, Scowcroft returned to Beijing, this time in a highly publicized mission to demonstrate U.S. ties. The administration even maintained China's most-favored-nation relationship—a commercial right not granted to the Soviets.

The Bush administration was convinced that its new policies were correct. Three decades of isolating China had not brought democratic reform after the Communist takeover in 1949; there was no reason to think that such an approach would work now. A punitive policy, according to the White House, would thoroughly alienate those in control and undermine U.S. interests in nuclear nonproliferation and the future of Asia. Early in 1990, China ended martial law in Beijing, drawing skepticism from most Americans but praise from Bush's supporters as the calculated result of his careful policy. A fair analysis, however, reveals that the White House once again pursued an uncertain course in foreign affairs, adopting one position before reversing itself and setting out on another. Whether prudence or indecision, such a waffling approach did little to assure allies of resolute U.S. leadership.

Latin America

The Bush administration also had to conduct relations with Latin America, where poverty remained the dominant reality and caused many problems that spilled over into neighboring countries. Many Latin Americans migrated northward, where they hoped to circumvent U.S. immigration laws and find employment above the Rio Grande. Others participated in the enormously profitable narcotics trade, prompting the Bush administration to send troops to help the governments in Colombia, Bolivia, and Peru combat powerful drug cartels that were producing and selling cocaine and crack. In addition, the United States tried to cut off the growing importation of marijuana and heroin from Mexico. When Americans complained that Mexico had become a virtual conduit for narcotics into their country, that government bitterly charged that it was U.S. demand and not Mexican supply that prolonged the problem.

Indeed, huge supplies of heroin came into the United States from the Middle East. Although various governments' efforts to halt the international drug traffic had led to scattered successes, they had been unable to destroy either its sources or its demand.

In Central America, the Bush administration boldly broke with its predecessor's policies by lifting the United States's heavy hand in that region and thereby encouraging an end to the long struggle between Nicaragua and El Salvador. Secretary Baker drew on the ideas expressed in the Arias peace plan of 1987 by halting U.S. assistance to the contras and urging the Sandinistas to permit free elections in February 1990. Then, with Soviet cooperation, he intended to put pressure on the Salvadoran government to work out its differences with the leftist rebels. The key to success was Nicaragua. Baker felt confident that its people would turn out the Sandinistas—a belief encouraged by Gorbachev's secret assurances that he would stop military assistance to Nicaragua and put pressure on Daniel Ortega to accept the popular verdict.

The Bush administration's diplomacy led to some measure of success. In the elections of early 1990 that former President Jimmy Carter and other international observers certified as honest, Ortega and the Sandinistas suffered a crushing defeat. Eleven years of incompetent rule by the Sandinistas had combined with sustained economic hardship throughout Nicaragua to account for this result. The United States's economic embargo on Nicaragua had further devastated its economy and forced Ortega into a retrenchment program that had cut the country's budget more than forty percent and left thousands of government workers unemployed. Ironically, the winner was Violeta Chamorro, the widow of Pedro Joaquín Chamorro, the slain editor of *La Prensa*. Her husband's writings had helped drive the Sandinistas into overthrowing Somoza's oppressive regime.

In February 1992 the rightist government of President Alfredo Cristiani in El Salvador met with the insurgents and arranged a cease-fire that established only a fitful peace. After twelve years of fighting and the loss of 75,000 lives, the beleaguered country now entered what contemporaries aptly called "the crisis of peace." Both Nicaragua and El Salvador were a long way from a true reconciliation of the warring parties.

Despite the diplomatic approach to the Salvadoran-Nicaraguan imbroglio, the Bush administration had returned to the use of military force in Latin America when it dealt with Panama. On December 20, 1989, the president approved an invasion by 27,000 U.S. troops whose objectives, according to Bush, were to safeguard the canal and U.S. citizens in the area and to stop the passage of drugs through the country by unseating their chief sponsor, dictator Manuel Noriega. Skeptics argued that the real reason for such a massive military strike was personal: Noriega had alienated both Reagan and Bush. Throughout much of the decade, Noriega had helped the contras while also working undercover for Cuba's Fidel Castro. Noriega had actually been in the secret employ of the CIA since the 1960s, which raised questions about how many of his activities Bush knew about after becoming CIA director in 1976. During the Reagan years, the Panamanian strongman played both sides of the drug scene as well, on the one hand cooperating with dealers from Colombia and other countries and on the other hand working with the U.S. Drug Enforcement Agency in seizing drug shipments.

By the time Bush became president, Noriega's history of personal and government corruption had embarrassed the United States. In early 1988 two grand juries in Florida indicted him for drug-running activities that included smuggling the Colombian product into the United States, accepting bribes for laundering drug money in his country's banks, and permitting Colombians to produce cocaine inside Panama. Revelations of Noriega's venal conduct soon became known in Panama, inciting demonstrations against his rule that led to a brutal government crackdown. As was the case with Ferdinand Marcos in the Philippines, the Reagan administration put pressure on Noriega to resign. But economic sanctions did not work, nor did a suspension of both economic and military aid. During the presidential campaign of 1988, Bush came under constant questioning about how the White House could allow Noriega to deal with drug lords.

As Bush settled into the presidency, the pressure heightened to remove Noriega. Elections in Panama (that former President Carter and other international observers attested as fraudulent) went against the general in May 1989, awarding victory to the vice presidential candidate, Guillermo Endara. Noriega, however, nullified the results and proclaimed his candidate the victor. Bush protested that "the Panamanian people have spoken. And I call on General Noriega to respect the will of the people." Noriega ignored the plea and ordered his personal police force, the Dignity Battalions, to use an iron bar in administering a public beating to Endara. American television and news magazines highlighted the bloody affair that turned Endara's white shirt to crimson. President Bush angrily called on Panamanians to throw out Noriega and "his Doberman thugs," and Americans in Panama urged officers in his Panamanian Defense Force (PDF) to rise in rebellion. But a coup attempt in October failed, partly because its leaders received no U.S. assistance against the soldiers who remained loyal to Noriega. As the news carried stories of the officers' executions, critics denounced Bush as a "wimp" for refusing to act.

Then, in mid-December 1989, the Bush administration decided to oust Noriega after he proclaimed himself Panama's "maximum leader" and declared that the two American nations (Panama and the United States) were in a "state of war." The president approved "Operation Just Cause," which sought to depose Noriega by U.S. military action. But the intervention proved more difficult than expected, leading to massive destruction in an already economically ravaged country. Only after several days of fighting did the Noriega regime fall, leaving behind a death list that included twenty-four U.S. soldiers, 139 PDF troops, and more than 300 Panamanian civilians. In the wake of the PDF's collapse came widespread lawlessness and rampant looting. Hospitals overflowed with the injured, most of whom received inadequate care because of a severe shortage of food and medical supplies. Especially frustrating was Noriega's elusiveness. At long last, the Americans located him in the Vatican Embassy in Panama City, where he had sought refuge. After protracted negotiations, he agreed to surrender and was taken to Miami to stand trial, on the two indictments for drug trafficking.

The U.S. invasion of Panama was a revealing episode. For the first time in four decades, the United States carried out a forceful intervention that did not rest on Cold War considerations. The administration accomplished its main objective in removing Noriega: He ultimately stood trial in the United States and was convicted in April 1992 and sentenced to jail. Not surprisingly, the military action earned Bush extraordinarily high praise from most of his nation's people. But despite the assurances by Washington's leaders to assist the new Endara government in Panama City, they could do little because of the economic shortfall in the United States. As in the past, the new regime held on to power only with the assistance of the 13,500 U.S. soldiers who were on the scene before the invasion and remained behind after the others pulled out in February 1990.

And, as in the past, the image was that of a U.S. surrogate put in place by White House military action. Numerous Latin American observers criticized the United States's use of force, even as they welcomed the results. The Soviet Union questioned Bush's heavy-handed methods, particularly after Americans had criticized Moscow's use of military force in neighboring Afghanistan. West Europeans wondered about the wisdom of resurrecting the Roosevelt Corollary, particularly when the Soviet Union seemed to have buried its own policy-making apparatus—the Brezhnev Doctrine—in refusing to put down the anti-Communist movement erupting all over Eastern Europe. Both the OAS and the UN Security Council moved to condemn the U.S. intervention; the latter failed to do so only because of the veto exercised by the U.S. delegate.

In still another look backward, the president had sanctioned the invasion of Panama without consulting Congress. The War Powers Act of 1973 authorized that body to put restraints on unilateral military action by the president, and yet neither house in Congress challenged the measure or inquired into the reasons behind it. The explanation seemed clear: The move stirred up the martial spirit among Americans and drew widespread support because of the removal of an unpopular dictator. To question the president's action would have been politically unwise.

By the time Bush left the presidency, U.S. relations with Latin America had improved, however slightly. The White House had withdrawn from the conflict between Nicaragua and El Salvador, allowing it to end and thereby encouraging the growth of a democratic process that Latin Americans themselves had devised. The cease-fire in El Salvador had brought some semblance of peace to the economically destitute country. But in Panama, the U.S. military presence remained unmistakable, even as the two nations moved closer to the change in canal control scheduled in the year 2000. Economic problems remained dominant, which helped the drug business continue despite government efforts to close it down. In Cuba, Castro remained chief of state, though older and grayer and less active in pushing his revolutionary ideas in areas outside his own domain. He now stood as the only Communist dictator in office outside Asia, but, without Soviet assistance, his island was in dire economic straits and internationally isolated. Signs of growing disillusionment among Cuba's ruling elite led more than a few observers to believe that this was "Castro's final hour." In the meantime, the number of illegal aliens migrating from Mexico into the United States remained high, even while the two nations continued to work toward the proposed North American Free Trade Agreement (or NAFTA, signed by Canada, Mexico, and the United States in October 1992), aimed at bringing the same benefits afforded by the United States's free-trade agreement with Canada in 1988. The growing numbers of Haitian refugees entering the United States remained a hot issue, although signs pointed to the restoration of democracy and perhaps a greater chance of a settlement. And the drug problem persisted, even as the White House provided funds to help the Colombian government defeat the drug lords.

Beneath all these matters and more, however, the poverty that ran throughout Latin America required more attention from Washington. Indeed, by the close of the Bush administration, the United States was sending more economic assistance to Latin America than to all of Europe. As Western Europe and Japan moved toward a dominant economic position in each of their respective regions, so had Washington's policymakers finally come to realize that their nation's vital interests were also rooted in the region of its location—that is, North America and the Caribbean Basin—and that only economic improvement offered any hope for success.

The Gulf War in the Middle East

White House attention suddenly turned to the Middle East in autumn 1990, when on August 2 nearly 100,000 Iraqi forces, escorted by tanks and armed with Soviet weapons, Chinese missiles, and poison gas, invaded their oil-rich neighbor Kuwait and set off a crisis in the Persian Gulf that had global repercussions. Iraqi dictator Saddam Hussein attempted to justify this military move in several ways. His country had owned Kuwait until Western imperialists wrested it away many years earlier, leaving Iraq without adequate access to the sea. Kuwait's massive production of oil had driven prices down, preventing him from marketing his own oil at prices high enough to meet $80 billion of debts resulting from the arms and materiel acquired from the United States and other nations during his long war with Iran. No less critical was his need for money to re-

build his nation's economy and finance the huge army and police state that underpinned his stay in power. Most important, he could become leader of the Arab states. His armies had rolled on to the northeast border of oil-rich Saudi Arabia, seemingly poised to launch an invasion of the United States's longtime ally.

Until the very moment of his assault on Kuwait, Saddam remained confident that the Bush administration would take no action. The United States had not responded with force to either the Iranian hostage crisis or the killing of marines in Lebanon. Furthermore, he had both public and private assurances that the White House intended to stay out of the ongoing boundary crisis between Iraq and Kuwait. But after some initial hesitation, President Bush felt compelled to respond. Saddam's invasion of Kuwait had endangered international peace by threatening the world's oil flow. If he seized Saudi Arabia as well, Saddam would control more than one-half of the world's crude oil deposits. Aggression unchallenged, Bush declared in harkening back to the pre–World War II decade, fed upon itself and ensured wider conflict. "What is at stake," he insisted, "is more than one country, it is a big idea—a new world order" based on "peace and security, freedom and the rule of law." The United States, he declared, did not wish to be "the world's policeman." It sought to cooperate with other nations in combating the instability and disorder that imperiled the world community. As Bush saw it, Saddam was another Hitler whom the United Nations must stop.

Bush received surprising support from a large number of nations that feared a takeover of the Middle East's oil reserves by Saddam Hussein. The Iraqi ruler was a ruthless and mercurial tyrant who was willing to crush his neighbors and who chose Stalin (not Hitler) as his model in creating a personality cult based on fear and terror. Most members of the United Nations and all those on the Security Council approved strong action against Iraq. Among those in the U.S. camp were the Soviets (who needed Western economic assistance and broke with their longtime ally, Iraq),

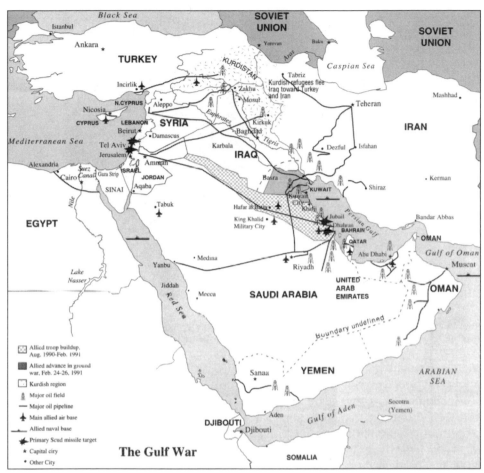

Map 29
A prime example of regional conflicts that developed in the post–Cold War period.

the British (who had oil interests in Kuwait), and the Chinese (who sought economic ties with the United States). Bush wanted to create and command a UN coalition of powers that would deliver a military response if necessary. What became clear was that the demise of the Cold War meant increased stature for the United Nations. No longer would the bitter U.S.-Soviet exchanges within the Security Council block its efforts to guarantee collective security. The United Nations gave Saddam until midnight of January 15, 1991, to withdraw his forces from Kuwait.

In the meantime, Bush mobilized a massive UN military force that had two objectives: to liberate Kuwait, and to protect Saudi Arabia. The allied powers first worked through the United Nations to impose an international economic boycott on Iraq that most Arab governments supported—including the Syrians, who had aligned with Iran in its war with Iraq and whose assistance the United States cultivated despite their longtime involvement in terrorism. Only Iran and the Palestinians in Jordan supported Iraq, the former because of territorial concessions offered by Saddam (withdrawal from all lands won in their recent war), and the latter out of a chance to destroy Israel. Bush persuaded Kuwait and Saudi Arabia to underwrite U.S. military costs in the

Iraqi Invasion of Kuwait
Exiled Sheik Jaber al-Ahmed of Kuwait discusses the Gulf crisis with
President George Bush in the White House on September 28, 1990.
White House Office Photos.

Middle East—although the Saudis simply raised their production of oil as prices escalated and then used half the income to meet financial obligations to the United States while keeping the rest.

Eventually President Bush masterminded the establishment of a highly unusual coalition of forty-eight countries from the Middle East, Europe, and Asia. To help finance the anticipated UN military operation, he put great pressure on several nations to make contributions—including Germany and Japan, both of whom drew heavily from the Middle East's oil supply and yet required considerable persuasion before promising billions in monetary assistance. U.S. war mobilization had meanwhile raised opposition at home, with thousands of marchers in New York City's Times Square chanting, "Hell, no, we won't go—we won't fight for Texaco." Others warned, "Speak Out Now—Remember Vietnam." Bush at first hesitated to ask the Democrat-controlled Congress to authorize him to use force. What if it rejected his request? He finally decided to seek congressional approval for participation in any military

action, although he would surely have followed the same course regardless of the outcome. The result of a long and bitter debate was a narrow victory for the president that proved vital to maintaining the shaky union of Americans, Europeans, Arabs, and Soviets. In many ways, Bush performed admirably as commander in chief of a unique mixture of allies.

Soon close to 250,000 U.S. combat troops (including a large number of activated reserves), along with planes and aircraft carriers, were en route to Saudi Arabia, the Persian Gulf, and the Red Sea. Their first tasks were to set up the defense of Saudi Arabia ("Operation Desert Shield") and establish a naval blockade of Iraq. In a pointed reference to a major command flaw during the Vietnam War, Bush assured the chair of the Joint Chiefs of Staff, General Colin Powell, that his military operations would encounter no political interference.

The deadline for the UN ultimatum came and passed without an Iraqi evacuation of Kuwait, thus activating a mammoth air and land campaign known as "Operation Desert Storm." To roll back the Iraqi offensive, General Powell orchestrated a month-long bombing of key Iraqi positions, including air defense and ground force command and control centers, which provided the vital prelude to a massive ground assault by 550,000 coalition forces under the command of General H. Norman Schwarzkopf, Jr. The land attack on Kuwait and eastern Iraq began on February 23, 1991.

As the UN forces headed into Kuwait, Saddam defiantly promised the "Mother of All Battles"; instead, his troops put up amazingly little resistance and sustained a crushing and humiliating defeat. In a vain attempt to draw Israel into the war, Saddam hit that country with ground-launched Scud missiles, confident that the Arab members of the UN coalition would switch sides if he converted the struggle into a contest between Arab and Jew. But Bush convinced Israeli leaders not to retaliate, probably by ensuring a quick victory and increased U.S. aid following the war. For more than a month three Cable News Network (CNN) reporters stayed bunkered in a Baghdad hotel, televising live shots of U.S. Tomahawk cruise missiles hammering Iraq (some within yards of the hotel) and U.S. Patriot missiles intercepting and downing the incoming Iraqi Scud missiles. American tank commanders found it surprisingly easy to maneuver through Iraqi minefields; Saddam's leaders had marked their own path through the area with wire that the invasion forces quickly discovered. "Once we found that," a U.S. officer declared, "the only thing missing was a neon sign saying 'start here.'" Coalition troops, meanwhile, advanced easily into the occupied kingdom of Kuwait, liberating it from quickly retreating Iraqi soldiers who had looted the country of nearly everything of value—even devouring most of the animals in the national zoo. In a spectacle of destruction, Saddam had ordered his departing troops to set fire to nearly 650 Kuwaiti oil wells, which unleashed a fiery holocaust that blackened the sky and took nearly nine months to extinguish. Not all enemy soldiers ran. They had undergone a terrific pounding from the bombing program and were so badly shell-shocked and demoralized

Secretary of Defense Richard Cheney and Gen. Colin Powell, Chair of the Joint Chiefs of Staff
Meeting with troops in Saudi Arabia on December 21, 1990. *U.S. Department of Defense.*

Kuwaiti Oil Fields Afire
U.S. Marines pushing into Kuwait found its oil fields ablaze as a result
of demolition charges set off by retreating Iraqi soldiers. *U.S. Army*

that thousands upon thousands surrendered with little or no opposition.

In less than one hundred hours of ground fighting, Iraq agreed to a UN cease-fire. The coalition had freed Kuwait and went on to take southern Iraq—at the cost of 148 American lives along with ninety-two allied soldiers. Even then, the Iraqis were not responsible for all coalition casualties. About one-quarter of its deaths resulted from "fratricide," or friendly fire caused by error. Despite the U.S. claims to pinpoint accuracy, nearly one-half of 167 laser-guided bombs dropped from F-117s during the first five nights of conflict missed their targets completely. Other errant air attacks hit oil tankers, milk trucks, and, according to the Iraqis, a factory that made baby formula. More than 100,000 Iraqis died, including numerous civilians. An epidemic of cholera and typhoid soon blanketed the Iraqi nation, adding to the horrid situation.

A wave of euphoria over the surprisingly easy victory momentarily threatened to widen the war's objectives. The coalition command underwent considerable pressure to order its troops into Baghdad to topple Saddam. During his long, tyrannical reign, he was responsible for numerous atrocities against his own people, particularly the authorization of chemical warfare against Kurdish rebels (including women and children) in northern Iraq and the ordering of thousands of young men into suicidal attacks on Iranians in the recent war. Then, in the Gulf War, supporters of the UN coalition were appalled by the brutalities committed by Iraqi soldiers on Kuwaiti civilians, by the Scuds lobbed indiscriminately on urban centers in Israel and Saudi Arabia, and by Saddam's decision to send Western captives (including women and children) as "human shields" to Iraqi military targets in an effort to prevent enemy bombing. Although British prime minister Margaret Thatcher ridiculed Saddam for "hiding behind women's skirts," he had to be taken seriously. Saddam possessed chemical and biological weapons and would probably develop his first atomic bomb within eighteen months. Most chilling, he had the will to use all his weapons.

President Bush wisely resisted the temptation to take the war into Baghdad. In comparing Saddam to Hitler, Bush had helped to bring on the overwhelming pressure needed to finish the military task in Iraq. Could there be anything less than unconditional surrender with an enemy accused of war crimes and thus not susceptible to negotiations? But Bush recognized the likelihood of the coalition's breakup if he pushed the war into Iraq's capital. He also realized the danger of becoming entangled in street fighting that might not even uncover Saddam, who was hidden, along with his military officers and commanders of his elite Republican Guard, somewhere deep beneath the city in heavily reinforced bunkers. Most of all, Bush knew that Iraq's destruction would automatically make Iran the chief Islamic power in the region. Had not General Powell told him that "our practical intention was to leave Baghdad enough power to survive as a threat to an Iran that remained bitterly hostile to the United States"? Besides, Bush hoped that Saddam's own soldiers

would overthrow him. This did not happen—partly because of videocassettes circulated in the Middle East that showed executed military officers hanging on meat hooks. Saddam held on to power, brutally squelching all opposition at home while defiantly proclaiming victory over his hated imperialist enemy.

The UN success had important repercussions. Security Council Resolution 687 sounded as if Iraq had suffered a great defeat. It had to respect Kuwait's border, permit UN peacekeepers along the Iraqi borders, and divulge and help to destroy all chemical, biological, and nuclear weaponry. Indeed, the UN inspection teams disposed of more than one hundred Scud missiles along with huge supplies of mustard gas and nerve gas, but they had only slowed the production of nuclear weapons that was well under way when the Gulf War erupted. Although the coalition had achieved its chief objectives of liberating

Cease-Fire Talks, March 3, 1991
Gen. H. Norman Schwarzkopf and the commander of Arab ground troops, Saudi Lt. Gen Prince Khalid (on left) meet with the Iraqi commanders (on right), Lt. Gen. Mohammed Abdez Rahman al-Dagitistani and Lt. Gen Sabin Abdel-Aziz al-Douri. *U.S. Army.*

Kuwait and safeguarding Saudi Arabia, Saddam's regime and country remained intact, providing him with stature in the Arab world as a leader who had warded off the U.S. imperialists. He thus remained a dire threat to his neighbors, adding more stress to the constant turmoil in the Middle East. Furthermore, much of Kuwait lay in ruins and bitterly torn between those Kuwaitis who had fled the country upon the Iraqi advance and those who had braved the invasion by remaining behind. In addition, thousands of Palestinians in Kuwait drew the wrath of its people because of PLO complicity with Saddam. But the Bush administration exploited the UN conquest and deep apprehensions over Saddam to salvage something of potential value: It arranged another round of Middle East peace talks. This time, however, there were two differences: The Israelis agreed to meet with the Arab states, but with the Palestinians (though not the PLO) in attendance as part of Jordan's delegation, and the United States permitted the Soviet Union to participate— a phenomenal turnaround from the past.

The Persian Gulf crisis had only temporarily diverted attention from the persistent Arab-Israeli tensions in the Middle East. The region had become a veritable armed camp, thanks to the great majority of weapons that came from the United States itself. Israel's continued refusal to meet with the PLO, combined with its severe military tactics in putting down the intifada in Gaza and the West Bank, had alienated Americans and in 1989 drew a harsh reprimand from the state department for violating human rights. In addition, Israeli domestic politics had become bitterly divided between Menachem Begin's hard-line Likud party, which rejected any form of compromise and called for a Greater Israel, and the Labor party, which supported Secretary of State George Shultz's earlier proposal of giving up occupied land for peace. By the middle of 1990 the chances for a settlement appeared impossible as the more radical wing of the PLO intensified its "holy war" (Jihad) against Israel and the Likud party assumed control of

the government in Tel Aviv. Israel's new prime minister, Yitzhak Shamir, staunchly proclaimed continued opposition to discussions with the PLO. Then, when Yasir Arafat refused to denounce an aborted terrorist attack on an Israeli beach by one of the PLO's factions, the Bush administration abruptly halted the talks in Tunis. It now hoped that the unity shown in the Gulf War would combine with the widespread fear of Saddam's reckless and brutal behavior to take precedence over ancient Arab-Israeli difficulties and drive both parties to the peace table.

In the Middle East, as in numerous other hot spots in the world, the United States found itself unable to control events. Secretary of State Baker urged the Israelis to negotiate with the PLO and accept, if not a sovereign state, at least its claim to self-government in the Israeli-occupied areas. A Greater Israel was unrealistic, he insisted. Local elections must take place in East Jerusalem, Gaza, and the West Bank. But Shamir rejected any concessions to the PLO and Israeli-American relations hardened. And yet the Bush administration could do nothing because of both domestic and foreign considerations. Not only did Israel enjoy widespread and effective support in the United States, but it was also the United States's closest ally in the Middle East.

As Bush left the presidency in 1993, the embittered Middle East stalemate showed few signs of coming to an end. The Cold War was over, which meant that the fear of Russian expansion into the region had greatly diminished. Indeed, the end of this intense international rivalry had the potential of encouraging a move toward peace in the Middle East, largely because the United States had provided most of Israel's arms while its chief enemies, Iraq and Syria, had received the bulk of their weapons from the now deceased Soviet Union. The Gulf War had driven Israel and the United States closer together again, but the wartime rapprochement had not resolved the underlying tensions. The Arab-Israeli-Palestinian problem remained, recently worsened by the arrival in Israel of thousands of Soviet Jewish

Map 30

The end of the Cold War encouraged a greater sense of interdependence among European nations along with their effort to become more independent of the United States.

immigrants, the Israelis' continuing intention to expand settlements and build a Greater Israel, and the Palestinians' desperate conditions in the occupied areas. The most feasible route to peace lay in some sort of settlement worked out by those two parties most actively enjoined in the dispute—Israel and the PLO.

The Post–Cold War Era: An Assessment

As in all great changes in history, the Cold War left a mixed legacy. On the positive side, the end of the East-West conflict greatly eased the chances of nuclear war. The arms race came to an end, and the two superpowers withdrew

their nuclear missiles from Europe. For the first time in more than four decades, the world's problems came under scrutiny on their own merits rather than through the funneled lenses of the Cold War. In addition, increasing numbers of peoples pursued the objectives of nationalism, leading to more demands for self-government and boosting the stature of the United Nations. Furthermore, the twelve-member European Community took a major step toward the economic and political integration of the continent when it established a single market in 1992. Indeed, the reconstruction of all Europe seemed possible because of the work of the thirty-five-nation Conference on Security and Cooperation in

Europe. Although the United States hoped to maintain a voice in Europe, particularly by preventing NATO's dissolution, the chances of Americans playing a central role in continental affairs had steadily diminished with the growth of European independence.

On the negative side, the heightening multi-polarity among nations meant the growth of what the Pentagon called "major regional conflicts" as increasing numbers of leaders competed for the world's limited resources. In Asia, more than a few governments had become concerned over a revived Japan, and others were apprehensive over North Korea's push for nuclear capabilities. The Middle East had already become the scene of two regional wars—one between Iraq and Iran, and the other in the Persian Gulf. Africa remained a hot spot primarily because of economic hardship. Apartheid continued in South Africa even though it had eased in intensity. On February 2, 1990, South African President F. W. de Klerk submitted to economic sanctions and worldwide moral pressure to lift a thirty-year ban on the African National Congress (ANC). Nine days later, as television covered an event watched all over the world, the ANC's leader, Nelson Mandela, became a free man after spending twenty-seven years in prison. In Europe the chief concern was whether a reunited Germany would again threaten its neighbors. Others wondered how the former Communist states in Eastern Europe would resolve their many national, ethnic, religious, and territorial differences. All observers anxiously awaited the final disposition of the former Soviet Union: Would it become Balkanized, pitting Russia against the other former members of the Soviet Union?

Critics have noted a sharply diminished U.S. foreign policy influence, which they have attributed to a general decline in power experienced by all great empires in the past. In March 1979, *Business Week* published an issue entitled "The Decline of U.S. Power" in which the writers pointed out that although the United States was the dominant world power in the mid-1940s, it had fallen victim to a "decay" that by 1980 prevented it from controlling the "radical economic and social change in the Third World." The Suez crisis of 1956, the writers declared, marked the key turning point. It was then that the United States broke with its allies, virtually inviting Soviet intervention in the Middle East and ensuring the West's steady loss of control over oil and, as a matter of course, over the direction of international affairs. Although the future was not as bleak as that portrayed in the *Business Week* article, many contemporaries realized that the United States could not determine history and would have to work more closely with other peoples than ever before.

Only for a brief time did leaders in Washington make a realistic attempt to deal with the great changes in the world's power structure. The Nixon administration had taken the proper step during the last years of U.S. involvement in Vietnam by recognizing that no single nation possessed sufficient resources to resolve the world's problems and by calling for help through partnerships. But this broadened approach soon lost favor as Americans turned inward after the Vietnam experience. According to historian Paul Kennedy in his bestselling work of 1987 and 1988, *The Rise and Fall of the Great Powers,* proof of the U.S. decline in global stature came in the government's sense of insecurity, which led to inordinate expenditures on defense rather than investment. How otherwise to explain the meteoric rise in the national debt during the Reagan years?

The Reagan and Bush administrations made little attempt to deal with the shifting realities in world power and concentrated instead on the impossible task of restoring the United States to its immediate post–World War II position of global leadership. The military and economic power of the world was now so diffused that no individual power could control both peoples and events. Anticommunism no longer remained a viable consideration in the formulation of U.S. policy; many observers noted the overweening importance of nationalism not only throughout the Third World but also in other regions now freed from outside control and seeking self-assertion. Reagan and Bush were unable to use military power as a remedy for the world's growing social, political, and economic problems. Their focus on foreign concerns further contributed to their own nation's domestic social and economic problems.

Bush was only partly correct in claiming a victory in the Cold War and attributing that outcome to containment. Kennan's ideas had surely worked to frustrate the Soviet Union's expansionist activities, raising searching questions among its subjected peoples about the effectiveness of the Communist regime and switching their concerns from foreign threats to domestic troubles. Moscow's leaders, Kennan had argued, would ultimately undergo pressure either to grant reforms or to clamp down on unrest and risk revolution. He was correct. Soviet hard-liners had resisted reforms so long that Gorbachev's introduction of *perestroika* and *glasnost* unleashed a long pent-up spiral of desperation that became revolutionary in intensity and proved impossible to stop, short of a brutal military crackdown that he had no interest in supporting. Such a move might have brought on another Russian Revolution far bloodier than the first.

Gorbachev recognized that the Soviet Union was in a serious state of internal and external decline. He was president of a powerful military state that had no sound economic base. Some critics characterized the Soviet Union as a Third World nation that could boast of a nuclear arsenal while having to admit that forty percent of its people were poverty-stricken, more than thirty percent lacked running water at home, the infant death rate was increasing, and males faced a steadily declining life expectancy. To rectify this potentially disastrous situation, he advocated economic and political reforms that would be astronomically expensive. Thus, the ever-heightening arms expenditures drove the already weak Soviet Union into a state of bankruptcy and dictated its retreat from the Cold War. In that regard, the Reagan administration's military buildup

contributed to the collapse of the Soviet Union and of communism itself.

Even more, however, is involved in accounting for the end of the Cold War. Admittedly, Gorbachev and others in Moscow recognized the impossibility of holding on to their client states in Eastern Europe, but this reality should not overshadow the long-standing determination of these peoples to throw off their Soviet captors and achieve independence. Not only did they hate Soviet oppression, but they also despised communism. That archaic system had called for strict one-party rule and the removal of national boundaries, and it ultimately self-destructed in the face of growing popular demands for self-determination. The Communist ideology had proved socially, politically, economically, and morally bankrupt, helping to pull down the entire system from within.

Proponents of a U.S. triumph in the Cold War often overlook both the costs and the results of that long ordeal. The United States emerged victorious in that Soviet communism had been toppled, but the responsibility for that outcome chiefly belonged to those people both inside and outside the Soviet Union who had long resisted Communist control and finally became free after 1989. The core of the once-extensive Soviet empire had imploded, the result of so many structural weaknesses and anachronisms that it was amazing that the collapse had not come earlier. In an article entitled "The End of History," Francis Fukuyama in the state department proudly declared that democracy had prevailed because of its superiority over communism. This vain self-praise ignored the many developments beyond U.S. control and unfairly diminished the vital role of the many individuals who had spent most of their lives under Communist regimes and now struck boldly for independence. Fukuyama's self-congratulatory approach also failed to deal with piercing questions about the United States's interventions in other countries. Cold War considerations had numerous times encouraged interventions that erased the crucial distinction between vital and secondary interests. In two of the most flagrant examples, Korea and Vietnam, civil wars erupting out of domestic problems had become vital parts of the Cold War struggle primarily because of exaggerated or erroneous perceptions by Washington of Soviet and Chinese Communist intentions. In the meantime, the United States's fears of Communist expansion had intensified a dangerous arms race that would culminate in either nuclear war and mass destruction or peace and two economically and morally drained superpowers. Fortunately, the latter development prevailed, but at the heavy cost of a flattened Soviet state and a vastly weakened American nation that found itself nearly $3 trillion in debt and in dire need of a greatly refurbished infrastructure. Such developments raise doubts that anyone should claim victory in the Cold War.

President Clinton: A New Direction in Foreign Policy?

Bush lost his bid for reelection in 1992 to Democratic Governor William Clinton of Arkansas, who sidestepped foreign policy issues and attacked the incumbent's inability to end the nation's longtime economic recession. Despite an eighty-nine percent approval rating following the successful Gulf War, Bush's popularity had plummeted because of the sluggish economy at home and his seeming bewilderment about what remedies to take. While Bush emphasized his victories in the Cold War and in Iraq, Clinton hammered away at diminished economic hopes and an unpromising future for the nation's youth. During the campaign, Clinton tied the failing U.S. economy to the troublesome global situation. The biggest problem was the huge federal deficit, which had fractured the nation's economy and undermined its foreign policy. The trade deficit with Japan alone stood at nearly $50 billion, which had crippled the United States's capacity to invest abroad and thereby generate more jobs at home. Japan had become a chief commercial rival of

the United States, and it had reemerged as both an economic and a military power in Asia. Perhaps Massachusetts Senator Paul Tsongas, a former Democratic presidential hopeful himself, expressed it best when he declared, "The Cold War's over. Japan won."

After achieving victory with only forty-three percent of the popular vote (Bush had thirty-eight percent, and nineteen percent went to billionaire Texas businessman Ross Perot), President Clinton insisted that the chief impetus to economic recovery at home and abroad was market expansion throughout the world. Reducing his own nation's gigantic budget deficit, he argued, was critical to this overall growth. With these goals in mind, he attended the annual economic summit of 1993, which convened in Tokyo during the summer and brought together the "Group of Seven" leading capitalist nations of Britain, Canada, France, Germany, Italy, Japan, and the United States. There, among other objectives, Clinton sought a broad commercial agreement with Japan aimed at lowering the U.S. trade deficit. He later participated in talks about global tariff reductions under the auspices of the General Agreement on Tariffs and Trade (GATT), established in 1947 to determine fair trade rules and now with 117 members. Finally, he encouraged the Senate to approve the North American Free Trade Agreement (NAFTA) worked out by Canada, Mexico, and the United States in December 1992.

Some progress took place toward the establishment of international reciprocity in trade. GATT's member nations agreed to a new commercial arrangement in Geneva during late December 1993. No less important than specific provisions was their decision to drop that unfortunate name—GATT—and replace it in 1995 with the more staid title of World Trade Organization. The new policy reduced tariffs on manufactured goods by an average of thirty-seven percent and encompassed agricultural products for the first time. The United States stood to profit from the total elimination of tariffs in a dozen industries it dominated. In addition, White House pressure had led to the congressional approval of NAFTA in November 1993, offering the hope of building greater commercial ties throughout North America. NAFTA's proponents had argued that it would create 130,000 new American jobs by 1995; instead, NAFTA was responsible for the loss of 125,000 jobs that, fortunately, the robust U.S. economy ameliorated by expanding the country's employment in other areas.

Clinton's policy also worked well in Asia, the location of nearly one-half of all foreign currency reserves and forty percent of the world's new markets. In 1993 fifteen national leaders from the Pacific region attended an Asia-Pacific Economic Cooperative (APEC) forum in Seattle that sought to establish a huge free trade zone. The following year, APEC met in Indonesia, where its members agreed to create a free-trading Pacific Rim by 2010. But on the issue of opening Japanese markets to U.S. industries (including auto parts), a final agreement remained elusive until in February 1994 the Clinton administration threatened commercial sanctions against Japan for violating a previous trade arrangement. The Tokyo government agreed to increase its imports of U.S. goods by eighty-five percent. Furthermore, the two nations negotiated the Japan-American Security Treaty in early 1995 that strengthened their ties and obligated Japan to assume seventy-five percent of the expense of maintaining at least 100,000 American troops in the Asia-Pacific area.

Clinton early demonstrated a greater awareness than did his predecessor of the interdependence of domestic and foreign problems facing the United States in the post–Cold War era. But this is not to say that he had developed a cohesive strategy in dealing with these world-shaking changes. At a White House policymaking meeting, the new president shook his head with wonderment and confusion. "You know," he moaned after listening to detailed discussions about the international issues facing his administration, "the problem is that in this post–Cold War period, the lines just aren't as clear as they were before." After

a pause, a telling response came from James Schlesinger, former defense secretary and now CIA director: "Mr. President, that is your fate. You will just have to get used to dealing with ambiguity."

If the United States had not entered a "brave new world," it certainly confronted what contemporaries have called a "Disorderly New World." The president, largely inexperienced in foreign affairs, preferred to leave those matters to subordinates. The result was a strange amalgam of idealism and Wilsonian internationalism that led to a confused and disoriented foreign policy. Only when public opinion demanded his leadership did he shift to a pragmatic "trial and error" approach. At the outset of his administration, Clinton prepared for summit meetings in Brussels, Prague, and Moscow that focused on three critical issues: NATO's future and whether the newly independent nations of Eastern Europe should become members; the aftermath of recent elections in Russia and the question of reform; and the continued economic stagnation in Europe. Somehow he had to convince Western Europe that the United States intended to remain involved in Atlantic concerns despite its recent focus on NAFTA and the Pacific Rim.

Most urgent to the new administration was the need to assure East Europeans, once part of the Soviet empire, that Russia under Boris Yeltsin posed no threat to their security. Toward this end, Clinton secured the U.S.-Russian-Ukraine Trilateral Statement and Annex in mid-January 1994, which provided for dismantling all 1800 long-range nuclear warheads in Ukraine—the third largest nuclear arsenal in the world. Later that same month, he and Yeltsin signed an agreement requiring the United States and Russia by May 30 to stop targeting their missiles at each other. By January 1997 the United States and Russia had cut more than 20,000 strategically placed warheads (their total as of 1990) to about 7000; Ukraine and Kazakhstan no longer had nuclear weapons, and neither would Belarus in a short time. The president went farther. On September 25, 1996, he informed the UN

Bill Clinton and Al Gore
Democratic presidential nominee Bill Clinton of Arkansas with vice-presidential running mate Al Gore of Tennessee. *Wide World Photos, New York.*

General Assembly that the United States would join fifty other nations—including China, France, Russia, and Great Britain—in signing the Comprehensive Test Ban Treaty (CTBT). Rejoicing over the pact proved premature: India refused to sign until the nations had abolished *all* existing nuclear weapons. The United States could not agree to such a proposition; nor would it impose sufficient political and economic pressure on the Indian government, given its opposition to free trade and its indecision regarding whether to join the Western alignment. Unlike Bush, however, Clinton had become actively engaged in reshaping the entire East-West relationship.

All this posed a formidable task. Many observers worried that dismantled nuclear weapons might come into the possession of what Washington called "rogue states" such as Cuba, Iran, Iraq, Libya, North Korea, or Syria, all of which threatened democracy. Improved technology now permitted the manufacture of nuclear devices small enough to carry in one hand, making it imperative to keep plutonium and uranium away from terrorists. West Europeans resented the Clinton administration's new emphasis on other sections of the world and had already begun formulating economic and political policies without consulting the United States. But Poland, Czechoslovakia, and Hungary remained concerned about the "security vacuum" stemming from the Soviet collapse and insisted that the Russians were die-hard imperialists and not born-again democrats. Although the United States sympathized with these recently liberated peoples, it could not risk alienating Russia. Any thought of inviting these and other East European states into NATO gave way to a gradualist process of membership in 1994 called "Partnership for Peace," which rested on limited military cooperation in an effort to avoid provoking the Russians.

The surprising shift from granting immediate NATO membership aroused great resentment in Eastern Europe. The Polish foreign minister angrily dismissed Clinton's program as a "buzz-off project" in which NATO members "ask us to talk and walk and act like a duck." The problem is "that after we've done all that's asked of us, NATO reserves the right to say, 'Well, now we want you to be a chicken instead.'" A spokesman of the Polish Institute of International Affairs in Warsaw renounced the "firm assumption in American policy that reformers will finally win in Russia." "All that is nonsense," stormed a high official in the Czech Defense Ministry. "Yeltsin is not a democrat. He is a Russian feudal lord." Former U.S. defense secretary Les Aspin (replaced by William Perry in early February 1994) nonetheless opposed the extension of NATO membership to East European countries, particularly while the United States was in the process of reducing its defense budget. If Poland were allowed into NATO, Aspin warned, "we would be saying that an attack on Poland would be the same as an attack on New York."

NATO continued to be a chief concern of the Clinton administration. The president called that organization the "bedrock" of security; Yeltsin warned that Europe had not yet freed itself of the Cold War and was "in danger of plunging into a cold peace. Why sow the seeds of mistrust?" Ironically, Yeltsin stated: "It is a dangerous delusion to suppose that the destinies of continents and the world community in general can somehow be managed from one single capital." In October 1996, Clinton recommended that in 1999, the fiftieth anniversary of NATO and the tenth anniversary of the destruction of the Berlin Wall, NATO should admit the first of the former members of the Warsaw Pact (disbanded in 1991). "If we fail to seize this historic opportunity to build a new NATO—if we allow the Iron Curtain to be replaced by a veil of influence—we will pay a higher price later." Russia, he urged, should approve NATO's expanded membership as a good-faith effort to "advance the security of everyone." It "[was] not directed against anyone. I know that some in Russia still look at NATO through a Cold War prism, but I ask them to look again. We are building a new NATO just as they are building a new Russia." The decisive factor was both parties' opposition to renewing the Cold War. "We are no longer enemies," Yeltsin had earlier declared, "but partners."

A multilateral approach to foreign policy became crucial as the president faced growing national, ethnic, and religious problems throughout the world that, as in the period before World War I, threatened to pull in outside nations. Regional conflicts became flashpoints, as the Middle East remained a severely troubled area and Bosnians and Serbs engaged in a genocidal war over control of a tattered and torn pocket of land still known as Yugoslavia. In the south Russian province of Chechnya, an Islamic-led movement for independence caused Yeltsin to use military force in a failing effort to salvage the oil in that area of the Caucasus Mountains and to prevent a precedent for similar such actions by other dissidents. The White House had worked closely with the United Nations in winning a war against Iraq during the Bush administration, and it now employed the same strategy in dealing with desperate Haitians seeking refuge in the United States. Economic destitution in Africa remained a major problem, most notably in Somali, where tribal wars caused such extreme hardship that the United Nations sponsored a massive humanitarian and pacification aid program intended to put down a local warlord, and the United States contributed materiel, gunships, and, until the spring of 1994, more than 4000 combat troops. Apartheid had continued to soften but all too slowly. South Africa's first open elections took place in April 1994, resulting in an overwhelming ANC victory that brought in Nelson Mandela as the country's first black president. The U.S. economic embargo on Cuba continued in force, hurting Clinton's efforts to improve relations. Finally, he wanted to resolve the longtime bitter fighting in Northern Ireland.

Given the novelty and magnitude of the foreign problems confronting the United States, the Clinton administration spent much of its first year in office groping its way through these matters. The new president had had little experience in foreign affairs, even though he was a graduate of Georgetown University's prestigious School of Foreign Service; a former staff member of Senator William Fulbright, chair of the Foreign Relations Committee; and a student at Oxford University in England, where he read in Russian and East European history. Clinton's publicly expressed interest in what some have called liberal internationalism, however, had not taken specific form except in general references to spreading democracy and freedom. In the first days of his presidency, he delegated foreign policy making to subordinates, freeing him to concentrate on domestic issues. This kind of standoffish approach could not last in a world undergoing such a profound and sudden transformation. The rapidly changing global situation dictated a flexible U.S. foreign policy that permitted adjustments to constantly changing realities. And yet, as the world stumbled toward a new order, the Clinton administration lacked a comprehensive strategy and proved itself incapable of effective leadership.

Clinton had campaigned on three foreign policy ideas in 1992, which a year later he pulled together in a strategy that became known as "enlargement." His presidency, he had predicted, would have to reshape and modernize the nation's military establishment (including the ending of discrimination against gays, which caused a tremendous uproar), deal with the growing impact of economics in foreign affairs (geoeconomics rather than geopolitics, with the latter's emphasis on military considerations), and encourage the worldwide spread of democracy ("pragmatic neo-Wilsonianism," according to National Security Adviser Anthony Lake). The growth of democratic states, Clinton insisted, ensured international prosperity and security. Enlargement strategy, according to Lake, would

"strengthen the community of market democracies," "foster and consolidate new democracies and market economies," "counter the aggression and support the liberalization of states hostile to democracy," and "help democracy and market economies take root in regions of greatest humanitarian reform." The United States felt no idealistic obligation to promote human rights and democracy all over the world. The new policy sought to protect the nation's strategic and economic interests by ridding the post–Cold War era of commercial barriers. World peace would grow out of a free-market economy that rested on law and economic freedom. The new administration intended to emphasize the establishment of economic ties with the emerging democratic states—including Russia. Clinton told Congress that he had put "economic competitiveness at the heart of our foreign policy." He soon created the National Economic Council under Secretary of the Treasury Robert E. Rubin to coordinate this new blend of domestic and foreign economic policies.

International Challenges of Post–Cold War Nationalism: Eastern Europe and the Balkans

The fallout from the end of the Cold War, meanwhile, unleashed deep-rooted forces of nationalism inside several countries, including those in the once powerful and sprawling Soviet empire, that now threatened to cause international problems. Traditional remedies were no longer available: The shaky economic situation in the United States precluded meaningful assistance to those people seeking change, and the collapse of the Soviet threat to European security greatly reduced NATO's importance. In a critical period that required innovative approaches to a European world no longer burdened by the Cold War, the new president at first reacted haphazardly and often in utter confusion. He initially favored a strong response to a war that broke out in Bosnia and then backed off when he received no European support. He first advocated the integration of the newly independent nations of Eastern Europe into NATO; but then, in December 1993, he abruptly changed course. In that year Russia's first democratic election in nearly eight decades brought an ultranationalist member of the neo-fascist Liberal Democratic party, Vladimir Zhirinovsky, to the lower house of Parliament. His election alarmed many in Eastern Europe that Russia would drop reform efforts at home and become more belligerent abroad, and it caused Clinton to fear that the incorporation of that region's nations into NATO might alienate the Russians by resurrecting Cold War boundaries. The White House therefore stunted NATO's growth, buying time by instituting more steps in the procedure of soliciting membership.

Zhirinovsky's election aroused strong strains of Russian nationalism that sent shock waves throughout Eastern Europe. In August 1991, just after the Gorbachev coup, Zhirinovsky had declared in the Kremlin: "I'll bury radioactive waste along the Lithuanian border and put up powerful fans and blow the stuff across at night. They'll all get radiation sickness. They'll die of it. When they either die out or get down on their knees, I'll stop." His campaign posters in 1993 had promised, "I will bring Russia up off her knees." To do this, he demanded the incorporation of Estonia, Latvia, and Lithuania into Russia, the carving up of Poland, the conquest of Finland, and, incredibly, the seizure of Alaska from the United States. Failing to gain satisfaction on these demands could lead to what Zhirinovsky ominously called "new Hiroshimas." Vice President Albert Gore denounced Zhirinovsky's views as "reprehensible and anathema to all freedom-loving people." Clinton refused to see Zhirinovsky during the summit trip to Moscow in 1993 and drew a characteristic verbal tirade. Clinton, Zhirinovsky accused, was a "coward" who should "play his saxophone instead of coming here and meeting with nobodies."

Most observers realized that Zhirinovsky himself posed no threat to world security, but they also recognized that his rise to power signaled the existence of deep unrest inside Russia that Yeltsin must address through reforms. Zhirinovsky's party had less than eighty seats in the 450-member lower house, whereas reformers numbered about twice that amount. Clinton saw no reason to expect a "big new dangerous direction in Russian policy." But Ambassador-at-Large Strobe Talbott (a Russian specialist and Clinton's close friend and college classmate at Oxford) considered it necessary to convince Congress that Russia needed more aid rather than less in the election aftermath. He also assured Russia's neighbors that the United States would protect them from this new outburst of Russian nationalism. Talbott insisted that the key to their safety was the continued political and economic reform of Russia.

The most explosive problem in Europe continued to be the Balkans, where Yugoslavia's recent dissolution had led to a civil war in 1991 that reopened a centuries-old struggle between Muslims and Christians in Bosnia and Herzegovina. Yugoslavia after World War I was similar to most other countries in Eastern Europe in that it was a mixed state of diverse nationalities and religions. The populace was primarily Serb (Eastern Orthodox), but it also included significant numbers of Slovenes and Croats (Catholic) along with Bosnians (Muslim). The Serbs headed the national government and armed forces in the capital city of Belgrade and tried in vain to stop the country's disintegration in the post–Cold War period. When the republics of Slovenia and Croatia declared independence in 1991, the European Union (EU) recognized the new nations. The Yugoslav army intervened with force in both areas, setting off bitter fighting that the EU attempted to mediate rather than turn to NATO and invite U.S. participation. All peace efforts failed.

On one side stood the internationally recognized government in Bosnia led by President Alija Izetbegovic, a Muslim; on the other side was Serbia's President Slobodan Milosevic, an outspoken proponent of a "Greater Serbia" free of Islamic fundamentalists. The United

Nations admitted both Slovenia and Croatia as member nations and branded Milosevic's Serbian government the aggressor. The Serbs then focused their military assaults on Bosnia-Herzegovina, which also threatened to declare independence. A vicious military campaign ensued, with the Bosnian Serbs pursuing a self-proclaimed policy of "ethnic cleansing" aimed at the majority population of Muslims.

Other nations throughout the world at first only watched these horrifying events unfold in the Balkans. Although Serbia's attacks on Bosnia and Croatia (which were in military alliance) had not endangered the strategic interests of either the United States or Europe, the refusal of outside countries to help Bosnia had the potential of alienating Muslims in friendly Arab states and thereby threatening the West's oil flow. The United Nations announced an arms embargo on all sides in the war, which originated out of an attempt to prevent the Russians from helping Serbia. Ironically, however, the Serbian forces already held the military advantage from having received weapons from the Yugoslav army, and the UN action actually augmented that superiority by denying arms to Bosnia. The United Nations also imposed economic sanctions—especially on oil—but one-half of Serbia's supply came from Russia and China, neither of which favored the oil sanction.

A brief respite in the war soon came, however. In November 1991 a UN Security Council delegation headed by Cyrus Vance, a former secretary of state in the Carter administration, negotiated an uneasy cease-fire between Yugoslavia and Croatia that left the Serbs holding nearly twenty-five percent of Croatian territory. Soon a UN peacekeeping team comprised primarily of British and French soldiers was en route to the troubled scene. In the following December, the situation sharply deteriorated when Germany ignored Vance's entreaties and extended recognition to Croatia and Slovenia. The remainder of the EU countries did the same, leading the United States to follow suit. Bosnia and Macedonia, the other two self-proclaimed republics, eventually won recognition from the Bush White House as well. Only a shell of Yugoslavia remained. Recognition, the president wishfully asserted, might help to stabilize the Balkans. By no means would he give in to the pressure for a U.S. military intervention that might, he feared, lead to another Vietnam. Nor would Britain or France consider air strikes or any form of stronger action; they realized that the UN peacekeeping forces already in place had become Milosevic's hostages. Yugoslavia, one state department official asserted, had become a "tar baby" that no one would touch. Bush's greatest fear was that Milosevic would set off a Balkan war by resuming the fighting, this time in Kosovo, a former Yugoslav (now Serb) province heavily populated with Albanians.

The cease-fire quickly crumbled despite several peace efforts, including a partition proposal that sought to divide Bosnia into ten districts under the nominal control of a governing body in Sarajevo. As fighting erupted anew in Bosnia, charges spread of genocide as Serbian forces burned and sacked villages, engaged in mass tortures of non-Serbs in concentration camps, systematically raped Muslim women, and laid a deadly siege on the Bosnian capital of Sarajevo that led to mass starvation. "Like pre-1914 Europe," brooded one French political analyst, "the new world order of George Bush died in Sarajevo." If not dead, the new world order had met its stiffest match: Ethnic violence in economically primitive areas has seldom proved subject to economic boycotts or sanctions. And rarely have appeals to compromise been effective when one of the central issues driving that ethnic conflict was nationalism and another was religion—the ancient dispute between Christians and Muslims.

The Clinton administration acted indecisively toward the Balkan crisis. It showed no interest in partition. Not only did such an idea violate the Wilsonian principle of self-determination, but it would also mark a concession to aggression that ignored the chief lesson of Munich. The president must not appear weak. He had already come under attack for his earlier opposition to the Vietnam War and for his appointing advisers characterized as soft on foreign policy issues. *The Economist* of London had declared in December 1992 that the United States under the new president must act as "world cop" by forcefully intervening as the most "humane response" to the Serbs' "systematic nastiness." Clinton, however, could not consider military intervention because Bosnia posed no threat to U.S. interests—a point emphatically made by public opinion polls that showed seventy percent opposition to American involvement. A *New York Times* editorial in February 1993 warned against the "slippery slope" of military involvement: "Is anyone around the Oval Office reading history books?" And yet, Clinton had to do something. Former British prime minister Margaret Thatcher had publicly denounced the West's refusal to adopt stronger measures. "I never thought I would see another holocaust," she said, leaving the implication that her successor, John Major, was repeating the pre–World War II mistakes of Neville Chamberlain. A call for negotiations without the leverage of force, Clinton likewise knew, would not work. Under great pressure from the European governments to support the partition plan, he agreed to do so only if all parties concerned did so first. The Bosnian Serbs rejected the proposal.

President Clinton recommended arming the Muslims, but this idea drew no support from European allies, and the United Nations tried again. It established a 14,000-member peacekeeping force from thirty countries (the first in Europe) to help the more than one million Muslims in the splintered country, most of them gathered in refugee camps euphemistically called "safe havens" and under UN troop protection. As the casualty lists soared and thousands died of starvation, the Security Council authorized NATO's military commanders to approve air strikes against Bosnian Serb forces, who had laid siege to tens of thousands of Muslims in eastern Bosnia. In the summer of 1993 the United Nations sent a peacekeeping unit to the old Yugoslav border

on the south to keep the conflict from spreading into neighboring Macedonia.

As the Muslims accused the Serbs of genocide, the problems steadily escalated until early 1994, when the United States joined other NATO countries in warning the Serbs of aerial assaults unless they called off their long siege of Sarajevo. The situation was desperate. In early January of that year, Bosnian Serbs had declared a cease-fire on the Bosnian capital, only to resume their barrage shortly thereafter. During the holiday season, both sides had violated the truce, killing more than one hundred civilians in the process. The commander of the UN peacekeepers in Bosnia resigned in disgust, and a disgruntled French general bitterly compared his troops to "goats tied to a stake."

There were no signs of a breakthrough to peace in what Secretary of State Warren Christopher called the "problem from hell." Limited air strikes finally quieted the siege guns, but the Bosnian Serbs denounced NATO for intervening on behalf of the Muslims and broke off contact with the United Nations. In August 1994, Bosnian Serbs raided a UN weapons depot west of Sarajevo, carting off a tank, two armored personnel carriers, and an antiaircraft gun. When NATO planes instantly responded by destroying a Serb motorized antitank weapon, the speaker of the Bosnian Serb parliament telephoned UN officials in Zagreb within two hours of the theft to assure them of the return of the UN weapons the next day. In the meantime, Milosevic accused the Bosnian Serbs of "insane political ambitions" and announced a political and economic break. Although he attributed this decision to the Bosnian Serbs' refusal to accept a UN peace plan, it more than likely resulted from the impact of the international trade embargo on his own country of Serbia. The Bosnian Serbs' assaults nonetheless continued, drawing more air strikes from NATO fighter-bombers that provoked the Serbs into seizing as hostages UN peacekeepers (later released) to embarrass the United Nations and force an end to the bombing.

In early 1995 several changes occurred that made peace a possibility. A UN withdrawal from Bosnia seemed imminent, raising talk of a U.S. military intervention ostensibly sent only to protect the UN forces as they pulled out. Democratic leaders in the United States warned that Bosnia was eating away at the presidency, threatening the chances for re-election. The Clinton administration secretly approved a Croatian proposal to import Iranian weapons, and Congress prohibited the U.S. Navy from supporting the UN arms embargo. By August the better-supplied Croatian forces had opened a successful assault against the Serbs that regained territorial losses and drew Muslim troop support. NATO then launched a massive bombing campaign that, combined with the ongoing embargo, seriously damaged the Serbian war effort. But the most important single development was the slaughter engineered by a Serb counteroffensive against UN forces at the safe havens of Srebrenica and Zepa. World public opinion was furious over the mass killings in Srebrenica. When the town fell, President Clinton stormed at his National Security Council leaders, "I'm getting creamed." Following the European lead, he angrily realized, had led to failure. He had placed the fate of his presidency in his allies' hands, and they had acted in their own interests by taking no decisive action. Especially galling was the snide remark made by French president Jacques Chirac after a June visit to Washington: The White House, he declared in a widely publicized quote, was "vacant."

By early September 1995 the chances for peace had brightened. The president had called on his advisers to formulate a "comprehensive peace settlement" that rested on recognition of Bosnia, Croatia, and Yugoslavia, followed by the lifting of economic sanctions after a cease-fire. Popular opposition in the United States to military intervention had lessened, adding teeth to his program. A *Washington Post* editorial in late May 1995 had warned that the "abandonment of Bosnia would rip at the threads of international order." Another Bosnian Serb bombardment of Sarajevo had killed more than thirty people, and NATO had responded with sustained air strikes on military targets. Clinton had put Assistant Secretary of State Richard C. Holbrooke in charge of negotiations, and he warned the White House that the Serb attack and NATO's bombings constituted the "most important test of American leadership since the end of the Cold War . . . not only in Bosnia but in Europe." Unlike the Vietcong, he insisted, the Bosnian Serbs would fold. Belgrade, he argued, would not support them. Milosevic wanted to see the sanctions lifted; the Bosnian Serbs could preserve the lands they had; and the Croatians could safeguard their recent territorial gains. NATO allies were now ready to enforce an agreement, particularly since Clinton had assured them of American troop participation in the peacekeeping mission.

On November 21, 1995, both sides agreed to a series of U.S.-mediated peace talks at Wright-Patterson Air Force Base near Dayton, Ohio, that resulted in an uneasy settlement of the forty-two-month-long Bosnian conflict. A cease-fire had gone into effect the previous October, about a month after Holbrooke had announced the main points of a settlement on September 8. Conditions were right. The Serbs wanted to solidify their gains for Bosnia and to halt the economic sanctions; the Croats sought to guarantee their new state and the security of their people elsewhere; and the Muslims demanded an end to their people's suffering and the establishment of a Bosnian state with strong Muslim representation. Three weeks of negotiations led by Holbrooke produced an agreement to divide Bosnia into two states: one a republic under Bosnian Serb control, the other a Croat-Muslim federation with Sarajevo as capital. Bosnian leaders immediately established a new government led by a three-member presidency, one from each ethnic group and all chosen in a national election. The White House three years earlier had opposed a Bosnian partition but now reversed its position. As a *New York Times* editorial put it on September 9, "The partition plan, imperfect as it is, offers the best hope for ending a war that has done grievous damage to Bosnia's people. It would be better if Bosnia were untouched and intact, but three years of vicious fighting have eliminated that possibility, and the Bosnians themselves are resigned to accepting a good deal less."

On December 14, in France, the presidents of Bosnia, Serbia, and Croatia signed the Paris Peace Accord, which enacted the Dayton agreements. To keep the peace, President Clinton joined Operation Joint Endeavor by pledging 20,000 U.S. ground troops as part of a NATO force of 60,000. The United States, Great Britain, and France would supervise the three zones until the civilian government could take over. America had "stood for peace in Bosnia," he proudly declared in his January 23, 1996, State of the Union address. "Remember the skeletal prisoners, the mass graves, the campaign to rape and torture, the endless lines of refugees, the threat of a spreading war. All these threats, all these horrors have now begun to give way to a promise of peace." Even though critics accused the West of reacting too slowly to the Balkan crisis, its actions had ended a terrible nightmare. In September 1996 elections in Yugoslavia resulted in Serb and Croatian majorities who advocated Bosnia's annexation of their peoples' territories and the establishment of a Muslim mini-state around Sarajevo. Muslim president Alija Izetbegovic won enough votes to become chair of the three-member presidency. In the following December, Clinton announced that U.S. forces would stay in Bosnia for an indefinite period.

Peace in the Balkans was short-lived, however. In 1999 violence erupted again when Milosevic ordered an ethnic cleansing of Kosovo, a Serbian province that was comprised primarily of Albanian Muslims but had enjoyed some measure of self-rule. The Kosovo Liberation Army (KLA) had launched a series of assaults on Serbian police in 1996, drawing a severe counteraction. By the spring of 1998 the KLA had intensified its fighting

with the aid of additional arms from inside Albania. The situation in Kosovo seemed less complicated than that in Bosnia, but this was not the case. The Serbs constituted nearly one-third of Bosnia's people; they were only a small minority in Kosovo. Bosnians spoke the same language; the Serbs and Albanians in Kosovo were distinctly different ethnic groups. Milosevic, who had turned his back on his Serbian allies in Bosnia, had built his nationalist reputation by taking away Kosovo's autonomy during the late 1980s. He and his cohort had been receptive to outside intervention in Bosnia; the Serbian military in Kosovo would oppose such a move, even at the risk of causing a military confrontation with peace-seeking powers. Whereas the violence in Bosnia remained within its boundaries, the intensified fighting in Kosovo threatened to spread into neighboring Albania and Macedonia. Kosovo was not a "second Bosnia," as many Europeans and Americans had surmised. The former U.S. ambassador to Yugoslavia, Warren Zimmermann, offered the most trenchant remark: "Inconceivable though it may seem, Kosovo is . . . a more complex problem than Bosnia."

The West again responded in a haphazard fashion. NATO warned Milosevic to respect Kosovo's sovereignty. The persecutions nonetheless continued, causing NATO's military leaders in March to order the bombing of Serbia's military and communication facilities. This step likewise proved ineffective. The United States reacted as indecisively as it had done at the onset of the Bosnian crisis. It denounced the KLA as "terrorists," a charge that might have been accurate but had the unintended impact of encouraging Milosevic to employ military force without fear of Western retaliation. It recommended economic sanctions, only to encounter rigid French and Russian opposition to a measure that had already proved empty in Yugoslavia. It failed at negotiations—including Clinton's meeting with pacifist Kosovar leader Ibrahim Rugova and Holbrooke's later conference with a KLA leader, effectively legitimizing the organization earlier branded as terrorist. The White House then abruptly reversed its policy and called for military force. The Serbs, meanwhile, continued to kill and rape ethnic Albanians, forcing the KLA into retreat and driving more than 800,000 refugees into the neighboring states of Albania and Macedonia.

Peace finally returned in the summer of 1999. Milosevic called off his brutal assault in June, but only when facing an aerial barrage, an oil embargo, and resistance from all the nations around him. He withdrew his Serb forces from Kosovo, allowed the refugees to return home, agreed to a NATO peacekeeping force, and authorized expanded autonomy to Kosovo. The atrocities committed by Milosevic's forces in Kosovo led to indictments against him and his top officers by the International War Crimes Tribunal at The Hague. According to a Western diplomat, Milosevic was "a python, slowly tightening his grip." National elections in September 2000, however, resulted in his overwhelming defeat by Vojislav Kostunica. Milosevic refused to concede, calling for a runoff that ignited student strikes and guaranteed further troubles.

By the spring of 2001, Yugoslav authorities had placed Milosevic under arrest, charging him with domestic crimes and leaving open the question of whether he would stand trial for international war crimes as well.

Clinton's Balkan policy deserves a mixed verdict. Peace in both Bosnia and Kosovo was his legacy, but had he acted quickly at the beginning of the Bosnian crisis in early 1993, he might have achieved the same cease-fire terms that came in the fall of 1995. Such resolute action might also have prevented the crisis in Kosovo. At the cost of thousands of lives, he had moved only when it became evident that continued inaction might damage his domestic program and hence his presidency.

The Middle East

In the midst of the Balkan troubles, a faint glimmer of peace came in the Middle East in September 1993, when Israel and the PLO

agreed to mutual recognition in an agreement that many contemporaries hailed as path breaking. On the South Lawn of the White House on September 13, President Clinton presided over an elaborate ceremony that featured a historic handshake between Israeli prime minister Yitzhak Rabin and PLO leader Yasir Arafat, dressed in his olive-drab uniform. "Enough. Enough blood and tears," Rabin had asserted. The "Declaration of Principles on Interim Self-Government Arrangements" was actually the culmination of a long peace process that had begun during the Yom Kippur War of 1973 and had seemingly concluded in Oslo, Norway, where two Israeli professors had contacted the PLO and by August 1992 (without U.S. input) had hammered out a text. Indeed, the White House had dismissed such talks as unimportant.

The Declaration provided a framework for a comprehensive peace, which meant that success was contingent on subsequent agreements with Israel's neighboring countries of Jordan, Lebanon, and Syria. In addition to mutual recognition, the Israelis would withdraw from Gaza and Jericho, but only after receiving security assurances for the 5000 Israeli settlers in Gaza. Under a Civil Administration of Palestinians, the PLO would control the Gaza Strip and the West Bank, both occupied by Israel since the Six Day War in 1967. Most important, the PLO renounced terrorism and Arafat promised a repudiation of its charter's call for Israel's destruction. Elections would take place among the nearly two million Palestinians on the West Bank and in Gaza, aimed at bringing self-government, first in the town of Jericho on the West Bank and then in Gaza before spreading into every other sector of the West Bank except for East Jerusalem. During a five-year interim period, the Palestinians were to gain autonomy over the lands and negotiations would begin with the Israelis in 1995 over a final settlement of the conflict that pointed to the establishment of a Palestinian homeland. The two sides would have until December 1993 to implement the September terms.

Why this progress? The PLO no longer could count on Soviet support because of the end of the Cold War. Arafat's ill-advised decision to support Saddam Hussein in the Gulf War had cost the PLO its longtime financial assistance from Iraq's enemy Arab kingdoms. Before these events, however, Arafat's control had come into question when he reacted with restraint to the intifada, which had broken out in December 1987 among the West Bank Palestinians in protest against Israeli occupation, and then announced in 1988 the establishment of a Palestinian "authority" in the troubled area, virtually recommending joint governing authority with Israel rather than its elimination. On the other side, Israelis were weary of the long conflict and feared that the intifada had won growing support from Palestinian extremists. Peace could bring economic stability in the region, which would profit everyone.

But the much-heralded September agreement in Washington constituted only another step in a long road to peace that lay cluttered with contentious issues. Arafat told reporters that the pact meant the "birth of Palestine" because self-rule provided the nucleus for a Palestinian state with Jerusalem as its capital. "He can forget about it," Rabin emphatically responded. Violence had erupted again—on the day *before* the agreement. In an incident of September 12 that proved to be the first of many to follow, Palestinian militants attacked Israelis in Gaza City, killing four. Meanwhile, in the occupied West Bank, protests against the accord led to a confrontation in which Israeli soldiers shot and killed two Palestinian youths while wounding eight others.

The December deadline came and passed, with no implementation of the September 1993 agreement. Rabin expressed concern about the safety of his people and opposed even a token withdrawal of Israeli troops from the Gaza Strip and Jericho. Arafat made new demands, most notably Palestinian control of the border crossings between the autonomous areas and Egypt and Jordan. Border control, he insisted, was a symbolic sign of sovereignty and would prevent humiliating interrogations and body searches by Israeli soldiers. But Israel feared that Arafat's hold on these checkpoints would bolster his claim to statehood and allow the infiltration of terrorists. Rabin assured the Knesset (Parliament) in mid-December that "no compromise is possible." In London, Arafat declared, "I haven't given up my dream [of a unified state]. But love cannot be one-sided."

What was the White House's position? Clinton hoped to facilitate an Israeli-PLO settlement by first securing agreements with the Arab states of Jordan, Lebanon, and Syria. During his visit to the Middle East in October 1994, he met with Syria's President Hafez al-Assad in Damascus, vainly attempting to lure him into the peace talks and bring an end to his country's support for international terrorism. Clinton had tried to persuade Syria to enter into a pact with Israel that included Lebanon (Syria's protégé) and would encourage peace along Israel's northern frontier. Since the Six Day War of 1967, Israeli troops had occupied the Golan Heights, a narrow strip of land along northern Israel that Islamic activists had used to launch attacks. Rabin and Assad reportedly favored the restoration of the Golan Heights to Syria in exchange for its recognition of Israel, but they took no initiative toward an agreement. In early May 1994 a series of autonomy agreements between Israel and the PLO transferred the administration of Jericho and most of the Gaza Strip to the Palestinians. Under this self-rule agreement, the 5000 Jewish settlers in the Gaza Strip would remain in their homes, protected by Israeli soldiers and PLO forces. In the following July, the White House canceled Jordan's foreign debt in exchange for its agreement to a treaty with Israel that provided mutual recognition. Jordan's King Hussein and Israel's Prime Minister Rabin also laid the basis for bilateral trade and tourist exchanges by agreeing to adjoining boundaries and dividing water rights and other natural resources. The Clinton administration authorized seed money for aid from Japan, Europe,

Scandinavia, and the Gulf Arab states, and it furnished assistance to the new Palestinian communities in the Gaza Strip and Jericho.

Sporadic outbreaks of violence in the Middle East continued to obstruct the erratic move toward a settlement. In late February 1995 trouble broke out on the West Bank when a Jewish extremist shot at least thirty Palestinians while at worship in Hebron and an angry mob beat him to death. The "Hebron massacre" once again drove home the tenuous nature of any Middle East settlement. One Israeli military spokesman observed, "You don't fire warning shots in a combat situation. All Gaza is a combat situation, all the time."

Then, on November 4, 1995, a right-wing Israeli student shot and killed Prime Minister Rabin at a peace rally in Tel Aviv, shocking the world and raising new questions about the possibilities of peace in this battle-scarred land. President Clinton demonstrated his unbroken pursuit of peace by heading a U.S. delegation to Rabin's funeral in Tel Aviv. "Those who practice terror must not succeed," he later declared. "We must root them out, and we will not let them kill the peace." More violence broke out during the Israeli election campaign in the spring of 1996, when Palestinian terrorists in less than two weeks carried out four suicide bombings that killed more than sixty Israelis and wounded more than two hundred others. Popular disenchantment with the peace process became clear when the voters narrowly selected a new prime minister, Benjamin Netanyahu, who headed the conservative Likud party and promised "peace with security" as an unmistakable warning that he would concede nothing to the Arabs without absolute guarantees of Israel's safety. In January 1997, with the area seething with tension, the White House joined other countries in exerting pressure on Israel to withdraw from Hebron.

This concession had a short-lived impact, however, because of the violent reaction to Netanyahu's call for new Jewish settlements in East Jerusalem, where many Palestinians resided. At a nine-day conference at Camp David, Maryland, in October 1998, Clinton oversaw agreements between Arafat and Netanyahu to withdraw from jointly held areas and to process the release of imprisoned Palestinians in exchange for Arafat's assurances (again) of an end to the PLO's demand for Israel's destruction. This was not enough for hard-liners in the Likud party, however, who turned against Netanyahu and forced a national election in the spring of 1999. He lost to Ehud Barak, who had campaigned for reopened negotiations with the Palestinians. In the summer of 2000, President Clinton attempted to broker a Middle East settlement between the Israelis and the Palestinians, but no treaty had developed by the September deadline. Late that same month, Israeli police killed and wounded a large number of Palestinians in a clash by a holy site in Jerusalem. Outbreaks of violence continued into the spring of 2001.

Peace in other parts of the Middle East also remained elusive. Saddam Hussein in late 1994 had again shown signs of ordering an invasion of Kuwait, leading the Clinton administration to send a huge military contingent to the Persian Gulf to maintain the peace. Before the World Jewish Congress in April 1995 the president announced his "dual containment" policy, which aimed to harness the ambitions of Iraq and Iran. Both countries "harbor terrorists within their borders," he declared. "They establish and support terrorist base camps in other lands. They hunger for nuclear and other weapons of mass destruction. Every day, they put innocent civilians in danger and stir up discord among nations. Our policy toward them is simple: They must be contained." Twice in 1998—in February and November—Clinton dispatched military forces into the Persian Gulf, only to call off attacks at the last minute when Saddam agreed to cooperate with inspection teams. In mid-December, however, Saddam again interfered with the inspection process, leading the president to approve "Operation Desert Fox," an air and missile assault that lasted for four days and again brought an uneasy peace. Critics, however, noted more than a coincidence in the president's resort to force in the midst of the House debate on impeachment over a sex scandal that resulted in an indictment and ultimately ended in a Senate acquittal.

The end of the Cold War had put a different complexion on U.S. interests in the Middle East. Containment and confrontation tactics had proved fruitless. Whereas in the Cold War the United States had used its influence to oppose Soviet expansion in the region while protecting Israel, it realized in the post–Cold War era that an Arab-Israeli conflict could not escalate into a U.S.-Soviet confrontation and thereby lost the sense of urgency in seeking a final settlement. The Oslo agreements had turned the emphasis toward the Palestinians, over whom the United States had little or no leverage, and away from the Arabs, who had been more malleable to its interests. Thus, as the peace focus shifted to the core issue of Palestinian autonomy, the peace process ground nearly to a halt and White House frustration turned more against the Israelis. This new tension between the United States and Israel received further impetus from the steady decline of U.S. influence in the region after the Gulf War. Indeed, French and Russian resistance to U.S. hegemony in the Middle East had caused some Arab states to inch closer to neutrality. Moreover, the growth of Arab nationalism and Islamic fundamentalism made it prohibitive for Arabs to support the United States in its continuing battle with Saddam Hussein, especially in view of Israeli-PLO troubles. In a bizarre reversal of form, Washington began courting Teheran in an effort to exert more pressure on Saddam.

The Arab-Israeli dispute was no longer the exclusive issue in the Middle East. The Soviets had lost their dominant control over the Caucasus and Central Asia, meaning that new forms of competition had assumed pivotal importance not only because of the region's rich oil reserves but also because of the fear of nuclear proliferation. What if archenemies Iran and Iraq developed nuclear power? Israel had already acquired such capacity while both India and Pakistan (age-old enemies) did the

same in the spring of 1998. If the end of the Cold War had pushed the Arabs and Israelis closer to a final resolution that included the Palestinians, it had also spawned a host of other regional problems that would continue to interfere with the search for a lasting peace.

East Asia and Other Matters

Clinton confronted equally serious problems in East Asia. Realizing that this region was fast becoming a commercial Mecca, the president made a major effort to establish better trade relations with its leaders. As noted earlier, the United States considered it critical to deal amicably with Japan and in early summer 1995 narrowly averted a commercial war by securing a trade agreement and then turning full circle from confrontational policies to economic and political engagement. China, too, presented a problem. Its continued human rights violations and sales of nuclear weapons technology to Pakistan and other nations raised questions about whether the United States should renew its most-favored-nation status with that Communist government. About forty percent of China's exports entered the United States, resulting in a $30 billion annual commercial surplus. But China refused to yield; instead, it cracked down on citizens who called for democratic changes and jailed Tibetans who sought independence for their country. In June 1993, however, the Clinton administration extended most-favored-nation commercial rights to Beijing in exchange for China's release of several imprisoned dissidents. In the next year, in May 1994, the White House formally separated human rights aspirations from commercial aims, admitting that their linkage had yielded few results and declaring that the old policy of engagement offered greater promise.

Sino-American problems remained. Tensions flared in March 1996 over elections in Taiwan when the Chinese government began an intimidation campaign that included its firing three missiles near the island and staging military maneuvers in the Taiwan Strait. Two

U.S. carrier task forces headed toward the troubled area. The crisis passed after the White House confirmed its support of "one China" and the Beijing government promised not to help terrorists. Beijing's leaders still claimed Taiwan as part of China and feared that the elections would bring in a new administration that demanded independence. In February 1997, Deng died, leaving a mixed legacy of human rights abuses, military expansion, and the clampdown on pro-democracy demonstrators at Tiananmen Square along with a massive opening of trade that led to China's economic upswing during the 1990s. Anxious Americans on July 1, 1997, joined others throughout the world in watching Hong Kong pass peacefully from British hands to China's. Although Hong Kong's residents totaled only 6 million in comparison with China's 1.2 billion, the former British colony furnished almost twenty percent of China's gross national product and would help the vast country be an even greater force in international affairs. China's new president, Jiang Zemin, visited the United States in October 1997, and in the following year he worked with Clinton to ease a crisis between India and Pakistan over nuclear testing. President Clinton reciprocated by traveling to China that same year, where he expressed the two nations' growing concern over Japan's stumbling economy. The administration's enlargement policy now included China as well as Japan.

In North Korea, the Clinton administration confronted its most dangerous issue when that Communist regime threatened to withdraw from the Non-Proliferation Treaty of 1985 and develop its own nuclear capacity. More serious, North Korea might sell nuclear weapons, which could cause a regional arms race and a major proliferation problem. As tensions soared throughout East Asia, President Clinton reaffirmed the U.S. troop commitment to South Korea during the summer of 1993 and in the following spring made preparations for implanting defensive missiles. The crisis soon passed when former president Jimmy Carter acted as intermediary in per-

suading Kim Il Sung's North Korean government to halt its nuclear program while talks were under way. Then Kim died in July 1994, leaving the country's leadership to his son Kim Jong Il, who continued the talks in Geneva. The result was a deal in October by which the United States, South Korea, and Japan provided North Korea with nearly $5 billion in energy assistance (including peaceful nuclear reactors), free oil for up to ten years, and diplomatic relations with Washington and Tokyo—all in exchange for its complying with the Nuclear Non-Proliferation Treaty by shutting down its plutonium reprocessing plant and permitting international inspection within eight years (promises made years earlier and broken). Chinese pressure had pushed Kim to relax tensions, primarily out of a desire to diminish the U.S. presence in Asia. Kim also recognized the questionable value in heading a rogue state. New hope for peace came in 2000, when North Korea and South Korea agreed to end their war that began in June 1950 and to move toward a reconciliation.

Vietnam also posed a major dilemma for the administration as the White House attempted to balance commercial potential with lingering hatreds stemming from the United States's longest war. In February 1994 the United States lifted its nearly two-decade-long trade embargo on Vietnam and, a little more than a year later, on July 11, 1995, extended diplomatic recognition. The move, argued President Clinton, would triple the trade between the countries to more than $8 billion by the end of the century, facilitate a settlement of the POW and MIA issues (more than 2200 American soldiers missing in action and still unaccounted for), and, by focusing on economic ties, help put the U.S.-Vietnam War in the past. To ease the angry fallout of such a move, he appointed as ambassador a former POW in Hanoi for seven years, Pete Peterson. Five years later, in the summer of 2000, the two nations reached a trade agreement that, if approved by Congress, would permit generally open commerce for the first time since the end of their war in 1973.

The Clinton administration also tried, with some success, to bring peace to Northern Ireland. It first argued that Sinn Fein, the political voice of the Irish Republican Army (IRA), deserved a seat in the negotiations over the status of Ulster. When the state department in Washington permitted Sinn Fein leader Gerry Adams to come to the United States, the British government angrily protested that he was a terrorist. Clinton nonetheless invited Adams to the White House in 1995, on St. Patrick's Day. The president's tactics resulted in Adams's attracting American support for his cause and then arranging for the IRA to announce a unilateral cease-fire later that same year. Clinton reciprocated with a visit to Belfast, where he assured a cheering public of U.S. support if the Irish people worked toward peace. The result was a truce agreed to by the British government, the Ulster Defense Association, and the IRA.

Although IRA bombings in London soon broke the truce in April 1996, new talks began in September that culminated twenty-one months later in the Good Friday Peace Accord of April 10, 1998. In Belfast, Northern Ireland, British prime minister Tony Blair and Northern Ireland's prime minister, Bertie Ahern, ended three decades of fighting by approving a peace pact that resulted from a long series of arduous negotiations chaired by former U.S. Senator George Mitchell. To satisfy the Irish unionists, mostly Catholic, who want the British province integrated into a united Ireland, and the Irish republicans, mostly Protestant, who wish to continue British rule in Northern Ireland, the British and Irish governments agreed that Northern Ireland would remain within the United Kingdom unless Irish majorities voted for unity. In late May 1998, Irish voters overwhelmingly approved the pact, setting in motion the machinery for implementing the Good Friday Peace Accord. President Clinton encouraged peace with a visit to Northern Ireland in September. Scattered instances of violence have occurred as the peace process continues.

Perhaps the biggest barometer of whether the Clinton administration had taken a new direction in foreign policy was its attitude toward intervention. In Haiti, the White House took an interventionist course when it exerted pressure on strongman Raoul Cédras and his military clique to leave the island after their coup in 1991. With the help of President Carter as intermediary (again), along with General Colin Powell and Senator Sam Nunn, the president achieved Cédras's departure without serious incident. In September 1994, Clinton approved "Operation Uphold Democracy," which authorized U.S. troops to facilitate the peaceful return of ousted President Jean-Bertrand Aristide. The United States and the United Nations then cooperated with the Haitian government in arranging a series of national elections that led to the first democratic change of presidents in that nation's history—the election of René Preval in December 1995. The thirty-nation force had already withdrawn from Haiti in March, leaving the peacekeeping responsibility to the United Nations. This careful approach, along with the restraint that characterized the U.S. involvement in the Balkan and Irish crises, reflected how well the U.S. experience in Vietnam had demonstrated the dangers of an interventionist foreign policy. To the Russians, President Clinton declared over live television that "it's all we can do to deal with our own problems. We don't have time to try to dictate your course."

Prospects of a New World Order

As the United States entered the twenty-first century, it became clear that the chief legacy of the Cold War was a distinctly different global order in which no single power was dominant. Franklin D. Roosevelt's vision of a half century earlier had seemingly emerged: a world order based on the principle of collective security exercised through the United Nations. His World War II aims had finally reached fulfillment with the United States's important position in international affairs, its resolution of differences with the countries once part of the former Soviet Union, its recognition of China's integral role in a peaceful world, and the collapse of colonial rule. So had the Yalta Declaration on Liberated Europe manifested itself through the democratization of Eastern Europe. The end of the Cold War had brought to a close that long and bitter U.S.-Soviet rivalry in the Security Council, thus allowing the United Nations to become an active guardian of peace.

But the image was considerably different from the reality. The bipolar world of 1945 had rested on military power but had now given way to new power alignments based primarily on economics. The world remained bipolar in terms of nuclear weaponry and delivery mechanisms, but it had divided into three distinct regional blocs. Western Europe had moved toward a union of states by the establishment of the European Common Market in the early 1990s. East Asia was the scene of unparalleled economic growth with Japan leading the way and only the Philippines lagging behind. And third was the bloc taking shape in North America, led by the United States and including Canada, the Caribbean Basin, and Mexico. The North American Free Trade Agreement had promoted the economic integration of the continent, making it necessary to speak of superblocs rather than superpowers in discussing international leadership. Clinton had made his nation's domestic economy the measure of his success, but he had done so only by securing free-trade agreements that created new jobs and strengthened the dollar. Secretary of State Madeleine Albright, Warren Christopher's successor in 1997 following Clinton's reelection in 1996, pointed to one of the most salient facts of the administration: "Thanks to over 200 new market agreements we have created 1.6 million American jobs."

Clinton's foreign policy had a mixed success. He had moved from an idealistic approach that resulted most often in chaos and indecision, to a policy based on pragmatism and some sense of strategy built on expanding global trade. He had achieved the expan-

sion of NATO to include three East European members by March 1999—Poland, Hungary, and the Czech Republic—and had redefined the meaning of European security while maintaining an active U.S. involvement. The downside, of course, was the disintegration of the "strategic partnership" with Russia that resulted not only from the NATO issue but also from a revived Russian nationalism and a continued reluctance by the West to extend economic assistance. His economic enlargement strategy had succeeded in opening new commercial avenues, but at the cost of near silence on environmental needs in the face of corporate pressure against government regulations. Most telling, the moral stature of the presidency had suffered a devastating blow not only from the indecision and backtracking of the administration's foreign policy but also from the personal scandals that repeatedly rocked the White House.

Free trade had remained Clinton's guiding star in spreading democracy by placing the United States into the middle of the economic integration of the Pacific Rim, the European continent, and the Western Hemisphere. "With our help, the forces of reform in Europe's newly free nations have laid the foundations of democracy," the president declared. "We've helped them to develop successful market economies, and now are moving from aid to trade and investment." Martin Walker wrote in *The New Yorker* that "the age of geopolitics has given way to an age of what might be called geo-economics." Clinton's new world order had "abandoned the militarized slogans of the past to the commercial realities of the future." Not only had the United States become the world's military *and* economic leader, but it had also contributed to the global spread of democracy. In the mid-1970s about twenty-five percent of the world's independent nations chose their leaders by democratic elections. As the new millennium began, that percentage had doubled. Problems remained in China and Bosnia, the environment was in danger, global terrorism was a recurring threat, and Russian prospects for democracy and economic reforms remained elusive as former Cold Warrior and KGB officer Vladimir Putin succeeded the aged and worn Yeltsin as president in the elections of March 2000. The tenets of a free-market democracy had taken hold in several countries, however. In early December 1996, *New York Times* columnist Thomas L. Friedman highlighted the key element in Clinton's enlargement strategy: "No two countries that both have a McDonald's have ever fought a war against each other."

War will doubtless remain an instrument of policy because of the unavoidable differences between nations. The most obvious examples have been the wars between Iraq and Iran and between Iraq and Kuwait. But during the 1990s, guerrilla conflicts erupted all over the world—in Bosnia, Cambodia, El Salvador, Ethiopia, Liberia, Mozambique, Nigeria, Peru, Sierra Leone, and Sri Lanka (formerly Ceylon). Some argued that in the post–Cold War era these problems were subject to analysis on the basis of their own issues: No longer were quarreling peoples mere pawns of the two chief Cold War rivals. Others argued just as convincingly that the two chief Cold War antagonists had repeatedly kept small countries from engaging in civil wars out of concern that they could draw in the major powers and become part of a larger conflict. In that regard, perhaps, veteran Cold Warriors on both sides could claim that they had recognized the insanity of nuclear war and had successfully kept localized conflicts from escalating into world war.

The end of the Cold War had freed U.S. allies from the Communist threat and allowed them to focus on other, long-neglected needs; so did it have a similar impact on the United States. To continue its role in a new world order based on the spread of market-based democracies and a diffusion of power, the United States must recognize its limitations at home and away, control its arms sales abroad, enforce the renewed Treaty on the Non-Proliferation of Nuclear Weapons of 1995, deal with terrorists and their easy access to weapons, implement the call of the Chemical Convention of 1993 to destroy all chemical weapons by 2005, and establish a sound relationship with China, Germany, Japan, and Russia. The United States must also welcome the former Soviet states and other fledgling countries into the new global system, repair relations with Asia after its brush with financial and economic disaster during the late

George W. Bush Inauguration
George W. Bush taking the oath as president on January 20, 2001, as his family and other dignitaries observe the proceedings. *Wide World Photos, New York.*

1990s had drawn belated U.S. assistance, and help Latin America to resolve its economic problems, particularly after the White House regained considerable credibility by turning over the Panama Canal to Panama on schedule in 2000. In addition, the United States must maintain its balanced budget and continue its revived economy, improve education at home, stimulate developmental research, become a better steward of the environment, seek fair treatment of women and minorities worldwide, work to disseminate the new plethora of computer-generated information afforded by the Internet, and resolve the domestic problems caused by drugs, guns, and violence. Most important, the United States must cooperate with other nations in establishing an international economic and financial network that will facilitate the development of a global market system conducive to a higher standard of living, the spread of self-determination, and the peaceful settlement of international disputes.

All these problems and more confront Clinton's successor in the new millennium, President George W. Bush, who narrowly defeated Vice President Al Gore in the hotly contested election of 2000.

Selected Readings

Ambrose, Stephen E., and Brinkley, Douglas G. *Rise to Globalism: American Foreign Policy since 1938*. 8th ed., 1997.

Amos, Deborah. *Lines in the Sand: Desert Storm and the Remaking of the Arab World*. 1992.

Arnson, Cynthia. *Crossroads: Congress, the President, and Central America, 1976–1993*. 1994.

Ash, Timothy G. *In Europe's Name: Germany and the Divided Continent*. 1994.

———. *The Magic Lantern: The Revolution of '89 Witnessed in Warsaw, Budapest, Berlin, and Prague*. 1990.

Aslund, Anders. *Gorbachev's Struggle for Economic Reform: The Soviet Reform Process, 1985–1988*. 1989.

Atkinson, Rick. *Crusade: The Untold Story of the Persian Gulf War*. 1993.

Barnet, Richard J., and Cavanagh, John. *Global Dreams: Imperial Corporations and the New World Order*. 1994.

Benedick, Richard E. *Ozone Diplomacy: New Directions in Safeguarding the Planet*. 1998.

Berman, William C. *America's Right Turn: From Nixon to Clinton*. 2nd ed., 1998.

Beschloss, Michael R., and Talbott, Strobe. *At the Highest Levels: The Inside Story of the End of the Cold War*. 1993.

Brands, H. W. *The Devil We Knew: Americans and the Cold War*. 1993.

Brown, Archie. *The Gorbachev Factor*. 1996.

Buckley, Kevin. *Panama: The Whole Story*. 1991.

Buckley, Roger. *U.S.-Japan Alliance Diplomacy, 1945–1990*. 1992.

Burrows, William E., and Windrem, Robert. *Critical Mass: The Dangerous Race for Superweapons in a Fragmentary World*. 1994.

Bush, George, and Scowcroft, Brent. *A World Transformed*. 1998.

Calleo, David P. *Beyond American Hegemony: The Future of the Western Alliance*. 1987.

Chace, James. *The Consequences of the Peace: The New Internationalism and American Foreign Policy*. 1992.

Cheng, Chu-yüang. *Behind the Tiananmen Massacre: Social, Political, and Economic Ferment in China*. 1990.

Cohen, Warren I. *America's Response to China: An Interpretive History of Sino-American Relations*. 2000.

Cox, Michael. *U.S. Foreign Policy after the Cold War: Superpower without a Mission?* 1995.

Cronin, James E. *The World the Cold War Made: Order, Chaos, and the Return of History*. 1996.

Dobbs, Michael. *Madeleine Albright: A Twentieth-Century Odyssey*. 1999.

Doder, Dusko, and Branson, Louise. *Gorbachev: Heretic in the Kremlin*. 1990.

Dukes, Paul. *The Last Great Game: USA Versus USSR*. 1989.

Ehrman, John. *The Rise of Neoconservatism: Intellectuals and Foreign Affairs, 1945–1994*. 1995.

Evangelista, Matthew. *Unarmed Forces: The Transnational Movement to End the Cold War*. 1999.

Freedman, Lawrence, and Karsh, Efraim. *The Gulf Conflict, 1990–1991: Diplomacy and War in the New World Order*. 1993.

Freney, Michael A., and Hartley, Rebecca S. *United Germany and the United States*. 1991.

Friedman, Norman. *Desert Victory: The War for Kuwait.* 1991.

Gaddis, John L. "The Tragedy of Cold War History," *Diplomatic History* 17 (1993): 1–16.

———. *The United States and the End of the Cold War: Implications, Reconsiderations, Provocations.* 1992.

Garthoff, Raymond L. *The Great Transition: American-Soviet Relations and the End of the Cold War.* 1994.

Gati, Charles. *The Bloc That Failed.* 1990.

Gerner, Deborah J. *One Land, Two Peoples: The Conflict over Palestine.* 1991.

Gittings, John. *China Changes Face: The Road from Revolution, 1949–1989.* 1989.

Gow, James. *Triumph of the Lack of Will: International Diplomacy and the Yugoslav War.* 1997.

Graham, Otis L., Jr. *Losing Time: The Industrial Policy Debate.* 1992.

Graubard, Stephen R. *Mr. Bush's War: Adventures in the Politics of Illusion.* 1992.

Grayson, George W. *The North American Free Trade Agreement: Regional Community and the New World Order.* 1995.

Greene, John R. *The Presidency of George Bush.* 2000.

Greider, William. *Fortress America: The American Military and the Consequences of Peace.* 1998.

Hanson, Jim M. *The Decline of the American Empire.* 1993.

Harding, Harry. *A Fragile Relationship: The United States and China since 1972.* 1992.

Haselkorn, Avigdor. *The Continuing Storm: Iraq, Poisonous Weapons and Deterrence.* 1999.

Hiro, Dilip. *Desert Shield to Desert Storm: The Second Gulf War.* 1992.

Hoffmann, Stanley. *World Disorders: Troubled Peace in the Post–Cold War Era.* 1998.

Hogan, Michael J., ed. "The End of the Cold War: A Symposium," *Diplomatic History* 16 (1992): 45–113, 223–318.

———, ed. *The End of the Cold War: Its Meanings and Implications.* 1992.

Homer-Dixon, Thomas F. *Environmental Scarcity and Global Security.* 1993.

Hosking, Geoffrey A. *The Awakening of the Soviet Union.* 1991.

Hough, Jerry F. *Democratization and Revolution in the USSR, 1985–1991.* 1997.

Hunter, F. Robert. *The Palestinian Uprising: A War by Other Means.* 1993.

Hyland, William. *Clinton's World: Remaking American Foreign Policy.* 1999.

Kaiser, Robert G. *Why Gorbachev Happened: The Man and His Revolution.* 1991.

Karsh, Efraim, and Rautsi, Inari. *Saddam Hussein: A Political Biography.* 1991.

Kaufman, Burton I. *The Arab Middle East and the United States: Inter-Arab Rivalry and Superpower Diplomacy.* 1996.

Kaufmann, William W. *Glasnost, Perestroika, and U.S. Defense Spending.* 1990.

Kennedy, Paul. *The Rise and Fall of the Great Powers: Economic Change and Military Conflict from 1500 to 2000.* 1987.

Kuisel, Richard F. *Seducing the French: The Dilemma of Americanization.* 1993.

LaFeber, Walter. *America, Russia, and the Cold War, 1945–1996.* 8th ed., 1997.

———. *The Clash: A History of U.S.-Japan Relations.* 1997.

Lebow, Richard N., and Stein, Janice G. *We All Lost the Cold War.* 1994.

LeoGrande, William M. *Our Own Backyard: The United States in Central America, 1977–1992.* 1998.

MacArthur, John R. *Second Front: Censorship and Propaganda in the Gulf War.* 1992.

Maier, Charles S. *Dissolution: The Crisis of Communism and the End of East Germany.* 1997.

Mandelbaum, Michael. *The Dawn of Peace in Europe.* 1996.

Mann, Jim. *About Face: A History of America's Curious Relationship with China from Nixon to Clinton.* 1999.

Matthews, Ken. *The Gulf Conflict and International Relations.* 1993.

McMahon, Robert J. *The Limits of Empire: The United States and Southeast Asia since World War II.* 1999.

Melanson, Richard A. *American Foreign Policy since the Vietnam War: The Search for Consensus from Nixon to Clinton.* 2000.

Miller, Judith, and Mylorie, Laurie. *Saddam Hussein and the Crisis in the Gulf.* 1990.

Mueller, John E. *Policy and Opinion in the Gulf War.* 1994.

Nau, Henry R. *The Myth of America's Decline: Leading the World Economy into the 1990s.* 1990.

Oberdorfer, Don. *From the Cold War to a New Era: The United States and the Soviet Union, 1983–1991.* 1998.

———. *The Turn: From the Cold War to a New Era. The United States and the Soviet Union, 1983–1990.* 1991.

Palmer, Michael A. *Guardians of the Gulf: A History of America's Expanding Role in the Persian Gulf.* 1992.

Parmet, Herbert S. *George Bush: The Life of a Lone Star Yankee.* 1997.

Paterson, Thomas G. *On Every Front: The Making and Unmaking of the Cold War.* 1992.

Pérez, Louis A., Jr. *Cuba and the United States: Ties of Singular Intimacy.* 1997.

Prados, John. *Presidents' Secret Wars: CIA Pentagon Covert Operations from World War II through the Persian Gulf.* 1996.

Quandt, William B. *Peace Process: American Diplomacy and the Arab-Israeli Conflict since 1967.* 1993.

Raat, W. Dirk. *Mexico and the United States: Ambivalent Vistas.* 1996.

Remnick, David. *Lenin's Tomb: The Last Days of the Soviet Empire.* 1993.

Rosecrance, Richard N. *America's Economic Resurgence: A Bold New Strategy.* 1990.

Ruggie, John G. *Winning the Peace: America and World Order in the New Era.* 1996.

Sayigh, Yezid. *Armed Struggle and the Search for State: The Palestinian National Movement, 1949–1993.* 1997.

Schaller, Michael. *Altered States: The United States and Japan since the Occupation.* 1997.

Schoenbaum, David. *The United States and the State of Israel.* 1993.

Schoutz, Lars. *Beneath the United States: A History of U.S. Policy toward Latin America.* 1998.

Scranton, Margaret E. *The Noriega Years: U.S.-Panamanian Relations, 1981–1990.* 1991.

Sigal, Leon V. *Disarming Strangers: Nuclear Diplomacy with North Korea.* 1998.

Smith, Gaddis. *The Last Years of the Monroe Doctrine, 1945–1993.* 1994.

Smith, Jean Edward. *George Bush's War.* 1992.

Smith, Patrick L. *Japan: A Reinterpretation.* 1997.

Solomon, Robert. *Money on the Move: The Revolution in International Finance since 1980.* 1999.

Spanier, John W., and Hook, Steven W. *American Foreign Policy since World War II.* 14th ed., 1998.

Stares, Paul B. *Global Habit: The Drug Problem in a Borderless World.* 1996.

Steel, Ronald. *Temptations of a Superpower.* 1995.

Stern, Jessica. *The Ultimate Terrorists.* 1999.

Szabo, Stephen F. *The Diplomacy of German Unification.* 1992.

Treverton, Gregory F. *America, Germany, and the Future of Europe.* 1992.

Tucker, Robert W., and Henrickson, David C. *The Imperial Temptation: The New World Order and America's Purpose.* 1992.

Ulam, Adam B. *The Communists: The Story of Power and Lost Illusions, 1948–1991.* 1992.

Van Crefeld, Martin. *Nuclear Proliferation and the Future of Conflict.* 1993.

Weissman, Stephen R. *A Culture of Deference: Congress's Failure of Leadership in Foreign Policy.* 1995.

Woodward, Bob. *The Commanders.* 1991.

Woodward, Susan L. *Balkan Tragedy: Chaos and Dissolution after the Cold War.* 1995.

Wyden, Peter. *Wall: The Inside Story of Divided Berlin.* 1989.

Yergin, Daniel. *The Prize: The Epic Quest for Oil, Money, and Power.* 1991.

INDEX

Note: Page numbers in *italics* indicate illustrations. Page numbers followed by letter *m* indicate maps.

modern, development of, 2–3
recruiting posters for World War
 I, *87*
world cruise (1907–1909), 48, 49
post-World War I, 117
Nazis
 in Austria, 148
 in Germany, 136–137, 144, 155
Nazi-Soviet Nonaggression Pact
 (1939), 157, *158*, 159, 163
 Tripartite Pact and, 172
NDEA. *See* National Defense Edu-
 cation Act
Near East
 Cold War and importance of, 237
 U.S. intervention in, Cold War
  and, 228, 242
 See also specific countries
Nehru, Jawaharlal, 287
Netanyahu, Benjamin, 518
Netherlands
 and Brussels Treaty (1948), 249
 German invasion of, 165
 at Washington Naval Conference
  (1921–1922), 119, 120
Neutrality
 Act of 1935, 146, 150
 Act of 1936, 147, 150
 Act of 1937, 150, 157
 Act of 1939, 165, 180
 Act of 1941, 181
 in World War I, 69, 70, 71, 75,
  76
 pre-World War II, 146–152, 155
 in World War II, 163, 165, 167,
  171
New Deal program, 138, 148, 154,
 247
New Freedom program, 53
New Granada. *See* Colombia
New International Economic Order
 (NIEO), call for, 452
New Left, 367
New manifest destiny, 1, 5
"New Order" in East Asia, Japan
 and, 152–153, 172
New Panama Canal Company, 30,
 31, 32, 33, 34, 35
New world order, prospects of,
 521–522
New York Journal, 9
 and U.S. imperialism, 4–5, 7, 12
New York Times
 on Balkan crisis, 513, 514–515
 on Cold War, 229
 on Iranian hostage crisis, 436
 on *Lusitania* sinking, *74*
 and peace efforts of 1920s, 122
 on Sino-U.S. relations, 397
 on Vietnam War, 358, 367, 390,
  403
New York World
 and Panama Canal, 33
 and U.S. imperialism, 4, 5, 21

New Zealand
 in Tripartite Security Treaty
  (ANZUS), 279
 Vietnam War and, 371
Nhu, Madame, 346
Nhu, Ngo Dinh, 346, 347, 348
Niagara Conference (1914), 63
Nicaragua
 Bush administration policies
  toward, 493
 canal route through, considera-
  tion of, 31, 32, 57
 contras in, *463*
  U.S. support for, 462,
   465–467, 476, 493
 Cuban exiles in, and Bay of Pigs
  invasion, 327
 dollar diplomacy in, 42
 Gorbachev's policies toward, 458,
  493
 insurrections of 1911 and 1912, 43
 Reagan's policies toward, 461
 Sandinistas in, 116, 428, 458,
  459, 461, 463, 466, 493
 settlement with El Salvador, 478
 U.S. intervention in
  (1912–1925), 43, 57, 116
Nicholas II, Czar, 16, 88
NIEO. *See* New International Economic Order
Nigeria, 424
Nimitz (U.S. carrier), 441
Nine-Power Treaty (1922), 120,
 129, 150, 151
Ninth International Conference of
 American States (1948), 248
Nitze, Paul, 253, 435
Nixon, Richard M., 355
 China policies of, 395–396, 397
 and détente, 386, 387, 391,
  395–396, 397
 on First Indochinese War,
  292–293
 Formosa crisis of 1954 and, 299
 Guam speech (1969), 390–391
 on Kissinger, 387
 kitchen debate with Khrushchev,
  314
 Latin American policies of,
  409–411
 Middle East policies of, 407–409
 and Pahlavi (Shah of Iran), *437*
 in presidential election of 1952,
  280
 in presidential election of 1960,
  316
 in presidential election of 1968,
  380, 381
 and Red Scare of 1950s, 243
 and Vietnam War policies,
  389–390, 391–392, 393,
  394, 399, 401, 402–403
 visit to China (1972), 397–398,
  398

 visit to Latin America, 316
 visit to Soviet Union (1972), 314,
  400, *401*
 and Watergate scandal, 406, 411
Nixon Doctrine, 390, 391, 442
NLF. *See* National Liberation Front
Nobel Peace Prize
 for Briand, 122
 for Gorbachev, 489
 for Kellogg, 124
 for Kissinger and Le Duc Tho,
  404
 for Roosevelt (Theodore), 47, 50
 for Sánchez, Oscar Arias, 478
 for Walesa, 488
Nomura, Kichisaburo, 174, 175,
 177, 181, 186, 187
Nonpartisan Committee for Peace
 through Revision of the Neutrality Act, 165
Non-Proliferation Treaty (1985),
 520
Nonrecognition
 of China, People's Republic of,
  265, 266, 295
 of East Germany, 300, 311
 of Manchukuo, 129, 131, 132,
  149
 Manchurian crisis and, 129, 131,
  132
 of Soviet Union, 141–142
 Stimson Doctrine of, 129, 131
Noriega, Manuel, 476, 494, 495
Normandy Beach, Allied invasion
 of, 200
Norris, George, 81, 104, 145
North, Oliver, 476, 477, 478
North African campaign, World War
 II, 191, 194–195, 196
North American Free Trade Agree-
 ment (NAFTA), 495–496, 506,
 507, 522
North Atlantic Treaty (1949), 251
North Atlantic Treaty Organization
 (NATO), 228
 Berlin crisis of 1958 and, 311, 312
 Bosnian war and, 513, 514
 Carter administration and, 423
 Clinton administration and, 509,
  511
 post-Cold War, 507, 508, 509
 expansion of, 522
 formation of, 251
 Kennedy and, 349
 Kosovo crisis and, 515
 purpose of, 253
 reunited Germany in, 489
 U.S. membership in, 252
 West Germany in, 300
Northern Ireland, Clinton adminis-
 tration and, 521
North Korea
 Bush administration policies
  toward, 491